First Edition Published November 1996 (P. E. Standley, N. J. Bucknell, Andy Swash, Ian Collins)
Second Edition Published November 2013 by Birds of Berkshire Atlas Group (BBAG)

BBAG, c/o 63 Hamilton Road, Reading RG1 5RA

British Library Cataloging-in-Publication Data is available

ISBN 978-0-9529297-1-0

Production and design by Robert Still, Eye on the Ball Ltd., Old Basing, Hampshire UK.
Printed in Poland by Drukarnia DIMOGRAF Sp. z. o. o.

10 9 8 7 6 5 4 3 2 1

*The following organisations contributed £1,000 or more towards the Atlas project:*

**Bracknell Forest Unitary Authority**

**Eton College**

**John Spedan Lewis Foundation**

**Royal Borough of Windsor & Maidenhead**

**Syngenta**

**The Earley Charity**

**West Berkshire Council**

Little Ringed Plovers with chicks by Robert Gillmor.

# Contents

# Figures and tables

## Tables in the species accounts (Chapter 6)

# Sponsors of the *Birds of Berkshire Atlas* Project

*The following organisations contributed £1,000 or more towards the Atlas project:*

Bracknell Forest Unitary Authority

Eton College

John Spedan Lewis Foundation

Royal Borough of Windsor & Maidenhead

Syngenta

The Earley Charity

West Berkshire Council

*In addition to the many species sponsors acknowledged in the species accounts, the following contributed up to £1,000 towards the Atlas project:*

Berkshire, Buckinghamshire and Oxfordshire Wildlife Trust

Berkshire Ornithological Club: Birds of Berkshire Conservation Fund

Blackwater Valley Countryside Trust

Bucklebury Parish Council

Chartered Institute of Builders

Compton Parish Council

Council for the Protection of Rural England

County Ornithological Services

Englefield Trust

Holybrook Parish Council

J&F Farnsworth

Kings Hall Trust

Duncan Spence

West Berkshire Countryside Society

Everyone, who has contributed to this splendid work, deserves the highest praise. It could only have been produced with the cooperation of a great number of dedicated volunteers. It is a highly valuable contribution to the ever-changing record of breeding bird species seen in Berkshire.

Probably the most valuable aspect of this record is the chance it offers to compare numbers and densities with previous surveys, and to speculate on the causes of changes. It might help to establish whether some of the recent changes are due to the unintentional introduction of exotic species, and to the re-introduction of previously resident species.

I have no doubt that future generations of bird-watchers will greatly value this book, and I hope it will help them, and all who are interested in the general conservation of nature, to encourage the introduction of measures, which will help to ensure that our rich ornithological legacy is maintained for the pleasure and instruction of future generations.

# CHAPTER 1

# Introduction and acknowledgements

## About *The Birds of Berkshire* and its compilation

This book is the second edition of a book which, when first published in 1996, was the first publication covering the birds of Berkshire exclusively, either within former or current boundaries. Previous avifaunas have covered Berkshire together with Oxfordshire (Radford, 1966) and with Buckinghamshire (Clark Kennedy, 1868). Further details of these are included in the following chapter which provides a history of birdwatching and recording in the county, and a summary of the ornithological literature published prior to 1974, when the current boundaries of the county were largely established by a re-organisation of local government, and the year for which a separate annual county report was first published for Berkshire.

The roots of the first edition of this book were twofold. The first was the establishment of the Berkshire Atlas Group which grew out of a conversation between Ian Collins, then the county's British Trust for Ornithology (BTO) representative, and Andy Swash, at the 1986 BTO/Wader Study Group Conference at Swanwick. Both wanted to remedy the lack of local fieldwork and comprehensive local information on the county's birds. Berkshire faced severe development pressure, and information for conservation use was needed on a more detailed basis than was available from the casual records collated annually for the county bird report.

Many other counties had either started or completed tetrad-based breeding bird surveys, in which the presence of birds is recorded during the breeding season in each tetrad within the area being studied (a tetrad being a square of 2 km × 2 km based on the National Grid kilometre squares familiar to users of Ordnance Survey maps). Berkshire seemed ripe for such a project and in the early months of 1987 Ian and Andy assembled a co-ordinating group to organise such a survey. That summer saw the first of three years' fieldwork resulting in the breeding distribution maps and ancillary information for 1987–89 set out in this book. Some 250 observers organised through a network of local co-ordinators took part. The Group acquired the computer software originally written for a similar survey carried out in Devon (Sitters, 1988). Much of Andy Swash's spare time in the three winters after each summer's fieldwork was taken up with entering the data onto a computer. Data was exchanged with the groups undertaking similar projects in Oxfordshire and Hampshire. The group's intention was to publish the results as a breeding bird atlas of Berkshire.

At the same time another project was being undertaken. Peter Standley, who had been County Recorder since 1966, was, with the assistance of Paul Andrew, collating the bird records for the county which had been collected in the 40 years since the founding of the Reading Ornithological Club (ROC), for a publication to mark its 40th anniversary. When Peter Standley's project came to the attention of the Atlas Group it was realised that, after a quarter of a century without any county avifauna, two competing publications might appear simultaneously, with adverse consequences for both. The two projects came together to produce a complete county avifauna, the information was pooled, and the task of writing the species accounts began.

It was decided at an early stage to illustrate each species. Robert Gillmor, at the time President of both the Society of Wildlife Artists and the ROC, kindly volunteered to be art editor, and obtained work without charge from all the past winners of the British Birds Bird Illustrator of the Year competition, apart from Crispin Fisher who tragically died shortly after his acceptance was received. Robert also contributed over 60 illustrations himself.

The task of writing and producing the book itself took longer than originally envisaged. After a number of problems and delays, the Group decided to publish privately, retaining Quetzal Communications to provide the technical expertise needed. Backing was given by the ROC. Funds were raised, marketing organised, design and production proceeded (notwithstanding further setbacks!) and, thanks to the assistance of Rob, Len and Penny Still of Quetzal Communications, the first edition of this book was finally published in November 1996.

In 2004, the BTO announced its intention to undertake a third national Atlas project, and to organise it so that, not only could records be submitted on line, but local tetrad atlases could also use the BTO's website to collect, store and retrieve their data too. However the new BTO atlas would also include a winter survey with timed tetrad counts in both seasons, and it would be possible to use the BTO's facilities to cover every tetrad in the county or other area any local group wanted to cover. Chris Robinson, the county's then BTO regional representative, assembled a new group to organise the fieldwork for a repeat atlas survey in Berkshire. The decision was made to undertake atlas surveys in both seasons in all tetrads in the county, and to incorporate the results in a second edition of The Birds of Berkshire. The project was supported by both the Berkshire Ornithological Club (BOC) and the Newbury District Ornithological Club (NDOC).

The support of the BTO, and the on line facilities that they made available, helped achieve the objectives set by the group. All tetrads within the county were covered by four two-hour counts, two in the breeding season and two in winter. The results of these timed surveys were supplemented by "roving records", gathering information on breeding status to repeat the 1987–89 survey and provide information on species not seen in the timed survey visits. A fuller account of the survey methods is set out in Chapter 4.

The next task was to produce the book. Once again a team of volunteers was assembled, now to revise and update the species accounts from the first edition. The team had to incorporate the new survey data, the published records for the period since publication of the first edition, and compare the local trends with information published nationally on bird population trends. Details of the team that has worked to complete this edition are set out in the Acknowledgements section at the end of this chapter.

Not only was there much more advance planning for the second edition, but the opportunity was taken to start fund raising as soon as possible. The intention was to raise sufficient funds to largely cover the production costs, so that the sales could fund local conservation schemes, as had been the outcome of sales of the first edition once production costs had been repaid from sales income. This objective has been achieved, so sales will generate funds for bird-related conservation schemes in the county.

## An introduction to Berkshire

The modern county of Berkshire, as created by the local government re-organisation of 1974, is the second smallest non-metropolitan county. With a population of 862,000 (2011 Census) in an area of 125,901 hectares, it is relatively densely populated, and has experienced considerable urban and suburban development since 1945, especially in the centre and east of the county. At first sight this would not seem a promising prospect for the birdwatcher, but Berkshire does boast a wide variety of habitats within its boundaries, including high open downland, coniferous plantations, river valleys and relict heathland. The Kennet Valley still has many relatively unspoilt wetland areas, and Thatcham Marsh is the largest inland reedbed in Britain outside East Anglia.

Development has also created new habitats in the county. Early in the 20th century the attraction of old-fashioned sewage farms with open settling beds for birds was discovered by birdwatchers. The spread of gravel extraction has resulted in a network of lakes in the river valleys and created a variety of habitats which have attracted new breeding species to the county, including Ringed and Little Ringed Plover, Oystercatcher, Cetti's Warbler and Common Tern. These areas have also provided havens for established breeding species, such as Grey Heron and Mute Swan and have attracted many vagrants. In the far east of the county is the Queen Mother Reservoir at Datchet which is the westernmost of London's reservoirs. It is situated close to the main reservoir complex at Staines, an area which has long been recognised for its attraction to wintering wildfowl and migrants. In east Berkshire, the Crown Estate has had an important influence on birds. The woodlands and ornamental lakes of Windsor Great Park, which extend into Surrey, have created a refuge for a number of species and provided the base from which the introduced Mandarin has begun to colonise Britain.

Whilst a full account of the habitats in Berkshire appears in Chapter 3, their diversity is reflected in the total species list of birds for the county which now stands at over 310. This is higher than the 294 species recorded in neighbouring Oxfordshire, even though Oxfordshire is over twice the area of Berkshire and has a considerably smaller population of about 684,500.

## Changes to the county boundary

In sifting through the records to produce the species accounts in this book, a number of problems were encountered as a result of the county boundary changes in 1974 and further minor revisions since. A number of old records had been simply ascribed to Berkshire, making it unclear whether the site in question lay in the considerable area in the north-west of the old county which passed to Oxfordshire in April 1974. There were also a number of records from the Downs where it is unclear whether they fall within the present county boundary. Prior to 1974, observers had no reason to be particular about records in the area around Churn, Lowbury Hill and Compton Downs, which was frequented by birdwatchers, as it then lay entirely within Berkshire. Now, however, it lies on the county boundary. Although areas of old Berkshire that lay adjacent to the city of Oxford passed to Oxfordshire in 1974, including such sites of ornithological interest as Wytham Wood and Farmoor Reservoir, the same logic was not applied to those areas of Oxfordshire immediately adjacent to Reading. Thus records from Henley Road Gravel Pits in Reading are not included, even though the site is surrounded on three sides by Berkshire and access is normally gained to the site from the adjoining built-up area of Caversham, situated in Berkshire.

The 1974 boundary changes did bring Slough and the area around Wraysbury, Horton and Datchet into Berkshire.

This has resulted in earlier records from Slough Sewage Farm and the gravel pits in the lower Colne Valley being added. These boundary changes also brought part of Wraysbury Reservoir into Berkshire, although this was a temporary feature since the boundary was revised again in 1991 to exclude all of the Reservoir! Reference to the site has been retained where it is felt appropriate. Apart from the loss of Wraysbury Reservoir, post-1974 adjustments to the county boundary have had little impact on local bird records. One adjustment was to change the boundary with Oxfordshire and Buckinghamshire along the Thames. Here the boundary used to switch from bank to bank, but now runs down the middle of the river. No attempt has been made to attribute records from the Thames to a particular county and all records for the river which were submitted for publication in Berkshire have been taken into account in the analyses of records included here. The most recent change to the county boundary took place in 1995, when an area around Colnbrook, Poyle and Old Slade was transferred from Buckinghamshire and Surrey to Berkshire.

As can be seen from the description of the Tetrad Survey methodology in Chapter 4, the tetrad maps inevitably include records from neighbouring counties. If a tetrad overlapped the county boundary all of its area was surveyed even if part, or in many cases most, lay outside Berkshire. Similar considerations apply when the results of national surveys co-ordinated by the BTO and other organisations are discussed.

## The species included

The information in this book is based on all available records up to the end of 2012, with some later records. An account has been included for all species known to have occurred in a truly wild state, or which are recognised introduced species with self-sustaining populations included on the British Ornithologists' Union's (BOU) Category 'C' list. The book does, however, contain accounts for four introduced species, Black Swan, Bar-headed Goose, Wood Duck and Chukar, where breeding has occurred in the county or (in the case of Bar-headed Goose), nearby, even though these species may not maintain self-sustaining populations in the wild. Records which are likely to relate to escaped pets, livestock or aviary birds, such as Reeve's Pheasant, which are often recorded but have not yet been reported breeding outside captivity in Berkshire, have been omitted from the species accounts. As complete a list as possible of the escaped or introduced species which have been recorded in Berkshire since 1974 is included in Category 'D' species and Escapes (page 478), together with details of one species which is included on the BOU Category 'D' list i.e. there is reasonable doubt that it occurred in a truly wild state.

There are also accounts for two species, Marsh Sandpiper and Chough, which have been published elsewhere, but which are not regarded as proven records, and for Black Grouse, which was the subject of two unsuccessful introduction attempts in the 19th century. Whilst the tetrad survey maps include all records for the tetrad, including those outside the county boundary in border tetrads, the avifauna includes only records within the current boundary of Berkshire.

## The value and importance of surveys of local birds

Shortly after the first edition of this book was published the County Council was abolished, leaving the Districts as single-tier local authorities. Berkshire though remains as a geographic unit and has been retained for some, mostly ceremonial, purposes. The problems faced by birds within the county are unlikely to diminish, however. It is hoped that the second edition of this book, as well as providing the most complete account so far of Berkshire's birds and acting as a reference source for those involved in wildlife conservation, will stimulate interest in the changing populations of local birds. The material published here, especially the tetrad maps, show changes in the county's bird life in the two decades since the first tetrad survey, and provide a benchmark against which future changes in the numbers and distribution of breeding and wintering species in the county can be monitored.

It was apparent when the first edition was being prepared that there had been less local fieldwork carried out in Berkshire than in many other counties. Since the 1970s, much of the increase in interest in birds had been focused on identification and in chasing rarities. The success in generating support for the BTO's Breeding Bird Survey (BBS) in the county since 2000, and the participation by a larger number of volunteers in the more demanding survey work of the second county atlas, provide encouraging evidence that this is no longer the case. Hopefully this effort will continue, and the county's birdwatchers will continue to contribute to supporting the gathering of data to support conservation locally and nationally. National schemes run by the BTO have produced evidence of the effect of the use and control of pesticides between the 1950s and the 1970s, the impact of hard winters, such as that of 1962/63 and, more recently, the problems generated by current agricultural practices and the use of selective pesticides. Only a large band of willing amateur volunteers can produce such a volume of information.

In 1996 the Royal Society for the Protection of Birds (RSPB) published the UK's first 'Red List' of 36 bird species of high conservation concern (RSPB, 1996). Of these, 23 were included on the list because their breeding populations had declined by 50% or more over the preceding 25 years. Some 15 of these species breed regularly in Berkshire although three, Stone Curlew, Woodlark and Nightjar, have very restricted ranges. Others, such as Grey Partridge, Tree Sparrow and Corn Bunting, which were formerly widespread, have either disappeared entirely in recent decades or their range within Berkshire has reduced considerably, although the extent of this cannot always be determined by the records appearing in the county reports. Major gaps clearly still exist in the information available on the distribution and populations of many of the birds in Berkshire, a deficiency which is being addressed by a good level of participation in the BBS, and has also been addressed by the second county tetrad atlas project. We do though live in a changing world, and the factors driving changes in our wildlife, locally, nationally and internationally and their impact, are still only partly understood. This second atlas has given a first opportunity to compare the distribution of the county's breeding birds against a previous comparable survey to ascertain changes between the two atlas surveys. The Timed Tetrad Visit (TTV) data now collected and presented in this second edition also provide a benchmark against which general changes in abundance can be measured. Hopefully this book will encourage another generation of citizen scientists to continue the work presented here to help monitor the fortunes of the county's and the nation's birds.

N. J. Bucknell

## Acknowledgements

This book, in both its first and second editions, is the culmination of the work of a large number of unpaid volunteers. We are grateful to all concerned for their assistance since without their help a book of this nature would not have been possible. We hope that everybody who has contributed is acknowledged below but if anyone has been omitted this is entirely inadvertent and we offer our sincere apologies.

Two of the main contributors to the first edition deserve special mention. Peter Standley's work in collecting together the historical information and compiling the species accounts for the non-breeding species still forms the basis of these accounts in this edition. The hard work put in by Andy Swash in carrying out the final editing of the first edition has given us an excellent basis upon which this second edition has been compiled.

The core of this second edition is the presentation of the results of the second Berkshire bird atlas project. The scale of this project can be appreciated by comparison of the number of records collected for each project. The first atlas only recorded breeding distributions and status, and 22,989 records were collected, which Andy and Gill Swash manually entered onto their computer. The second survey repeated the breeding distribution survey, but also involved four two-hour timed counts – two in the breeding season, two in winter – in each tetrad, with ancillary casual records to complete the coverage. This produced a total of 275,115 records to analyse! None of this would have been possible without the on-line facilities provided by the BTO, and we are grateful to them for their vision and generosity in enabling BBAG (and over 40 other local groups) to use them without charge. Particular thanks are due to the BTO's atlas team, Dawn Balmer and Simon Gillings, for being friendly, patient and helpful contacts, and Ian Downie for his behind the scenes work leading the Information Technology team which created and managed the Atlas website.

The fieldwork for the second atlas was coordinated by the BBAG committee, whose inspiration and first chair was Chris Robinson, the BTO's regional representative in Berkshire until he moved to Herefordshire in 2009, where he is now the BTO regional representative and organising a local bird atlas. He set the project on its way, and has remained involved notwithstanding his move. The group initially comprised Brian Clews, Renton Righelato, Jim Burnett, Colin Wilson and Neil Bucknell. When Chris moved to Herefordshire, the group was joined by his joint successors as Berkshire BTO regional representatives, Ken and Sarah White, and Ken Moore from the Berkshire Records Committee (BRC). Ken and Sarah White oversaw the considerable task of record validation, while Ken Moore was helpful in a number of ways, as set out below. Jim Burnett resigned from the committee as a result of a change in personal circumstances, and was replaced by John Swallow as NDOC's representative.

The fieldworkers were coordinated by a network of 10 km square organisers who were responsible for recruiting volunteers in their area and monitoring coverage, many taking on a substantial part of the survey work in their areas personally. They were-

| | | |
|---|---|---|
| Roy Alliss | Tim Ball | Neil Bucknell |
| Jim Burnett | Brian Clews | Patrick Crowley |
| Dave Glover | Barry Howes | Jan Legg |
| John Lerpiniere | Bill Nicoll | Renton Righelato |
| Chris Robinson | John Swallow | Andy Tomczynski |
| Colin Wilson | | |

The benchmark against which the changes revealed by the breeding season distribution survey of the 2007–11 project were measured was the first Berkshire Atlas survey undertaken between 1987 and 1989. This was co-ordinated by the Berkshire Atlas Group comprising Andy Swash, Ian Collins, Debby Reynolds, Neil Bucknell and Steve Abbott. A total of 250 observers contributed records to the first Berkshire Atlas, whilst 437 contributed breeding season records (of whom 135 undertook timed tetrad counts) and 325 contributed winter records (of whom 146 undertook timed tetrad counts) for the second atlas. The contributors to both tetrad atlas surveys are listed in Appendix I.

The atlas contributors' records have been supplemented by those from other sources as mentioned in Chapter 4. We are also grateful to the organisers of the atlas surveys in adjoining counties for their cooperation in coordinating coverage, and their work in validating records within the parts of Berkshire that fall within 10km grid squares that are in adjoining BTO regional representatives' areas.

Once fieldwork had been completed, the task of revising the species accounts to incorporate the results of the second atlas survey and records for the period since the publication of the first edition began. Ken Moore of the Berkshire Records Committee helpfully reviewed the county list and identified which species had not been recorded since or (for scarcer species) the years in which records had occurred, thereby saving considerable time in reviewing the county reports.

To produce this edition, the species accounts written for the first edition have been updated to incorporate the results of the 2007–11 Atlas survey and records for the intervening period. The accounts for the breeding species in the first edition were prepared by a number of authors who are fully acknowledged later, notable contributions being made by Jim Walling and Gordon Wilson. Most of the non-breeding species accounts were drawn up by Peter Standley, who carried out much research into pre-1947 material to ensure that the information was as comprehensive as possible.

The ringing information in this edition is derived from the county information now published on the BTO's website. It should be noted that there a some records shown in the Berkshire summary on the website which appear to relate to birds ringed or recovered in adjoining areas of Oxfordshire that were in the old county of Berkshire before 1974, and no attempt has been made to eliminate these from the summaries in the species accounts.

As for the first edition, a team of volunteers was assembled to revise the species accounts in this edition. Advances in information technology helped considerably in organising the task. Renton and Jason Righelato set up a password protected website, onto which were posted the maps and data from the two Atlas surveys, the species accounts from the first edition, copies of county reports, habitat maps derived from data supplied from the Thames Valley Environmental Records Centre (TVERC) and links to sources of other relevant information, notably the BTO's Bird Facts and ringing summaries. The hard work they put in setting up this on-line resource made the process of research for revising and updating the species accounts set out in this book considerably easier and have enabled this edition to be published within a little more than two years after fieldwork for the second atlas project was completed. Thanks are also due to Bill Nicoll, who carried out work updating some of the data tables from the first edition, to Nigel Wardell who digitised the data from the maps in the first edition, for which there was no electronic record, to Keith Chard for scanning the text of the first edition and converting to Word to enable the revisers to edit it, to Giles Sutton who provided advice on map generation and Marek Walford who both provided advice and helped with data collection through his Berksbirds website. Jason Righelato has also been responsible for designing and setting up the Birds of Berkshire website, which hosts further supplementary information and other facilities as explained below.

Each species has been illustrated by a drawing specially commissioned for this new edition, and thanks are due to Colin Wilson for undertaking the task of commissioning the drawings, overseeing the consideration of them by the panel, and putting in place arrangements with the artists for the sale of artwork as part of the fundraising for the book. Colin also co-ordinated Chris Heard, Brian Clews and Neil Bucknell who acted as the panel to consider the submissions. We are also grateful to Ken Moore and Chris Heard of the Berkshire Records Committee for reviewing and commenting upon the draft revised species accounts, and to Peter Standley for drawing to our attention some errors in the first edition for correction. John Westmacott kindly volunteered to undertake proof reading, completing the task efficiently and in a timely manner to help us adhere to our publication timetable. The complete list of original authors, revisers and artists who have produced the drawings can be found in Table i (*pages 15–20*)

Brian Clews drafted the "Where to Watch Birds" section that appears in Chapter 5 and checked and expanded the gazetteer. John Swallow analysed the records of escapes and hybrids, to produce the basis of the summaries which appear at the end of the main species accounts (*page 478*). The original material for the latter will be available on website (see *page 20*). The other appendices were drafted by Renton Righelato. Marek

Table i *Birds of Berkshire* Artists, original authors and revisers.

| Species | Original author | Reviser | Artist for 2nd Edition |
|---|---|---|---|
| Mute Swan | N. J. Bucknell | N. J. Bucknell | Dafila Scott |
| Black Swan | — | N. J. Bucknell | Rob Still |
| Bewick's Swan | P. E. Standley | N. J. Bucknell | Dafila Scott |
| Whooper Swan | P. E. Standley | N. J. Bucknell | Dan Powell |
| Bean Goose | P. E. Standley | N. J. Bucknell | Richard Allen |
| Pink-footed Goose | P. E. Standley | C. Robinson | Rob Still |
| White-fronted Goose | P. E. Standley | N. J. Bucknell | Richard Allen |
| Greylag Goose | N. J. Bucknell | N. J. Bucknell | Richard Allen |
| Bar-headed Goose | — | N. J. Bucknell | Richard Allen |
| Snow Goose | P. E. Standley | N. J. Bucknell | Richard Allen |
| Canada Goose | N. J. Bucknell | N. J. Bucknell | Richard Allen |
| Barnacle Goose | N. J. Bucknell | N. J. Bucknell | Dafila Scott |
| Brent Goose | P. E. Standley | N. J. Bucknell | Richard Allen |
| Red-breasted Goose | P. E. Standley | C. D. R. Heard | Ernest Leahy |
| Egyptian Goose | N. J. Bucknell | N. J. Bucknell | Ernest Leahy |
| Ruddy Shelduck | P. E. Standley | N. J. Bucknell | Ernest Leahy |
| Shelduck | P. E. Standley | N. J. Bucknell | Ernest Leahy |
| Wood Duck | N. J. Bucknell | N. J. Bucknell | Ernest Leahy |
| Mandarin Duck | K. J. Herber | N. J. Bucknell | David Thelwell |
| Wigeon | N. J. Bucknell | R. Righelato | David Thelwell |
| American Wigeon | P. E. Standley | B. D. Clews | David Thelwell |
| Gadwall | N. J. Bucknell | R. Righelato | David Thelwell |
| Teal | N. J. Bucknell | R. Righelato | David Thelwell |
| Green-winged Teal | — | N. J. Bucknell | David Thelwell |
| Mallard | N. J. Bucknell | R. Righelato | David Thelwell |
| Pintail | N. J. Bucknell | R. Righelato | David Thelwell |
| Garganey | N. J. Bucknell | R. Righelato | David Thelwell |
| Blue-winged Teal | P. E. Standley | *not amended* | David Thelwell |
| Shoveler | P. E. Standley | R. Righelato | David Thelwell |
| Red-crested Pochard | P. E. Standley | N. J. Bucknell | David Thelwell |
| Pochard | N. J. Bucknell | R. Righelato | David Thelwell |
| Ring-necked Duck | P. E. Standley | B. D. Clews | David Thelwell |
| Ferruginous Duck | N. J. Bucknell | S. S. White | David Thelwell |
| Tufted Duck | N. J. Bucknell | R. Righelato | David Thelwell |
| Scaup | P. E. Standley | R. Reedman | David Thelwell |
| Lesser Scaup | — | N. J. Bucknell | David Thelwell |
| Eider | P. E. Standley | R. Reedman | David Thelwell |
| Long-tailed Duck | P. E. Standley | R. Reedman | David Thelwell |
| Common Scoter | P. E. Standley | R. Reedman | Ernest Leahy |
| Velvet Scoter | P. E. Standley | B. D. Clews | Rob Still |
| Goldeneye | P. E. Standley | C. R. Wilson | Peter Sewell |
| Smew | PE. Standley | R. Reedman | David Thelwell |
| Red-breasted Merganser | N. J. Bucknell | R. Reedman | David Thelwell |
| Goosander | P. E. Standley | R. Reedman | David Thelwell |
| Ruddy Duck | N. J. Bucknell | N. J. Bucknell | David Thelwell |
| Black Grouse | P. E. Standley | *not amended* | Ernest Leahy |
| Chukar | J. J. Walling | N. J. Bucknell | Ernest Leahy |
| Red-legged Partridge | P. E. Standley | R. Murfitt | Ernest Leahy |
| Grey Partridge | J. J. Walling | R. Murfitt | Ernest Leahy |
| Quail | J. J. Walling | R. Murfitt | Rob Still |
| Pheasant | J. J. Walling | N. J. Bucknell | Ernest Leahy |
| Lady Amherst's Pheasant | P. E. Standley | N. J. Bucknell | Ernest Leahy |
| Golden Pheasant | J. J. Walling | R. Reedman | Ernest Leahy |
| Red-throated Diver | P. E. Standley | T. Rogers | Dan Powell |
| Black-throated Diver | P. E. Standley | T. Rogers | Dan Powell |
| Great Northern Diver | P. E. Standley | T. Rogers | Dan Powell |
| Fulmar | P. E. Standley | N. J. Bucknell | Dan Powell |
| Manx Shearwater | P. E. Standley | R. Righelato | Dan Powell |
| Storm Petrel | P. E. Standley | N. J. Bucknell | Dan Powell |
| Leach's Petrel | P. E. Standley | R. Righelato | Dan Powell |
| Gannet | P. E. Standley | T. Rogers | Dan Powell |
| Cormorant | N. J. Bucknell | N. J. Bucknell | Dan Powell |
| Shag | P. E. Standley | T. Rogers | Dan Powell |

| Species | Original author | Reviser | Artist for 2nd Edition |
|---|---|---|---|
| Bittern | P. E. Standley | T. Rogers | David Thelwell |
| Little Bittern | P. E. Standley | *not amended* | David Thelwell |
| Night Heron | PE. Standley | *not amended* | David Thelwell |
| Cattle Egret | — | N. J. Bucknell | David Thelwell |
| Little Egret | P. E. Standley | N. J. Bucknell | Robert Gillmor |
| Great White Egret | — | N. J. Bucknell | David Thelwell |
| Grey Heron | N. J. Bucknell | N. J. Bucknell | David Thelwell |
| Purple Heron | P. E. Standley | N. J. Bucknell | Robert Gillmor |
| White Stork | P. E. Standley | C. R. Wilson | Rob Still |
| Glossy Ibis | P. E. Standley | N. J. Bucknell | Dan Powell |
| Spoonbill | P. E. Standley | C. R. Wilson | Dan Powell |
| Little Grebe | N. J. Bucknell | N. J. Bucknell | Dan Powell |
| Great Crested Grebe | N. J. Bucknell | N. J. Bucknell | Dan Powell |
| Red-necked Grebe | P. E. Standley | N. J. Bucknell | Dan Powell |
| Slavonian Grebe | J. J. Walling | N. J. Bucknell | Dan Powell |
| Black-necked Grebe | RE. Standley | N. J. Bucknell | Dan Powell |
| Honey Buzzard | P. E. Standley | R. Righelato | Jan Wilczur |
| Black Kite | — | N. J. Bucknell | Jan Wilczur |
| Red Kite | P. E. Standley | R. Righelato | Jan Wilczur |
| White-tailed Eagle | P. E. Standley | *not amended* | Jan Wilczur |
| Marsh Harrier | P. E. Standley | T. Rogers | Jan Wilczur |
| Hen Harrier | P. E. Standley | T. Rogers | Jan Wilczur |
| Montagu's Harrier | P. E. Standley | T. Rogers | Robert Gillmor |
| Goshawk | P. E. Standley | R. Righelato | Jan Wilczur |
| Sparrowhawk | M. J. Taylor | N. J. Bucknell | Jan Wilczur |
| Buzzard | C. D. R. Heard | R. Righelato | Jan Wilczur |
| Rough-legged Buzzard | P. E. Standley | S. White | Jan Wilczur |
| Spotted Eagle | P. E. Standley | *not amended* | Jan Wilczur |
| Golden Eagle | P. E. Standley | *not amended* | Jan Wilczur |
| Osprey | P. E. Standley | T. Rogers | Jan Wilczur |
| Kestrel | N. J. Bucknell | N. J. Bucknell | Jan Wilczur |
| Red-footed Falcon | J. J. Walling | S. White | Jan Wilczur |
| Merlin | P. E. Standley | T. Rogers | Jan Wilczur |
| Hobby | M. J. Taylor | M. J. Taylor | Jan Wilczur |
| Gyr Falcon | P. E. Standley | *not amended* | Jan Wilczur |
| Peregrine | P. E. Standley | R. Righelato | Jan Wilczur |
| Water Rail | J. A. Horsfall | R. Murfitt | Robert Gillmor |
| Spotted Crake | P. E. Standley | N. J. Bucknell | Ernest Leahy |
| Sora Rail | P. E. Standley | *not amended* | Ernest Leahy |
| Baillon's Crake | P. E. Standley | N. J. Bucknell | Ernest Leahy |
| Corncrake | P. E. Standley | C. R. Wilson | Ernest Leahy |
| Moorhen | J. A. Horsfall | R. Murfitt | Ernest Leahy |
| Coot | J. A. Horsfall | R. Righelato | Ernest Leahy |
| Crane | P. E. Standley | T. Rogers | Robert Gillmor |
| Little Bustard | P. E. Standley | N. J. Bucknell | Dan Powell |
| Great Bustard | P. E. Standley | R. Righelato | Dan Powell |
| Stone Curlew | D. Foskett | N. J. Bucknell | Dan Powell |
| Black-winged Stilt | P. E. Standley | *not amended* | Dan Powell |
| Avocet | P. E. Standley | T. Rogers | Dan Powell |
| Oystercatcher | P. E. Standley | R. Righelato | Dan Powell |
| Golden Plover | P. E. Standley | R. Righelato | Robert Gillmor |
| Grey Plover | P. E. Standley | R. Righelato | Ernest Leahy |
| Sociable Plover | P. E. Standley | C. D. R. Heard | Ernest Leahy |
| Lapwing | G. E. Wilson | R. Righelato | David Thelwell |
| Little Ringed Plover | G. E. Wilson | R. Righelato | Dan Powell |
| Ringed Plover | G. E. Wilson | R. Righelato | Dan Powell |
| Killdeer | P. E. Standley | *not amended* | Dan Powell |
| Kentish Plover | P. E. Standley | *not amended* | Dan Powell |
| Dotterel | P. E. Standley | T. Rogers | Ernest Leahy |
| Whimbrel | P. E. Standley | N. J. Bucknell | Robert Gillmor |
| Curlew | B. D. Clews | N. J. Bucknell | Jan Wilczur |
| Black-tailed Godwit | P. E. Standley | C. R. Wilson | David Thelwell |
| Bar-tailed Godwit | P. E. Standley | C. R. Wilson | David Thelwell |
| Turnstone | P. E. Standley | T. Rogers | Dan Powell |

| Species | Original author | Reviser | Artist for 2nd Edition |
|---|---|---|---|
| Knot | P. E. Standley | R. Righelato | David Thelwell |
| Ruff | P. E. Standley | J. Baker | Robert Gillmor |
| Sharp-tailed Sandpiper | P. E. Standley | N. J. Bucknell | David Thelwell |
| Broad-billed Sandpiper | P. E. Standley | N. J. Bucknell | Jan Wilczur |
| Curlew Sandpiper | P. E. Standley | R. Righelato | Jan Wilczur |
| Temminck's stint | P. E. Standley | R. Righelato | Ernest Leahy |
| Sanderling | P. E. Standley | R. Righelato | David Thelwell |
| Dunlin | P. E. Standley | R. Righelato | Jan Wilczur |
| Purple Sandpiper | P. E. Standley | T. Rogers | Ernest Leahy |
| Little Stint | P. E. Standley | R. Righelato | David Thelwell |
| Least Sandpiper | P. E. Slandley | *not amended* | Ernest Leahy |
| Pectoral Sandpiper | P. E. Standley | N. J. Bucknell | Robert Gillmor |
| Wilson's Phalarope | P. E. Standley | *not amended* | David Thelwell |
| Red-necked Phalarope | P. E. Standley | N. J. Bucknell | David Thelwell |
| Grey Phalarope | P. E. Standley | J. Baker | David Thelwell |
| Common Sandpiper | P. E. Standley | T. Rogers | Dan Powell |
| Green Sandpiper | P. E. Standley | T. Rogers | Dan Powell |
| Spotted Redshank | P. E. Standley | T. Rogers | Dan Powell |
| Greenshank | P. E. Standley | J. Baker | Dan Powell |
| Lesser Yellowlegs | P. E. Standley | N. J. Bucknell | Dan Powell |
| Marsh Sandpiper | P. E. Standley | *not amended* | Dan Powell |
| Wood Sandpiper | P. E. Standley | T. Rogers | Dan Powell |
| Redshank | G. E. Wilson | T. Rogers | Dan Powell |
| Jack Snipe | P. E. Standley | N. J. Bucknell | David Thelwell |
| Woodcock | B. D. Clews | N. J. Bucknell | David Thelwell |
| Snipe | B. D. Clews | N. J. Bucknell | David Thelwell |
| Great Snipe | P. E. Standley | N. J. Bucknell | David Thelwell |
| Black-winged Pratincole | P. E. Standley | N. J. Bucknell | Dan Powell |
| Pomarine Skua | P. E. Standley | M. Turton | David Thelwell |
| Arctic Skua | P. E. Standley | T. Rogers | David Thelwell |
| Long-tailed Skua | P. E. Standley | M. Turton | David Thelwell |
| Great Skua | P. E. Standley | M. Turton | Ernest Leahy |
| Puffin | P. E. Standley | N. J. Bucknell | Simon Gillings |
| Razorbill | P. E. Standley | *not amended* | Simon Gillings |
| Little Auk | P. E. Standley | R. Crawford | Simon Gillings |
| Guillemot | P. E. Standley | *not amended* | Simon Gillings |
| Little Tern | P. E. Standley | A. Taylor | Simon Gillings |
| Caspian Tern | P. E. Standley | N. J. Bucknell | Steph Thorpe |
| Whiskered Tern | — | N. J. Bucknell | Simon Gillings |
| Black Tern | P. E. Standley | A. Taylor | Peter Sewell |
| White-winged Black Tern | P. E. Standley | N. J. Bucknell | Simon Gillings |
| Sandwich Tern | P. E. Standley | A. Taylor | Simon Gillings |
| Common Tern | J. J. Walling | M. Turton | Simon Gillings |
| Roseate Tern | P. E. Standley | N. J. Bucknell | Simon Gillings |
| Arctic Tern | P. E. Standley | A. Taylor | Simon Gillings |
| Sabine's Gull | P. E. Standley | M. Turton | David Thelwell |
| Kittiwake | P. E. Standley | A. Taylor | Richard Allen |
| Bonaparte's Gull | — | N. J. Bucknell | Richard Allen |
| Black-headed Gull | J. J. Walling | M. Turton | David Thelwell |
| Little Gull | P. E. Standley | T. Rogers | David Thelwell |
| Laughing Gull | — | N. J. Bucknell | David Thelwell |
| Mediterranean Gull | P. E. Standley | T. Rogers | David Thelwell |
| Common Gull | P. E. Standley | M. Turton | Richard Allen |
| Ring-billed Gull | P. E. Standley | M. Turton | Robert Gillmor |
| Lesser Black-backed Gull | P. E. Standley | M. Turton | Richard Allen |
| Herring Gull | P. E. Standley | T. Rogers | Richard Allen |
| Yellow-legged Gull | P. E. Standley | N. J. Bucknell | Richard Allen |
| Caspian Gull | — | N. J. Bucknell | Richard Allen |
| Iceland Gull | P. E. Standley | M. Turton/C. D. R. Heard | Richard Allen |
| Glaucous Gull | P. E. Standley | A. Taylor | Steph Thorpe |
| Great Black-backed Gull | P. E. Standley | R. Crawford | Richard Allen |
| Pallas's Sandgrouse | P. E. Standley | C. D. R. Heard | Ernest Leahy |
| Feral Pigeon | J. J. Walling | S. White | Dan Powell |
| Stock Dove | J. J. Walling | S. White | Dan Powell |

| Species | Original author | Reviser | Artist for 2nd Edition |
|---|---|---|---|
| Woodpigeon | J. J. Walling | S. White | Dan Powell |
| Collared Dove | J. J. Walling | S. White | David Thelwell |
| Turtle Dove | J. J. Walling | S. White | David Thelwell |
| Ring-necked Parakeet | C. D. R. Heard | B. D. Clews | David Thelwell |
| Cuckoo | P. Gipson | S. White | David Thelwell |
| Barn Owl | G. E. Wilson | R. Righelato | David Thelwell |
| Little Owl | M. J. Taylor | R. Righelato | David Thelwell |
| Tawny Owl | M. J. Taylor | R. Righelato | David Thelwell |
| Long-eared Owl | M. J. Taylor | R. Crawford | David Thelwell |
| Short-eared Owl | P. E. Standley | R. Righelato | David Thelwell |
| Tengmalm's Owl | P. E. Standley | N. J. Bucknell | David Thelwell |
| Nightjar | N. Cleere | R. Righelato | David Thelwell |
| Swift | G. E. Wilson | R. Righelato | David Thelwell |
| Alpine Swift | P. E. Standley | R. Righelato | David Thelwell |
| Kingfisher | P. Gipson | N. J. Bucknell | David Thelwell |
| Roller | P. E. Standley | N. J. Bucknell | David Thelwell |
| Hoopoe | P. E. Standley | A. Taylor | Robert Gillmor |
| Wryneck | P. E. Standley | A. Taylor | David Thelwell |
| Green Woodpecker | M. J. Taylor | T. Rogers | David Thelwell |
| Great Spotted Woodpecker | M. J. Taylor | T. Rogers | David Thelwell |
| Lesser Spotted Woodpecker | M. J. Taylor | T. Rogers | David Thelwell |
| Golden Oriole | P. E. Standley | N. J. Bucknell | Dan Powell |
| Red-backed Shrike | P. E. Standley | A. Taylor | Dan Powell |
| Great Grey Shrike | P. E. Standley | B. D. Clews | Dan Powell |
| Woodchat Shrike | P. E. Standley | N. J. Bucknell | Dan Powell |
| Chough | P. E. Standley | *not amended* | Dan Powell |
| Magpie | C. E. Wilson | N. J. Bucknell | Dan Powell |
| Jay | C. E. Wilson | N. J. Bucknell | Dan Powell |
| Nutcracker | P. E. Standley | N. J. Bucknell | Dan Powell |
| Jackdaw | N. J. Bucknell | B. D. Clews | Dan Powell |
| Rook | G. E. Wilson | B. D. Clews | Dan Powell |
| Carrion Crow | G. E. Wilson | B. D. Clews | Dan Powell |
| Hooded Crow | — | B. D. Clews | Dan Powell |
| Raven | P. E. Standley | B. D. Clews | Dan Powell |
| Goldcrest | R. Still | R. Murfitt | Dan Powell |
| Firecrest | P. E. Standley | R. Murfitt | Dan Powell |
| Penduline Tit | P. E. Standley | N. J. Bucknell | Dan Powell |
| Blue Tit | D. J. White | B. D. Clews | Dan Powell |
| Great Tit | D. J. White | B. D. Clews | Dan Powell |
| Coal Tit | D. J. White | B. D. Clews | Dan Powell |
| Willow Tit | J. Legg | J. Legg | Dan Powell |
| Marsh Tit | J. Legg | J. Legg | Dan Powell |
| Bearded Tit | J. Legg | J. Legg | Dan Powell |
| Short-toed Lark | P. E. Standley | N. J. Bucknell | David Thelwell |
| Woodlark | G. E. Wilson | T. Rogers | Ernest Leahy |
| Skylark | P. E. Standley | T. Rogers | Ernest Leahy |
| Shore Lark | N. J. Bucknell | A. Taylor | Ernest Leahy |
| Sand Martin | G. E. Wilson | B. D. Clews | David Thelwell |
| Swallow | G. E. Wilson | B. D. Clews | David Thelwell |
| House Martin | G. E. Wilson | B. D. Clews | David Thelwell |
| Red-rumped Swallow | B. D. Clews | B. D. Clews | David Thelwell |
| Cetti's Warbler | I. L. G. Weston | T. Rogers | Rob Still |
| Long-tailed Tit | A. R. H. Swash | N. J. Bucknell | Dan Powell |
| Pallas's Warbler | — | N. J. Bucknell | David Thelwell |
| Yellow-browed Warbler | P. E. Standley | A. Taylor | David Thelwell |
| Western Bonelli's Warbler | P. E. Standley | N. J. Bucknell | Dan Powell |
| Wood Warbler | G. E. Wilson | T. Rogers | Dan Powell |
| Chiffchaff | G. E. Wilson | T. Rogers | Dan Powell |
| Willow Warbler | G. E. Wilson | T. Rogers | Dan Powell |
| Blackcap | R. Still | T. Rogers | David Thelwell |
| Garden Warbler | R. Still | T. Rogers | David Thelwell |
| Lesser Whitethroat | R. Still | L. Daniells | David Thelwell |
| Whitethroat | R. Still | L. Daniells | David Thelwell |
| Dartford Warbler | P. E. Standley | T. Rogers | David Thelwell |

| Species | Original author | Reviser | Artist for 2nd Edition |
| --- | --- | --- | --- |
| Grasshopper Warbler | P. Gipson | T. Rogers | Ernest Leahy |
| Savi's Warbler | P. E. Standley | N. J. Bucknell | Dan Powell |
| Icterine Warbler | P. E. Standley | N. J. Bucknell | Dan Powell |
| Melodious Warbler | P. E. Standley | N. J. Bucknell | Dan Powell |
| Aquatic Warbler | P. E. Standley | N. J. Bucknell | Ren Hathway |
| Sedge Warbler | N. J. Bucknell | L. Daniells | Ernest Leahy |
| Paddyfield Warbler | — | N. J. Bucknell | Dan Powell |
| Marsh Warbler | P. E. Standley | N. J. Bucknell | Dan Powell |
| Reed Warbler | I. L. G. Weston | L. Daniells | Dan Powell |
| Great Reed Warbler | P. E. Standley | N. J. Bucknell | Dan Powell |
| Waxwing | P. E. Standley | B. D. Clews | David Thelwell |
| Nuthatch | J. J. Walling | N. J. Bucknell | Dan Powell |
| Treecreeper | J. J. Walling | N. J. Bucknell | Dan Powell |
| Wren | LL. G. Weston | C. R. Wilson | David Thelwell |
| Starling | J. J. Walling | N. J. Bucknell | Dan Powell |
| Rose-coloured Starling | P. E. Standley | N. J. Bucknell | Dan Powell |
| Dipper | P. E. Standley | N. J. Bucknell | David Thelwell |
| Ring Ouzel | P. E. Standley | T. Rogers | David Thelwell |
| Blackbird | G. E. Wilson | R. Reedman | Ernest Leahy |
| Black-throated Thrush | — | N. J. Bucknell | Ernest Leahy |
| Fieldfare | G. E. Wilson | R. Murfitt | Ernest Leahy |
| Song Thrush | G. E. Wilson | R. Reedman | Ernest Leahy |
| Redwing | G. E. Wilson | N. J. Bucknell | Dan Powell |
| Mistle Thrush | G. E. Wilson | T. Rogers | Dan Powell |
| Spotted Flycatcher | N. J. Bucknell | N. J. Bucknell | Dan Powell |
| Robin | G. Webb | C. R. Wilson | David Thelwell |
| Nightingale | P. Martin | R. Crawford | Robert Gillmor |
| Bluethroat | P. E. Standley | N. J. Bucknell | David Thelwell |
| Pied Flycatcher | P. E. Standley | R. Righelato | Dan Powell |
| Black Redstart | G. E. Wilson | R. Righelato | David Thelwell |
| Redstart | P. E. Standley | R. Righelato | David Thelwell |
| Whinchat | G. Webb | R. Reedman | David Thelwell |
| Siberian Stonechat | N. J. Bucknell | N. J. Bucknell | Ian Lewington |
| Stonechat | G. Webb | R. Righelato | David Thelwell |
| Wheatear | P. E. Standley | R. Reedman | David Thelwell |
| Wheatear (Greenland) | — | — | David Thelwell |
| Dunnock | I. L. G. Weston | C. R. Wilson | David Thelwell |
| House Sparrow | J. J. Walling | N. J. Bucknell | David Thelwell |
| Tree Sparrow | J. J. Walling | R. Righelato | David Thelwell |
| Yellow Wagtail | I. C. Bell | N. J. Bucknell | David Thelwell |
| Grey Wagtail | I. C. Bell | N. J. Bucknell | David Thelwell |
| Pied Wagtail | I. C. Bell | C. R. Wilson | David Thelwell |
| Richard's Pipit | P. E. Standley | C. R. Wilson | Simon Gillings |
| Tawny Pipit | RE. Standley | N. J. Bucknell | Simon Gillings |
| Olive-backed Pipit | P. E. Standley | *not amended* | Simon Gillings |
| Tree Pipit | I. C. Bell | B. D. Clews | Simon Gillings |
| Meadow Pipit | I. C. Bell | B. D. Clews | Simon Gillings |
| Red-throated Pipit | P. E. Standley | N. J. Bucknell | Simon Gillings |
| Rock Pipit | P. E. Standley | R. Murfitt | Simon Gillings |
| Water Pipit | P. E. Standley | R. Murfitt | Simon Gillings |
| Buff-bellied Pipit | — | N. J. Bucknell | David Thelwell |
| Chaffinch | R. J. Godden | N. J. Bucknell | David Thelwell |
| Brambling | P. E. Standley | N. J. Bucknell | David Thelwell |
| Greenfinch | R. J. Godden | N. J. Bucknell | David Thelwell |
| Serin | I. L. G. Weston | N. J. Bucknell | David Thelwell |
| Goldfinch | R. J. Godden | N. J. Bucknell | David Thelwell |
| Siskin | P. E. Standley | N. J. Bucknell | Ernest Leahy |
| Linnet | J. J. Walling | N. J. Bucknell | Ernest Leahy |
| Twite | P. E. Standley | N. J. Bucknell | Ernest Leahy |
| Lesser Redpoll | P. E. Standley | N. J. Bucknell | Ernest Leahy |
| Common Redpoll | — | N. J. Bucknell | Ernest Leahy |
| Two-barred Crossbill | P. E. Standley | N. J. Bucknell | Ernest Leahy |
| Crossbill | P. E. Standley | J. Baker | Ernest Leahy |
| Parrot Crossbill | P. E. Standley | R. Righelato | Ernest Leahy |

| Species | Original author | Reviser | Artist for 2nd Edition |
|---|---|---|---|
| Common Rosefinch | — | N. J. Bucknell | David Thelwell |
| Pine Grosbeak | P. E. Standley | *not amended* | Ernest Leahy |
| Bullfinch | J. J. Walling | N. J. Bucknell | David Thelwell |
| Hawfinch | P. E. Standley | N. J. Bucknell | David Thelwell |
| Snow Bunting | P. E. Standley | N. J. Bucknell | David Thelwell |
| Lapland Bunting | P. E. Standley | N. J. Bucknell | David Thelwell |
| Yellowhammer | J. J. Walling | N. J. Bucknell | David Thelwell |
| Cirl Bunting | P. E. Standley | N. J. Bucknell | David Thelwell |
| Ortolan Bunting | P. E. Standley | N. J. Bucknell | David Thelwell |
| Little Bunting | P. E. Standley | N. J. Bucknell | David Thelwell |
| Reed Bunting | J. J. Walling | N. J. Bucknell | David Thelwell |
| Corn Bunting | I. D. Collins | N. J. Bucknell | David Thelwell |

Walford of the Berksbirds website gave permission for the Berkshire List, as published on that site, to be used as the basis for Appendix V, and Ken Moore gave assistance in producing the final version.

In addition, we are grateful to the photographers who have made available the images of some key species, or which have been used in the final design and layout of the book, including the illustrations of habitats and sites in Chapters 3 and 5, and whose names appear by their pictures. In addition thanks are due to Novotel Reading Centre and Mesrihel Dell'ovo for their assistance in obtaining the photographs of Reading town centre.

The BBAG committee once again approached Rob Still to design the book and oversee its final production. Since his work on the first edition, Rob and Andy Swash have gained much praise for the attractive **WILD***Guides* series of specialist field guides and associated publications that they have produced. Since production of the first edition in 1996 there have been considerable advances in electronic design and publication, and once again Rob has brought vision and flair to the process to produce an attractive full colour publication.

We are also grateful to our families for their support during the process of organising and undertaking the fieldwork, attending committee meetings and presentations to local clubs and groups promoting the project and writing up this book. Both the Berkshire Ornithological Club and the Newbury District Ornithological Club have also provided valuable assistance, by promoting the project and assisting in fund raising.

Finally, we must thank the sponsors. Funds for the first edition were raised entirely during the last year of production, and it is largely thanks to the generosity of the Environment Agency (who provided almost half the sponsorship) and a number of commercial sponsors that it was produced as a private publication, and eventually a surplus produced which has funded a number of local conservation projects. It was decided at an early stage of the second atlas project to use it as a focus for fundraising, and to produce this publication to raise further funds. It was fortunate that an early start was made, as the period during which most of the fieldwork for the project and subsequent production of this book has coincided with a prolonged period of economic stress. Particular credit is due to Brian Clews for his efforts in approaching and following up prospective sponsors, and for administering the "sponsor a species" scheme under which members of the public have provided donations as sponsors of the species accounts in this book. Each sponsor is acknowledged in the relevant account, and we are grateful to them for their support. We are also grateful to Mary Jacobs for her advice at the outset of the fundraising campaign. We are particularly grateful to Eton College, Syngenta, West Berkshire Council, the Earley Charity and the John Spedan Lewis Foundation for their substantial contributions and to the other sponsors who have contributed, who are listed on page 8.

## The Birds of Berkshire Website

One of the decisions the BBAG had to make early in the planning of the project was the form in which the results were to be published. One of the important factors that resulted in the decision to publish a book was that it would be something tangible that could be sold to raise money, but it was recognised that there are limits to what can be done with a traditional paper publication. As a supplement to this book, BBAG is establishing a website which will contain electronic versions of the atlas and habitat maps and some of the underlying data. The website will enable users of this book to compare the distribution of different species, and also the distribution of a species with habitat distribution, as well as to gain access to some of the underlying statistics which would be difficult to publish in full in this book.

## www.berkshirebirdatlas.org.uk

# A history of bird recording in Berkshire

## Introduction

The history of recording birds in Berkshire, covering a period of some two hundred years, reflects the wider pattern for Britain. Until the end of the 19th century, much of the emphasis was on the procurement of rare and unusual specimens for mounting and display in collections. It was not until the start of the 20th century, with improved optical equipment, the first attempts at bird ringing, and the implementation of legislation for the protection of birds, that the emphasis changed to one of systematic study and recording. More recently, there is a suggestion that things have swung full-circle, and the early enthusiasm with which the unusual was pursued in order to shoot it has been replaced with the equally enthusiastic pursuit of the unusual in order to list it. However, the growing popularity of organised surveys has resulted in much amateur effort producing a wealth of information from which trends in bird populations can be effectively monitored.

For the purpose of this review, the development of bird recording in Berkshire is considered under five main headings, with the 18th and 19th Centuries dealt with individually, and then the present century subdivided into three periods, each of which represents a distinct era in the development of ornithology in the county.

## The 18th Century – the first records

The earliest surviving attempt to produce a complete list of the birds of Berkshire dates from the end of the 18th century. This is a paper by Dr Charles Lamb of Newbury entitled *Ornithologia Bercheria*, which was written in 1814. It is based upon his observations and recollections of the period from about 1790. In his account, a respectable 160 species, excluding escapees, can be identified, which appear to have occurred within present county boundaries. Identification problems make it necessary to exclude from his list Golden Eagle, the records for which may well refer to immature White-tailed Eagle, and Montagu's Harrier, which was not separately identified from Hen Harrier until 1802 (Lamb's record dated from 1790). There is inevitably some bias in the records towards west Berkshire and the Newbury area, but Lamb's account provides an interesting insight into the diversity of species to be met with in the county two centuries ago. Unlike more recent systematic lists, there is an underlying thread of anatomical detail. This results from Lamb's obvious interest in the postmortem examination of specimens brought to him for mounting and inclusion in what must have been a large personal collection of locally obtained birds. His account contains many interesting observations, such as a stranded Little Auk diving for and catching minnows, "stomach contents five minnows", a Cuckoo found to be carrying two eggs "one in the ovarium, the other in the vagina", and information about the boom of the Bittern "from repeated dissections I found the male alone had the loose membrane on the internal side of the trachea, joined by a strong ligament, which passing into the lungs, authors conclude, can be filled with air and exploded at pleasure". Observations of a non-medical nature vary from the detailed, "Crossbills on arrival in July placing the sides of their bills against the sides of the leaves of a Cherry tree to sweep them clear of Aphids", to the enigmatic, "Woodlark: since the extravagant price of timber, rare".

Although the account was written in 1814 and apparently sent at the time to the Linnean Society for publication in their *Transactions*, the manuscript appears to have been lost or mislaid during the move of that Society from one premises to another. Its existence was referred to in Matthews' account of *The Birds of Oxfordshire and its Neighbourhood* which appeared in *The Zoologist* in 1849, but it was not until 1880 that a copy was obtained for publication, appearing in *The Zoologist* in August of that year. While there appears to have been an assumption in previous accounts of Berkshire's birds that delay in publication until 1880 prevented earlier access to Lamb's records, this is not in fact the case. The Rev F. O. Morris, author of *A History of British Birds* (1851–57), was well aware of Lamb's collection of mounted specimens, referring to several of Lamb's records in his own work. As Morris was residing in west Berkshire for some time around 1826 at the vicarage in East Garston, his awareness of Lamb's records, if not of his paper, is not surprising.

## The 19th Century – the era of lists and county avifaunas

### Accounts of downland birds and of the birds of the Henley area

A Victorian obsession with listing produced a succession of county avifaunas from about 1850. These included *Ornithological Rambles in Sussex* by Knox in 1849, *Birds of Somersetshire* by Crotch in 1851 and *Birds of Middlesex* by Harting in 1866, and these were accompanied by a number of local lists of species from particular localities within counties. For Berkshire, the first published reference to the birds of a local area, albeit brief, appears in the *The History of the Hundred of Compton*, written by W. Hewett Jr in 1844. Four species of "rare occurrence" are mentioned, including Dotterel, and nine as "commonly to be found" in the Compton area, including Stone Curlew, Nightjar, [Red] Kite and Hen Harrier. A much more comprehensive account of the birds of the Downs, however, is provided by the notes made by the author's father, Dr W. Hewett, who lived for some 35 years at East Ilsley and was a keen observer of the wildlife of the area.

By good fortune, many of Dr Hewett's observations survived as annotations in his personal copy of Knapp's *Journal of a Naturalist* and were reproduced, as written, in the *Transactions of the Newbury District Field Club* for 1895 to 1911. His notes were made around 1861 and provide a glimpse of the wealth of bird life which then existed on the Downs around East Ilsley. Most evocative is his calendar of the local birds observed each month throughout the year. Describing May he writes: "The Downs and gorse etc. are now all alive with birds. Linnets build in great numbers, as do Wheatears, Peewits, Red-backed Shrikes, Quails, Corncrakes, Corn Buntings, Skylarks, Meadow Pipits and some Stone Curlews. Dotterels leave after resting about a fortnight. There are a few pair of Nightingales and many Stonechats. This might be called the sitting month".

His autumn notes also reveal an equally rich density of birds and contain references to parties of 40–60 Stone Curlews and of up to 60 Dotterel, and by November to immense flocks of Skylarks and "large wings" of Golden Plovers. He also mentions the considerable commercial exploitation of this richness, with thousands of Skylarks being caught yearly and sent to London and other cities. Slightly more than 50 species are referred to, including a number that Hewett had observed in other parts of the county. His passing reference to the passage in April of "stints (small sandpipers)" is a good 60 years before the first official county record of Little Stint at Reading Sewage Farm in 1922. His earliest recollection, and the most remarkable, concerns the bitter winter of 1814 when "the Thames was frozen over, there was a fair on the ice at London Bridge, and the frost did not break up till April, with deep snow". He notes that, in that spring, the Fieldfares remained for longer in the local woodland and he found many of their nests in young fir trees before they left, although he did not see an egg.

A few years later, in 1867, Charles E. Stubbs wrote a paper entitled *A Slight Sketch on the Ornithology of Henley-on-Thames*, where he had lived for many years. Information about this work has been difficult to obtain, but there is a reference to it in an account by O. V. Aplin of the birds of Oxfordshire which appeared in *The Zoologist* in 1903. This reveals that Stubbs had formed an extensive collection of the eggs of British birds and that he had catalogued these in a carefully prepared

"Egg Book", in which he also sketched the history of the different species, with particular reference to their status in the Henley area. His *Slight Sketch* was inserted at the end of the Egg Book and was apparently written just after the winter of 1867/68. After his death in 1872, his Egg Book passed into the possession of Heatley Noble, who drew upon its content for his own work published in 1906 (see below). Stubbs includes a number of records from the Berkshire side of the Thames in his paper, providing information on the status of several species, including the first county reference to Dartford Warbler, which he had observed near Maidenhead.

### The first county avifauna

The first comprehensive account of the birds of Berkshire, written and published as a county avifauna, appeared in 1868, an early date for such a work. Covering two counties, *The Birds of Berkshire and Buckinghamshire* by Alexander W. M. Clark Kennedy was a remarkable book in two respects. It was written by Clark Kennedy while he was still only 16 years old and a schoolboy at Eton, and it was illustrated by hand coloured photographs, apparently the first natural history book anywhere to be illustrated in this manner. This medium was still relatively new for book illustration and required the preparation of individual prints, to which colouring had to be added by hand before being pasted into each copy of the book. As cameras at that time were not able to take photographs involving movement (and were not able to do so for about another twenty years), the four illustrations, of Long-eared Owl, Royston [Hooded] Crow, Black Tern and Hoopoe are of mounted specimens.

It is clear from several of the species accounts that Clark Kennedy was well-acquainted with local taxidermists and it is likely his attendance at Eton helped considerably in making contact with a number of ornithologists and notable collectors of mounted specimens, from whose collections, recollections and writings he draws much information. These include extracts from *Birds of Great Britain* by Gould and *The History of British Birds* by Morris. He was, however, unaware both of Lamb's ornithological records (the only examples of which had appeared via the work by Morris) and of the paper by Stubbs, whilst Hewett's notes on the Compton district had still to be published. With Clark Kennedy's book covering two counties, Eton then being in Buckinghamshire, general comments about the status of some species have to be treated with reservation where it is not clear to what extent the species occurred within the current boundaries of Berkshire. There is also a bias towards records from the east of the county, which were best known and most easily accessible to the author.

In this respect his work helps to complement the earlier paper by Lamb. For the scarcer species there is also a bias towards the period from about 1860, for which the records of birds passing through the hands of local taxidermists were most readily available.

A total of 225 species is listed as occurring in the two counties. After excluding those which appear only to have occurred outside present county boundaries *e.g.* Scops Owl and Bee-eater, those which were at that time escapees *e.g.* Black Swan, Virginian Colin, Egyptian Goose, Canada Goose and Mandarin, and those about which some doubt properly exists *e.g.* Golden Eagle and Great Auk (!), his avifauna raises the county list by a further 35 species to 196. Clark Kennedy's earliest record, which if correct would be the earliest dated county record, is of a pair of Red-breasted Mergansers shot near Reading "as early as 1785", but these are presumably the birds which Lamb records as shot in 1795. The inclusion of Mandarin among escapees is of more significance than might appear today, as this was the first wild-living specimen to be shot in the British Isles (Lever, 1987).

### The Newbury District Field Club and accounts of the birds of the Newbury area

Shortly after Clark Kennedy's avifauna was published, the first county society to embrace ornithology was established. In January 1870 the Newbury District Field Club was founded in order to "combine the study of antiquity with that of natural history". The Society's first *Transactions* covered the years 1870 and 1871 and included an article entitled Notes on some of the rarer birds observed in the neighbourhood of Newbury by W. H. Herbert. In all, Herbert mentions 57 species, including three acceptable additions to the county list, namely Gannet, Rough-legged Buzzard and Pomarine Skua (the latter found in a taxidermist's shop where it had been sent to be made into a fan!). The *Transactions* of the Newbury District Field Club for 1872 to 1875 carry an update by Herbert of additional records of rare birds observed in the Newbury area, but none involved species new to the county.

A more comprehensive listing of the birds of the Newbury area was provided in 1886 by Dr M. H. C. Palmer who contributed four long articles on Birds of Newbury and District for the *Newbury Weekly News*, apparently an hitherto untried medium for the dissemination of local ornithological information. In these articles Palmer lists 157 species, but only extends the county list by one, Manx Shearwater, to bring it to 200. Although Palmer's articles are interesting for their inclusion of information on the arrival dates of spring migrants and for general observations on status (*e.g.* the Bullfinch is "a jolly sight too common for buds"), they are largely a catalogue of birds caught or shot in the area, either because of their rarity or some aberration of plumage. There are also several references to the practice at that time of attempting to keep alive in captivity some of the birds caught in the wild, even those with specialised food requirements. After six young Kingfishers were brought to him "which if released might have starved", he describes the problem of feeding them: "all the little urchins bringing minnows, numerous twopences to pay, every one's friends pestered and bothered for minnows and when my supply ran short the boy was sent to the Angling Association water bailiff for a supply". His three months supply of minnows cost him £3 and he ends his account "Moral - Don't try and keep Kingfishers".

While clearly possessing a considerable collection of stuffed specimens, on several occasions Dr Palmer expresses a concern for the protection of birds: "I have little doubt that I should not be willing to destroy the house [of the Chiffchaff] which must have cost the little architect such an endless amount of labour, also the anguish the robbing of its contents would cause the before happy little pair". Such sentiments were to receive national expression with the founding five years later of the Society for the Protection of Birds.

One other 19th century writer whose work includes a number of references to birds in Berkshire deserves mention. This is W. H. Hudson, whose *Birds in a Village*, 1893, updated in *Birds in Town and Village*, 1919, contains much descriptive material about the commoner birds then to be found in and around Cookham, as well as an account of the London bird-catchers sent there to hunt them (recently updated by Clews (2006)).

### The emergence of school Natural History Societies

This outline of bird recording in the 19th century would not be complete without mentioning the emergence of school societies and field clubs, which encouraged the study of natural history at an early age. At least three such societies produced accounts of their activities and observations, The Leighton Park School Natural History Society, The Wellington College Natural Science Society and Eton College Natural History Society. Whilst the Wellington College report for 1890 contains the first county record of Two-barred Crossbill, these accounts are most valuable for the fore-taste they provide of the emerging systematic observation and recording of birds by organised groups.

The manuscript *Curator's Reports* of the Leighton Park School NHS for 1895 records the then unusual occurrence of a winter influx of gulls to the Reading area. After one was seen in early February that year, "a rare bird in this neighbourhood", the report for March included the following observation: "I notice that Topp's window is full of Gulls just now, no doubt driven inland by the severe weather and shot as curiosities or whatever else those who killed them considered them as". Topp's was presumably the town taxidermist's shop and the entry hints at an early sensitivity towards the shooting of birds. The entry for June 1895 records the early use of artificial nest sites by Sand Martins, birds being observed "flying in the pipes of the bridge over Sonning Cutting".

The recording of natural history in the field was not without its problems however. An interesting insight into the impact that excursions into the field by members of these societies could have is provided by the following extract from a report by the Natural Science Society which appears in the Wellington College Year Book for 1906: "We record the death of the Field Club. Popularity killed it. Some 50 fellows, all professedly naturalists, let loose on any one's property had rather a deleterious effect, for they acted as a small tooth comb and nothing escaped them; and the land was as the garden of Eden before them, and behind them a desolate wilderness".

## A time for systematic study and recording – 1900 to 1945

### The Victoria County History
Previous records, apart from those in the notes by Dr W. Hewett which had still to be published, were conveniently amalgamated at the start of the 20th century by Heatley Noble, who provided the section on birds in the *Victoria County History of Berkshire* published in 1906. Noble's account, which was written in 1902 with an Appendix for records up to the end of 1905, goes well beyond the repetition of the records of Lamb, Herbert, Palmer, Stubbs and Clark Kennedy. He had corresponded widely with other county ornithologists and collectors and makes extensive use of their observations, examples including the first reported breeding of Dippers in 1891 and of Grey Wagtail in 1898. He also expanded his search of potential sources of additional records to include museum collections, relevant national periodicals of the time – *The Zoologist* and *The Field*, in which Berkshire records had occasionally appeared – and, for the first time, the reports of the Wellington College Natural Science Society.

To the records of others Noble adds his own notes and recollections from 30 years of bird study in the county, largely confined to the area between Reading and Maidenhead. His wide-ranging personal observations include finding the eggs of the Song Thrush on 14th February in the mild spring of 1894, use by Nuthatches of the same nest hole for 14 consecutive years, and

measurement of the incubation period of the Cuckoo (12 days 2 hours, as he proved by placing the egg in an incubator!). Numerically, his account added a further nine species to the county list, to bring it to 209 (excluding sub-species, escapees and uncertain records). Historically, it marked the end of the era of the somewhat erratic recording of birds (and the far from erratic shooting of them) and heralded a new era of more systematic recording and sympathetic study. This was given impetus by improvements in optical aids and legislation for the protection of birds. Ironically however, for the reviewer of records, the replacement of collected specimens by sight records can introduce uncertainty into the correct identification of scarce species, summed up in the well-known comment "what's hit is history, what's missed is mystery".

### The first national monthly bird journals
The publication from June 1907 of a national monthly magazine, *British Birds*, which was devoted solely to the study of birds, played a significant part in encouraging the more systematic approach to bird study and recording and, in due course, to a level of record adjudication. In June 1908 its editors proposed a plan for the systematic "marking" of birds with rings in order to determine their subsequent movements. Berkshire was represented from the start by Dr N.H. Joy of Bradfield, who had the second highest total of birds ringed in the scheme's first three full years of operation from 1910 to 1912. His decision to concentrate on the ringing of Starlings was to be well rewarded, particularly as he was able to ring such large numbers (no less than 1,696 between May 1910 and February 1912 within one mile of his house at Bradfield). In April 1912 a bird he had ringed on 31st January that year was found dead in Finland, 1,200 miles east-north-east. This was the first such British recovery over such a distance, and the first from Finland.

Berkshire also featured in a number of the sightings submitted for publication in British Birds in the period up to 1915, when the county was to have its own report. These included many reports of the successful breeding of Crossbills following the great invasion of 1909, as well as three new additions to the county list: Pintail and Little Owl in 1907 and Marsh Warbler in 1909.

In January 1909 a second national monthly magazine, *Wild Life*, appeared. Although not devoted specifically to birds, this magazine was to carry a number of ornithological articles, some of which contain information on the status in Berkshire for selected species (*e.g.* Redpoll).

## The start of annual County Bird Reports

The next major step towards the systematic recording of birds in Berkshire occurred with the establishment in 1921 of the Oxfordshire Ornithological Society (OOS) and with the decision of that Society to publish an annual bird report, covering not just Oxfordshire but also Berkshire and Buckinghamshire. The first report, which appeared in 1924 and was edited by the Rev F. C. R. Jourdain and Bernard W. Tucker, covered records for the years from 1915 to 1922. Although this and subsequent reports inevitably had a bias towards records from the Oxford area, the reports provide an important source of county records from 1915 to 1945, a period during which birdwatching remained largely an individual pursuit and the gathering together of observers' records was still only being done on a limited basis.

Although significant county sightings still continued to be submitted for inclusion in *British Birds*, the availability of a county report opened the way to the publication of far more detail about the number, variety and distribution of the county's birds together with information on the dates of arrival and departure of migrants, on the weather and on ringing recoveries.

By fortunate coincidence, publication of these regular annual reports coincided with the discovery by N. H. Joy in 1922 of the rich bird life of Reading Sewage Farm. As a result, we have considerable detail about the number and variety of species observed on the Farm's then 400 acres of irrigated old-style sewage beds including, in its year of discovery, the addition to the county list of Black-winged Stilt and four other wader species. In 1923 there were three more county additions from the Farm, including most notably the identification of a Water Pipit by H. G. Alexander at a time when this species had been rarely identified inland and was thought by many ornithologists inseparable in winter from Rock Pipit.

The debt we owe the small group of ornithologists responsible for founding the OOS is considerable. Their foresight led not only to formalised arrangements for the collection, adjudication and publication of county records on an annual basis, but also to the first coordinated surveys into the distribution of selected species, beginning in 1929 with a selection of eight species including Tree Sparrow, Redpoll and Corn Bunting.

## The 1930s: Increases in observer coverage and further accounts of local birds

Despite the annual publication of county reports, the level of observer coverage within Berkshire was initially extremely low. Until 1929, there were no more than three such observers listed among the 30 or so contributors to the county report, but following a drive in that year for wider coverage to improve the comprehensiveness of the annual surveys of selected species, a peak of 52 contributors was achieved in 1931, of which at least ten lived within present Berkshire boundaries. They included J. Duncan Wood, who in 1931 produced an account with F. R. Barlow of the *Birds of Leighton Park School Grounds and Neighbourhood*, and J. L. Hawkins, who in 1933 contributed an account of the *Birds in the Neighbourhood of Reading* for publication in the first *Proceedings* of the newly-established Reading and District Natural History Society. With an increase in contributors, the content of county reports was expanded to include a number of articles, important among which was *Bird Life at Reading Sewage Farm 1922–1932*, a comprehensive review by H. M. Wallis and J. D. Wood. There was also a series of articles on the results of the surveys of selected species. Among the less detailed accounts of birds in Berkshire to appear in print at this time were *Bird Haunts in Wild Britain* by R. N. Winnall and G. K. Yeates in 1932 and *Birds in an Eton Garden* by H. M. Bland in 1935. The former includes chapters on the birds of the Berkshire Downs (of interest for its references to breeding Wheatears and the flushing in June of a Short-eared Owl) and on the bird life of a Berkshire lake. Bland's book contains recollections of bird life in an Eton College master's garden from about 1908, the garden checklist (of 50 species) including Wryneck, Reed Warbler, Hawfinch and, at times of flood, Little Grebe!

The Reading and District Natural History Society (RDNHS) was to follow the much older Newbury District Field Club (NDFC), founded in 1870, in having an ornithological section. Indeed the RDNHS created a post of recorder of ornithology responsible for presenting an annual ornithological report. Both the *Proceedings of the RDNHS* and the *Transactions of the NDFC*, in which bird records had appeared from time to time, provide a further source of information on the local status of many species in the period up to 1945.

There were some observers, who were part of this expansion in the recording of local birds, whose records were to span a life-time. The County Report for 1935 contains the first published Berkshire record of Great Black-backed Gull provided by Basil Parsons, who contributed records for over 60 years to county reports. In all, from 1915 to 1945, a further 30 new species for Berkshire appeared in county reports. These included a much belated record for 1872 of a Spotted Eagle, and two introduced species (Canada Goose and Mandarin) which had begun to breed on a sufficiently large scale to merit addition to the list. By the end of 1945 the county list had reached 242 species.

Anticipating the wider horizons of the ornithologists of the second half of the 20th century, the era to 1945 was to end on an international note with the addition to the county list in 1944 of Pectoral Sandpiper, identified at Slough Sewage Farm by an American army sergeant who was birdwatching while "over here".

## Local bird clubs and improvements in recording – 1946 to 1973

The main features of this fourth phase in the development of bird recording in Berkshire were the formation of local societies dedicated solely to ornithology, and the publication of the second avifauna for the county.

### The Reading Ornithological Club
### (now Berkshire Ornithological Club)

The first local society to be established solely to promote organised ornithological field work and to systematically collect bird records for its area was the Reading Ornithological Club (ROC). Following a successful public meeting in November 1946, at which over 40 people signed a paper indicating their interest in forming an ornithological society, a committee was formed which agreed in January 1947 to form the ROC. The inaugural meeting took place the following month, under the chairmanship of J. Duncan Wood.

The ROC recorder, a post first filled jointly by C. C. Balch and C. E. Douglas, effectively subsumed, and considerably extended the activities of the bird recorder of the RDNHS. From 1947, records from the ROC's main recording area, a radius of five miles from the centre of Reading, were published in detail in the ROC annual reports, together with the more interesting records from a wider area of Berkshire and south Oxfordshire. To provide a baseline, the ROC published a *Provisional List of the Birds of the Reading Area* in 1951, compiled by Clive Balch from records prior to 1947. A total of 197 species are listed. The Club continued to publish annual reports until the county boundary changes in April 1974 and to maintain a comprehensive card index of all the records of its members, not just of those that appeared in its annual reports.

As mentioned below, the ROC took on responsibility for publishing the Berkshire county report from 1974. It continues to provide a programme of talks during the autumn and winter period, mostly held at the University of Reading. In 2007, in recognition of the lack of any bird club serving the east of Berkshire and the desirability of extending its appeal beyond the central part of Berkshire, the club changed its name to the Berkshire Ornithological Club (BOC).

### The Middle-Thames Natural History Society

Also in 1947, the Slough Natural History Society was founded, producing annual reports from that year under the title of *The Middle-Thames Naturalist*. Following a decision to widen its area, from five miles around Slough to all of Berkshire east of the River Loddon together with Buckinghamshire south of the Lower Icknield Way, the Society renamed itself the Middle-Thames Natural History Society (MTNHS) and established a separate Bird Section. A. C. Fraser was appointed as the first recorder and comprehensive bird reports appeared in *The Middle-Thames Naturalist*, until the demise of the Society in 1983. From 1953 these reports covered the whole of Buckinghamshire, as the county was no longer covered by the OOS reports.

The MTNHS actively encouraged the local study of birds, established a ringing group and pressed the Local Authority to have Slough and Ham Sewage Farms made into reserves. In 1954, the Society published an annotated checklist, *The Birds of the Middle-Thames* by A. C. Fraser, which was updated in 1967. An extended edition under the new title *The Birds of Buckinghamshire and East Berkshire* compiled by A .C. Fraser and R. E. Youngman (Bird Recorder for both the MTNHS and Buckinghamshire), appeared in 1976.

### The Newbury District Ornithological Club

In west Berkshire, occasional ornithological records had continued to appear in the Transactions of the Newbury District Field Club until 1939, when it appears that the Ornithological Section briefly lapsed before being subsequently reformed in 1949. Its revival was marked in 1950 by the "communication to the Club" of *A History of the Birds of the Newbury District* by Denis Summers-Smith, which appeared in the *Transactions* of the Field Club for that year (the "Newbury district" being a region of approximately ten miles around the town). This comprehensive account drew upon the earlier records of Hewett, Herbert, Palmer and Noble, as well as on those of the Club and less obvious sources, such as *The Newbury Weekly News*. A total of 189 species were recorded of which 68 had been observed on fewer than ten occasions (35 of these with no records since 1930). A further account by the same author covered the period from 1951 to 1953, with additions and corrections to the earlier list and mentions the new habitat of gravel workings created at Aldermaston (Summers-Smith, 1954). Annual reports were produced from 1950.

At the end of 1958 the Ornithological Section of the Field Club was disbanded following the founding, in January 1959, of the Newbury District Ornithological Club (NDOC) devoted solely to the recording and study of birds. To mark this change, L. R. Lewis produced a final account on the birds of the district for the Field Club, covering the period from 1954 to 1958.

The NDOC adopted the same recording area, ten miles radius from Newbury, which included parts of north Hampshire as well as downland to the north of Newbury that now lies in Oxfordshire. The club produced annual reports from 1958 to 1963 (those for 1960 and 1961 appearing independently of the Club) followed by quarterly reviews from 1964 to 1969. Annual reports recommenced from 1970 and are still published by the Club. Ian Weston was the NDOC recorder and report editor continuously from 1963 until 2012.

An important development in 1967 was the formation of the Newbury Ringing Group, which has consistently ringed birds in the Thatcham area and more recently also in the Hungerford area, providing detailed information on the breeding populations of such species as Reed and Sedge Warbler and, in the process, adding Savi's Warbler to the county list in 1968. A remarkable total of over 142,000 birds of 105 species were ringed by the Group in the 27 years to 1993.

Additional information on the birds of the area can be found in a number of *Bird Bulletins* dealing with the status of local birds and published by the Borough Museum, Newbury, in the 1960s, as well as in detailed accounts of the birds and plants of Freeman's Marsh (1970–1979) and of Hungerford Common (1980–1984) by Richard Frankum.

### A first checklist for the county and a second avifauna
In 1952 the OOS published *An Annotated List of the Birds of Berkshire* by W. B. Alexander. The 241 species listed include five subsequently "lost" to Oxfordshire and excludes several later to be gained from Buckinghamshire as a result of boundary changes. The list is notable for containing a considerable amount of information on the recovery of ringed birds.

In 1966 the county's second avifauna was published. Written by Dr Mary Radford of the OOS, it covered the birds of both Berkshire and Oxfordshire, and the author was able to capitalise on the increased level of observer cover already existing by the early 1960s. Radford examined the bird life of the two counties and the changes that had taken place over the preceding century. There are informative essays by E. L. Jones on the Lambourn Downs, by L. R. Lewis on the Kennet Valley and its birds, and by R. South on Windsor Great Park and its neighbourhood. For the Berkshire element of the systematic list, records from 1915 were drawn largely from county reports, which meant that for the 1950s and 1960s some records appearing only in the reports of the ROC, NDOC and MTNHS were omitted.

## The popularisation of birdwatching – 1974 to the present

### The first annual bird reports devoted solely to Berkshire records
Although the most interesting records from the ROC, NDOC and MTNHS had continued to find their way into the annual county reports, it was becoming clear by the 1960s that not all the important records in any year were certain to reach the OOS. To ensure better coverage it was agreed in 1966 that the county report should be jointly edited by the OOS and ROC recorders. This effectively established county recorders for Oxfordshire and Berkshire and, in that latter capacity, P. E. Standley helped to edit the two-county reports from 1966 until 1973, liaising with the NDOC and MTNHS recorders to do so.

Following the revision of county boundaries in 1974, the OOS decided to restrict its annual report only to records from Oxfordshire and from 1974 the ROC undertook to sponsor and publish an annual bird report, the *Birds of Berkshire*, devoted solely to county records. The ROC ceased then to produce its own annual report, although the NDOC and the MTNHS continued with theirs. The editor of the county report from 1974 has had the advantage of being able to draw directly upon the records of the ROC, the NDOC and, until 1983, of the MTNHS, as well as upon those appearing in the reports of the London Natural History Society, for the Wraysbury area, and in the Hants and Surrey Borders Bird Reports, for the Sandhurst/Eversley area.

From 1986, the gap left by the demise of the MTNHS was more than filled by a comprehensive monthly bulletin, *The East Berks Bird Bulletin*, edited by Brian Clews. This in due course became a county-wide publication, and is still published and distributed electronically. The annual county bird reports include records from this source, as well as from the monthly reports of the Runnymede Ringing Group (active in east Berkshire), from the bird reports published by the Theale Area Bird Conservation Group and Dinton Pastures Country Park, from organised surveys such as the winter wildfowl counts, and directly from observers who are not members of any society. This greater diversity in the sources of records significantly increased the volume of information available at the county level. Contributors to annual county bird reports reached about 130 by the mid-1990s, a far cry from the peak of around ten contributors in the 1930s.

The advent of the internet opened up a new method of receiving and publishing records. Many local groups and individuals started local birdwatching websites, and in Berkshire Marek Walford, a web developer, set up the

Berksbirds website (www.berksbirds.co.uk) in 2000. It provides up to the minute information on sightings submitted over the web and other bird related material on an attractively designed and easy to use site.

## Participation in national and local surveys, and the pursuit of rarities

The increased interest in birdwatching which has occurred since the 1960s has not only produced many more records, but has provided volunteers willing to participate in active fieldwork. In particular, they have been able to participate in national surveys organised by the British Trust for Ornithology (BTO), both of selected breeding species, such as Nightjar, regular annual surveys and counts such as the Wetland Bird Survey (WeBS) counts, and national ringing and nest recording schemes. The BTO organised a national atlas survey of all breeding birds in the summers of 1968–72 and again from 1988–91, and of all wintering birds in the winters of 1981/82 to 1983/84. In the summers of 1987 to 1989 the first Tetrad Survey of the county's breeding birds was carried out, and a repeat of this survey combined with county-wide timed counts in both breeding seasons and winter was undertaken between November 2007 and August 2011 as described in Chapter 4. The first county atlas survey was organised by the Berkshire Atlas Group and provided much new information on the distribution of species within the county, and the second by the Birds of Berkshire Atlas Group. These surveys have shown how the distribution of breeding species has changed in the intervening 20 years, and the Timed Tetrad Surveys provide a new benchmark against which numbers can be assessed in future years.

The need for as much carefully collected data to be gathered to monitor trends in bird populations at a regional as well as a national scale, has resulted in the development by the BTO of the Breeding Bird Survey (BBS) to replace the Common Bird Survey (CBC) which had been running since the early 1960s. The BBS was introduced in 1995, and by reducing the number of visits required each breeding season from at least eight to two was intended to increase participation considerably. At first take up in Berkshire was slow. Chris Robinson, who was then the BTO regional representative for Berkshire, brought together a group of interested members of the birdwatching community in the county who organised a simplified version of the BBS survey in 2000. Take up of the survey was strong, and despite the access problems caused by the outbreak of foot and mouth disease in farm livestock and restriction of access to the countryside the following year, it remained so. The decision was taken to merge the survey into

the full BTO BBS survey, so that by 2006 Berkshire was contributing over 100 BBS squares to the national survey, one of the highest levels of coverage in Britain. Originally an annual report on the survey locally (The Berkshire Bird Index) was published with the assistance of grants from the local authorities. However this lapsed during the years of the 2007–11 Atlas survey.

There are now (2013) three formal ringing groups in the county, the Newbury Ringing Group, the Berkshire Downs Ringing Group and the Runnymede Ringing Group whose area of activity overlaps the eastern part of Berkshire. Reading and Basingstoke Ringing is an informal group that covers the centre of the county and also runs a major Black-headed Gull colour-ringing project, and another group rings at Silwood Park and Ascot Heath.

Not only has the number of observers increased in recent years, but there has been a significant increase in their ability to identify, as well as to search for, uncommon or rare species. This is in no small way due to a combination of improved optical aids, better field guides, and the opportunity to travel widely abroad to gain experience of species which are otherwise only rare vagrants to this country. At the local level there is now more information available on the most productive sites to visit, following publication in 1987 of a guide on *Where to Watch Birds in Bedfordshire, Berkshire, Buckinghamshire, Hertfordshire and Oxfordshire*, the Berkshire section of which was written by Brian Clews. The latest edition of this book (now entitled *Where to Watch Birds in the Thames Valley and Chilterns*) was published in 2002. There is now also up-to-the-minute information on the local occurrence of scarce species through websites such as Berksbirds and through electronic pagers. Sponsored annual twenty-four hour bird races which have been held in May for many years have shown that skilled observers with good communications can now locate over one third of the species on the county list in just a day. The present 24-hour record stands at a very respectable 121 species and was set by Andy Swash, Steve Abbott, Neil Bucknell and Ian Collins on 12th May 1990 and equalled by Fraser Cottington, Adam Bassett and Andy Johnson on May 13th 2006.

This wider observer coverage, allied to higher levels of expertise, has led to some unexpected additions to the county list, and improved mobility and better communications between observers has often allowed many to share in these records. In Berkshire, these additions have included such exotic garden sightings as Olive-backed Pipit, Yellow-browed Warbler, Scarlet Rosefinch and Black-throated Thrush, while from gravel pits, reservoirs and sewage farms there have been records of Blue-winged Teal, Bonaparte's Gull, Red-rumped

Swallow, Short-toed Lark, Buff-bellied Pipit and Little Bunting. A graphic illustration of how popular the pursuit of rarities had become is provided by the Olive-backed Pipit in 1984 which, during its winter stay in and around a garden in Bracknell, attracted over 3,000 observers from all over the country.

In the 50 years from 1946 to 1995 there were 65 additions to the county list, if Snow Goose, Egyptian Goose, Ruddy Shelduck, Ruddy Duck, Golden Pheasant, Lady Amherst's Pheasant, Feral Pigeon and Ring-necked Parakeet are included. In addition, two introduced species which are not included on the British List have bred in Berkshire: Wood Duck and Chukar. The most additions in any one year was four, in 1975, 1976 and again in 1987. County checklists of species appeared in the county reports for 1974 and 1985 and a checklist for the NDOC area, by Debby Reynolds, in their 25th Anniversary Report for 1984. With these 65 additions, the county total had reached 307 when the first edition of this book was published in 1996. Since then 17 more species have been added. Eleven of these are species seen for the first time, which include three added to the list between December 2012 and May 2013 as the text of this second edition was being prepared for publication. The other six result from decisions by the taxonomic sub-committee of the BOU to upgrade six taxa previously regarded as races of other species to full species status.

### The adjudication of county records

Before new species are added to the county list they are subjected to a process of adjudication to assess their acceptability, a process which applies also to records of locally rare species. The Berkshire Records Committee (BRC) was established to consider the records for the 1990 annual report and originally comprised the county recorder (Peter Standley), Chris Heard, John Lucas and Andy Swash. The preparation of the first edition of this county avifauna provided an opportunity to reconsider, with the benefit of hindsight and improved identification criteria, county records of rare species. Where this resulted in doubts being exposed about the reliability of records this has been indicated in the species accounts in Chapter 5. As a consequence, Red-breasted Goose, Marsh Sandpiper and Chough have not been included in the County List of fully acceptable records. Currently (2013) the BRC comprises Chris Heard, Ken Moore and Derek Barker.

### Birdwatching with a purpose – supporting conservation and science

Since the 1950s bird recording has acquired a new and increasingly important purpose. Over this period there has been considerable loss of bird habitat in Berkshire, beginning with the ploughing up of downland in the early 1940s, followed by the adoption of more intensive farming practices, loss of habitat to residential, commercial and recreational development, and to infrastructure projects. There has been an increasing appreciation that changes in land use and management can have adverse effects on bird life. This has created a need for site-based bird records which indicate the ornithological importance of those areas either under threat from development, or in need of preservation and conservation. It has become important for county bird records to have increasing depth as well as width.

These factors reflect changes at a national and global level. Changes in agriculture are driven by national and international market forces and policy decisions. Our summer visiting breeding birds rely on different habitats overseas for survival in winter, and on migration and many have declined in recent decades. Equally our winter visitors' fortunes will be affected by habitat and climate change in their breeding sites and stop-over sites on migration routes. Nationally, the resource that thousands of willing volunteer birdwatchers represent has been harnessed with increasing effectiveness in recent decades. The Berkshire Atlas surveys, BBS squares, WeBS counts, ringing records and other contributions to national BTO surveys, provide much data for analysis to help identify the factors driving changes in bird populations.

The completion of the second Berkshire Bird Atlas survey marks a milestone in the capture and use of information on Berkshire's Birds. The increasing use of the internet and information technology has transformed the process. This is likely to continue to develop in the coming years, hopefully to provide assistance in the formulation of local planning and wildlife conservation policies, and the raw data from which some of the challenges facing birds can be analysed and addressed.

*P. E. Standley*
*(updated by N. J. Bucknell 2013)*

Looking north into Berkshire from
West Woodhay Down.
*Andy Tomczynski*

# CHAPTER 3

# The physical geography, habitats and climate of Berkshire

## Geology and topography

Berkshire is an entirely land-locked county which is roughly an elongated rectangle in shape, some 75 km (47 miles) east to west, but only between 12 km and 25 km (seven to 15 miles) north to south. It lies mostly in the Thames Basin, with only a small area in the far south-west of the county lying at the northern edge of the Hampshire Basin. Figure i shows a simplified geological map of Berkshire and Figure ii a topographical and drainage map.

The western and northernmost parts of Berkshire lie on the band of Cretaceous chalk that sweeps from north-east to south-west across England. The scarp slope of the main area, the Berkshire Downs, lies on the north-west side to the west of the Goring Gap, now largely falling just over the county boundary in Oxfordshire, following local government boundary changes in 1974. The highest hills in the Berkshire Downs are generally near the northern county boundary and are around 200 metres above mean sea level. The outskirts of Caversham run up into the Chilterns, and to the south-east, separated from the Chilterns by the Thames Valley, there are lower chalk hills from Sulham Hill running into west Reading, around Sonning and between Wargrave and Maidenhead. Here, the highest elevation is at Ashley Hill (144 metres). In the south-west, part of the northern scarp of the Hampshire Downs falls within Berkshire. This area includes Walbury Hill which, at 297 metres above sea level, is the highest chalk hill in England.

Much of this chalk downland has the typical rolling landscape characteristic of the Downs of southern England. The permeable chalk results in a general absence of surface streams and rivers, with only the rivers Pang and Lambourn running south off the Berkshire Downs. Dry valleys, thought to be the result of surface drainage in periglacial conditions, are typical. There are, however, considerable areas where Plateau

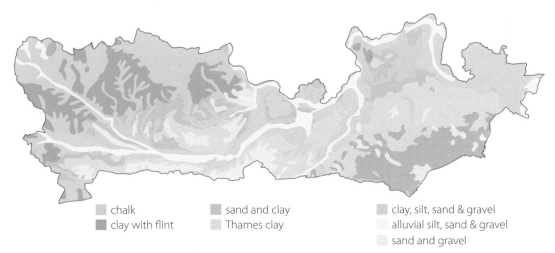

| | | |
|---|---|---|
| ▨ chalk | ▨ sand and clay | ▨ clay, silt, sand & gravel |
| ▨ clay with flint | ▨ Thames clay | ▨ alluvial silt, sand & gravel |
| | | ▨ sand and gravel |

**Figure i  A simplified geological map of Berkshire (Contains British Geological Survey materials © NERC, 2013).**

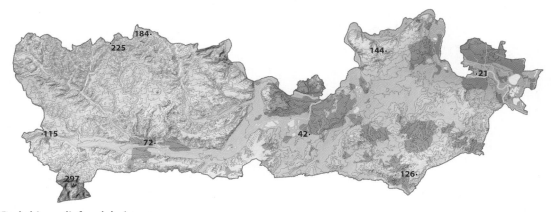

**Figure ii  Berkshire: relief and drainage.**

The chalk downland in the west is drained by the Kennet, Lambourn and Pang into the Thames. The Blackwater and Loddon drain the flatter, lower clay, and and gravel of the east of the county into the Thames. Spot heights in metres are shown for Walbury Hill (297m), Farnborough Down (225m), Ashley Hill (144m), Lower Star Post (126m) and sample points in the main river valleys.

Gravels or clay with flint overlie the chalk. This results in relatively flat, elevated areas, such as the area to the south of Aldworth and west of Ashampstead and the area to the west of Tilehurst through to Sulham.

The south and east of the county are dominated by Eocene deposits; Bagshot, Bracklesham and Reading Beds and London Clay. These series consist of a variety of clays, gravels and sands. To the west, these deposits are confined to the floor of the Kennet Valley but their extent from north to south generally increases from west to east. The landscape of these areas is generally flatter and low-lying, although to the south-east of Bracknell it rises to 120 metres above sea level near the Surrey border at Olddean Common. There are also some considerable areas of Plateau Gravels overlying the Eocene deposits, especially in the Mortimer and Burghfield areas.

The areas of Eocene deposits are drained by a number of the minor tributaries of the Thames, Kennet and Loddon. The Enborne runs south of and parallel to the Kennet along the southern boundary of the county from Ball Hill, west of Newbury, until it swings north at Brimpton to join the Kennet at Aldermaston. The Blackwater, which follows the county boundary from Sandhurst and then joins the Loddon at Swallowfield, is the largest tributary in the east.

The principal river valleys are a significant feature. The Thames once marked the northern boundary of the county, although following the 1974 boundary changes it is only the case from Streatley eastwards to the edge of urban Reading and east from Reading to Slough. Between Streatley and Reading, the Thames runs through the Goring Gap where the valley floor is no more than 0·5 km to 1 km wide. At Reading the valley widens out, where firstly the Kennet and then, at Wargrave, the Loddon join the main river. From Wargrave to Cookham, the Thames runs between the Chilterns and the chalk hills east from Wargrave to Winter Hill in a valley about 2 km wide, before broadening out past Maidenhead into the lower Thames plain.

The Kennet is the second largest river in Berkshire. It runs from west to east and its valley widens steadily, from less than 0·5 km where it passes into the county from Wiltshire to the west of Hungerford, to some 3 km shortly before it turns north to join the Thames at Reading. The Thames and Kennet Valleys are linked by a gap running north from Theale to Pangbourne, which narrows from 2·5 km to 1 km and includes the lower Pang Valley. The Loddon and Blackwater rivers run in valleys less marked than the Thames and Kennet, but their alluvial plains tend to be about 2 km to 2·5 km wide where they run through Berkshire. On the eastern boundary of the county, the Thames flood-plain is further augmented by that of the Colne Brook and River Colne. The main river valleys are characterised by deposits of alluvium, loam and Valley Gravel. The extensive gravel deposits of the middle and lower Kennet, the Blackwater, Lower Loddon, the Thames around Maidenhead and the lower Colne have been extensively exploited for construction aggregates.

Thurle Down and Streatley Warren.
*Andy Tomczynski*

## The principal habitats

In common with the rest of the British Isles, the landscapes and habitats in Berkshire are the result of many centuries of human influence. The landscape is highly fragmented, with most tetrads containing many types of habitat. Although the county is still predominantly agricultural, the built area, particularly in central and east Berkshire, continues to expand, farming is diminishing and areas managed for conservation are increasing.

Analysis of Berkshire's habitats has been greatly facilitated by the Thames Valley Environmental Records Centre's (TVERC) detailed mapping exercise, completed in 2008 and covering 80% of the land area, most of the remainder being built areas and gardens. Based on habitat surveys and aerial photography (carried out between 1999 and 2003), habitat areas greater than 0·25 hectares have been assigned to one of 45 categories. The habitat maps shown here are based on the TVERC mapping, which has generously been made available to us. The copyright for these data is held by the TVERC. For simplicity of display, the habitat categories have been aggregated as described in Appendix VI. An analysis of habitat types by tetrad can be found on the Birds of Berkshire website (www.berkshirebirdatlas.org.uk).

Some of the recent changes in land use and habitats and their impact on bird populations are discussed below in the context of the individual habitats.

### Farmland

Berkshire still has a considerable area devoted to agriculture: 65,580 hectares in 2010, representing 52% of the land area of the county. Although much of east and central Berkshire is now heavily and increasingly urbanised, the west of the county is still predominantly rural. The changes in agricultural practice and their impact on Britain's bird populations, particularly since the 1960s, have been well documented elsewhere (*e.g.* O'Connor and Shrubb (1986), Marchant *et al.*, (1990), Lack (1992) and Shrubb (2003)). In lowland England, there has been a tendency towards increased concentration of arable cultivation in the east of England, and of intensive livestock farming in the west. This has resulted in a reduction in the diversity of the farmed environment, which is increasingly seen as a factor contributing to the decline in farmland birds in addition to changing agricultural practice (Shrubb, 2003). Berkshire falls within the area of Britain which has seen an increasing concentration on arable farming since the Second World War, but the picture is far from simple.

Arable farming predominates in the downland areas to the west of the county and on the clay soils to the north of Bracknell, occurring less widely elsewhere (Figure iii). The area of arable land, which after the county boundary changes in 1974 was 51,000 hectares had fallen to about 35,000 hectares by 2010. The main crops are wheat, barley and increasingly, oilseed rape (Figure iv), but the

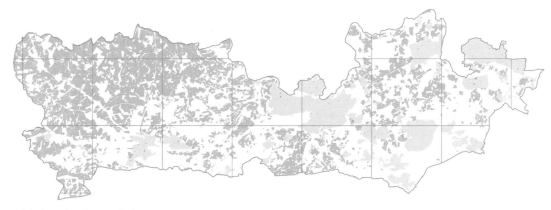

**Figure iii  Arable farmland in Berkshire.**
The area of land used for arable farming had fallen to 34,000 hectares by 2010, most of it in the west and north of the county.

cultivation of other crops including field beans, linseed. poppies for pharmaceutical use and fuel crops such as miscanthus has also increased.

The change from spring-sown to predominantly winter-sown cereals is likely to have had an effect on many of the commoner species, both through loss of suitable open breeding habitats (*e.g.* Lapwing, Skylark) and loss of winter stubbles (*e.g.* sparrows, finches and buntings). Some of the changes in arable cropping though seem to have had some beneficial effects on some species. The spread of oilseed rape and other alternative crops has apparently benefitted species which otherwise are in decline, and may account for an increase in the number of tetrads occupied by Yellow Wagtail, a species in serious decline nationally and formerly associated with damp pastures, which now breeds almost exclusively in arable crops in Berkshire, and the increase in the number of tetrads occupied by Linnets and Reed Buntings on the Downs. It is assumed that the different structure of these crops bring diversity to the arable landscape, mitigating, some of the effects of modern farming practices.

The area of farm grassland in the county, 24,000 hectares in 2010, has changed little since 1975. However most

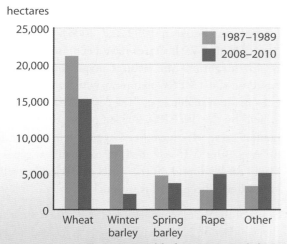

**Figure iv  Arable farming in Berkshire: area of cultivation of crops in hectares: averages 1987–89 and 2008–10.**

The total area of arable land fell from 41,000 to 35,000 hectares over the 21 year period. Cereal production fell and the areas of oilseed rape and other crops, such as linseed and biofuel grasses, grew. Defra farm statistics

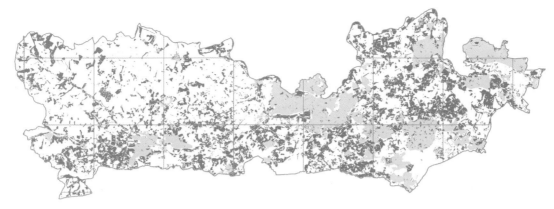

**Figure v  Berkshire: grassland.**

TVERC habitat data. The total area of grassland, which includes both farm and non-farm grassland, is approximately 32,000 hectares, over 95% of which is classed as improved.

has been agriculturally improved, a process which accelerated in the latter half of the 20th century with reseeding using commercial grass varieties and the use of artificial fertilizers and silage or hay-making occurring early in the season. These are conditions which are not conducive to biodiversity or the successful breeding of most ground-nesting birds. Some consider that its adverse ecological impact may have been greater than the changes to arable farming, as indicated by the dramatic decline of many traditional farmland birds in the western parts of the British Isles between the first and second BTO Atlas, the surveys for which were carried out in 1967–72 and 1988–91 respectively (Shrubb, 2003). Nonetheless, close grazing by sheep and cultivation and reseeding to grass in the spring can produce areas suitable for ground nesting species.

The number of mixed farms has declined, and livestock numbers have fallen substantially in recent decades (Figure vi), animal husbandry being increasingly focused in fewer, larger units. Dairy farming used to be a significant part of the agricultural scene in Berkshire, and in the early 20th century the fresh milk trade supplying London by rail was important.

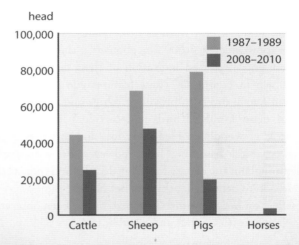

**Figure vi  Farm animals in Berkshire: averages 1987–89 and 2008–10.**

Despite decreases of 44%, 31% and 75% respectively in cattle, sheep and pigs, the area of farm grassland (24,000 ha in 2010) has changed little. The number of horses had increased to 3,395 in 2010 from 1,720 in 1975, the figure for 1987–89 is not available. Defra Farm Statistics.

Extensive fields of arable crops, such as at Cow Down, are an intrinsic part of the West Berkshire landscape.
*Andy Tomczynski*

The number of dairy farms has fallen dramatically, and if anything the decrease has accelerated since 2000. The number of dairy farms fell from 35 to 24 between 2005 and 2010 alone. The significant decline in pig numbers reflects the substantial change to the pig industry resulting from the outlawing of farrowing crates and the move away from indoor intensive production to more extensive outdoor pig rearing, and a return to the previous pattern of pig fields with pig huts, bringing some greater diversity to the rural landscape in the late 1990s and early 2000s (Shrubb, 2003). Muddy pig fields provide a feeding habitat favoured by crows and gulls, particularly in winter.

Farmland also contains patches of scrub, hedgerows and other linear features, such as tracks or shelter breaks. From aerial photographs, the total length of hedgerows and similar linear features in Berkshire was measured as approximately 1,600 km, about two thirds of which contained trees; an indication of their distribution is shown in Figure vii. These features add to the floral and faunal diversity, providing refuge and nesting sites for many farmland birds and corridors linking larger areas of woodland. Hedgerow loss and unsympathetic mechanical trimming have, however, been apparent throughout the county for many decades and there is no reason to believe that this has not had the same adverse effect on hedgerow breeding birds as has been observed elsewhere (O'Connor and Shrubb, 1986).

In winter, both downland and low-lying cultivated and grassland areas still provide feeding areas for flocks of Lapwings, crows, gulls, Woodpigeons, Starlings, thrushes, small numbers of Meadow Pipits and, in favoured areas, Golden Plover. However, large feeding flocks of seed-eating species are less frequently encountered.

Many farmers and estates in the county have encouraged the rearing of gamebirds, either for their own sport or for additional income from the letting of shooting. Pheasant and Red-legged Partridge are the main species involved. Chukars were present in the 1987–89 surveys, though their introduction was banned in 1992 and they have since died out. Gamebird-rearing may benefit some native species to some extent in encouraging the retention of areas of cover. However, control of predators, including the illegal persecution of birds of prey, is sometimes associated with game-keeping. In Berkshire there has not been much evidence of this being the problem that it has been in the north of England and parts of Scotland, and it has not prevented the spread of the Buzzard's breeding range or the re-establishment of the Red Kite in the county (*page 193*). It remains to be seen if it may affect other potential colonizers, such as Raven and Goshawk.

Although the Downs were amongst the earliest areas to be cultivated, as their light soils were easy to work before the development of farm implements (Fleure and Davies, 1951), for much of early modern history this was primarily an area of sheep-rearing. A combination of factors changed this situation in the first half of the 20th century. The blockades of both World Wars

Livestock farming has declined and is concentrated in fewer units, mostly in the west of the county.
*Cattle at Sulhamstead  Anya Still*

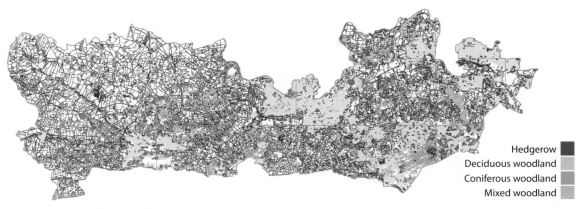

Hedgerow
Deciduous woodland
Coniferous woodland
Mixed woodland

**Figure vii  Approximate distribution of hedgerows.**

Field boundaries, 90% of which are hedgerows, are used here to indicate the relative densities of hedgerows across the county. Woodland is also shown: deciduous (green tint); mixed (brown tint); coniferous (turquoise tint).

brought a considerable area under the plough and the advent of artificial fertilisers and heavy machinery meant that it could be kept under cultivation thereafter. However the Downs still have a mosaic of different habitats, arising from the presence of the old broad droveways, the Ridgeway and the Fairmile and their verges, gallops for racehorse training and remaining sheep pasture. The Downs provide the remaining stronghold for some of the county's rarer breeding birds. Stone Curlews still breed in small numbers, and helped by co-operation between farmers and the conservation bodies their numbers have recovered modestly in recent decades (see *page 223*). Quail are still regular and Corn Buntings continue to breed, apparently in good numbers, though declining elsewhere, and the Downs provide a significant proportion of the range of many of the species traditionally associated with open farmland in Berkshire, such as Lapwing, Grey Partridge, Yellowhammer and Meadow Pipit. The Downs also support a small wintering population of scarcer predators of the open country – Hen Harrier, Short-eared Owl and occasional Merlin.

Berkshire has also experienced a loss of traditional farm buildings as these have been abandoned in favour of modern, more efficient buildings which tend to be less attractive to wildlife. As the number of farms has reduced due to consolidation into a smaller number of larger farms, even more recent farmyards have been abandoned, or reduced to temporary use. Redundant buildings are often demolished or converted into dwellings. Through the latter part of the twentieth century, this is believed to have contributed to the decline of at least one species in Berkshire, the Barn Owl, a decline that has been dramatically reversed by widespread installation of nest-boxes over the last twenty years (*page 314*). The reduction in farmsteads with traditional barns, which provided nesting niches and a food resource from both the insects associated with livestock and stored

grain, may partly explain the considerable reduction in some species previously considered successful exploiters of the man-made environment, such as House Sparrow and Starling, in rural Berkshire.

Between the two Berkshire Atlas surveys there was a major change in the regulation of agriculture in Britain, following a review of the EU's Common Agricultural Policy at the end of the 20th century. This resulted in a change in the previous emphasis on subsidies for production, to a subsidy system which included payments that were available for carrying out management aimed at increasing the wildlife quality of the farm. In 2003, this became the Environmental Stewardship scheme, with payments made for a number of prescribed management measures and different levels of participation, including a basic Entry Level, Organic and Higher Level Stewardship. Many measures are (understandably) not specifically targeted at birds, but currently (2013) they include Skylark plots, retaining stubble in winter and supplemental bird feeding, and hedgerow restoration and improvement. The farming industry has also responded to the prospect of greater government intervention by launching the Campaign for the Farmed Environment in 2009 to encourage participation in the scheme.

Notwithstanding some positive developments in the two decades between the two Berkshire Bird Atlas surveys in 1987–89 and 2007–11, it seems that the national trend of a continued decline in farmland birds disclosed by the national CBC and BBS surveys, albeit possibly at a slower rate since the 1990s, applies in Berkshire too. This is reflected in the decline in the number of tetrads occupied by breeding Lapwing, Skylark, Grey Partridge, Yellowhammer, Corn Bunting and Linnet. It should be borne in mind that this only shows a contraction in range, and the actual decline in numbers is likely to be greater.

Coniferous woodland at Padworth Common. *Anya Still*

Agricultural practice will continue to be a key factor in the health of our avian population. Some of the mistakes of the past have been corrected: the elimination of organochlorine pesticides in the 1960s and the subsequent recovery of bird of prey populations, set a precedent. However, a range of other pesticides and herbicides destroy key food resources (Newton, 2013) and higher agricultural commodity prices increase the pressures for intensive farming. The position is clearly complex, with a few species such as Woodpigeon flourishing, some such as Chaffinch remaining relatively constant in numbers but many still in decline. It is to be hoped that the range of Environmental Stewardship measures help reverse earlier damage, but there can be no guarantee that the current subsidy system will be permanent, or that other economic pressures may not result in a return to a system more focused on increasing production than encouraging biodiversity.

## Woodland, Scrub and Heathland

Woodland occurs widely in Berkshire, with almost all tetrads containing at least 25 hectares (Figure viii). The few exceptions are found either on the higher parts of the Downs or in urban Reading. Since the neolithic clearance of the deciduous forest that covered the south of England following the last Ice Age, the woodlands in what is now Berkshire have waxed and waned. Woodland areas tend to be neglected by birdwatchers, so the surveys for the atlases have provided a valuable opportunity to establish the distribution of a number of species, which may not have been fully reported in the annual county reports. Monitoring these species is especially important as many woodland specialists have declined in recent decades, particularly in southern England, for example: Woodcock, Lesser Spotted Woodpecker, Marsh Tit, Willow Tit, Wood Warbler and Hawfinch. Since the 1980s two of these, Hawfinch and Wood Warbler, appear to have been lost from Berkshire as breeding species.

Little of the woodland in Berkshire can be regarded as climax vegetation – the community that would have developed had there been no human intervention. However, a number of sites have been identified as "Ancient Woodland", *i.e.* woodland that has been in continuous existence since at least 1600 (Spencer and Kirby, 1992), including parts of Combe Wood, Snelsmore Common, Bowdown Wood, Bisham Wood and Windsor Forest.

Much of Berkshire's woodland comprises mixed broadleaf tree species, predominantly oak *Quercus* spp, Beech *Fagus sylvatica* and Ash *Fraxinus excelsior*, with Silver Birch *Betula pendula* on more acid soils. By the early 20th century, traditional woodland management had largely been abandoned. Coppicing, usually of hazel under oak, was commonly practiced from the Middle Ages until the 19th century, when a combination of factors, including the replacement of the forest products by cheap manufactured goods and coal as fuel, and the loss of labour from the countryside resulted in its decline and eventual abandonment by the early decades of the 20th century (Rackham, 2006). During the middle decades of the 20th century woodland management tended to consist of removal of native broadleaved trees and their replacement with plantations of introduced species of conifers. This is reflected in the widespread distribution of mixed woodland in the county (see Figure viii). In the 1980s it was realised that coppicing, although no longer commercially viable, created a good variety of micro-habitats for wildlife during the rotational cutting and regeneration that the regime involves. The canopy is opened on cutting, bringing to life a ground flora which is lost as the coppiced trees regrow, creating a shrub layer favoured by birds such as Nightingale, and then lost again as growth continues, but because a coppiced wood will usually have patches at various stages in a 15 to 30 year coppice cycle, suitable habitat should always be available. The Berkshire, Buckinghamshire and Oxfordshire Wildlife Trust (BBOWT) reinstated coppice management at its reserve at Moor Copse, near Tidmarsh, and has encouraged similar management elsewhere. The area under such management remains small, and more recently a new threat to woodland habitat has emerged, namely increased grazing by deer which has resulted in a loss of the field and shrub layers of vegetation, as the deer population in England has increased considerably since the 1970s (Fuller *et al.*, 2007). The lack of management and degradation by overgrazing may be a factor in, for example, the loss of Nightingales from many Berkshire woodlands (*page 418*).

There are a number of extensive areas of forestry on the Plateau Gravel areas, from Wickham Heath and Snelsmore Common in the west, through Fence Wood, Hermitage, Bucklebury Common and the Yattendon Estate in the Pang Valley and from Wasing Wood through to Burghfield Common along the southern county boundary. By far the largest area, of largely coniferous forest, runs west to east from Finchampstead Ridges to Ascot and north to south from Bracknell to Camberley. A considerable part of this area falls within the Crown Estate and much lies on areas of acid gravels. These coniferous areas support species such as Crossbill, Siskin and, in the more open areas, possibly Redpoll, which are largely absent as breeding species from the rest of the county. The Swinley Forest, south of Bracknell, is also the stronghold of the Redstart and of the Firecrest, which, whilst still scarce, has been expanding westwards

A deciduous bluebell wood at Warren Row *Andy Tomczynski*

in Berkshire. The edges of many of the coniferous plantations have been planted with broadleaved species which add to the diversity of bird species, especially if Silver Birch has been planted for shelter.

The forestry cycle makes an important contribution to the avian diversity of Berkshire. Mature woods tend to have a simple vegetation structure with fewer niches for birds, supporting fewer species and a lower density of birds than do managed woods (Fuller, 1982). A number of species that are not found in mature woodland, such as Nightjar, Woodlark, Tree Pipit, Willow Warbler, Yellowhammer and Whitethroat, breed in areas that have been cleared as part of a rotational management regime for coniferous forestry.

Windsor Great Park makes an important contribution to the diversity of woodland habitats in Berkshire. Only a small part is regularly open to the public, and this had long been known to birdwatchers as one of the 'reliable' sites for Hawfinches until the species disappeared in the 1990s. The mixture of native tree species and exotics make this area very attractive to most typical woodland species, and the trees and shrubs around the ornamental lake were amongst the first in the county colonized by the expanding populations of Mandarin and Ring-necked Parakeet.

Small areas of scrub are present in most tetrads, often associated with linear features such as roads, paths and railway lines (Figure viii). Scrub areas are ephemeral in the absence of management, growing on to woodland, but represent an important element in many of Berkshire's

habitats. As a bird habitat, it is similar to hedgerow and woodland edges, with species such as Bullfinch, Blackcap, Dunnock, Wren, Whitethroat and Lesser Whitethroat breeding. Hawthorn and other berries may provide a winter food resource for thrushes and it can offer roosting sites for thrushes and finches. Scrub areas on the edges of droveways and gallops on the Downs provide breeding habitat for Yellowhammers, Linnets, Whitethroats and Willow Warblers and winter roosts for Short-eared Owls. Scrub areas around mature gravel pits in the lower Kennet valley at Theale and Burghfield hold most of the county's remaining Nightingales. Scrub areas around derelict land south of Reading produced records of breeding Stonechat and Meadow Pipit in the first Berkshire Bird Atlas survey in 1987–89. These areas have since been grubbed out as the area has been redeveloped, and both species lost to this part of the county.

Scrub areas provide a challenge for conservation habitat management. Scrub invasion can lead to a loss of valuable dry grassland or heath habitat. The scrub areas around the Kennet valley gravel pits will mature into woodland if not managed, and this process could lead to the loss of Berkshire's Nightingales which are increasingly looking like an anomalous outlier in the UK range of the species as its range retreats.

Most of Berkshire's heath is on the sand and gravel along its southern border (Figure ix). The heaths along the south eastern boundary of the county lie within the Thames Basin Heaths Special Protection Area (SPA), most of which lie in Hampshire and Surrey.

Grazing and a rotational regime of cutting of heather and gorse maintains Greenham Common as open heathland that attracts Stonechat and Dartford Warbler and ground-nesting species such as Ringed and Little Ringed Plovers, Lapwing and Woodlark.

*Andy Tomczynski*

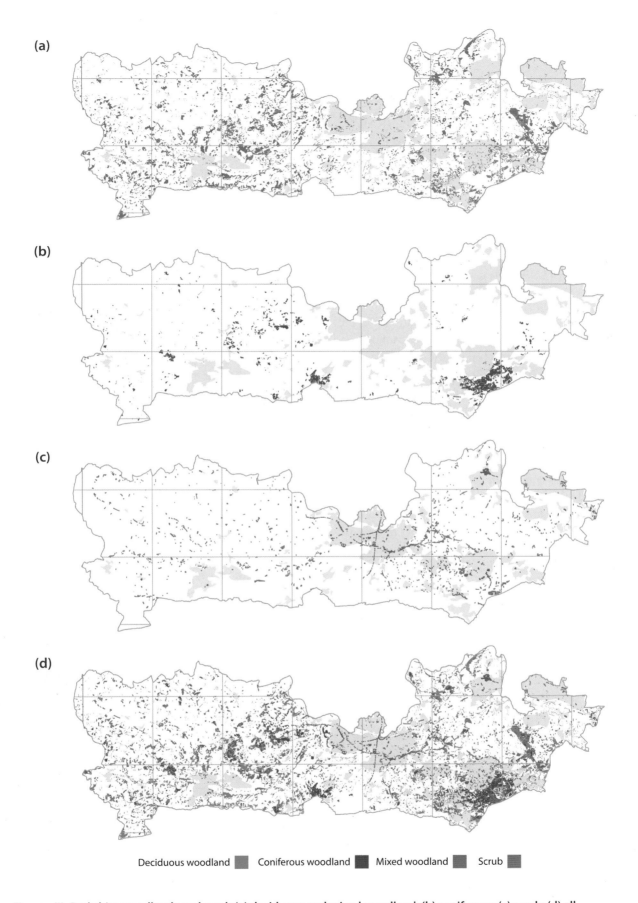

Deciduous woodland ■   Coniferous woodland ■   Mixed woodland ■   Scrub ■

**Figure viii  Berkshire woodlands and scrub (a) deciduous and mixed woodland; (b) coniferous; (c) scrub; (d) all.**

The total area of woodland and scrub in Berkshire is approximately 19,000 hectares, 57% deciduous, 17% coniferous and 18% mixed, with 8% scrub. With the exception of Windsor forest, Swinley forest and the Bucklebury, Hermitage, Yattendon area, most woodland is in fragments of less than 100 hectares. Scrub corridors can be seen following major roads, railways and pathways.

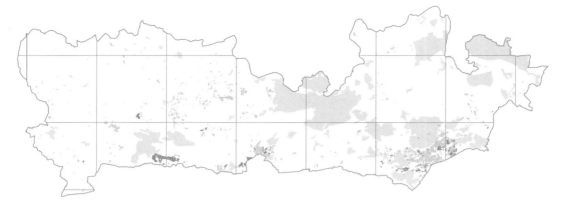

**Figure ix  Heathland. Berkshire's heathland (purple) is restricted to the south of the county.**

The Thames Basin Heath comprises Snelsmore, Greenham Common and the heaths along the Hampshire and Surrey borders. Much of the area has been planted with coniferous forest (green tint).

The lowland heaths of southern England have been recognised as a threatened but internationally important habitat. Lowland or maritime heath is confined to limited areas on the western fringes of Europe where the combination of poorly drained sand or gravel substrata and mild climate produces areas of heather, gorse and bracken, valley mires and impoverished soils overlying an impermeable layer of leached minerals which prevent water draining. These areas are important for Dartford Warblers, which have one of Europe's most restricted ranges, Nightjars and Woodlarks. In the past such areas were regarded as of little value, being agriculturally poor. As a result large areas have been lost to development and forestry, and the abandonment of traditional low level grazing threaten further loss through scrub encroachment. Fires, sometimes set maliciously, also are a threat to heathland birds. However such incidents can counteract scrub invasion.

The designation of the SPA in 2005 under the European Commission's Wild Bird's Directive followed a long process, and the formulation of planning measures to safeguard the SPA have proved controversial. While local naturalists supported funding for on-site management work as a condition of any planning permission for new housing in the designated zones around the SPA where development would be permitted, English Nature adopted a policy of obtaining payments to fund the acquisition of areas outside the SPA to provide alternative areas for recreation (SANGS, or Suitable Alternative Natural Greenspace) to mitigate the increased recreational pressure such development is likely to cause. Whether the public will use such areas in the absence of restrictions on access to the heaths remains to be seen. Within the SPA, BBOWT has a reserve at Wildmoor Heath near Sandhurst. The Ministry of Defence also controls areas from which the public is largely excluded at Wishmoor Bottom on the Surrey border and around Sandhurst, thereby helping safeguard these too.

Outside the SPA there are other heathland fragments, including the BBOWT reserve at Decoy Heath near Aldermaston and the Snelsmore Common Country Park north of Newbury. When the US Air Force left Greenham Common in 1997, the area was handed over to the Greenham Common Trust. Working in conjunction with West Berkshire Council, the old runways were removed, and the area was sown with heather. A management regime of rotational cutting of heather and gorse and grazing has been established to maintain the newly created heath, greatly enhancing the county's stock of this threatened habitat.

The heaths host a number of species rarely encountered elsewhere in Berkshire. Dartford Warblers, which first bred in Berkshire in 1991, now breed from Wishmoor Bottom in the east to Greenham Common in the west. Stonechat, Woodlark and Nightjar have expanded and now breed on most heaths and take advantage of the transient clear fell areas created in the forestry cycle. At Greenham Common open gravel areas have also been created, providing breeding sites for Ringed and Little Ringed Plover. However, the Tree Pipit, which also makes use of recently cleared areas, has, like many other trans-Saharan migrants, suffered a major decline in range and abundance, perhaps related to factors outside the breeding season.

### Rivers, streams, wetlands and water bodies

Although much of Berkshire lies in the river valleys of the Thames basin, the valleys have been extensively drained. Areas of open water have been created by the excavation of gravel, sand and clay, which has left numerous small lakes, and by the construction of a large reservoir. The importance to avian diversity of the open water and associated wetlands is clearly demonstrated by the species richness maps (Chapter 4, *page 56*), which show many more species to be present in the river valleys than in other areas.

The management of Berkshire's rivers for flood defence and the drainage of adjacent wet areas for agriculture has had an adverse effect on the bird life of these areas in the past. Ordnance Survey maps for the early part of the 20th century indicate that the low-lying land alongside the Thames was "liable to flooding". After the disastrous floods of the winter of 1946/47, river management works were undertaken which significantly reduced the risk of flooding to riverside areas. Field drainage has also long been a feature of agricultural land management. There are now few areas of marsh or fen vegetation left and those which do remain are often fragmented (Figure x).

Areas alongside the Loddon at Arborfield, Fobney Meadows to the south of Reading and other areas that flood during the winter can attract large flocks of wildfowl, gulls and Lapwing and smaller numbers of other waders. There are also areas of marsh or regularly waterlogged land in the Lambourn and Kennet Valleys in West Berkshire, and in exceptionally wet periods, such as the late autumn 2000 or the winter of 2013, when the water table is high, transient floods occur in the otherwise dry valleys of the Downs. However, these areas are now not sufficiently wet in summer to support the breeding species typical of wet meadows, such as Redshank and Snipe. Conversely, the chalk streams and associated marginal areas can dry out entirely leading to the temporary loss of wet habitats in the upper Lambourn and Pang valleys. This may explain the reduction in records of some of the other species typical of such habitat, such as Reed Bunting, Sedge Warbler and Grey Wagtail, from these areas in the 2007–11 Berkshire Tetrad Survey, which coincided with a prolonged period of below average rainfall in the county between 2009 and 2011.

The River Lambourn at Easton is a typical shallow chalkbed stream *Andy Tomczynski*

In recent decades there has been a growing appreciation of the value of the wet area which has been lost. When flood alleviation works in the Windsor to Maidenhead area were proposed in the 1990s, the design included the creation of new wetland areas for wildlife, the Dorney Wetlands. Another scheme, the Fobney Island Wetland Reserve has been created alongside the Kennet south of Reading as a result of cooperation between the Environment Agency, Thames Water, Reading Borough Council and the Thames Restoration Trust, with advice from the BOC, and was opened in 2013.

Of the waterways themselves, the largest, the River Thames, provides a breeding habitat for those waterbirds able to cope with the pressure from recreational activities. This pressure is greatest during the summer months, when motorboating, canoeing and rowing are at their peak and the towpaths are extensively used by walkers and anglers. Some light river traffic occurs throughout the year, however, and the upsurge in interest and participation in rowing means that winter waterborne traffic has increased since the 1980s. The wash from motorboats adds to the perils of waterbirds that nest in riverside vegetation or birds such as the Sand Martin, which nests in river banks. The additional hazard of anglers' lead weights, which at one time appeared to be threatening the Mute Swan, was eliminated by the ban in 1987 (*page 106*). Unsurprisingly, those species which have a close association with man, such as Mallard, Mute Swan and Canada Goose, seem to make good use of many of the areas used for recreation. Others, such as Great Crested Grebe, Coot and Heron appear to have adapted to the pressures and Mandarin, Egyptian Goose and Black Swan have begun to breed alongside the river.

Two species, Kingfisher and Grey Wagtail, are particularly closely associated with waterways and others, such as Moorhen, Coot, Mute Swan, Pied Wagtail, Sedge Warbler and Reed Bunting, occur most frequently along rivers and streams. Little Grebes, however, seem to avoid the busier waters and seldom breed on the Thames except on stretches with sheltered backwaters. Dredging and drainage improvement works have been carried out to many watercourses, particularly in the developed areas to the south and east of the county. In many cases this has led to the loss of riparian habitats and their associated bird species.

Of the marshland sites in the Kennet Valley one, Thatcham Marsh, is of particular importance. This site is one of the largest inland reedbeds in southern England yet its future has often seemed precarious. In the late 1970s, gravel extraction resulted in a lowering of the water table and the invasion of scrub, and the drought of 1989 to 1992 had a similar effect. It has, however, attracted a number of notable species, both as wintering visitors or breeding birds, including Bittern, Bearded Tit, Water Rail, Cetti's Warbler and Grasshopper Warbler. The site has now become a local nature reserve and a new visitors' centre was opened in 1995. Further west, Hungerford and Freeman's Marshes alongside the Kennet and Avon Canal, and the Dun, a tributary of the Kennet, west of Hungerford together provide another valuable site, part being managed as a reserve by BBOWT.

The spread of gravel extraction created a considerable range of new wetland habitats in the second half of the twentieth century and in Berkshire this is one wildlife habitat that is increasing in extent. The main concentrations of gravel pits are in the Kennet, Loddon,

As gravel extraction has been completed at Moor Green Lakes, Eversley, an extensive wetland area has been created.
*Jerry O'Brien*

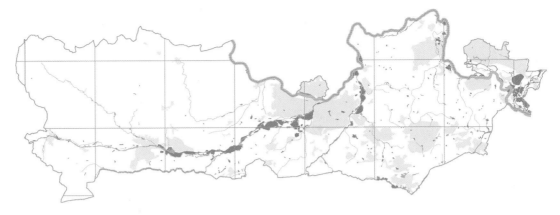

**Figure x  Rivers, water bodies and wetland.**

Although there are small ponds in most tetrads, larger water bodies are restricted to the gravel pits of the Kennet, Blackwater and Loddon valleys and Queen Mother Reservoir in the east. There are small amounts of marsh and reed-beds (orange), totalling only 350 hectares, along the rivers and on some old gravel workings.

Blackwater, and Lower Colne Valleys. In the Kennet Valley, there are extensive gravel workings from the east of Newbury to Thatcham, around Brimpton, Woolhampton and Beenham and in the Theale and Burghfield areas. The Loddon Valley contains the Woodley and Twyford Gravel Pits and the Blackwater Valley the Eversley and Yateley Gravel Pits which straddle the Hampshire county boundary. The Summerleaze and Bray Gravel Pits are in the Thames Valley either side of Maidenhead and the Wraysbury, Horton and Yeoveney Gravel Pits are in the lower Colne Valley.

In the past, many low-lying gravel workings, which had generally been kept dry by pumping, were simply left to flood following extraction. In the 1970s and 1980s, however, the demand for landfill tipping sites for household waste resulted in many being back-filled with refuse. Despite this, there is a considerable area of open water in Berkshire, as illustrated by the map in Figure x, and many of the flooded gravel workings are now important as breeding sites for wetland birds and wintering sites for wildfowl.

The open, bare, gravelly areas with pools of water, silt or mud are created during gravel extraction and are attractive to breeding and migrant waders. They have led to a number of species becoming established in the county as breeding birds, including Little Ringed and Ringed Plovers, Common Tern and, most recently, Oystercatcher, as well as providing breeding sites for other species, such as Redshank and Lapwing. In addition, the associated wetland vegetation has provided breeding habitats for species such as Sedge and Reed Warblers, Reed Bunting and occasionally attract other unusual breeding species and rare vagrants. This has made such areas particularly popular with local birdwatchers. As the vegetation around disused pits has developed, the scrub and woodland become suitable for many other species. The Theale and Burghfield pits hold good populations of Nightingales as mentioned above and such areas also support good

Reedbeds, often created on disused gravel workings, attract breeding Sedge and Reed Warblers and wintering Bitterns
*Thatcham Discovery Centre  Robert Still*

breeding populations of Cetti's Warbler, Whitethroat, Chiffchaff and Bullfinch for example. They also provide a winter refuge for many woodland birds, and the Alders *Alnus* that often fringe the water can produce large winter Siskin flocks with smaller numbers of Redpoll.

In winter, many wildfowl occur in good numbers on old gravel workings throughout Berkshire. Counts of Gadwall, Tufted Duck, Wigeon and Coot regularly exceed 200 at a number of sites, and Pochard, Teal, Shoveler, Canada Geese, Greylag Geese and Great Crested Grebes also occur in good numbers. The most common wintering wildfowl species is Tufted Duck and one area, Wraysbury Gravel Pits, has regularly produced counts of over 1,000 – over 1% of the national population. Dinton Pastures and Burghfield Gravel Pits are also sites where nationally important numbers of Gadwall have been recorded; and small but nationally important numbers of Smew, one of Britain's scarcer wintering ducks, have been recorded at Wraysbury and Twyford Gravel Pits. Cormorants and roosting gulls also occur in considerable numbers in winter. The gravel pits of the lower Kennet valley at Theale and Burghfield produced the largest inland winter roost counts for Lesser Black-backed Gulls in the UK during the Wintering Gull Roost survey of 2003–06 and the second largest in the UK (Burton *et al.*, 2013), although subsequently numbers at these sites have reduced, and higher counts have occurred at Moor Green Lakes.

Flooded gravel workings also attract water-related recreation. Sailing, water-skiing, jet-skiing, wind-surfing and angling all occur widely, creating varying levels of disturbance for breeding and wintering birds. However, since the late 1970s there have been a number of encouraging developments, as the wildlife value of these areas began to be appreciated and reflected in conditions imposed in new planning permissions granted for mineral extraction.

The wildlife conservation measures at gravel pits have been influenced by a combination of action by volunteers and wildlife groups and action by local authorities. For example, an area was set aside as a nature reserve and a birdwatching hide built when Wokingham District Council created the Dinton Pastures Country Park on old gravel workings between Woodley and Hurst. After many years of negotiation, BBONT (now BBOWT) secured a reserve at Twyford, which is now their Loddon Nature Reserve, and they also have a reserve at Bray Gravel Pits. In the late 1980s, measures aimed at creating habitats to benefit wildlife were incorporated into the proposal for new gravel workings at Woolhampton. The Newbury District Ornithological Club works with Tarmac Southern Ltd to manage conservation work and a hide at Lower Farm Gravel Pit near Newbury.

Three other voluntary conservation groups have been established to manage old gravel workings in Berkshire which deserve special mention. When a nature conservation area was proposed at Lavell's Lake adjacent to Dinton Pastures in the mid-1980s, a number of local groups were consulted and a management plan drawn up, which included the provision of wader scrapes, floating nesting platforms and two hides. A voluntary group, The Friends of Lavell's Lake (FOLL), which was established to manage the site with the help of Wokingham District Council, has since extended the conservation area northwards by taking in Lea Farm Gravel Pit in an agreement with Summerleaze Ltd. In 1988, a group of birdwatchers, led by Brian Uttley formed the Theale Area Bird Conservation Group, which carried out conservation work at Theale Gravel Pits. Both groups have cleared islands for ground-nesting birds, established reedbeds and provided hides or screens. Both have been rewarded with Bitterns and Bearded Tits in the winter and Redshank, Little Ringed Plover, Oystercatcher, Cetti's and Reed Warblers in the breeding season. After many years spent promoting the site by the Theale group, Hosehill Lake was designated a local nature reserve by Newbury District Council and it is now the focus of the Group's work.

At Eversley Gravel Pits, Ready Mix (now CEMEX plc) established a nature reserve at Moor Green Lakes. A voluntary group, the Moor Green Lakes Group, was established in 1993 with the objectives of improving the area for wildlife, providing facilities for visitors and recording the wildlife at the site. Management and habitat creation has been undertaken, including creating reedbeds and pools and the reserve now forms the largest wetland conservation area in Berkshire.

In addition to the difficulties involved in ensuring the appropriate management of gravel pit complexes for the benefit of birds, a number of the areas have been threatened by development proposals. In the 2000s Prudential Insurance promoted a scheme known as Kennet Valley Park, which would have resulted in the loss of much of the eastern part of Theale Gravel Pits and most of Burghfield Gravel Pits, for designation as a major strategic development in the Regional Spatial Strategy for the South East of England. After a campaign supported by a variety of local groups including wildlife groups this failed, but the area remains without formal wildlife conservation designation. However, many are now designated as local nature reserves and the Wraysbury complex is part of the South-west London Water Bodies Important Bird Area (IBA), and part of it is designated a Site of Special Scientific Interest (SSSI).

The Queen Mother Reservoir at Datchet in the far east of the county is the westernmost of the large reservoirs serving Greater London and the largest area of open water in the county. Although like many of the gravel pit complexes it is used heavily for recreation, it has been notable for attracting migrant waders, storm-driven seabirds and other vagrant birds. It also acts as a refuge for wintering water birds in hard weather, when the gravel pits nearby freeze.

The presence of ornamental lakes has contributed to the diversity of bird life in Berkshire and these areas have often produced records of scarcer wildfowl. Particularly notable are the lakes in Windsor Great Park: Virginia Water and Great Meadow Pond. The trees adjacent to ornamental lakes often hold heronries, such as at Englefield Park, which for many years was the only heronry in central Berkshire.

No account of the wet habitats in Berkshire would be complete without mention of the open sewage works settling beds in the county, of which only one, Slough Sewage Farm, remains. Reading, Iver and Ham Island sewage farms having been modernized. The old-style settling beds on these works have been particularly important for attracting vagrant waders.

### Urban and built-up areas

Berkshire has experienced continued population growth since the late 19th century. In the late 1930s, the population of the county was about 350,000; by the 2011 UK National census it had more than doubled to 862,000. Research carried out for the unitary local authorities and other local bodies in 2009 predicted growth by a further 10% to 912,000 by 2026. Considerable areas of central and eastern Berkshire are heavily urbanized (Figure xi), although there are still areas outside the main urban areas of Reading, Wokingham, Bracknell, Ascot, Maidenhead and Slough, which lie in the Metropolitan Green Belt around London, which retain a rural character. Most of the recent development has been around the periphery of the larger towns and villages, for suburban housing and industrial estates. The west of Berkshire is still predominantly rural away from the Newbury and Thatcham conurbation, though few tetrads have no buildings.

A few species favour buildings as nesting sites and most of these, such as Feral Pigeon, Swift, House Martin, Swallow and House Sparrow, are widespread. One rare breeding species, which is associated with buildings and occurs in Berkshire is the Black Redstart. This species has bred on buildings in Windsor, Maidenhead, Bracknell, Reading, Newbury and at the Atomic Weapons Establishment, at Aldermaston; it was last confirmed to have bred in 2010. However they often rely on the niches created by lack of repair or dereliction. Despite the increase in built area, three

Ledges and rooftops provide nesting opportunities for scarce species such as Peregrine (*inset*) and Black Redstart, and for Herring Gulls, which have begun to colonise inland towns such as Reading.
*Robert Still, with thanks to Hotel Novotel Reading Centre*

Peregrine, 3M building, Bracknell *Jerry O'Brien*

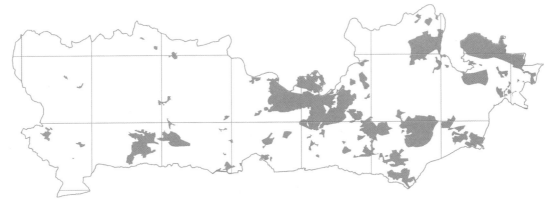

**Figure xi  Built areas.**

species associated with buildings have suffered declines: House Sparrow, Starling and Swift. The increased prosperity of the area leads to higher standards of repair of the housing stock, and gaps under eaves are filled as roofs are renewed. The emphasis on concentrating development in previously developed or "brownfield" land has resulted in the removal of much older industrial development, an example being the demolition of the old Courage Brewery and its replacement by flats in the 1980s, and the Oracle Development in the late 1990s which together resulted in the removal of most of the traditional industrial landscape of central Reading. Modern flat roofed or high rise development though appears to suit some species. In the first decade of the 21st century, three species that had not hitherto bred in Berkshire began to breed in our towns: Lesser Black-backed and Herring Gulls and the Peregrine, the breeding ranges of all three species having spread to inland sites nationally. Some species also take advantage of buildings as roost sites, notably Pied Wagtails and (in the past) Starlings. The railway station and the Royal Berkshire Hospital have provided roost sites for Pied Wagtails in Reading in recent decades.

Parks, gardens and the landscaping around housing developments and industrial estates occupy a similar area to that of buildings and form an important habitat for several woodland and farmland species. Perhaps because of the heterogeneity of parks and gardens and supplemental feeding by Man, they can hold high densities of species, such as Blackbird, Robin, Wren, Blue and Great Tits, Greenfinch and Goldfinch. Indeed the abundance of some "woodland" species such as the Blackbird, and "farmland" species such as Greenfinch, show stronger correlations with gardens and the built areas than they do with woodland and farmland respectively.

Supplemental feeding has been shown to enhance both winter survival and breeding success in several garden species (Robb *et al.*, 2008) and the correlation between abundance and built areas exhibited by some wildfowl (*e.g.* Mute Swan, Mallard) may be due in part to artificial feeding in parks. However, the fact that continental Blackcaps wintering in the UK are recorded largely through their visits to garden feeders may simply reflect that they are easier to see here whereas they are more difficult to detect in woodland or scrub.

Whilst most bird-watchers leave the towns in search of birds, many bird species have adapted well to the urban environment and it is notable that the species richness of built areas is similar to that of the county as a whole: the average summer species richness for urban tetrads was 55 (Berkshire average 63); winter 57 (56). Parks gardens and neglected brownfield sites can offer richly mixed habitats. Even in town centres and on industrial estates, there is some vegetation which is exploited by birds. Thus in Reading, Mistle Thrushes sing from isolated trees, and wintering thrushes raid Buckthorn *Rhamnus catharticus* bushes around the Police Station in winter. Wintering Waxwings often occur in urban sites, feeding on trees and bushes in suburban areas or around supermarkets.

For many, more specialist, species, however, the spread of development in Berkshire has little to offer. The woodland specialists, the breeding birds of wet meadows and the ground-nesting birds deprived of feeding and breeding areas by modern agricultural practice have little or nothing to gain from further development. They are further threatened by disturbance caused by growing leisure use of the countryside by an increasing population. The development pressure on the urban areas of central and eastern Berkshire remains. This area is sandwiched between the North Wessex Downs Area of Outstanding Natural Beauty and the Metropolitan Green Belt and is an area of continued economic growth. Further development seems bound to occur, and more study of the effectiveness of mitigation measures would undoubtedly benefit Berkshire's birds in future.

*N. J. Bucknell and Andy Swash,*
*revised and updated by Renton Righelato*

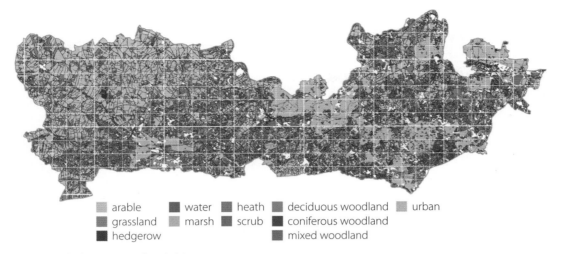

arable    water    heath    deciduous woodland    urban
grassland    marsh    scrub    coniferous woodland
hedgerow    mixed woodland

**Figure xii  Composite habitat map of Berkshire.**

TVERC mapping assigned habitat categories to 79% of the area of the county; gardens occupy 9%, most of the remainder being buildings and roads.

## The future for Berkshire's habitats – threats and opportunities

It can be seen that Berkshire has within its modest area a wide variety of habitat, which is reflected in the variety of its birdlife. Its farmland has seen significant changes, and development has spread. Its heathland fragments face a number of threats, and its wet areas are mostly in areas not generally appreciated as being of conservation value to those not interested in wildlife. Much of the wildlife value depends upon active management to maintain it, whether keeping nesting islands clear of vegetation, preventing scrub encroachment on heaths, maintaining scrub and understory by periodic cutting or providing suitable open nesting areas for ground nesting birds in arable land by leaving areas uncultivated.

It has become clear to the wildlife conservation movement that acquiring reserves and managing them could not address many of the threats to Britain's wildlife. In the early years of the 21st century, the concept of "Living Landscapes" evolved. The idea was to work together with the community, landowners, local government and other local groups to improve an area for wildlife by encouraging sympathetic land management practice, providing advice and organising conservation fieldwork to enhance habitat across a larger area – landscape scale conservation action.

In Berkshire, one such area is being promoted, the West Berkshire Living Landscape. It encompasses an area bounded by the Enbourne to the south and east, the A4 main road to the north and the southern and eastern boundaries of Thatcham and Newbury built up areas to the west and north west. It includes the commons at Greenham and Crookham, the wooded slopes at Bowdown and the gravel pits at Woolhampton

and Thatcham and the reedbeds at Thatcham. The compilation of the second edition of this book highlights that there are other areas with special characteristics which appear to merit consideration for future projects. The flooded gravel pits of the lower Kennet valley, the valleys of the Kennet, Lambourn and Pang, the Berkshire Downs, the valleys of the Loddon and Blackwater, the heaths of south east, Windsor Great Park and the lakes of the Colne valley all face challenges but have features worth preserving and enhancing.

## The climate of Berkshire

Like much of central southern England, Berkshire enjoys a relatively benign climate, protected by its inland position and away from the more extreme temperatures of the eastern counties. Monthly temperature, rainfall and sunshine data for 1991–2010, from Heathrow, the nearest Met Office station, are summarized in Figure xiii.

There has been a significant warming trend over the last fifty years of around 0·3 °C/decade (Figure xiv), resulting in a springtime temperature advance of one to two weeks in March/April between the 1950s and the first decade of the 21st century. There has been little change in autumn temperatures, but midwinter temperatures were around 2 °C warmer in the last twenty years (1990–2010) than in the preceding period (1971–1990). Notably, the incidence of freezing weather has decreased significantly (Figure xv). Over the same period there has been no trend in annual rainfall, though there is some suggestion of an increase in total annual sunshine (Figure xvi).

The trend to warmer winters may have contributed to the recent expansions in Berkshire of a number of

**Table ii Median earliest arrival dates in Berkshire of some summer migrants.** Data from Annual reports.

| Species | 1980–89 | 2000–09 | Change (days) |
|---|---|---|---|
| Cuckoo | 12th April | 9th April | −3 |
| Swift ** | 22nd April | 16th April | −6 |
| Sand Martin * | 16th March | 10th March | −6 |
| Swallow ** | 2nd April | 21st March | −12 |
| House Martin * | 3rd April | 25th March | −9 |
| Yellow Wagtail ** | 4th April | 27th March | −8 |
| Wheatear | 14th March | 14th March | 0 |
| Nightingale ** | 12th April | 4th April | −8 |
| Sedge Warbler ** | 8th April | 1st April | −7 |
| Reed Warbler ** | 22nd April | 16th April | −6 |
| Lesser Whitethroat | 22nd April | 21st April | −1 |
| Whitethroat * | 15th April | 7th April | −8 |
| Willow Warbler | 26th March | 25th March | −1 |

* advance significant at p < 0·05; ** at p < 0·01

resident species at the northern limit of the European range, such as Little Egret, Stonechat, Dartford Warbler, Cetti's Warbler and Firecrest. Fewer freezes, as well as more reed-beds, may have contributed to an increasing number of winter records of Bittern. However, these species can be vulnerable to extended freezing weather, as was exemplified by the fall in the Stonechat population following the hard winters of 2008/09 and 2009/10 (*page 427*).

Warmer winter and early spring temperatures have caused an advance in plant growth and the timing of invertebrate hatches to which bird species tend to adapt by nesting earlier. For migrant species this would imply arriving earlier and it has been noted that arrival times have advanced for some species, though more so than laying dates (Thackeray *et al.*, 2010). The earliest arrival dates of the majority migrant species shown in Table ii have advanced by 6–12 days between 1980–89 and 2000–09, whilst for the Cuckoo, Wheatear, Lesser Whitethroat and Willow Warbler there has been no significant change. The northward shift in the national distribution that has been observed for some species, including the Cuckoo and Willow Warbler (1988–91 BTO Atlas), may be an alternative response to a warming climate.

There have been several analyses of arrival times showing advances over recent decades (*e.g.* Jonzen *et al.*, 2006), though the extent to which earlier arrival is due to evolving migration strategies in response to resource availability in the breeding areas, or conditions in wintering grounds or en route is by no means clear. The reasons for the differences between species in earliest

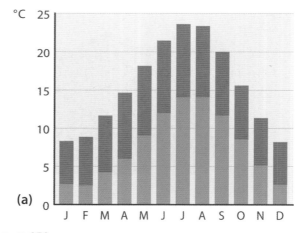

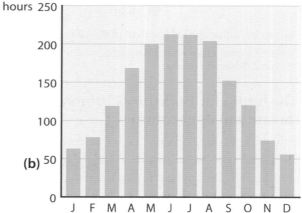

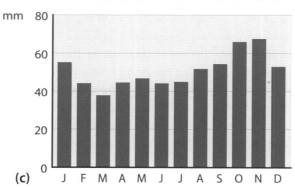

**Figure xiii Temperature, sunshine and rainfall at Heathrow.**

Monthly averages 1991–2010:
(a) temperature (daily minima – blue; maxima – red);
(b) sunshine hours; (c) rainfall. (Met Office data)

arrival time observed here are not obvious: both the species showing advance and those showing no trend include birds wintering in the Sahel, in West Africa and in southern Africa and include earlier and later migrants.

With continuing global warming, we can expect further changes to the local climate in Berkshire and changes to the conditions our summer and winter migrants experience elsewhere, though the detail of these changes and their impact on our avifauna is uncertain.

*Renton Righelato*

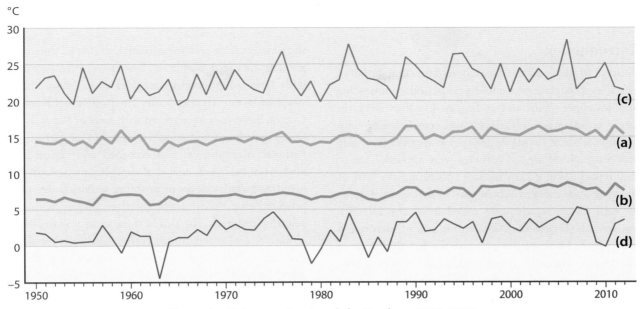

**Figure xiv Air temperature trends for Heathrow 1950–2012.**

Annual average of daily maximum temperatures (a) and minimum temperatures (b).
July maximum (c) and January minimum temperatures (d) are also shown.
There is a significant upward trend of approximately 0·3 °C per decade in all the measures shown. (Met Office data)

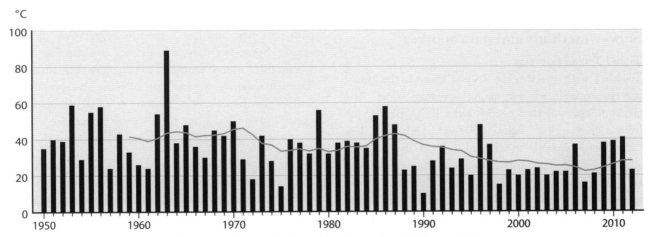

**Figure xv Days of air frost at Heathrow 1949/50 to 2012/13.**

There have been significantly fewer hard winters since 1990 ($p<0.05$). The rolling 10 year average is shown.

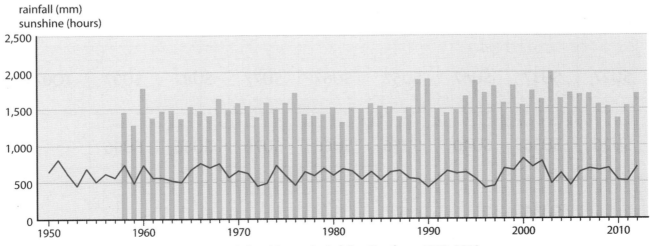

**Figure xvi Sunshine and rainfall at Heathrow 1950–2012.**

Whilst there has been a small upward trend in sunshine hours, there has been no discernible trend in rainfall.

# The surveys of breeding and wintering birds in Berkshire

## Introduction

Surveys to gather all the data required for compilation of the atlas took place over a four-year period, commencing in November 2007 and ending in October 2011. In order to maintain consistency and comparability with the first Birds of Berkshire atlas the same rules regarding the geographical area of coverage were applied. That is, any tetrad (2 km × 2 km square) containing any part of Berkshire was counted as being part of the county. Tetrads in each 10 km square were coded using the DINTY convention (Figure xvii). The entire area of each tetrad was included in the survey, despite the fact that some of the species recorded may not actually have been in or bred in Berkshire. In total, 99 tetrads (25%) overlap the county boundary. It should be noted that, due to changes in boundaries, Berkshire has "won" three more tetrads since the first atlas, taking the total from 391 to 394, although, apart from a little extra survey work, this appears to have made no material difference to the results.

## Survey methods and data sources

### Timed Tetrad Surveys:

Together with the Roving Record surveys, the timed surveys constituted the main surveying effort. The methodology was that used for the BTO/BirdWatch Ireland/SOC Bird Atlas 2007–11 and the data contributed to both the Berkshire and the national atlases. Timed Tetrad Visits (hereinafter referred to as TTVs) entailed two surveys of each tetrad in the summer and two in the winter in any of the four years of the survey period. Visits lasted two hours and surveyors were asked to cover as much of the tetrad as possible in

the time available and, in particular, to visit all the major habitats included within it. Surveyors were provided with aerial photographs and land cover maps kindly supplied by the Thames Valley Environmental Records Centre. Surveyors were issued with a set of paper TTV forms (produced and supplied by BTO as part of the national atlas project) and recorded and counted all birds seen or heard during their 2-hour visits. In the breeding months, notes of breeding activity were taken provided that this did not interfere unduly with the counting progress. The aim of these visits was to obtain a more or less standardized count from each tetrad so that comparisons of the relative numbers of each species could be made between squares. The data from these visits provided the basis for the relative abundance maps accompanying species accounts. TTV surveying started on November 1st 2007 and finished on July 31st 2011 with each year being divided into two "seasons" – Winter (start of November to end of February) and Breeding (start of April to end of July). Each survey season was further subdivided into "early" and "late" visits, these being the first and last 2 months respectively of the season. Surveyors were able to pick any suitable date within the 2 month windows to complete their surveys. The vast majority of each "pair" of visits was completed within the same survey season. A small number of surveys (1%) used a one hour survey period; for these, counts were doubled to provide the 2 hour estimate.

Volunteers for TTVs were recruited by a team of sixteen "Squaremasters" who were responsible for liaising with their volunteers, handling any queries and ensuring that tasks were carried out on time. They are listed in the Acknowledgements in Chapter 1.

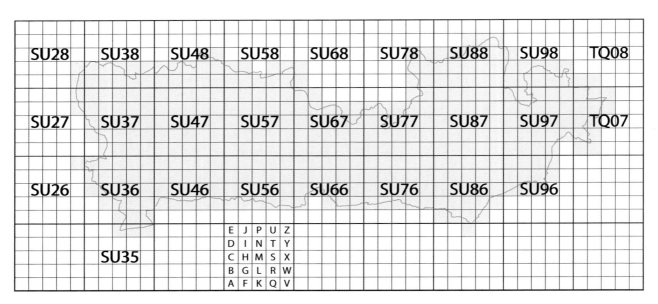

**Figure xvii  The 10 km square and tetrad map of Berkshire.**

Overall administration of Squaremasters and online square allocation for the whole county was overseen by the BTO Bird Atlas administrator (the then BTO Representative, Chris Robinson) as part of the national Bird Atlas 2007–11 project.

### Roving Record Surveys:

Of different but equal importance were the Roving Record surveys. These were less structured surveys and could be submitted from any time of year from any birdwatcher from any tetrad within the county. Submissions varied from a single casual observation (sometimes from a visitor to the county) to multiple species lists gathered as part of a dedicated survey visit by an individual birdwatcher. Their purpose was to gather data on extra species which might have been missed during a TTV and, during the breeding months, to gather evidence of breeding. Because of the time constraints on TTVs, they provided insufficient opportunity to gather much breeding evidence, so the majority of breeding status records were obtained through subsequent Roving Records. Indeed, as the fourth and final breeding season approached, it became apparent that there were a number of tetrads which had few (or even no) species confirmed as breeding despite having received a thorough TTV. Roving Record "hit squads" or individual enthusiasts then visited poorly covered parts of the county in order to improve the recording of breeding status.

### BTO BirdTrack:

BirdTrack is an online bird recording tool set up by the BTO and was created some years before Bird Atlas 2007–11. Although the recording methodology is somewhat different to atlas requirements, early in the Atlas period modifications were made to BirdTrack to enable users to submit data compatible with the Atlas requirements. This resulted in some 27,000 winter and 33,000 breeding records being added to the Berkshire database.

### BTO Nest Record Scheme:

The Nest Record Scheme (NRS) is a long-running BTO survey which provided additional information to the Atlas database. Although only adding a further 265 records to the Berkshire dataset, nearly all were "confirmed" breeding records with only 8 being "probable" breeding.

### BTO ringing records:

Similar useful breeding status information was obtained from ringing records. 382 breeding season records (all but one confirming breeding) and 1,613 winter records were transferred to the Berkshire dataset from the BTO Ringing Scheme.

### BTO Heronry Census:

All the accessible known heronries within Berkshire have been monitored annually as part of the long-running BTO Heronry Census and records from this provided useful confirmation of breeding for this species with 54 records being transferred to the Berkshire atlas dataset.

### Breeding Bird Survey:

The BTO/JNCC/RSPB Breeding Bird Survey (BBS) has been running continuously since 1994. As its main purpose is to monitor population changes, it does not report breeding evidence, though may supplement species richness data. It was found that the data duplicated information recorded in other ways, so only BBS data from 2008 and 2009 were transferred to the Atlas database (9,700 individual records).

### County bird records database:

The county database includes records sourced from Berkshire Bird Bulletin (BBB), the Berksbirds website, NDOC and direct submissions. All records of rare and uncommon species from this database, after scrutiny if necessary by the appropriate Rare Birds Committee, were uploaded to the main Atlas database for use on both the national and county atlases. Over 12,000 breeding and nearly 9,000 winter records were shared in this way.

### Miscellaneous sources:

A small number of records came from two other sources. Records from neighbouring counties' bird clubs included in the BTO dataset were accepted as Roving Records. Those from the website Birdguides, a website where birders may post information about rare or unusual bird sightings, were included in the BTO dataset, but not used here as the observer was not identified and hence the records were not verifiable.

## Data Management

### Data Entry:

A major benefit of synchronising the county atlas with the national atlas was that surveyors were able to submit their data online using the BTO Atlas website. Records entered as part of a county atlas survey thus became useable for the national atlas and vice versa. Submission on traditional paper forms was available for those unable to use the internet but by the end of the 4-year survey period the great majority of surveyors were submitting their data electronically. The key data recorded were location (tetrad or grid reference), species, count and breeding code (**Table iii**).

| Category | Evidence | Code letter(s) |
|---|---|---|
| NON-BREEDER | Flying over | F |
| | Migrant | M |
| | SUmmering | U |
| POSSIBLE BREEDER | Observed in suitable nesting Habitat | H |
| | Singing male | S |
| PROBABLE BREEDER | Pair in suitable nesting habitat | P |
| | Permanent Territory (many individuals on 1 day or 1 individual over 1+ week) | T |
| | Courtship and Display | D |
| | Visiting probable Nest site | N |
| | Agitated behaviour | A |
| | Brood patch of Incubating bird | I |
| | Nest Building or excavating | B |
| CONFIRMED BREEDER | Distraction Display | DD |
| | Used Nest or eggshells found from this season | UN |
| | Recently FLedged young or downy young | FL |
| | Adults entering or leaving nest-site indicating Occupied Nest | ON |
| | Adults carrying Faecal sac or Food for young | FF |
| | Nest containing Eggs | NE |
| | Nest with Young seen or heard | NY |

**Table iii  Categories of breeding evidence and codes used, ranked from the least to the best evidence of breeding.**

## Data Validation

An essential requirement, once records had been entered, was that they be validated. The task of validation was initially assigned to the Atlas Administrator in each BTO region (the Berkshire BTO Rep, Chris Robinson, in this case) but it was quickly realized that the role needed to be shared. Ken White (later to become one of the Berkshire BTO Representatives when Chris left the county) took on the task and was responsible for the great majority of validation. Although the vast majority of records were immediately and obviously acceptable there were occasional instances where one needed to be queried. Queries fell into four possible categories:-

**Location:**
*Did the grid reference (tetrad letter) given by the observer correctly match the area of survey?*

**Identity:**
*Was the bird really the species being claimed?*

**Breeding status:**
*If the observer was claiming that the bird was attempting breeding, was it likely for that species or on the date claimed?*

**Number:**
*Was the number of birds being recorded likely for that species?*

Most queries arose from data entry errors and were quickly resolved through an email exchange system built into the validation system. The other main source of query arose with species that were either county or national rarities; for these the Atlas Steering Group adopted a policy of not validating any such records until they had been approved by the appropriate Rarities Committee. At the end of the 4-year survey period, all outstanding non-validated records were assessed en bloc by a team comprised of Ken White, Renton Righelato and Ken Moore.

Migrant species that did not, so far as we know, breed in Berkshire but that had been given breeding codes were reviewed by Neil Bucknell and Renton Righelato and the codes (H, S, T, D, P) removed where the record was in the migration season or the bird was more appropriately recorded as summering (U). Records with no tetrad assignment were also removed.

## Final dataset

**Breeding season:**
A total of 164,774 records from all sources were included in the final breeding dataset. Breeding season records were submitted by 437 individuals whose contributions ranged from 1 to many thousands of records.

Breeding season TTVs were carried out by 138 surveyors, many of them completing two or more tetrads.

### Winter:

A total of 120,665 records from all sources were included in the final winter dataset. Winter records were submitted by 325 individuals and, as with breeding records, their contributions varied widely, ranging from 1 to many thousands of records. Winter TTVs were carried out by 146 surveyors, many of them completing two or more tetrads.

## Data presentation

### Breeding:

As in the previous atlas, evidence of breeding was divided into three levels, as shown in Table iii, to indicate whether a species was possibly breeding, probably breeding or confirmed to have bred. The maps which accompany the species accounts in this book are based on these three categories and show the best evidence of breeding recorded for each species in each tetrad over the four years of the survey, small-sized dots being used to indicate possible breeding, medium-sized dots to represent probable breeding and large-sized dots to show confirmed breeding. Details for each species are included in the species accounts and the accompanying distribution maps. As the breeding seasons covered by the 2007–11 comprise those in 2008 to 2011 inclusive, data for the breeding seasons during the second Berkshire Atlas are presented as "2008–11".

A complete list of the species recorded during the four years of the breeding survey is shown in Appendix III. Table A1 (*page 490*) shows the number of tetrads in which each species was confirmed to have bred, to have probably bred or to have possibly bred, and how these numbers compare with the first Atlas counts. Table A2, Appendix III (page 492) shows the number of species which occurred in each tetrad in the summer and winter periods. Table A3 (page 500) provides a 'league table' of the percentage of tetrads in which each species occurred in winter and Table A4 (page 501) a league table for the breeding season. The percentage of occupied tetrads has been rounded to the nearest whole number. Supplementary data are provided at **http://berkshirebirdatlas.org.uk/**.

### Abundance:

The timed tetrad surveys allowed approximate relative abundance estimates to be made. For the maps, the highest count of individuals of a species observed during either survey was divided by the average for all occupied tetrads; this relative abundance measure was used to assign the count to one of six categories, represented by increasing depth of colour tint: relative abundance $>0–0.5$; $>0.5–1.0$; $>1.0–1.5$; $>1.5–2.0$; $>2.0–2.5$; $>2.5$. Tetrads in which the species was not recorded during the timed survey, but had been found to be present at other times, are shown in the palest tint. The abundance measure is subject to potentially large errors and individual tetrad abundance estimates should be viewed with caution. However, for many species, the overall patterns disclosed in the abundance maps show the expected relationships with habitat, and population estimates derived from the county total abundance correlate well with independent estimates (Appendix IV).

### Migrants:

For migrant species that pass through Berkshire regularly but do not breed in the county, maps of their relative abundance are shown, measured by the number of birds recorded in a tetrad each day during the spring migration (March–June) and the autumn migration (July–October). The data are inevitably biased towards those tetrads visited most frequently.

*Chris Robinson and Renton Righelato*

Tufted Duck  *Alan Rymer*

Wren  *Graham Carey*

**Figure xviii  Breeding species richness.**

**(a)**
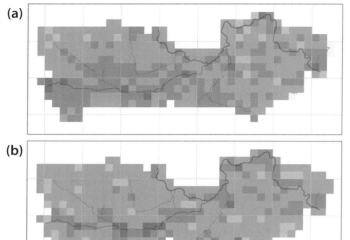
**(b)**

**Figure xix  Confirmed breeding species richness.**

**(a)**
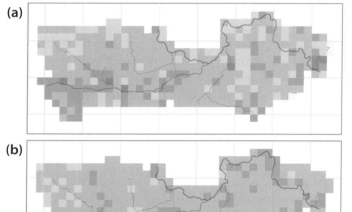
**(b)**

**Figure xx  Summer season species richness.**

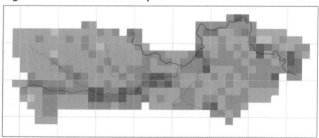

**Figure xxi  Winter season species richness.**

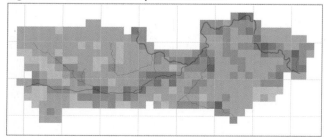

## Species richness

The total number of species recorded during the four breeding season years of the survey was 202 and of these 121 were confirmed to have bred. A further 11 species probably bred and 4 others were recorded as possibly breeding. Four species were recorded in all tetrads (Woodpigeon, Blackbird, Wren and Great Tit) and a further five species were recorded in 99% of the tetrads (Blue Tit, Blackcap, Chaffinch, Robin and Dunnock), see Appendix III, Table A4. A total of 187 species were recorded during the four year winter survey period.

**Figure xviii  Breeding species richness.**
**(a) 1987–89; (b) 2008–11**

All species showing any evidence of breeding are included. In the 2007–11 surveys, 29 tetrads (7% of those in the county) produced counts of more than 70 species, 10 tetrads (2.5 %) had more than 80 and 24 (6%) fewer than 40. The median of all species showing evidence of breeding was 52, somewhat lower than the median 59 observed in the 1987–89 survey.

**Figure xix  Confirmed breeding species richness.**
**(a) 1987–89; (b) 2008–11**

Breeding was confirmed for 40 or more species in 70 tetrads (18%), for 50 or more species in 15 tetrads (4%) and for 60 species in one tetrad (SU67F, Englefield/Wigmore Lane). The results suggest reasonable comparability of effectiveness of surveying between the 1987–89 and 2008–11 breeding data: the median of confirmed breeding species per tetrad was 30 in both periods and, for species confirmed in both atlas periods, the ratio of confirmed species to species with any breeding evidence was similar in both, 49% in the 2008–11 survey and 45% in the 1987–89.

**Figure xx  Summer season species richness.**

All species recorded, including summering birds and migrants recorded from April to July, are included. For 20 tetrads, the species richness exceeded 100 (some by a large margin) with the three highest being: SU77W (Lavell's Lake) with 125 species, SU56T (Woolhampton GPs) wth 126 and SU46Y (Lower Farm) with 129 species. In only 17 tetrads (4%) were fewer than 45 species recorded, suggesting that the overall level of coverage across the county was excellent. The median of all species, including migrants, across the whole county was 60 species per tetrad.

**Figure xxi  Winter season species richness.**

All species recorded in a tetrad for the months of November to February for the winters of 2007/08 to 2010/11 are included. The median winter species richness was 53. 58 tetrads (15%) recorded more than 70 species, 35 tetrads (9%) had more than 80 and 19 (5%) more than 90. Nine tetrads held 100 or more species with the five highest being: SU88T (Little Marlow GP) and SU97J (Dorney Wetlands) with 108 species, SU77W (Lavell's Lake) and SU86B (Moor Green Lakes) with 109 species and TQ07D (Queen Mother Reservoir) with 113 species. In 36 tetrads (9%) there were fewer than 40 species recorded but only 2 held fewer than 30.

# CHAPTER 5

# Birdwatching in Berkshire

Though entirely land-locked, the Royal County of Berkshire nonetheless contains a range of different habitats as summarised in Chapter 3. Despite a relatively high population density and small size, the county's bird list of species on the BOU's British List is a very reasonable 317 species (May 2013) and consistently over 200 species are recorded each year.

Within the County there are, with some overlap of designations, 38 Local Nature Reserves, 71 Sites of Special Scientific Interest, 13 Wildlife Trust reserves, three National Trust reserves, eight Special Areas of Conservation and one RAMSAR site (Wraysbury). There are also no fewer than 764 Wildlife Sites (previously Wildlife Heritage Sites), representing 8% of the county land area, but which have very little formal protection.

This chapter sets out details of some of the better known or well visited sites in the county, and some less well-known which might be of interest. The sites are described, access details are given and an indication of the species that may be encountered is supplied. They provide a variety of birdwatching experiences, from urban fringe sites, through small nature reserves to places that afford some of the finest landscapes and views in central southern England.

Please note that the details are current at the date of writing (2013), but may change over the years, and may repay checking from on-line sources as time passes. Some current web addresses of relevant organisations are given.

While these sites regularly hold or attract the scarcer and more 'interesting' birds, the fieldwork for the two Berkshire Bird Atlas projects and the records summarised in the species accounts in this book show the variety of birds that can be found in any suitable habitat in Berkshire. Any patch of woodland, wetland or scrub is worth exploring, and there are plenty of opportunities to spend time in a local patch away from the sites listed below and find species of interest. Sometimes rare and interesting birds turn up in unlikely locations, and Berkshire records include a Puffin found on a golf course, a Black-throated Thrush in a housing estate and an Olive-backed Pipit and a Yellow-browed Warbler in suburban gardens.

Observers are encouraged to submit all sightings at **www.berksbirds.co.uk**, or to the Berkshire Bird Bulletin, BirdTrack or directly to the County Recorder.

**Sources:- NBN Gateway web site**
**Natural England web site**
**TVERC web site**

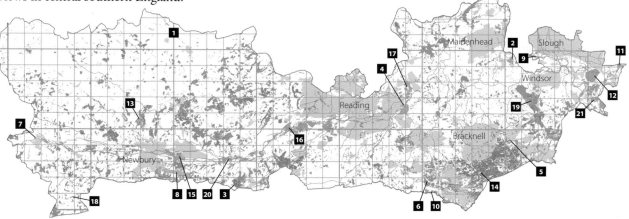

## Key to the sites

| | | |
|---|---|---|
| **1** The Berkshire Downs | **8** Greenham Common & Bowdown Woods | **15** Thatcham and Lower Farm |
| **2** Bray Gravel Pits | **9** Jubilee River | **16** Theale and Lower Kennet Lakes |
| **3** Burghfield and Padworth Commons | **10** Moor Green Lakes | **17** Twyford Lakes |
| **4** Dinton Pastures, Lavell's Lake & Lea Farm | **11** Old Slade Lakes | **18** Walbury Hill |
| **5** Englemere Pond | **12** Queen Mother Reservoir | **19** Windsor Great Park |
| **6** Finchampstead Ridges and Heath Lake | **13** Snelsmore Common | **20** Woolhampton Gravel Pits |
| **7** Freeman's Marsh | **14** Swinley Forest and Wishmoor | **21** Wraysbury Lakes |

**Key to the maps**

**Water features**

∿ Stream  ∿ Canal  ∿ River  ⬭ Water

**Features**

⌂ Reserve  Woodland  Area of interest  Notable habitat  Built up area

**Roads and paths**

Motorway  A-road  B-road  C-road  Unclassified road or track  - - - Footpath

**Symbols**

🅿 Parking  ⵜ Church  ● Station  ∥ Footbridge  ■ Building  ■ Hide

# The Berkshire Downs

The northern scarp slope of the Berkshire Downs runs for nearly 25 kilometres west of Streatley. The Ridgeway Trail follows close to the line of the escarpment. Since 1974, the boundary between Berkshire and Oxfordshire cuts back and forth across the Ridgeway and the scarp. East of the A34 the Ridgeway lies either on the boundary or just within Berkshire, but west of Bury Down and Cow Down above West Ilsley the county boundary lies to the south of the trail and escarpment. This is open country, with vantage points offering magnificent views northeast along the Chiltern escarpment, north over the Vale of White Horse, west along the escarpment itself and south over the dip slope and beyond to the Hampshire Downs. The scarp slope rises and falls with steep slopes in places on the escarpment itself and has dry valleys which cut into it, such as at Thurle Down (SU 570 815), the Devil's Punchbowl (SU 355 850) and in the Lambourn area (SU 365 785). There is a mix of habitat. Little chalk grassland remains, although the wide margins of the Ridgeway and the Fair Mile provide some unmanaged grass areas. Arable cultivation is interspersed with gallops for the many racing stables in the area, and sheep and some outdoor pigs provide a variety of farmed land. There are also a number of woodlands and copses, and areas of scrub notably at Cow Down.

Access is limited for vehicles following the closure of most of the Ridgeway west of the A34 to vehicular traffic in 2006, although the trail is still open to vehicles between April and October between Churn and Streatley. The usual access points to the most-visited eastern areas involve parking at the end of Rectory Road in Streatley or Ambury Road Lane in Aldworth, driving south out of Blewbury down Bonham's Road, or parking at one of the car parks either side of Bury Lane which leads north out of West Ilsley. Unfortunately this means some of the best areas are inaccessible for those with limited mobility.

This area still supports good numbers of some of the birds of arable areas that have declined or vanished from the rest of the county. It is the stronghold of Corn Bunting, Yellowhammer, Linnet, Skylark, Meadow Pipit, Yellow Wagtail and Grey Partridge. It also holds a small population of Stone Curlew, but please take care if you find them as they are very sensitive to disturbance. Lapwings occur all year, either as winter flocks or in smaller numbers, on well grazed sheep pasture or late emerging

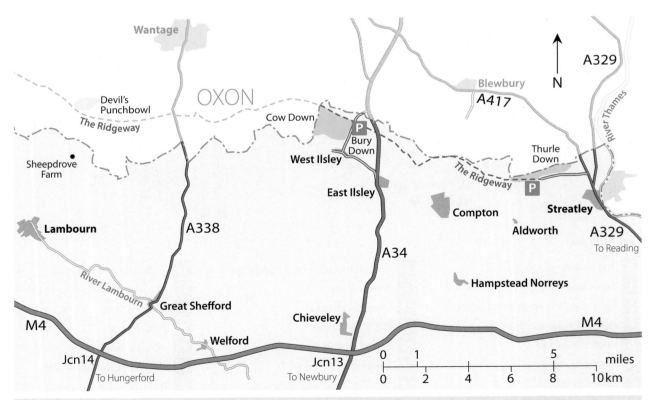

**Access:** There are formal car parks at Rectory Road, Streatley (SU 567 813) and Bury Down (SU 479 841). Ordnance Survey Explorer Map 170 or Landranger map 174 are essential for planning a trip and finding your way.

**Facilities:** Much of the area is well away from established settlements and services. The nearest pub is probably The Bell at Aldworth which has nesting Swifts in its roof! Take suitable clothing and footwear at all times.

**Web Information:** The National Trails website (www.nationaltrail.co.uk) has a section on the Ridgeway, with information on the wildlife, history, access and nearest services.

spring sown crops as a scattered breeding bird. This is also the best area for Quail, which in good Quail years such as 2011, may be widespread. A few Curlew also remain in most summers. Rectory Road leading out of Streatley is a reliable site for Spotted Flycatcher – check the gardens of the cottages along the road. The Downs also support a good Willow Warbler population.

In winter the resident Kites and Buzzards are joined by Merlins and occasional Peregrines, Hen Harriers and varying numbers of Short-eared Owls. In some years large flocks of Fieldfares, Redwing or Starlings may be encountered. Flocks of finches, buntings or sometimes both can occur on stubbles. Golden Plover may join Lapwings in winter or on passage. Muddy pig fields may attract large flocks of gulls, especially Lesser Black-backed, and there are a number of sites where local Rooks and Jackdaws gather in their hundreds. Barn Owls are relatively numerous, Sheepdrove Farm, north-east of Lambourn, being one regular site, and Great Grey Shrike has occurred more than once. Passage can bring small flocks of Wheatears and Whinchats, scattered records of Ring Ouzel, Redstart, Marsh Harrier and occasional Dotterel.

The valley of the Lambourn should not be overlooked. For water birds, places such as Great Shefford in the south (SU 390 750) may produce Kingfishers and Little Egrets, and in January 2011 a Great White Egret was present with a Dipper at nearby Welford.

## Species

**Resident:** Farmland species, some scarce elsewhere in Berkshire, including Grey Partridge, Barn and Little Owl, Stock Dove, Skylarks and Meadow Pipits, Pied Wagtails, Yellowhammer, Corn Bunting, Bullfinch, huge numbers of Rooks, Crows and Jackdaws.

**Summer:** Stone Curlew, Curlew, Quail, Corn Buntings, many breeding warblers, Spotted Flycatchers. Montagu's Harriers have occurred in the past.

**Winter:** Large groups of corvids, gulls and winter thrushes. Gatherings of Corn Buntings and other finches in significant numbers, wandering Hen and Marsh Harriers, Merlin, possible Great Grey Shrike, Short-eared Owls, Stonechat.

**Spring/Autumn passage:** Wheatears, Redstarts, Yellow Wagtails and Ring Ouzels on passage, chance of overflying waders, raptors.

**Scarcer visitors:** Great White Egret (Jan 2011), Dipper (Jan 2011), Great Grey Shrike, Dotterel.

TOP TO BOTTOM:
Short-eared Owl *Jerry O'Brien*; Dipper *Jerry O'Brien*;
Thurle Down and Streatley Warren *Andy Tomczynski*.

# Bray Gravel Pits

This pleasant site is a 20 hectare (50 acre) area of lakeland comprising two main pools, separated by the Bray Cut stream, surrounded by maturing scrub and bushes, which provides something of interest at any time of year. The largest lake is used extensively for water sports, and angling points proliferate around much of its shoreline. Consequently, it is mostly occupied by varying numbers of waterfowl, the highest numbers occurring in winter. To the north, and accessed by means of a footbridge, is a quieter lake, where rafts of ducks and geese can be found, and the surrounding dense shrubs hold numerous passerine species whose territorial song is characteristic of the site. The Cut itself should be checked for the resident Kingfishers. Its bankside hedges are also a regular location to detect the loud (but difficult to see) Cetti's Warbler which has spread here, possibly from its main county strongholds in the Kennet and Loddon valleys. Several calling birds can be located around these lakes. Finally, at the western-most end of the main lake there is a small Wildlife Trust reserve, mainly noted for its flora, but incorporating another tiny pool.

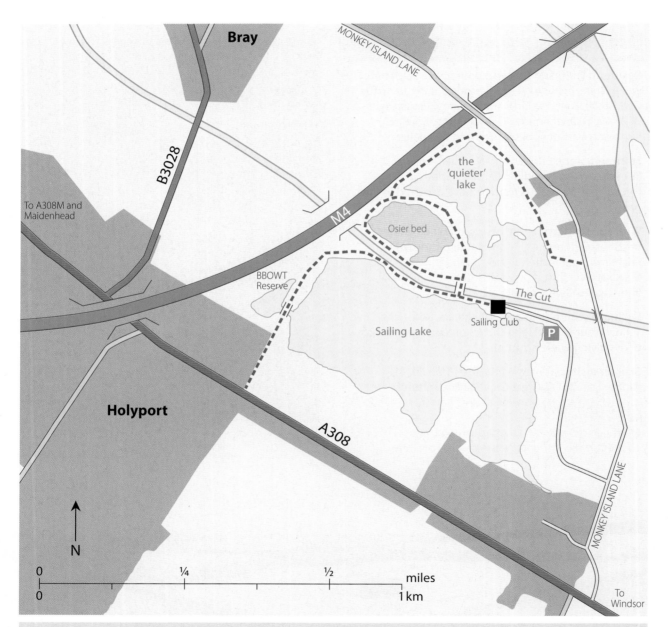

**Access:** North of the A308 Maidenhead to Windsor road, via Monkey Island Lane and forking left after 150m into the sailing club entrance, the free car park being on the left after another 200m (SU 913 787). Continuing along this track on foot accesses the main lake on the left, the footbridge over the stream further along on the right, and the Wildlife Trust site at the very end.

**Facilities:** Sailing club shop and beverage counter, with toilet.

**Web Information:** Check the BBOWT website – **www.bbowt.org.uk**.

### Species

**Resident:** Little and Great Crested Grebes, Water Rail, Herons, all the commoner duck and passerine species, Ring-necked Parakeets regular. Sparrowhawk and Kestrel, Kites and Buzzards often overhead. Cetti's Warbler calling at any time.

**Summer:** Most common warblers, including Whitethroat, Blackcap, Chiffchaff, Reed, Sedge, and Cetti's. Large gatherings of hirundine (though no nesting sites for Sand Martin), Common Tern fishing (no nesting rafts), Hobby, Cuckoo.

**Winter:** Large mixed rafts of Pochard, Wigeon, Tufted, Teal and Mallard ducks, occasionally interspersed with Goldeneye and Smew. Rarer grebes have been noted and large flocks of mixed tits and finches can gather. Both winter thrushes regular.

**Spring/Autumn passage:** Passage terns (mainly Arctic and Common) and waders (primarily Little Ringed Plover, Redshank and Common Sandpiper, although anything could potentially call in), occasional Garganey, Willow Warbler.

**Scarcer visitors:** Whilst not noted as a great site for rarities, scarcer visitors have included Green-winged Teal (March 2004), and Ferruginous Duck (Feb 2012).

TOP TO BOTTOM: Little Grebe *John Absolom*; Kingfisher *Jerry O'Brien*; the 'quieter' lake *Jerry O'Brien*.

# Burghfield and Padworth Commons

Between the villages of Mortimer, Burghfield, Padworth and Ufton Nervet lies 300 hectares (750 acres) of woods and common-land, surrounded by farmland, which are worthy of a birdwatching walk. The Englefield Estate woodland comprises coniferous stands of varying ages, interspersed with more open areas of carr and saplings. Padworth Common itself is a Local Nature Reserve and a Wildlife Heritage site and comprises approximately 30 hectares of open heathland, birch, gorse, shrubs and ponds, noted for its flora and insect communities as much as for its birds. The coniferous sectors reward visitors with Goldcrest, Treecreeper, and roving tit flocks which will include Coal Tits. Both Green and Great Spotted Woodpeckers are encountered at the woodland edge, adjacent agricultural land affording the chance to find Little Owl, Yellowhammer and, in season,

winter thrushes. A small pond in the middle of these woods can hold Moorhen and Little Grebe but any strange 'crake-like' calls emanating from its direction are almost certainly due to its frog community. Siskins and Crossbills, which breed in small numbers, are more likely to be encountered during winter-time. Padworth Common is perhaps best in spring and summer when parachuting Tree Pipits, calling Cuckoos, Spotted Flycatchers and churring Nightjars can be seen or heard. The songs of all the commoner summer warblers can be heard, while overhead hunting Hobbies are likely. After dusk, listen for Tawny Owls, Nightjars and roding Woodcock. Barn Owl is occasionally recorded. Reed Buntings and Linnet can be found and the Oval Pond has hosted Little Grebe and Mandarin. A small roost of Meadow Pipits can often be found in winter.

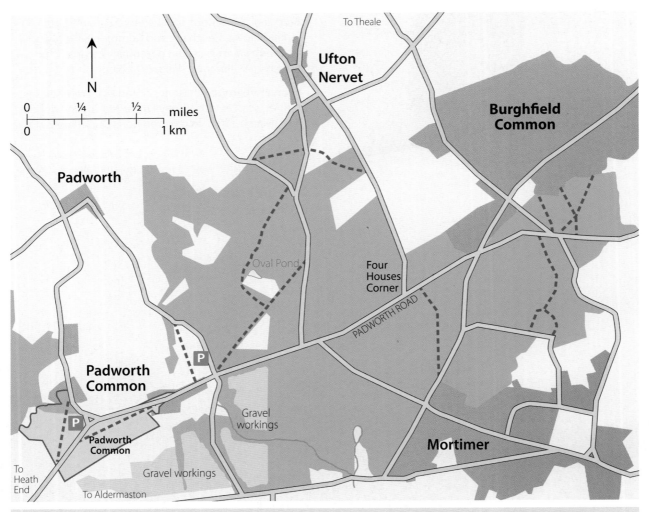

**Access:** The coniferous plantations of the Englefield Estate lie to the west and north of Four Houses Corner (SU 644 658) on the road from Burghfield Common to Heath End, with several road-side pull-offs available for parking on this, and the two roads going north to Ufton Nervet. Padworth Common lies to the south of the same road (SU 624 648) and has a network of footpaths criss-crossing the area.

**Facilities:** None.

**Web Information:** Padworth Common is a local nature reserve, and details can be found on West Berkshire's website – **www.westberks.gov.uk**, currently under Environment and Planning-Countryside / Nature Reserves and Commons. Management is about to pass to BBOWT (2013), so checking their website (**www.bbowt.org.uk**) might be worthwhile.

## Species

**Resident:** Little Grebe and Moorhen on the ponds, Woodcock, Tawny and Little Owl, all three woodpeckers possible, common tits and finches, Treecreeper, Nuthatch.

**Summer:** Cuckoo, Willow and Garden Warblers, Whitethroat, Chiffchaff, Blackcap, Hobby and Nightjar, with potential for Nightingale and Grasshopper Warbler. Tree Pipit, Reed Bunting, Spotted Flycatcher.

**Winter:** Potential for Golden Plover and Snipe, increased numbers of Siskin and Lesser Redpoll, flocks of Redwing and Fieldfare, occasional Crossbills.

**Scarcer visitors:** Pied Flycatcher (Apr 2010), Mealy Redpoll (Jan 2011).

TOP TO BOTTOM: Tree Pipit; Marsh Tit; Padworth Common *Jerry O'Brien.*

# Dinton Pastures, Lavell's Lake and Lea Farm

The lakes, scrub and tree-lines of Dinton Pastures Country Park soon became a favourite area for birdwatchers after opening in the 1980s. Subsequently, the Lavell's Lake Conservation Area, with its two hides, was established on the northern edge. Still further north along the Loddon, an additional lake with scrape areas was created at Lea Farm, and a hide built, the key to which is available to members of the Friends of Lavell's Lake (www.foll.org.uk for details). Dinton Pastures' lakes hold the greater concentrations of ducks in winter, occasionally including rarer species such as Scaup and Pintail, and Smew in smaller numbers. In spring, Sandwich, Arctic and Black Terns pass through, and a few Common Terns remain for the summer. The denser scrub holds the few remaining Nightingales in the Loddon valley, as well as commoner summer visitors. The country park's golf course often has Green Woodpeckers and numbers of Pied Wagtails amongst the grazing Canada and Egyptian Geese, and the adjacent Loddon River and Emm Brook provide excellent opportunities to see Grey Wagtails and Kingfishers. Lesser Spotted Woodpecker is also regular here, and the list of species recorded is 210 over the years.

Lavell's Lake is fringed with reeds, and typically produces over 130 species per year, attracting a variety of waterfowl, terns and reed specialists, the most notable being wintering Bitterns and Water Rail. Nightingales, Common Terns, Reed and Sedge Warblers can also be found here, and Hobbies may be seen hunting among the hirundines overhead. Small scrapes in front of the two hides draw Green and Common Sandpipers, alongside Snipe, Dunlin, Lapwings and Redshank, plus less usual species such as Greenshank, Temminck's Stint, Jack Snipe and Wood Sandpiper. Lea Farm, with its quieter, shallow pool, muddy scrapes, and Sand Martin bank, attracts Yellow Wagtail on passage, and waders preferring more open areas, such as Little Ringed Plovers, Godwits, Ruff, Curlew and Whimbrel. Shelduck and Little Egrets are frequent, and have even been joined by Spoonbills on one occasion. Large numbers of geese, corvids and gulls gather here and it is worth checking for Mediterranean, Yellow-legged and Caspian Gulls. Red Kites and Buzzards are regularly noted. Combined, these three sites offer good birding all year.

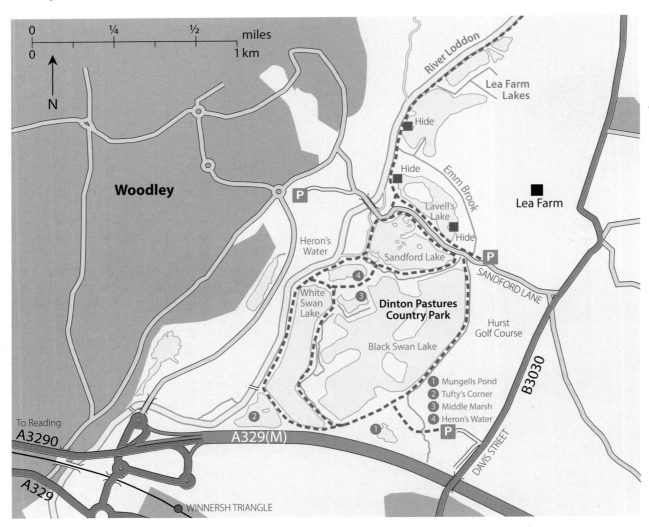

**Access:** The main pay-and-display car-park for Dinton is off Davis Street (SU 784 720) whilst Lavell's Lake has a separate car-park along Sandford Lane (SU 786 727) and pay-and-display tickets are available from the car park at the club house opposite. Lea Farm (SU 784 735) is approached on foot along the Loddon-side footpath from the western end of Lavell's Lake Conservation Area, and best viewed from the members-only hide.

**Facilities:** Toilets, café and education centre at Dinton Pastures.

**Web Information:** The Friends of Lavell's Lake has its own website, **www.foll.org.uk**. For access details and car park charges at Dinton Pastures, go to Wokingham Borough Council's website – **www.wokingham.gov.uk**, following the link to Parks and Countryside / Parks and play areas / Country Parks.

## Species

**Resident:** Grey Heron, all the common grebes, waterfowl, finch and tit species, Kestrel, Sparrowhawk, Stock Dove, all three woodpeckers, Kingfisher, Grey Wagtail.

**Summer:** Breeding warblers, Reed Buntings, Nightingale, Cuckoos and occasional Grasshopper Warbler, Common Terns, many nest boxes used, including Barn Owls. Hobbies regular.

**Winter:** Bitterns in the reedbeds at Lavell's and White Swan Lakes, Goldeneye, Smew, occasional Goosander and Scaup. Rafts of commoner waterfowl. Siskins and Lesser Redpolls flock in riverside Alders. Large groups of winter thrushes. Lapwings and Golden Plover at Lea Farm.

**Spring/Autumn passage:** Passage terns, waders, hirundines and Swifts.

**Scarcer visitors:** A good list including, over the years, records of Gannet, Purple Heron, Spotted Crake, Spoonbill, Ferruginous Duck, Wilson's Phalarope, Red-footed Falcon and Great White Egret.

TOP TO BOTTOM: Spotted Crake *Michael McKee*; Bittern *Jerry O'Brien*; Black Swan Lake *Ray Reedman*.

# Englemere Pond

This 28 hectare (68 acre) Local Nature Reserve lies to the east of Bracknell. Although nominally a nature reserve with a management plan, the site is also managed for public access, and investment is being made in facilities for public access as part of the SANGS (Suitable Alternative Natural Greenspace) programme, funded by developers' contributions, to reduce recreational pressure on the nearby Thames Basin Heaths.

The site comprises a small acidic reed-lined lake surrounded by Alder carr and mixed woodland, belonging to the Crown Estate. Stands of conifers abut oaks and Hornbeams, Rowan and Cherry, edged with a small area of heath. This results in an interesting mix of bird species for such a small area. The pond is an SSSI and was once one of the largest reedbeds in East Berkshire, with interesting plants such as Round-leaved Sundew. A sinuous boardwalk forms much of the waymarked trail round the lake, and several footpaths cross the small woodland area. The site is well known for Grass Snakes,

bats and dragonflies in addition to the birdlife, which is more varied during spring and summer. Willow Tits no longer occur and even Marsh Tit has become far less common, but visitors should encounter Treecreeper, Coal Tit, Goldcrest, Siskin and Great Spotted Woodpecker. Nuthatch is less frequent, but may join mixed flocks of tits in winter. Green Woodpecker and Mistle Thrush favour the boundary adjacent to the golfing range while Wrens and Pied Wagtails nest amongst the piles of planks in the woodyard area. Sparrowhawk has bred here, but the resident Jays may pose more risks for the passerine nesters of Englemere. The now-mature trees around the pond restrict visiting waterfowl to small numbers of Mallard, Tufted Ducks, and occasional Teal, Pochard and Shoveler. Moorhen, Coot and Water Rail are resident. Small groups of Black-headed Gulls loaf during winter days whilst the setting is also perfect for Reed and Sedge Warblers in summer. There are no habitat elements suiting waders to speak of but Snipe continue to be reported here.

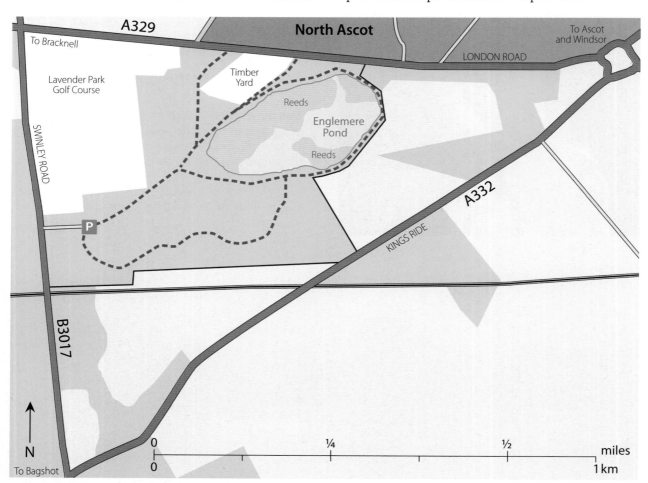

**Access:** A small car-park is available off the B3017 Swinley Rd (SU 902 686). The long-distance Three Castles Path runs through the reserve.

**Facilities:** None.

**Web Information:** Details can be found on Bracknell Forest Borough Council's website (www.bracknellforest.gov.uk), following links to Leisure & culture / Parks & countryside / Parks to visit / Englemere Pond. A reserve leaflet and ramblers' map are available to download.

### Species

**Resident:** Little Grebe, common ducks, Water Rail, Green and Great Spotted Woodpeckers, Coal Tits, Long-tailed Tits, Goldcrest, Nuthatch, Treecreeper, Jay, common finches and Reed Bunting.

**Summer:** Chiffchaff, Blackcap, Garden Warbler, Reed and Sedge Warblers, possible Cuckoo. Occasional Spotted Flycatcher and hunting Hobby.

**Winter:** Tawny Owl heard occasionally. Mixed feeding flocks of tits and finches gather, including Siskin and Lesser Redpoll. Crossbill possible. Small numbers of ducks that may include Gadwall, Pochard, Shoveler and Teal.

**Scarcer visitors:** Wood Warbler (April 2007).

TOP TO BOTTOM: Reed Bunting *Marek Walford*; Sedge Warbler *Dave Bartlett*; Englemere Pond *Jerry O'Brien*.

# Finchampstead Ridges and Heath Lake

Shaped during the Ice Age, and formerly a royal hunting forest, this tranquil, open-access 24 hectare (60 acre) woodland lies between Finchampstead and Crowthorne on the southern side of the B3348. Its soils being very acidic, it contains areas of gorse, heathers and bracken. Pines and birch trees have encroached over the decades but a heathland reclamation scheme in the 1990s has ensured there is sufficient variety of habitat to attract a range of birds and other wildlife. Spout Pond has a good reputation for dragonflies and, at higher locations, panoramic views of parts of Berkshire, Surrey and Hampshire can be enjoyed, and the adjacent avenue of striking Wellingtonias, planted by John Walter in 1863, is another significant feature.

Further habitat variety is available on the other side of the B3348 in the form of the deciduous Simons Wood, managed by the National Trust, to the north of which lies Heath Lake, sitting alongside The Devil's Highway, the old Roman Road between London and Silchester. Boardwalks have been constructed in the more permanently boggy areas. The naturally-formed Heath Lake is home to small numbers of Little Grebes, Moorhen, Coots and Canada Geese, whilst the small nesting island also often holds one or two terrapins, which no doubt predate smaller ducklings. Mandarins are occasional visitors and the lake is just large enough for the occasional Goosander in some winters. Toads are another regular user of the lake. Wood Warblers and Willow Tits may have been lost, but the site is worth a visit all year round. Wandering flocks of mixed tits will often contain Goldcrests or Nuthatches, and Great Spotted Woodpeckers are present in good numbers. This is a site where Firecrests can be found.

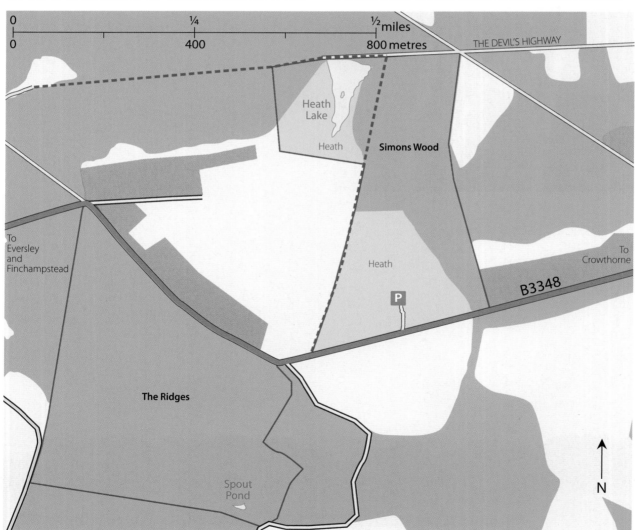

**Access:** Car park for some 50 vehicles in Simons Wood on the north side of the B3348 (SU 813 637). Easily-followed tracks and trails in both woods.

**Facilities:** None.

**Web Information:** There is currently nothing on the National Trust's website (2013). There is a limited entry on the Woodlands Trust's Visit Woodlands website (**www.visitwoods.org.uk**).

## Species

**Resident:** Little and Great Crested Grebes, common waterfowl, occasional Egyptian Geese and Mandarin, Sparrowhawk, Red Kite, Buzzard, Kingfisher, Great Spotted Woodpecker, Pied and occasional Grey Wagtails. Goldcrest, Coal Tit, Nuthatch, Treecreeper.

**Summer:** Most common warblers, possible nesting Grey Heron, nesting grebes, Hobby, potential for Spotted Flycatcher.

**Winter:** Rafts of Canada Geese, groups of Cormorants, Shoveler, Teal, Pochard, Siskin and Lesser Redpoll. Brambling and Crossbill possible.

**Spring/Autumn passage:** Passage hirundines and Swifts over the lake.

**Scarcer visitors:** Occasional Common Sandpiper, Firecrest (since 2002), Waxwing (Mar 2005).

TOP TO BOTTOM: Siskin *Alan Rymer*; Treecreeper *Jerry O'Brien*; Finchampstead Ridges *Colin Wilson*.

# Freeman's Marsh and Hungerford Marsh

This area runs about a mile, east to west, north of the Kennet and Avon Canal in the valley of the River Dun, a tributary of the Kennet to the west of Hungerford. It comprises wet grassland, shrubs and open marsh, through which run the river and its side channels. A network of footpaths runs through the site from the small Wildlife Trust reserve at the town end of the marsh to the Ford Gate access at the western end. Stark, leafless Willows in winter give way to brilliant spring blossom on the numerous Hawthorn bushes and the Yellow Iris around the water's edge in summer.

Over 130 species have been recorded here. Residents include Little Grebes, Water Rails, Kingfishers, Bullfinches, Pied and Grey Wagtails, and this is a good site for Little Egret and Green Sandpiper. In winter, small numbers of Teal may be present with Tufted Ducks and Coots, and flocks of Lapwing and Golden Plover often pass overhead. Winter finch flocks, especially at the town end, should be checked for Brambling. Parties of Fieldfare and Redwings are attracted to the Hawthorn bushes. Spring brings the sights and sounds of Common and Lesser Whitethroats, Blackcaps and Chiffchaffs. This used to be a good site for Grasshopper Warblers and Turtle Doves, but they are now scarce. Cetti's Warblers have however become established. Nesting Dunnocks and Meadow Pipits attract Cuckoos. The site attracts scarcer species such as Jack Snipe and Garganey. With Water Voles along the canal, regular reports of Otter, an excellent botanical record, and this wide range of birdlife, the site usually provides something for a visiting naturalist.

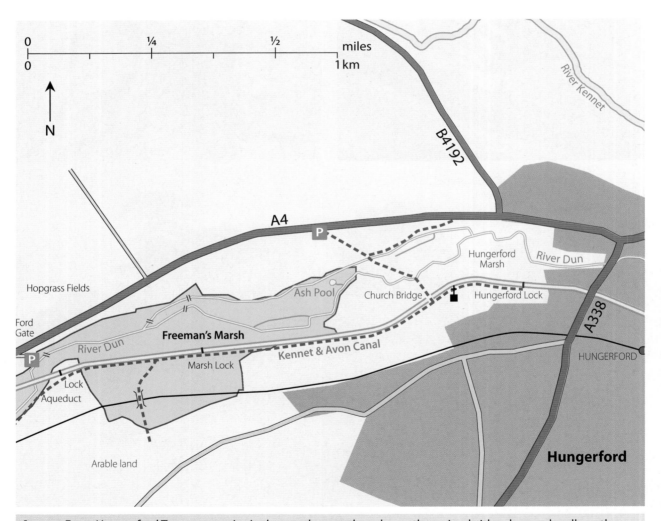

**Access:** From Hungerford Town, access is via the canal towpath and over the swing bridge, known locally as the Church Bridge (SU 334 686). There are also pull-over places on the A4 with access footpaths at SU330 689 and SU320 685 (The Ford Gate).

**Facilities:** Toilets and shops in Hungerford and refreshments at Cobb Farm Shop near the Ford gate.

**Web Information:** Hungerford Marsh is a BBOWT reserve, and details can be found on their website (www.bbowt.org.uk). Freeman's Marsh is owned by the Town and Manor of Hungerford, whose website includes a page with details about the site and conservation measures there – see www.townandmanor.co.uk.

## Species

**Resident:** Little Grebe, Grey Heron. Little Egret regular. Common ducks, Water Rail, Red Kite, Buzzard, Sparrowhawk, Kestrel, Skylark, Pied and Grey Wagtail, Cetti's Warbler, Bullfinch, Reed Bunting.

**Summer:** Nesting warblers, including Reed and Sedge Warblers, Hobby regular, large numbers of Swallows, House Martins and Swifts from neighbouring town. Spotted Flycatcher possible.

**Winter:** Snipe, Redshank, Green and Common Sandpipers. Possible Jack Snipe and Curlew. Lapwing and Golden Plover. Winter thrushes, Brambling, Siskin, Lesser Redpoll.

**Spring/Autumn passage:** Waders possible, Yellow Wagtail, occasional Grasshopper Warbler, Cuckoo.

**Scarcer visitors:** Dipper (Dec 1980), Spotted Crake (Feb 1984), Glossy Ibis (Dec 2010).

TOP TO BOTTOM: Glossy Ibis *Gary Loader*; Water Rail *John Absolom*; Freeman's Marsh *Jerry O'Brien*.

# Greenham Common and Bowdown Woods

The restoration of the former US airbase at Greenham Common to create a new heathland habitat is one of the conservation success stories in Berkshire since 1990. 95 hectares of two-foot thick concrete was removed, the soil was seeded with gorse and heather, left to settle, and elsewhere open areas of gravel and ponds were created. The site is not solely a nature reserve, but was also intended to provide an open area for recreation. However, a management plan was implemented with a grazing and cutting regime to maintain the optimum heath habitat, and attempts have been made to control access in a way that maintains public access while protecting ground nesting birds.

To the north lies the BBOWT woodland reserve of Bowdown, which lies on the northern slope of the plateau on which Greenham Common sits.

The result is a new heath providing a breeding habitat for Linnets, Stonechats and Dartford Warblers. The gravel bars and seasonal pools attract Ringed and Little Ringed Plovers, and occasional Shelduck. Alder-lined gullies draw groups of Siskins and Lesser Redpolls. The more open areas attract breeding Woodlarks, Stonechats, Tree and Meadow Pipits, Whitethroats and Willow Warblers, Redstarts, Nightingales and Tree Pipits regularly occupy the surrounding birch woodland in summer. Although Dartford Warblers are resident, severe winters, such as those of 2010/11 and 2011/12 can take their toll. Overhead, look out for Kites and Buzzards. Evening visits in summer often produce a hunting Hobby, a handful of roding Woodcocks or a churring Nightjar or two. Spring and autumn passage usually produces Whinchat, Wheatears and Yellow Wagtails, with large flocks of Swifts and hirundines feeding on insects overhead. In winter, huge numbers of corvids fly over from adjacent farmland, flocks of various species of gulls loaf around the pools and gravel strips, flocks of Goldfinches, Linnets and other flocking birds occupy the scrub, and Great Spotted Woodpeckers, Nuthatch and Treecreepers will be easier to find in the surrounding leafless woods.

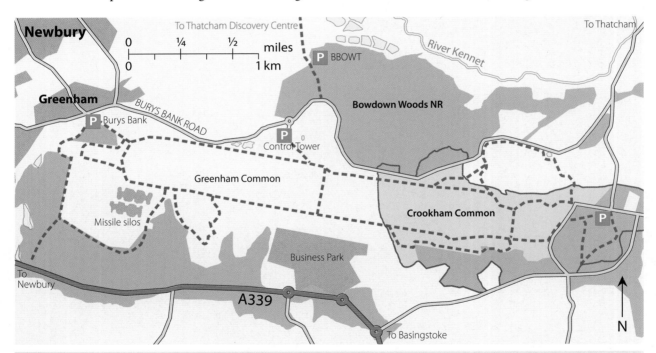

**Access:** Crookham Common, centred at SU 523 643, is encircled by narrow lanes, with parking at SU 533 646 off the Brimpton-Bishop Green Road. Greenham Common to the west has footpath entrances at Burys Bank Road on the northern edge of the Common, but most visitors park at the Control Tower car-park (SU 500 650 – check for closing times, currently (2013) 8pm) or at Burys Bank car-park at the western end (SU 484 653) which often fills at weekends. Footpaths include the 2 km long Taxiway Walk. Summer wardens direct visitors away from sensitive breeding birds. Early morning is often the best time here.

**Facilities:** None, although the old control tower is currently (2013) being sold, and community groups have expressed an interest in acquiring it for use as a possible visitor centre.

**Web Information:** Greenham and Crookham Commons are local nature reserves, and details can be found on West Berkshire's website – www.westberks.gov.uk, currently under Environment and Planning / Countryside / Nature Reserves and Commons. Management is about to pass to BBOWT (2013), so checking their website (www.bbowt.org.uk) might be worthwhile. The Greenham Common Trust has a website that gives a brief history of the site (www.greenham-common-trust.co.uk). Details of access to Bowdown Woods can be found on the BBOWT website, www.bbowt.org.uk.

## Species

**Resident:** Little Grebe, common ducks, Sparrowhawk and Common Buzzard, Tawny Owl, Green and Great Spotted Woodpecker, Skylark, Woodlark, Stonechat.

**Summer:** Tree Pipit, common warblers, Spotted Flycatcher, Woodlark, Dartford Warbler, Stonechat, Ringed Plover, Little Ringed Plover breeding. Hobby, Cuckoo.

**Winter:** Gulls and small numbers of duck, Snipe and possibly Jack Snipe, on the pools and flashes, Stonechat and Dartford Warbler on the heath, Siskins, Lesser Redpolls and winter thrushes in Bowdown Woods.

**Spring/Autumn passage:** Yellow Wagtails and Wheatears. Possible (but increasingly scarce) Turtle Dove. Variety of passage waders.

**Scarcer visitors:** Alpine Swift (Apr 2006), Ring Ouzel (Apr 2009), Mealy Redpoll (Mar 2009), Wryneck (Sep 2010).

TOP TO BOTTOM: Dartford Warbler *Jerry O'Brien*; Little Ringed Plover *Roger Milligan*; Greenham Common *Jerry O'Brien*.

# Jubilee River

This 11 km flood relief channel was constructed in the 1990s and completed in 2002 to divert Thames floodwaters away from Windsor and Maidenhead. It runs through open countryside north of the Thames between Boulter's Lock at Maidenhead and Slough, and was designed to recreate a natural river with both reed-beds and new plantations. In one particular area, known as Dorney Wetlands, the channel was widened and designed as a wildlife refuge with many features for waterfowl and reed-bed specialists. Here, a number of scrapes and islands, new plantations, scrub and grassland provide a wide range of habitat.

Dorney Wetlands is worth a visit throughout the year. Bitterns and Bearded Tit have overwintered since the site was established, and the same habitat holds numerous Reed and Sedge Warblers and Reed Buntings in summer, and good numbers of Water Rails all year round. Little Ringed Plover have bred occasionally, along with Redshank and Lapwing, and over twenty species of wader have been recorded, primarily during spring passage. Wintering Golden Plover have numbered up to 1,000. Common Terns breed, but are often predated by resident Mink. The grasslands have attracted Skylarks and Meadow Pipits to breed and both Barn and Short-eared owl are noted regularly. This slow-flowing river is popular with waterfowl and larger numbers build up when nearby lakes freeze over. Such groups have included small numbers of Goldeneye, Smew and Goosander, occasional Scaup, and, more rarely, Common Scoter, Ruddy Duck, Eider and Red-crested Pochard. Regular passage birds include Wheatears and Yellow Wagtails, while common species of warbler breed in the maturing shrubs and vegetation, including Lesser Whitethroat.

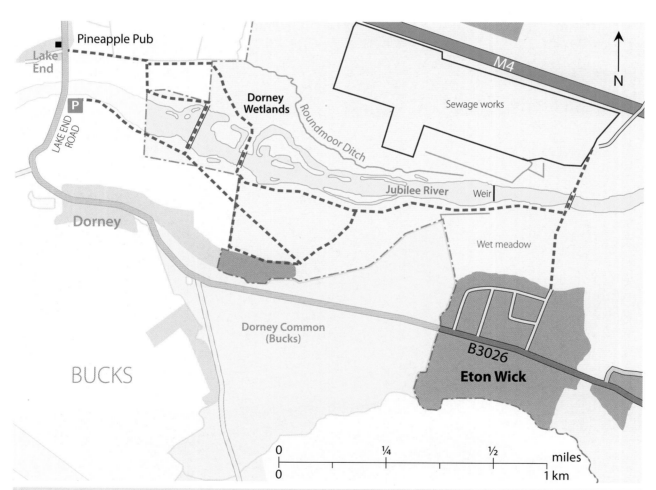

**Access:** Car park in Lake End Road, Bucks, (SU 929 795) or side roads in Eton Wick and take the county boundary footpath northwards (SU 943 786). Footpath and cycleway all along southern bank; short circular walk using two bridges 500 m east of Lake End Road (SU 935 795).

**Facilities:** on site: several viewing screens and information boards. Toilets at nearby Pineapple Pub 200 m north of car park.

**Web Information:** A map and brief details of Dorney Wetlands appear on the website www.birdsofberkshire.co.uk. There are also brief details of the Thames path section of the National Trails website – www.nationaltrail.co.uk, following the links Thames Path / Planning a Trip / Local Information / Jubilee River.

Both Willow Warbler (an uncommon breeding bird in this part of the county) and Grasshopper Warbler have held territory on more than one occasion. Maturing habitat has attracted Cetti's Warbler, with up to eight territories in 2013. Flood meadows opposite the weir near Eton Wick (SU 945 789) have attracted rarer waders amongst large numbers of Lapwings and several Snipe.

TOP TO BOTTOM: Roseate Tern *Marek Walford*;
Bearded Tit *Michael McKee*; Looking west *Jerry O'Brien*.

## Species

**Resident:** Great Crested Grebe, Grey Heron and occasional Little Egret, Mute Swan, common goose and duck species, Water Rail, Sparrowhawk, Kestrel, Red Kite, Buzzard, Kingfisher, Ring-necked Parakeet, Pied and Grey Wagtails, Skylark, Cetti's Warbler, Reed Bunting.

**Summer:** Tufted Duck and Gadwall, Common Tern, Lapwing and Redshank breed occasionally. Breeding passerines include Skylark, Meadow Pipit (occasional); Reed, Sedge and Garden Warbler, Whitethroat, Lesser Whitethroat, Blackcap and Chiffchaff, Reed Bunting. Hobby and Cuckoo are both regular. A post breeding Starling flock is occasionally 1,000-strong.

**Autumn/Winter:** Bittern, Shelduck, occasional White-fronted Geese, Scaup, Common Scoter, Goldeneye, Smew, Goosander, Snipe and Jack Snipe, up to 1000 Golden Plover. Mediterranean Gull, occasional Short-eared Owl and Waxwing. Floods at Eton Wick have attracted Temminck's Stint, Ruff, Greenshank, Common and Green Sandpiper and Grey Plover.

**Spring/Autumn passage:** Passage Dunlin, Grey Plover, Black-tailed and Bar-tailed Godwits, Oystercatcher, Greenshank, Common and Green Sandpiper. Garganey, Little Gull, Arctic Tern, Wheatear, Yellow Wagtail and occasional Whinchat pass through. Steady movement of hirundines and swifts. Hobbies regular, often up to eight or more. Willow and Grasshopper Warblers sometimes singing into late May.

**Scarcer visitors:** Spotted Crake (Aug 2000), Green-winged Teal (February 2004), Spoonbill (May 2007), Bearded Tit (since 2011), Roseate Tern (May 2011), Red-footed Falcon (May 2012), Pectoral Sandpiper (Sep 2012 and Aug 2013).

# Moor Green Lakes

Following half a century of gravel extraction in the Blackwater valley around Eversley on the Berkshire/Hampshire border, a 36 hectare (90 acre) nature reserve was created around Colebrook and Grove Lakes, each of which has a viewing hide. Together with the adjacent Horseshoe Lake, used for sailing, there is a significant area of water, with riverbank, scrub, paddocks and lines of trees, providing suitable habitat for a wide range of birdlife. Some 210 species have been recorded, of which typically 70 breed. Ringing is undertaken, a nest-box scheme is in place and a large extension to the reserve is (2013) being constructed to the west of the site.

The footpath running south from the Lower Sandhurst Road car-park to the river overlooks the Colebrook Lakes and its breeding islands to the east, and gives a view of the emerging scrapes and gravel bars of the new (2013) extension to the west. A hide half-way down the path provides a viewpoint for the breeding activity on three small islands on the north lake, and also looks over Long Island, which separates the north and south lakes. A viewing screen further down the path provides a view of two small islands on the south lake. Numerous Little and Great Crested Grebes, geese (including feral Barnacle and Snow Geese) and ducks are joined by breeding Redshank, Little Ringed Plovers, Lapwings, Common Terns and Black-headed Gulls in summer. A wide variety of waders pass through on passage. Turning left (east) on the riverside pathway takes one through bank-side Alders where Treecreepers, Goldfinches, Siskins and Lesser Redpolls may be seen, and Kingfishers are active along the river. After 1 km, another hide looks over Grove Lake, which is perhaps more renowned for waterfowl than waders. This lake, and Horseshoe Lake to the east, hold most of the winter Goosanders for which the site is renowned. A footpath goes north then east between Grove and Horseshoe Lake, and, as you pass along the north side of Horseshoe Lake, Little Owls often occur in

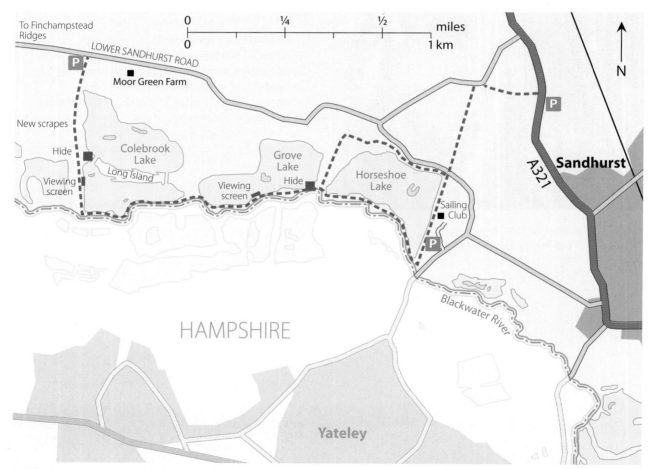

**Access:** At the western end, there is a small car park off Lower Sandhurst Road (SU 805 628), and at the eastern end, the Activity Centre car-park off Mill Lane (SU 821 620). Currently (2013) the closing times are 8pm, but please check the Moor Green Lakes Group website and signs on site.

**Facilities:** None at western end car-park. At Mill Lane Activity Centre, snacks and drinks vending machines, and toilets (for customers only). Basic café opening 2013.

**Web Information:** The Moor Green Lakes Group maintains a website (**www.mglg.org.uk**) which includes access and parking details and a site map.

hedgerows on the left. There is access between the north side of Horseshoe Lake and Lower Sandhurst Road if you wish to return along the lane to the car-park. Overall, the site attracts many passage waders, including Little and Temminck's Stints, Spotted Redshanks, Curlew Sandpipers and Whimbrel in addition to the commoner species, while in winter good numbers of Goldeneye and sometimes Smew join the Goosanders.

Following the River Blackwater to the west, a footpath gives views over the new wetland area, in which a number of rare species have been found, including Pectoral Sandpiper, Red-footed falcon, Great Grey Shrike and, in 2013, a summering Marsh Harrier. Berkshire's only Pallas's Warbler wintered along this stretch of the river in 2012/3.

TOP TO BOTTOM: Goosander *Jerry O'Brien*;
Pallas's Warbler *Ken White*; Colebrook Lake *Ray Reedman*.

## Species

**Resident:** Little and Great Crested Grebes, Little Egret, feral Barnacle and Snow Geese, Egyptian Goose, Sparrowhawk, Buzzard are often overhead, Barn and Little Owl, Kingfisher, possible Lesser Spotted Woodpecker, Stonechat, Linnet, Reed Bunting, Bullfinch, Yellowhammer.

**Summer:** Many common warblers breeding, Mandarin, Little Ringed Plover, Lapwing, Black-headed Gulls and Common Terns breeding. Hobby ever-present.

**Winter:** Possibility of Short-eared Owl. Goosander, Goldeneye, Smew, Brambling.

**Spring/Autumn passage:** Garganey regular, Yellow Wagtail, Cuckoo. Turtle Dove possible, passage warblers and waders.

**Scarcer visitors:** Species generally rare in Berkshire turn up here, such as Red-crested Pochard, Ferruginous Duck, Common Scoter, Scaup, Little and Glaucous Gulls, Little Tern. Osprey and Honey Buzzard have been noted. True rarities have included Shorelark (1998), Lesser Yellowlegs (2001), Pectoral Sandpiper (2003), Whiskered Tern (2005), Ring-necked Duck (2006), Red-footed Falcon (2006 and 2007) and Pallas's Warbler (2012/3).

# Old Slade Lakes

This site comprises four main lakes, with a fifth nearby in Thorney Country Park (Buckinghamshire). It lies immediately adjacent to and to the south west of one of Britain's busiest motorway junctions, where the M4 and M25 meet. It is close to a busy commercial truck centre and under the approaches to Heathrow Airport and, perhaps because of this, is somewhat under-watched. But lakeland birds thrive here, whilst emerging reed-beds and bank-side vegetation provide cover for waterfowl, and Hawthorn scrub supports a range of passerine species. The adjacent sewage treatment works has been modernised but small areas of boggy reed-bed attract Water Rail, occasional Green Sandpipers and nesting Moorhens. The main lake holds good numbers of common ducks, grebes and Cormorants, with rafts of loafing gulls at various times, and with scarcer gulls such as Iceland, Glaucous, Caspian and Mediterranean often seen at nearby Queen Mother Reservoir, it is worth checking for these amongst the Black-headed, Common and Herring Gulls here. Arctic Tern occurs on passage, Common Tern hunt in summertime and Kingfisher can be expected at any time over the lakes or along the Colne Brook running through the complex. Three smaller lakes can provide closer views of the Teal, Gadwall and occasional Goldeneye among the commoner species, and Little Egret has also been noted. Scrubland abutting the sewage works host mixed flocks of tits, finches and Goldcrest in winter and Blackcaps,

ABOVE: Gadwall; BELOW: Orlitts Lake;
OPPOSITE: Ferruginous Duck.
*Jerry O'Brien*

## Species

**Resident:** Great Crested and Little Grebes, common waterfowl including good numbers of Gadwall, Water Rail, Kestrel, Sparrowhawk, Lapwing, Kingfisher, Pied and Grey Wagtail, Green and Great Spotted Woodpecker, Skylark, Bullfinch, Reed Bunting, Yellowhammer.

**Summer:** Grebes and Coots nesting. Common Terns feeding. Large numbers of Swifts and hirundines, breeding warblers include Reed and Sedge, Blackcap, Chiffchaff and Whitethroat. Nest boxes around Sewage Works perimeter in use.

**Spring/Autumn passage:** Wheatear and Yellow Wagtail possible on grazing area. Cuckoo and occasional Turtle Dove may pass through. Small tern passage. Occasional Willow Warbler briefly.

**Scarcer visitors:** Velvet Scoter (Nov 1994), Ferruginous Duck (Nov 2002).

Chiffchaffs and Whitethroats in summer, when both Reed and Sedge Warblers can be found in surrounding reed-beds. Adjacent rough pasture holds good numbers of overwintering geese, Skylarks, Meadow Pipits, Fieldfares and Redwings. A visit to the 20 hectare (50 acre) Thorney Country Park (Buckinghamshire) to the north-east is worth combining with a visit here. A more manicured site than the Old Slade complex, its single lake hosts Smew, Goldeneye and Goosander and occasional Red-necked Grebe and Little Egret in winter, and Kingfisher and Grey Wagtail all year. The extensive path-side scrub holds singing males of all the commoner warblers in summer.

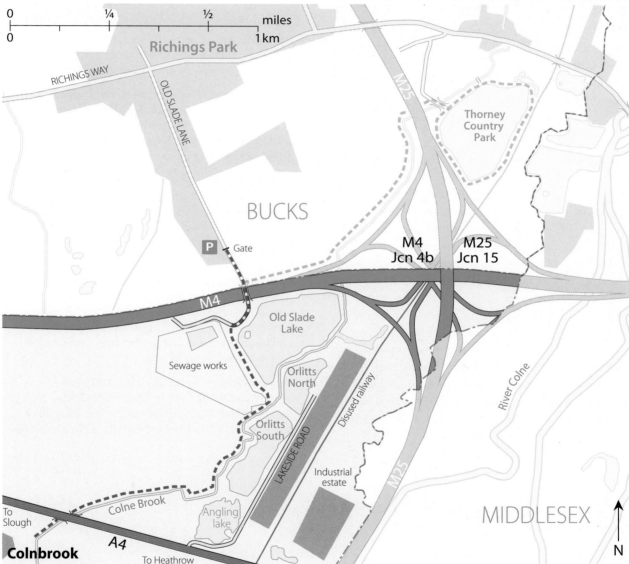

**Access:** No formal parking at either site. It is prudent to park outside swing gate (to avoid getting locked in) along Old Slade Lane (TQ 037 784). The southbound footpath gives access to Old Slade and the eastbound footpath around the field provides access to Thorney Country Park alongside the River Colne under the M25.

**Facilities:** None. View main lake from elevated road. Viewing screens alongside sewage works to view created mire.

**Web Information:** The Old Slade Lake is a private carp fishing lake, and it might be worth checking the owner's website – **www.boyer.co.uk**, following links / Our Waters / Old Slade Lake, for information on parking, and warnings about the consequences of not observing their requirements. Alternatively, for gaining access from Thorney Country Park, try Buckinghamshire County Council's website – **www.buckscc.gov.uk**, following the links / Leisure and culture / Country parks and green spaces / Thorney.

# Queen Mother Reservoir

Without doubt one of the county's premier sites for rarer species, this 140 hectare (350 acre) concrete lined reservoir also provides a raised vantage point from which to scan adjacent farmland for winter geese and raptors. A visit at any time of the year can prove rewarding.

The large area of open water attracts a substantial proportion of the county's records of divers, phalaropes, skuas, rarer gulls (including Glaucous, Iceland, Caspian, Yellow-legged, Ring-billed and Mediterranean), sea duck (including Eider, Scoter and Long-tailed Duck) and vagrant seabirds, including Guillemot and Little Auk, Kittiwakes, the first Sabine's Gulls (in the 1987 storm), Leach's and Storm Petrels, Manx Shearwaters, and Gannets. More common wintering duck, grebes and other water birds occur in good numbers. Terns of all the usual species occur on passage. There is a substantial mixed winter gull roost, and in the 2003–2006 Winter Gull Roost survey it recorded the 11th highest maximum site count in Britain.

Waders are attracted on passage, both to the shore of the water and flying over. Both Ringed and Little Ringed Plover are regular, Dunlin, Sanderling and Oystercatcher are frequent; Greenshank, Turnstone, Avocet, Knot, Curlew Sandpiper, Bar-tailed and Black-tailed Godwits and Little Stint have occasionally been found. Bank-side grasslands and trees are always worth checking. Wheatear, Yellow Wagtail, White Wagtail and Black Redstart occur in spring and autumn on passage, Rock Pipit, Lapland Bunting and Snow Bunting might be found in winter. Huge numbers of Swifts can gather low over the embankments. There is a resident pair of Peregrine Falcons who often create turmoil as they swoop across the area. The site has been well watched and regularly produces good records. Unusual records have included Wryneck, Great Bustard and two Buff-bellied Pipits in the winter of 2012/13.

## Species

**Resident:** Great Crested Grebes, Cormorant, Mute Swan, common geese, Shelduck, common ducks, Kestrel, Peregrine, Green Woodpecker, Pied Wagtail.

**Summer:** Relatively quiet, breeding Shelduck, Egyptian Geese, but still prospects of waders such as Dunlin, Curlew, Sanderling, Common Sandpiper, with Ringed and Little Ringed Plovers visiting from adjacent breeding sites.

**Winter:** Autumn and winter are the main seasons for mass accumulation of gulls and windblown vagrants. Potentially Shag, all three divers, five grebe species, Goosander, Red-breasted Merganser, Smew, Eider or Long-tailed Ducks, and wrecks of gulls or auks. Rock Pipit, Snow Bunting, Black Redstart.

**Spring/Autumn passage:** Major passage movements of terns and waders, occasional Kittiwakes, arrival of Yellow Wagtails and Wheatears, possibility of Whinchat. Large numbers of Swifts and hirundines. Returning Whimbrel, Godwits and Greenshanks by end of July.

**Scarcer visitors:** Spoonbill (Nov 2003), Lesser Scaup (Nov 2008), Grey-headed Wagtail (May 2009), Kumlien's Gull (Mar 2010), Roseate Tern (May 2011 and May 2012), Buff-bellied Pipit (Dec 2012 – first for Berks).

ABOVE: Great Skua *Jerry O'Brien*;
BACKGROUND: Queen Mother Reservoir *Andy Tomczynski*;
OPPOSITE: Gull roost with Iceland Gull *Marek Walford*.

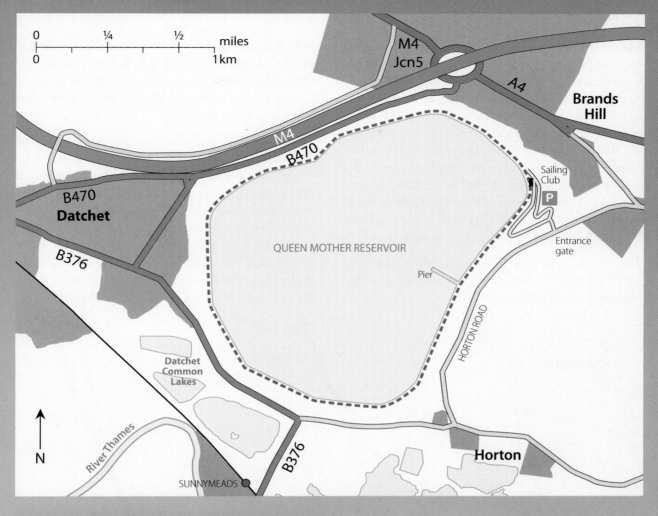

Map showing Queen Mother Reservoir with labels: M4 Jcn5, M4, A4, Brands Hill, B470, Datchet, B376, Sailing Club, P, Entrance gate, QUEEN MOTHER RESERVOIR, HORTON ROAD, Pier, Datchet Common Lakes, River Thames, N, B376, Horton, SUNNYMEADS. Scale bar showing 0–½ miles and 0–1 km.

**Access:** Access is by permit, and these are only available to members of the Berkshire Ornithological Club. The club though may organise limited access if an exceptional rarity occurs under the agreement they have with Thames Water, the owner and operator of the site as happened when the Buff-bellied Pipits occurred in 2012/13. All visitors are required to observe the terms of their permits or of any temporary access arrangements; failure to do so or unauthorised access by birdwatchers may result in termination of the current (2013) arrangements by Thames Water. Entry is usually from dawn to one hour after sunset, 7 days a week (TQ 017 771). The walk around the rim is 6 km long.

**Facilities:** None except in sailing club hours (**www.dwsc.co.uk**), when the club makes its toilets and café available to permit-holders.

**Web Information:** See the Berkshire Ornithological Club website – **www.berksoc.org.uk** for details of permit arrangements.

# Snelsmore Common

Snelsmore Common is a country park and nature reserve north of Newbury of about 100 hectares (250 acres). It comprises one of the larger areas of lowland heath in the county, with associated valley mires and bogs, and has been managed to remove woodland which encroached after traditional common grazing ceased in the 20th century. The site is now actively managed to control bracken and encourage heather and gorse, and grazing resumed in 1998. As well as heathland birds, a wide range of other fauna and flora typical of heaths can be found, such as Bog Bean, Sundew, Bog Asphodel, and White Admiral and Purple Emperor butterflies.

The site is at its best in summer, when displaying Tree Pipit may be seen during the day and churring Nightjar and roding Woodcock heard or seen at dusk.

Woodlark are scarce, but singing warblers, including Willow Warblers, are plentiful. It was probably the last Berkshire site to regularly host breeding Wood Warblers, until around 2000. Hobbies and Buzzards might be seen overhead.

In the autumn, flocks of Long-tailed, Blue, Great and Coal Tits, along with Goldcrests and occasional Chiffchaffs, can be encountered. Great Spotted and Green Woodpeckers are always present and Lesser Spotted has been seen at the car-park feeding station. Tawny Owl is often reported, and Collared Doves are plentiful. Winter visitors to the woods include flocks of wintering thrushes, Siskins, Lesser Redpolls and Bullfinches, with occasional records of Crossbill, whilst the open areas may hold a Stonechat or two.

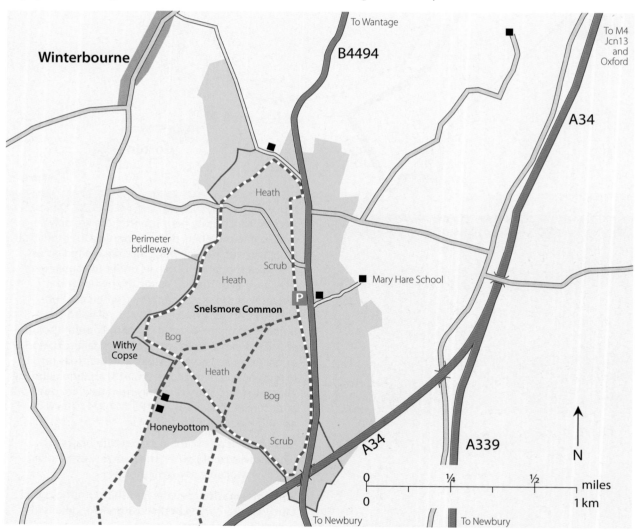

**Access:** The car park and picnic area is 2½ miles north of Newbury on the B4494 Wantage Road, (SU 463 713). The site is crossed by footpaths and tracks, whilst a bridleway encircles the outer edge.

**Facilities:** Car park, toilets and picnic area. The site is an SSSI and a Country Park.

**Web Information:** Snelsmore Common is a local nature reserve and country park, and details can be found on West Berkshire's website – **www.westberks.gov.uk**, currently under Environment and Planning / Countryside / Nature Reserves and Commons. Management is about to pass to BBOWT (2013), so checking their website (**www.bbowt.org.uk**) might be worthwhile.

## Species

**Resident:** Sparrowhawk, Kestrel, Woodcock, Collared Dove, Tawny Owl, potential for all three woodpeckers, Goldcrest, Nuthatch, Treecreeper, Jays, occasional Yellowhammer or Reed Bunting.

**Summer:** Possible Hobby and Nightingale, occasional Cuckoo, many singing Chiffchaffs, Willow Warblers, Whitethroats, Blackcaps and Garden Warblers, Tree Pipits, Woodcock, Nightjars and Linnets. Possibility of Turtle Dove.

**Winter:** Winter thrushes regular, with Siskins and Lesser Redpolls frequent. Crossbills occasional, Stonechat possible.

**Scarcer visitors:** Firecrest (Oct 2006)

TOP TO BOTTOM: Wood Warbler *Michael McKee*; Woodcock; Snelsmore Common. *Jerry O'Brien*

# Swinley Forest and Wishmoor

This 2,000 hectare (5,000 acre) area comprises a substantial part of the Thames Basin Heaths in the county, with compartments of richly-mixed deciduous and coniferous woodland interspersed with open heath and birch-encroached gorse-land, with mires and bogs, woods and open heathland between Bracknell and Camberley. A considerable part falls within the Crown Estate lands, and has been open to public access, which has given rise to the potential for conflict between wildlife conservation and recreation, particularly as this is a popular area for mountain biking. The Crown Estate has recognised the conflict, and in 2013 published a revised map of cycle routes designed to reduce it. In its publicity material for the area, the importance of visitors keeping dogs under control is stressed. The area is also used by the nearby Royal Military Academy at Sandhurst for exercises, so be prepared to see fully-armed and camouflaged soldiers on your visit! There is much for birdwatchers and other naturalists looking for typical heath species to find at any time of the year in the public areas such as Crowthorne Woods, Caesar's Camp, Wishmoor Bottom and Olddean Common. On the east of the site lies Rapley Lake, large enough to attract Little Grebes, but mainly noted for its dragonfly community.

The area has been studied comprehensively for some years. It holds a substantial population of Firecrests, and of Dartford Warblers, which peaked at around 40 pairs before the cold winters of 2009/10 and 2010/11 reduced numbers to one or two individuals.. In winter this is the best area for wintering finches, with Crossbills, Siskins and Lesser Redpolls likely, and it is worth checking Chaffinch flocks for the regular Bramblings. These species can occur in very substantial numbers, often late in winter or in early spring. Areas of open heath and bracken may still hold a few Stonechat and Reed Bunting and this is one of the more reliable sites for Great Grey Shrike, which has occasionally over-wintered.

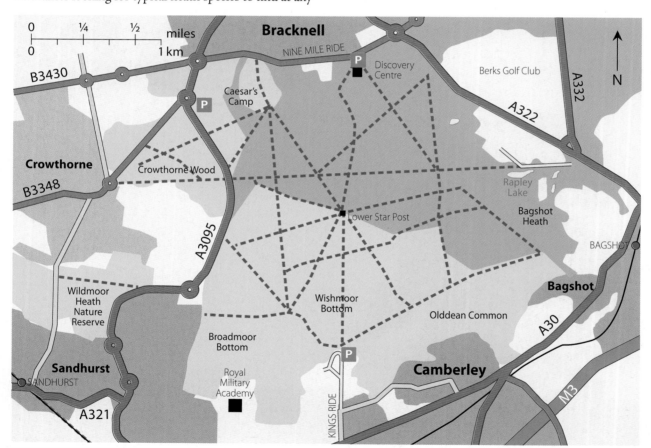

**Access:** Car park at the Look Out Discovery Centre of the B3430 to the north of the site (SU 877 662). Charges apply, closed early in the evening – do not use for Nightjar hunts. Alternatively, kerb-side parking in Kings Ride, Camberley (SU 875 622) and there is a small car park near Caesar's Camp (SU 854 655).

**Facilities:** toilets, snacks and coffee shop at the Discovery Centre.

**Web Information:** Bracknell Forest Borough Council publishes information about parking on its website (**www.bracknellforest.gov.uk**) following the links Leisure and culture / The Look Out Discovery Centre / The Look Out general information. The Crown Estate has a section on its Windsor estate which includes the Swinley Forest on its website (**www.thecrownestate.co.uk**, following the links Windsor / Forestry) but currently (2013) no access information is set out.

Breeding season surveys have disclosed 25 to 30 pairs of Redstarts in most years, with a similar number of Tree Pipit territories, 20 or so pairs of Stonechats and 30 or so pairs of breeding Woodlarks in addition to the Firecrests and Dartford Warblers. An evening visit might produce churring Nightjars, up to 38 pairs of which have been counted, roding Woodcock and calling Tawny Owls.

## Species

**Resident:** Tawny Owl, Green and Great Spotted Woodpeckers, Stonechat, Dartford Warblers (numbers vary greatly), common tits, including Coal Tit, Nuthatch, Treecreeper, Linnet.

**Summer:** Nightjar, Woodlark, Woodcock, Redstart, Spotted Flycatcher, Firecrest, occasional Hobby.

**Winter:** Wandering Crossbill, chance of Brambling, variably sized flocks of Siskin and Lesser Redpoll. Redwings and Fieldfares.

**Spring/Autumn passage:** Cuckoo, Tree Pipit, Willow Warbler.

**Scarcer visitors:** Wryneck (May 2001), Great Grey Shrike (several winters), Hen Harrier (Oct 2011).

TOP TO BOTTOM: Stonechat *Jerry O'Brien*; Woodlark *Dave Rimes*; Wishmoor Bottom *Andy Tomczynski*.

# Thatcham Marsh, Nature Discovery Centre & Lower Farm Gravel Pits

This complex of sites offers a variety of wetland birdwatching experiences throughout the year. The Nature Discovery Centre hosts a number of organised events for all the family. In summer, the lake in front of the centre has displaying Great Crested Grebes, a raft for breeding Common Terns and an artificial Sand Martin bank, and may hold late-staying Gadwall or Pochard. In winter the usual wintering wildfowl can be found with Red-crested Pochard often present. Long Lake to the south of the centre has attracted such scarcer species as Great Northern Diver and Osprey. A track runs south from the centre to the west of these lakes and leads to a level crossing across the railway, the path giving access to an area of scrub and reeds, the state of which has fluctuated over the years depending on the level of the water table. In the 1970s this area was one of the first in Berkshire to be occupied by Cetti's Warbler, which are now widespread in suitable habitat in this part of the Kennet valley. The reed and scrub is also occupied by Reed and Sedge Warblers in summer, and Reed Buntings and Water Rails throughout the year although

the latter will be easier to hear at night or see in winter. A trail leads west along the canal where Kingfisher and Grey Wagtail might be seen, while bank-side vegetation attracts warblers such as Garden, Whitethroat and Lesser Whitethroat, together with occasional Bullfinches. Siskin and Lesser Redpoll can also occur in winter.

The canal side path crosses the railway. Shortly after, two paths diverge. One leads north back towards Lower Way, where a subsequent right turn leads between the sewage treatment works and two more small pools, where once again Cetti's Warblers can be encountered, together with Cuckoo and Hobby in summer, and another right turn takes you back towards the Discovery Centre. The second continues west a little before another path joins from the south to lead back over the canal. Turn back east after crossing the canal and further waters can be seen. Race Course Gravel Pit [now Lower Farm Trout Lake] on the left generally holds commoner species including Little Grebe, and additional Water Rails, and perimeter vegetation attracts Lesser Whitethroats and Grasshopper Warblers. Scanning the race-course grassland to the west often reveals numbers of Golden Plover in winter. The lake to the west is known as Lower Farm, which attracts a wide variety of waterfowl and wetland species, and has been one of the best sites for passage wading birds in the vicinity. A hide is available but sadly problems with vandalism means that it is sometimes closed and locked. On spring passage, Green Sandpiper, Redshank, Greenshank and Curlew pass through. Both Ringed and Little Ringed Plover have bred here. Common Terns occur in summer, with other tern species on passage. In winter, look out for Goldeneye. Smew have also occurred, and Garganey is possible on passage. Scarcer visitors have included Temminck's Stint, Curlew Sandpiper and Osprey.

ABOVE: Grasshopper Warbler *Jerry O'Brien*;
BACKGROUND: Lower Farm Gravel Pit *Jerry O'Brien*.

## Species

**Resident:** Little and Great Crested Grebes, common geese and ducks, plus Shelduck, Sparrowhawk, Kestrel, Kingfisher, Grey Wagtail, Cetti's Warbler

**Summer:** Ringed Plover may breed. Many breeding warblers, Cuckoo and Hobby active.

**Winter:** Large flocks of Lapwing and Golden Plover possible. Wintering wildfowl.

**Spring/Autumn passage:** Waders including Dunlin, Oystercatcher, Greenshank, Green and Common Sandpiper, Sedge, Reed Warbler and Whitethroat in good numbers. Lesser Whitethroat and Turtle Dove may pass through. Autumn wader passage may include Black-tailed Godwit and Curlew.

**Scarcer visitors:** Great Reed Warbler (May 1970), Paddyfield Warbler (1997), Kumlien's Gull (March 2004), Grey Phalarope (November 2005), Cattle Egret (October 2007), American Wigeon (Nov 2008), Spoonbill (May 2011).

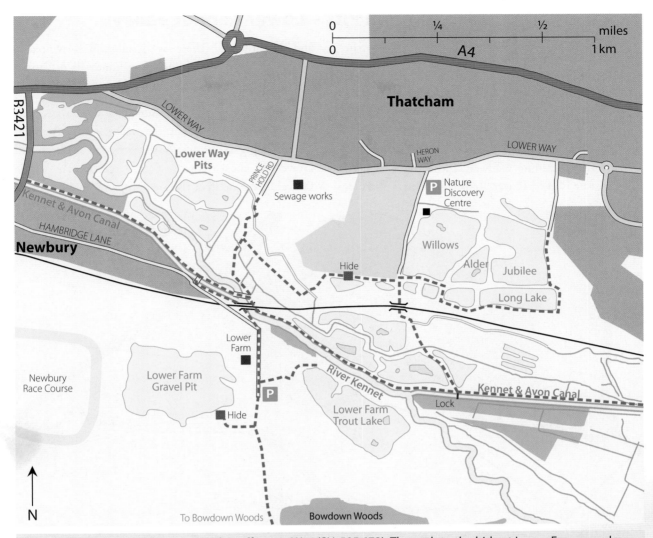

**Access:** The Discovery Centre car park is off Lower Way (SU 505 672). The path to the hide at Lower Farm can also be reached from the eastern end of Hambridge Lane.

**Facilities:** toilets and café at the Nature Centre during opening hours. Hide at Lower Farm Lake (SU 498 662).

**Web Information:** Access and opening details for the Nature Discovery Centre together with details of events can be found on West Berkshire's website – **www.westberks.gov.uk**, currently under Environment and Planning / Countryside / The Nature Discovery Centre. Management is about to pass to BBOWT (2013), so checking their website (**www.bbowt.org.uk**) might be worthwhile. Details also appear on the RSPB's website under the reserves section. The NDOC website has details of access to the Lower Farm hide and a map (**www.ndoc.org.uk**, click on the link for Lower Farm Hide).

# Theale and Burghfield Gravel Pits – Lower Kennet Valley

The string of flooded former gravel workings in the Kennet valley running over four miles from south west Reading to Sulhampstead rank amongst the most important wildlife areas in Berkshire. The area has consistently attracted some of the county's rarest birds and the largest gatherings of many commoner species. The combined area includes breeding sites for locally scarce birds, including Gadwall, Little Egret, Ringed Plover, Little Ringed Plover, Redshank, Cetti's Warbler and Nightingale. There is a substantial wintering population of wildfowl, including hundreds of Tufted Duck, Gadwall and Wigeon.

The naming of the various waters has not always been consistent. In this account, the waters east of the road from Reading to Burghfield are referred to as Burghfield Gravel Pits, those to the west (the larger area) as Theale Gravel Pits. Not all of the area is open to public access,

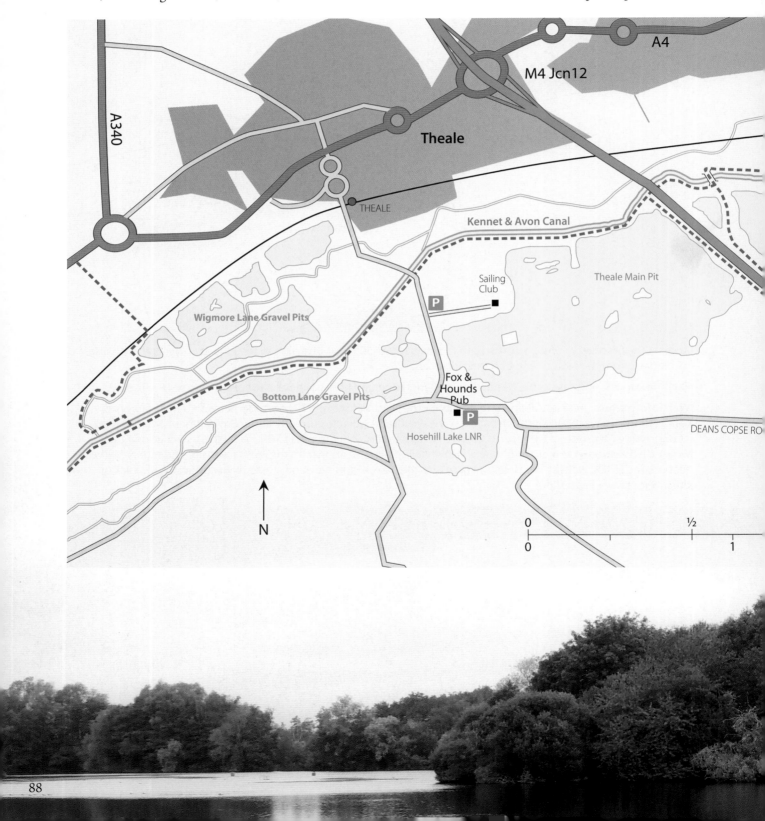

**Access:** Small area for five cars between the lakes along Deans Copse Road (SU 651 698) or park in adjacent Fox and Hounds car park, after seeking permission. For Main Pit only, use the sailing club car park (SU 650 704). For Burghfield Gravel Pits, park just inside Water Ski entrance (SU 670 703), or in the small lay-by on the east side of Searles Farm Lane near its junction with Berrys Lane (SU 685 700). Refer to *Where to Watch Birds in Thames Valley* (Clews and Trodd, 2002) for more details of surrounding lakes.

**Facilities:** refreshments (and hence patrons' toilet facilities) are available at the Fox and Hounds pub opposite Hosehill Lake or the Cunning Man opposite the junction between Pingewood Lane and Burghfield Road.

**Web Information:** Hosehill Lake is a local nature reserve, and details can be found on West Berkshire's website – **www.westberks.gov.uk**, currently under Environment and Planning / Countryside / Nature Reserves and Commons. Management is about to pass to BBOWT (2013), so checking their website (**www.bbowt.org.uk**) might be worthwhile. The Theale Area Bird Conservation Group's website at **www.tabcg.webs.com** gives details of all the areas west of the M4 and access information

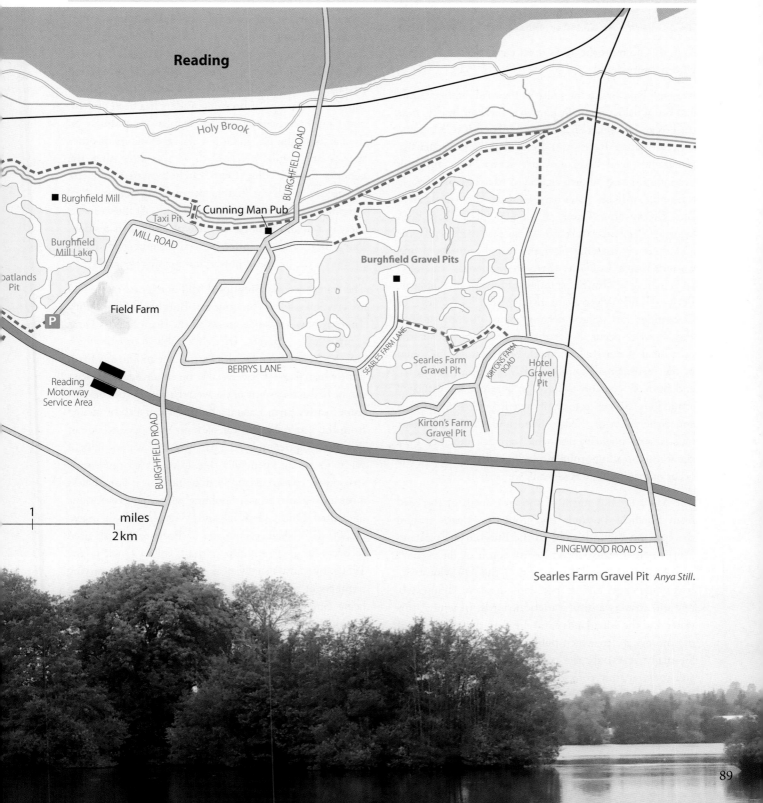

Searles Farm Gravel Pit *Anya Still*.

so in this account the areas most easily visited are dealt with in more detail.

Hosehill Lake lies to the south of the road linking Theale and Burghfield. Originally known to local birdwatchers as the Fox and Hounds Pit, after the pub opposite, it became a Local Nature Reserve in 1998. It possesses extensive phragmites reed beds, a wader scrape, tern and gull nesting rafts and an artificial Sand Martin bank, largely the result of many years hard work by the Theale Area Bird Conservation Group. Over 160 species have been recorded. A circular walk around the perimeter is possible and there are viewing platforms on the northern and western banks. In winter there are numerous waterfowl and loafing gulls. Substantial numbers of Gadwall, Pochard and Wigeon are regular, and Goldeneye or Goosander can appear among them. Groups of Teal and Shoveler occur in the shallower sections, while the occasional Water Rail, and even Bittern, might be found in the reeds. Small numbers of Snipe occur in winter, and waders occur on passage. In summer the principal attractions are the colony of breeding Common Terns and Sand Martins, Sedge, Reed and Cetti's Warblers, plus singing Nightingales, which are accompanied by a clamorous breeding group of Black-headed Gulls. Waders occur on passage, and Redshank sometimes breed.

The Main Pit fills much of the area north of the road from Sheffield Bottom (the group of houses around the Fox and Hounds pub) to the Burghfield Road and Pingewood (Deans Copse Road), south of the Kennet and Avon Canal and south west of the M4 Motorway. It is much larger and deeper, with an active sailing club, but still attracts a great variety of birds. In winter, this water and the Moatlands Gravel Pit on the other side of the motorway (to which public access has been limited for many years) are the centre of a substantial winter gull roost, mainly comprising Black-headed and Lesser Black-backed Gulls. The pits at Theale and Burghfield together held the second largest winter concentration (and largest inland concentration) of Lesser Black-backed Gulls in Britain during the BTO's Winter Gull Roost

Survey undertaken between 2003 and 2006, and large numbers can be seen flying in from feeding areas at dusk. The gull flock produces occasional records of Berkshire's scarcer species, including Mediterranean, Caspian or Iceland Gulls. Disturbance from sailing results in a lower density of wintering duck than some other waters, but the considerable expanse of water has attracted a variety of scarce wildfowl, and vagrant water and sea birds over the years, including Gannet, Little Auk, Great Skua, divers and Leach's Storm Petrel. A few Red-crested Pochards, which sometimes breed locally, may be seen all year.

Spring and autumn passage draws Common, Arctic, Black and Sandwich Terns and a few Little Gulls. Since the flooding of the area on the south side known as the Wader Pit, which produced many good wader and passage records in the 1980s, the amount of habitat suitable for passage or breeding waders has been limited, but Common Sandpipers are regular on passage on the banks of the pit, and a few passage waders of other species are regularly recorded. It was here that the county's first breeding Oystercatchers nested in 2010. As the area is well watched the surrounding areas produce a good variety of records of passage birds. At the west end there is a small Heronry. The area also supports resident Peregrines, which can often be seen occupying one of the pylons on the overhead power line crossing the area.

The waters around Burghfield Mill north east of the M4 are less accessible, as are much of Burghfield Gravel Pits. There is however some access to the main Searles Farm complex at two points. There is a public footpath which crosses the site from Searles Farm Lane to Kirtons Farm Lane which passes between lakes on either side, and views can be had across some of the western part of the complex from Searles Farm Lane itself. Access can also be gained from the water ski club car park on the opposite side of this water. The complex is a patchwork of waterbodies of varying sizes and generally thickly vegetated causeways, so comprehensive coverage is difficult. This is nonetheless a rewarding area to visit, holding wintering populations of Tufted Duck, Gadwall and Wigeon well in excess of 200 each, smaller numbers of Pochard (which used to occur in greater numbers than Tufted Duck in the 1980s, but now usually peak at less than 100), varying numbers of Shoveler, and Goldeneye. Hard weather can bring Smew, Goosander or Black-necked Grebe; and Shelduck, Pintail and Scaup occasionally occur. The trees which surround the pits frequently attract flocks of over 50 Siskins in winter, and Water Rail or Woodcock are possible in winter. In the breeding season, this is a good site for Nightingales and Lesser Whitethroat and there is a substantial heronry. Cetti's Warblers are present all year around, and Mandarin Duck and Egyptian Goose have become more frequent in recent years.

OPPOSITE: Nightingale; *John Absolom.*
TOP TO BOTTOM: Arctic Tern *Marek Walford*;
Greylag Geese *Linda Garner-Langham*;
Hosehill Lake *Robert Still.*

## Species

**Resident:** All the common waterfowl, grebes and gulls, tits and finches, and both Pied and Grey Wagtails. Kestrel, Sparrowhawk, Peregrine, Water Rail, Kingfisher, Green and Great Spotted Woodpeckers, Cetti's Warbler.

**Summer:** Breeding Common Terns can be found on rafts, waders such as Redshank, Dunlin, Oystercatcher, Little Ringed and Ringed Plovers, Sedge and Reed Warblers, and Reed Buntings are plentiful. Scrub hosts numerous warbler species and is the main area in Berkshire for Nightingale.

**Winter:** Large numbers of gulls, wildfowl, winter thrushes and Siskin, potential for Bittern, scarcer wildfowl and grebes. Chance of divers on Main Pit.

**Spring/Autumn passage:** A significant passage of gulls, terns, wading birds and passerines, with the possibility of Osprey, Garganey, Turtle Dove and Grasshopper Warbler. Large numbers of Swifts and hirundines possible.

**Scarcer visitors:** There have been many, but highlights include Bittern, Red-rumped Swallow (1992), Spoonbill (2001), Ring-necked Duck (2001, 2006) and Ferruginous Duck (2007), Great White Egret (2004), Crane (2002) and Yellow-browed Warbler (2003) and in past decades, Melodious Warbler, Roseate Tern, Sharp-tailed Sandpiper and Caspian Tern.

# Twyford Gravel Pits and Loddon Reserve

This group of worked-out gravel pits, west of Twyford and dissected by a railway line, is worthy of a visit at any time of year. Angling disturbance on some waters tends to concentrate most wildfowl to the north-eastern (BBOWT Loddon Reserve) and most southerly (Hurst Green) lakes, but all should be checked as well as the intervening hedgerows, paddocks and scrub that have turned up scarce vagrants including Wryneck, Hoopoe and Pied Flycatcher. In addition to the regular duck species, Goosander, Goldeneye and Smew can be expected in winter, the latter often lurking under overhanging branches amongst the Teal. Rafts of commoner ducks such as Wigeon, Pochard and Shoveler should be checked for Pintail, and both Scaup and Common Scoter have been recorded amongst the numerous Tufted Ducks. Red-breasted Merganser and Great Northern Diver have been recorded at Park Lane East Lake in the past, so it should not be ignored. Shelduck and Egyptian Geese are likely among the Canada and Greylag geese and the rarer grebes are possible, particularly in spring. When the Loddon, which runs through the complex, over-tops its banks in wet seasons, the resulting flood-water attracts Lapwings, Golden Plover and even more Wigeon.

Features for wading birds are limited, but Snipe, Redshank and Dunlin can sometimes be found on the small islands on the BBOWT reserve, which also produced the second ever breeding of Oystercatchers in the county, in 2011. Common Terns nest here also, and a variety of warblers and other small birds breed in the lakeside vegetation. Nuthatch, Treecreeper and Coal Tit are often amongst them and Bullfinch is frequent. Kingfisher occur throughout the area.

This is a site worth visiting in winter when reduced foliage aids visibility across the lakes, after floods when wet meadows attract numbers of ducks, geese and winter thrushes, and in the breeding season when the variety of breeding species is impressive.

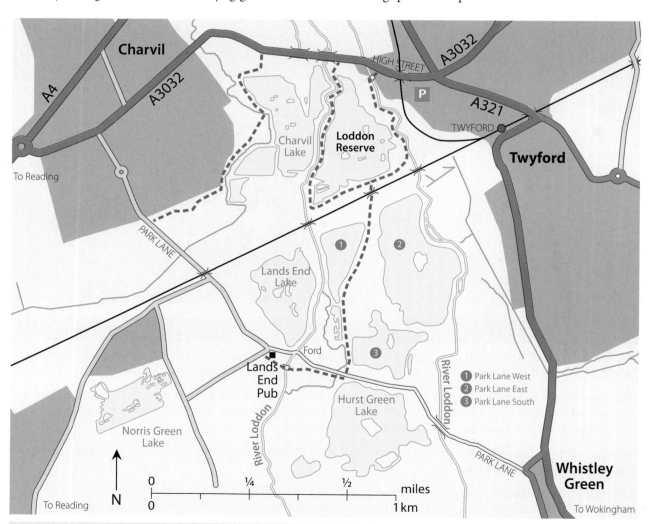

**Access:** Car Park off High St, Twyford, 200 m away (SU 786 760).

**Facilities:** None.

**Web Information:** The reserves section of the BBOWT website has a page for the Loddon reserve (www.bbowt.org.uk / reserves / Loddon-Nature-Reserve) which also has a link to events at the site.

## Species

**Resident:** Great Crested and Little Grebe, Egyptian Geese, Sparrowhawk, Kestrel, occasional Little Owl, Green and Great Spotted Woodpeckers (occasionally Lesser Spotted Woodpecker), Nuthatch, Treecreeper, Bullfinch.

**Summer:** Oystercatcher, Redshank and Common Terns on island territories, Cuckoo, hirundines and Swifts, most common warblers.

**Winter:** Goldeneye, Smew, Goosander all likely. Scaup possible amongst increasing rafts of commoner duck species. Snipe, Water Rail more obvious, winter thrushes, possible Stonechat.

**Spring/Autumn passage:** Possibility of the rarer grebes on passage and several passage waders, such as Green and Common Sandpiper, Ringed Plover, Greenshank, Ruff.

**Scarcer visitors:** Great Northern Diver (Jan 2002), Hoopoe (Aug 2000), Pied Flycatcher (Apr 2001).

TOP TO BOTTOM: Goldeneye; Oystercatcher; The Loddon Reserve.

*Jerry O'Brien*

# Walbury Hill

Walbury Hill is, at nearly 300 m above sea level, the highest chalk hill in Britain. It is worthy of a visit just for its tremendous views, north across the Kennet valley to the dip slope of the Berkshire Downs and northeast and east over Newbury and towards Reading and beyond, giving an unparalleled panorama of Berkshire. Its flat top, the site of an ancient hill fort, and well-wooded slopes, open farmland, scattered bushes and wind-blown trees attract a number of interesting species. West Woodhay Down on the northern slope also attracts many of the same species and, indeed, the whole ridge from here west to the Combe Gibbet and on to Inkpen Hill is worth exploring. On the top Grey Partridges and Corn Buntings are now scarce, but there are still plenty of Yellowhammers and Meadow Pipits. You can look down on soaring Red Kites and Buzzards. It is the county's best site for Ravens, numbers of which have built up since the turn of the millennium and

groups of between 10 and 20 are often seen. To these are added Merlins and occasional Short-eared Owls in winter, and Great Grey Shrike has been recorded. At this time huge numbers of Fieldfares and Redwings or flocks of buntings and finches can sometimes be seen. These may include Bramblings and potentially even rarer species such as Snow Bunting. During migration the hilltop and areas of scrub will often yield Wheatear, Whinchat, Ring Ouzel and Redstart and, potentially, Turtle Doves and Hen Harriers.

At the bottom of the southern slope is Combe Wood, which not only hosts most of the usual woodland species but also a number which are now difficult to find elsewhere in Berkshire. It is fast becoming the only site for breeding Willow Tits in the county. Lesser Spotted Woodpecker has been recorded, along with Crossbills, Tree Pipit, Spotted Flycatcher, and even Hawfinch.

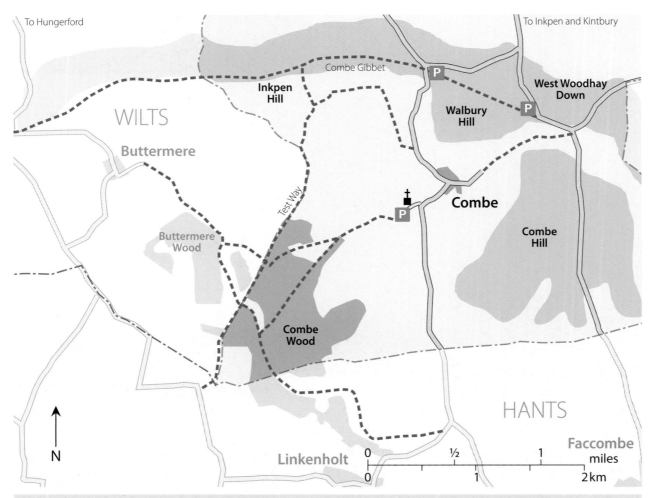

**Access:** park at West Woodhay ridge (SU 378 617) or nearer Combe Gibbet (SU 371 620). Do not use the connecting track in wet weather. For Combe Wood, park near church (SU 368 607).

**Facilities:** None.

**Web Information:** The Visit Newbury website (www.visitnewbury.org.uk) has up to date information, including car parking conditions, which may differ from those shown above.

TOP TO BOTTOM: Raven *Jerry O'Brien*; Willow Tit *Peter Stronach*; Walbury Hill. *Jerry O'Brien*

## Species

**Resident:** Grey Partridge, Kestrel, Sparrowhawk, Red Kite, Buzzard, Tawny, Barn and Little Owl, Skylark, Willow Tit, Raven, Yellowhammer.

**Summer:** Common woodland species breeding in Combe Wood, plus Willow Tit. Spotted Flycatcher near church. Chance of Hobby, occasional Cuckoo.

**Winter:** Good numbers of Meadow Pipit, Linnet, Skylark, Yellowhammer. Merlin, Short-eared Owl, Brambling.

**Spring/Autumn passage:** Hen Harrier, possible Turtle Dove, Wheatear, Whinchat, Redstart, Ring Ouzel.

**Scarcer visitors:** Rough-legged Buzzard (Mar 1995), Goshawk (Jul 2004), Snow Bunting (Nov 2004), Great Grey Shrike (Apr 2007), Hawfinch (Winter 2012/13).

# Windsor Great Park

The vast 1,920 hectares (4,800 acres) of Windsor Great Park fills most of the area between the town of Windsor to the north, Old Windsor and Egham to the east, and Ascot and Virginia Water to the south. The area is part of the Crown Estate, with substantial areas open to the public. It features a mixture of woodland, open grassland, farms and waterbodies of various sizes. It has been managed as a royal estate since it was enclosed as a royal hunting reserve in the 13th century. This continuity means that it supports some of the oldest standing trees in southern England, including some notable veteran oaks. The south east corner, comprising the Savill Gardens and the eastern half of Virginia Water lake lie over the county border in Surrey. It is separated from the less wild Home Park which lies to the east of Windsor and north of the Great Park by the A308.

The area is too large to be covered comprehensively on foot in a single day. In the northern part, open parkland with scattered copses rises to the south, with access along the Long Walk, or the parallel Queen Anne's Ride. At the south of this section lies The Village (SU 955 725), where small pools add variety to both scenery and wildlife. The open areas with dispersed trees should be checked for Stock Doves, Green Woodpeckers, Ring-necked Parakeets and Mistle Thrushes and (potentially) Spotted Flycatchers. Nuthatches, Goldcrests and, in winter, thrushes and roving mixed flocks of finches, are plentiful. Any small, single bird in undulated flight needs checking as Lesser Spotted Woodpeckers are a good prospect almost anywhere within the Park. An evening visit in the summer may be rewarded with Barn Owl or roding Woodcock.

The Village pools host Little Grebe, Mallard, Gadwall, Tufted Duck, Coot, Moorhen, and occasional Mandarin, joined in winter by small numbers of Egyptian Geese,

## Species

**Resident:** Common waterfowl including Little Grebe and Mandarin. Woodcock, Barn, Tawny and Little Owl, Ring-necked Parakeet, Lesser Spotted Woodpecker, Marsh Tit, many Jackdaws.

**Summer:** Hobby, Nightjar, Cuckoo, Spotted Flycatcher. Raven has bred.

**Winter:** Large numbers of corvid species, flocks of Woodpigeons, Collared and Stock Doves. Wandering groups of mixed finches; Brambling likely.

**Spring/Autumn passage:** Wheatear, Yellow Wagtail.

**Scarcer visitors:** Great Reed Warbler (May 1990), Lapland Bunting (Oct 1990), Gannet (Jul 2005).

Teal and Pochard. Many of these birds alternate between these pools and the much larger, but inaccessible, Great Meadow Pond in the centre of the Park. Further south and east lie the Savill Gardens, Obelisk Pond and Smith's Lawn polo ground (SU 972 703), and this area

TOP TO BOTTOM: Lesser Spotted Woodpecker; Windsor Great Park.

*Jerry O'Brien*

is more densely wooded than the north. However open areas like the polo ground sometimes attract passage Wheatears, and Pied Wagtails are numerous. Little Owls nest in the vicinity.

Further south still, from Norfolk Farm (SU 960 702) to Blacknest Gate (SU 962 687), mixed woodland flanks the widening stream which feeds into Virginia Water. Jays, Treecreepers, Siskins and Lesser Redpolls, common tits and finches occur with Kingfishers and Mandarin Ducks along the stream. On the main lake itself where Grey Heron, good numbers of common ducks and Cormorants can be found, Mandarin sometimes emerge from the waterside vegetation and the occasional Goldeneye, Smew or Goosander are seen in winter. Throughout the park in summer, birdsong is both varied and persistent, adding greatly to the magic of the place. And everywhere, Buzzards and Red Kites may be seen soaring overhead. Just outside the Park and west of the A332, is Cranbourne Chase, also worthy of exploration as this somewhat scrubby area, surrounded by farmland, adds still more variety to the potential list of species, including warblers.

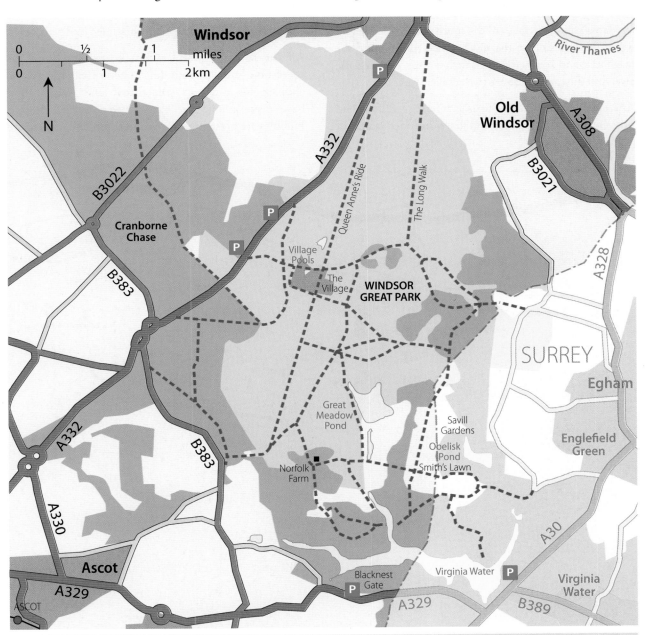

**Access:** Free car parks on A332 (SU 952 734 & SU 945 727). Pay Car Parks are provided at Blacknest Gate (SU 961 686) and across the county boundary on the A30 London Road next to the Wheatsheaf Hotel (SU 980 689).

**Facilities:** None in the Berkshire part of the site, but there are WCs in the Valley Gardens, Savill Gardens and Virginia Water car park in Surrey, where refreshments may be obtained.

**Web Information:** The Crown Estate's website has a section devoted to the Windsor Estate which includes the Great Park – see **www.thecrownestate.co.uk**, and click on "Windsor". There is a wealth of information for visitors, including a number of maps and guides which can be downloaded.

# Woolhampton Gravel Pits

One of the more recent sites created by flooding of a former gravel extraction quarry, these pits sit between and to the south of the Kennet & Avon Canal and the River Kennet and the site readily becomes flooded after heavy rain. Access to the site from the east is along a 400 m track through a wooded area, which is the best place for Siskins and Lesser Redpolls in winter and singing warblers, including Cetti's, in summer. Water Rail call along this section, Lesser Spotted Woodpecker and Nightingale have been recorded, and it can be a good spot for Bullfinch. The first lake is the largest, the Rowney Predator Lake, which lies to the south of the Kennet, and a path branches off to the south which runs around the lake's east and southern side. Further west, between the river and the canal there are two smaller waters.

The open waters hold the usual wintering wildfowl and other water bird species, and have included some of the rarer species found in Berkshire including Black-necked and Red-necked Grebes, Scaup and Lesser Scaup. Fewer species remain to breed, but this is a site where the colourful Red-crested Pochard can sometimes be seen. There is some suitable habitat for waders, including wintering Snipe, passage Greenshank, Green and Common Sandpiper, Redshank and Dunlin, and summer visiting Little Ringed and Ringed Plover. Common Terns may visit in summer or occur on passage, when Black or Arctic Terns are also possible. Little Egrets may be seen, and Spoonbill has been recorded. The site remains one of the few regularly occupied by Turtle Dove.

All the common warblers can be expected and the vegetation and surrounding open area should be checked for migrants. Bluethroat and Water Pipit have been among the rarer species recorded here. Hobbies are present in spring and summer but these too

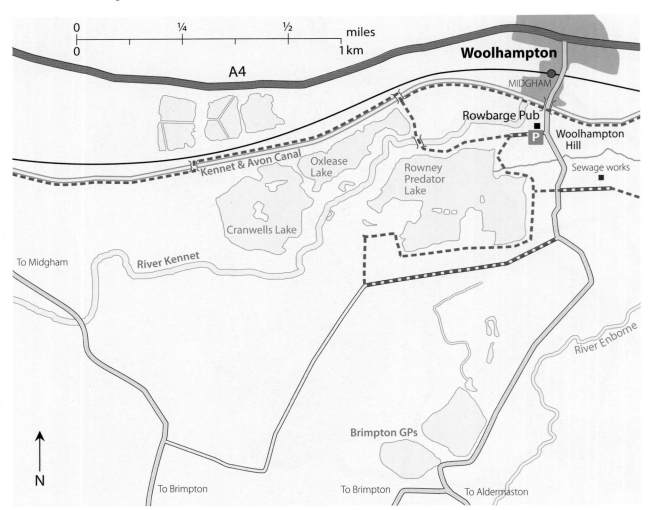

**Access:** Park at Rowbarge Pub (SU 573 665) where the car park has space set aside for visitors to the canal. Midgham Station is a short walk away. Cranwells Lake is difficult to view, but the Wasing Estate is planning a path around the Rowney Predator Lake with hides or blinds.

**Facilities:** The Rowbarge is a popular pub, other village services are available in Woolhampton.

**Web Information:** Currently (2013) there is a brief section on the NDOC website (**www.ndoc.org.uk** / sites / brimptonpits).

should be studied as Red-footed Falcon, an increasingly regular bird in Berkshire, has been recorded here. On return to the car park, a quick check of the sewage works further east might produce Yellow Wagtail or Little Owl, while Grey Wagtail and Kingfisher are likely around the canal crossing. If leaving towards Brimpton, it might be worth checking the old Brimpton Gravel Pit site to the south, which produced a number of notable records when an actively worked pit.

### Species

**Resident:** All the common waterfowl, Little Owl, Water Rail, Kingfisher, Grey Wagtail, Cetti's Warbler, Goldcrest, Nuthatch, Treecreeper, possible Marsh Tit, Bullfinch, Reed Bunting.

**Summer:** Breeding waterfowl including Shelduck. Turtle Dove, Cuckoo, possible Spotted Flycatcher.

**Winter:** Goose and duck numbers increase, potential for scarcer species. Lapwings and Golden Plover in the area.

**Spring/Autumn passage:** possibility of the rarer grebes, variety of wader species, Black Tern, Hobby, Yellow Wagtail, Whinchat, Wheatear, Nightingale.

**Scarcer visitors:** Lesser Scaup (Oct 2007), Red-footed Falcon (May 2008), Bluethroat (Apr 2009), Spoonbill (Jun 2011).

TOP TO BOTTOM: Little Owl *Brian Winter*; Cetti's Warbler *Jerry O'Brien*; Rowney Predator Lake. *Jerry O'Brien*

# Wraysbury, Horton and Yeoveney Gravel Pits

The flooded old gravel workings around Wraysbury are mature sites, and one of the longer established of such areas in Berkshire, long known to, and watched by, local birdwatchers. The area comprises 12 main waters between Horton Pits to the north of the railway line and Hyde End by junction 13 of the M25. Between the lakes there are mature hedgerows, tree-lines and an important area of scrub (TQ 015 735). The Colne Brook River runs through the complex, often used by resident Kingfishers. Some fishing and sailing is undertaken, but there are sufficient undisturbed areas to ensure good birdwatching at any time. On any of the waters, the usual common geese and duck species, which can include many hundred Tufted Duck, are supplemented by good numbers of Goldeneye and Smew in winter. Disturbance however may be responsible for reduced numbers of visiting Goosander in recent winters. Nonetheless, the various pools have attracted Slavonian, Red-necked and Black-necked Grebes, all three diver species, Long-tailed Duck and Red-breasted Merganser. This group of lakes perhaps has the most extensive areas of reed, in which Sedge and Reed Warblers, and Reed Buntings can be found breeding. In the same section, river-side scrub and mature trees draw in several summering warbler species and Nightingales, plus many Siskins and Lesser Redpolls in winter, and Treecreepers, Goldcrests and Chiffchaffs all year round. The scrub has traditionally been a good area for Grasshopper Warbler,

ABOVE: Jack Snipe; BELOW: Hythe Lake *Jerry O'Brien*.

### Species

**Resident:** Little and Great Crested Grebes, Heron, Little Egret, Egyptian Goose, Gadwall (numerous), Buzzard, Water Rail, Ring-necked Parakeet, Kingfisher, Grey Wagtail, Reed Bunting.

**Summer:** Most common warblers, possible summering Nightingales, and Grasshopper Warblers, Cuckoos, many Swifts and hirundines.

**Winter:** Substantial numbers of gulls and commoner wintering duck and waterbirds, especially Tufted Duck and Gadwall, and some scarcer species, notably Goldeneye and Smew. Chiffchaffs, substantial winter thrush flocks and other wintering passerines. Notable roosts of Jackdaws and Ring-necked Parakeets.

**Spring/Autumn passage:** Possible Garganey, Hobby, variety of passage waders, Turtle Dove, Nightingale, Wheatear, Whinchat.

**Scarcer visitors:** Ortolan Bunting (Sep 2007), Lesser Scaup (Oct 2008), Long-tailed Duck (Nov 2008), Red-rumped Swallow (Apr 2010).

Lesser Whitethroat, Linnet, Bullfinch and occasional Stonechat, whilst in winter it holds large numbers of Redwing and Fieldfares.

The few areas suited to waders are around the Horton lakes, where Green and Common Sandpipers, Redshank, Ringed and Little Ringed Plovers and Snipe are regularly seen, and Jack Snipe is recorded fairly often. Red-footed Falcon has been noted here and Hobbies, sometimes in good numbers, can occur anywhere throughout the site.

Passage terns might include Arctic, Sandwich and Black, and Cuckoos parasitize local nesting birds. The main Ring-necked Parakeet roost is no longer at Wraysbury, but this noisy and conspicuous bird is almost always present, sometimes in hundreds. In addition to the numbers of ducks and gulls on the open waters, and birds of the densely-vegetated areas, the site and surrounding area attracts winter roosts of Jackdaws, Fieldfares and Redwings which can be seen gathering at dusk.

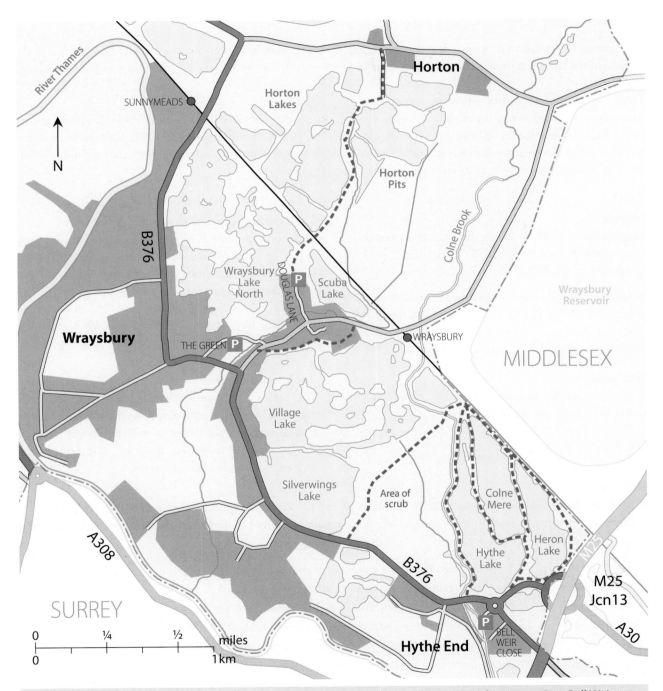

**Access:** Car park The Green (TQ 003 742). Kerb-side along Douglas Lane (TQ 007 745) for Horton Pits. Bell Weir Close (TQ 019 726) for Hythe Lake etc. The Waterloo to Windsor railway line runs through the site, with convenient stations at Wraysbury and Sunnymeads.

**Facilities:** Local shops and pubs.

**Web Information:** There is a brief summary on the Berkshire Nature Conservation Forum website www.berkslnp.org/index.php/colne-valley-gravel-pits-and-reservoirs.

# The species accounts

## Introduction

The species accounts which follow are based on all published records in reports produced by the Middle-Thames Natural History Society, Newbury District Ornithological Club, Oxfordshire Ornithological Society and the Berkshire (formerly Reading) Ornithological Club, as well as the Hants/Surrey Borders Bird Reports and other sources available to the authors. The Berkshire Ornithological Club's database has been used for records up to the end of 2012, and some notable records for the months of 2013 prior to final checking of these accounts prior to publication have been added. It should be noted that some records for recent years have not been considered and validated by the Berkshire Records Committee. Where these are not supported by published photographs or were not seen by many observers, the species account mentions that such records are subject to such checking.

The criteria for inclusion of species and the geographical area covered have been dealt with in the Introduction. At the end of the species accounts, there is a list of the escapees recorded in Berkshire, and a summary of hybrid records.

### Order of species accounts – finding a species

The species accounts follow the taxonomic order set out in the version of the British List currently (2013) published by the BOU on its website. Following the advances in DNA analytical techniques since the 1990s, the taxonomic order has been subject to considerable change, and is likely to change further. For those unfamiliar with the taxonomic order, or recent changes, an alphabetic index is given at the end of the book.

## Text

### Names

**English Names** – these follow the English vernacular names used in the current (2013) British List published by the BOU.

**Scientific Names** – these follow the binomial used in the current (2013) British List published by the BOU. The scientific names of non-avian species are given wherever such species are mentioned in the accounts

### Gazetteer

A gazetteer of all the sites in Berkshire mentioned in this book appears in Appendix II.

### Conventions used in the text

References to periods of time are denoted in the texts of the species accounts with a dash (−) to denote the start and end of a defined time period or with an oblique (/) to denote a winter season, e.g. the period from 1962 to 1963 inclusive would be shown as 1962−63, whereas the winter from the end of 1962 into 1963 would be shown as 1962/63.

### Tables and Figures

The Tables and Figures included in the species accounts are numbered consecutively. Data have been derived from county annual reports and the county records database unless otherwise specified. The caption for each explains basis of presentation.

### References

A complete list of the references used can be found on *pages 512–515* and these are referred to in the text in the conventional manner. A small number of texts which are regularly referred to have been given abbreviated, italicised names throughout the species accounts:

| | |
|---|---|
| *1968-72 BTO Atlas* | *The Atlas of Breeding Birds in Britain and Ireland* (Sharrock 1976). |
| *1981-84 BTO Winter Atlas* | *The Atlas of Wintering Birds in Britain and Ireland* (Lack 1986). |
| *Population Trends* | *Population Trends in Britain's Breeding Birds* (Marchant et al. 1990). |
| *1988-91 BTO Atlas* | *The New Atlas of Breeding Birds in Britain and Ireland* (Gibbons et al. 1993). |
| *Historical Atlas* | *The Historical Atlas of Breeding Birds in Britain and Ireland 1875-1900* (Holloway 1996). |
| *Migration Atlas* | *The Migration Atlas: movements of the birds of Britain and Ireland* (Wernham et al, 2002). |
| *County Report* | The annual (or biennial) reports produced by the Oxford Ornithological Society (OOS) for Berkshire, Buckinghamshire and Oxfordshire (later only Berkshire and Oxfordshire) until 1973 and by the Berkshire (formerly Reading) Ornithological Club for Berkshire since 1974. |

In addition, *The Handbook of the Birds of Europe, the Middle East and North Africa: the birds of the Western Palearctic* Volumes I–IX (Cramp *et al.* 1977–94) is referred to throughout as *BWP*, followed by the relevant volume number given in Roman numerals.

## Abbreviations and terms

The following abbreviations and terms have been used in this book:

| | | | |
|---|---|---|---|
| Abundance Maps | Maps produced from results of timed tetrad surveys and other records (see Chapter 4) | ROC | Reading Ornithological Club (now Berkshire Ornithological Club ) |
| BBOWT | Berkshire, Buckinghamshire and Oxfordshire Wildlife Trust Ltd. | RRG | Runnymede Ringing Group |
| | | RSPB | Royal Society for the Protection of Birds |
| BBRC | British Birds' Rarities Committee. | 10km square | A National Grid square of 10km × 10km (100 km²) |
| BBS | Breeding Bird Survey of the BTO. | | |
| BOC | Berkshire Ornithological Club (formerly Reading Ornithological Club) | Tetrad | A square of 4 km² (2 km × 2 km) comprising four National Grid 1 km squares (see Chapter 4). |
| BOU | British Ornithologists' Union. | | |
| BTO | British Trust for Ornithology. | Tetrad/ Tetrad Atlas Survey | Surveys based on presence/absence or timed counts of birds in tetrads (see Chapter 4). |
| CBC | Common Bird Census of the BTO. | | |
| LNHS | London Natural History Society. | TTV | Surveys based on counts of all species present in a tetrad during a set period, usually two hours (see Chapter 4). |
| MTNHS | The Middle-Thames Natural History Society (now defunct). | | |
| NDOC | Newbury District Ornithological Club. | TVERC | Thames Valley Environmental Records Centre. |
| NRG | Newbury Ringing Group. | WeBS | Wetland Bird Survey. |
| OOS | Oxford Ornithological Society. | Winter Map | Abundance Map produced from TTVs in winter during 2007–11 Atlas Survey. |
| | | WWT | The Wildfowl and Wetlands Trust. |

# Maps

Maps derived from the two Berkshire Atlas surveys in 1987–89 and 2007–11 are used throughout the species accounts. These are in two sizes, the larger, at a double column width, are the breeding distribution maps derived from both surveys, the smaller, a single column width, are the abundance and migration maps derived from the 2007–11 survey.

## Breeding Distribution Map

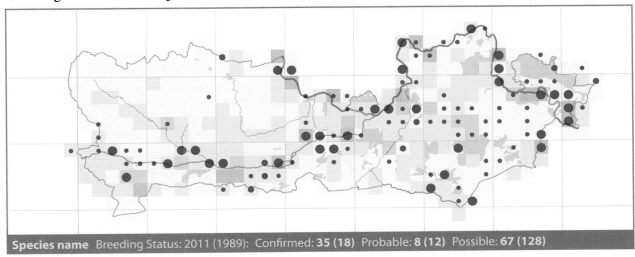

**Species name** Breeding Status: 2011 (1989): Confirmed: **35 (18)** Probable: **8 (12)** Possible: **67 (128)**

The results of the 2007–11 are shown overlaid on the results of the 1987–89 survey for ease of comparison. The results of the 2007–11 survey are shown by red dots. The size of the dots used indicates the category of breeding evidence recorded from the best evidence obtained during the 2007–11 survey in a tetrad (see Chapter 4) as follows:- possibly breeding (•), probably breeding (●), or confirmed breeding (●). The information for the 1987–89 survey are shown by the background orange shading in a tetrad, possible breeding is shown by the palest shading (   ), probable breeding by medium shading (   ) and confirmed breeding by the darkest shading (   ). No dot means that no breeding evidence was obtained in the 2007–11 survey in that tetrad, and no background shading means no breeding evidence was obtained in that tetrad in the 1987–89 survey.

The captions summarise the number of tetrads in each category – the numbers in each category for the 2007–11 survey (referred to as 2011) are shown in **bold text**; those for the 1987–89 survey (referred to as (1989)) are shown as bold text within brackets (**bold text**).

*Maps are shown for all species for which breeding evidence has been obtained, except Stone Curlew, as the species' vulnerability to disturbance is considered to justify not publishing a map. Some dots have also been moved in the Peregrine map in the interest of protecting vulnerable breeding sites.*

## Abundance Maps

**Species name**  Breeding season abundance
Tetrads occupied: **145** (232) Average of occupied tetrads: **1·9**

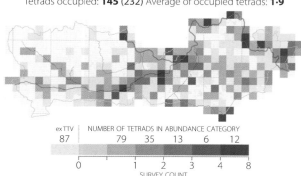

| exTTV | NUMBER OF TETRADS IN ABUNDANCE CATEGORY | | | | |
|---|---|---|---|---|---|
| 87 | 79 | 35 | 13 | 6 | 12 |

0    1    2    3    4    8
SURVEY COUNT

**Species name**  Winter abundance
Tetrads occupied: **148** (232) Average of occupied tetrads: **2·2**

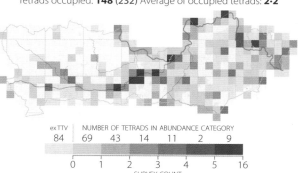

| exTTV | NUMBER OF TETRADS IN ABUNDANCE CATEGORY | | | | |
|---|---|---|---|---|---|
| 84 | 69 | 43 | 14 | 11 | 2 | 9 |

0    1    2    3    4    5    16
SURVEY COUNT

These are based on the results of the 2007-11 Atlas survey, and show the relative number of birds recorded during the timed tetrad counts and casual records collected indicating presence of birds not recorded during the timed counts.

Each tetrad from which the species has been recorded is shown by shading.
**Green** shading is used in the breeding season maps, **blue** shading in the winter maps.

The palest shade ( for summer and  for winter) shows tetrads for which records were only obtained outside the timed surveys. The six darker shades indicate the relative abundance category derived from the two-hour counts.

Chapter 4 sets out the basis upon which the six categories of abundance have been ascertained, as derived from the timed two-hour counts, shown by the darkness of the shading ( , , , , , for summer and , , , , , for winter).

The captions above the map show the number of tetrads in which the species was recorded – the **bold** figure is the number of tetrads in which the species was recorded in timed counts in each season, the figure in brackets the number in which it was recorded in both timed counts and roving or casual records. The **bold** figure that follows "Average of occupied tetrads" is the sum of the higher of the timed survey counts (TTVs) for each tetrad divided by the number of tetrads in which the species was recorded in the TTVs.

The key below the map shows the following:

| | |
|---|---|
| SURVEY COUNT | the number of birds represented by the boundaries of the abundance categories in which birds were recorded in the timed surveys. |
| NUMBER OF TETRADS IN ABUNDANCE CATEGORY | the number of tetrads with counts in each category. |
| exTTV | records from outside the timed counts. |

## Migration Maps

**Species name**  Spring migration occurrence
Tetrads used: **14** Average of used tetrads: **1·4**

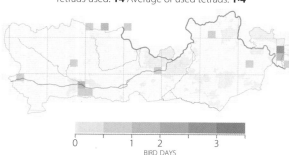

0    1    2    3
BIRD DAYS

**Species name**  Autumn migration occurrence
Tetrads used: **18** Average of used tetrads: **2·0**

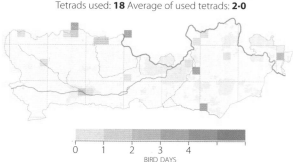

0    1    2    3    4
BIRD DAYS

These are based on records received during the spring (March to June) and autumn (July to October) periods of the 2007–11 Atlas survey (2008 to 2011) for species which occur in most years on migration but which do not regularly breed in Berkshire.
The aggregate of the numbers of birds recorded on each day (BIRD DAYS) was calculated for each tetrad. The darkness of the shading indicates the relative numbers of bird-days, using six categories as with the abundance maps, the spring maps using **green** shading ( , , , , , ), and the autumn maps **brown** shading ( , , , , , ).

The figures above the map show the number of tetrads in which the species was recorded and average of the bird-days during the survey period for the tetrads in which it was found. The key below the map show the number of bird-days represented by the upper boundaries of the categories used in the map.

Great Crested Grebes, Dinton Pastures *Tony Harden*

# The Birds of Berkshire

# Mute Swan

Green

*Cygnus olor*

*Widespread resident*

The Mute Swan is now a widespread resident in suitable habitat in Berkshire, although its recent history provides an illustration of the way in which practical conservation measures can influence the success of a species.

The Tetrad Survey breeding distribution maps show that Mute Swans were present on all the river systems in the county in both surveys, with an increase in the number of tetrads with proven and probable between the 1987–89 and 2007–11 surveys. The species' requirement for a sufficiently long 'runway' to enable it to take off appears to limit its use of standing water bodies to those which are relatively large. Some two-thirds of records were of confirmed breeding in the 1987–89 survey and four fifths in 2007–11, as would be expected for such a conspicuous species.

Information on breeding numbers and success in the county reports is limited. The Mute Swan was the focus of much attention in the early 1980s following a number of surveys which indicated that many birds were dying from lead poisoning. Anglers' lead shot weights were identified as the cause, the swans taking in lead shot with

vegetation when feeding. A campaign to ban the use of lead fishing weights followed and a swan rescue service 'Swan Life-Line' was established locally. This service took in stricken birds, used a fibre optic endoscope to remove the lead, and then kept and rehabilitated the birds prior to release back to the wild. Voluntary bans on the use of lead shot were followed by a national ban from 1st January 1987. Subsequent analysis showed a dramatic decline in lead poisoning deaths on the Thames, from 50–60% of all deaths investigated prior to 1987 to 5% of all adult deaths in 1988 (Sears, 1989). A national survey of Mute Swans carried out by the BTO in 1983 found 43 pairs possibly breeding in Berkshire. It is difficult to be certain whether the 1987–89 Tetrad Survey results indicated an increase in the population in the intervening period or simply reflect an improvement in coverage.

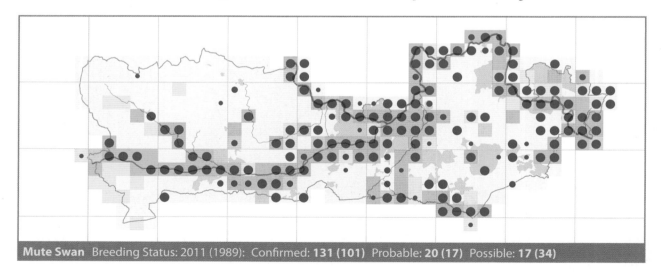

**Mute Swan**  Breeding Status: 2011 (1989): Confirmed: **131 (101)**  Probable: **20 (17)**  Possible: **17 (34)**

**Mute Swan**  Breeding season abundance
Tetrads occupied: **138 (184)** Average of occupied tetrads: **8·2**

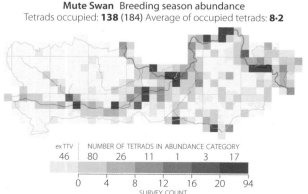

| exTTV | NUMBER OF TETRADS IN ABUNDANCE CATEGORY | | | | | |
|---|---|---|---|---|---|---|
| 46 | 80 | 26 | 11 | 1 | 3 | 17 |

0   4   8   12   16   20   94
SURVEY COUNT

**Mute Swan**  Winter abundance
Tetrads occupied: **147 (175)** Average of occupied tetrads: **9·8**

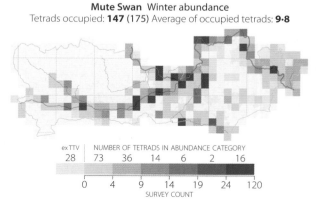

| exTTV | NUMBER OF TETRADS IN ABUNDANCE CATEGORY | | | | | |
|---|---|---|---|---|---|---|
| 28 | 73 | 36 | 14 | 6 | 2 | 16 |

0   4   9   14   19   24   120
SURVEY COUNT

Non-breeding birds form flocks of varying sizes both during and outside the breeding season. The winter map indicates that flocks can be found anywhere in the river valleys. Considerable numbers are attracted to urban riverside areas, such as Reading, Henley and Windsor, where the public provide swans with food. Unfortunately, for many years few counts from these areas have been submitted to the county reports. Sears (1989) reported taking blood samples from 181 individuals in the Windsor flock between 1983 and 1986 and in the winter of 1990/91 up to 138 were counted at Reading. More recently the flock at Windsor has been counted more regularly, and this site produced the county's highest count of 342 in June 2006. There were also 324 there in January 2004, and 319 in April 2009. The only other site to record a count of over 300 is Thameside Promenade, Reading where there were 310 in January 1997.

Elsewhere, flocks of 20 to 100 birds often occur on gravel pits or in riverside meadows although their distribution often changes as birds move between sites as the winter progresses. Counts of more than 100 have been almost annual since the mid-1990s at such sites,

with such counts being most frequent from Wraysbury, Burghfield and Theale Gravel Pits. The increase in flock counts since the 1980s locally reflects a doubling of the UK population between the early 1980s and the first decade of the 21st century (Holt *et al.*, 2011).

Ringing recoveries indicate that movements occur throughout the country and there have been recoveries in Berkshire of birds which were ringed at Abbotsbury, Dorset; Alvaston, Derbyshire; Tredegar, Gwent; Hertfordshire; Sussex and Enfield, Middlesex. Birds ringed at Pangbourne and Caversham have been reported from Coventry and Bristol respectively. There have though been no records of movements of more than 100 km since 1990.

Nationally, Mute Swan numbers have remained stable since the increase in the last two decades of the 20th century. It may mean that the population has now reached the level where most of the available breeding sites are occupied now that the problems apparently caused by lead shot have been eliminated.

*Sponsored by Swan Life Line*

Mute Swan, River Thames *Dickie Duckett*

# Black Swan

## Cygnus atratus

*Escaped introduced resident in small numbers, has bred*

The Black Swan is a native of Australia and New Zealand, which has been bred in captivity as an ornamental bird. It is not yet regarded as having a self-sustaining population in Britain, and is not on the British List. However a small breeding population has apparently become established in Berkshire in recent years.

Once escaped introduced species began to be reported in the County Reports, the species was occasionally recorded from gravel pits, rivers and other waterbodies throughout the county in most years from 1974 to 1994, and annually since then, with records from ten or more sites in most years since 2005. The majority of records have been of single birds although two birds together have been reported frequently, and they often associate with Mute Swans. Apart from the recently established breeding group at Reading and family parties elsewhere, there have also been other higher counts, of which the highest were five at Twyford Gravel Pits on 28th December 1976, and five at Dinton Pastures in December 2003.

There was a probable juvenile at Dinton Pastures in August 1982, an immature bird there from 17th to 20th October 1983 and an adult and two cygnets at Theale Gravel Pits from 11th to 12th November 1989, but no evidence that breeding took place there. Breeding was eventually proved at Great Meadow Pond, Windsor Great Park in 2004, and a pair was reported breeding there every year until 2009. Success was poor. Although cygnets were seen in most years, successful fledging was not confirmed until 2007.

Elsewhere a pair raised three young at the mouth of the Kennet in Reading in 2005. The following year a pair bred in Newbury, but at least one pair have bred every year from 2008 to 2011 at Reading, three in 2010, although as the nest site was not found in 2008 it is possible that it might have been in Oxfordshire. The area between Thameside Promenade and the mouth of the Kennet has become a regular haunt, with highest counts of ten on 9th May 2009 and 1st July 2010. A family party with four cygnets at Sonning on 3rd May 2010 was presumably one of the Reading families.

*Sponsored by Amy McKee*

# Bewick's Swan

Amber   Sch. 1

## Cygnus columbianus

*Uncommon passage migrant and winter visitor*

The Bewick's Swan was first recorded in Berkshire in March 1950 when two birds were seen at Burghfield. Since then it has become a regular passage migrant during the winter months and has occurred in small numbers in most years.

Since 1962, Bewick's Swans have been recorded in the county every year apart from 1972, 1977, 1988, 1994, 2001, and 2004 to 2006. Some 480 birds in total were seen up to the winter of 1993/94. However there was a decline in the number of birds recorded during the spell of mild winters from 1987/88 to 1993/94 when only 43 were seen, compared with the preceding seven winters in which 181 were observed. There then followed an exceptional period from the winter of 1995/96 to 1997/98 when there were records involving at least

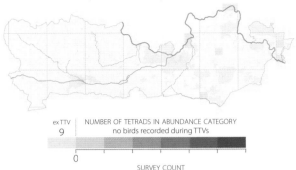

**Bewick's Swan** Winter abundance
Tetrads occupied: **0** (9) Average of occupied tetrads: **0**

ex TTV | NUMBER OF TETRADS IN ABUNDANCE CATEGORY
9 | no birds recorded during TTVs

0
SURVEY COUNT

200 birds. After this there was a spell with very few records, with no more than 23 between 1998/99 and 2008/09, followed by something of a recovery in numbers with records of a further 20 birds in the three winters 2009/10 to 2011/12.

The exceptional period in the mid- to late 1990s included two winters, 1995/96 and 1996/97, when flocks were present in the Kennet Valley to the west of Theale from early January to 17th March (in 1996) and 20th February (in 1997), involving up to 20 birds in the first winter and 29 in the second. There was also an exceptional count of 42 in flight over Reading on 10th March 1996.

Except for this period, the pattern of records parallels the fluctuating fortunes in the wintering population at the WWT refuge at Slimbridge, Gloucestershire and elsewhere in the south of England, with a decline in numbers during the 1990s and early years of the 21st century which has not been matched in the East of England or the Netherlands, possibly indicating that in milder winters they winter further east (Holt *et al.*, 2011). This suggests that weather conditions are an important factor in determining the movements of the species through Berkshire. It is likely that the bulk of the Berkshire records relate to birds on passage between sites to the south and west of Berkshire and eastern Europe. This was indicated by a bird with a coloured neck ring seen at Theale Gravel Pits in December 1996, which had been ringed in north eastern European Russia in August 1994, and which was seen in the Netherlands three days before it arrived at Theale, and arrived at Slimbridge two days after it was last seen at Theale. It was also reported from Germany the following March.

In the 1950s and 1960s a small number of birds remained in the county for up to a month but apart from the flocks which overwintered in 1995/96 and 1996/97, most records since have been of over-flying birds or of short stays of up to five days. The earliest arrivals have been recorded in October, the earliest date being 7th October in 1984, and immigration appears to continue until January. Return passage generally occurs

during February and March although there has been a decline in the number of February and March records since the 1970s. The latest post-winter departure date recorded in the county was of a bird on the Thames between Cookham and Bourne End which was present until the end of April 1962. A summary of the arrival dates of Bewick's Swans in Berkshire since the winter of 1949/50 is shown in Figure 2.

The majority of sightings have been of small, sometimes family, groups of up to ten birds. Larger numbers have occurred on only 15 occasions up until the winter of 2010/11, the largest flocks being 47 and 34 at Theale in February and March 1970 respectively, the 42 over Reading in March 1996 noted above and 30 over Windsor in February 1980. The largest number of records has come from the Kennet Valley and the Thames Valley in east Berkshire.

*Sponsored by Roger and Pat Brown*

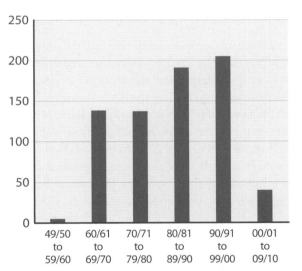

**Figure 1: Bewick's Swan: all birds recorded 1949–2010, by decade.**
Includes all of the two flocks wintering west of Theale in 1996 and 1997 although numbers increased after January.

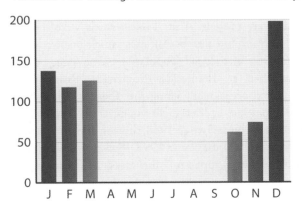

**Figure 2: Bewick's Swan: all records 1949–2010, by month of arrival.**
Includes all of the two flocks wintering west of Theale in 1996 and 1997 although numbers increased after January.

# Whooper Swan

Amber | Sch. 1

*Cygnus cygnus*

*Scarce winter visitor, small introduced resident population*

The Whooper Swan is a scarce winter passage migrant to Berkshire with 25 records in the 20th century up to 1982, when a small introduced population became established. For the next 20 years it was unclear how many records were genuine wild birds. Since the introduced populations apparently died out in 2002, there have been 10 further records until the winter of 2012/13.

The earliest 20th century record was a pair at Slough Sewage Farm from 26th March to 2nd April 1939. This was followed by further records of one or two birds in 1940, 1944 and 1945 which were presumed to be wild. The 1944 record involved a bird which remained at Ham Island from March until 25th April and formed a close association with a breeding pair of Mute Swans. It moved to Slough Sewage Farm following the destruction of the Mute Swans nest and was present there until 3rd May.

The next records were of a single bird in 1958 and a flock of 23 over Bray in January 1959. An unprecedented influx occurred during the severe winter of 1962/63, when there were up to 15 on the River Kennet at Marsh Benham from mid-February to early March, with 19 flying over on one occasion, and 37 flew south-east over Bucklebury Ford on 23rd March. Smaller parties of up to four birds were also seen at various localities and it is believed that the influx involved at least 62 birds. In contrast, the period from 1964 to 1982 only produced records of up to five birds, with the exception of parties of 24 over Windsor in December 1964 and 20 in January 1967, although the latter flock could have included Bewick's Swans.

Pairs of free-flying Whooper Swans were present on private lakes in east Berkshire in the 1980s. They started to breed in about 1986 and by 1990 eight birds were present. After 1982 records were received regularly from a number of sites which involved birds from this introduced population. One pair became established at Thameside Promenade, Reading and wandered occasionally along the Thames Valley. From 1988 to 1994, at least eight young were raised by the introduced birds: two in 1988, three in 1989 and singles in each of 1990, 1992 and 1993. However, at least some of these young apparently dispersed, as the maximum number of adults remained at five (in 1992 and 1994) or six (in 1991 and 1993). There were no records after 1994. Another population established itself in the Warfield/Windsor area, with young noted in 1994, 1998, and from 1999 to 2002. However no reports were

received from the area after 2002. While the introduced population was present it was difficult to determine which, if any, records of Whooper Swans in Berkshire were of wild birds. A party of four over Brimpton Gravel Pits in February 1987 was considered truly wild, as were records from Theale Gravel Pits in October 1995 and four at Burghfield Mill in December 2000.

There were no records after 2002 until two records on 3rd October 2008 involving one flying over Windsor Marina and four at Woolhampton. Most of the subsequent records have been from the Kennet valley, with three records of one or two from Lower Farm Gravel Pits at Thatcham, and four at Woolhampton, again on 3rd October in 2009.

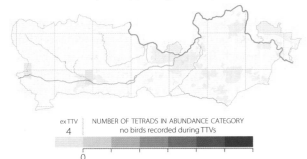

**Whooper Swan** Winter abundance
Tetrads occupied: **0** (4) Average of occupied tetrads: **0**

ex TTV | NUMBER OF TETRADS IN ABUNDANCE CATEGORY
4 | no birds recorded during TTVs

0

SURVEY COUNT

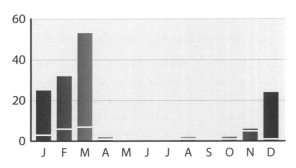

**Figure 3: Whooper Swan: all records 1939–1982, by month of arrival.** Bar – birds; white line – records.

Two flew over West Ilsley on 22nd October 2010, and three flew over Maidenhead on 26th January 2009. Two were in the Beenham and Lower Padworth area from 18th February to 28th March 2013.

The month of arrival of birds from 1939 to 1982, before the pattern of records was affected by the presence of introduced birds, but excluding the possible mixed flock in 1967, is shown in Figure 3. Nearly all records were of over-flying birds, the only long-staying individual being a juvenile which joined a flock of Mute Swans at Caversham Bridge, Reading in January 1966 and which remained until June. The August record was of two seen over Brimpton in 1977 which, in view of the date, may not have been wild birds. With the exception of these records, the extreme dates for arrival and departure in Berkshire have been 3rd October in 2008 and 2009 and 1st April in 1974.

Prior to 1900, Lamb (1880) recorded two Whooper Swans shot near Reading in 1795 and Clark Kennedy (1868) and Noble (1906) list ten records of 18 birds between 1831 and 1866, including a party of five near Cookham in 1855.

*Sponsored by David Lloyd*

# Bean Goose Amber

## *Anser fabalis*

### *Rare winter visitor*

Bean Geese were not recorded in Berkshire in the 20th century until 1976, when there were two at Purley from 13th December 1976 until 2nd January 1977 and again on 5th February 1977. The next record came the following year when one flew over Wraysbury Gravel Pits on 31st December 1978. Two were present at Wellington Country Park, Hampshire, from 3rd to 25th February 1979 and crossed into Berkshire occasionally. The next

records were in 1985: singles at Dinton Pastures and one flying towards Wraysbury Reservoir, both on 13th January, and two near Datchet from 20th to 21st January.

Since the mid-1990s there has been an increase in the number and frequency of records. In 1996 there was one at Eversley Gravel Pits from 14th to 17th December, and two (first seen in Buckinghamshire) were seen near Eton Wick on 21st to 23rd December. There were four at Wigmore Lane, Theale from 5th to 15th January 1997 and another at Cockmarsh from 5th to 12th December 1998. Berkshire shared in influxes into Britain in 2003 and 2004, with 17 over Queen Mother Reservoir, Datchet on 24th February and five at Pingewood Gravel Pits the following two days in 2003, and another flock of 17 at Coldharbour on 13th and 14th December 2004. The flock comprised 15 adults and two juveniles, and one carried a numbered neck collar that was put on in the Netherlands in 2002. It was seen in Staffordshire on the 15th. There was one at Remenham from 2nd to 8th January 2007 and another flying over Dinton Pastures on 8th December 2010.

Two races of the species occur in Britain, *A. f. fabalis*, referred to as Taiga Bean Geese which breed from Scandinavia east to the Urals, and *A. f. rossicus*, known as Tundra Bean Geese which breed in the tundra of northern Russia and northwestern Siberia. Most records in Britain

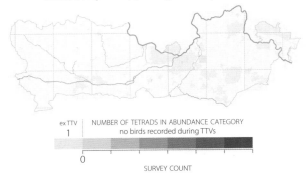

**Bean Goose** Winter abundance
Tetrads occupied: **0** (1) Average of occupied tetrads: **0**

ex TTV **1** | NUMBER OF TETRADS IN ABUNDANCE CATEGORY
no birds recorded during TTVs
**0**
SURVEY COUNT

are believed to be the latter, and the Theale birds in 1997, the five at Pingewood in 2003, 17 at Coldharbour in 2004 and the Remenham bird in 2007 were all identified as this race. The only birds identified as Taiga Bean Goose were the two at Eton Wick in 1996.

Prior to 1900, the only specific references to Bean Geese are of several killed near Windsor and Maidenhead in the hard winter of 1866/67 (Clark Kennedy, 1868) and one shot on the Thames near Henley in 1850 (Aplin, 1889). Stubbs (1867) also refers to records from the Henley area and Clark Kennedy (1868) states more generally that "a few [are] shot almost every winter" but gives no further details.

*Sponsored by Colin Wilson*

# Pink-footed Goose   Amber

## *Anser brachyrhynchus*

*Scarce winter visitor*

The Pink-footed Goose is a scarce winter visitor to Berkshire, with most records from the Kennet Valley and the Thames Valley.

The first county record was of a bird shot in about 1890 at Catmore, which was preserved initially at the Fox and Cubs Inn at Lilley (Noble, 1906). The next record was not until four birds visited a collection of wildfowl at Bulmershe briefly on 29th October 1938. There was then a gap of 17 years before a single bird was seen at Burghfield Gravel Pits in February 1955. Since then, Pink-footed Geese have been observed in 20 of the 54 winters from 1959/60 to 2012/13, most frequently in the 1970s, although there was more than one sighting in only four of these years. Of the 95 birds observed between 1955 and 2011, 48 occurred in two passing skeins of 33 in February 1972 and 15 in January 1984. All the other records were of singles, or flocks of eight birds or fewer. Between 1994 and 2013 there have only been five years when the bird was recorded and in three of those (all single sightings) it is likely

**Pink-footed Goose** Winter abundance
Tetrads occupied: **0** (6) Average of occupied tetrads: **0**

ex TTV **6** | NUMBER OF TETRADS IN ABUNDANCE CATEGORY
no birds recorded during TTVs
**0**
SURVEY COUNT

that they related to escaped birds. Apart from four records of single birds between 11th and 17th April in 1966, 1975, 1979 and 1982, which may have been individuals on return passage, most observations apart from that in 1938 have been of birds first seen either in January or February. This suggests that hard weather may be responsible for many records in Berkshire. The earliest winter record was 4th December 2009 and the latest post-winter departure date was 17th April 1975. The occasional records of single birds in Berkshire from May to November indicate that escapes from collections do occur.

Most records have been of passage birds seen only for one day. Singles present on the Thames below Marlow from 13th February to 10th March 1963, at Chamberhouse Marsh from 28th February to 16th April 1982, and near Maidenhead from 1st February to 27th March 1992 may have been escapees or ailing birds. No other stays have exceeded six days with the exception of a single bird at Streatley on 4th January 2009 which stayed until 15th March, three birds at Lower Farm from 9th April to 4th May 2011 and one at Theale Gravel Pits which stayed from 24th February until 10th April 2013.

*Sponsored by Neil Bucknell*

# White-fronted Goose

Green

*Anser albifrons*

*Uncommon passage migrant and occasional winter visitor*

The White-fronted Goose was a rare vagrant to Berkshire prior to 1953, with just seven records. Since then the species has been seen in every winter except for 1956/57, 1964/65, 1990/91, 1992/93, 1994/95, 2000/01 and 2007/08. Numbers have varied widely from year to year due to the occasional occurrence of over-flying skeins, the largest of which have been about 120 over the Downs in March 1968, 120 over Cippenham, Slough on 21st December 2010, about 140 over Upper Woolhampton in February 1979 and about 250 over Hungerford in February 1979. However, fewer than 25 birds have been recorded in more than half the winters since 1953 and over two-thirds of the records have been of ten or fewer birds.

Figure 4 shows the monthly totals of White-fronted Geese in Berkshire over ten-year periods since the winter of 1944/45 and Figure 5 an analysis by monthly arrival. The decline in records since the 1970s reflects a decline in numbers wintering in Britain over this period, as more birds winter further east in continental Europe, especially the Netherlands (Holt *et al.*, 2011). The earliest arrivals were one at Winkfield on 16th October 2010 and five at Ham Island on 19th October 1958, and the latest post-winter departure date involved one at Summerleaze Gravel Pits from 8th to 11th April 1986 (a bird which remained there to 14th July 1986 was injured). Occasional records of single birds from May to September are presumed to relate to escaped captive bred birds.

Nearly all the observations of White-fronted Geese in Berkshire have been along a broad line from the Kennet Valley eastwards through Reading to Windsor and Wraysbury. It is likely that most of the birds recorded were passing through the county en route to, or from,

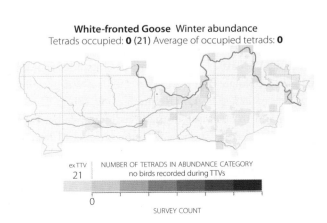

**White-fronted Goose** Winter abundance
Tetrads occupied: **0** (21) Average of occupied tetrads: **0**

| ex TTV | NUMBER OF TETRADS IN ABUNDANCE CATEGORY |
|---|---|
| 21 | no birds recorded during TTVs |

0

SURVEY COUNT

their wintering areas in the south of England. However, records during mid-winter may be due to hard weather movements of birds from farther afield. There have been few records of birds staying for longer than a week, only four of which have been for longer than a month: eight in the Theale/Burghfield area from 28th January to 18th March 1979, one near Maidenhead from 9th February to 27th March 1992, a flock of between 27 and 60 in the area north of Maidenhead between 4th December 1998 and 9th March 1999, and four at Pingewood from 29th January to 8th March 2011.

The Berkshire records of White-fronted Geese prior to 1953 were of one shot near Reading in January 1795 (which Lamb (1880) gives, probably erroneously, as Lesser White-fronted Goose *Anser erythropus*), an adult male shot near Kintbury in December 1879 (Noble, 1906), an adult female shot near Langley in February 1929, four at Reading Sewage Farm in January 1935, one shot at Purley in January 1939, 89 on the River Thames at Boveney in February 1940 during severe weather and one shot at Aldermaston in January 1945.

*Sponsored by Neil Bucknell*

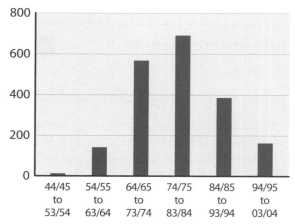

**Figure 4: White-fronted Goose: birds recorded by decade**

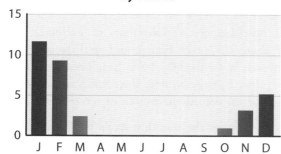

**Figure 5: White-fronted Goose: birds recorded by month of arrival.** Annual average 1944/45–2003/04.

# Greylag Goose

Amber

*Anser anser*

*Increasing introduced resident*

The Greylag Goose is an introduced resident in Berkshire. Since the 1980s the UK population has expanded rapidly, with one estimate that during the 1990s it was growing at a rate of 12% per year (Rehfisch *et al.*, 2002). This is reflected in the increase in the breeding range between the two local Atlas surveys, with the number of tetrads with confirmed breeding increasing from 12 to 54, and probable breeding increasing from six to 24 tetrads. The species now breeds along most of the Thames, lower Kennet and Loddon rivers and in Windsor Great Park.

114

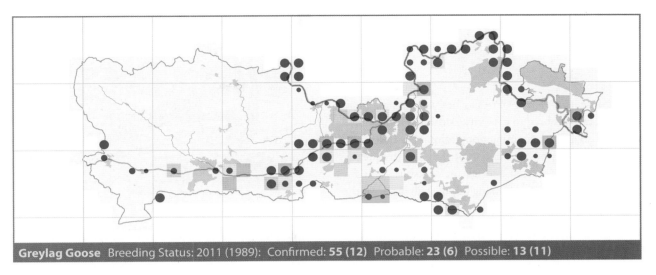

**Greylag Goose** Breeding Status: 2011 (1989): Confirmed: **55 (12)** Probable: **23 (6)** Possible: **13 (11)**

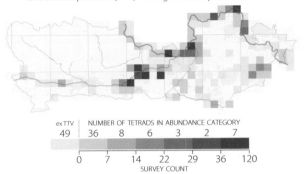

**Greylag Goose** Breeding season abundance
Tetrads occupied: **62 (111)** Average of occupied tetrads: **14·8**

| ex TTV | NUMBER OF TETRADS IN ABUNDANCE CATEGORY | | | | | |
|---|---|---|---|---|---|---|
| 49 | 36 | 8 | 6 | 3 | 2 | 7 |

0    7    14    22    29    36    120
SURVEY COUNT

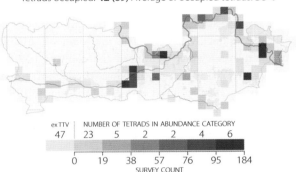

**Greylag Goose** Winter abundance
Tetrads occupied: **42 (89)** Average of occupied tetrads: **38·4**

| ex TTV | NUMBER OF TETRADS IN ABUNDANCE CATEGORY | | | | | |
|---|---|---|---|---|---|---|
| 47 | 23 | 5 | 2 | 2 | 4 | 6 |

0    19    38    57    76    95    184
SURVEY COUNT

There are only a small number of records of birds possibly originating from the wild population, which has been confined to the northwest of Scotland since the late 18th century (*Historical Atlas*). Clark Kennedy (1868) refers to one obtained near Cookham and another shot out of a flock of seven near Boveney Lock, but gives no dates. Noble (1906) includes a reference to two birds which had been killed near Remenham in February 1854.

A flock of at least 30 free-flying birds was present, and bred, in Windsor Great Park from the late 1960s. The first Berkshire records of confirmed breeding outside this area were from Aldermaston and Theale Gravel Pits in 1975. The next breeding records were of two broods at Windsor Great Park in 1978, followed by a pair at Bearwood Lake in 1982 and 1983 and a pair at Burghfield Gravel Pits in 1983. By the late 1980s the Thames Valley region had one of the highest concentrations of Greylag Geese in southern England (*1988–91 BTO Atlas*).

The Winter Abundance Map shows a similar distribution to the breeding season map during the 2007–11 Atlas survey, with highest numbers at the main waterbodies or along the principal river valleys.

Non-breeding flock counts increased after the early 1970s as the local population began to increase. It was not until 1977 that counts in double figures appeared in the county reports, when 30 were reported over Earley in June, and this total was not exceeded until 1983. As the population increased, so the maximum counts have increased too. The first count over 100 was of 114 at Burghfield Gravel Pits on 17th September 1988. The first count of over 200 was 205 at Padworth Lane Gravel Pit in August 2003, soon exceeded by 243 at Hosehill Lake, Theale on 16th September that year. Padworth Lane retook the record on 27th September 2008 when 321 were present. The following year 346 were at Windsor Great Park on 23rd August, which remains the county record. Like Canada Geese, Greylags tend to form mobile flocks in winter so WeBS counts are not so useful for monitoring numbers. However Windsor Great Park has produced the highest counts in recent years.

There have been eight local ringing recoveries of Greylag Goose, the furthest travelled birds being two from Kent. One which originated from the Sevenoaks Wildfowl Reserve in Kent was recovered at Mortimer in 1988, another also ringed at Sevenoaks in June 1987 was recovered eight years later in June 1995 at Arborfield.

With plenty of suitable habitat in the county, there seems every prospect of Greylag Geese continuing to increase and spread in Berkshire in the future.

*Sponsored by Renee Grayer*

# Bar-headed Goose

*Anser indicus*

*Introduced species*

This goose is a native of Asia, but is popular as an ornamental bird bred in captivity. Although it has failed to establish a self-sustaining population in Britain from escapes from captivity, it is one of the most frequently encountered introduced species in Berkshire, and for some years there was a breeding population just over the Hampshire border.

Bar-headed Geese were reported almost annually from 1974 to 1990, and every year since and in all months of the year. Most records are of single birds or occasionally two together, often associating with Canada Geese, and from all areas of the county with rivers or waterbodies. There are occasional higher counts, and from 1998 until 2006 a flock was present in the Maidenhead and Cookham areas which produced the county's highest count (up to 2012) of ten. Elsewhere the highest count was eight at Theale Gravel Pits on 20th August 1995. The number of records received for the county report increased during the 1990s, with records received from 20 sites in 2003.

There has been no evidence of courting display or nesting, but in 2005 three adults with three young were at Summerleaze Gravel Pit, Maidenhead on 28th July, and juveniles have been noted several times since; these may have originated from a private collection at Winter Hill (Chris Heard *in litt.*). It was considered likely that many of the birds in Berkshire came from the population at Stratfield Saye in Hampshire where between 1983 and 1997 up to three pairs have bred each year and 25 were counted in September 1983 (Clark and Eyre, 1993). This population has subsequently disappeared, being considered extinct by 2006 (Keith Betton, *pers. comm.*).

*Sponsored by Blackwater Valley Countryside Trust*

# Snow Goose

*Anser caerulescens*

*Occasional escapee which has bred*

Prior to 1974 county reports did not include sightings of escapees from wildfowl collections and the first published record of Snow Goose for Berkshire is of one to two birds between Reading and Aldermaston from March to May 1975. Since then, the species has been reported annually, with the exception of 1978 and 1984.

The first small party of Snow Geese in Berkshire occurred in 1979 when there were five at Reading Sewage Farm in January. Five were seen again at Lower Basildon from December 1981 to January 1982 and in 1983 there were 14 at Dinton Pastures in March. Although there was a suggestion at the time that the flock of 14 birds might have come from the WWT reserve at Slimbridge, the bulk of the Berkshire records from about 1977 until the early years of the 21st century relate to a flock originating from Stratfield Saye in Hampshire, whose history was recorded by Clark (2009). In 1977, seven birds were present at this site and breeding, resulting in free-flying young, occurred there in 1979, 1986, 1987 and 1991, by which time the flock comprised up to 34 birds. Birds from this site started to winter across the

border at Eversley Gravel Pits, where maximum counts increased to a maximum of 39 in March 1994. In that year seven pairs nested on an island in one of the lakes. Although young were seen they failed to fledge. Snow Geese bred at this site again in 1995 when there were at least four nests. Breeding occurred again in 1996, 1997 and 2000, but breeding success was very poor, as at Stratfield Saye itself. The population as a whole

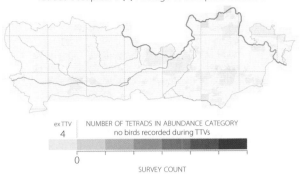

**Snow Goose** Breeding season abundance
Tetrads occupied: **0** (4) Average of occupied tetrads: **0**

| ex TTV | NUMBER OF TETRADS IN ABUNDANCE CATEGORY |
| 4 | no birds recorded during TTVs |

0

SURVEY COUNT

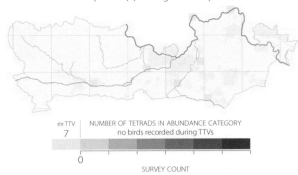

**Snow Goose** Winter abundance
Tetrads occupied: **0** (7) Average of occupied tetrads: **0**

| ex TTV | NUMBER OF TETRADS IN ABUNDANCE CATEGORY |
| 7 | no birds recorded during TTVs |

0

SURVEY COUNT

dwindled from the mid-1990s and by 2012 just one bird was left at Eversley.

Elsewhere there are records of small numbers received from a number of sites, with at least one site producing records away from Eversley every year, and a maximum number of ten sites in 2009. There are occasional reports of larger flocks. There were 24 flying high in a chevron over Burghfield Gravel Pits in October 1986, 31 at Beech Hill on 24th September 1992 and a flock of 19 arrived at Theale Gravel Pits on 14th February 2008, 17 of which moved to Dinton Pastures the following day. Most of the birds reported are of the white morph, but there are regular records of birds of the grey and white blue morph, including four of the mobile 2008 flock.

*Sponsored by Blackwater Valley Countryside Trust*

# Canada Goose

*Branta canadensis*

*Widespread introduced resident*

The Canada Goose is a common resident in the river valleys and gravel pits of Berkshire. Although the species had been kept in wildfowl collections since at least the end of the 17th century, records outside collections were rare until the last quarter of the 19th century. Clark Kennedy (1868) notes that "it is an extremely rare visitant", noting one bird being shot on the river near Windsor in the summer of 1867. The *Historical Atlas* also shows it as uncommon in Berkshire. There are few other references until the 1930s when there were several nests on different waters in the Reading area, breeding occurred at Aldermaston Court and there was a count of about 70 at Cranemoor Lake in 1935. The first flock to exceed 100 birds was of 136 at Cranemoor Lake in August 1950.

The Thames Valley is now one of the strongholds of the species nationally. Owen *et al.*, (1986) estimate a population of 2,790 in 1976 for the region, out of a national population of 19,120. This represented an increase from 163 in the Thames Valley in 1953 and 700 in 1968. The centre of this regional concentration is the middle Thames Valley and north Hampshire and adjacent parts of the Kennet, Loddon and Blackwater Valleys (*1988–91 BTO Atlas*). The 1991 census of introduced geese, which was carried out in the moulting season, produced a count of 3,666 Canada Geese for the county. The largest single count was 350 at Dinton

Pastures, although a total of 768 was found along the Thames between Henley and Hurley (Delaney, 1992).

The Tetrad Survey maps show that the species is widespread in Berkshire, occurring in most tetrads where there is open or flowing water, with similar distributions in summer and winter. Once the winter flocks have broken up in February and March, Canada Geese disperse widely. Being conspicuous both whilst on the nest and once the young have hatched, a high proportion of confirmed breeding records was achieved. There is little evidence of any further spread of the species between the 1987–89 and 2007–11 surveys, but the number of tetrads in which breeding was confirmed increased from 116 to 146.

Communal nesting occurs in gravel pit complexes with islands, and creches of young are frequently encountered, the highest count of goslings being 83 at Dinton Pastures in May 1981. Although Canada Geese

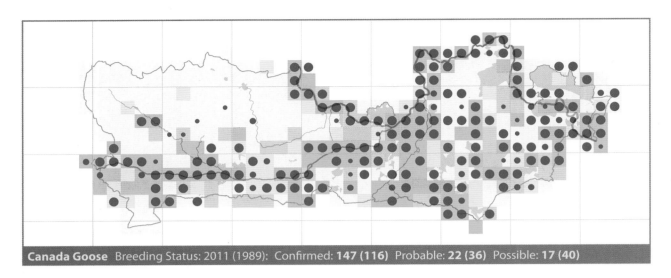

**Canada Goose** Breeding Status: 2011 (1989): Confirmed: **147 (116)** Probable: **22 (36)** Possible: **17 (40)**

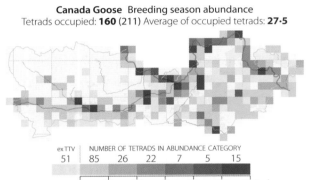

**Canada Goose** Breeding season abundance
Tetrads occupied: **160 (211)** Average of occupied tetrads: **27·5**

| exTTV | NUMBER OF TETRADS IN ABUNDANCE CATEGORY | | | | | |
|---|---|---|---|---|---|---|
| 51 | 85 | 26 | 22 | 7 | 5 | 15 |

0    13    27    41    55    68    286
SURVEY COUNT

**Canada Goose** Winter abundance
Tetrads occupied: **129 (177)** Average of occupied tetrads: **45·5**

| exTTV | NUMBER OF TETRADS IN ABUNDANCE CATEGORY | | | | | |
|---|---|---|---|---|---|---|
| 48 | 61 | 31 | 9 | 6 | 5 | 17 |

0    22    45    68    90    113    339
SURVEY COUNT

form moulting flocks in late June and early July, the highest counts tend to be in the autumn from August to October. Six counts of 600 or more were recorded in the period 1974 to 1988, and four more in just the next three years. The highest counts ever were in December 1976 when about 1,000 where reported from Binfield, in the Cookham area in July and August 1991, when similar numbers were reported, and between 800 and 1,000 at Spencers Wood in September 2008. Perhaps surprisingly there have been just two other counts in excess of 600 since 2000, although this may simply reflect the fact that observers are not bothering to count large flocks. The highest counts tend to be in Central and East Berkshire, but counts of over 200 have been regular from sites in the Kennet valley in the west of the county since the 1990s.

Canada Goose flocks can be mobile in the winter, which tends to limit the usefulness of winter WeBS counts for monitoring the population increase. Whereas annual breeding-season monitoring through BBS has shown a continuing increase in the UK population since the 1980s, the winter monitoring by WeBS has shown little change since 2001 (Holt *et al.*, 2012).

There are a number of ringing records indicating movements beyond south east England, with birds ringed in Berkshire recovered in Merseyside and Nottinghamshire, and a bird ringed in Staffordshire has been recovered in Berkshire. Most remarkably, three birds ringed on 2nd July 2003 at Caversham were all recovered in the Exe estuary in Devon over the next 18 months, on 2nd January, 10th and 24th December 2004.

There have also been records of birds which may be of some races other than *B. c. canadensis*, the nominate race, from which the northern European population is derived. One at Summerleaze Gravel Pit in December 1989 appeared to be a large dark bird of the race *B. c. interior*, while a small bird at Lower Farm Gravel Pit in December 2007 may have been of the race *B. c. parvipes*. There have also been records of birds which appeared to be Cackling Geese, now regarded by some authorities as a separate species, but none have been regarded as wild birds.

The large numbers of non-breeding birds present in Berkshire in the summer may indicate that lack of breeding sites is limiting further increases. Concern has been expressed at the adverse impact of the high number of geese on crops and the problems caused by fouling of waterside recreation areas. Although shooting has been suggested as a means of controlling numbers, Canada Geese are not popular as a quarry species as they are relatively tame and make poor sport.

*Sponsored by Neil Bucknell*

# Barnacle Goose

Amber

*Branta leucopsis*

*Rare vagrant and recently introduced resident*

The Barnacle Goose was formerly a rare vagrant to Berkshire, although recently birds of introduced origin have become established in the county and have bred since 1988. All records in the 20th century are likely to relate to birds of introduced origin, with the possible exception of a family party of four at Horton Gravel Pits in January 1990, whose arrival coincided with the arrival of wild flocks in Essex and Suffolk.

Since the first record of a Barnacle Goose in the Reading area in the winter of 1950/51, there have been a number of records of single birds and occasional reports of small flocks. Eight fully-winged individuals were released into Windsor Great Park in the early 1970s. Until 1989, the highest counts were of 19 at Burghfield and Theale Gravel Pits on 17th and 18th March 1981 and of 18 at Windsor Great Park from mid-November 1983 to January 1984. After 1989, Eversley Gravel Pits attracted increasing numbers during the winter, which formed part of a flock which originated from Stratfield Saye in Hampshire. The history of this population was described by Clark (2009). Although the main breeding

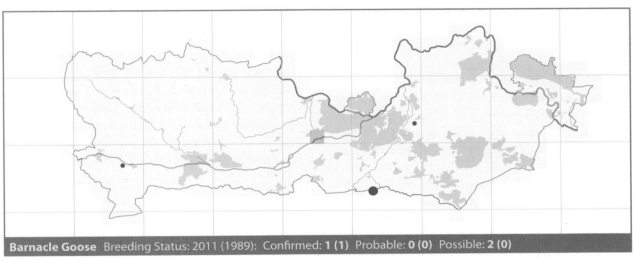

**Barnacle Goose**  Breeding Status: 2011 (1989):  Confirmed: **1 (1)**  Probable: **0 (0)**  Possible: **2 (0)**

**Barnacle Goose**  Breeding season abundance
Tetrads occupied: **2 (19)** Average of occupied tetrads: **7·5**

| ex TTV | NUMBER OF TETRADS IN ABUNDANCE CATEGORY | | |
|---|---|---|---|
| 17 | 0 | 1 | 1 |

0    3    7    11
SURVEY COUNT

**Barnacle Goose**  Winter abundance
Tetrads occupied: **2 (19)** Average of occupied tetrads: **8·5**

| ex TTV | NUMBER OF TETRADS IN ABUNDANCE CATEGORY | | |
|---|---|---|---|
| 17 | 1 | 0 | 1 |

0    4    8    12    17
SURVEY COUNT

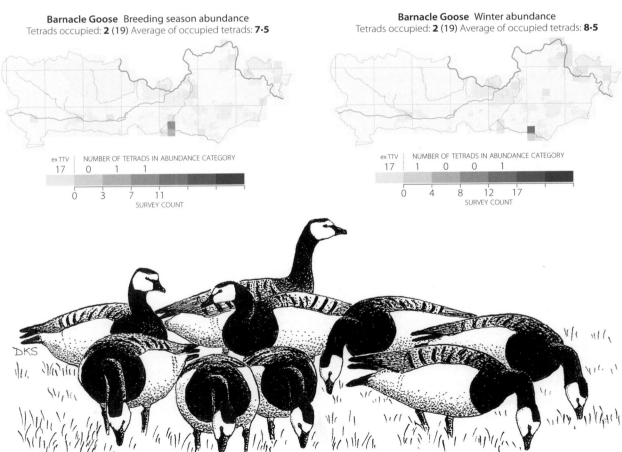

centre of the population was at Stratfield Saye, Eversley Gravel Pits became the main wintering site in the 1990s. In 1995 the number of Barnacle Geese at Eversley Gravel Pits reached 121 in December, and the highest count recorded was 311 in January 1997. Winter counts of over 200 were recorded from every year up to 2003, after which numbers declined rapidly, with annual maximum counts of just 17 or 18 from 2009 to 2012.

Barnacle Geese were proved to breed for the first time in Berkshire during the 1987–89 Tetrad Survey when a pair, which had remained at Theale Gravel Pits since January 1988, was seen with two young on 25th June. Another pair subsequently raised young at Eversley Gravel Pits in 1990 and the number of breeding pairs recorded at this site has subsequently varied between one and eight (in 2004). Breeding success has always been poor. Clark (2009) postulates that poor breeding success in the population in northeast Hampshire and the neighbouring border areas of Berkshire and Surrey may be caused by inbreeding in an ageing population, although his paper also gave examples of both immigration into and emigration out of the population. This included a flock of 45 at Ibsley, in the Avon Valley south of Salisbury which arrived in January 2006 at the time a marked reduction was noted at Eversley, which

was identified as being from Eversley due to the presence of a distinctive leucistic (pale) individual.

Elsewhere, records of small numbers of birds continue to occur, with occasional larger flocks of up to 20 birds reported. There were counts of 146 and 185 from the Binfield area in 2000 and 2002 respectively, but little further information on any population in the area has been published in the County Reports. Despite the apparent failure of the population in the Blackwater Valley to establish itself, nationally the population of introduced Barnacle Geese has grown rapidly in the last 40 years (Holt *et al.*, 2011), so Berkshire may yet be colonised by another successful introduced species of wildfowl.

Although claimed by Lamb (1880) to have been "frequently seen about Newbury in severe weather" prior to 1814, the only specific 19th century records of Barnacle Geese in Berkshire are of one shot near Datchet a few years before 1868 and one killed on the Thames near Maidenhead (Clark Kennedy, 1868). The next record was not until the presumed escapee in the Reading area in the winter of 1950/51.

*Sponsored by Iain Oldcorn*

# Brent Goose Amber

## *Branta bernicla*

*Scarce passage migrant*

The Brent Goose was a rare vagrant to Berkshire prior to 1969 with just three 20th century records: one at Reading Sewage Farm in January 1933, one shot at Bucklebury in January 1961 and one over Ham in January 1967. Subsequently, the species has become much more regular and was recorded in 14 of the 23 winters from 1969/70 to 1991/92, including successive winters from 1981/82 to 1987/88, and in every year since 1992. The number of records up to the winter of 2011/12 is 89, 52 of which are since 1994/95. The increase in the occurrence of the species in the county in recent years has coincided with a considerable expansion in its British wintering population (Stroud and Glue, 1991).

Most of the records were of single birds or of groups of less than ten. The largest parties recorded were 26 over Holyport in October 1989, about 50 over Queen Mother Reservoir on 9th March 1983 and, on 5th November 1994, an unprecedented passage over Queen Mother Reservoir, with five parties totalling 89 and, later, a party of 72 which may have been additional birds.

**Brent Goose** Winter abundance
Tetrads occupied: **0 (5)** Average of occupied tetrads: **0**

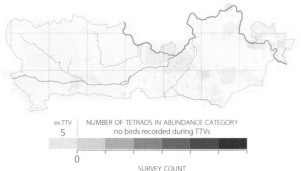

ex TTV | NUMBER OF TETRADS IN ABUNDANCE CATEGORY
5 | no birds recorded during TTVs

0

SURVEY COUNT

Since then, the highest counts were 48 at Cockmarsh on 19th February 1999, 42 at Queen Mother Reservoir on 28th October 2000 and 30 over Purley on 24th March 1996.

A summary of the arrival dates from the winter 1969/70 to winter 2011/12 is shown in Figure 6. Although there have been many records of single birds, the fact that they have occurred during the typical periods of arrival and departure of the species in southern England suggests that they were of wild, rather than captive, origin. The earliest arrival date was on 4th October in 1992 and the latest post-winter departure on 10th May in 1988. A record of a bird at Thatcham Marsh in August and September 1985 has been omitted from the analysis as its origin is uncertain.

The majority of records of Brent Geese in Berkshire have been of over-flying birds and more than two-thirds have been single-day sightings. The longest stay was an individual which lingered at Theale Gravel Pits from 10th November to 17th December 1982. Where sub-specific identification has been possible, all birds apart from one were of the dark-bellied race *B. b. bernicla* which winters in southern Britain and western France.

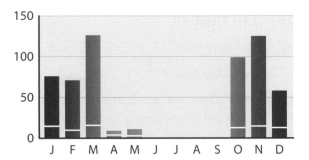

**Figure 6: Brent Goose: all records 1969/70–2011/12, by month of arrival.** Bar – birds; white line – records.

The exception was a single pale-bellied bird of race *B. b. hrota* (which in Britain winter around the Irish Sea) at Theale Gravel Pits on 16th and 17th March 2005.

Historically, there are records of two Brent Geese shot near Datchet in 1865, one killed near Eton, one near Cookham and two near Maidenhead, with many more seen, during the hard winter of 1866/67 (Clark Kennedy, 1868), and one killed near Remenham in 1880 (Noble, 1906). There are also references by Stubbs (1867) and Aplin (1889) to birds shot on the Thames near Henley.

*Sponsored by BOC Norfolk 2013 Trip*

# Red-breasted Goose

## *Branta ruficollis*

*Rare vagrant, or possible escapee*

The Red-breasted Goose is a rare vagrant to Berkshire, having been recorded on just two occasions. The first record was an immature male found dead after hitting overhead wires at Enborne on 21st October 1963. The second record was of a bird flying north-east over Summerleaze Gravel Pits, calling on 24th December 1981. In view of the early date of the 1963 record and the absence of reports of the species from elsewhere in Britain during the winter of 1981/82, there is some uncertainty as to whether either of these records relate to genuinely wild birds. Neither record was submitted to BBRC for scrutiny.

A more recent sighting involved a report of 14–15 on a private estate at Wokingham on 23rd Oct 2008 reported to the county recorder by the landowner.

If correctly identified, these would undoubtedly have been escapes; at the last count there were at least three waterfowl collections containing Red-breasted Geese in the county.

*Sponsored by Colin Wilson*

# Egyptian Goose

*Alopochen aegyptiaca*

*Increasing introduced resident*

The Egyptian Goose is an introduced species in Britain, and Berkshire supports a growing, free-flying population. In the period between the 1987–89 and 2007–11 Tetrad Surveys in Berkshire it has expanded its breeding range, and now occurs throughout most suitable habitat in the centre and east of the county.

The two established breeding centres in Berkshire were shown by the 1987–89 Tetrad Survey map. The first was at Lower Basildon, in the vicinity of the Child-Beale Wildlife Park. Breeding was first recorded there in 1976, when two nests and one brood were reported. The second was at Dinton Pastures, where breeding was first reported in 1979 and a breeding pair was present throughout the 1980s. In 1988, a pair also bred successfully at Twyford Gravel Pits nearby. However, at Lower Basildon breeding was not reported again until 1984. In the years of the 1987–89 Tetrad Survey a possible nest site was reported from further east and in 1990 breeding was confirmed at a third location, Bill Hill Park.

The 1991 WWT census of introduced geese located 12 birds in Berkshire, the most important concentration outside Norfolk, where the first British self-sustaining population was established (Delaney, 1992). Of these, ten were at Lower Basildon, three of which were juveniles, and two were at Dinton Pastures. Thereafter during the 1990s breeding was reported at an increasing number of sites. In the 2007–11 Atlas Survey breeding was confirmed in 87 tetrads compared to only four in

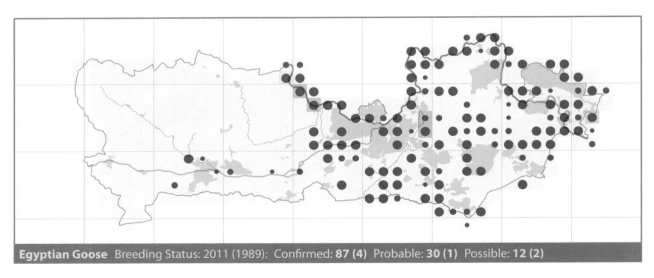

**Egyptian Goose**   Breeding Status: 2011 (1989):   Confirmed: **87 (4)**   Probable: **30 (1)**   Possible: **12 (2)**

**Egyptian Goose**  Breeding season abundance
Tetrads occupied: **76** (142) Average of occupied tetrads: **4·2**

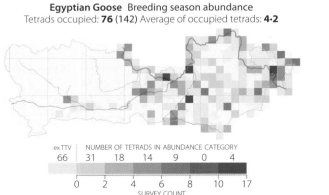

| exTTV | NUMBER OF TETRADS IN ABUNDANCE CATEGORY | | | | | |
|---|---|---|---|---|---|---|
| 66 | 31 | 18 | 14 | 9 | 0 | 4 |

0   2   4   6   8   10   17
SURVEY COUNT

**Egyptian Goose**  Winter abundance
Tetrads occupied: **80** (142) Average of occupied tetrads: **4·3**

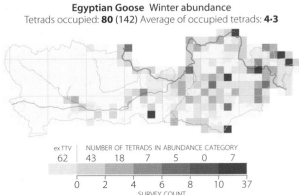

| exTTV | NUMBER OF TETRADS IN ABUNDANCE CATEGORY | | | | | |
|---|---|---|---|---|---|---|
| 62 | 43 | 18 | 7 | 5 | 0 | 7 |

0   2   4   6   8   10   37
SURVEY COUNT

1987–89. The only apparently suitable area where the species has yet to establish itself in significant numbers is the Kennet Valley west of Theale, where breeding was only proved in two tetrads.

Towards the end of the 1990s counts of over 20 were reported from Binfield (25 in December 1998) and Cockmarsh. The latter site produced the first count in excess of 50 in December 2002. Counts of 20 to 50 are now regular in east and central Berkshire after the breeding season when autumn flocks can be found on waterbodies or feeding on stubble nearby. Numbers are lower in the Kennet Valley west of Theale, where counts of over 10 adults are still unusual, a pattern confirmed by the Winter distribution map. Two sites regularly produce high counts, Eversley Gravel Pits, where there were 177 on 1st October 2009 and 180 on 18th September 2011, and the area around Cookham and north of Maidenhead. There were 171 on 26th September 2008 at Cookham.

Noble (1906) refers to occasional escapees from collections having been killed and there is a record of two at Reading Sewage Farm on 4th May 1935.

The Egyptian Goose has proved one of the most successful birds in Berkshire since the late 1980s, and there seems no reason to doubt that it will colonise the remainder of the suitable river valley areas of the west of the county in the near future.

*Sponsored by Brian Boyland*

Egyptian Goose, Dinton Pastures *Tony Harden*

# Ruddy Shelduck

*Tadorna ferruginea*

*Rare vagrant and sometime resident, probably of introduced origin*

The Ruddy Shelduck is an accidental visitor to Britain and has been reported on several occasions in Berkshire. It is likely, however, that most if not all the records relate to escapees or the offspring from birds of introduced origin breeding on the near continent. There are a number of records of hybrid birds (usually crossed with Cape Shelduck *T. cana*), although a bird at Dinton Pastures in July 2004 was identified as an Egyptian Goose *Alopochen aegyptiacus* × Ruddy Shelduck hybrid.

The first records for the county came from Slough Sewage Farm, where a bird was present in March and September 1940 and three were seen in March the following year, one of which stayed into May. A bird clearly of doubtful origin was seen at Bearwood Lake in June 1942, and in 1944 another was seen at Bulmershe Lake. In May 1950, one was at Burghfield Gravel Pits and in January 1973 a pair circled Theale Gravel Pits.

There has been an increase in sightings since 1982, when one flew south-east over Wraysbury in September. This was followed in May 1983 by a male among buildings at the Burghfield Royal Ordnance Factory and a female which was seen frequently at Theale Gravel Pits from October 1987 and throughout 1988. A single bird was also seen at Northcroft in April 1988. Between 1990 and 1995, a pair of cross-bred birds (possibly hybridised with Cape Shelduck *T. cana*) frequented various waters

throughout east Berkshire, hatching young in Windsor Great Park in both 1992 and 1993, and on the Thames at Windsor in 1994. Most of the subsequent records come from the east of the county, although breeding has not been subsequently recorded. Records have been received every year since then apart from 2003 and 2010. Influxes of one or more birds apparently occurred in the autumn of 1997, early spring of 1998 and autumns of 1999, 2006 and 2009, when records were received from central and west Berkshire, and there were two at Newbury Racecourse on 25th February 2012. These clusters of records may however simply reflect the conspicuous nature of the species and that once arrived they often remain for weeks or even months. The highest count was six at Theale Gravel Pits on 23rd September 1997.

*Sponsored by Ian Tarr*

---

# Shelduck                    Amber

*Tadorna tadorna*

*Uncommon passage migrant, winter visitor and scarce breeding summer visitor*

The Shelduck is an uncommon passage migrant, winter visitor and scarce summer visitor to Berkshire. Nationally it showed an increase in breeding numbers in the 20th century and has spread inland to breed in small numbers. This pattern is reflected in the species' recent history in Berkshire.

The 1987–89 Tetrad Survey map showed a clear concentration of records in the east of the county, where all five tetrads in which breeding was confirmed were located. By the time of the 2007–11 Tetrad Survey confirmed breeding had increased to 16 tetrads and had spread further west to a number of locations in the

Kennet valley from Theale to Kintbury. Breeding was also confirmed from the Thames valley and Jubilee River area and Eversley Gravel Pits.

The surveys confirm the trend that had emerged from previous records. Breeding was suspected in east Berkshire at Ham Island and Great Meadow Pond from 1950 to 1953, but was only proved at the latter site in 1954 when a pair with six young was found. Breeding was not proved thereafter until 1974 when a pair bred at Wraysbury Gravel Pits. Subsequently, pairs bred at that site in three years and were suspected to have bred in two other years prior to the 1987–89 Tetrad Survey, and breeding has continued since. In 1982 a pair was present at Theale Gravel Pits from January to May. In 1991 a pair summered at Racecourse Gravel Pit, Newbury and breeding occurred there in 1995 with eight young being seen in July. There is a possibility that these, and some other casual records, may relate to escaped birds as the species is popular in collections. Since the late 1990s the County Reports have recorded breeding from between two and eight sites annually, with an apparent decline noted after 2002. The latest Tetrad Atlas results either indicate a recovery or the results of more systematic recording.

Throughout the year, the pattern of records reflects the Shelduck's annual pattern of movement. After the breeding season, firstly non-breeding adults, then breeding adults and young leave to go to the moulting grounds in the Wadden Sea in the southern North Sea. Wintering birds start to return in November or December.

In Berkshire, most non-breeding records have been of fewer than five birds and, although the species can be encountered anywhere, they used to be more numerous further east in the county. However, the abundance maps and recent County Reports reveal that counts in the Kennet valley now equal or exceed those in the east. Both the number of records and maximum counts have increased since the early 1960s when an apparent decline in records occurred. There were no records at all in 1962 and only one in both 1964 and 1965. By the mid-1980s, records were received from at least seven or eight sites throughout the year, with the larger gravel pit complexes often providing two or more records annually. Since then the number of sites reporting Shelduck has increased to between 25 and 49 in the years between 2000 and 2008.

Between 1947 and 1985, there were seven records of between ten and 15 birds: four from the Wraysbury and Horton Gravel Pits, two from Queen Mother Reservoir and one from Reading Sewage Farm. Until 1998 the highest count was 15, recorded at Reading Sewage Farm in September 1965, Wraysbury Gravel Pits in May 1985

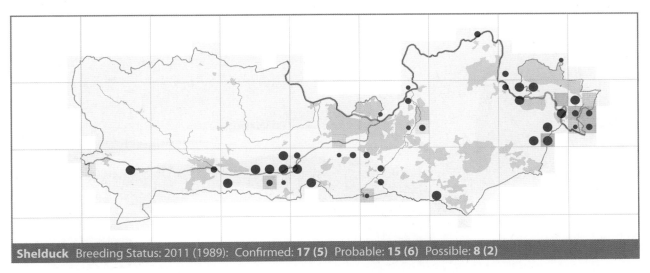

**Shelduck** Breeding Status: 2011 (1989): Confirmed: **17 (5)** Probable: **15 (6)** Possible: **8 (2)**

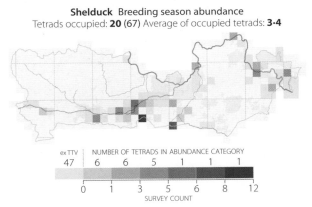

**Shelduck** Breeding season abundance
Tetrads occupied: **20** (67) Average of occupied tetrads: **3·4**

| ex TTV | NUMBER OF TETRADS IN ABUNDANCE CATEGORY | | | | | |
|---|---|---|---|---|---|---|
| 47 | 6 | 6 | 5 | 1 | 1 | 1 |

0   1   3   5   6   8   12
SURVEY COUNT

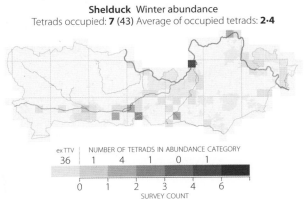

**Shelduck** Winter abundance
Tetrads occupied: **7** (43) Average of occupied tetrads: **2·4**

| ex TTV | NUMBER OF TETRADS IN ABUNDANCE CATEGORY | | | | |
|---|---|---|---|---|---|
| 36 | 1 | 4 | 1 | 0 | 1 |

0   1   2   3   4   6
SURVEY COUNT

and Queen Mother Reservoir in May 1997. Since then the highest counts have been 29 at Pingewood Gravel Pits in June 2001, 23 at Slough Sewage Farm on 21st May 2012 and 21 at Padworth Lane Gravel Pit in June 2007. The Pingewood and Padworth Lane counts both included young birds fledged that year, while the Slough flock also included an additional hybrid with another unidentified *Tadorna* species.

The earliest reference to Shelducks in Berkshire is of one shot near Newbury in 1806 (Lamb, 1880). Clark Kennedy (1868) records that one was shot on the Thames near Cookham some years before 1868 and one was seen in the neighbourhood for several days in the winter of 1867/68. The earliest 20th century record

appears to be one at Reading Sewage Farm, on 8th November 1926. The next record was also from this site in 1932, when two were seen on two dates, with further records in 1934 and 1935. The species appeared annually at Slough Sewage Farm from 1934 to 1944 and there were records of nine at Bulmershe on 9th September 1938, nine at Cookham on 25th February 1940 and two at Ham Island Sewage Farm in May 1943.

Although the national population of Shelduck has declined from a peak in the mid-1990s, this handsome species has become established alongside the other wetland species which have taken advantage of the new habitats created by gravel extraction in Berkshire.

*Sponsored by Sarah and Ken White*

Shelduck, Dinton Pastures *Tony Harden*

# Wood Duck

## *Aix sponsa*

*Localised introduced species*

Although the Wood Duck is not on the British List, as there is doubt that its national population is self sustaining, it is included here because it has bred in Berkshire. Records of this attractive ornamental duck are received annually, mostly from Windsor Great Park, the Loddon and Kennet Valleys and the Goring Gap.

During the early 1970s, up to three fully-winged Wood Ducks were present at any one time at Virginia Water in Windsor Great Park. The original three birds, one drake and two ducks, came from a small captive waterfowl collection at nearby Titness Park. They regularly returned there for some years to feed on grain, which also attracted up to 100 Mandarins. They did not appear to move far from this area, although they were once seen with a party of Mandarins at Rapley Lake. One of the ducks disappeared but the group was soon joined by another drake. Broods of ducklings were first seen at Virginia Water in 1972 when there were four on 13th May. In 1973, another brood of four was seen on 20th and 29th May. The last year when young were seen was 1974, when there were eight on 24th June. The population seems to have died out in the early 1980s.

Elsewhere in Berkshire, the Thames between Purley and Streatley produced records in ten years between 1974 and 1994, including an unpaired, free-flying drake present in the springs of 1991 to 1993 inclusive. There have only been three records since from this area. These records may relate to birds from the Child-Beale Wildlife Park.

Since 1993, nestboxes have been erected for Barn Owls by the Hawk and Owl Trust in the Loddon Valley. In 1995, three of these were occupied by Wood Duck and in 1996 two were occupied. Although eggs were laid

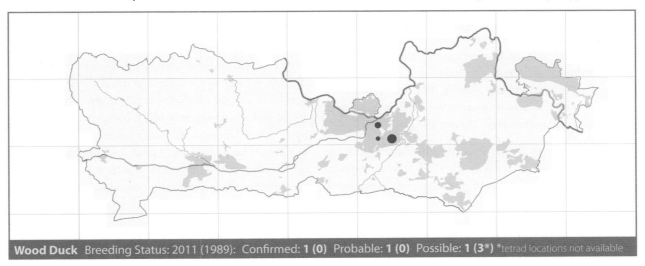

**Wood Duck** Breeding Status: 2011 (1989): Confirmed: **1 (0)** Probable: **1 (0)** Possible: **1 (3*)** *tetrad locations not available

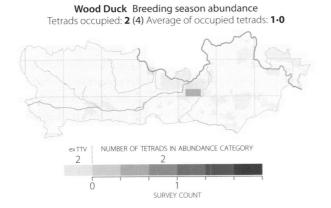

**Wood Duck** Breeding season abundance
Tetrads occupied: **2 (4)** Average of occupied tetrads: **1·0**

ex TTV | NUMBER OF TETRADS IN ABUNDANCE CATEGORY
2 | 2

0                    1
SURVEY COUNT

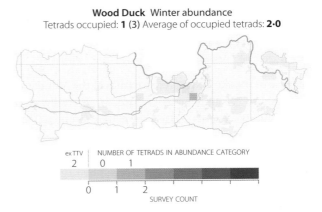

**Wood Duck** Winter abundance
Tetrads occupied: **1 (3)** Average of occupied tetrads: **2·0**

ex TTV | NUMBER OF TETRADS IN ABUNDANCE CATEGORY
2 0 | 1

0        1        2
SURVEY COUNT

in four cases, young successfully fledged from only one nestbox. Since 1999, a small population has apparently become established in the area around the south east of Reading, with records from both Whiteknights Park and Maiden Erleigh Lake. Breeding occurred at the former site in 2005, when a brood of eight was noted on 20th April, and at the latter site in 1999 when a pair with ducklings was noted. These sites have also produced Berkshire's highest counts: ten at Maiden Erleigh on 8th March 2004 and nine at Whiteknights on 13th June 2001 and 2nd May 2005. There have however been no counts in excess of two at either site since 2008, save for five at the latter site early in January 2012.

There have been a number of other records of one or two from a number of other sites between Summerleaze Gravel Pits in the east and Hungerford in the west, the highest count being four on the Thames near Bray in January 1985. Most records are of drakes. Females may have been overlooked, due to their similarity to female Mandarins and an albino at Pangbourne on 3rd April 1990 could not be attributed to either species.

*Sponsored by Val Tarr*

# Mandarin Duck

## *Aix galericulata*

### *Localised and increasing introduced resident*

The Mandarin Duck, a native of eastern Asia, is now an established introduced resident in Britain. The British population first became established in south east England, principally in Berkshire and Surrey. In Berkshire, its stronghold was in the east of the county but in recent decades it has spread to colonise several areas to the west.

The species first became established in Berkshire in 1932, where Windsor Great Park, which straddles the Berkshire/Surrey border, provided the ideal habitat of mature, open broadleaved woodland with secluded ponds and streams and overhanging Rhododendron *Rhododendron ponticum* for shelter. Berkshire features in the early history of the species, the first recorded specimen of a Mandarin shot in the wild in Britain being from Cookham in May 1866 (Lever, 1987).

Comparison between the breeding distribution maps from the 1987–89 and 2007–11 atlas surveys shows the expansion of the breeding range in Berkshire into the centre of the county from the strongholds where breeding was confirmed in the earlier survey, in and around Windsor Great Park, the areas around Swallowfield and Arborfield, near or along the River Loddon and Brimpton. The breeding range now extends to most of the Thames valley and lower Kennet and into urban Reading, and Eversley Gravel Pits. It remains scarce west of Newbury.

Because of the shy and secretive nature of the Mandarin, it is almost certainly under-recorded, especially after regular WeBS counts ceased in Windsor Great Park in 1994. Its preference for secluded, undisturbed and often private waters adds to the problems of accurate recording, particularly during the breeding season. This makes it hard to form any conclusions about its absence

D.A.Thelwell.

or breeding status in some apparently suitable tetrads (Davies, 1988).

The distributions shown by the abundance maps, both breeding and winter seasons, generally match the county records during recent years. With the preference the species shows for a habitat of mature, open broadleaved woodland, especially that which comprises oak *Quercus* spp., Sweet Chestnut *Castanea saliva* and Beech *Fagus sylvatica*, which provides a source of nesting sites and an autumn and winter food source, it is unsurprising that the breeding distribution correlates well with that of broadleaved woodland and river valley systems. The greatest concentrations were from Windsor Great Park, the Thames in east Berkshire and the area to the east and south east of Reading.

Few Mandarin were reported before 1970 away from their main stronghold in east Berkshire, Aldermaston Gravel Pits being the farthest west the species was recorded. Thereafter, they possibly bred at Swallowfield in 1971 and were confirmed to have bred at Bearwood Lake in 1977, maybe earlier, and on the River Whitewater in 1980. Mandarins were thought to have established a small colony in the Brimpton and Aldermaston area in 1984. Significant numbers of pairs have bred along the Thames since the late 1980s, especially in the east of the county. A total of 58 young was counted in June 1993

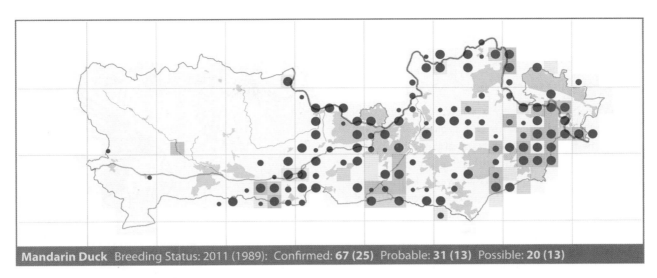

**Mandarin Duck** Breeding Status: 2011 (1989): Confirmed: **67 (25)** Probable: **31 (13)** Possible: **20 (13)**

**Mandarin Duck** Breeding season abundance
Tetrads occupied: **47 (141)** Average of occupied tetrads: **3·4**

**Mandarin Duck** Winter abundance
Tetrads occupied: **19 (62)** Average of occupied tetrads: **5·7**

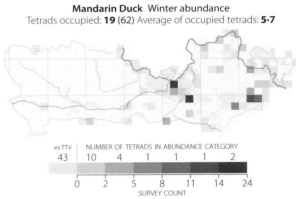

| ex TTV | NUMBER OF TETRADS IN ABUNDANCE CATEGORY | | | | | |
|--------|----|----|---|---|---|---|
| 94 | 14 | 19 | 5 | 2 | 3 | 4 |

0   1   3   5   6   8   13
SURVEY COUNT

| ex TTV | NUMBER OF TETRADS IN ABUNDANCE CATEGORY | | | | |
|--------|----|---|---|---|---|
| 43 | 10 | 4 | 1 | 1 | 2 |

0   2   5   8   11   14   24
SURVEY COUNT

between Romney Lock and Old Windsor. In 1994, there were 17 pairs between Cookham and Maidenhead in May, and 90 young from 15 broods were counted in the Runnymede area in July, and in 2003 70 young were counted as having hatched from 96 eggs in nestboxes at Eversley Gravel Pits, another site which has become a stronghold for the species. In south east Reading, Whiteknights Lake has become a regular urban breeding site, although the failure rate of breeding attempts has been reported as high.

In Britain, seasonal movements of Mandarin are relatively local, yet in their natural range, the Eastern Palearctic, the species is migratory and dispersive (*BWP I*). In 1990, there was an exceptional movement of a bird ringed in Berkshire which was recovered in Pskov in north-east Russia (Dudley, 1991). Most of the other ringing recoveries relate to movements within the county or neighbouring counties, but four ringed at Sunninghill have been recovered in Kent.

*Sponsored by Sarah and Ken White*

Mandarin, Moor Green Lakes *Roger Milligan*

# Wigeon

## *Anas penelope*

*Widespread winter visitor and rare summer visitor*

The Wigeon is principally a winter visitor in rather variable numbers to Berkshire. It is typically encountered on lakes or flooded gravel pits, or grazing beside them although, as shown on the winter map, it can occur on rivers or in adjacent meadows anywhere in the county, especially when hard weather influxes occur. With the creation of many artificial water bodies as a result of gravel extraction, particularly where they are alongside grassland, the area of wintering habitat suitable for Wigeon has been increasing in Berkshire.

Britain's breeding population of Wigeon was only about 140 pairs in 2009, most of which occur in the north. Although Berkshire is very much on the edge of the species' breeding range (*BWP I*, Owen *et al.*, 1986, Holling *et al.*, 2011), breeding has occurred at two sites: Windsor Great Park and Sunninghill Park Lake. It was first confirmed to have bred at both sites in 1950 and continued until 1957, although in no year were more than three pairs found. Breeding was again confirmed in 1962, annually from 1965 to 1968 and in 1973 and 1974, with only one pair each year except 1967 when two pairs bred. Since then breeding has not been confirmed, although pairs were present throughout the summer in east Berkshire in 1976. Summering Wigeon have been recorded in the period May to July most years since 1980 and each year since 2000; these are usually single birds, sometimes with evidence of injury that may have prevented migration. Wintering birds usually start to arrive in small numbers in late August and reach a peak between December and February (Figure 7). Most depart in March and only a few stragglers remain into April or May. Opportunities to observe passage migration are limited in Berkshire, but on the morning of 5th November 1994 five flocks totalling 160 birds flew west over Queen Mother Reservoir.

Around 440,000 Wigeon winter in the UK (Musgrove *et al.*, 2011), in greatest numbers near the coast, where counts at regular strongholds such as the Ouse Washes and Lindisfarne are often in the range 20,000–40,000. Only a small part of this population is found in Berkshire, where peak winter counts total 1,000–2,000. The highest counts at individual sites in Berkshire have been about 1,000 at Bulmershe South Lake on 27th February 1938, about 900 at Wraysbury Gravel Pits in January 1986, 828 at Twyford in January 1997 and 800–1,000 at Lea Farm Gravel Pit in December 2010. In the 1930s, Great Meadow Pond regularly recorded over 100 with a minimum of 415 on 26th December 1932. In line with the national trend, which shows a twofold increase

in the WeBS index between 1980 and 2010, Berkshire counts show a strong increase in recent decades. Counts at four sites for which there are WeBS data during the 1980s and the period 2000–2009, Dinton Pastures, Twyford Lakes (Loddon Nature Reserve), the Theale Gravel Pits and Burghfield (Searles Farm) Gravel Pits, showed an average increase of nearly three-fold over this 20 year period. Counts of over 100 Wigeon are now recorded most years in the winter months at many of the gravel pit complexes across the county, with Lower Farm, Theale, Burghfield, Eversley, Dinton Pastures, Lea Farm, Twyford and Wraysbury showing maxima in excess of 300 in the last 20 years.

There is one Berkshire recovery of a Wigeon ringed abroad, a bird ringed at Harsbeeg, Noord Brabant in the

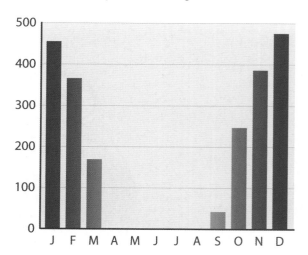

**Figure 7: Wigeon: average monthly counts.**
WeBS standard counts for Berkshire in 2000–2010 (2001 excluded because of poor coverage due to foot and mouth disease).

**Wigeon** Breeding season abundance
Tetrads occupied: **3** (29) Average of occupied tetrads: **3·0**

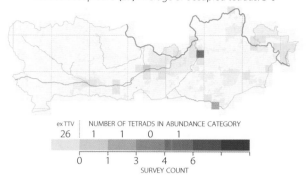

| ex TTV | NUMBER OF TETRADS IN ABUNDANCE CATEGORY | | | |
|---|---|---|---|---|
| 26 | 1 | 1 | 0 | 1 |

0   1   3   4   6
SURVEY COUNT

**Wigeon** Winter abundance
Tetrads occupied: **36** (78) Average of occupied tetrads: **46·8**

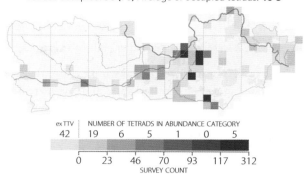

| ex TTV | NUMBER OF TETRADS IN ABUNDANCE CATEGORY | | | | | |
|---|---|---|---|---|---|---|
| 42 | 19 | 6 | 5 | 1 | 0 | 5 |

0   23   46   70   93   117   312
SURVEY COUNT

Netherlands on 26th December 1967 being recovered at Reading on 31st December 1969. A drake ringed in Littleborough, Nottinghamshire, on 20th February 2000 was shot near Reading on 9th November 2002.

Historically, the Wigeon was an occasional winter visitor to Berkshire in limited numbers in the mid-19th century (Clark Kennedy, 1868) and annual in small numbers by 1900 (Noble, 1906).

*Sponsored by Mike Turton*

# American Wigeon

## *Anas americana*

*Rare vagrant, some records probably refer to escapees*

The American Wigeon is a rare vagrant to the UK with typically five or so records per year (Fraser *et al.*, 2006). In Berkshire, eight records have involved about 15 birds. The presence of apparently escaped birds from waterfowl collections, and the occurrence of hybrids resembling American Wigeon, cast doubt however on a number of the records.

On 26th November 1985 a party of four birds, two first-winter males and two females, was discovered at Thatcham Gravel Pits and was seen there and at Theale Gravel Pits subsequently until the end of December. One of the males and one female remained until 26th January 1986. They were assumed to be of wild origin in view of their arrival date and the record was accepted by BBRC.

The initial record of four birds was then followed by reports from the Kennet Valley (from Thatcham to Theale) of a female in March 1986, two males in February 1987, a female and a first-winter male in November 1987 and two males in December 1987. Only the two birds in November 1987 were submitted to BBRC and accepted. In 1988, there were several reports of an apparent hybrid male and female at Theale in February, September and December and of a pair of apparently escaped American Wigeon on the Thames near Pangbourne in October and December. The Theale hybrids returned again in 1989, accompanied by a second male. There is a possibility that the apparent hybrids were Gadwall × Chiloe Wigeon, which show

a close resemblance to American Wigeon. The latter has occurred as an escapee on a number of occasions in Berkshire (see Appendices). An adult male was located at Lower Farm Gravel Pits on 19th November 2008 which stayed until 28th January 2009, and this became only the third fully acceptable record for the county. Another was reported just beyond the Thames at Sonning Eye in September 2009 during a WeBS count, but was not observed to cross the county boundary into Berkshire.

More recently, during March 2013, a first-winter drake American Wigeon × Wigeon hybrid was discovered among a large flock of Wigeon at Lea Farm Gravel Pit.

Small parties of American Wigeon have occurred elsewhere in Britain and in the stormy winter of 1986/87 there was another first-winter male in Oxfordshire in February 1987. There have been significant influxes to UK in 2000 (30) and 2002 (23) indicating a steady increase in arrivals nationwide over recent years. Nonetheless, there must be some doubt over the origin of some of the birds reported in Berkshire.

*Sponsored by Amy McKee*

# Gadwall

*Anas strepera*

*Increasingly widespread winter visitor and scarce breeder.*

The Gadwall is primarily a regular winter visitor to lakes and flooded gravel pits in Berkshire and has increased considerably in numbers in recent years. Small numbers remain to breed at suitable wetland sites.

The species' recent history in Berkshire reflects its status nationally. A scarce duck fifty years ago, the UK wintering population has increased to around 25,000 (Musgrove *et al.*, 2011). The British breeding population has also increased rapidly since the 1960s and is now over 2,000 pairs (Holling *et al.*, 2011). Fox and Salmon (1989) attributed the increase in Gadwall in part to wild stocks being supplemented by hand-reared birds by wildfowlers until the early 1970s and in part to the increasing use by the species of nutrient-rich artificial water bodies.

The first county record was of a pair shot at Maiden Erleigh in 1915, followed by two seen at Virginia Water in 1933. By the 1950s records were annual but single figure counts were the norm until the mid-1970s when maximum counts began to increase, initially in the east of the county. Numbers reached 38 in December 1977 at Wraysbury Gravel Pits and exceeded 60 there

in October 1978. Thereafter, Dinton Pastures became a major wintering site, with maximum numbers rising from 43 in 1979 to 115 in 1981 and to 161 in 1982.

In the mid-1970s, December counts were considerably lower than October counts, but by 1982 they were regularly comparable and for the last decade midwinter counts have been substantially higher than autumn numbers (Figure 8), reflecting the national pattern.

Wintering numbers at most sites increased rapidly throughout the 1980s and 1990s and more slowly thereafter. Figure 9 shows the counts at the sites with the largest concentrations in the county, the gravel pits

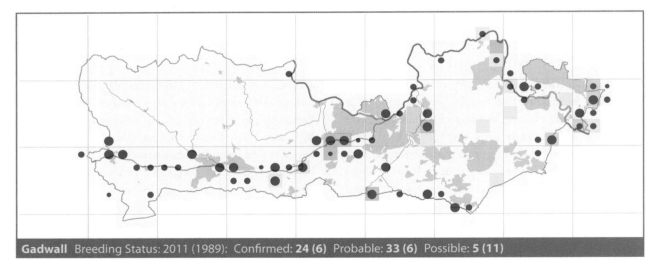

**Gadwall**  Breeding Status: 2011 (1989):  Confirmed: **24 (6)**  Probable: **33 (6)**  Possible: **5 (11)**

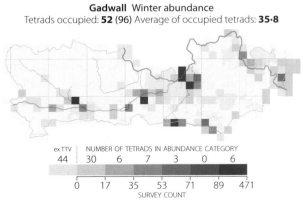

**Gadwall**  Breeding season abundance
Tetrads occupied: **33 (70)** Average of occupied tetrads: **5·9**

| ex TTV | NUMBER OF TETRADS IN ABUNDANCE CATEGORY | | | | | |
|---|---|---|---|---|---|---|
| 37 | 13 | 9 | 5 | 2 | 0 | 4 |

| 0 | 2 | 5 | 8 | 11 | 14 | 26 |

SURVEY COUNT

**Gadwall**  Winter abundance
Tetrads occupied: **52 (96)** Average of occupied tetrads: **35·8**

| ex TTV | NUMBER OF TETRADS IN ABUNDANCE CATEGORY | | | | | |
|---|---|---|---|---|---|---|
| 44 | 30 | 6 | 7 | 3 | 0 | 6 |

| 0 | 17 | 35 | 53 | 71 | 89 | 471 |

SURVEY COUNT

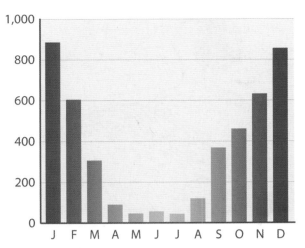

**Figure 8: Gadwall: monthly maximum counts.**
Average of the monthly maxima reported in Annual Reports
for 2000–08.

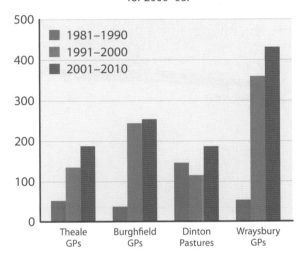

**Figure 9: Gadwall: trend in annual maximum counts at four main sites.** Decadal averages of annual maxima reported in Annual Reports.

Gadwall, Lower Farm Gravel Pits *Dave Bartlett*

at Wraysbury, in the lower Kennet valley at Burghfield and Theale and Dinton Pastures. The highest counts have been at the Wraysbury Gravel Pits, with a peak of 1004 in December 2011. In that year the peak winter count for the sites in Figure 9, which account for the majority of Gadwall in Berkshire, was 1,720, consistent with the winter population estimate for the county of 1,500 (Appendix IV). In contrast to the increases elsewhere, numbers at Dinton Pastures declined following a programme of weed removal in the 1990s, and have remained at about the same level since. The dramatic increase in wintering Gadwall in Berkshire that continued through the second half of the twentieth century and more slowly in the first decade of the 21st century, reflects the national trend (Holt *et al.*, 2012).

Gadwall were first proved to breed in Berkshire at Windsor Great Park in 1976. They subsequently bred at Dinton Pastures in 1983, were thought to have bred at Summerleaze Gravel Pits in 1984 and bred at Theale in 1988. The number of tetrads where breeding was proved increased from six tetrads in the 1987–89 survey to 26 in the 2007–11 survey and, as the tetrad maps show, it is now established through the Kennet, Loddon and Colne valleys, along the Blackwater and in the Dorney area. Breeding is probably substantially under-recorded as Gadwall breed secretively in rank vegetation and young ducklings usually remain secluded. With apparently plenty of suitable breeding habitat left to colonise, it seems likely that the Gadwall will continue to spread as a breeding species in Berkshire.

There have only been two ringing recoveries of Gadwall for Berkshire, one ringed at Slimbridge, Gloucestershire in December 1978, shot at Bray two months later, and a first year male ringed near Peterborough in December 1999, shot a year later near Padworth.

*Sponsored by Neil Bucknell*

# Teal

*Anas crecca*

*Widespread winter visitor and rare summer visitor*

Teal occur principally as winter visitors to Berkshire and occasionally breed. As a species that favours upland bog and coastal salt marsh in Britain, the numbers in the county form only a small part of the national population at any time of the year.

In winter, Teal occur widely throughout the river valleys, as indicated by the Winter Map. Open areas of gravel, sand, mud, pools of water and scattered vegetation at any gravel pit seem to be favoured. They also make use of flooded fields and can be found along rivers, streams and ditches. Numbers build up from August, reaching a peak in December and January, when many gravel pit sites may hold over 100 birds: since 2000 these include the pits at Wraysbury, Bray, Dorney, Dinton Pastures, Lea Farm, Eversley, Theale and Lower Farm. For many years in the late 1970s and during the 1980s the unflooded area of abandoned gravel workings at Theale Gravel Pits, known locally as the 'Wader Pit', was the county's prime site with peak counts of over 200 in each year from 1978 to 1985 and with a maximum of about 600 in January 1980. However, as a result of

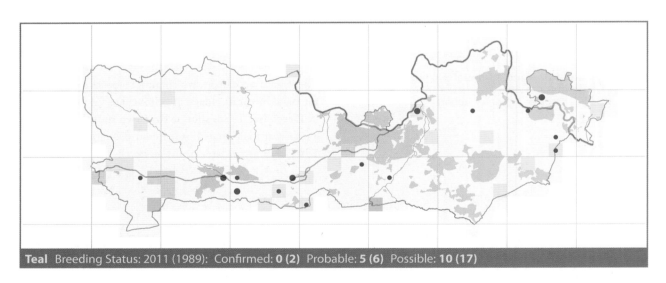

**Teal** Breeding Status: 2011 (1989): Confirmed: **0 (2)** Probable: **5 (6)** Possible: **10 (17)**

**Teal** Breeding season abundance
Tetrads occupied: **7 (44)** Average of occupied tetrads: **3·3**

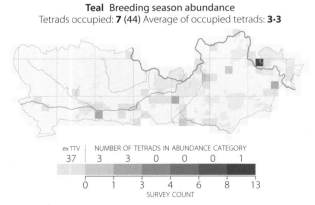

| ex TTV | NUMBER OF TETRADS IN ABUNDANCE CATEGORY | | | | | |
|---|---|---|---|---|---|---|
| 37 | 3 | 3 | 0 | 0 | 1 | 1 |

| 0 | 1 | 3 | 4 | 6 | 8 | 13 |
|---|---|---|---|---|---|---|

SURVEY COUNT

**Teal** Winter abundance
Tetrads occupied: **31 (104)** Average of occupied tetrads: **21·1**

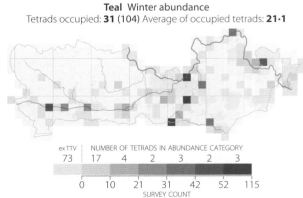

| ex TTV | NUMBER OF TETRADS IN ABUNDANCE CATEGORY | | | | | |
|---|---|---|---|---|---|---|
| 73 | 17 | 4 | 2 | 3 | 2 | 3 |

| 0 | 10 | 21 | 31 | 42 | 52 | 115 |
|---|---|---|---|---|---|---|

SURVEY COUNT

back-filling with waste, the area became less attractive. The highest recorded count since 2000 was at least 500 on the ice at Woolhampton in December 2010. From the data recorded in the Wetland Bird Survey and from the county reports, there is no evidence of a long term trend in numbers in Berkshire. Nationally, following slow growth from 1960 to 1980, the wintering population has changed little in subsequent years (Holt *et al.*, 2011).

By April, most of the wintering birds have left, though in most years some individuals and pairs remain through the summer. There are occasional small influxes of Teal in May and June, perhaps late northward passage. The return movement starts in August, though there was an unusual arrival of Teal at Pingewood Gravel Pits in July 2007, when numbers rose from 21 to 88 overnight.

Although summering birds can be found in most years, breeding in Berkshire has not been confirmed since the 1987–89 Atlas Survey, when confirmation was obtained in two tetrads, one based on a distraction display in the West Woodhay area and one involving fledged young being seen in the Loddon Valley. Nesting was also reported in Hamstead Park in 1987 and 1988 and in the Theale and Wraysbury areas in 1988. Breeding had previously been noted in only three years since 1974, at Silwood in 1975, Easthampstead in 1976 and Slough Sewage Farm in 1985. Breeding was also suspected at Wraysbury Gravel Pits in 1976. In the breeding seasons during the 2007–11 Tetrad Survey, most records of possible or probable breeding birds are likely to have been passage migrants or stragglers from the wintering population. However, summering pairs were present at four sites where breeding may have been attempted. Breeding is not easy to confirm as Teal nest in dense vegetation, usually away from open water.

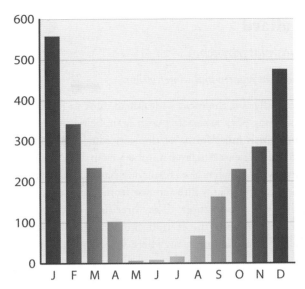

**Figure 10: Teal: average monthly counts.** Average for 2000–2008 of the aggregated monthly maxima at main sites reported in Annual Reports: Lower Farm GP, Thatcham GPs, Padworth Lane GP, Theale GPs, Pingewood GPs, Dinton Pastures, Dorney Wetlands, Bray GPs, Eversley GPs, Great Meadow Pond, Wraysbury GPs.

A similar pattern emerges from records earlier in the 20th century, with artificial sites such as Slough and Reading Sewage Farms, the Bulmershe Lakes and Great Meadow Pond producing the highest counts, including the highest ever of 1,030 at Bulmershe North Lake on 21st February 1937. Breeding was reported from near Reading in 1921, Kintbury in 1932 and Slough Sewage Farm in 1935, where two or three may have bred in 1946 and a pair bred in 1967. The Teal was recorded by Lamb (1880) as an annual visitor to marshes near Newbury around 1800 and it remained a regular winter visitor throughout the 19th century. Noble (1906) recorded breeding at Kintbury in 1880, Great Meadow Pond in 1896 and Thatcham Marsh in 1900.

*Sponsored by Moor Green Lakes Group*

# Green-winged Teal

## *Anas carolinensis*

*Rare vagrant – three records*

There have been three records in Berkshire of this North American duck, which used to be regarded as a subspecies of the Common Teal (*A. crecca*). The first was a drake seen briefly at Burghfield Gravel Pits on 21st April 1990. The second was another drake which was first seen at Moor Green Lakes, Eversley Gravel Pits on 17th November 2001 and which was last seen on 27th January 2002. The most recent record, also a drake, was first seen at Slough Sewage Farm on 23rd February 2004, and seen at Dorney Wick and back at Slough

Sewage Farm before last being seen at Bray Gravel Pits on 4th March.

*Sponsored by Hattie Spray, WSP Environment & Energy*

# Mallard

Amber

*Anas platyrhynchos*

*Abundant resident and winter visitor.*

The Mallard is the most widespread duck in Berkshire. It has long been associated with man, being the species from which most forms of domestic duck are derived, and is also released in large numbers from captive-reared stock by wildfowlers. As a result, it is hard to differentiate the effects of man's interference from the state of the truly wild population. The breeding distributions revealed by both the Tetrad Surveys show that the Mallard breeds almost anywhere where open water or watercourses occur, however small a proportion of the tetrad these may constitute. Even on the dry downland areas in the north west of the county small ponds or farm reservoirs can provide adequate open water for breeding. Although the nests, which are usually away from open water, may not be conspicuous, once the brood has hatched and made its way to open water it is comparatively easy to confirm breeding.

The results of the Common Bird Survey and Breeding Bird Survey have shown that the increase in the breeding population of the Mallard in Britain in the 20th century (*1968–72 BTO Atlas*) has continued more

slowly, but steadily between 1970 and 2010, although little information is available on the population trend in Berkshire. The breeding season abundance map shows the Berkshire population to be densest along the major rivers, particularly close to towns, where supplemental feeding by man may be a factor. Based on the abundance surveys, the Berkshire population is estimated to be 1,200 pairs (Appendix IV).

The much larger UK winter population, swollen by immigration from the east and north, declined 40% in between 1990 and 2010 (Holt *et al.*, 2011). For this

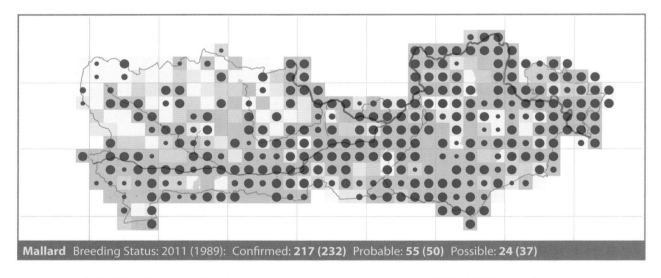

**Mallard** Breeding Status: 2011 (1989): Confirmed: **217 (232)** Probable: **55 (50)** Possible: **24 (37)**

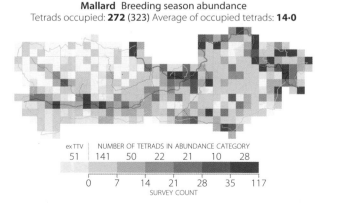

**Mallard** Breeding season abundance
Tetrads occupied: **272 (323)** Average of occupied tetrads: **14·0**

| exTTV | NUMBER OF TETRADS IN ABUNDANCE CATEGORY | | | | | |
|---|---|---|---|---|---|---|
| 51 | 141 | 50 | 22 | 21 | 10 | 28 |

| 0 | 7 | 14 | 21 | 28 | 35 | 117 |
|---|---|---|---|---|---|---|

SURVEY COUNT

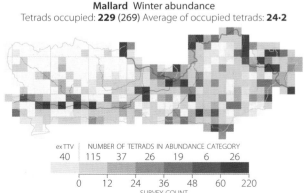

**Mallard** Winter abundance
Tetrads occupied: **229 (269)** Average of occupied tetrads: **24·2**

| exTTV | NUMBER OF TETRADS IN ABUNDANCE CATEGORY | | | | | |
|---|---|---|---|---|---|---|
| 40 | 115 | 37 | 26 | 19 | 6 | 26 |

| 0 | 12 | 24 | 36 | 48 | 60 | 220 |
|---|---|---|---|---|---|---|

SURVEY COUNT

reason the Mallard has been put on the Amber List of species of conservation concern (Eaton *et al.*, 2009). In Berkshire peak numbers occur from early autumn to mid-winter (Figure 11). Years with an early autumn peak may reflect the increase in population from local breeding success outweighing the increase due to the immigration of continental wintering birds.

The winter abundance map shows a similar distribution pattern to summer abundance, though the counts of early winter tetrad surveys (4,196) was 48% higher than that for the June/July surveys (2,842). As Mallard are widespread, the monthly totals of counts from the Wetland Bird Survey's Berkshire sites, which were between 187 and 676 for the recent Atlas survey period, and those recorded for major sites in County annual reports account for only a small proportion of the population.

Counts of over 100 are recorded most years at several sites across the county, and regularly at sites where ducks are fed by visitors, such as Thatcham Marsh, Black Swan Lake at Dinton Pastures and Windsor Esplanade. Unusually high totals of 750 and 700 were counted in Windsor Great Park in September 1961 and December 1978 respectively and 660 were counted there in November 1982. Elsewhere, 644 at Burghfield in January 1982 is the highest recorded count. Consistent with the decline in the national winter population, peak counts have been lower since 2000, the highest being 402 at Windsor Esplanade in October 2005.

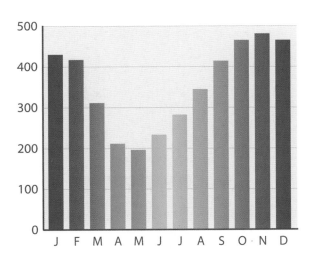

**Figure 11: Mallard: average monthly counts.** Average of aggregated monthly maxima for Dinton Pastures, Dorney Wetlands, Thatcham Discovery Centre and Lower Farm Gravel Pit, 2004–2008.

There has been one overseas recovery of a Mallard ringed in Berkshire, a drake which was ringed at Silwood Park on 14th February 1950 being recovered on the west coast of Jutland, Denmark on 12th October 1951. Other notable recoveries were of a bird ringed at Pangbourne in June 1931, which was recovered at Holme, Norfolk in December 1932, and one ringed at Langley in October 1962, which was recovered near Evesham the following January.

*Sponsored by Renee Grayer*

# Pintail

## *Anas acuta*

*Uncommon winter visitor and passage migrant*

The Pintail is a scarce winter visitor to Berkshire and is usually recorded from gravel pits and shallow flooded areas in the east or centre of the county, although it has been recorded at other areas of open water, such as the settling beds of open sewage works. Though there are occasional breeding records elsewhere in inland counties of southern England (Holling *et al.*, 2012), it is not known to have bred in Berkshire.

One shot near Henley on 30th March 1850 (Noble, 1906) would be the first record for Berkshire if it had been obtained on the Thames. In 1922, one was recorded at Cranemoor Lake, Englefield Park and, after 1924, the species was reported from Twyford, Virginia Water, Windsor Great Park, Ham Island and Bulmershe Lakes. On 6th June 1937 a pair visited Bulmershe Lakes, an unusual mid-summer record. Since the 1940s there has been a notable increase in records. The actual numbers present in any winter are difficult to assess because of the mobility of birds between different waters, but

Figure 12 shows the five yearly totals estimated for birds arriving in the county. The increase in numbers in the 1970s may reflect the doubling of numbers wintering

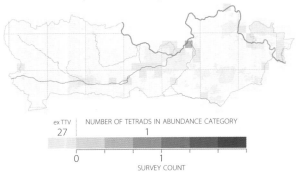

exTTV | NUMBER OF TETRADS IN ABUNDANCE CATEGORY
27 | 1

0        1
SURVEY COUNT

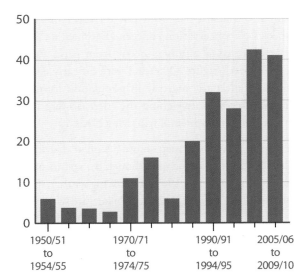

**Figure 12: Pintail: arrivals from 1949/50–2009/10.**
Five-yearly totals of estimated numbers of birds arriving.
An exceptional influx of approx. 200 birds in February 2003
is excluded.

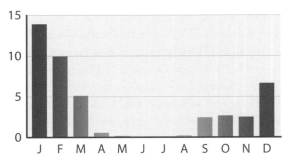

**Figure 13: Pintail: average monthly counts.** Average of
totals of Pintail from winter 1990/91–2009/10, based on
numbers of birds recorded in the month. An exceptional
influx of approx. 200 birds in February 2003 is excluded.

in the UK between 1968/9 and 1974/5, since when the national population has not changed substantially (Holt *et al.*, 2001). Subsequent increases in the numbers recorded in Berkshire may, in part, reflect an increase in the number of observers and the area of open water in the county.

A few passage birds occasionally pass through in late August and most years single birds or small parties are recorded in September and October. Wintering birds, often staying for several weeks, occur from November to March. They may be found on open water or flooded fields or ditches anywhere in the county, the main sites being gravel pits at Wraysbury, Dinton Pastures, Lea Farm, Theale, Woolhampton and Lower Farm. Numbers vary widely from year to year: the median for January and February from 1990 to 2000 was 12, but this included months with no records and one with an exceptional influx of 200 birds. Most records have been of single birds, or of small groups of less than ten. The appearance of larger numbers of these elegant birds in Berkshire is probably largely dependent on conditions in their normal wintering grounds. The influx of about 200 Pintail in February 2003, with 150 in one flock on Fobney Meadows, coincided with hard weather across the country following extensive flooding. Prior to that, the highest Berkshire count was 28 over Horton Gravel Pits on 31st December 1974. Other counts greater than twenty were 22 over Dinton Pastures in March 1992 and 22 at Smallmead Farm Gravel Pit in January 1993.

Pintail are rarely seen after April and the few records in May, July and August (a total of 16 between 1950 and 2010) may be very late or early passage birds or may have come from collections or possibly from one of the few breeding sites in southern England.

*Sponsored by David Hastings*

Pintail *Tony Harden*

# Garganey

*Anas querquedula*

*Uncommon passage migrant and rare summer visitor.*

The Garganey is an annual but scarce passage migrant through Berkshire, which has also bred on two occasions. The Garganey is on the Amber List of birds of conservation concern because of its relatively small and declining European population (Eaton *et al.*, 2009).

Garganey were first reported in Berkshire in the 20th century from Reading Sewage Farm in April 1923. After two more records in 1926 and one in 1933, the species was recorded annually from 1935 to 1940 and in 1944 and 1945, with most records from Slough and Ham Island Sewage Farm, and from Bulmershe Lakes. The species was then recorded annually from 1946 to 2011, with numbers ranging from one (in 1963) to 37. Only three records have been of ten or more birds: 20+ at Windsor Great Park in August 1950, 17 at Bulmershe in March 1959 and 11 at Manor Farm in August 1969. The next highest counts were of eight on floods at Dorney Common in August 1999, seven at Wraysbury in August 1979 and in the Theale area in August 1994. Despite the increase in observer coverage and in the available habitat for the species, there was no indication of an increase in Garganey records in the county between the mid-1940s and the mid-1990s (Figure 14), reflecting perhaps the declining European population, although there has been an increase since the mid-1990s.

Figure 15 summarises the records for the period from 1995 to 2011 by month of arrival and shows peaks corresponding to spring passage in April and autumn passage in August, though annual total numbers vary widely from year to year: from five in 1996 to 37 in 1999. Spring passage commences in March, sometimes as early as the 6th, as in 1988, and continues through to early June. Records are normally of single birds or pairs, which may stay for a week or more. Autumn passage begins in July, when birds are frequently in eclipse, and often extends into October. Exceptionally birds remain into November: in 1989 a juvenile at Wraysbury Gravel Pits stayed from 17th September to 5th November, and

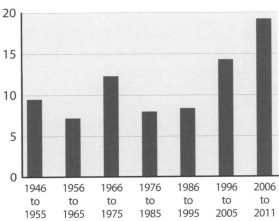

**Figure 14:  Garganey: average number of birds recorded per year.**

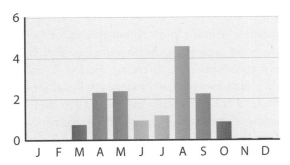

**Figure 15:  Garganey: count by month of arrival.** Average 1995–2011.

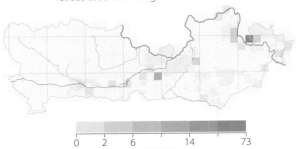

**Garganey**  Spring migration occurrence
Tetrads used: **19** Average of used tetrads: **7·1**

0   2   6      14      73
BIRD DAYS

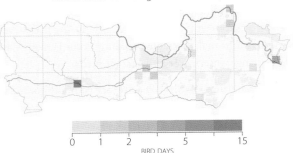

**Garganey**  Autumn migration occurrence
Tetrads used: **10** Average of used tetrads: **3·3**

0   1   2      5      15
BIRD DAYS

in 2005 a bird remained at Dorney from 9th October to 11th November. There have been three winter records: one at Ham Island Sewage Farm in January 1952, a drake seen at Theale Gravel Pits, Slough Sewage Farm, Wraysbury Gravel Pits and Windsor Great Park between 26th November 1987 and 6th February 1988, sightings which presumably relate to the same bird, and a drake at Lower Farm on 14th December 2008.

The first breeding record was at Burghfield in 1975, when a brood of small young was seen in July. The only other confirmed breeding record was revealed by the 1987–89 Tetrad Survey in Foliejon Park where fledged young were seen in 1988. Described by the *1968–72 BTO Atlas* as an opportunistic breeder, it seems unlikely that the Garganey will ever be more than an erratic breeding species in Berkshire.

Prior to 1900, the only records of Garganey in Berkshire were of one shot at Maidenhead in very severe weather in January 1795 (Lamb, 1880), a pair shot at Kintbury in 1874 (Palmer, 1886) and a male shot at Theale in December 1898 (Noble, 1906).

*Sponsored by Andrew Kitching*

# Blue-winged Teal

*Anas discors*

*Rare vagrant, recorded twice*

There are only two records of Blue-winged Teal for Berkshire, both in spring. The first was on 19th May 1988, when a drake was with a pair of Shoveler from 7.30 am to 9.30 pm at Theale Gravel Pits. Another drake was located at the same site by the same observer on 19th April 1990.

*Sponsored by Brian Uttley*

# Shoveler

Amber

*Anas clypeata*

*Regular winter visitor and uncommon breeder*

In Berkshire, as in the UK as a whole, the Shoveler is primarily a winter visitor. Although summering birds are recorded most years, the Shoveler has yet to become firmly established as a breeding species. It was first confirmed to have bred in the county at Reading Sewage Farm in 1922 and again in 1925, 1926 and 1927. Breeding also occurred sporadically at Slough Sewage Farm in the 1930s and 1940s.

The two confirmed breeding records during the 1987–89 Tetrad Survey came from Theale Gravel Pits and from Windsor Great Park, where breeding was also confirmed in 2002 and 2005. Breeding was not confirmed in any tetrads in the summers of 2008 to 2011 during the 2007–11 Tetrad Survey, though summering pairs were present at seven sites across the county during the survey period. Additional "probable breeding" records may relate to lingering wintering or late passage birds.

Small gatherings of Shoveler are occasionally found in late June and early July: in 1994 there were at least 20 Shoveler in Windsor Great Park as early as 10th July, and 12 at Twyford on 1st July 2008: whether these are passage birds or gatherings of local post or non-breeding birds is unclear.

Most records in August and September probably relate to passage birds. It appears that most continental birds only stop briefly in Britain when passing through on autumn migration, and there have been recoveries in Berkshire of birds ringed in Denmark and the Netherlands. Britain is outside the main wintering area of this species (*1981–84 BTO Winter Atlas*), and the majority of the breeding population moves out into south western Europe. Occasionally, large flocks are encountered in September, such as 325 at Wraysbury Gravel Pits in 1995, 99 at Great Meadow Pond in 1968, and 85 at Theale in 2006.

The winter abundance map shows the main concentrations of Shoveler to coincide with the gravel pits in the east of the county and along the main river valleys. Figure 16 shows the averages of peak counts for the main wintering sites in Berkshire which are covered by the WeBS winter wildfowl counts. Although the winter distribution and numbers are more variable than for most of the regular wintering wildfowl species, there is no evidence of a long term trend in the data. The highest counts have tended to be associated with hard weather, especially in the run of cold winters in the 1980s, when the highest recorded count of 422 was made at Queen Mother Reservoir in January 1985. Nearby, Wraysbury Gravel Pits have often returned counts in excess of 100, with 300 in January 2005. In central Berkshire, the highest count was 351 at Theale Gravel Pits in January 2010. In west Berkshire, counts tend to be lower, the highest being 120 at Thatcham Marsh Gravel Pits in February 2006.

Prior to 1900, the Shoveler appears to have been a scarce winter visitor to Berkshire, with Clark Kennedy (1868) only mentioning males shot at Datchet in 1855 and at Burnham in the winter of 1862/3, and a female at Wraysbury in late September 1867.

*Sponsored by Renee Grayer*

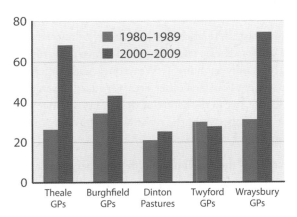

**Figure 16: Shoveler: average winter maxima.** WeBS data – all Berkshire sites.

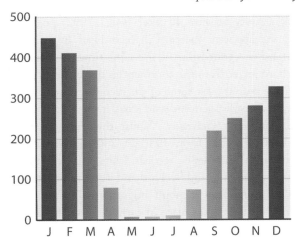

**Figure 17: Shoveler: average of monthly counts.** Annual Reports 2000–2008 – all Berkshire sites.

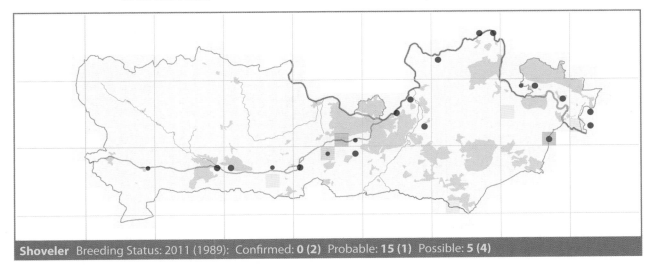

**Shoveler** Breeding Status: 2011 (1989): Confirmed: **0 (2)** Probable: **15 (1)** Possible: **5 (4)**

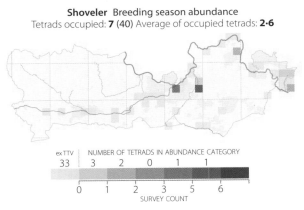

**Shoveler** Breeding season abundance
Tetrads occupied: **7 (40)** Average of occupied tetrads: **2·6**

| exTTV | NUMBER OF TETRADS IN ABUNDANCE CATEGORY | | | | | |
|---|---|---|---|---|---|---|
| 33 | 3 | 2 | 0 | 1 | | 1 |

| | | | | | | |
|---|---|---|---|---|---|---|
| 0 | 1 | 2 | 3 | 5 | 6 |
SURVEY COUNT

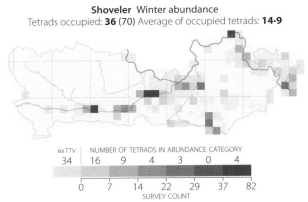

**Shoveler** Winter abundance
Tetrads occupied: **36 (70)** Average of occupied tetrads: **14·9**

| exTTV | NUMBER OF TETRADS IN ABUNDANCE CATEGORY | | | | | |
|---|---|---|---|---|---|---|
| 34 | 16 | 9 | 4 | 3 | 0 | 4 |

| | | | | | | |
|---|---|---|---|---|---|---|
| 0 | 7 | 14 | 22 | 29 | 37 | 82 |
SURVEY COUNT

# Red-crested Pochard

## *Netta rufina*

*Scarce but increasing winter visitor, has bred*

The Red-crested Pochard is a primarily a scarce but increasing winter visitor to Berkshire. In recent years the number of records has increased, with birds remaining all year, and breeding has been recorded.

The origin of the birds in Berkshire is unclear, as this attractive duck is kept in collections and there is an introduced breeding population at the Cotswold Water Park, Gloucestershire. Brucker *et al.,* (1992) postulate that the apparent increase in records of Red-crested Pochard in Oxfordshire at the same time as wintering Pochard arrive from the continent in the autumn, could indicate that at least some of the records relate to birds from the nearest genuine wild stock in the Netherlands and north-east Germany. Whilst the analysis of the Berkshire records from 1946 to 2005 indicates that there are a number of records from June to August, before most wintering Pochard and Tufted Duck arrive, *BWP I* notes that a moult migration of adult males and immatures takes place in early June, so this arrival pattern is not necessarily inconsistent with wild status. Of the sites where Red-crested Pochard were most frequently recorded up to 1985, Wraysbury Gravel Pits with 11 records and Windsor Great Park with five are in east Berkshire, farthest from Gloucestershire. The others, Theale and Burghfield Gravel Pits, together recorded only as many as Wraysbury, with six and five respectively. Fourteen other sites were used, seven in east Berkshire, five in the centre of the county and two in the west. For only two of the records were birds reported as being tame.

Since 1985, the distribution of records between east and central Berkshire has been reversed, with 59 birds seen in east Berkshire and 103 in the centre of the county in the 20 years up to 2005, but few from west Berkshire.

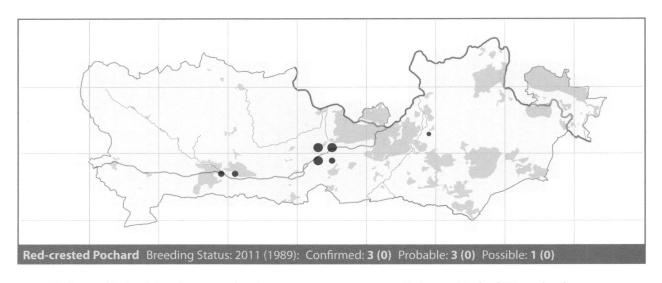

**Red-crested Pochard**  Breeding Status: 2011 (1989):  Confirmed: **3 (0)**  Probable: **3 (0)**  Possible: **1 (0)**

**Red-crested Pochard**  Breeding season abundance
Tetrads occupied: **2 (8)** Average of occupied tetrads: **2·5**

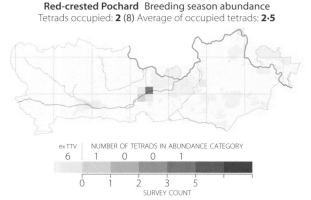

| ex TTV | NUMBER OF TETRADS IN ABUNDANCE CATEGORY | | | | |
|---|---|---|---|---|---|
| 6 | 1 | 0 | 0 | 1 | |

0    1    2    3    5
SURVEY COUNT

**Red-crested Pochard**  Winter abundance
Tetrads occupied: **2 (28)** Average of occupied tetrads: **1·5**

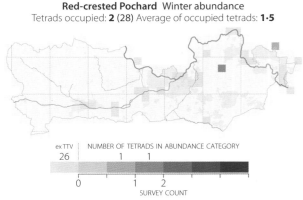

| ex TTV | NUMBER OF TETRADS IN ABUNDANCE CATEGORY | |
|---|---|---|
| 26 | 1 | 1 |

0    1    2
SURVEY COUNT

This might indicate that at least some of the birds seen in Berkshire originate from the introduced breeding population at the Cotswold Water Park. Since 2005 more records have been received from sites further west in the Kennet Valley, with records from the gravel pits between Theale and Newbury now regular.

There has been a marked increase in recent years, particularly since 1996. Birds began to remain all year in the early years of the 21st century, with birds present at Burghfield Gravel Pits all year in 2002 and 2003. Eventually breeding was proved at Wigmore Lane Gravel Pit, Theale in 2008 when three young were seen on 28th June. Another brood of five was noted at Bottom Lane Gravel Pit, Theale and nearby Sulhampstead in June 2011.

Notwithstanding the increase in the number of records, counts are generally low. There was an unprecedented party of four males and four females at Theale Gravel Pits in January 1994, a total not equalled until 2008 when another count of eight occurred also at Theale on 4th December, and finally exceeded when nine were at Queen Mother Reservoir on 30th December 2010.

*Sponsored by Brian Clews*

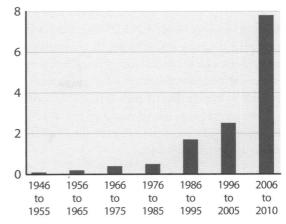

**Figure 18:  Red-crested Pochard: trend in peak annual count.** Average of the counts of the month in each year with the highest number of records.

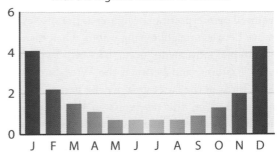

**Figure 19:  Red-crested Pochard: average of monthly counts.** Data from annual reports, 1996–2010.

# Pochard

Amber

## *Aythya ferina*

*Common winter visitor and passage migrant, rare summer visitor and breeding species.*

In Berkshire, the Pochard is a common wintering duck on flooded gravel pits, but no more than an occasional breeder in the county.

The 2007–11 Tetrad Survey shows three confirmed breeding records during the four years of fieldwork, one of which was just outside the county boundary, compared to just one confirmed record in the 1987–89 survey. In both surveys, possible and probable records almost certainly relate to late lingering wintering birds, or early returning autumn arrivals.

Although summering Pochard are recorded annually, usually as single birds or pairs, and small parties including juveniles are not infrequently recorded in July, confirmation of breeding within the county is sporadic. Figure 20 shows the pattern of breeding records since 1950. The exceptional total of 14 for east Berkshire in the 1960s includes two consecutive years when six pairs bred in Windsor Great Park, accounting for 12 of the 14 records. In the 20 years to 2009, breeding was confirmed at Great Meadow Pond, Old Slade Gravel

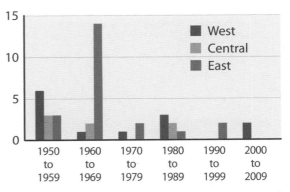

**Figure 20:  Pochard: distribution of breeding records per decade from 1950.**

143

Pit and Lower Farm and again at Lower Farm in 2010 and Great Meadow Pond in 2011. Given the availability of suitable habitat, it is surprising that breeding is not more widespread in Berkshire, although the species' requirement for dense cover near water indicates that it is vulnerable to human disturbance. If this is the case, then the heavy recreational use of many of the waterbodies in the county may limit the range of the Pochard as a breeding species in Berkshire.

The Winter Map indicates that Pochard occur throughout the river valleys with gravel pits in winter, with occasional birds on the Thames. Numbers peak in December and January (Figure 21). Figure 22 shows the peak counts at the principal wintering sites over the 10 years to 2009/10 compared with the 1980s. Some care is required in interpreting the figures as the species tends to move between neighbouring waters when disturbed. For example, movements occur between Twyford and Dinton Pastures, and between the Wraysbury waters. Indeed, birds in the latter area may be part of the larger group centred on the reservoirs in the Staines area, which had an average maximum winter count of 460 between 1960 and 1982 (Owen *et al.*, 1986). Wraysbury Gravel Pits produced the county's highest count of 900 on 19th February 1995, and 790 were counted there the previous month. Away from these sites, Virginia Water

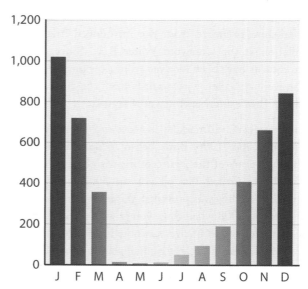

**Figure 21: Pochard: average monthly counts.**
Average of monthly maxima for 1998–2008 for all sites reported in Annual Reports.

formerly held the highest numbers in the late 1940s, with over 800 in November 1948 and 400 in December 1950. In the west of the county, Donnington Grove returned counts of 200 or more in the late 1970s and early 1980s, with a maximum of 270 in January 1980. Apart from the count at Virginia Water in 1948, there have been few records of over 500 birds: 650 at Theale

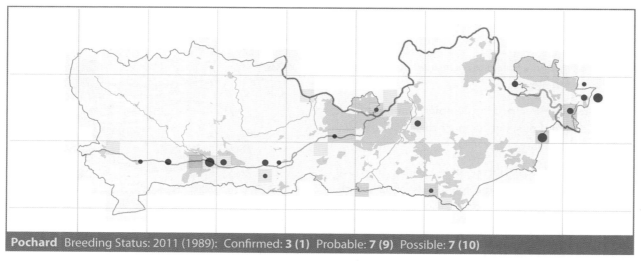

**Pochard**  Breeding Status: 2011 (1989):  Confirmed: **3 (1)**  Probable: **7 (9)**  Possible: **7 (10)**

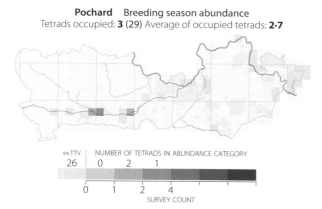

**Pochard**  Breeding season abundance
Tetrads occupied: **3 (29)** Average of occupied tetrads: **2·7**

| exTTV | NUMBER OF TETRADS IN ABUNDANCE CATEGORY | | |
|---|---|---|---|
| 26 | 0 | 2 | 1 |

0   1   2   4
SURVEY COUNT

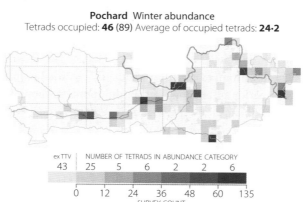

**Pochard**  Winter abundance
Tetrads occupied: **46 (89)** Average of occupied tetrads: **24·2**

| exTTV | NUMBER OF TETRADS IN ABUNDANCE CATEGORY | | | | | |
|---|---|---|---|---|---|---|
| 43 | 25 | 5 | 6 | 2 | 2 | 6 |

0   12   24   36   48   60   135
SURVEY COUNT

Gravel Pits in December 1970, 506 at Burghfield Gravel Pits in December 1986, 561 at Theale Gravel Pits in February 1987 and 510 at Wraysbury in December 2005.

Nationally wintering Pochard numbers have fallen by nearly half since 1998 (Holt *et al.*, 2011). In Berkshire the numbers recorded by the regular WeBS Counts (formerly Wildfowl Counts) carried out every winter have shown a mixed picture. Numbers at central Berkshire sites have fallen since the 1980s. Theale and Burghfield Gravel Pits produced 18 counts in excess of 350 between 1970 and 1990, just one between 1991 and 2010. However counts in east Berkshire have not shown this pattern. This may though reflect a change in the local distribution of the population on the west London reservoirs referred to above, rather than reflecting an increase in this population.

Evidence of the continental origin of some of the Pochard wintering in Berkshire was provided by the recovery of two birds ringed at the same site in Latvia. One was recovered at Maidenhead on 20th January 1975 and one was shot at West Woodhay on 5th December 1987.

Prior to 1900, the Pochard was a winter visitor only in "very limited numbers" (Noble, 1906), with most occurrences in severe winters, as in 1792 when many

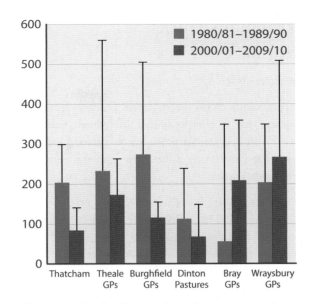

**Figure 22: Pochard: annual maximum counts.** Average of annual maxima at sites with an average maximum count of >100 in the 1980s and 2000s. Bars indicate the highest counts. Data from annual reports.

were shot near Reading (Lamb, 1880). Breeding first occurred in 1915 when nests of 12 and eight eggs were found at Great Meadow Pond on 9th May. Pochard subsequently bred regularly at this site and at Hay Mill Pond in the 1930s.

*Sponsored by Graeme Stewart*

# Ring-necked Duck

## *Aythya collaris*

*Rare vagrant, with nine county records*

The first Berkshire record of Ring-necked Duck, which was only the second for Great Britain, (the first being in Gloucester in 1955) was of a drake at Burghfield Gravel Pits from 19th to 27th April 1959. Since that time, there has been a significant increase in records nationwide, with 25% of all records arising since 2007. Berkshire appears to have had its fair share of these (although none since 2007) commencing with a drake at Theale and Burghfield Gravel Pits from 24th December 1977 to 9th April 1978. A female at Lower Farm Gravel Pit on 26th March 1999 was joined by another on 3rd April. They remained together until 10th April, after which one stayed until 26th April. There was a female or immature at Virginia Water on 17th January 2001, followed by a first winter female at Searles Farm Gravel Pit, Burghfield on 23rd November 2001 which stayed until 29th December. Possibly this same bird was seen at Burghfield Gravel Pits on 20th January 2002, a drake was then found at Pingewood Gravel Pits on 13th May, moving to Moatlands Gravel Pit, Theale where it remained until 13th June 2002. Presumably the same

individual was seen later in the year in eclipse plumage at Moatlands Gravel Pit on 12th September. A drake was present at Theale from 24th March to 1st April 2006 and females at Moor Green on 19th November 2006 and Dorney Wetlands and Slough Sewage Farm from 17th to 26th April 2007.

With no fewer than 48 records across UK in 2001 alone (Fraser & Rogers, 2006), and an increasing proportion of modern sightings being of first-year birds, more records of this species in Berkshire seem likely.

*Sponsored by Marek Walford*

# Ferruginous Duck

*Aythya nyroca*

*Rare winter visitor*

The true status of the Ferruginous Duck in Berkshire is unclear due to the possibility of hybrids occurring between this species and Pochard or Tufted Duck, the latter being notoriously difficult to separate from 'pure' Ferruginous Ducks.

The earliest county record is of a male at Bulmershe on 17th April 1938, followed by one again there in September that year. Tame birds were present in the area at the time, however. A drake was at Ham Island Sewage Farm on 14th and 15th October 1944 and an immature, which was considered to be an escapee was at Wraysbury Gravel Pits on 7th December the same year. Subsequently, singles were at Virginia Water from 29th December 1949 to 5th March 1950 and at Burghfield on 25th October and 30th November 1952, a pair was at Virginia Water on 7th October 1956, and single drakes were at Theale Gravel Pits on 7th February 1960 and at Marsh Benham on 29th October 1966.

There was a spate of ten records between 1970 and 1976, from Wraysbury/Horton and Theale Gravel Pits, Reading Sewage Farm and Purley. Other than a pair on the Thames at Purley in April 1976, which were tame and swam towards the observer who threw gravel into the river to simulate supplemental feeding, all subsequent sightings have been of single birds.

There were a further ten records from 1985 to 1988. Three in the autumn of 1985 were of single birds at Eversley, Thatcham and Theale/Burghfield Gravel Pits, the latter being joined by three further birds which were apparently hybrids. The bird at Eversley remained until 16th March 1986 and singles were seen at Dinton Pastures from 21st to 30th November 1987, Theale on 9th December 1987, and again at Dinton Pastures on 22nd and 23rd December 1987. There is, however, some doubt that the bird at Dinton Pastures in November 1987 was pure bred. In 1988, a female was at Dinton Pastures from 13th February to 11th March, and a male was at Theale Gravel Pits on 4th October.

A drake at Burghfield Gravel Pits that arrived on 29th December 1995 was the first apparently-wild bird since 1988, and was seen until 8th January 1996. The following winter, on 29th December 1996, a drake was found at Bray Gravel Pits; it stayed at least until the end of January 1997 after which it was believed to have relocated to the nearby Taplow Lake, Buckinghamshire, on 22nd February 1997.

A female was at Knight's Farm Gravel Pit, Burghfield from 28th December 1999 until 9th January 2000.

Nearby, an adult male found at Searles Farm Gravel Pit, Burghfield on 29th December 2000 stayed until February 2001, and then returned on 2nd December 2001 and, though proving elusive at times, stayed until 23rd February 2002.

A juvenile bird was found at Wraysbury Gravel Pits on 1st October 2002, but then moved to Staines Reservoir, Surrey. It was subsequently relocated at Harmondsworth Moor Country Park but had moved back into Berkshire at Old Slade by 1st November, where it remained until 23rd November.

A presumed "escaped" male, found on the Jubilee River on 12th December 2005, appeared intermittently in the Dorney Wetlands throughout 2008, 2009 and 2010, regularly coming for bread.

A five-year absence of genuinely-wild birds in the county was finally broken by the appearance of a female at Wigmore Lane Gravel Pit on 15th November 2007, also appearing at Sheffield Bottom Lake, and was last seen 5th January 2008. In 2009 a genuinely-wild drake was seen for just one day at Sandford Lake, Dinton Pastures on 2nd December. A first-winter female found at Horton Gravel Pits on 3rd January 2010 subsequently moved to Wraysbury Gravel Pits on 7th January but departed after another day or so.

In November 2011 a first-winter drake was found at Dinton Pastures, moving to Woolhampton Gravel Pit in January 2012 and then, before departing the county, stopping off at Bray Gravel Pits in February.

Of all these records, including tame birds, arrival dates have most frequently been in October and December. Since October is the peak month for autumn migration for the wild eastern European population of Ferruginous Duck (*BWP I*), it seems likely that at least some of the records relate to wild birds.

*Sponsored by Ian Tarr*

# Tufted Duck

Amber

*Aythya fuligula*

*Common winter and summer visitor, possibly resident*

The Tufted Duck is the most widespread and numerous diving duck in Berkshire. It breeds widely in suitable habitat, but numbers are swollen in winter by birds from north and east Europe.

In Berkshire, breeding was first confirmed in Berkshire in 1921 at Cranemoor Lake, and then between Hungerford and Newbury in 1928 and at Great Meadow Pond in 1934. By the time of the first tetrad atlas survey in 1987–89, the Tufted Duck was well-established across the county, breeding on gravel pits along the Kennet, Loddon and Thames valleys and other shallow water-bodies, and in some places on the River Thames. The recent tetrad survey shows a small decrease in the number of tetrads in which breeding was confirmed, suggesting perhaps a loss of suitable habitat as flooded gravel workings have been back-filled and with increasing recreational pressure on many water-bodies. This is in contrast to national trends from CBC and BBS data, which indicate that there has been a long term increase in the breeding population that has continued at about 10% per decade since the 1970s. However as the 1987–89 Tetrad Survey did not include

any timed counts, the apparent contraction in range may not mean that overall numbers have fallen. The counts of Tufted Duck in the breeding season surveys for the 2007–11 Atlas indicate a summer population of at least 600 adult birds in Berkshire.

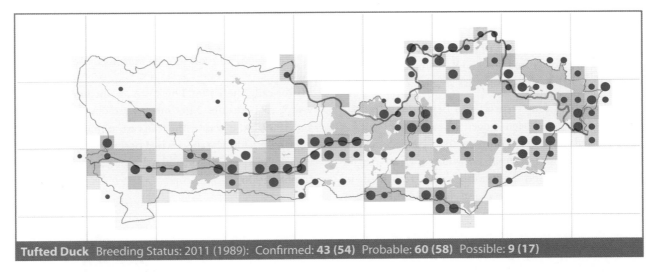

**Tufted Duck** Breeding Status: 2011 (1989): Confirmed: **43 (54)** Probable: **60 (58)** Possible: **9 (17)**

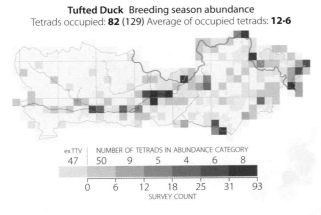

**Tufted Duck** Breeding season abundance
Tetrads occupied: **82 (129)** Average of occupied tetrads: **12·6**

| exTTV | NUMBER OF TETRADS IN ABUNDANCE CATEGORY | | | | | |
|---|---|---|---|---|---|---|
| 47 | 50 | 9 | 5 | 4 | 6 | 8 |

0   6   12   18   25   31   93
SURVEY COUNT

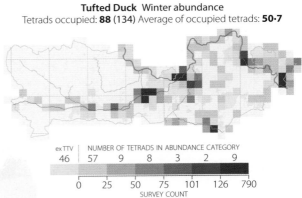

**Tufted Duck** Winter abundance
Tetrads occupied: **88 (134)** Average of occupied tetrads: **50·7**

| exTTV | NUMBER OF TETRADS IN ABUNDANCE CATEGORY | | | | | |
|---|---|---|---|---|---|---|
| 46 | 57 | 9 | 8 | 3 | 2 | 9 |

0   25   50   75   101   126   790
SURVEY COUNT

Information in the county reports seldom shows more than ten broods present at any one site. At Dinton Pastures breeding success is reportedly very low, possibly due to predation by Pike *Esox lucius* although on the Thames at Purley, where breeding was usually only detected when young appear, broods of at least three were noted every year between 1985 and 1988. In 1974, 68 young were recorded from 15 broods at Wraysbury Gravel Pits.

The breeding and winter distributions of the Tufted Duck are similar, and show some marked differences to those of the Great Crested Grebe (see *page 187*), another species whose expansion has been linked to the spread of flooded gravel workings in the county. The Tufted Duck is more widespread than the Great Crested Grebe, which is largely absent from the west of the county, where there is a predominance of small, shallow water-bodies.

In winter, Tufted Duck numbers peak in November to January (Figure 23). The largest numbers usually occur on the Wraysbury Gravel Pits complex, where the highest recorded count was 2,303 in February 2003 and counts frequently exceed 1,000. Elsewhere, the largest concentrations occur on the gravel pits in the Loddon and Kennet Valleys to the south-east and west of Reading respectively, and smaller numbers may occur on any water-body or river. In addition, movements to rivers and reservoirs occur during hard weather, when still water-bodies freeze. The tetrad survey winter counts totalled 3,666 birds, over 5% of the UK population.

Although varying from year to year, numbers at principal wintering sites for Tufted Duck in Berkshire have shown no significant trend in recent years (Figure 24).

There have been nine recoveries in Berkshire of Tufted Ducks which have been ringed elsewhere in Britain and involved movements of more than 100 kilometres. Birds ringed in the autumn or winter in East Anglia between March and September were recovered in Berkshire between October and January, three from Abberton Reservoir in Essex. There have been three overseas recoveries of birds ringed in the county. All were ringed at Sunninghill in February or March; two were shot in the Cherepovets region in Russia in April and September and one at Lake Vileiski in Belarus in August. A bird colour-marked at Sao Jacinto Dunes Nature Reserve, Aveiro, Portugal in November 2005 was seen a year later at Lower Farm Gravel Pit.

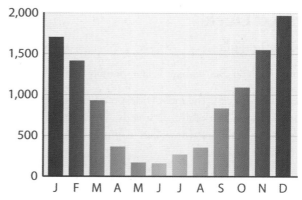

**Figure 23: Tufted Duck: average monthly counts.** Average of monthly maxima for 1998–2008 for all sites reported in Annual Reports.

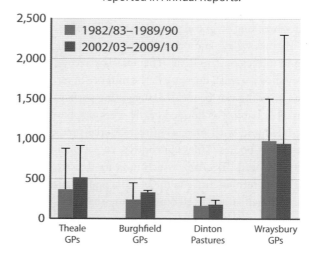

**Figure 24: Tufted Duck: winter counts at four main sites.** Columns show the average winter maxima and bars the highest count recorded for the eight year periods to 1989/90 and 2009/10. Data from annual reports.

Historically, the Tufted Duck was an uncommon winter visitor to Berkshire. Specimens were obtained in 1794 and 1809, but it was considered rare at that time (Lamb, 1880). By 1900, the species had become a regular winter visitor which was considered to be increasing in numbers (Noble, 1906).

*Sponsored by Berkshire Ornithological Club*

Tufted Duck, River Thames *Dickie Duckett*

# Scaup

Red | Sch. 1

*Aythya marila*

*Uncommon passage migrant and winter visitor*

The Scaup is an almost annual passage migrant and winter visitor to Berkshire and has been recorded every year since 1946 except 1951, 1955, 1961, 1962, 1967 and 1984.

The earliest known record is of one shot at Reading in January 1794 (Lamb, 1880), followed by a female shot at Wargrave in 1888 (Noble, 1906). A female was present at Virginia Water on 10th December 1932 and four were reported from there on 11th January 1935. In 1938, there was a drake at Slough Sewage Farm and one at Bulmershe which, although believed to be wild, was accompanying three Scaup which were apparently tame thus casting doubt on the record. From 1955, the number of records increased steadily. There were 13 from 1955 to 1964; 17 from 1965 to 1974; 28 from 1975 to 1984; 71 from 1985 to 1994; 58 from 1995 to 2004 and 54 from 2005 to 2011. A marked increase in the number of records in the late 1980s resulted in annual totals of 19 in 1988 and 14 in 1991. 1997, 1999, 2008 and 2010 also produced 10 or more records. Conversely, 1998, 2000, 2004 and 2006 produced only one or two records each.

Most records have been of one or two birds, with the highest count being nine at Horton Gravel Pits on 20th November 1988, at least four of which remained in the Horton/Wraysbury area into February 1989. Six birds were on the Thames at Boveney Lock during an influx of 11 birds into Berkshire in February 1991. In the winter of 1999–2000, another group of six gathered at Heron Lake, Wraysbury, with the earliest pair of these noted on 20th December and the last sighting of the flock on 20th March. A total of six birds was present in the same area from 25th November 2008, and remained into 2009, when a seventh bird joined them at Queen Mother Reservoir on 11th January.

The founders of the winter flock of 1999–2000 achieved a record stay of 91 days. An immature female, also at Wraysbury, stayed for 86 days, between 22nd January and 22nd April 1995. Most unusually, a summer female, found at Queen Mother Reservoir on 21st June 1999, was seen intermittently there and at Horton Gravel Pits until 12th September, a total of 75 days.

Figure 25 summarises the records of Scaup in Berkshire by month of arrival from 1946 to 2011, although the numbers given are approximate due to undetermined movement between sites. The spring and autumn migrations of Scaup occur over a relatively long period, in spring from February to May and in autumn from August to late October (*BWP I*). The autumn migration clearly accounts for many of the records of the species in Berkshire, whilst mid-winter records may reflect hard weather movements out of the Baltic and Dutch wintering areas, as in February 1991.

Well over 40% of records of Scaup in Berkshire are from the reservoirs, lakes and gravel pits in the east of the county, with Theale and Burghfield Gravel Pits providing a further 30%. Records have also come from Dinton Pastures, Eversley Gravel Pits, Bray Gravel Pits, Dorney Wetlands, Sandhurst and the River Thames. Records from the west of Theale were rare before 1990: a female at Donnington Grove in September 1964, a drake at the Blue Pool, Stanford Dingley in March 1985 and two females at Brimpton Gravel Pits on 22nd October 1990. Since then there have been ten further records from Woolhampton and Brimpton Gravel Pits, but only two from further west: an injured female,

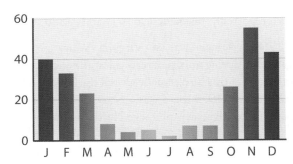

**Figure 25: Scaup: all birds recorded 1946–2012, by month of arrival.**

Scaup Winter abundance
Tetrads occupied: **2** (22) Average of occupied tetrads: **1·0**

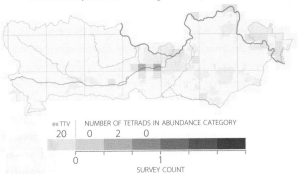

| exTTV | NUMBER OF TETRADS IN ABUNDANCE CATEGORY | | |
|---|---|---|---|
| 20 | 0 | 2 | 0 |

0                    1
SURVEY COUNT

considered to have been an escape, in the Lower Farm area of Newbury from 9th February to 15th April 2002, and a female there on 22nd March 2009.

Scaup are held in some wildfowl collections and escapes and hybrids occasionally occur.

*Sponsored by Brian Hayward.*

# Lesser Scaup

## *Aythya affinis*

*Rare vagrant – two records*

The first Berkshire record of this North American diving duck was an adult drake at Woolhampton between 27th October and 16th November 2007. The following year there was an adult drake at Wraysbury Gravel Pits on 5th October, then at Queen Mother Reservoir, Datchet from 8th to 15th October. Care needs to be taken with records of this species as hybrid *Aythya* ducks often resemble them, and confirmation of the first record was delayed by the presence of such a hybrid at Woolhampton at the same time.

*Sponsored by Ken Moore*

# Eider

Amber

## *Somateria mollissima*

*Rare vagrant, twelve records*

The Eider is a rare vagrant to Berkshire, with only twelve records, all but one of which has been since 1968. The first record was in the 19th century when a bird was shot near Sonning Mill, presumably on the River Thames, in a severe winter some time before 1814, which reportedly "tasted delicious" (Lamb, 1880).

In 1968, a female was at Virginia Water on 15th September during north-easterly gales, although it is not clear whether this bird actually visited the Berkshire end of the lake. In 1973 there was an exceptional record of a party of 26, all brown-plumaged birds, which flew low to the west over Silwood on 30th November. A female was at Wraysbury Gravel Pits from 6th December 1975 to 29th February 1976 and an immature male was at Theale Gravel Pits from 8th to 17th February 1976. Four, including an immature male, were seen at Queen Mother Reservoir on 8th November 1980 and a female was recorded at the same site from 4th November 1985. This bird was later seen at other waters in east Berkshire, where it remained until 17th June 1986 before crossing the county boundary to Wraysbury Reservoir where it was last reported on 23rd August 1986. There was a female at Theale Gravel Pits on 6th November 1993. In December 1995 five birds, including two immature males, were seen at Bray Gravel Pits. A drake arrived at Theale Main Pit on 26th December 1996 and stayed right through until 30th March 1997. An un-seasonal

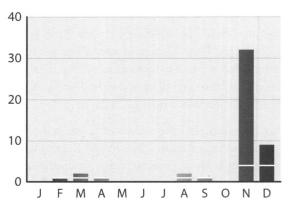

**Figure 26: Eider: all birds recorded 1968–2012, by month of arrival.** Bar – birds; white line – records.

150

female was at Lea Farm Gravel Pit on 22nd and 23rd April 2003. On 4th December 2010 a female and an immature male were present at Dorney Wetlands.

The small number of records of Eider in Berkshire is not particularly surprising as the species has an exclusively coastal distribution outside the breeding season, birds occurring inland mainly after rough weather (*1981–84 BTO Winter Atlas*).

*Sponsored by Bill Nicoll*

# Long-tailed Duck   Sch. 1

## *Clangula hyemalis*

*Rare winter visitor*

The Long-tailed Duck is a rare winter visitor to Berkshire, with just 19 confirmed records. Apart from a record of a "Harlequin Duck" shot on the River Thames near Maidenhead in the winter of 1866/67 (Clark Kennedy, 1868), which Noble (1906) felt was probably a Long-tailed Duck, all records have been since 1961 and reflect the considerable increase in the extent of open water in the county in recent years.

After an isolated record of a female at Hambridge Lake on 21st November 1961, there were no records until a small influx in the winter of 1979/80. A female at Theale Gravel Pits from 19th November 1979 was joined by a second on 22nd November and a third on 2nd December. The three birds were present until 15th December and one remained until 6th January 1980. Another female was in Windsor Great Park on 30th and 31st December 1979. These records formed part of a wider influx of Long-tailed Ducks into south-east England at this time.

The following winter there was a female at Thatcham Gravel Pits from 7th December 1980 to 31st January 1981, and then at Burghfield Gravel Pits from 4th to 14th February. In 1983, a female was at Dinton Pastures on 26th January. In the winter of 1985/86 there was a second small influx, with two first-winter females at Wraysbury Gravel Pits from 20th November 1985 to 22nd February 1986, one of which stayed until 6th May, and an adult male was on Queen Mother Reservoir from 23rd February to 2nd March 1986 and at waters nearby until 19th March. In 1992 there was a male at Wraysbury Gravel Pits from 13th to 15th February and, exceptionally, a female or first-summer bird at Eversley Gravel Pits from 21st to 28th July. 1996 provided two more records: an immature male at Theale Main Pit on 27th January, and an adult in winter plumage on 29th March at Queen Mother Reservoir. The winter of 1998/99 was another good one for this species. A female or juvenile was at Queen Mother Reservoir on 7th November 1998. A female arrived at Wigmore Lane Gravel Pit, Theale on 29th December and was seen there, and on two other Theale sites, until 26th January 1999. Meanwhile another female

ᴅ.A.Thelwell.

was seen at Sunnymeads Gravel Pit and at Wraysbury Village Pit on 1st January 1999, and reappeared at Heron Lakes on 17th January. A juvenile was again at Wraysbury Village Pit on 30th November 2008. Another juvenile bird, which was first recorded at Moatlands Pit on 11th November 2009, remained there until 20th December. A long staying bird was found at Queen Mother Reservoir on 26th November 2012 and remained until 26th March 2013, moving to Wraysbury Gravel Pits before leaving the county on 31st March.

Of the 19 birds recorded in Berkshire, seven have stayed for over four weeks and one for over five months. November is the peak month of arrival (Figure 27), with five of the eight November arrivals being between the 19th and the 21st. Peak numbers in Britain in winter do not usually occur until late December or early January and individuals or small groups only occasionally occur inland (*1981–84 BTO Winter Atlas*).

*Sponsored by Val Tarr*

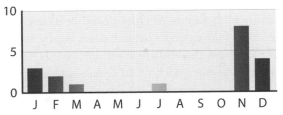

**Figure 27: Long-tailed Duck: all birds recorded winter 1961/62–2012/13, by month of arrival.**

# Common Scoter

**Red** | **Sch. 1**

*Melanitta nigra*

*Scarce passage migrant and rare winter visitor*

The Common Scoter is an uncommon but regular passage migrant and occasional short-staying winter visitor to Berkshire. Only sporadically recorded prior to the 1960s, it has been almost annual since and seen in increasing numbers towards the end of the 20th century (Figure 28). The increase in records is probably due to the increase in the area of open water in the county and to greater observer coverage. There are no reliable national trend data available: numbers recorded overwintering vary considerably, as most winter at sea and counts may reflect counting conditions rather than numbers present (Holt *et al.*, 2011).

The first 20th century record was not until one was seen on the Thames at Reading for about a week in August 1930. The first small party of Common Scoter for the county, which comprised three males and two females, was seen on Great Meadow Pond on 19th June 1935. A male was seen on the Kennet and Avon Canal at Burghfield on 30th January 1941, and subsequently birds were recorded in 29 of the 48 years from 1947 to 1994 and annually since 1982, with the exception of 1987 and 2001. Records have come from a variety of waters, but since 1971 most have come from Queen Mother Reservoir, with a substantial number from Theale Gravel Pits, and Woolhampton Gravel Pits, Eversley Gravel Pits and Dinton Pastures all featuring more than once.

Common Scoter have occurred most frequently in Berkshire either singly or in groups of up to three and, until 1993, the only higher counts were of five birds in June 1935, April 1971, April 1984 and September 1990, and six, on Queen Mother Reservoir, in January 1986. In 1993, however, a flock of 30 males was found at Theale Gravel Pits on 25th April where they remained together throughout the day in dull, calm weather conditions. A second large count occurred on 5th November 1994, when flocks of nine and five flew over Queen Mother Reservoir. The latter site subsequently attracted a flock of eleven on 21st August 2000. However, all of these counts were eclipsed by one exceptional sighting on 8th November 2004, when a flock of 90 female and immature birds flew in to Queen Mother Reservoir at noon. After four attempts to land, disturbed by aircraft from Heathrow, the birds flew off northwards half an hour later. Another flock of 15 female and immature birds was recorded at the same site on 18th November 2008. These groupings often reflect the fact that several duck species winter in single age or single sex flocks.

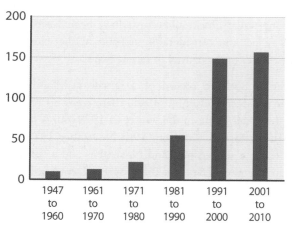

**Figure 28: Common Scoter: all birds recorded 1947–2010, by decade.** A flock of 90 over Queen Mother Reservoir in November 2004 is not included.

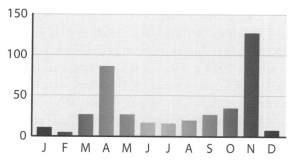

**Figure 29: Common Scoter: all birds recorded 1947–2010, by month of arrival.** A flock of 90 over Queen Mother Reservoir in November 2004 is not included.

Although Scoter may occur at any time of year, there are marked peaks in April, coinciding with the movement to their northern breeding grounds, and in November when birds are moving to the wintering grounds around the UK coasts (Figure 29). Relatively few of the Common Scoter recorded in Berkshire stayed for longer than one day. An immature female, which was at Theale Gravel Pits from 3rd February to 3rd March 2006, and a female at Woolhampton Gravel Pits from 5th to 21st March 2009, were quite exceptional. Other lingering birds were individuals at Theale Gravel Pits from 12th to 22nd April 1974; Queen Mother Reservoir from 7th to 17th October 1990; and again at Queen Mother Reservoir from 8th to 19th November 2011, and Padworth Lane Gravel Pit from 9th March to 10th April 2012. Of the records where the sex of the birds has been reported there have been about equal numbers of males and females. Not surprisingly, males and females have been frequently noted together during April passage, but are seen together much less frequently in all other months.

Historically, Lamb (1880) reports a pair shot on the Thames near Reading in October 1792; Palmer (1886) refers to a pair at Aldermaston in 1860; Clark Kennedy (1868) records that birds were shot at Datchet in the winter of 1862, at Cookham in the winter of 1865 (a male) and near Reading in July 1867; Herbert (1871) notes one shot at Newbury in March 1870; and Noble

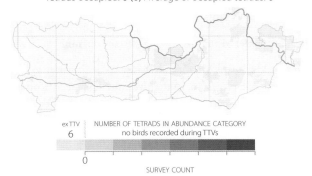

**Common Scoter** Winter abundance
Tetrads occupied: **0** (6) Average of occupied tetrads: **0**

ex TTV | NUMBER OF TETRADS IN ABUNDANCE CATEGORY
6 | no birds recorded during TTVs

0

SURVEY COUNT

(1906) refers to a male shot at Clewer Point, Windsor in March 1879. A decline in shooting resulted in a decline in records with no further published reports after 1879 until the August 1930 record.

*Sponsored by Ray Reedman*

# Velvet Scoter

Amber  Sch. 1

## *Melanitta fusca*

*Rare winter visitor*

The Velvet Scoter is a rare winter visitor to Berkshire, which has been recorded on 14 occasions involving at least 20 birds since 1900.

Apart from a report of two shot near Wargrave in January 1795 (Lamb, 1880), all other records of Velvet Scoter in Berkshire are confined to two periods: 1855 to 1876 and 1954 to 2011. The 19th century records involved six birds killed in one week in 1855 (Noble, 1906), and single drakes killed at Cookham in the severe winter of 1866/67 (Clark Kennedy, 1868), near Newbury on 2nd January 1871 (Herbert, 1871) and at Welford in 1876 (Palmer, 1886). The six in 1855, not 1885 as quoted by Summers-Smith (1951), appear from the wording used by Noble to have been killed near Newbury, but as the record comes from an account by Stubbs (1867) of birds in the Henley area this is the more likely location.

It was 78 years before the next record when two males were seen on the Thames at Ham on 10th February 1954, with one on 13th. Another gap of 21 years ensued followed by nine more 20th century records, one of which was from the River Kennet at Burghfield where a single bird was present from 19th December 1975 to 9th January 1976. The majority of records were from Queen Mother Reservoir: a male on 24th December 1981, a female or immature from 25th December 1981 to 24th January 1982, a first-summer male on 1st May 1984, two immatures from 16th to 27th January 1985 and a male and a female from 19th February to 2nd March the same year; two females on 22nd December 1994 and the first

ever October bird was a female or immature bird on 31st October 1999. Elsewhere there were three immature birds at Old Slade Nature Reserve (a site which was transferred to Berkshire in 1995) on 29th November 1994.

21st century records commenced with a report of 17 birds at Queen Mother Reservoir on 17th April 2002, some of which were accepted by the county records committee as being Velvet Scoters. This group is included in the county total of 20 mentioned above as one record. Queen Mother Reservoir was the site of the next record of a female on 15th and 16th January 2008 followed by a female or juvenile on 8th December 2008. The most recent report was of another at this site, an adult female, from 29th December 2010 to 21st January 2011.

In contrast to the Common Scoter, the Velvet Scoter is almost exclusively a winter visitor to Berkshire, once regarded as only expected between December and February, when over 50,000 over-winter in the North Sea. But in recent years, birds have been noted as early as October and as late as April. These records are likely to result from severe weather conditions, the four birds in early 1985 arriving as part of a larger influx into the London area during freezing conditions (Moon, 1985).

*Sponsored by Robin Dryden*

# Goldeneye

Amber

*Bucephala clangula*

*Regular winter visitor and spring passage migrant*

The Goldeneye is an annual visitor to deep water gravel pits and reservoirs in Berkshire and has been known to occur on rivers, usually during hard weather. The changes in the numbers recorded reflect the trend in Britain generally, with increases from the mid-1960s until the mid-1990s with marked annual fluctuations. Since that time numbers have been in general decline, although locally the decline does not seem as marked as that nationally, with numbers in the UK having returned to the levels of the 1960s. (Holt *et al.*, 2012).

There were few published records of Goldeneye in Berkshire in the 20th century until coverage of Windsor Great Park from 1925 produced a number of sightings, including a peak of 21 in January 1934. In Berkshire since 1946, there has been an increase in the wintering population as new gravel pits and reservoirs have been created. Up until about 1980, although Goldeneye were being quite widely reported, concentrations at particular sites rarely exceeded ten, with the sole exception of Wraysbury Gravel Pits where there was a peak count of 39 birds in March 1979.

In subsequent decades, numbers at favoured gravel pits and complexes have often exceeded 20 and occasionally reached 40 or more. The Wraysbury and Horton Gravel Pits complex has produced the highest counts, with an exceptional count in hard weather of 159 on 28th December 2012 and a second highest count of 90 in March 2004. Theale Gravel Pits have also provided notable counts. There were 61 there in January 1995, 53 at Hosehill Lake in December 1997 and 48 at Moatlands in December 1997. There were 43 at Dinton Pastures in January 2003, and Queen Mother Reservoir had a count of 35 in November 1995. Other locations such as Twyford and Burghfield gravel pits have held 20 or more birds from time to time, although counts of this order have been infrequent since the middle of the first decade of the 21st century. In the west of the county numbers rarely exceed ten, and from Brimpton Gravel Pits westwards counts of over five are unusual, a pattern confirmed by the 2007–11 Winter Tetrad Map.

Goldeneye usually first arrive in Berkshire in mid-October although occasionally birds occur much earlier. The earliest arrival date recorded was 27th July 1995 when an immature bird appeared at Queen Mother Reservoir and stayed for two days. The previous year, on August 12th 1994 an immature or female arrived at Moatlands Gravel Pit, Theale, these dates being consistent with experience at the West London reservoirs at that time. Numbers increase during the winter and

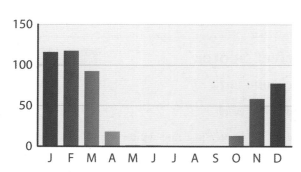

**Figure 30:  Goldeneye: average monthly counts.**
Average monthly maxima for all sites recorded in annual reports from 2001–2010.

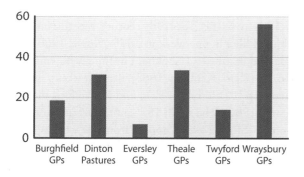

**Figure 31:  Goldeneye: peak counts at main sites.**
Average of the annual peak counts recorded in annual reports from 2000–2010.

**Goldeneye** Winter abundance
Tetrads occupied: **10** (35) Average of occupied tetrads: **6·9**

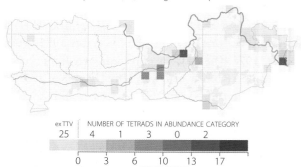

| exTTV | NUMBER OF TETRADS IN ABUNDANCE CATEGORY | | | | |
|---|---|---|---|---|---|
| 25 | 4 | 1 | 3 | 0 | 2 |

0   3   6   10   13   17
SURVEY COUNT

Goldeneye, Queen Mother Reservoir *Michael McKee*

the highest counts are often in February and March, possibly because numbers are swollen by returning passage birds. Most birds have departed by mid-April, although there are indications that departure dates were getting later when counts were higher, with records for 1st May 1993, 2nd May 1998, 7th May 1989, 13th May 2000 and 21st May in both 1984 and 1986. Although a female summered in the Theale/Burghfield area in 1983, this may have been an injured bird. Where observations indicate the number of males and females or immatures present, females or immatures invariably predominate.

Prior to 1900, the Goldeneye appears to have been a regular winter visitor to Berkshire, Lamb (1880) reporting that many were shot near Reading in the winter of 1791 and Clark Kennedy (1868) noting that "scarcely a winter elapses in which a few are not shot on the Thames". As is the case today, records then were fewer for the Kennet Valley, with just one at Thatcham Marsh in December 1808 (Lamb, 1880) and a pair near Newbury in January 1871 (Herbert, 1871).

*Sponsored by Natalie Newport*

# Smew

Amber

*Mergus albellus*

*Scarce, localised winter visitor*

Smew are annual but local winter visitors to Berkshire in small, but nationally significant, numbers, with Wraysbury Gravel Pits recording the highest average annual peak count nationally (18) as recorded by WeBS counts between 2006/07 and 2010/11 (Holt *et al.*, 2012).

From 1900 to 1945 there were scattered records of from one to five birds, mostly in January to March, with higher counts of six at Whiteknights Lake in 1924, up to eight at Virginia Water in 1931, and seven at Theale Gravel Pits in December 1938. Since the winter of 1946/47, Smew have been recorded annually in Berkshire, with the exception of the winters of 1949/50 and 1964/65, reflecting the steady increase in the number of open water sites. As arrivals can occur throughout the winter and because there can be frequent movements of birds between different waters, precise numbers are difficult to assess. Until the late 1970s, however, the totals appear

to have remained fairly constant, then rose substantially over the next two decades, though have fallen over recent winters (Figure 32).

From 1946/47 to the 1970s, there was an average wintering population of Smew in Berkshire of around 12, with extremes of none in 1949/50 and an exceptional count of about 37 in the severe winter of 1946/47. Virginia Water and the gravel pits at Theale, Burghfield

155

and Aldermaston were the most frequently used sites. The first record for Wraysbury Gravel Pits was in the winter of 1957/58. Subsequently, Wraysbury has had peak counts of at least 40 in 1965/66 (still the county maximum) and 36 in 1978/79. The count of 36 in the hard weather of early 1979 coincided with an influx into the country of about 400 Smew, four times the usual number at that time (*1981–84 BTO Winter Atlas*).

An increase in numbers and a trend towards earlier arrival occurred in the 1980s, the average number of birds increasing to 38 in the ten years 1996/97 to 2005/06, with a peak of 51 in 1997. The earliest arrival was of a red-head (female or juvenile) on 25th October 1997, at Moatlands Gravel Pit, Theale; the second-earliest record was five birds seen on 13th November 1999 at Twyford. Birds were more widely dispersed, with Wraysbury Gravel Pits attracting only around two-thirds of those recorded. In early 1985, birds were particularly widespread with records from as far west as Kintbury and a count of 11 males and three 'red-heads' (females or immatures) at Burghfield Gravel Pits and others at Theale, Twyford and Eversley.

Fewer Smew have arrived in Berkshire in recent years, with just one November arrival in 2008, and only six to 10 birds recorded in December in the years from 2006 to 2009. The highest January total for Berkshire in 2008 was only 13 birds, with just 16 birds in January 2009. This coincided with a national decline in numbers, attributed to the increasing availability of ice-free water in the Baltic Sea in winter, which encouraged increasing numbers of Smew and other ducks to winter to the north-east of their traditional ranges (Holt *et al.*, 2012). Harsh weather in the winters of 2009/10 and 2010/11 saw numbers rise again.

Despite fluctuating numbers, the Wraysbury Gravel Pits complex has remained the main site for wintering Smew, with Twyford Gravel Pits also hosting a smaller number every year. Bray and Theale Gravel Pits also regularly produce records, with occasional records from Dinton Pastures, Eversley Gravel Pits, and other sites in the centre and the west of the county. The use of the rivers by Smew, particularly the Thames, is now noted regularly: these sites can be important when other waters are frozen over, such as in 1987 when up to nine birds were reported from the Thames between Hurley and Maidenhead. In the harsh winter of 2010 there was a high proportion of records from the both the Thames and the Jubilee River.

Most birds leave by the middle of March but a few stragglers have remained into the last week of the month. There are few records of later departures: a red-head was noted at Great Meadow Pond on 14th April 1959; four birds lingered into April 1996 at Twyford, with the last leaving on 21st; and an exceptionally late male was at Moatlands Gravel Pit, Theale on 21st May

2010. There were records from three sites in the cold late spring of 2013.

Of the historical records of Smew in Berkshire prior to 1900, Lamb (1880) records a male shot near Newbury in January in about 1814 and Clark Kennedy (1868) describes the Smew, or "White Nun", as a rare visitor linked to severe weather with the majority of birds shot being immatures. He gives three examples of adult males being taken: near Boveney Lock in the winter of 1850/51, near Reading a few years before 1868 and, undated, near Monkey Island, Bray, the latter being sold for a sovereign by the wildfowler. Noble (1906) adds further records from Hennerton (undated), a party of four at Sonning and one near Kintbury, all apparently during the winter of 1890/91.

*Sponsored by Kathryn & Mike Horsepool*

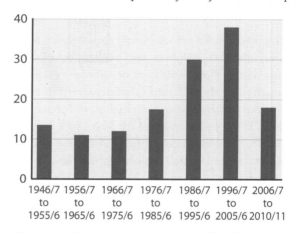

**Figure 32: Smew: average number of birds per year 1946/47–2010/11.**

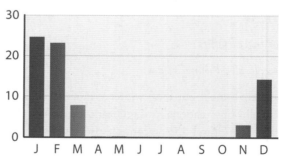

**Figure 33: Smew: by month of arrival.** Average of monthly counts of arrivals from 1978–2011.

**Smew** Winter abundance
Tetrads occupied: **2** (20) Average of occupied tetrads: **3·0**

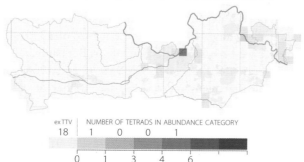

# Red-breasted Merganser

Green

*Mergus serrator*

*Scarce winter visitor*

The Red-breasted Merganser is a scarce winter visitor to Berkshire in very small numbers. In recent years the number of records has declined, although previously records had been almost annual.

An increase in observer coverage and a steady increase in the number of open water sites after the 1940s probably accounts for the increasing frequency of records of Red-breasted Mergansers in the county, with records in 32 of the 45 winters from 1949/50 to 1993/94 and records were annual from 1978/79 until 2005/06 apart from 1990/91. In spite of the greater coverage and the increase in suitable sites, however, there was no significant increase in the number of records between the 1960s and early 1990s (Figure 34). The above-average count for the subsequent decade was almost entirely due to unusually high counts in November 1994, and the first winter of 1996. Records fell away significantly in the first decade of the new century, with no January or February records after 2003 and no records at all in 2006, 2007 and 2008. This is consistent with national trends disclosed by WeBS surveys, which have recorded a fall in numbers since 1990. There has also been a general decline in the European population over 40 years (Holt *et al.*, 2012). There have however been records in each year from 2009 to 2013.

The occasional sightings in March, April and November, may involve passage migrants as the peak passage along the south coast occurs at these times in some years (Clark & Eyre, 1993). The only September record, a juvenile at Theale Gravel Pits from 19th to 25th in 1993, is exceptionally early for an inland record in southern England, the next earliest being an exceptional count of 14 on Queen Mother Reservoir on 5th November 1994, also the highest count for the species in the county. The latest departure was a female or immature at Lower Farm Gravel Pit on 28th April 2001, nine days later than the next latest records, three individuals in 1967, 1968 and 2005. The isolated June record, a female at Wraysbury Gravel Pits on the 15th in 1974, is exceptional for an inland site, although one or two are recorded most years on the Hampshire coast in June, July or August (Clark & Eyre, 1993).

Otherwise, Red-breasted Mergansers are winter visitors to Berkshire, invariably during periods of severe weather; with the bulk of the records involving from one to five birds, mostly females or immatures. Larger parties have occurred on a few occasions with the 14 in 1994 referred to above, ten, including five drakes, at Virginia Water in December 1968, six, including two drakes, at Queen Mother Reservoir in January 1987 and seven, including

five drakes, at Eversley Gravel Pits in December 1991. There was also an exceptional influx in February 1979 apparently involving 22 different birds, the largest party being 11, including three drakes, at Wraysbury Gravel Pits. These birds were part of a national influx involving at least 420 birds (*1981–84 BTO Winter Atlas*).

Nearly all records relate to birds which remain for just one to three days. Records of longer stays include a 'red-head' (female or immature) at Theale Gravel Pits from 14th February to 21st March 1976, up to two males and two females at Dinton Pastures from 17th February to 4th March 1979, between one and four birds at Queen Mother Reservoir on many dates from 11th January to 13th February 1987. In the 1990s a number of long staying birds were noted: Brimpton hosted one bird from 22nd February to 23rd March 1996, and a female at Theale between 17th November and 26th December the same year was followed by long stays by individual red-heads (possibly the same bird) at that site in the winters of 1998/99 and 1999/2000.

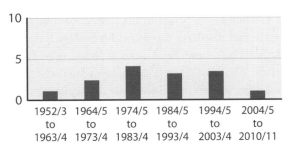

**Figure 34: Red-breasted Merganser: average number of birds recorded per year 1952/53–2010/11.**

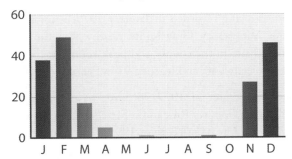

**Figure 35: Red-breasted Merganser: all birds recorded 1952/53–2010/11, by month of arrival.**

Historically, the Red-breasted Merganser appears always to have been a scarce winter visitor to Berkshire, particularly associated with severe weather. Lamb (1880) records a male and a female shot near Reading in 1795 and Clark Kennedy (1868) observed that birds were occasionally shot on the Thames in winter, citing as examples a female at Wraysbury in 1854 and one near Cookham a few years before 1868. His record of a pair killed near Reading in 1785 is almost certainly a misquotation of Lamb's record of 1795. Noble (1906) adds records of a female shot on the Thames near Henley in January 1848, one at Culham Court in 1879 and, away from the Thames, a male and two females shot at Bulmershe in 1883. There was then a gap in published records, no doubt reflecting the decline in duck-shooting on the Thames, until a report of one shot at Reading Sewage Farm "a few years before 1932" (Wallis and Wood, 1933).

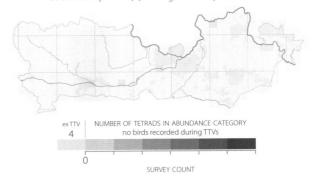

**Red-breasted Merganser** Winter abundance
Tetrads occupied: **0 (4)** Average of occupied tetrads: **0**

ex TTV 4 | NUMBER OF TETRADS IN ABUNDANCE CATEGORY
no birds recorded during TTVs

0

SURVEY COUNT

*Sponsored by Andrew Taylor*

# Goosander

Green

## *Mergus merganser*

*Uncommon winter visitor that has summered in recent years*

The Goosander is a regular winter visitor to Berkshire, that usually occurs on gravel pits and reservoirs, especially in the east and south of the county. Since 1929, Goosander have been recorded annually apart from four winters during the 1940s and in 1964/65 and 1974/75. They typically occur in numbers varying from about 20 to 60 each winter, with larger numbers during severe winters.

The existence of winter concentrations of Goosander on waters in adjacent counties seems to have had an important influence on the species' distribution within Berkshire. As long ago as 1929, county reports noted that Goosander "now occur annually, no doubt arising from the fact that large numbers visit Staines Reservoir" and that birds have been "seen to leave over Egham towards Windsor Great Park". Throughout the 1930s there were parties of Goosander on either Virginia Water or Great Meadow Pond, with as many as 30 at the latter site in March 1934. The building of the Queen Mother Reservoir resulted in an increase in county records. It also provides an alternative to the Thames to which birds can move when shallower waters freeze over, 65 being recorded in January 1979. Prior to the 1990s Wraysbury Gravel Pits nearby was the most favoured site in the county and peak counts at this site often exceeded 40, and reached 91 in February 1987.

Since the winter of 1977/78, birds have wintered at Wellington Country Park and at Stratfield Saye in north-east Hampshire (Clark & Eyre, 1993). This resulted in an increase in the frequency of records from Eversley Gravel Pits where, after the winter of 1988/89, Goosander roosted in increasing numbers. By the mid-1990s this

D.A. Thelwell.

had become the site with the largest numbers, with high counts of 134 in February 1996 and 184 in January 1997. Occasional individuals, or small groups, occur every winter on gravel pits throughout the county or on the Thames, even in the absence of hard weather. The Theale gravel pit complex provides regular sightings with occasional winter counts of ten or more, and a highest count of 102 in January 1987. Smaller numbers occur in west Berkshire, where the highest number of Goosander seen was 15 over Brimpton Gravel Pits in December 1988.

The mobility of birds during the winter makes it difficult to establish either the length of time birds spend in the county or the size of the wintering population. Severe weather is a major factor influencing the number of Goosander wintering in Berkshire, when it is thought that the regular wintering population in south east England, originating from the British breeding population, is augmented by birds from the continent (Holt *et al.*, 2012). The most extreme example of this was during the bitter weather of early 1963, when even

**Goosander** Breeding season abundance
Tetrads occupied: **1** (6) Average of occupied tetrads: **2·0**

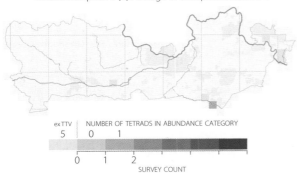

| ex TTV | NUMBER OF TETRADS IN ABUNDANCE CATEGORY | |
| --- | --- | --- |
| 5 | 0 | 1 |

0   1   2
SURVEY COUNT

**Goosander** Winter abundance
Tetrads occupied: **10** (58) Average of occupied tetrads: **5·1**

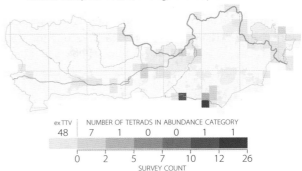

| ex TTV | NUMBER OF TETRADS IN ABUNDANCE CATEGORY | | | | | |
| --- | --- | --- | --- | --- | --- | --- |
| 48 | 7 | 1 | 0 | 0 | 1 | 1 |

0   2   5   7   10   12   26
SURVEY COUNT

stretches of the River Thames froze. Prior to 1963, the highest count had been of 30 birds but in February of that year an estimated 100–150 Goosander took refuge on an unfrozen section of the Thames at Cliveden Reach. In contrast, the highest count during the following winter was six.

Figure 36 shows the maximum Berkshire-wide count in each winter from 1946/47 to 2010/11. This follows the trend of the wintering population in Britain, comprising British breeders and continental visitors, which rose steeply from the late 1960s to the mid-1990s, but has since fallen back to 1980s levels (Holt *et al.*, 2012). In the harsh winters of 1995/96 and 1996/97 numbers were exceptionally high in the county, with totals of 148 and 277 birds respectively. The first decade of the new millennium saw more modest counts, though numbers once again exceeded 100 in the colder winter of 2010/11.

As the wintering population increased in the 1980s and 1990s the winter arrival dates became earlier and departure dates later. Until the 1990s the first Goosander to arrive in Berkshire were usually seen in early November. Larger parties did not normally occur until December, with the highest counts usually being in January and February before numbers fell away again during March. Prior to the winter of 1985/86, October arrivals were exceptional, with records only in 1956 and 1967, both on the 31st, and on the 24th in 1957. In contrast, there were October arrivals in five of the six winters from 1988/89 to 1993/94, the earliest being on the 21st in 1989, but only four between 1994 and 2011. There were, though, records of three at Cookham on 9th August 2007, a September record at Wraysbury in 1996

and two at Hosehill Lake, Theale on 16th September 2007. There was also an exceptional early count of ten at Wraysbury on 3rd October 2010.

There had been only about seven April departure dates up to 1985, the latest being on 23rd in 1938, but in eight of the nine winters from 1985/86 to 1993/94 and 11 of the years between 1994 and 2010 Goosanders remained into April. In 1988 a male was seen over Wraysbury Gravel Pits on 14th May, and a female was present there during the summer of 1993, and a male throughout the summer of 1994. A female or immature was at Queen Mother Reservoir on 3rd May 2003, and another flew over Brimpton on 13th May 2006. There was also a female at Eversley on 20th June 1996, and another which stayed at Wraysbury into June 1998.

On most occasions the number of 'red-heads' (females and immatures) exceeds the number of adult males, with some parties composed almost entirely of the former, as in January 1989 when there were only nine adult drakes in a flock of 76 at Bray Gravel Pits.

Although records of Goosander in Berkshire were sparse before 1929, it is likely that a few occurred most winters even if published records are lacking. The earliest record is of "many shot near Reading in winter 1791" (Lamb, 1880) which clearly relates to an influx during hard weather. Unfortunately, 19th century records reveal only the level of fatalities and not the number of birds likely to have been present. Clark Kennedy (1868) notes that "scarcely a winter elapses in which a few are not shot on the Thames" and cites six specific instances from 1847 to 1867 of birds being obtained along the Thames between Cookham

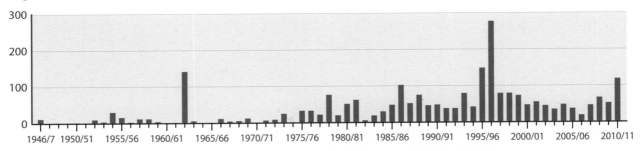

**Figure 36: Goosander: annual maximum counts 1946/47–2010/11.**

and Wraysbury. Noble (1906) noted that there had been several records of birds which had been captured, usually immatures, and describes the Goosander as an occasional visitor to the Thames. The only early record for west Berkshire comes from Herbert (1871), who reports that three immatures were killed near Newbury in 1871, two in January and one in February.

*Sponsored by Moor Green Lakes Group*

# Ruddy Duck

## *Oxyura jamaicensis*

*Introduced scarce winter visitor and rare breeder, now being eradicated.*

The Ruddy Duck is an introduced species which increased in numbers and started to breed in Berkshire before a controversial eradication campaign commenced in 2003. In its native North America, the species is successful and widespread. However its closely related European counterpart, White-headed Duck *Oxyura leucocephala* is a threatened species with a fragmented range. As feral birds spread from Britain to Spain where the nearest White-headed Duck population is found, the two species began interbreeding giving rise to concerns that the vigorous introduced species might threaten one of Europe's most vulnerable species. As a result it was decided to eradicate Britain's growing feral population.

After an early record of one at Theale Gravel Pits in December 1957, there were occasional records from

1969 until a drake summered at Windsor Great Park in 1976. Most records in the late 1970s and early 1980s were in the winter. Between 1976 and 1984 there were 25 records in December, 34 in January, 24 in February and 28 in March. Most records were from gravel pits, especially in the east and centre of the county, or from the lakes in Windsor Great Park. Nationally the species underwent a population explosion in the mid- and late–1970s, resulting in a ten-fold increase in peak winter

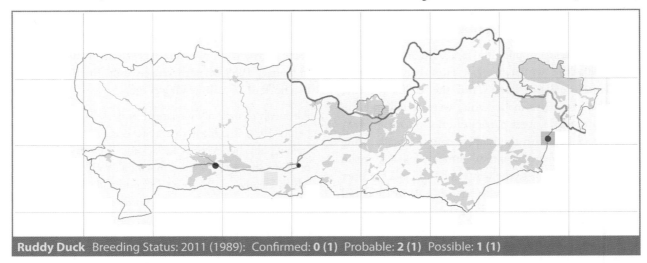

**Ruddy Duck** Breeding Status: 2011 (1989): Confirmed: **0 (1)** Probable: **2 (1)** Possible: **1 (1)**

**Ruddy Duck** Breeding season abundance
Tetrads occupied: **1 (5)** Average of occupied tetrads: **1·0**

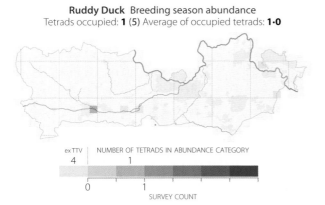

| exTTV | NUMBER OF TETRADS IN ABUNDANCE CATEGORY |
|---|---|
| 4 | 1 |

0       1
SURVEY COUNT

**Ruddy Duck** Winter abundance
Tetrads occupied: **3 (22)** Average of occupied tetrads: **3·3**

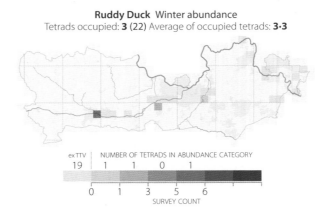

| exTTV | NUMBER OF TETRADS IN ABUNDANCE CATEGORY |
|---|---|
| 19 | 1 1 0 1 |

0  1  3  5  6
SURVEY COUNT

counts between 1974/75 and 1984/85 as recorded by the WWT winter wildfowl counts (Cranswick *et al.*, 1995).

After a number of summer records in Berkshire between 1976 and 1984, nine in June and 11 in both July and August, breeding was confirmed in Windsor Great Park in 1985 and 1986. During the 1987–89 Tetrad Survey there was a further record of confirmed breeding, at Great Meadow Pond in 1987. Although often recorded there in summer, confirmation of breeding was only infrequently obtained. A second breeding population was established in the Kennet valley east of Newbury, with breeding confirmed at Woolhampton in 1998 and Lower Farm Gravel Pit from 2001.

Winter counts also increased, with a highest ever count of 53 at Old Slade Gravel Pit in the eastern-most part of the county on 9th January 1997. There then followed something of a decline in highest annual counts until 40 were counted at Wraysbury Gravel Pits in 2004 and 2005. In 2006 and 2007 there were no counts in excess of 11, and since then most records are only of one or two, presumably reflecting the success of the control campaign. Breeding was last confirmed in Windsor Great Park in 2007. It now seems likely that this briefly successful alien will soon be lost to Berkshire.

*Sponsored by Sally Wearing*

# Black Grouse

*Tetrao tetrix*

*Introduced and extirpated in the 19th century*

The Black Grouse was introduced into Berkshire during the 19th century, after which breeding took place until the 1880s. The species appears never to have been indigenous to the county and has never been recorded with any certainty as a vagrant.

Two releases have been documented by Clark Kennedy (1868). The first in 1815 involved birds turned out between Dorking and Guildford which subsequently strayed as far as Finchampstead. The second occasion was in the mid-1860s when several were released "in the royal preserves at Windsor" from where they moved to Ascot Heath and other locally suitable areas. It appears from an account in *The Field* for 5th October 1867 that they bred freely in Berkshire that summer, a number being killed. The last of these birds to be seen within the county boundary were a cock and a hen at Easthampstead in the spring of 1884 (Noble, 1906).

A male seen in a young plantation at Wickham in west Berkshire on 4th November 1981 was presumably an escapee, there being no other sightings which would support the possibility of further releases having been made.

*Sponsored by Renton Righelato*

# Chukar

*Alectoris chukar*

*Introduced species, possibly extinct*

The Chukar does not form part of the official British List, as its introduced population has probably never been self-sustaining. Indeed, the free-flying population of Chukar has been largely supported by frequent releases of captive-bred birds, but this practice was banned in 1992. However, it is included here because it was recorded breeding in several locations during the tetrad survey for the First Edition of this book and, because of identification problems, the presence of Chukar may have obscured the status of the Red-legged Partridge in the county.

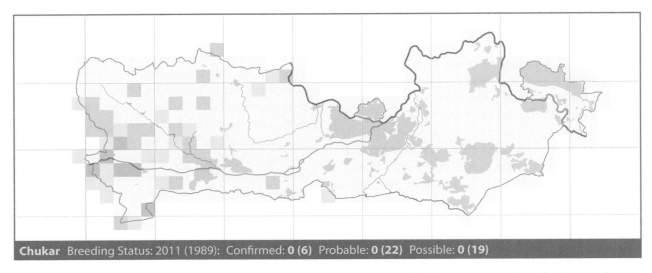

**Chukar** Breeding Status: 2011 (1989): Confirmed: **0 (6)** Probable: **0 (22)** Possible: **0 (19)**

It is probable that Tetrad Survey fieldworkers were not always able to differentiate between the Red-legged Partridge and Chukar, a problem compounded by frequent hybridisation between the two species. Indeed many hybrids were reared for release until this was banned as a result of the withdrawal of a general licence under the Wildlife and Countryside Act 1981. The presence of Chukar was first noted by the NDOC in the far south-west corner of the county in 1982. Breeding was confirmed in six tetrads in this area during the 1987–89 Tetrad Survey and birds probably bred in 22 others. Records in the county report include a September count of 29 at Streatley in 1988. These populations, whether pure Chukar or hybrid, were clearly sustained by releases of captive-bred birds and since no such releases apparently took place to the east of Reading, and the Chukar is a sedentary species, it has not been recorded from that part of the county.

In December 1992, the release of captive bred Chukars and Chukar × Red-legged Partridge hybrids into the wild was prohibited in order to maintain the viability of the national Red-legged Partridge population. Thereafter the number of records of Chukar declined. In 1994 Chukars were only reported from two locations, but the following year birds with Chukar characteristics were still reported from five localities (County Reports). Four were at Combe Hill on 16 May 1998, and the latest record was of four Red-legged Partridge × Chukar at West Woodhay on 11 November 2001.

*Sponsored by Renton Righelato*

# Red-legged Partridge

*Alectoris rufa*

*Widespread resident*

The Red-legged Partridge was introduced to this country in the 18th century and was rare in Berkshire before 1814, one shot in 1810 being considered to be an escapee (Lamb, 1880). However, by the end of the 19th century it appears to have been thinly, but probably widely, distributed (Noble, 1906). According to Palmer (1886) it was the practice of keepers to destroy all the eggs of this species in order to protect the Grey Partridge. The Red-legged Partridge is now a widespread resident of Berkshire, where it is commonest on agricultural land and chalk downland. It also occurs in river valleys, at both active and worked-out gravel pits and occasionally in woods with large glades or wide rides.

Populations of Red-legged Partridge nationally have fluctuated considerably since it was introduced from mainland Europe. The long-term UK trend since 1970 from the CBC and BBS indicates a gentle population decline of 14% between 1970 and 2009, but the more recent trend shows a significant increase of 27% from 1995 to 2009. The Berkshire Bird Index also showed a

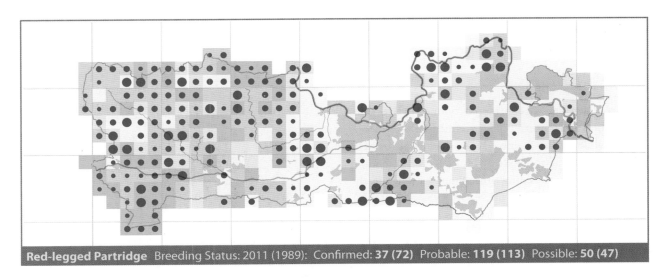

**Red-legged Partridge** Breeding Status: 2011 (1989): Confirmed: **37 (72)** Probable: **119 (113)** Possible: **50 (47)**

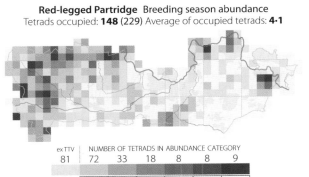

**Red-legged Partridge** Breeding season abundance
Tetrads occupied: **148 (229)** Average of occupied tetrads: **4·1**

| exTTV | NUMBER OF TETRADS IN ABUNDANCE CATEGORY | | | | | |
|---|---|---|---|---|---|---|
| 81 | 72 | 33 | 18 | 8 | 8 | 9 |

| 0 | 2 | 4 | 6 | 8 | 10 | 28 |
SURVEY COUNT

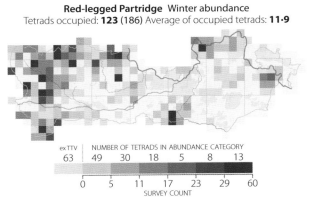

**Red-legged Partridge** Winter abundance
Tetrads occupied: **123 (186)** Average of occupied tetrads: **11·9**

| exTTV | NUMBER OF TETRADS IN ABUNDANCE CATEGORY | | | | | |
|---|---|---|---|---|---|---|
| 63 | 49 | 30 | 18 | 5 | 8 | 13 |

| 0 | 5 | 11 | 17 | 23 | 29 | 60 |
SURVEY COUNT

statistically significant increase in abundance from 2000 to 2008. However, the Breeding Distribution Map from the 2007–11 Atlas Survey indicates some reduction in range, in Berkshire, with 12% fewer tetrads occupied during the breeding season compared to the 1987–89 Tetrad map. Comparison of the maps for the two surveys shows a broadly similar distribution, with the stronghold being in the west of the county and some shrinkage of range in the east since the 1987–89 Atlas Survey. In central and east Berkshire greater urbanisation has reduced the amount of suitable breeding habitat, though the species does breed on the edges of some urban areas. However, it is absent from the conifer woodlands of south-east Berkshire. The Red-legged Partridge is no less sedentary than the Grey, so the autumn and winter distribution is very similar to that of the summer.

The Red-legged Partridge is largely vegetarian and less dependent upon insect food than its native counterpart, the Grey Partridge, and this in part will explain why the former has coped much better with the impact of agricultural intensification and the loss of insect food

from farmland. The Red-legged Partridge population is regularly augmented by birds reared and released for shooting, with 6·5 million birds released annually in the UK in recent years (PACEC, 2006). The release of birds for shooting is evident from high autumn counts such as 750 in the Aldworth/Compton area of the Downs in September 2003, 56 in Windsor Great Park in September 2006 and 81 at Remenham in September 2010. Their supposed preference for drier situations is clearly met at several gravel pits in central Berkshire, successful breeding being reported from Theale, Pingewood, Brimpton and Lower Farm.

The future status of the Red-legged Partridge in Berkshire will depend on a variety of factors. Climate change and agri-environmental measures such as unsprayed grassy margins, overwintered stubbles etc. could prove beneficial, whereas further residential and industrial development could prove detrimental. The popularity of the species as a game-bird is apparently variable, so the future impact of shooting pressures and the release of captive-bred birds are unpredictable.

*Sponsored by Blackwater Valley Countryside Trust*

# Grey Partridge

*Perdix perdix*

*Localised, declining resident*

The Grey Partridge was considered common in Berkshire during the 19th century (Clark Kennedy, 1868, Noble, 1906), while earlier Lamb (1880) had considered it abundant in the period up to 1814. However, in modern times it has been declining throughout its range in the western Palearctic since the early 1950s (*BWP II*), and the UK breeding population has declined by 91% between 1970 and 2009.

The Grey Partridge has, not surprisingly, also been in decline in Berkshire. The Breeding Distribution Map from the 2007–11 Atlas Survey shows a total of 86 tetrads with evidence of breeding, compared to 251 tetrads in the 1987–89 survey, representing a 66% reduction in range across the county. Furthermore, in the 2007–11 Atlas Survey breeding was confirmed in only around 20% as many tetrads as in the 1987–89 survey. Comparison of the distribution maps for the two surveys shows that since the 1987–89 Atlas Survey, the Grey Partridge has disappeared from the very eastern part of Berkshire and also from much of southern and central areas of west Berkshire. Its range is now becoming increasingly confined to the downland areas of north-west Berkshire, with small pockets remaining elsewhere, particularly around Englefield in central Berks and Jealott's Hill in east Berkshire.

The Grey Partridge is one of the most studied farmland birds in the UK and there is convincing evidence that the main cause of decline is reduced chick survival as a result of decreased food availability caused by agricultural intensification (Southwood & Cross, 1969; Potts, 1980; Aebischer & Potts, 1998).

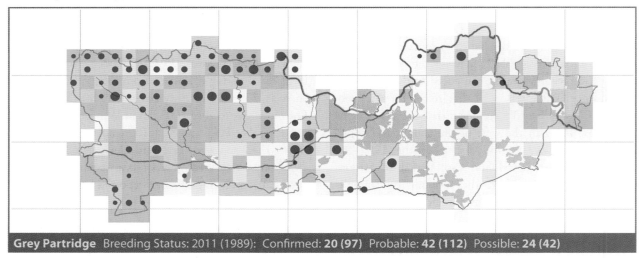

Grey Partridge Breeding Status: 2011 (1989): Confirmed: **20 (97)** Probable: **42 (112)** Possible: **24 (42)**

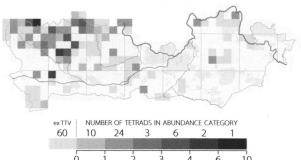

**Grey Partridge** Breeding season abundance
Tetrads occupied: **46 (106)** Average of occupied tetrads: **2·4**

| exTTV | NUMBER OF TETRADS IN ABUNDANCE CATEGORY | | | | | |
|---|---|---|---|---|---|---|
| 60 | 10 | 24 | 3 | 6 | 2 | 1 |

0   1   2   3   4   6   10
SURVEY COUNT

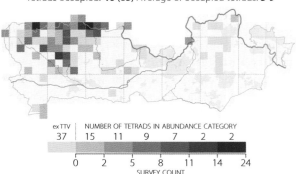

**Grey Partridge** Winter abundance
Tetrads occupied: **46 (83)** Average of occupied tetrads: **5·9**

| exTTV | NUMBER OF TETRADS IN ABUNDANCE CATEGORY | | | | | |
|---|---|---|---|---|---|---|
| 37 | 15 | 11 | 9 | 7 | 2 | 2 |

0   2   5   8   11   14   24
SURVEY COUNT

Grey Partridge, Sheepdrove Farm *Jerry O'Brien*

As it is difficult for observers to undertake fieldwork in cereal fields in spring and summer, some breeding birds may have been overlooked during the Atlas Survey. Since the Grey Partridge is one of our most sedentary species (*1981–84 BTO Winter Atlas*), its presence in autumn and winter is likely to imply that it bred in the locality, hence the winter map closely reflects the summer distribution shown by the breeding maps.

The population size of Grey Partridge seems to vary considerably between years, possibly connected to releases of birds reared for game shooting. For example, 1976 was considered a good year for the species in Berkshire, with more autumn coveys than usual being recorded. Examples of sizeable coveys on the Downs include 19 at Chaddleworth in January 1983 and 40 on the Compton Downs in January 1991. More recent high counts include 38 at Snelsmore in September 2000 and 44 at Bury Down in December 2007. The highest counts away from the Downs used to regularly exceed 20, for example 21 at Brimpton Gravel Pits in October 1984 and 26 at Cookham in December 1994. However, now even double-figure counts outside the Downs strongholds, such as the 20 seen at Tilehurst in December 2009, are becoming rare.

The increased emphasis on agri-environment schemes in UK farming holds out some hope for Grey Partridge populations in Berkshire, as options such as unsprayed margins, wildbird seed plantings and overwintered stubbles, where taken up by farmers, can enhance feeding opportunities and potential nesting places for this species. Future population trends for this species in Berkshire will depend upon whether these schemes can turn around the fortunes of this and other farmland birds, as well as other factors such as changing climate and, especially in the west of the county, the balance between the pressure of shooting and artificial replenishment of wild stock.

*Sponsored by John Lloyd-Parry*

# Quail

Amber · Sch. 1

*Coturnix coturnix*

*Uncommon summer visitor, regular only on downland*

The Quail is a scarce but annual summer visitor to Berkshire, now reported regularly only from its traditional downland habitat. The former abundance of Quail in central southern England is attested by White (1768): "Quails crowd to our southern coast, and are often killed in numbers by people that go on purpose." Lamb (1880) stated that it had been plentiful in Berkshire up to about 1780–90, but that by 1814 it was rare. However, Clark Kennedy (1868) reported that a few were shot every year

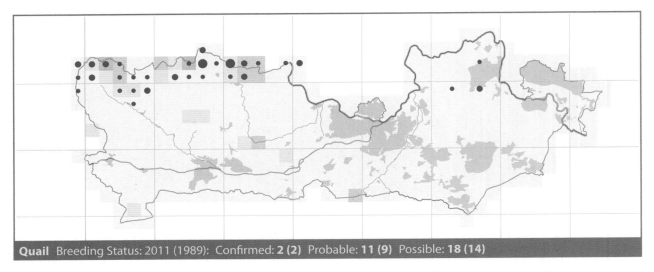

**Quail** Breeding Status: 2011 (1989): Confirmed: **2 (2)** Probable: **11 (9)** Possible: **18 (14)**

and, in mentioning birds shot at Warfield in both 1861 and 1862, indicates that the species was more widely distributed then than it is today. This is reinforced by Noble (1906) who records a nest with 11 eggs found at Remenham in June 1868, and Palmer (1886) who mentions breeding at Boxford in 1875.

Most reports of Quail are of calling males, but such records do not constitute proof of breeding as unmated birds may wander considerable distances. The county boundary changes of 1974 took most of the areas in Berkshire where Quail were known to breed into neighbouring Oxfordshire. Since that date, the number of reports of confirmed breeding Quail in Berkshire has not exceeded five in any one year, although the number of calling birds may be more than double that figure. In good years, termed 'Quail years', new areas may become colonised temporarily, but often for one season only. Such Quail years occurred in 1953, 1964, 1970, 1989, 1994, 1997, 2005 and 2011. Numbers of calling males reached 21 on the Berkshire Downs in 1997 and were as high as 38 in 2011. Confirming breeding by Quail usually involves observing young, very difficult for such a skulking species which spends its time under cover in crops or grassland, so breeding is rather rarely confirmed. However, with the vast acreage of suitable habitat on the Downs of north-west Berkshire, it is very probable that breeding occurs in most years but remains unproven.

The Breeding Distribution Map from the 2007–11 Atlas survey shows a lot of similarities to the 1987–89 Tetrad map, with the majority of records, as expected, from the Downs of north-west Berkshire. Breeding was confirmed from two tetrads on the Downs, as in the 1987–89 Atlas Survey. The 11 probable breeding tetrads (9 in 1987–89 Atlas Survey) are all also in the same general area of the Downs, except for one near Maidenhead. There were more tetrads occupied on the Downs in the 2007–11 Atlas Survey compared to the 1987–89 Atlas Survey, but none of the scattered records across west Berkshire

**Quail** Breeding season abundance
Tetrads occupied: **7 (37)** Average of occupied tetrads: **1·6**

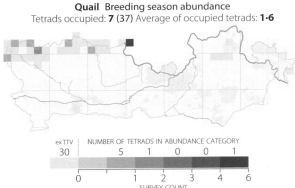

| exTTV | NUMBER OF TETRADS IN ABUNDANCE CATEGORY | | | | |
|---|---|---|---|---|---|
| 30 | 5 | 1 | 0 | 0 | 1 |

0  1  2  3  4  5  6
SURVEY COUNT

outside of the Downs seen in the previous survey (at least seven tetrads). However, the Breeding Distribution Map shows a small cluster of occupied tetrads in east Berkshire that were not seen in the 1987–89 Atlas Survey.

In some years there are very few records. For example, in 1988 there were no reports from the Downs. Isolated records away from the Downs continue to occur, like those in east Berkshire on the Breeding Distribution Map, and there was a series of records from Slough Sewage Farm in 1992, 1995, 1996 and 1998, though none since.

The Quail is normally present in Britain from late April to October. There is, however, a surprising record of two birds which were present at Manor Farm, on 15th December 1970, one of which remained until 21st January 1971 when it was last heard calling. One brought in by a cat at Cookham Rise on the highly unusual date of 15th January in 2002 was thought to have been an escape from captivity. Most records are of birds calling in June or July, with the earliest and latest dates since 1974 being 20th March 1999 and 11th October 1998 respectively.

In addition to changes in the Quail's preferred downland habitat, remote factors, like climate change and levels of shooting around the Mediterranean during the migration periods, may have significant long-term effects on the population.

*Sponsored by Andy Tomczynski*

# Pheasant

*Phasianus colchicus*

*Widespread, locally abundant resident*

The Pheasant is a conspicuous and widespread resident in Berkshire. Its preferred habitat is farmland or parkland with hedgerows and scattered, small, broadleaved woodlands. It is especially abundant in those areas of the county where it is bred and released for sporting purposes. It has been estimated that up to 35 million birds are released into the wild each year in Great Britain (PACEC, 2006) so the species must be considered as semi-domesticated. However, in Berkshire, as elsewhere, sizeable populations appear to thrive quite independently of released birds.

The Tetrad Survey maps from the 1987–89 and 2007–11 surveys indicate that the wild breeding population may have diminished considerably in the intervening 20 years. The number of tetrads in which breeding was confirmed fell from 216 to 94, although the species was still widespread, and the abundance maps show that Pheasants were present in most suitable habitat throughout the year. In both surveys there was more confirmed breeding in the western half of the county, with confirmation in well over 90% of the tetrads in 1987–89. In central and east Berkshire, its distribution is patchy

and it is absent from the larger conurbations, with the exception of Maidenhead, and scarce in most suburban areas, although occasional records of breeding in urban areas reach the county reports. The species is also absent, or sparsely distributed in some of the tetrads to the south and east of Bracknell where the habitat, predominantly coniferous woodland, is apparently unsuitable.

The Pheasant is a very sedentary species and, as a consequence, its winter distribution, as shown by the Winter Map, does not differ significantly from that of summer. The decline in the extent of the wild breeding population, which appears to be revealed by the Atlas surveys, may indicate that the population is increasingly dependent on the release of captive reared birds.

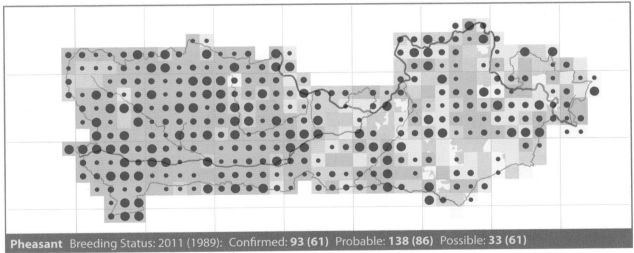

**Pheasant** Breeding Status: 2011 (1989): Confirmed: **93 (61)** Probable: **138 (86)** Possible: **33 (61)**

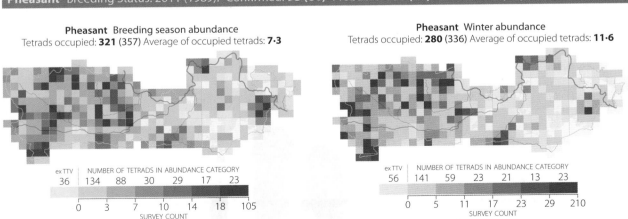

**Pheasant** Breeding season abundance
Tetrads occupied: **321 (357)** Average of occupied tetrads: **7·3**

| ex TTV | NUMBER OF TETRADS IN ABUNDANCE CATEGORY | | | | | |
|---|---|---|---|---|---|---|
| 36 | 134 | 88 | 30 | 29 | 17 | 23 |

| 0 | 3 | 7 | 10 | 14 | 18 | 105 |
|---|---|---|---|---|---|---|

SURVEY COUNT

**Pheasant** Winter abundance
Tetrads occupied: **280 (336)** Average of occupied tetrads: **11·6**

| ex TTV | NUMBER OF TETRADS IN ABUNDANCE CATEGORY | | | | | |
|---|---|---|---|---|---|---|
| 56 | 141 | 59 | 23 | 21 | 13 | 23 |

| 0 | 5 | 11 | 17 | 23 | 29 | 210 |
|---|---|---|---|---|---|---|

SURVEY COUNT

There seems little doubt that shooting interests will continue to replenish losses sustained in the annual 'bag'.

Most introduced males show the white neck-ring of the subspecies *P. c. torquatus*. However, several other races have been introduced and much inter-breeding occurs.

Lamb (1880) writing in 1814, refers to both *P. colchicus*, then numerous around Newbury, and the then recently introduced *P. c. torquatus*, of which a specimen was shot at Burghfield in October 1792.

*Sponsored by Duncan Spence*

# Lady Amherst's Pheasant

## *Chrysolophus amherstiae*

*Rare introduced resident, two records*

There have been two Berkshire records of this exotic, introduced pheasant, which is naturalised in parts of Britain. The first was a male at Sonning Golf Course on 31st October 1989, the second one at High Wood, Woodley on 16th October 2012.

*Sponsored by Amy McKee*

# Golden Pheasant

## *Chrysolophus pictus*

*Rare and localised introduced resident*

The Golden Pheasant is a localised, introduced species in Britain that has established viable populations in some areas. In Berkshire, there have been occasional records from a few localities but there is no suggestion of a stable population anywhere. During the 1987–89 Tetrad Survey it was confirmed to have bred at Eastwick in south-west Berkshire and probably bred near Stanford Dingley. This followed reports of releases on the Avington Estate in 1987.

The first county records of the species were from Maidenhead Thicket and Barkham in April and May 1976. There were two more records from Maidenhead Thicket in April 1978 and one at Freeman's Marsh from January to April that year. In April 1982, a male was seen and heard calling on several dates at Lower Basildon, and in 1985 there was a sub-adult at East Hampstead Forest on 30th April and a male at Dinton Pastures in October. One was at North Standen in March 1986. On 28th January 1999 an un-ringed bird appeared in a Maidenhead garden. One was seen in Whiteknights Park

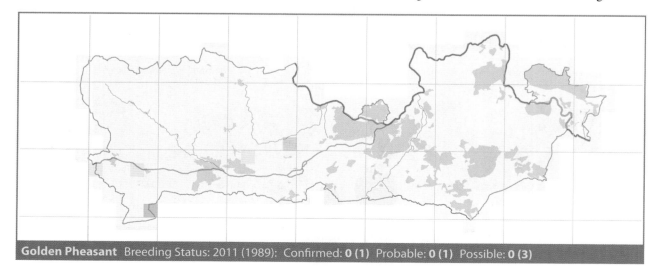

**Golden Pheasant** Breeding Status: 2011 (1989): Confirmed: **0 (1)** Probable: **0 (1)** Possible: **0 (3)**

on both 3rd and 16th February, 2005, and a pair was there on 29th March of that year. In 2006 there were two separate sightings near Streatley on 28th April, a male at Wraysbury on 14th May, and a pair was seen in the Harris Gardens in Whiteknights Park in mid-August.

*Sponsored by Duncan Spence*

# Red-throated Diver `Sch. 1`

## *Gavia stellata*

*Rare winter visitor*

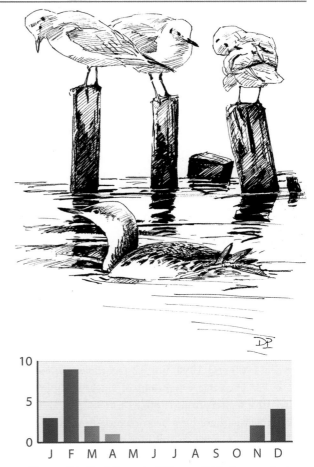

The Red-throated Diver is a rare winter visitor to Berkshire, with just 18 records in the 20th century and four further records since 2000. All records have been of single birds, the first being in 1936. Red-throated Divers have occurred on the Thames, on lakes, gravel pits and reservoirs, but since 1994 all records have come from reservoirs and gravel pits and, since 2000, records have only come from Queen Mother Reservoir.

Arrival dates have ranged from 11th November in 1997 at Bray Gravel Pits to 22nd April in 1996 at Theale Gravel Pits. A summary of the arrival dates since 1900 is shown in Figure 37. The length of stay has varied from a day to four weeks, with nearly half of the birds recorded remaining for between one and four weeks. In 2013, one was still making occasional visits to Queen Mother Reservoir in late May, having first been seen there in December of the previous year. This bird also visited other west London reservoirs.

Although severe winter weather appears to be the cause of some records of Red-throated Diver, the relatively high number of arrivals in February is likely to involve British breeding birds returning north towards the end of the winter.

Clark Kennedy (1868) indicated that in the mid-19th century some Red-throated Divers were killed "nearly every winter" and that most records involved immature birds. He gives seven examples, four of which were in the

**Figure 37: Red-throated Diver: all birds recorded 1900–2012, by month of arrival.**

1850s and 1860s. Thereafter, Noble (1906) only cited one later 19th century record, a bird killed on Maiden Erleigh Lake in about 1880. The next record was one at Virginia Water on 15th January 1936.

*Sponsored by Sunniva Taylor*

# Black-throated Diver `Sch. 1`

## *Gavia arctica*

*Rare winter visitor*

The Black-throated Diver is a rare winter visitor to Berkshire, which has been recorded on 28 occasions. After the first record in 1935, the next was not until 1950. Since then a further 26 have been recorded, 22 since 1978, seven since 1995 and four since 2000. 13 of the 22 records since 1978 have come from the Queen Mother Reservoir, which provides a large open stretch of deep water for birds driven inland during severe weather. Other recent records have come from Wraysbury and Twyford Gravel Pits.

Arrival dates have ranged from 20th October in 1979 to 13th May in 1986, both from Queen Mother Reservoir, with the remaining records ranging from 7th December to 24th April. The bird in May 1986 was last seen on 16th, and represents the latest recorded departure date. Two were seen together in 1979, 1982, 1985 and 1987, the last record involving an adult and a first-winter bird. A summary of the arrival dates is shown in Figure 38.

There have been four records of birds remaining for over two months, with the longest staying from 16th January to 9th May 1987 at Queen Mother Reservoir and attaining full summer plumage before departing.

The Black-throated Diver is the rarest of the three wintering diver species occurring in southern England. The first county record occurred in unusual

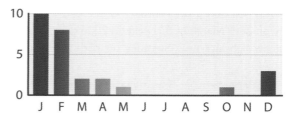

**Figure 38: Black-throated Diver: all birds recorded 1935–2012, by month of arrival.**

circumstances, the bird being caught on a trimmer baited with Dace *Leuciscus leuciscus* to catch Pike *Esox lucius* on the River Enborne on 5th March 1935 (Brown, 1935). Another unusual record was a bird found on the Bath Road at Aldermaston on 29th March 1963. It was caught and later released.

*Sponsored by Chris Bignal*

# Great Northern Diver  Amber  Sch. 1

## *Gavia immer*

*Rare winter visitor*

While the Great Northern Diver remains a rare winter visitor to Berkshire, there has been a noticeable increase in more recent winters. There were just 18 records between 1900 and 1994, but 32 records between 1995 and 2012. There were sightings of single birds in eight consecutive winters from 1980/81 to 1987/88, and from 1994 onwards there have been records in most winters. Although most sightings continue to involve single birds, occasionally two birds have been seen together, most notably in the winter of 2008/09 when one of the two juveniles present at Queen Mother Reservoir had unusual and distinctive crossed upper and lower mandibles.

The first 20th century record was one at Bearwood Lake in December 1929. There were only four records between 1946 and 1980, but the construction of the Queen Mother Reservoir led to a marked increase in the species' frequency in the county, with 28 of the 42 birds since 1980 having been seen on the reservoir, typically juveniles arriving during December. Fourteen of these birds remained for 22 days or longer, one being present from 8th December 2006 until the end of March 2007. Away from Queen Mother Reservoir, Theale, Brimpton and Horton Gravel Pits have also held birds in recent years, while one at Twyford Gravel Pits in early January 2002 was seen to be trapped in a small area of ice-free water and was believed to have perished.

Until recent years the Great Northern Diver had an earlier and narrower range of arrival dates in Berkshire than either the Red- or Black-throated Divers, but from the mid-1990s there were a number of late winter or early spring arrivals in April and May, and an even later

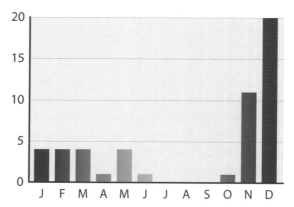

visitor to Queen Mother Reservoir on 1st June 1996. The earliest winter arrival was on 29th October 1992 at Brimpton Gravel Pits. Figure 39 shows the pattern of arrival dates since the first 20th century record.

Prior to 1900, there were at least ten records of Great Northern Diver in Berkshire. Lamb (1880) recorded

**Figure 39: Great Northern Diver: all birds recorded 1929–2012, by month of arrival.**

two at Maidenhead and one at Pangbourne in January 1794, and one at Newbury in 1810. Clark Kennedy (1868) notes that one taken at Virginia Water on 4th February 1851 was mounted and exhibited at The Great Exhibition and then given to Eton College Museum by Prince Albert. Noble (1906) cites a record of one killed on the Thames at Temple Island in 1865, and Palmer (1886) reports one shot at Ilsley in 1875, and three or more killed in the Newbury area in the ten years prior to 1886, although he gives no further details.

*Sponsored by Caroline Sellick*

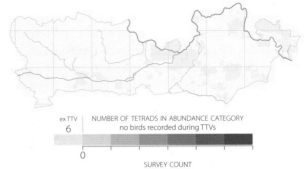

**Great Northern Diver**  Winter abundance
Tetrads occupied: **0** (6) Average of occupied tetrads: **0**

exTTV | NUMBER OF TETRADS IN ABUNDANCE CATEGORY
6 | no birds recorded during TTVs

0

SURVEY COUNT

# Fulmar  Amber

## *Fulmarus glacialis*

*Rare vagrant, four county records*

The Fulmar is a rare vagrant to Berkshire, having been recorded on just four occasions. The first record for the county was one seen flying over the Grassland Research Centre, Hurley on 23rd May 1971. The second was a bird flying south-east over Theale and Burghfield Gravel Pits on 17th March 1985 and the third was one flying over the Thames into Berkshire at Cliveden on 6th September 1989. The fourth was one found freshly dead at Old Bath Road, Newbury on 9th July 2003. These records coincide with a significant national increase in breeding numbers, although the low number of records indicates that the species is less likely to be blown inland by gales than other seabirds.

*Sponsored by John Burleigh*

# Manx Shearwater  Amber

## *Puffinus puffinus*

*Rare vagrant*

The Manx Shearwater is a rare vagrant to Berkshire, having been recorded on just 16 occasions in the 20th century. These records have all been of single birds and have occurred either in June, July or September.

There have been four records in June or July: a bird flying WSW over Cookham on 9th June 1970, one at Burghfield Gravel Pits from 11th to 12th June 1983 (which evaded attempts to capture it for subsequent release at the coast), one found dead at Wraysbury Gravel Pits on 29th July 1984, and one flying SSE over the same site on 23rd June 1987.

Most records have been in September. An immature female was shot at Sindlesham on 8th September 1909 (Noble, 1909), one was found at Pangbourne on 10th September 1983 (which was released at Cardiff), and

there were two on 1st September 1985, when one flew over Wraysbury Reservoir into Berkshire and one flew south-west over Wokingham. A recently dead bird was found at Upper Bucklebury on 5th September 1988, and one found alive at Spencers Wood a week later, which was taken to the Solent and released. A bird was found dead at Highstanding Hill, Windsor on 9th September 1997. A grounded bird was found in Shaw, Newbury on 9th September 2002 following heavy rain and released the next day. Another, found grounded in Kings Road, Reading on 19th September 2006, died two days later. Single birds were seen at Queen Mother Reservoir on 16th and 25th September 2007 and another two were seen in 2011, one at Horton Gravel Pits on 7th September and another at Queen Mother Reservoir on 17th September. A decomposed corpse of this species, which may have been present for some weeks, was found at Combe in October 1955. The concentration of records in early September coincides with the departure of most Manx Shearwaters from British waters (Brooke, 1990). This matches the pattern in some other inland southern counties such as Oxfordshire (Brucker et al., 1992).

Prior to 1900, Palmer (1886) cites an undated record of a corpse found near Winterbourne in 1883. Noble (1906) also refers to two records of birds found dead or exhausted: one, undated, from "near the Hampshire border" in 1893 and one at Reading in October 1899.

*Sponsored by Peter Roberts*

## Storm Petrel Green

*Hydrobates pelagicus*

*Rare storm-blown vagrant, recorded eight times*

The Storm Petrel is a rare vagrant to Berkshire and has occurred on just eight occasions, invariably after storms. Six of the records have been in the 20th or 21st century: a female found dead at Arborfield sometime between 8th and 14th December 1929, one found dead at Barkham on 30th November 1954 after gales, one over Burghfield Gravel Pits on 16th December 1956 and one found dead at Inkpen Common on 29th December 1989. Another was also at Burghfield Gravel Pits after gales on 30 October 2000 before being taken by a Sparrowhawk, and the most recent was taken by a Peregrine at Queen Mother Reservoir, Datchet on 2 December 2003.

There are two 19th century records: one caught after flying over gravel pits at Clewer "about the year 1855" (Clark Kennedy, 1868) which is noteworthy as being the first known record from a gravel pit, and one picked up near Newbury in about 1865 (Palmer, 1886).

*Sponsored by David Harrold*

## Leach's Storm-petrel Sch. 1

*Oceanodroma leucorhoa*

*Rare storm-blown vagrant*

The Leach's Storm-petrel is a rare vagrant to Berkshire with 21 records involving 22 birds. The species is subject to 'wrecks' across southern England following severe weather, and the majority of the county records are of birds which have been found after gales. All but two of the records have been between September and December.

The first Leach's Storm-petrel to be recorded in Berkshire in the 20th century was one found dead at Binfield Manor in December 1905 (Noble, 1906). The next was 45 years later when one was found dead at Hampstead Norreys in October 1950. Gales in the autumn of 1952 led to an influx into southern England, and three birds were found in Berkshire: one picked up at Reading Cattle Market on 31st October, one found dead at Beenham on 4th November and one flying over Wash Common on 21st November. There were two further records of casualties

in the 1960s: one found injured at Caversham on 2nd November 1967 and one found dying at Swallowfield on 13th October 1968. All records since then have been of live, uninjured birds: one flying west over Henley Road Gravel Pits into Berkshire on 8th November 1970, two at Queen Mother Reservoir on 3rd September 1983, after gales, and single birds at the same site on 1st October 1989, 30th October 2000, 16th October 2004, 9th November 2005 and 7 December 2006. Single birds were at Theale Gravel Pits on 27th September 1989, 4th October 1990 and 3rd October 1999.

Most unusually for this species, for which Spring records are rare, one was found on 1st April 2011, feeding at Theale Gravel Pits, during a period of relatively calm weather.

Prior to 1900 there were three records of Leach's Storm-petrel in the county: one found alive "fluttering against a lamp" at Eton after gales in the summer of 1847 or 1848 (Clark Kennedy, 1868), one shot near Newbury in November 1872 (Herbert, 1875), and one found dead under telegraph wires at Hurst in November 1899 (Noble, 1906).

It is not clear why nearly all records up to 1968 were of dead or dying birds but subsequent records have been of birds in flight. It may reflect the increase in open water sites which are now well watched by observers.

*Sponsored by Debby Reynolds*

# Gannet Amber

## *Morus bassanus*

### Rare vagrant

The Gannet is a rare vagrant to Berkshire with just 33 records up to the end of July 2013, although it has been observed with increasing frequency in recent years. There has been at least one record in each year between 2004 and 2011, except in 2006. With exception of two birds sighted over Aldworth Downs on 28th September 2007, all the records have been of single birds, which have invariably occurred following gales. Of the records where the age of the bird was recorded, approximately half were adults and four were immatures.

The first 20th century record was an adult male taken at Grazeley on 20th May 1902 (Noble, 1906). The next was one found at Aldermaston and released on the lake there on 13th March 1917 (Lewis, 1958). There was then a gap of 35 years until an adult was found exhausted near East Ilsley on 15th October 1952. A second-summer bird, which was believed to have been dead for about two weeks having possibly been shot, was found in a stubble field at Hermitage on 1st October 1958. A juvenile was picked up injured at Basildon on 22nd September 1971, and a fourth-year bird was picked up at Jealott's Hill on 26th May 1972.

In contrast to these older records, most recent observations have been of birds in flight, although one was found dead at Wigmore Lane, Theale on 2nd August 2001, having died apparently after flying into a deer fence. The increase in the frequency of records in recent years is probably a reflection of observer coverage, illustrated by the number of records from Queen Mother Reservoir (which has had records from four of the five years up to 2012), as well as the increase in UK Gannet populations which have risen by 77% between 1986 and 2010 (Eaton *et al.*, 2011).

A summary of the records of Gannets in Berkshire since 1900 is shown in Figure 40 and shows that they have occurred in most months of the year, but with more records during the migration periods, especially autumn.

Prior to 1900 there were records of Gannets found exhausted near Newbury in 1865 (Herbert, 1871), shot at Sandleford in 1875 (Palmer, 1886), captured near Reading on 25th March 1876, and seen near Hungerford on 14th April 1876 (Herbert, 1875).

*Sponsored by Ruth Angus*

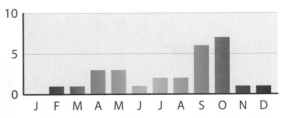

**Figure 40: Gannet: all birds recorded 1900–2012, by month of arrival.**

# Cormorant

## Phalacrocorax carbo

*Common winter visitor, which first bred in 1996*

The Cormorant is now a regular winter visitor to Berkshire, with small numbers remaining throughout the year and a growing breeding population, albeit at a few sites only. It can be found on lakes, flooded gravel pits and reservoirs and in smaller numbers in the main river valleys. This distribution is reflected in the distribution maps for both seasons in the 2007–11 Atlas survey.

Prior to the late 1950s, there was typically no more than one record of Cormorant in Berkshire each year, usually during spring or autumn migration, and before 1940 records were infrequent, with one in 1928 and four in the 1930s. Before 1957 the highest count was of seven at Theale in October 1950. In the winters of 1957/58 and 1958/59, up to 40 were counted at Wraysbury, but records reverted to a few each year, mostly in spring or autumn, until the winter of 1968/69. Since 1968 there has been a steady westward colonisation of Berkshire by the wintering population. The Queen Mother Reservoir began to be used regularly by wintering birds from 1977, and this site and nearby Wraysbury Gravel Pits have produced the county's highest counts. At the

former site, when the reservoir is partially drained, Cormorants occur in large numbers, apparently because the fish stock becomes concentrated and presumably easier to catch. Such conditions produced the highest ever counts so far for the county in the autumn of 2003, with 1,480 on 31st October and an estimated 1,500 on 2nd November, and the next highest count of 720 on 18th November 1997.

In mid-Berkshire numbers remained low until 1978/79, although by then Cormorants were regular in winter at most gravel pits. In 1978/79, a flock of up to 26 gathered at Dinton Pastures, attracting adverse comments in the media from anglers who expressed concern at

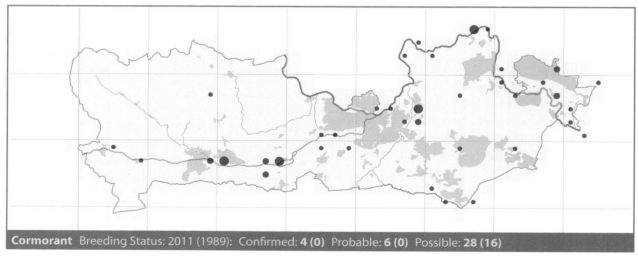

Cormorant  Breeding Status: 2011 (1989):  Confirmed: **4 (0)**  Probable: **6 (0)**  Possible: **28 (16)**

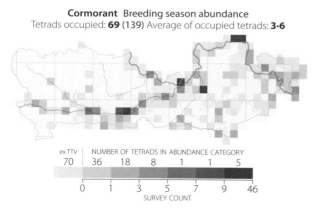

**Cormorant**  Breeding season abundance
Tetrads occupied: **69 (139)** Average of occupied tetrads: **3·6**

| exTTV | NUMBER OF TETRADS IN ABUNDANCE CATEGORY | | | | | |
|---|---|---|---|---|---|---|
| 70 | 36 | 18 | 8 | 1 | 1 | 5 |

0   1   3   5   7   9   46
SURVEY COUNT

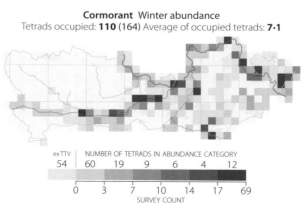

**Cormorant**  Winter abundance
Tetrads occupied: **110 (164)** Average of occupied tetrads: **7·1**

| exTTV | NUMBER OF TETRADS IN ABUNDANCE CATEGORY | | | | | |
|---|---|---|---|---|---|---|
| 54 | 60 | 19 | 9 | 6 | 4 | 12 |

0   3   7   10   14   17   69
SURVEY COUNT

the possible impact on fish stocks. The following year numbers reached 38 and by January 1986 a peak count of 118 was recorded. A roost was established at Sonning Eye Gravel Pits, Oxfordshire, east of Reading at the same time. Maximum numbers here grew from 15 in 1978 to 82 in 1985 (Brucker *et al.*, 1992). In 1980/81, numbers at Theale Gravel Pits reached 42 and since then counts of over 50 have regularly been recorded from the Theale and Burghfield Gravel Pits (with a maximum of 180 in December 1990), and from other gravel pit sites throughout the county. In 1982, 80 were counted flying over Reading in one day in February, indicating that Cormorants feeding in the Kennet valley by day probably roosted at Sonning Eye. Similar numbers occur regularly every winter on the flooded gravel pits in the Thames, Kennet and Loddon Valleys and smaller numbers on most other water-bodies and rivers.

The seasonal pattern varies somewhat between years. In some years the highest numbers are recorded in the autumn. In others there appears to be a mid-winter influx. Most birds depart in March or April, although small numbers now remain through the summer at most wintering sites, with numbers building up again from August.

There is evidence that many of the Cormorants wintering in Berkshire are not from the British coastal breeding population, which grew from about 8,000 pairs in 1969–70 to 10,400 pairs in 1985–87 (*BWP I*, Lloyd *et al.*, 1991). The population in the Netherlands has also grown, from 1,500 pairs in 1971 to 13,600 pairs (Lloyd *et al.*, 1991) and white-headed birds, indicating birds of the race *P. c. sinensis* that breeds on the continent, are regularly reported. The spread up the Thames Valley mirrors a similar colonisation up the Ouse in Cambridgeshire

since 1970 (Bircham, 1989), and wintering birds from the Danish and Dutch breeding populations re-colonised inland France in the 1980s (Reille, 1993). Although these factors indicate that continental breeding birds are likely to be found in Berkshire in winter, only two of the 18 ringing recoveries since 1980 have involved birds from overseas, one from Denmark and one from Sweden. Of the UK ringed birds recovered in Berkshire, three were from St. Margaret's Island, Dyfed; there were two from each of Anglesey and the Farne Islands, and one from North Berwick, Scotland.

Following the growth of the inland breeding colony at Abberton Reservoir in Essex, which totalled some 355 pairs in 1990 (Moon, 1990), breeding spread across south-east England, and occurred for the first time in Berkshire in 1996 at Aldermaston Gravel Pits where two pairs raised young. There is no indication whether these are birds that have wintered in the area or are summer immigrants. Since then breeding has been reported from this site in most years, numbers of nests growing to 16 in 1998, and 27 in 2001. Records of breeding have not always been submitted, but in 2006 a second breeding site was reported in the County Report. The 2007–11 breeding distribution map confirmed breeding in four tetrads. The birds breeding at the Aldermaston colony are of the continental race *P. c. sinensis*. This is consistent with the national pattern, with over 2,000 pairs now breeding inland, generally of this race (Newson *el al.*, 2007).

There were only two records of Cormorant in Berkshire prior to 1900; one killed near Newbury in November 1803 (Lamb, 1880) and one shot at Hennerton on 14th April 1871 (Noble, 1906).

*Sponsored by Renee Grayer*

Cormorant, Sashes Island, Cookham *Michael Vogel*

# Shag

*Phalacrocorax aristotelis*

*Uncommon autumn and winter visitor*

As an uncommon visitor to Berkshire, mostly in the autumn and winter, the Shag has occurred almost annually in recent years. Prior to 1962, however, it was a rare vagrant having been recorded with certainty on only two occasions.

A bird which was possibly this species was seen on the spire of St Giles' Church, Reading on 31st May 1927, but the first authenticated 20th century record was of one found on the Thames at Maidenhead on 8th July 1956. When caught on 10th August, the bird was found to be ringed and the ringing return showed that it had been ringed on Bass Rock the previous July. It was later found in a wood near Marlow on 23rd September and then released on Staines Reservoir, but it subsequently died. In 1962 there was a remarkable influx during March involving an immature found dead at Virginia Water on the 19th and a total of 35 birds on the Thames at Reading. The Reading birds took to roosting on the town gas holder by the river. Twenty-seven remained into April and then numbers dwindled to two by July. These birds were part of a wider influx into the counties bordering the Thames.

The period from 1963 to the winter of 1973/74 produced a further four records of eight birds. These records, which occurred in three out of the 11 years in this period, fit the pattern of apparently storm-blown birds described in the *1981–84 BTO Winter Atlas*, singles being found in August, September and October, and a party of four adults and an immature on the Thames near Reading in March 1969.

An apparent change in the status of the Shag in Berkshire took place after 1973, with birds being recorded in four of the years from 1974 to 1982 and, with the exception of 1987, annually from 1982 to 1994. In more recent years, the pattern is similar, with records from 12 of the 18 years from 1995 to 2012, with a gap of three years from 2002 to 2004. Birds have arrived in every month except June, with most records being of single individuals. However parties of two or three birds have been recorded on several occasions, with the largest parties being of eight in January 1984 and seven in November 1985. A summary of the arrival dates from 1963 to 2012 is shown in Figure 41.

The reason for the increase in records from 1974 is unclear, but greater observation along with an increase in the extent of open water in the county, especially gravel pits and reservoirs such as Queen Mother Reservoir, seem likely factors, although the Thames has played host to a number of birds over the period.

In addition to the recovery in autumn 1956 of a bird ringed on the Bass Rock, two birds were recovered in the east of the county in November 1985. Both had been ringed as nestlings that year, one on the Farne Islands and one on the Isle of May, and the two more recent recoveries, both young birds found dead (in February of 1996 and February 2005) were also ringed as nestlings on the Isle of May, pointing to a regular north to south movement during the winter and the possibility of overland passage. Nationally, Shag numbers have declined, falling by 33% between 1986 and 2010, the species seemingly slow to recover from severe weather events in 1994 and 2005 (Eaton *et al.*, 2011).

The first long-staying birds came from the flock of 35 that occurred in 1962, the last of which were seen four months after arrival. Since then, a number of long stays have been recorded: an immature at Bearwood Lake from August 1974 to May 1975, one on the Thames at Medmenham from October 1975 to March 1976, one of a flock of eight birds which arrived at Theale Gravel Pits in January 1984 was last seen in June 1984, up to seven at Queen Mother Reservoir from November 1985 which stayed until at least June 1986, and an immature which lingered on the Thames at Maidenhead from June 1991 until March 1995, a remarkable period of almost four years.

Prior to the 20th century there was only one record of a Shag in Berkshire, a bird reported to have been killed near Pangbourne in 1794 (Lamb, 1880).

*Sponsored by Mike & Mary Taylor*

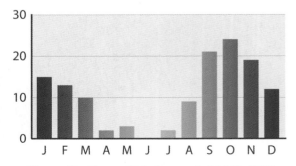

**Figure 41: Shag: all birds recorded 1963–2012, by month of arrival.**

# Bittern

*Botaurus stellaris*

*Scarce winter visitor*

The Bittern was a resident breeding species in Berkshire until about 1780, but subsequently became a rare winter visitor. Since 1945, the number of sightings in the county has increased. At the time of the 1987–89 Atlas Survey one or two birds were being seen annually, but since the mid-1990s numbers have continued to increase with many years having numbers into double figures. The species showed a marked decline throughout western Europe between 1970 and 1990, although numbers have since stabilized. In the UK, due to intensive work on habitat creation and management, breeding Bitterns have shown a marked increase (approaching 400%) between 1995 and 2010.

A summary of the ten-yearly totals for Berkshire from the winter of 1945/46 to the winter of 2004/05 is given in Figure 42.

Dinton Pastures Country Park has become the premier site for wintering Bitterns in recent years, hosting up to four birds in some winters, with the newly constructed

**Bittern** Winter abundance
Tetrads occupied: **0** (23) Average of occupied tetrads: **0**

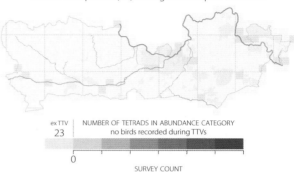

ex TTV   NUMBER OF TETRADS IN ABUNDANCE CATEGORY
23   no birds recorded during TTVs

0

SURVEY COUNT

Bittern, Moor Green Lakes *Roger Milligan*

Dorney Wetlands on the Jubilee River near Windsor also frequently holding more than one bird. As the winter map shows, other sites around the county have also held single birds in recent winters, including Windsor Great Park, the Kennet Valley from Hungerford to Reading, and Wraysbury Gravel Pits. The origin of Berkshire's wintering Bitterns is not clear, although some certainly originate from north west Europe. One individual that arrived at Lavell's Lake, Dinton Pastures during the second winter of 2002 unusually stayed on through the summer of 2003. When it was found dead in September 2003 it was carrying a French ring. Figure 43 shows a monthly summary of the records since 1945. The great majority of birds arrive during the winter months, coinciding with the onset of harder weather, but the spring and autumn arrivals suggest that Bitterns occasionally occur in Berkshire on passage. The significant rise in numbers has coincided with the increase in the UK breeding population and may also now involve some post breeding dispersal.

The duration of stay of Bitterns is often difficult to establish due to the retiring nature of the species, but, apart from the unusual over-summering bird of 2002/03, more typically, another bird that arrived at Dinton Pastures on October 13th 2006 was seen on many occasions through to March 27th 2007, when it was seen to fly off northwards. Booming birds have been heard at two sites during May, in 1982 and 1991, providing some hope that Bitterns may one day return to breed in Berkshire.

Lamb (1880) reported that until about 1780 Bitterns used to be common between Reading and Newbury but that "since the peat has been so much dug out they are

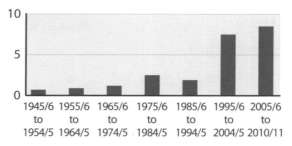

**Figure 42: Bittern: average number of birds recorded per year.** 198 Bittern were recorded from 1945/6–2010/11.

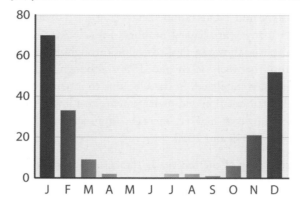

**Figure 43: Bittern: all birds recorded 1945/46–2010/11, by month of arrival.**

become very rare". Clark Kennedy (1868) and Noble (1906) give only seven records of nine birds for the period between 1855 and 1900 and there were only four more from 1900 to 1946, all in January or February, in 1917, 1937 and two in 1939. This suggests that greater observer coverage has also added to the increase in records in recent years.

*Sponsored by Friends Of Lavell's Lake*

# Little Bittern    `Sch. 1`

*Ixobrychus minutus*

*Rare vagrant*

The Little Bittern is a rare vagrant to Berkshire with only one 20th century record, a female seen by the River Kennet near Padworth on 18th and 19th April 1972.

In contrast, there were records of seven birds in the 19th century. The presence of two immature birds near Windsor in the summer of 1826, one of which was shot, led to speculation that breeding might have occurred. Further birds were shot near Newbury in about 1848 and in the Maidenhead and Windsor area in about 1856–58, and again in summer 1860 and August 1865. The last record was of a female with eggs in the process of formation which was taken at Wargrave in 1867, indicating that breeding may again have been attempted (Clark Kennedy, 1868).

*Sponsored by Jane Campbell*

# Night Heron

*Nycticorax nycticorax*

*Rare vagrant, three records*

The Night Heron is a rare vagrant to Berkshire with just three records. The first record was a juvenile which was present at Southcote Lock from 16th January to 4th March 1976, and the second was of an adult male at Wraysbury Gravel Pits from 4th May to 8th May 1983. The most recent record was another juvenile seen at Thatcham Marsh from at least 30th July to 6th August 1987 and again from 30th August to the end of September. The unusual date of the 1976 record led to speculation that it may have come from the colony of 'feral' breeding birds in Edinburgh, although there is no evidence that this is the case.

*Sponsored by Ian Tarr*

# Cattle Egret

*Bubulcus ibis*

*Rare vagrant*

Cattle Egrets have been spreading north through Europe for many years, with numbers occurring in Britain increasing in recent years and a pair first breeding in Somerset in 2008 (Holling *et al.*, 2012). The first accepted wild record in Berkshire was one at Lower Farm Gravel Pit, Thatcham on 14th October 2007. Subsequently there was one at Padworth Lane Gravel Pit on 30th and 31st July 2009, then, in 2010, two birds were photographed in a horse field at Sulhamstead on 4th December, the sighting only coming to light after photographs were posted on the internet. Most recently, one remained in the Theale Gravel Pits area from 20th March to 30th April 2012.

*Sponsored by Roger Stansfield*

# Great White Egret

*Egretta alba*

*Scarce vagrant*

The European range of this species has expanded in recent years, culminating in the first successful breeding in the UK in 2012 (Holt, 2013). Berkshire's first record was one seen flying over Theale Gravel Pits on 25th February 2003. Another flew off towards Calcot having been flushed at Field Farm Gravel Pit, Burghfield on 27th April 2004. One flew over Queen Mother Reservoir on 24th December 2007. 2009 produced three records, one at Stockcross on 8th February, one at Dinton Pastures on 5th November, and one at Borough Marsh, Charvil on 3rd and 4th December. Eventually one remained long enough to be seen by many observers, when one was at Great Shefford between 21st December 2010 and 11th January 2011. There were further individuals at Lavell's Lake on 15th April 2011 and at Hungerford on 22nd January 2012. These last two records await consideration by the Berkshire Records Committee.

*Sponsored by Alison Stares*

# Little Egret

*Egretta garzetta*

*Uncommon visitor and rare breeding species*

The Little Egret is an uncommon but increasing visitor to Berkshire, which has started to breed in the county. The 2007–11 Tetrad Survey produced records from most of the river valleys in the county, but with more recorded and from a wider area in winter. During the breeding seasons covered by the survey (2008 to 2011) breeding was proved in two tetrads.

The species was first recorded in Berkshire as recently as 1991. The species spread northwards through France in the 1970s and 1980s, following which it was recorded in increasing numbers in southern Britain; there were just 12 records prior to 1952 but over 700 from 1952 to 1990 (Dymond *et al.*, 1989, Rogers *et al.*, 1992).

It is somewhat surprising that the Little Egret was not recorded in Berkshire until 1991 and, being a rather conspicuous species, it seems unlikely to have been overlooked previously. The first record was of a bird flushed from a ditch near Hurst on 18th February 1991 which was seen again briefly, in misty conditions, at Dinton Pastures the following morning. This was followed by single birds on the river Kennet at Hungerford

from 8th to 12th May 1992, at Brimpton Gravel Pits on 1st August 1993, at Twyford Gravel Pits on 15th May 1994, and at various localities in east Berkshire from 6th to 30th July 1995. After none in 1996, and one at Lower Farm Gravel Pit, Thatcham on 16th November 1997, records increased in frequency, with six records in 1998, eight in 1999 (including the first records of more than one bird: four at Bottom Lane, Theale in May and between Kintbury and Hungerford in July), 32 records from 17 sites in 2000 and 106 records from 14 sites in 2001. By 2007 the number of records had reached 415 at 44 sites. By this time a clear pattern emerged of more

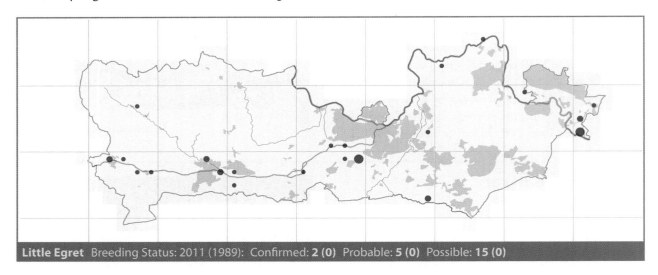

**Little Egret** Breeding Status: 2011 (1989): Confirmed: **2 (0)** Probable: **5 (0)** Possible: **15 (0)**

**Little Egret** Breeding season abundance
Tetrads occupied: **5 (47)** Average of occupied tetrads: **1·0**

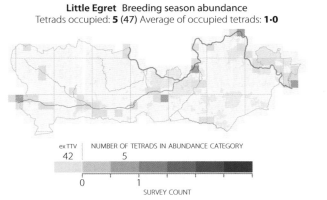

| exTTV | NUMBER OF TETRADS IN ABUNDANCE CATEGORY |
|-------|------------------------------------------|
| 42    | 5                                        |

0          1

SURVEY COUNT

**Little Egret** Winter abundance
Tetrads occupied: **22 (101)** Average of occupied tetrads: **1·7**

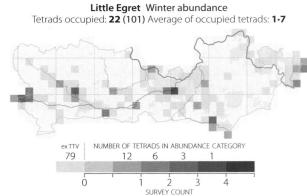

| exTTV | NUMBER OF TETRADS IN ABUNDANCE CATEGORY | | | |
|-------|------|------|------|------|
| 79    | 12   | 6    | 3    | 1    |

0          1          2          3          4

SURVEY COUNT

records in the winter than during the summer. Most records are of single birds, and the first records of counts in double figures did not occur until 2011, when 10 were at Great Shefford on 11th January, records of 10 and 12 at two breeding sites and 12 together at Freeman's Marsh, Hungerford on 22nd December.

Outside the breeding season, birds tend to be mobile, moving from site to site frequently. There has been one ringing recovery, involving a bird ringed as a nestling in May 2009 which was found dead at an unusual site, Warren Farm, Lambourn, the following March.

Breeding was first reported from a site in the east of the county in 2006 when three juveniles were reported in July. Since then breeding has been confirmed or suspected in most years at up to three sites, indicating that the species has become an established part of the breeding avifauna of Berkshire.

*Sponsored by Blackwater Valley Countryside Trust*

# Grey Heron Green

*Ardea cinerea*

*Locally common resident and winter visitor in small numbers*

The Grey Heron is a familiar resident in Berkshire, which is not only found by rivers and lakes, but is also seen flying over urban areas. Although the species is the subject of the longest running national census of any species, the BTO Heronries Census, the *1987–89 Tetrad Survey* provided the first opportunity to obtain a comprehensive picture of its status in the county since the *1968–72 BTO Atlas*.

During the breeding season birds range over a considerable area to feed, hence the distribution of 'possible' breeding records during the Tetrad Surveys, and the distribution in the Abundance Map, probably indicate their feeding areas, with low-lying river valleys being favoured. Heronries are normally found in woodland, situated close to open water and rivers, a pattern followed in Berkshire as comparison with the

Habitat maps shows. Ground nesting on islands has, however, been reported from at least one gravel pit site, at Burghfield Gravel Pits. During the 1987–89 Tetrad Survey, breeding was proved in a total of 18 tetrads and in three more 10 km squares than in the *1968–72 BTO Atlas*, indicating an extension in range. The 2007–11 Tetrad Survey showed a marked increase in the number of tetrads with confirmed breeding to 34. The fact that breeding was not confirmed in 2007–11 in 12 of the tetrads in which it was confirmed in 1987–89 indicates that many heronries are transient.

The national population of the Grey Heron has been monitored by the BTO Heronries Census since 1928. It appears to have increased since the severe setback of the 1962/63 winter to higher levels than before the 1940s, and the *1988–91 BTO Atlas* showed a considerable population growth since the *1968–72 BTO Atlas*. If the wider distribution reflects an increase in numbers, then the pattern in Berkshire would seem to follow the national trend. Mature gravel pits have evidently assisted in the expansion of the species' breeding range, with breeding proved from such sites in the Kennet, Colne and Loddon Valleys.

Although the information available from county reports and the BTO Heronry Census in Berkshire is clearly incomplete when compared to the Tetrad Survey, a number of heronries have been counted for many years, although coverage has been intermittent at many (Robinson, 2006). Heronries appear to fluctuate in size, with traditional sites sometimes being deserted. The largest was at Coley Park, which began with one nest in 1829 and reached about 50 in 1949. In the mid-20th century there were four counts of between ten and 20 nests, the last being 14 in 1962, the year before the site was deserted after the 1962/63 winter. The heronry in Englefield Park had one nest in 1949 and in recent years has varied between four and 16 occupied nests. A third mid-Berkshire site at Burghfield has recorded over ten occupied nests in recent years, with 23 in 2002, and 29 in 2006. In that year up to 118 individuals were counted at this colony in March. In east Berkshire, a heronry noted as far back as 1872 in the Windsor area relocated to Virginia Water by 1903. Fifty-one nests were counted in 1945, but it moved again to Fort Belvedere in Surrey in 1949. A further site at Wraysbury, apparently established in the 1940s, reached 36 nests in 1961 but has only been used (or perhaps counted) intermittently since 1965. 96 were counted there in March 2006.

The Winter Tetrad map confirms the tendency for the Grey Heron to favour river valleys and open water. Winter roosts are commonly reported from gravel pits throughout Berkshire and the river valleys in the west

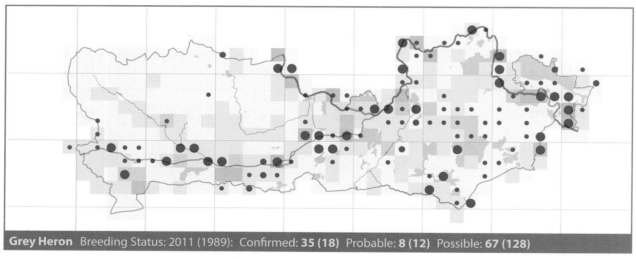

**Grey Heron**  Breeding Status: 2011 (1989): Confirmed: **35 (18)**  Probable: **8 (12)**  Possible: **67 (128)**

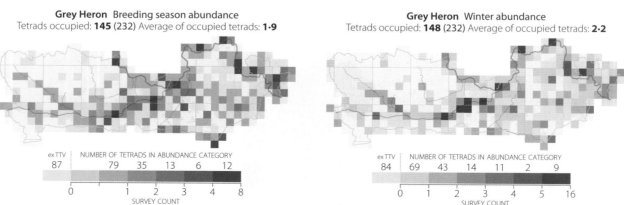

**Grey Heron**  Breeding season abundance
Tetrads occupied: **145 (232)** Average of occupied tetrads: **1·9**

| ex TTV | NUMBER OF TETRADS IN ABUNDANCE CATEGORY | | | | |
|---|---|---|---|---|---|
| 87 | 79 | 35 | 13 | 6 | 12 |

0  1  2  3  4  8
SURVEY COUNT

**Grey Heron**  Winter abundance
Tetrads occupied: **148 (232)** Average of occupied tetrads: **2·2**

| ex TTV | NUMBER OF TETRADS IN ABUNDANCE CATEGORY | | | | |
|---|---|---|---|---|---|
| 84 | 69 | 43 | 14 | 11 | 2 | 9 |

0  1  2  3  4  5  16
SURVEY COUNT

of the county. Counts of about 20 are frequent, with maxima of 64 at Wraysbury Gravel Pits in December 2006 and 51 in a field roost at Lower Denford in 1979.

Four Herons ringed as young in the nest in Europe have been recovered in Berkshire. One was ringed at Lac de Grand Lieu, west France, the others came from Norway, Sweden and Denmark. These last three provide evidence of the influx of wintering birds from the continent and Scandinavia.

*Sponsored by Hayley Douthwaite*

# Purple Heron Sch. 1

*Ardea purpurea*

*Rare vagrant, six records*

The Purple Heron is a rare vagrant to Berkshire and has been recorded on just six occasions. The first record was of an immature female killed at White Waltham in September 1861 (Clark Kennedy, 1868). The remaining five records have all been since 1972: one at Reading Sewage Farm from 17th August to 2nd September 1972, a second-year bird at Twyford Gravel Pits on 12th September 1976, an immature at Beenham on 9th August 1981, an adult at Wraysbury Gravel Pits on 15th May 1984, and one at Lavell's Lake, Winnersh on 5th and 6th April 2000. The bias towards autumn records contrasts with the general pattern of occurrence nationally, where the species most often occurs during the spring.

*Sponsored by Dick Haydon*

# White Stork

*Ciconia ciconia*

*Rare vagrant*

The White Stork is a rare vagrant to Berkshire and records of wild birds have been accepted on four occasions. The first was of a bird flying east over Ham Island on 2nd November 1968. The second record involved a bird watched flying west by members of a ROC outing to Walbury Hill on 16th March 1975. There were no further records until 2000, when one was seen soaring over Englefield on 22nd May. A first summer bird produced a number of records starting on 31st March 2004 with a brief sighting by a driver over the M4 motorway, the same bird then being seen several times around east Berkshire the following day. This bird was believed to be the same as that which had been regularly sighted in Kent between August 2003 and July 2004. (Heard, 2008). Escapees occur occasionally: a ringed adult seen south of Reading in August 1978 proved to be from a zoo in the Netherlands, and two near Thatcham in August 1990 followed an escape of White Storks from Whipsnade Zoo.

*Sponsored by Hugh Netley*

# Glossy Ibis

## *Plegadis falcinellus*

*Rare vagrant, three 21st century records and one 18th century record*

The Glossy Ibis is a rare vagrant to Berkshire. Prior to 2010 there was a single definite record from the 18th century. A male was shot a few miles from Reading in September 1793 whilst flying over the Thames in company with a second bird (Lamb, 1880).

An immature female, which was shot at Sonning Eye on the Oxfordshire side of the Thames on 11th May 1916, had been present in the area for about two weeks and may have entered Berkshire during its stay. This specimen is now in the Reading Museum collection.

After over 200 years, there were three records in short succession in 2010 and 2011. The first was one which remained from 9th December 2010 to 14th January 2011 at Freeman's Marsh, Hungerford during a cold spell, giving many observers good views. This was followed by one at Dinton Pastures on 7th May 2011, and another at Horton on 22nd and 24th October 2011.

*Sponsored by Debby Reynolds*

Glossy Ibis, Freeman's Marsh, 8th January 2011  *Michael McKee*

# Spoonbill

Amber  Sch. 1

*Platalea leucorodia*

*Rare passage migrant*

The Spoonbill is a rare passage migrant in Berkshire appearing in increasing numbers in recent times, all records being since 1940. Many of the 29 Berkshire birds recorded up to 2012 have been singles occurring during spring from May to June and in autumn from October to November, but the largest group appeared in September. The May and June records are consistent with the pattern of summer arrivals in other southern counties, presumed to be mainly failed breeders, and those in October coincide with dispersal periods from European breeding colonies, as disclosed by ringing recoveries (*Migration Atlas*).

The spring records have been of one at Slough Sewage Farm on 8th May 1940, four that circled Ham Sewage Farm on 19th May 1945, one in the Cockmarsh area on 11th May 1969, an adult over Wraysbury Gravel Pits on 7th May 1977, and one at Lower Farm Gravel Pit, Newbury on 7th and 8th June 1982. An immature appeared at Lower Farm Gravel Pit on 28th May 2000, and two flew over Finchampstead on 7th May 2003. Two birds seen at Lea Farm on 14th May 2007 may have contributed to a party of three seen at Dorney Wetlands two days later. In 2011, single birds were seen at Lower Farm on 8th May and Woolhampton on 16th June. The only summer record was a bird in non-breeding plumage at Wraysbury Gravel Pits on 5th July 1986.

The autumn records have been of one circling Ham Island and departing to the north on 20th October 1968,

an immature at Theale and Burghfield Gravel Pits from 14th to 15th November 1979, one at Dinton Pastures on 21st October 1983, which departed to the south west, and an immature at Summerleaze Gravel Pit on 10th October 1986. An immature was found at Queen Mother Reservoir on 2nd November 2003 and remained there until 25th. There was an outstanding record of five birds found at Pingewood Gravel Pits on 10th September 2001, flushed by a juvenile Osprey. These birds were relocated several times locally until the last one, that remained at Moatlands Gravel Pit, departed on 17th September. One of this group was colour-ringed as a nestling on 7th June in The Netherlands and was recorded at six locations in England before being found dead after hitting wires near Cheshunt, Hertfordshire on 16th September 2001. In 2011, a single bird was seen at Lower Farm on 9th and 21st October. The latest recorded date was a juvenile at Dorney Wetlands on 13th December 2007.

*Sponsored by Kate Dent*

# Little Grebe

Amber

*Tachybaptus ruficollis*

*Widespread resident*

The Little Grebe is a widespread resident of smaller rivers, streams and water bodies in Berkshire. Although many waterbirds have fared well in recent decades in Berkshire, the breeding distribution maps produced by the 1987–89 and 2007–11 Atlas surveys indicate a marked contraction in the local breeding range. In the earlier survey, breeding was proved in 83 tetrads, but in the later survey only 43.

Comparison with the habitat maps shows that while, in general, areas with either standing or flowing water are favoured, there are some gaps in the species distribution even in the 1987–89 Tetrad survey, notably along the Thames. In 12 years of a Waterways Bird Survey from 1979 to 1990 on the Thames at Purley, the species was only been proved to breed once, whereas up to eight

Great Crested Grebe territories were recorded every year. Additionally, the species tends to avoid urban areas during the breeding season. The absence of the species from the Thames probably reflects the popularity of the river for both boating and waterside recreation. In the period between the two surveys, the number of occupied tetrads has reduced considerably in the Kennet Valley. The reopening of the Kennet and Avon Canal in 1990 may have had an adverse impact. The most recent survey also coincided with a period of low rainfall, and falling river levels, particularly for the Pang, which may have reduced available breeding sites.

The species tends to conceal its nest site well, but the noisy and distinctive, shrill call means that locating the striped young is relatively easy when they leave the nest and associate with adults. As a consequence, it seems likely that the results from the survey provide an accurate reflection of the breeding distribution of the species during both surveys.

As mentioned in the *1981–84 BTO Winter Atlas* and indicated by the winter tetrad map, some redistribution of the population occurs in winter, with birds tending to congregate on larger waters. Little Grebes were recorded from most of the Thames and Kennet in the winter survey. Counts of flocks outside the breeding season may provide an indication of local population levels, although these could also include passage birds or winter visitors. From 1949 to 1970, there were no records of more than 20 birds. This figure was exceeded in 1971 and 1973, and again in 1974 when there were 27 at Wraysbury Gravel Pits. In 1976, 51 were counted at Dinton Pastures on 5th September, the second highest count for the county. From 1976 to 1981, and again since 1987, one or two sites have regularly returned counts of over 20 birds, with

the highest count for Berkshire being 54 on the Berkshire section of the Jubilee River on 16th November 2005. The wide distribution of sites with high counts, from Wraysbury to Thatcham Gravel Pits, suggests that the pattern of winter movements may vary from year to year.

Clark Kennedy (1868) stated that the species "is common on our ponds, streams and lakes, and on the river Thames" and the *Historical Atlas* shows it as common in Berkshire at the end of the 19th century. Radford (1966) stated that the species declined in Berkshire from the 1930s to the 1950s but recovered thereafter. *Population Trends* notes an apparent peak at a national level in the late 1970s after a long run of mild winters, followed by an apparent slight downward trend during the early and mid-1980s when there were several cold winters, but no such definite pattern can be gleaned from local breeding records. In more recent years, it appears that the local status matches national trends. A decline of between 25% and 50% in the breeding population since 1974 has resulted in the species being placed on the Amber List of Birds of Conservation Concern (Baillie *et al.*, 2012), although winter numbers monitored by the national WeBS counts have shown a slight upward trend (Holt *et al.*, 2011). This indicates that numbers in winter are augmented by wintering birds from overseas.

*In memory of Ian Bell*

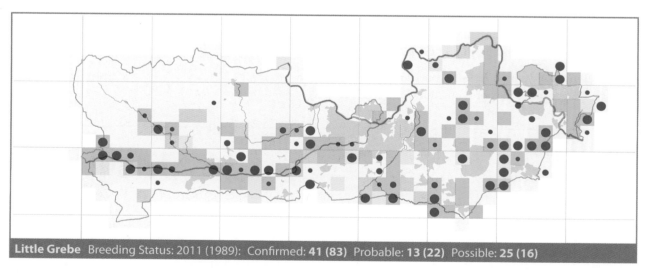

**Little Grebe** Breeding Status: 2011 (1989): Confirmed: **41 (83)** Probable: **13 (22)** Possible: **25 (16)**

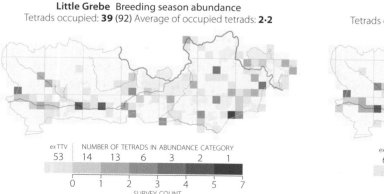

**Little Grebe** Breeding season abundance
Tetrads occupied: **39 (92)** Average of occupied tetrads: **2·2**

| exTTV | NUMBER OF TETRADS IN ABUNDANCE CATEGORY | | | | | |
|---|---|---|---|---|---|---|
| 53 | 14 | 13 | 6 | 3 | 2 | 1 |

0    1    2    3    4    5    7
SURVEY COUNT

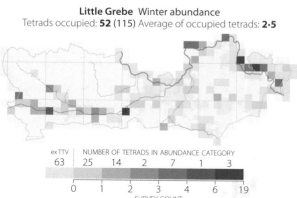

**Little Grebe** Winter abundance
Tetrads occupied: **52 (115)** Average of occupied tetrads: **2·5**

| exTTV | NUMBER OF TETRADS IN ABUNDANCE CATEGORY | | | | | |
|---|---|---|---|---|---|---|
| 63 | 25 | 14 | 2 | 7 | 1 | 3 |

0    1    2    3    4    6    19
SURVEY COUNT

# Great Crested Grebe

*Podiceps cristatus*

*Common resident and winter visitor*

The Great Crested Grebe is conspicuous on flooded gravel pits, reservoirs and the Thames, being both a resident and winter visitor in Berkshire. This has not always been the case as Clark Kennedy (1868) described it as occasionally occurring in the county, and the *Historical Atlas* indicated that it was rare at the end of the 19th century. The recovery of the species in Britain, after its near extinction in the 19th century through persecution, was one of the first successes for bird conservation and has been widely documented. Berkshire has been well placed to take advantage of this recovery due to the increase in the number of open water sites since the 1940s.

Table 1 gives the results for Berkshire of national surveys of Great Crested Grebes carried out in 1931, 1965 and 1975 and shows a marked increase in the number of occupied waters and in the population. This is also confirmed by the *1988–91 BTO Atlas* which showed that Berkshire is one of the species' strongholds in the south of England. Some of this increase may be attributable to its tolerance of human disturbance, as noted by the *1981–84 BTO Winter*

|  | 1931 | 1965 | 1975 |
|---|---|---|---|
| No. of waters holding birds | 11 | 17 | 40 |
| No. of adult birds | 58 | 141–150 | 302–340 |

**Table 1**: **Great Crested Grebe: BTO survey results for Berkshire**

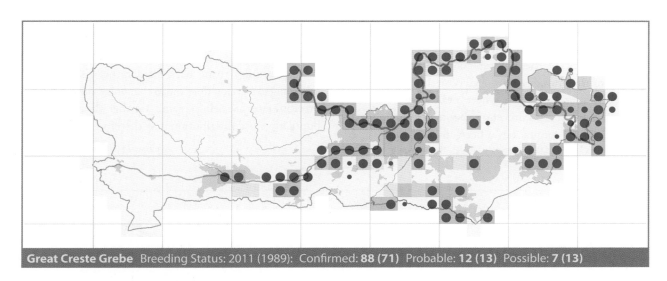

Great Creste Grebe  Breeding Status: 2011 (1989):  Confirmed: **88 (71)**  Probable: **12 (13)**  Possible: **7 (13)**

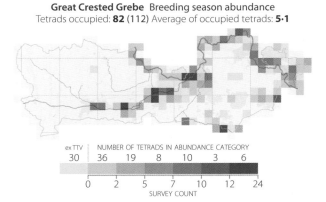

**Great Crested Grebe**  Breeding season abundance
Tetrads occupied: **82** (112) Average of occupied tetrads: **5·1**

| exTTV | NUMBER OF TETRADS IN ABUNDANCE CATEGORY | | | | | |
|---|---|---|---|---|---|---|
| 30 | 36 | 19 | 8 | 10 | 3 | 6 |

| 0 | 2 | 5 | 7 | 10 | 12 | 24 |

SURVEY COUNT

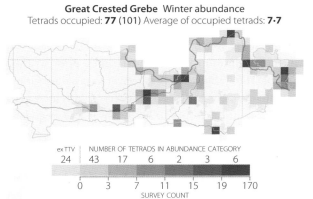

**Great Crested Grebe**  Winter abundance
Tetrads occupied: **77** (101) Average of occupied tetrads: **7·7**

| exTTV | NUMBER OF TETRADS IN ABUNDANCE CATEGORY | | | | | |
|---|---|---|---|---|---|---|
| 24 | 43 | 17 | 6 | 2 | 3 | 6 |

| 0 | 3 | 7 | 11 | 15 | 19 | 170 |

SURVEY COUNT

*Atlas* and county reports. Unlike the Little Grebe, the Great Crested Grebe apparently does not avoid urban areas.

Comparison of the Tetrad Survey maps for both seasons, and the habitat maps for open water areas, shows that the available area of open water is an important factor affecting the Great Crested Grebe's distribution. The distribution of the species closely matches that of the largest lakes and flooded gravel pits and the Thames. The species' preference for larger water bodies is mentioned frequently in the literature and it is therefore understandable that the widest river in the county, the Thames, has been colonised. The 1987–89 Tetrad Survey found Great Crested Grebes breeding in two 10 km squares in which they were not recorded during the *1968–72 BTO Atlas* and where the only open water is the Thames. County reports indicate that its use of the river was first recorded in the dry summer of 1976, when 16 pairs attempted to breed in areas where none were recorded during the 1975 BTO survey. The 2007–11 Tetrad Survey map shows a very similar distribution throughout the county, and the species was well established along the river in Berkshire, and the winter map shows a similar distribution. Nationally it appears the long term increase in this species may have peaked in the early years of the 21st Century, and may have declined slightly since (Baillie *et al.*, 2012)

The status of the Great Crested Grebe outside the breeding season has been monitored nationally since 1982 by the WeBS counts (formerly the WWT winter wildfowl counts). The highest counts have generally been from the gravel pits around Wraysbury and from Queen Mother Reservoir, where peak winter counts sometimes exceed 100. In central Berkshire, the highest regular winter counts have been from Theale and Burghfield Gravel Pits, which usually have peak winter counts in excess of 60 and 40 respectively. Other sites regularly producing counts in excess of 20 include Bray Gravel Pits, Thatcham Gravel Pits, Twyford Gravel Pits, Virginia Water and Woolhampton Gravel Pits.

In winter some flocking and movement occurs. National count figures show an autumn peak, followed by a trough in mid-winter and a recovery during the spring. The *1981–84 BTO Winter Atlas* states that whilst there may be an influx of continental birds in mid- winter, this is more than offset by the movement of birds out to the coast and beyond. The Queen Mother Reservoir, which normally holds less than 70 birds in winter, has recorded the highest counts for Berkshire in hard weather: 290 in February 1978 and 300 in February 1986. These counts have coincided with the freezing over of shallower gravel pits and lakes. Freezing conditions can result in most birds leaving the county. In the cold spell of February 1986 there were no sites, apart from Queen Mother Reservoir, where more than eight birds were recorded.

The WeBS counts have revealed a wintering population of some 350 birds on those open waters regularly counted. A 2·5 km stretch of the Thames at Purley, the only stretch regularly counted, usually holds between three and seven birds. If this density is representative, then the 80 km of the Thames along the county boundary could hold another 100–200 individuals.

The Great Crested Grebe's tolerance of human disturbance should enable it to sustain its present population levels, but the increasing tendency for gravel workings to be back-filled rather than flooded following extraction does mean that fewer new potential breeding sites are being created. Further expansion of its population and distribution may therefore be limited.

*Sponsored by John & Susan Palmer*

# Red-necked Grebe  Amber

## *Podiceps grisegena*

*Scarce winter visitor and passage migrant*

The Red-necked Grebe was, until 1966, a rare vagrant to Berkshire, the only records being of one shot at Burghfield in 1792 (Lamb, 1880), and one shot at Greenlands, presumably on the Thames, prior to 1867 (Stubbs, 1867). Since one was seen at Wraysbury Gravel Pits in November 1966, it was observed with increasing frequency until the mid-1990s, but was less frequently encountered in the first decade of the present century, as illustrated in Figure 44.

As records increased in the 1980s, Red-necked Grebes showed a growing tendency for early arrival and longer

stays. The earliest record was of a first-winter bird at Dinton Pastures on 13th September 1989, and

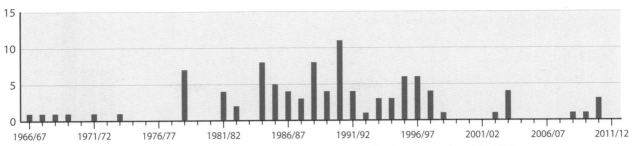

Figure 44:  Red-necked Grebe: birds recorded each winter 1966/67–2011/12.

there were later September arrivals in 1996 at Queen Mother Reservoir on the 22nd and Wraysbury on the 29th, and at Theale Main Pit on 29th September 2012. The first bird to stay for longer than two months was in the winter of 1981/82 and the first for longer than three months in 1984/85. The longest stay was a bird which arrived at Queen Mother Reservoir in November 1993 and remained throughout the following summer until November 1994. In the winter of 1988/89 there were intermittent records of a bird at Queen Mother Reservoir from 3rd October to 17th March, and another was at Woolhampton Gravel Pits from 28th November 2002 to 6th May 2003. Most wintering birds depart towards the end of February or early in March, with April records probably relating to returning passage birds. A summary of arrival dates between the winters of 1966/67 and 2010/11 is shown in Figure 45. Most early winter records have been of immature birds, and many of the birds which have lingered into late winter have attained full summer plumage before departure. The latest post-winter departure dates have been 14th May in 1996 at Dinton Pastures and at Wraysbury in 2004.

*Sponsored by Peter Standley*

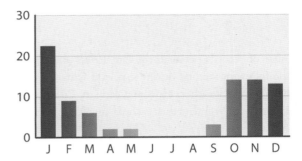

Figure 45:  Red-necked Grebe: all birds recorded 1966/67–2011/12, by month of arrival.

# Slavonian Grebe

Amber   Sch. 1

*Podiceps auritus*

*Uncommon winter visitor and passage migrant*

The Slavonian Grebe is an uncommon winter visitor and passage migrant to Berkshire, which showed an increase in numbers in the 1980s and 1990s. Most records have been from the lakes and gravel pits in east Berkshire, notably the Queen Mother Reservoir, where 34 of the 73 birds recorded from 1981 to July 2013 occurred. The majority of records have been of single birds, with the highest counts being four at Queen Mother Reservoir in October 1987, three there in November 1994, November 1997 and November 2011, and at Hambridge Lake in January 1966. The five-yearly totals of Slavonian Grebe records from 1945 to 2009 are shown in Figure 46. As with Red-necked Grebe, there was a decline in the

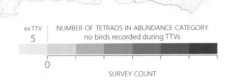

**Slavonian Grebe** Winter abundance
Tetrads occupied: **0** (5) Average of occupied tetrads: **0**

ex TTV | NUMBER OF TETRADS IN ABUNDANCE CATEGORY
5 | no birds recorded during TTVs

0

SURVEY COUNT

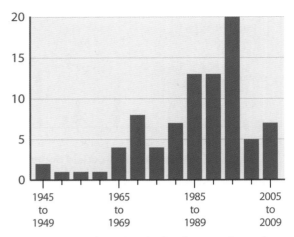

**Figure 46: Slavonian Grebe: five-yearly totals, 1945–2009.**

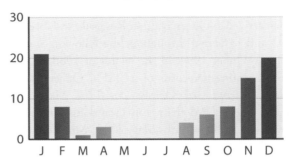

**Figure 47: Slavonian Grebe: all birds recorded 1945–2009, by month of arrival.**

number of records between the late 1990s and the end of the following decade during a period with few spells of hard winter weather. However, January 2010 to July 2013 provided eight further records involving a total of 11 birds.

Figure 47 provides an analysis of the dates when birds were first seen from 1945 to 2012. The county records reflect the national picture, Slavonian Grebes being primarily winter visitors to Britain with some limited passage along the east coast in spring and autumn (*1981–84 BTO Winter Atlas*). The earliest autumn arrival date was on 20th August in 1970 at Burghfield Gravel Pits and the latest post-winter departure was on 27th April in 1971 at Theale Gravel Pits.

The duration of stay has varied from one day to over two months, the longest apparently being of birds seen intermittently from 20th August to 6th December 1970 at Burghfield Gravel Pits and from 1st December 1986 to 17th February 1987 in the Wraysbury area.

The only 19th century records of Slavonian Grebe in Berkshire were of single birds shot in 1858, 1861 and 1865 (Clark Kennedy, 1868), and two shot at Newbury in February 1870 (Herbert, 1871).

*Sponsored by Liz Wild*

# Black-necked Grebe   Amber   Sch. 1

*Podiceps nigricollis*

*Uncommon winter visitor and passage migrant*

The Black-necked Grebe is an uncommon winter visitor and passage migrant to Berkshire, which has occurred almost annually in recent years. The first record for the county was from Virginia Water on 6th December 1936 and there were further, scattered records thereafter from December 1945 until 1969. The increase in the area of open water in Berkshire from 1970 led to an almost four-fold increase in the number of records, with annual sightings from 1979 to 1989. Inexplicably, none were recorded from 1990 to 1993, although there were three in 1994. Thereafter records have remained at or above the higher levels of the late 1980s. Two years have produced more than ten records: 1998, when there were 14, and 1999, when there were 11. A summary of the records for five-year periods from 1945 to 2009 is given

in Figure 48. Most records have been from gravel pits, with only five of the 44 records between 1980 and 1994 coming from Queen Mother Reservoir, although this site has produced about 20% of the records since.

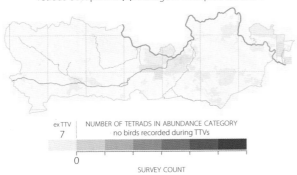

**Black-necked Grebe** Winter abundance
Tetrads occupied: **0** (7) Average of occupied tetrads: **0**

exTTV
7

NUMBER OF TETRADS IN ABUNDANCE CATEGORY
no birds recorded during TTVs

0

SURVEY COUNT

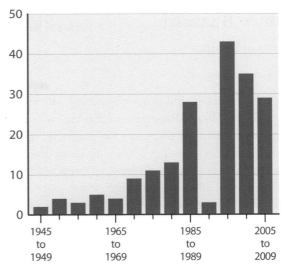

**Figure 48: Black-necked Grebe: five-yearly totals, 1945–2009.**

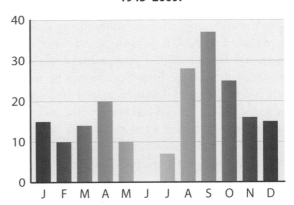

**Figure 49: Black-necked Grebe: all birds recorded 1945–2009, by month of arrival.**

A summary of the arrival dates of Black-necked Grebes in Berkshire is shown in Figure 49 and indicates that this species, unlike Slavonian and Red-necked Grebes, is predominantly a passage migrant through the county. The duration of stay also tends to be shorter, there having been only one bird which has stayed for longer than a month. This was an exceptional record of one at Theale Gravel Pits from 12th November 1986 to 2nd June 1987. The relatively low number of records in January and February is not unexpected, as the species is less tolerant of cold weather than are other grebes and tends to move south onto the continent at this time of year (*1981–84 BTO Winter Atlas*).

The highest number of birds which have occurred together in the county is four at Queen Mother Reservoir on 26th April 2009 and again there on 26th April 2013. There have been six or seven records of three together up to July 2013, all at gravel pits: Burghfield in August 1971, Wraysbury in April 1975, Theale in August 1984 and three at Woolhampton from 17th to 25th March 2011, which may be the same three that were at Moatlands Gravel Pit, Theale on the 28th March 2011. The spring of 2013 produced records of three again at Woolhampton from 24th March to 10th April 2013, and at Theale from 24th to 27th March. Most records, however, are of singles. The earliest arrivals have been at Dinton Pastures on 14th

July 1999, Ham on 19th July 1960 and two at Wraysbury Gravel Pits on 20th July 1971. Apart from the long-staying individual mentioned previously, the latest post-winter departure date was one at Lower Farm Gravel Pit, Thatcham from 27th to 29th May 2000. Full summer plumage has been attained by some late departing or passage birds from March onwards.

*Sponsored by Ray Reedman*

Black-necked Grebe, Rowney Predator Lake *Josie Hewitt*

# Honey Buzzard

**Amber** **Sch. 1**

*Pernis apivorus*

*Rare summer migrant*

There is a small breeding population of around 40 pairs of Honey Buzzards in Britain, mostly in central and southern counties (Holling *et al.*, 2011), however, in Berkshire, the Honey Buzzard has been recorded only on passage. It was not reported in the county in the 20th century until 1964, since when there were records in a further 11 years to the end of the century and in six years from 2000 to 2011. Records have usually been of single birds except for a remarkable passage involving at least 30 individuals in late September and early October 2000.

During the last 10 days of September and the first week of October 2000, approximately 2000 Honey Buzzards were recorded in the UK, most in south east England (Fraser and Rogers, 2002), presumably displaced on their southerly passage from Scandinavia by easterly winds in that period. In Berkshire, at least 30 birds were recorded, mostly in the east and centre of the county and heading southwards, and 19 of the records came from the Cookham and Maidenhead area, including eight on the 25th September, which included three separate records of two together.

All other records have been isolated, single day sightings, usually lone birds. Individuals were seen over Ham Sewage Farm on 4th September 1964, at Silwood on 8th July 1965, over Swinley on 16th September 1968, and again there on 3rd May 1975, over Whiteknights Park on 8th May 1976 being mobbed by Rooks, and flying south over Theale Gravel Pits on 2nd September 1979. In 1980, the only other record of more than one bird was obtained when two birds were seen flying north over Midgham on 1st June. Thereafter, singles were seen in Windsor Great Park on 13th June 1981 and again on 22nd September 1984 flying south mobbed by crows, over Crowthorne on 8th May 1989, over Eversley Gravel Pits on 3rd August 1991, flying north-west over central Reading on 19th July 1993 and near Bracknell on 4th June 1994, flying south over Eversley Gravel Pits on 18th September 1995. One landed in a tree at Eversley Gravel Pits on 12th July 1997. One was seen mobbed by crows at Theale 20th September 1998; one flew south-east over Bray 21st September 2001; one flew southwest over Pingewood on 7th September 2002; one flew west over Caversham on 1st May 2006; one flew south over Moatlands Gravel Pit, Theale on 15th September 2006 and one headed north-west over Dorney Wetlands on 9th June 2011. Where the direction in which the birds were flying was noted, the birds seen in May to July were

flying in a northerly direction and all those in August and September were flying south or south-west.

Prior to 1900, there are just three records of Honey Buzzard in Berkshire: a female shot near Reading in 1793 (Lamb, 1880), one trapped in Windsor Forest in 1860 (Clark Kennedy, 1868) and one shot at Bucklebury in 1875 (Palmer, 1886). Two records which were formerly attributed to Berkshire have been omitted from the above account, one of which was a bird referred to by Clark Kennedy (1868), as a "Montagu's specimen which was shot in Berkshire" but which was actually obtained at Highclere in Hampshire, and the other of two birds at a wasp's nest in August 1949 which were actually observed at Ashmansworth in Hampshire.

So far records of Honey Buzzards in Berkshire appear to have been birds on passage. However, with areas of suitable habitat in the south and west of the county and an increase in recent years in the UK breeding population, we can perhaps look forward to the Honey Buzzard joining the growing list of raptor species breeding in the county.

*Sponsored by Michael Taylor*

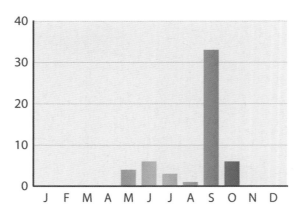

**Figure 50: Honey Buzzard: all birds recorded 1964–2011, by month.** Includes 24 in an exceptional passage in September 2000.

# Black Kite

*Milvus migrans*

*Rare vagrant, one record*

The only accepted record of this species, whose usual range extends north to central France, was one seen for about 40 minutes at Hodcott Down, West Ilsley on 26th June 2001.

*Sponsored by James, Alex and Emily Dryden*

# Red Kite

Amber  Sch. 1

*Milvus milvus*

*Widespread resident following a recent re-introduction*

Formerly resident in Berkshire, the Red Kite was eliminated by persecution in the 18th century, and had since been a rare vagrant until a recent reintroduction programme by the Joint Nature Conservation Committee and the RSPB starting in the Chilterns in 1989. Between 1989 and 1994, kites from Spain were imported and released at a site in the Chilterns, where they started breeding in 1992. The introduction was very successful and the population in southern England

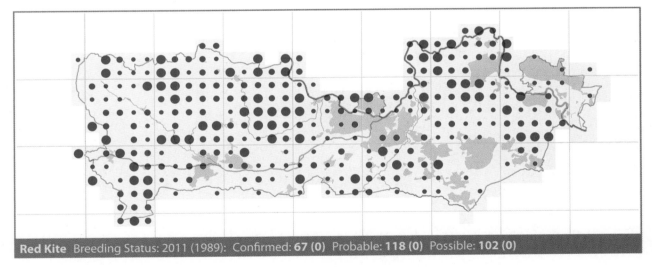

**Red Kite** Breeding Status: 2011 (1989): Confirmed: **67 (0)** Probable: **118 (0)** Possible: **102 (0)**

**Red Kite** Breeding season abundance
Tetrads occupied: **256 (360)** Average of occupied tetrads: **3·0**

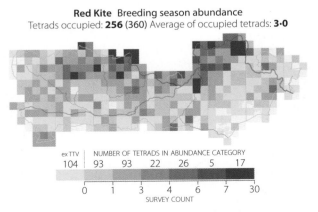

| ex TTV | NUMBER OF TETRADS IN ABUNDANCE CATEGORY | | | | | |
|---|---|---|---|---|---|---|
| 104 | 93 | 93 | 22 | 26 | 5 | 17 |

0   1   3   4   6   7   30
SURVEY COUNT

**Red Kite** Winter abundance
Tetrads occupied: **241 (354)** Average of occupied tetrads: **3·9**

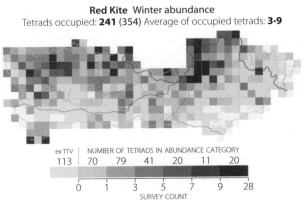

| ex TTV | NUMBER OF TETRADS IN ABUNDANCE CATEGORY | | | | | |
|---|---|---|---|---|---|---|
| 113 | 70 | 79 | 41 | 20 | 11 | 20 |

0   1   3   5   7   9   28
SURVEY COUNT

in 2010 was estimated to be around 800 pairs (Holling *et al.*, 2012).

Marked birds from the Chilterns introduction were first seen in Berkshire in 1990 and sightings increased rapidly over the succeeding decade. Breeding attempts in Berkshire were first recorded in 2000 near Great Shefford, where a pair nested but failed to raise young, and the Woolley Down/Farnborough Down area, where a pair were seen mating. In 2006 the ROC and NDOC organised a county-wide survey of Buzzards and Red Kites. It was estimated from the results that 51 pairs bred or attempted to breed in the county (Robinson, 2007). The 2007–11 Atlas surveys produced confirmed breeding in 67 tetrads and probable breeding in a further 118.

The breeding distribution map reflects the Red Kite's preference for nesting in areas of deciduous woodland and fields. Out of the breeding season, the birds range widely and can be found feeding on recently cut hay meadows, following ploughs, along roadsides and in suburban gardens. The summer and winter abundance maps show the Red Kite to have become almost ubiquitous in the county, with the greatest concentrations on the Berkshire Downs, where the winter roosts at Woolley Down and Sparrow's Copse held 122 birds in December 2008, and the Cookham area, where 86 were seen together in December 2010. Attracted perhaps by food provided for them in gardens, Kites are commonly seen in many residential areas, with 10 – 20 often seen in the air together in 2012 over the Woodley and Earley area.

Prior to the re-introduction programme the first 20th century record involved two birds seen over Unhill Wood on the Oxfordshire side of the county boundary in the spring of 1926, which are likely to have entered Berkshire. With improved observer coverage from the 1950s there have been occasional records, with single over-flying birds at Silwood in October 1951, at Wraysbury in April 1958, at Windsor in October 1964, at Crowthorne in July 1977 and at Emmbrook in October 1979. In the 1980s there were three further records: single birds near East Ilsley in May 1984, over Greenham in April 1986, and over Easthampstead Park in November 1988. The County records in the 1970s and 1980s occurred during a period when the Welsh Red Kite population had been steadily increasing and there had also been an increase in the continental population. As immature birds have a strong tendency to disperse once they fledge, Berkshire records up to 1989 are likely to have been of birds from either or both of those sources.

Historically, the only published references to Red Kites in Berkshire are by Lamb (1880) who indicates that they were frequent about Reading prior to 1784, and includes a specific record from that area in May 1795, and a somewhat vague statement by Clark Kennedy (1868) that one had been seen "many years ago" near Eton.

*Sponsored by Bob & Mary Jacobs*

Red Kite, Queen Mother Reservoir  *Michael McKee*

# White-tailed Eagle

Sch. 1

*Haliaeetus albicilla*

*Rare vagrant, five records involving six birds*

The White-tailed Eagle has not been recorded in Berkshire since 1927, prior to which there were four records involving five birds, four between 1851 and 1865. Additionally, there are two old Golden Eagle records, at Shottesbrooke in 1794 (Lamb, 1880) and at Billingbear before 1868 (Clark Kennedy, 1868), which seem more likely to have been immature White-tailed Eagles.

In 1851, one was shot near Windsor and exhibited at the Great Exhibition of that year before being presented to Eton College by the Prince Consort. A further bird was shot in Windsor Great Park in December 1856, and in the summer of 1865 two birds were present in the Park, an immature which was shot and a second bird which was wounded and captured (Clark Kennedy, 1868). According to the notice in the glass case in which this bird is preserved, it was kept alive for 33 years before it

"died in a fit" and Queen Victoria arranged for it to be preserved. It can now be seen in the entrance hall of the Crown Estate Office in the Park.

The remaining two records are of one shot at Rapley Lake in 1887 (Noble, 1906) and one seen at Combe a few days after being observed at Highclere, Hampshire on 18th December 1927. A record of one shot at Littlecote in 1847 (Radford, 1966) is properly attributable to Wiltshire.

*Sponsored by Maryanne Thomas*

---

# Marsh Harrier

Amber  Sch. 1

*Circus aeruginosus*

*Scarce passage migrant, recently wintering and summering*

The Marsh Harrier remains a scarce passage migrant through Berkshire, although it has increased in recent years and single birds have remained through the winter and summer. It bred in the county during the 18th and early 19th centuries, but persecution and habitat destruction reduced its status across Britain to a scarce vagrant until 1927 when it again began to breed regularly (*1981–84 BTO Winter Atlas*). The national decline and resurgence of the Marsh Harrier is reflected in the county records, there being no published 20th century records until 1948 when a harrier which was considered to be possibly this species was seen at Reading Sewage Farm on 24th July. A month later one was seen at Ham Fields from 26th August to 1st September. These records were followed by one at Slough Sewage Farm on

31st May 1954 and, in 1955, a first-year bird which was recovered on the "Newbury Downs" on or about 30th July which had been ringed as a nestling at Hickling Broad, Norfolk, a few weeks earlier on 19th June. It is assumed that the bird was found in the Combe area.

Records remained sporadic at about one every two years from 1960 to 1970, before declining in the 1970s to just single records in 1972 and 1975. This followed a national

**Marsh Harrier** Spring migration occurrence
Tetrads used: **14** Average of used tetrads: **1·4**

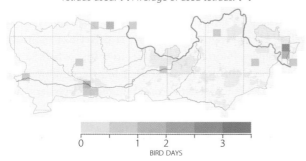

0   1   2   3
BIRD DAYS

**Marsh Harrier** Autumn migration occurrence
Tetrads used: **18** Average of used tetrads: **2·0**

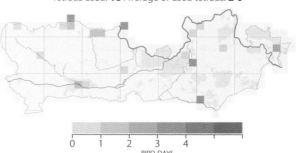
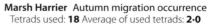

0   1   2   3   4
BIRD DAYS

decline in breeding pairs to just one in 1971 (*1981–84 BTO Winter Atlas*). County records then increased, with 14 sightings from 1981 to 1994, in line with the rise in breeding numbers nationally to 110 breeding females in 1990 (Spencer *et al.*, 1993). From 1982 to 1998, Marsh Harriers were recorded passing through the county in many years (the exceptions being 1985, 1988 to 1990, 1992, 1995 and 1996), but from 1999 onwards the number of records continued to increase, with at least three birds being recorded annually. (2004 had records of at least 11 birds, 2011 as many as 13). Again, this increase is broadly in line with the continued national increase in breeding birds, which reached an estimated 404 females in 2005–09 (Holling *et al.*, 2011).

Figure 51 shows the number of Marsh Harriers seen each month in Berkshire from 1948 to 2010. The increase in April to June records since 1981 probably involves birds returning to their breeding areas in eastern England from wintering grounds in South Wales, southeast Ireland, southern Europe and North Africa, areas where they are known to spend the winter (*1981–84 BTO Winter Atlas*). Sightings have come from various sites across the county, often, but not always, over bodies of water.

The great majority of Marsh Harrier records in Berkshire since 1900 have been of single birds, with a mixture of males, females and immature birds being reported, the exception being a report of a male and female seen together over Thatcham on May 7th 2006. There have been a few records of passage birds as early as mid-March, but the peak of spring movement occurs in April and May, while autumn migration starts as early as July, peaking in August and September (often involving immature birds). The first recorded wintering of Marsh Harrier since at least 1875 was in the Horton area in 2011/12, and in 2013 a female summered in the extended wetland area at Moor Green Lakes. These records may herald this charismatic bird's return to Berkshire as a breeding species in the near future.

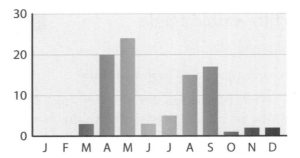

**Figure 51: Marsh Harrier: all birds recorded 1948–2010, by month of arrival.**

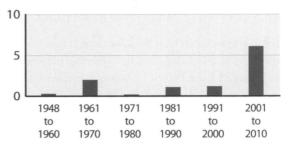

**Figure 52: Marsh Harrier: average number of birds recorded per year.**

Prior to 1900, Lamb (1880) stated that in 1814 Marsh Harriers were "the most common hawk in the marshes about Newbury" where they were "very destructive to the young wild ducks". Although Clark Kennedy (1868) assessed the species as "resident throughout the year" this was not supported by specific records and it remains unclear how far into the 19th century Marsh Harriers continued to breed in the Kennet Valley. By 1906, the species was considered a rare wanderer by Noble (1906). His only specific records were of one shot at Kintbury in 1875 on the unusual date of 13th January, which from the description provided was probably an adult female, and an adult male shot and injured at Swallowfield on 2nd October 1899, which was kept alive until March 1900 and is now in Reading Museum.

*Sponsored by Rodney Hill*

# Hen Harrier

`Red` `Sch. 1`

*Circus cyaneus*

*Scarce passage migrant and winter visitor*

The Hen Harrier is reported as a passage migrant in Berkshire, but the majority of sightings are of wintering birds, mainly from the downland areas in the west of the county. There were no published 20th century records of the species in the county until a female was seen on the Compton Downs in November 1925, followed by a single bird at Lower Whitley in December 1926, a male and a female in the Inkpen to Combe area in the winter of 1927/28 and a male at Caesar's Camp in November

1928. In the 1930s, four further birds were recorded from 1934 to 1937, including a male and a female at Pinkneys Green from 9th to 12th April 1937.

Figure 53 shows the estimated number of birds seen on passage or wintering in Berkshire from 1947/48 to 2010/11 and Figure 54 shows the pattern of monthly occurrence. Fourteen "probable" records, which arise from the difficulty in separating female or immature (ringtail) Hen Harriers from Montagu's Harriers, are not included in the figures.

The pattern of records of Hen Harrier in Berkshire changed significantly and abruptly from the winter of 1968/69. During the winters from 1947/48 to 1967/68 the species was only recorded in five winters, although there were records for several other years from the Oxfordshire side of the Downs. Since the winter of 1968/69, however, records have been annual, with the exception of 1977/78. The increase in the number of birds recorded was also significant, from none between 1963/64 and 1967/68 to five in 1968/69, three in 1969/70 and five, including two probables, in 1970/71. Some increase in records was not unexpected, as at this time there was a marked increase in numbers generally in East Anglia and south-east England (*1981–84 BTO Winter Atlas*). Improved observer coverage may also have played a part, but it is not clear why the increase in numbers after 1968 should have been so marked. Since 1969 there have been several winters when three to five birds have been recorded on passage or wintering, with peaks of eight in 1981/82, seven in 1982/83 and four to seven in the winters from 2007/08 to 2010/11, despite a recent decline in the British breeding population (Sim *et al.*, 2007a, Holling & RBBP 2011b).

Records away from the Downs since 1980 have come from a variety of sites, including wetland sites such as gravel pits, lakes and reservoirs, as well as commons and farmland, although these have mainly been passage rather than longer-staying birds, with the exception of a ringtail which was seen at Brimpton Gravel Pits on several dates from 14th December 1986 to 4th January 1987.

The earliest arrival dates in Berkshire have been of one at West Ilsley on 26th August 2009 and an adult female shot at Bisham on 31st August 1970, which pre-date by only a few days two subsequent arrivals in early September. Birds probably of this species were seen at Cookham on 24th August 1936 and at Burghfield on 19th August 1938, although the possibility that these were Montagu's Harriers cannot be ruled out.

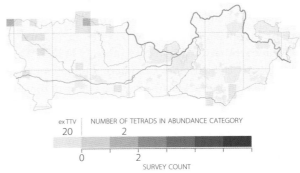

**Hen Harrier**   Winter abundance
Tetrads occupied: **2** (22) Average of occupied tetrads: **1·0**

exTTV | NUMBER OF TETRADS IN ABUNDANCE CATEGORY
20 | 2

0       2
SURVEY COUNT

A slight increase in records occurs from the second half of September and during October, with the main arrival of wintering birds in November. Passage records away from the Downs continue through December and January, supporting the suggestion by Watson (1977) that a westerly movement of birds into Britain occurs in mid-winter. Wintering birds often remain on the Downs well into March and occasionally into April, including a ringtail in the Compton to Aldworth area until 16th April 1983, ringtails at Catmore on 14th April and at Eastbury on 26th April in 1988, and three at Thatcham on 22nd April 2006. The latest spring date in Berkshire was of an adult male flying over Windsor Great Park on 29th May 2006. Most passage birds in spring have been recorded for one day only. The only summer record is of a male seen in the east of the county on 1st June 1990, but a ringtail harrier seen at Lambourn on 12th June 1989 was also thought to have been this species.

Of the 172 Hen Harriers recorded in Berkshire from 1947/48 to 2010/11, 42 were identified as adult, grey males, which, allowing for the fact that some records are unspecified, means that a significant majority of birds have been ringtails or females. Most records have been of single birds, although there have been records of two

birds together: a grey male with a ringtail on the Downs in February 1970, January 1982, December 1990, March 1993 and December 1993, and two ringtails on the Downs in January in 1983, 1985, 1994, in November 1995 and February 2012. In November 1990 there were two ringtails at Snelsmore Common, the only multiple record away from the Downs, except a report of three in April 2006 at Thatcham that does not appear to have been submitted to the Records Committee, and is not included within the analysis in this account. There are no records of larger numbers from within the present county boundary and no records of communal roosting which occurs quite widely elsewhere in Britain during the winter.

It is likely that Hen Harriers bred in Berkshire up to about the middle of the 19th century. Lamb (1880) records that a pair of harriers nested in "an extensive furze field" in June 1790, probably in the Newbury area, although he fails to mention the location. Both parents were caught and the young kept in captivity "for a long time in a garden and proved to be ringtails and Hen Harriers". This record must be questionable because it was not until 1802 that it was first suggested by George Montagu that Hen and Montagu's Harriers should be treated as separate species. A reference by Hewett (1844) to Hen Harriers breeding near Compton is unsupported by date or detail, but Hewett (1911) writing in the 1860s about the birds of the Compton district, refers to the arrival of Hen Harriers in March to breed and to them "having young ones in furze on the Downs" in June.

Clark Kennedy (1868) described the Hen Harrier as a resident but without providing supporting evidence.

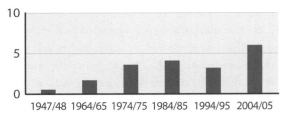

Figure 53: **Hen Harrier: average number of birds recorded per year.**

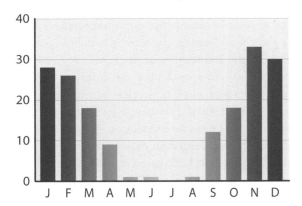

Figure 54: **Hen Harrier: all birds recorded 1947/48–2010/11, by month of arrival.**

Noble's (1906) description of the species as a rare visitor fits the pattern of available records from the middle of the 19th century, for which there are seven in the period 1855 to 1900. These include a male and a female flushed from heathland near Crowthorne in September 1886 and a male and a female seen at Earley in spring 1887. The remaining five records are of single birds, all shot, in 1855, 1857, 1859 or 1860, during the 1860s and in 1885. None of these birds were seen or procured on the Downs.

*Sponsored by Richard Capewell*

# Montagu's Harrier  Amber  Sch. 1

## *Circus pygargus*

*Rare passage migrant which has summered*

The Montagu's Harrier is a scarce summer visitor to Britain, typically arriving during April and departing during September and October. An average of 15 pairs were recorded as breeding in southern and eastern England in the years 2005 to 2009 (Holling *et al.*, 2011). It is the rarest of the harriers in Berkshire, with only 28 records involving 25 birds during the 20th century, although sightings have increased since 2000 coinciding with the presence of breeding birds in nearby Oxfordshire.

The first half of the 20th century produced only three records involving four birds: a female seen at Padworth on 16th August 1925, a pair on the Downs near West Ilsley in the summer of 1934, when attempted breeding was suspected, and one at Swallowfield on 16th July 1943.

An increase in the number of observers from the 1950s is no doubt partly responsible for the higher numbers recorded since, although there was an increase in the British breeding population in the late 1940s and early

1950s before numbers declined to a low level through the 1960s and 1970s (*1968–72 BTO Atlas*).

From 1950 to 2000 there was a further 25 records involving 21 birds, all but the following six records coming from the Downs: an adult male at Reading Sewage Farm on 20th April 1959; one, probably an adult female, at the same site on 10th September 1968; a male hunting over Snelsmore Common on 14th April 1970; a ringtail at a site in east Berkshire on 12th June 1988; an immature female over Wraysbury Gravel Pits on 2nd September 1995 and an immature bird at Lower Farm Gravel Pits on 9th August 1997. The successful breeding of a pair on the Oxfordshire side of county boundary in 1986, as detailed by Brucker *et al.*, (1992), generated several records in adjacent areas of Berkshire.

There has been an increase in Berkshire records since 2000, again coinciding with the summering of a pair across the border in Oxfordshire (present from 1995), with the majority of sightings being close to the county boundary. Away from the Downs, a female was seen over North East Reading on 24th June 2006 and a juvenile circled over Lea Farm Gravel Pit on 26th August 2007. Single birds of the rare melanistic form have been recorded twice in recent years, one at an undisclosed site and date in 2004 and a first-summer male at an undisclosed site from 16th July to 11th August 2005.

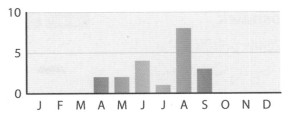

**Figure 55: Montagu's Harrier: all birds recorded 1925–2011, by month of arrival.** Excludes summering birds.

The monthly totals of Montagu's Harrier in Berkshire, excluding birds present throughout the summer, are shown in Figure 55. Although the number of sightings has been small, the records indicate some passage through the county in April/May and in August/September, with wandering birds probably accounting for the records during the summer months. It is possible that some of the nine ringtails recorded as probable Hen Harrier (*page 196*) occurring between April and September were in fact Montagu's Harriers.

Prior to 1900, the only specific 19th century references to the Montagu's Harrier, following its differentiation from the Hen Harrier in 1802, are of one "procured near Eton in the summer of 1867" (Clark Kennedy, 1868) and a male "of the dark variety" killed at Hall Place between Maidenhead and Hurley in September or October 1870 (Noble, 1912). A possible earlier record for 1790 (Lamb, 1880) is considered under Hen Harrier.

*In memory of Phil White*

Montagu's Harrier, Lambourn area *Jerry O'Brien*

# Goshawk

*Accipiter gentilis*

*Rare vagrant, may have bred.*

The Goshawk is a rare vagrant and occasional escapee in Berkshire, which may have bred or attempted to breed in recent years. Except when soaring, the Goshawk is generally very unobtrusive and easily overlooked in its preferred habitat of extensive woodland (*1968–72 BTO Atlas*). It is also an early nester, starting in March.

The Rare Breeding Birds Panel reported an increase between 1975 and 2010 from five to 295 confirmed breeding pairs in the UK (Spencer *et al.*, 1986, Holling *et al.*, 2012). The species is popular with falconers and the current UK population is probably derived exclusively from birds that have escaped or been released from captivity (*1981–84 BTO Winter Atlas*).

The first recorded sighting from within the present county boundary was in 1956 when one was seen well at Sunninghill on 15th and 16th October. There were no further sightings until the mid-1970s when it appears that breeding may have been attempted, a pair being seen displaying at one site in 1977. This was supported by claimed sightings of single birds from adjacent areas from 1975 to 1977. The increase in the frequency of sightings which has occurred since 1975 coincides with a similar increase in records for Oxfordshire (Brucker *et al.*, 1992). In Berkshire, after a gap in records from 1977 until 1982 when one was seen at Horton Gravel Pits in February, sightings have been reported most years, though the possibility of confusion with large female Sparrowhawks, a species that has expanded across the country along with Goshawks, has led to many records being regarded as "not proven". Goshawks may have attempted to breed again in Berkshire at one, perhaps two, sites in 1988, with display observed in spring at one of these. Neither of the 1988 sites were where birds were seen displaying in 1977.

Since 1990, there have been 11 records accepted by the BRC, two of which were presumed escapees, one bearing a ring, the other jesses. The other sightings were across the county: Combe Hill, Farnborough Down, Streatley, Eversley, the Reading area, the Windsor area and a bird on prey at Englefield. No evidence of breeding within Berkshire has been reported since 1988, though probable breeding has been recorded in the 2007–11 tetrad survey at two sites just outside the county boundary. The 1987–89 survey produced six records of individuals, but no evidence of probable or possible breeding, although identification is uncertain for the reasons set out above.

The only reports of prey taken involved a bird in 1987 which was watched and photographed in the garden of a house at Earley on 19th September with its kill of a Collared Dove (although not wearing jesses, in view of the suburban location of this record, the bird may have been an escapee), and a bird at Englefield on 14th December 1999 on unspecified prey.

Although it is a protected species, the Goshawk can be subject to the adverse attentions of egg collectors, falconers and keepers. This may further restrict its expansion in Berkshire and is the reason why the locations of possible breeding sites have not been included in this account.

*Sponsored by Linda & Roger Dobbs*

# Sparrowhawk

*Accipiter nisus*

*Widespread resident*

The Sparrowhawk is a widespread resident in Berkshire. It is primarily a species of mixed or coniferous woodland, but it is also found in farmland and even urban areas with sufficient tree cover. Sparrowhawks were fairly common during the 19th century (Noble, 1906) but persecution by gamekeepers and farmers kept their numbers low until the Second World War when the population increased due to reduced persecution.

However, the organochlorine pesticides disaster of the late 1950s and early 1960s reduced the Sparrowhawk numbers to such an extent that it became almost extinct in much of southern and eastern England. After these pesticides were banned in the 1960s the population recovered steadily and by the 1980s, Sparrowhawks were once again a familiar sight throughout the county, even in urban and suburban areas, and remains almost as familiar a sight as the Kestrel.

There was a quite rapid increase in numbers from the low point for the species in the 1950s. In 1958, there was just one record of three birds over Ham in October but, by 1974, 33 occupied nests were found during the regular monitoring of the species in east Berkshire on the Crown Estate.

The 2007–11 Tetrad Survey maps show that although Sparrowhawks remain widely encountered throughout most of the county, there has been an apparent reduction in the number of tetrads in which breeding occurs. In the 1987–89 survey, breeding evidence was recorded in 294 tetrads, compared to 230 in the latest survey. Nationally, the results of the CBC and BBS indicated that the population stabilised in the early 1990s, but has fallen by about 15% between 1999 and 2009 (Baillie *et al.*, 2012). However other factors may have affected the coverage and results. The 1987–89 survey took

place during an extensive survey of the forests of the Crown Estate in the south east of the county referred to above, which ran from the 1970s until 2001, so the local population in the area was well studied and well known locally. The end of this survey may be reflected in the reduction in the number of tetrads with confirmed breeding in the area from Sandhurst and Crowthorne through to Ascot and Virginia Water from 25 to 10 between the two tetrad surveys. There was also a dramatic reduction in the number of confirmed breeding records from 10 km squares SU26, 35 and 36 from 19 in 1987–89 to just one in the 2007–11 survey. Outside these two areas the number of tetrads with confirmed breeding increased slightly. There was also a fall of 38 tetrads in which possible breeding (generally presence in breeding habitat) was recorded, but presence without any category of breeding evidence was recorded in a further 45 tetrads in the latest survey. In the 1987–89 atlas survey there was no recording of presence with no breeding evidence, so some of the possible breeding records may simply relate to presence.

The Breeding Season TTV and Winter Maps indicate the Sparrowhawk's preference for woodland habitats, particularly the major areas of mixed and coniferous woodlands in the south and eastern parts of the county, but with higher densities in mixed rather than primarily

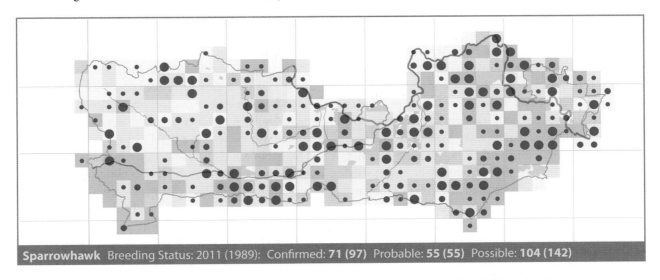

**Sparrowhawk** Breeding Status: 2011 (1989): Confirmed: **71 (97)** Probable: **55 (55)** Possible: **104 (142)**

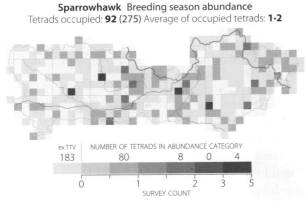

**Sparrowhawk** Breeding season abundance
Tetrads occupied: **92 (275)** Average of occupied tetrads: **1·2**

| exTTV | NUMBER OF TETRADS IN ABUNDANCE CATEGORY | | | |
|---|---|---|---|---|
| 183 | 80 | 8 | 0 | 4 |

0   1   2   3   5
SURVEY COUNT

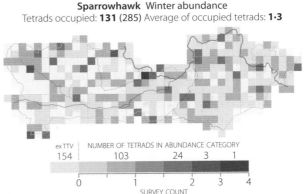

**Sparrowhawk** Winter abundance
Tetrads occupied: **131 (285)** Average of occupied tetrads: **1·3**

| exTTV | NUMBER OF TETRADS IN ABUNDANCE CATEGORY | | | |
|---|---|---|---|---|
| 154 | 103 | 24 | 3 | 1 |

0   1   2   3   4
SURVEY COUNT

coniferous areas. There are fewer records in the downland areas in the north-west of the county in the breeding season, indicating the relative lack of suitable habitat for breeding, but rather more in winter.

Although ringing has revealed some migration of Sparrowhawks between Britain and continental Europe, particularly from western Scandinavia, there have been no ringing recoveries involving movements between Berkshire and overseas. Most recoveries have been of locally ringed birds recovered in Berkshire, or exchanges with neighbouring counties, particularly Surrey. The longest movement involved a bird ringed in Windsor Great Park in June 1996 recovered the following November in Plymouth, 273 km away.

*Sponsored by Jim & Shirley Adams*

# Buzzard Green

*Buteo buteo*

### Widespread resident and uncommon passage migrant

In the 1980s, the Buzzard was a scarce migrant and localised breeding species in Berkshire at the easternmost edge of its breeding range in Britain. Since then it has spread rapidly eastward and is now present across the county throughout the year and breeding in all but one 10 km square.

Persecution, mostly attributable to game-keeping, was responsible for the virtual extermination of the Buzzard in Berkshire by the mid-20th century, in common with much of lowland Britain. A combination of legal protection and a reduction in keepering during and after the Second World War allowed the species to make a recovery but this was checked in the 1950s by the myxomatosis plague which almost eliminated its principal food source, the Rabbit *Oryctolagus cuniculus*. In addition, as with the Sparrowhawk, organochlorine pesticide residues are believed to have adversely affected its recovery (Marchant *et al.*, 1990). These threats diminished in the later decades of the 20th century and in common with several other raptors, Buzzard numbers increased in their strongholds in south west England and in Wales. Though little extension of their range had occurred up to the time of the 1983 BTO Buzzard Survey (Taylor *et al.*, 1988), some eastward expansion had become apparent in the 1988–91 national atlas.

In Berkshire, the county reports indicate that Buzzards bred in the Newbury area in 1953 and 1976 and were suspected to have bred in 1959. Family parties were also reported in 1979, 1981 and 1984, suggesting that birds had bred locally. Breeding was confirmed during the 1987–89 Tetrad Survey in three tetrads in the west of the county and probable breeding noted in a further four.

Since then, there have been increasing numbers of breeding records: around 10 pairs breeding in the county in 1997, including the first records in East Berkshire, increasing to at least 48 pairs in an incomplete county survey in 2006 (Robinson, 2007). The structure of the countryside in Berkshire provides Buzzards with the mix of farmland and

woodland patches that they prefer and the breeding map shows them to breed throughout the county except the built-up areas. The 2007–11 tetrad atlas survey confirmed breeding in 133 tetrads, with probable breeding in a further 129. In both winter and summer, Buzzards are commoner in the west than the east of the county. Territory size is generally much smaller than a tetrad (*BWP II*) and many tetrads probably contained more than one pair: three or more birds were recorded in 44% of the occupied tetrads in timed visits in the breeding season, indicating a breeding population for Berkshire of possibly 600 to 875 territorial pairs. There is no evidence, as yet, of a slowing of the recent rate of growth of the Buzzard population, though there are suggestions of renewed persecution.

Buzzards are essentially sedentary in Britain (*Migration Atlas*), as is reflected in the summer and winter abundance maps, which show a similar distribution and similar abundance in both seasons. However, some of the birds seen in autumn or spring, when counts of 10 or more together are not infrequent, may be migrants or individuals dispersing from elsewhere.

There have been two recoveries of ringed Buzzards in Berkshire: one which was ringed as a juvenile at Barrow Gurney, Avon in June 1986 being recovered at Bothampstead in September of the same year, and one ringed in the New Forest in June 1963 being recovered near Inkpen in October 1964.

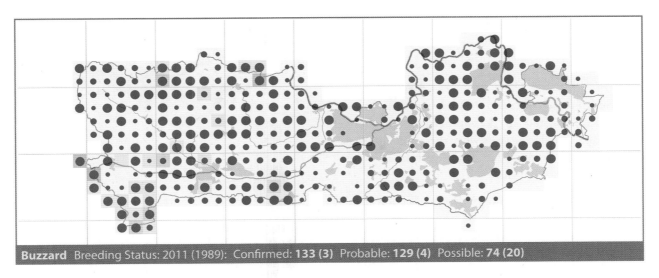

**Buzzard** Breeding Status: 2011 (1989): Confirmed: **133 (3)** Probable: **129 (4)** Possible: **74 (20)**

**Buzzard** Breeding season abundance
Tetrads occupied: **289** (368) Average of occupied tetrads: **2·7**

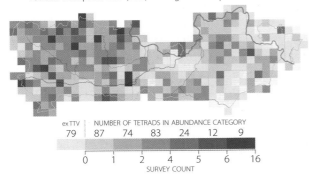

| exTTV | NUMBER OF TETRADS IN ABUNDANCE CATEGORY | | | | | |
|---|---|---|---|---|---|---|
| 79 | 87 | 74 | 83 | 24 | 12 | 9 |

0  1  2  4  5  6  16
SURVEY COUNT

**Buzzard** Winter abundance
Tetrads occupied: **277** (359) Average of occupied tetrads: **3·3**

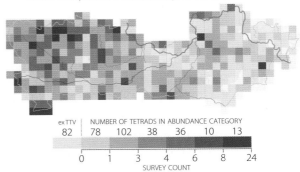

| exTTV | NUMBER OF TETRADS IN ABUNDANCE CATEGORY | | | | | |
|---|---|---|---|---|---|---|
| 82 | 78 | 102 | 38 | 36 | 10 | 13 |

0  1  3  4  6  8  24
SURVEY COUNT

Lamb (1880) describes the Buzzard as very common in Berkshire in 1814, but by the 1860s it had become uncommon, with Clark Kennedy (1868) mentioning only four birds taken between 1857 and 1866.

There were only two further records, one in 1866 (Herbert, 1871) and one in 1880 (Noble, 1906).

*Sponsored by Tony & Wendy Hayward*

Buzzard  *Ken White*

# Rough-legged Buzzard

*Buteo lagopus*

*Rare winter visitor and passage migrant*

The Rough-legged Buzzard is a rare winter visitor and passage migrant in Berkshire and occurs only sporadically, even during years when there is an influx of the species into Britain. Most of the Berkshire records have been from the Downs.

The Rough-legged Buzzard's preference for downland areas, which were well-keepered prior to the Second World War, was to its disadvantage and in an account in the 1934 county report, G. Brown of Combe recalled that there were two mounted specimens in the local keeper's house, which had been killed about 30 years before, and that the keeper had stated that three others had been killed by shooting parties in the period since then.

The first acceptable sight record of Rough-legged Buzzard in Berkshire was one seen in the Combe area on 18th October 1931 and for some time afterwards (Summers-Smith, 1951). This was followed by one seen at Cookham Dean on 4th November 1934. In spite of an increase in observer coverage from the 1950s, there were no further records until one was seen flying north-west over Windsor Great Park on 26th December 1970, apparently part of a hard weather movement, and a returning bird was seen over Slough Sewage Farm on 17th April 1971.

An influx of Rough-legged Buzzards into Britain in the winter of 1973/74 resulted, in Berkshire, in one seen flying north over Wraysbury on 17th October and a second bird which spent part of the winter, from 21st November to 21st December, on the West Ilsley Downs. The winter of 1974/75 produced some of the highest numbers of Rough-legged Buzzards ever recorded in Britain, with 85–100 birds wintering in England (Brown and Grice, 2005). However, Berkshire did not share in this influx until the spring, when up to three birds were present in the Combe and Inkpen area from 16th March to 6th April 1975, the first record for the county involving more than one bird.

There was an increase in records between the winters of 1978/79 and 1986/87, with eight birds recorded, four from the Combe area, including two together January to March 1981, and one each from Wraysbury Gravel Pits, Lowbury Hill, Summerleaze Gravel Pits and Shefford Woodlands. There were then seven winters, 1987/88 to 1993/94, with no records.

In 1995 a single bird was at Combe Hill on 4th January and 18th March, possibly the same bird seen there in December 1994. Despite a national influx in 1998/99, there were no Berkshire records that winter, and the next was not until 2005 when a probable adult female was reported from Frogmill, Hurley on 5th November. The next record was in February 2009, when a single bird was reported from the Combe area on 15th and 19th February and 8th and 13th March. A record from Compton, also on 19th February, was possibly the same bird. A juvenile near Warren Farm, Streatley, flew briefly into Berkshire on 17th March 2011.

Of the 20 birds recorded from 1931 to 2009, six were first recorded in December, four in January, one in February, three in March, two in October, three in November and one in April. The extreme dates for the Rough-legged Buzzard in Berkshire have been 17th October in 1973 at Wraysbury and 17th April in 1971 at Slough, both records relating to passage birds.

There are a number of sight records which, because of their date and the possibility of confusion with pale plumaged Buzzards, are now regarded as unreliable or doubtful in the absence of full documentation. These involve birds at Reading in 1895, Bradfield in 1898, Beenham in 1910, the Combe area in 1961 and Walbury Hill in 1981 and 1982.

The earliest county records of Rough-legged Buzzard were provided by Noble (1906): one shot at Ham Spray on 7th December 1876 and one killed at Culham Court near Maidenhead "many years" before 1905. As the hamlet of Ham Spray lies just within Wiltshire, it remains unclear whether this bird was seen in Berkshire before being shot.

*Sponsored by John and Fiona Farnsworth*

# Spotted Eagle

## Aquila clanga

*Rare vagrant, with one 19th century record*

A male Spotted Eagle which was shot at Wokingham on 2nd October 1872 is the only record for Berkshire. Noble (1906) was not aware of this record and it first appears in the county report for 1933 with the comment "The Rev F.C.R. Jourdain informs us that a male killed at Wokingham on 2nd October 1872 is now in the possession of Mr H. Whistler." The record was considered acceptable by Witherby *et al.*, (1939), who cited a paper entitled "Notes on British Records of the Spotted Eagle" (British Birds 14: 180, 209), but the Wokingham bird is not mentioned there!

*Sponsored by Ian Tarr*

# Golden Eagle          `Amber`

## Aquila chrysaetos

*Rare vagrant, one record*

The only acceptable record of the Golden Eagle in Berkshire is of one seen on the Downs near Fawley in July 1924, which was shot in Pinal Wood, Oxfordshire on 30th July. Subsequent examination of the specimen confirmed that it was this species and not an immature White-tailed Eagle. Earlier 'Golden Eagle' records, which now seem most likely to have been White-tailed Eagles, are considered under that species.

*Sponsored by Duncan Spence*

# Osprey          `Amber`  `Sch. 1`

## Pandion haliaetus

*Scarce passage migrant*

The Osprey is a scarce passage migrant in Berkshire, for which local records reflect the rising fortunes of the species in Britain over the last sixty years, from no breeding pairs before the mid-1950s to 180 in 2005–09 (Holling *et al.*, 2011).

The first Berkshire record in the 20th century was of one seen on the county boundary in the Cookham area in September 1938. Thereafter, one was seen entering Berkshire over the Fairmile on 31st August 1947, and in 1951 there was a surprising record of one spending most of July at a lake near Newbury. Ospreys were then seen in seven of the 16 years from 1951 to 1966 and then annually from 1967 to 2011 (apart from in 1975, 1986 and 1990). The first 20th century record of two birds in a year was in 1965, but since 2000 all years have seen at least eight birds passing through the county, with 2008 having as many as 16. Figure 56 shows the number of records from 1947 to 2010.

The monthly distribution of records from 1947 to 2011 is given in Figure 57, the extreme dates being 14th March in 2007 over Lower Farm, and a bird which stayed at Windsor Great Park from 16th November to 2nd December in 1956.

Recent records have shown a shift towards earlier arrival and departure, with an increase in the number of March records and significantly more records in April than in May. Return migration now peaks in August and

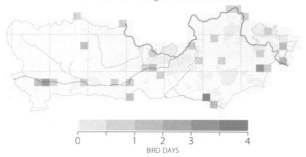

**Osprey** Spring migration occurrence
Tetrads used: **29** Average of used tetrads: **1·5**

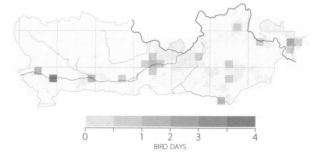

**Osprey** Autumn migration occurrence
Tetrads used: **18** Average of used tetrads: **1·5**

September, with very few birds passing in October and only very occasional late birds in November. The majority of records are of birds over open water at sites across the county, where passage birds sometimes pause to fish and also good observer coverage is likely to have influenced the number of sightings. Most birds appear to pass fairly quickly through the county, although one famous radio-tagged female (named Logie) was tracked through the county (although never actually seen), arriving on 13th April 2008, roosting at Virginia Water and by the Thames before finally heading north on the 15th, eventually reaching her nest site in Scotland on 23rd April. Another bird remained in the Marsh Benham area for about four weeks in 1988 from June into July, only the second time an Osprey has partially summered in the county. In autumn, again most have been single-day sightings of single birds, with the most recent exception being a juvenile bird which arrived in the Theale area on 30th August 2001 and was seen almost daily at various locations in the vicinity until 24th September, and two birds seen together briefly hunting at Eversley Gravel Pits before heading south on 16th September 2004.

Where the direction birds have been flying has been noted in spring, this has invariably been northerly. Birds have frequently been seen attempting to fish, but only occasionally has this been shown to be successful. A bird at Twyford Gravel Pits on 13th April 1988 was heard to 'whistle', the only such occasion this has been reported in Berkshire. One passing over Windsor Great Park on 30th July 1989 was observed to be in heavy moult.

Lamb (1880) reports that one was shot at Pangbourne before 1810. His record of one seen at Donnington in January 1810, however, appears unreliable in view of the

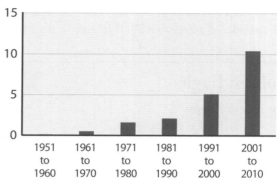

**Figure 56: Osprey: average number of birds recorded per year 1951–2010.**

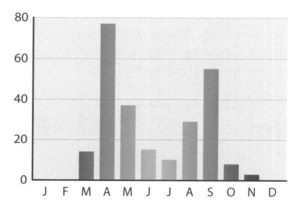

**Figure 57: Osprey: all birds recorded 1951–2010, by month of arrival.**

date. Clark Kennedy (1868) gives details of birds shot at Ditton Park, Slough in September 1863, at Cookham in October 1864 and in Windsor Great Park, also in 1864. Singles were seen over the Thames at Surley Hall near Maidenhead in 1865, 1866, 1867 and early 1868. The fact that Noble (1906) was not able to add to these records reflects the rapid decline in the Scottish breeding population in the second half of the 19th century.

*Sponsored by Ray & Janet Anstis*

Osprey, Queen Mother Reservoir *Jerry O'Brien*

# Kestrel

*Falco tinnunculus*

Amber

*Widespread resident and winter visitor*

The Kestrel was for many years the commonest and most widely distributed bird of prey in Berkshire. For many years before Sparrowhawks began recovering from the effects of pesticide poisoning in the 1970s, Kestrels were the only birds of prey regularly seen throughout the county. Its distribution in the county, as revealed by the Tetrad Surveys, is uneven. It appears that the resident population is joined by winter visitors from the north, although some local birds may also move out in winter.

Comparing both breeding tetrad surveys with the habitat maps shows few records from around Bracknell and Ascot where acid sand and gravels, with their associated heathland and coniferous woodland habitats, predominate. No clear pattern emerges for urban areas, however. Central Reading did not yield any probable or confirmed breeding records in either survey, although this was not the case in Slough, Windsor and Maidenhead in 1987–89. There seems to have been something of a contraction in range between the two surveys, with breeding evidence from 342 tetrads in the 1987–89 survey, and records in all categories (breeding evidence or only presence) from 331 in the breeding season surveys in 2007–11. However breeding was confirmed in more tetrads, 115 in 2007–11 compared with 92 in 1987–89. Nationally, Kestrel numbers as disclosed by the results of the CBC and BBS have declined in England by about 15% between 1984 and 2009 (Baillie *et al.*, 2012).

The *1981–84 BTO Winter Atlas* indicates that the pattern of movement of Kestrels in Britain out of the breeding season is complex, with birds moving away from upland areas and coming in from the continent in the autumn.

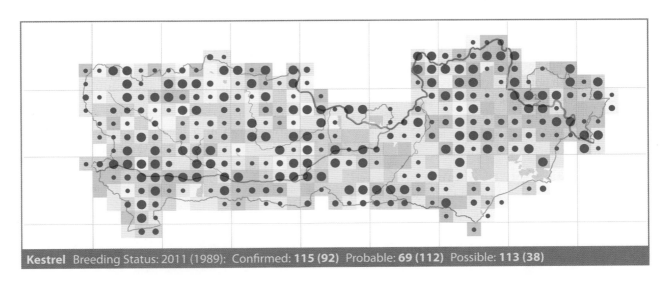

**Kestrel** Breeding Status: 2011 (1989): Confirmed: **115 (92)** Probable: **69 (112)** Possible: **113 (38)**

**Kestrel** Breeding season abundance
Tetrads occupied: **225 (331)** Average of occupied tetrads: **1·5**

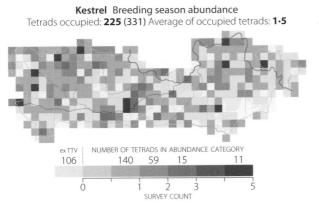

| exTTV | NUMBER OF TETRADS IN ABUNDANCE CATEGORY | | | |
|---|---|---|---|---|
| 106 | 140 | 59 | 15 | 11 |

0  1  2  3  5
SURVEY COUNT

**Kestrel** Winter abundance
Tetrads occupied: **256 (337)** Average of occupied tetrads: **1·7**

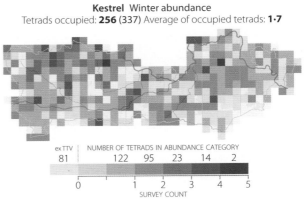

| exTTV | NUMBER OF TETRADS IN ABUNDANCE CATEGORY | | | | |
|---|---|---|---|---|---|
| 81 | 122 | 95 | 23 | 14 | 2 |

0  1  2  3  4  5
SURVEY COUNT

In the light of this, the recoveries of two birds ringed as nestlings in Berkshire, at Sunninghill Park in July 1950 and near Hungerford in 1972, during their first winters in eastern France are noteworthy in that they indicate a south-easterly dispersal of locally-reared birds. Other ringing recoveries reflect the more predictable pattern of birds from further north in Britain moving into Berkshire in winter, with recoveries of birds which were ringed in southern Scotland, Derbyshire and Lancashire. Birds ringed in Berkshire during the winter have been recovered in subsequent summers in Derbyshire and Cleveland. There has also been a winter recovery of a bird ringed as a nestling in Vastmanland, Sweden in June 2002 which was recovered having been hit by a car near Bracknell in October that year. The higher average counts in the results of the winter TTV survey compared to the breeding season TTV during the 2007–11 Atlas project also indicate net inward migration into Berkshire in winter.

Kestrels normally are only seen as individuals, pairs or small family parties. There have been a few counts of five or more, and just two since 1990 involving more than 10, both from the autumn of 1996 and the south west of the county. There were 12 in the Combe area on 14th September and 11 in the area around Combe and Inkpen Hill on 25th August.

*Sponsored by Renee Grayer*

# Red-footed Falcon

## *Falco vespertinus*

*Rare vagrant, nine records*

The Red-footed Falcon was not recorded in Berkshire until 1973, since when there have been nine records (involving 10 birds) of this rare, eastern vagrant to Britain. Five of these records occurred during notable invasions of the species, in 1973, 1992 and 2008.

In 1973, there was a female at Earley on 6th June and another female at Bracknell on 27th September. A male was at Mortimer on 4th June 1989; then a first-summer male was seen at Dinton Pastures on 3rd June 1992, and in 1999 a first-summer male was at Horton Gravel Pits from 11th to 14th June. The first July record was in 2003 when a first-summer male was at Pingewood Gravel Pits between the 4th and 9th July, but in 2006 there was another late record, of a juvenile female at Eversley Gravel Pits between 8th and 18th July.

The major spring influx of 2008, when over 60 birds were reported in Britain during May and June, was reflected in two Berkshire records, including the first multiple sighting for the county. On 30th and 31st May a first-summer male and female were present at Woolhampton Gravel Pits; from 1st to 5th June only the male was seen, the female being relocated on 7th June. Another female was feeding above the A4 at Colnbrook on 31st May.

Six of the nine Berkshire records occurred in late May and early June, typical of the national trend: of the 282 British records from 1958 to 1985, 75% were in spring with a marked peak in May and early June (Dymond *et al.*, 1989) while during the 1992 invasion, when 120 birds were recorded in Britain and Ireland, the vast majority occurred in the second half of May and June (Nightingale and Allsop, 1994). The September 1973 record, although not previously published in county reports, was accepted at the time by BBRC.

The record of a female Red-footed Falcon which was struck down by a Raven in Littlecote Park near Hungerford in the 1840s and mentioned by Radford (1966) is properly attributable to Wiltshire.

*Sponsored by Sarah and Ken White*

# Merlin

*Falco columbarius*

*Uncommon winter visitor and passage migrant*

In Berkshire, the Merlin may be encountered in winter and on passage almost anywhere in open country, although the area from the Kennet Valley to the Downs has produced most records.

The frequency of Merlin records in Berkshire increased between the 1950s and 1970s, and again since the 1990s, as shown in Figure 58. Birds were seen in eight of the 16 winters from 1950/51 to 1965/66, but have been annual since. Although this may, in part, reflect the greater level of observer coverage from the 1950s, the further increase in sightings in more recent years appears to result from a real increase in the number of passage or wintering Merlins reaching the county. At a national level, studies in the 1990s concluded that the UK breeding population had recently doubled to an estimated 1,291 pairs in Britain in 1993–94 (Rebecca & Bainbridge, 1998), but subsequent studies have shown the breeding population to have remained roughly stable, with an estimate of 1,162 breeding pairs in 2008 (Ewing *et al.*, 2011). This may indicate an overseas origin of some of our wintering birds.

The number of birds seen in successive winters is variable. For example, only one was recorded in 1975/76 yet there were ten sightings the following winter. The highest winter total to date was in 2008/09 when around 30 birds visited or over-wintered in the county, although, as with all totals in this account, it has been assumed that records from different locations relate to different birds.

The latest post-winter sighting was of one seen at Lower Farm, Newbury on the exceptionally late date of 19th June 2010, over a month later than the next latest recorded date, 13th May. On this date in 1999 a female was at Hosehill Lake, Theale and in 2006, another female was

**Merlin** Winter abundance
Tetrads occupied: **4** (43) Average of occupied tetrads: **1·0**

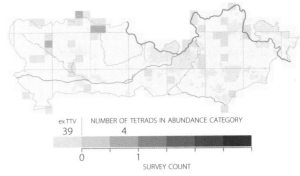

ex TTV | NUMBER OF TETRADS IN ABUNDANCE CATEGORY
39 | 4

0   1   SURVEY COUNT

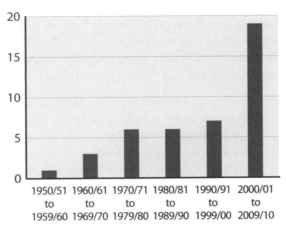

**Figure 58: Merlin: average number of birds recorded per winter, 1950/51–2009/10.**

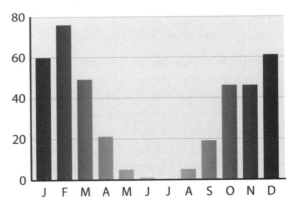

**Figure 59: Merlin: all birds recorded 1950/51–2009/10, by month of arrival.**

seen on the Downs. The earliest post-breeding records for the county have been in August, with the earliest being on the 15th at Hermitage in 1963, and there was a juvenile over Cow Down on 18th August 2009. A record of one at Streatley on 15th July 2012 awaits adjudication by the Berkshire Records Committee.

Merlins appear to roam quite widely during winter, which may have resulted in some duplication of records, although a site at Cold Harbour has proved to be an attractive wintering spot for Merlins, with regular sightings from 1998 onwards. The great majority of sightings involve single birds. Two birds were seen together at East Ilsley in December 1976, and an adult male and female over-wintered together in 2001/02 at Cold Harbour which were joined by another adult male for a few days in February 2002.

The great majority of records appear to have been single-day sightings, although birds do occasionally winter in the same area, examples being of one in the Wraysbury Gravel Pits area from 15th November 1968 to 25th January 1969, one in the Upper Bucklebury to Upper Woolhampton area from 30th December 1974 to 16th January 1975 and more recently the pair at Cold Harbour were present from 3rd November 2001 through to 1st March 2002. Wintering birds occur across Berkshire, but the Downs provide the most records where lower levels of observer cover could mean that they occur even more frequently than the records would indicate. The number of records where birds were identified as male or female or female/immature (given the difficulty in separating females from immatures in the field) show about twice as many records of females or immatures as males.

The earliest record was one shot near Reading on 25th January 1794 (Lamb, 1880). For the period from about 1855 to 1905 Clark Kennedy (1868) and Noble (1906) list some ten records, nearly all of birds shot, although one was killed at Wokingham against a rectory window, an early window-strike record. Where dates are given, all were between 1st January and 6th April. County reports during the period from 1917 to the winter of 1949/50 contain a similar number of records, 11, with five of these from 1943 to 1950.

*Sponsored by Peter Newbound*

# Hobby

Green · Sch. 1

*Falco subbuteo*

*Uncommon summer visitor and passage migrant*

The Hobby is an uncommon but increasing annual passage migrant and summer visitor to Berkshire. Hobbies have been traditionally associated with areas of dry heathland with scattered pine *Pinus* spp. trees, but now occur widely in rural Berkshire. Passage birds can occur almost anywhere although they are most regularly seen over gravel pits, where they may congregate in groups of up to 20 or more.

The Breeding Distribution Map from the 2007–11 Atlas Survey shows probable and confirmed breeding records spread across the county, with the confirmed breeding records mainly in the eastern half. Birds were recorded in 209 tetrads (55% of all tetrads), compared with 334 (84%) for the Kestrel and 275 (70%) for the Sparrowhawk. By comparison, the 1987–89 Atlas Survey recorded Hobby in only 17% of the tetrads. Breeding was confirmed in 11% (24) of the tetrads occupied during the three years of the survey, which is at least a twofold increase since the 1987–89 Atlas Survey. The 1987–89 Tetrad maps showed a strong correlation with the Hobby's favoured habitat of heathland with scattered trees, which is concentrated in the south-east of the county, but the distribution from the latest survey shows a spread to other habitats. There is a marked absence of records from areas of agricultural land

with few trees and from urban areas. There were also very few records from the downland areas to the north-west of the county, which is somewhat surprising since Hobbies breed in this type of habitat in neighbouring counties. This may, however, be a reflection of the difficulty involved in locating Hobbies in such areas.

Since Hobbies range over a wide area, birds seen hunting are not easily traced back to their breeding site. The low incidence of confirmed breeding is therefore not surprising. The majority of confirmed breeding records related to occupied nests or adults carrying food for their young and almost all corresponded to tetrads with more than 30 confirmed breeding species, those likely to have been covered most thoroughly during the survey.

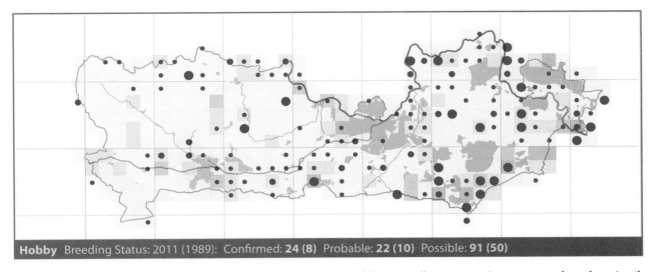

**Hobby** Breeding Status: 2011 (1989): Confirmed: **24 (8)** Probable: **22 (10)** Possible: **91 (50)**

**Hobby** Breeding season abundance
Tetrads occupied: **37 (217)** Average of occupied tetrads: **1·2**

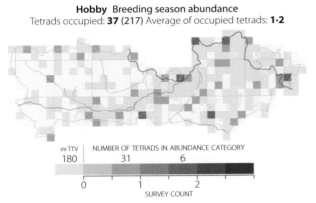

| ex TTV | NUMBER OF TETRADS IN ABUNDANCE CATEGORY | |
|---|---|---|
| 180 | 31 | 6 |

0      1      2
SURVEY COUNT

Hobbies were recorded in more 10 km squares during the 1987–89 Atlas Survey than in the *1968–72 BTO Atlas*, providing further evidence that their numbers have increased since the early 1970s. In Britain as a whole, there has been an increase in the Hobby population in recent decades after what was believed to be a long-term decline. This may be due to a succession of warm summers as well as a growing number of experienced observers. The population reported to the Rare Breeding Birds Panel has increased in recent years and is now estimated at between 200 and 1,200 pairs in Britain. Reports from Berkshire usually mentioned around five or six pairs in any one year in the 1980s, and breeding evidence from only 10 to 20 sites in the 2000s. If even only a small proportion of the possible or probable Tetrad Survey records relate to breeding pairs, previously published figures are likely to have underestimated the true status of Hobby in the county.

There has been a big increase in the number of sightings noted in the county reports since the 1970s: in 1991, for example, sightings came from 36 localities within the county with records most widespread in May, from 14 sites and August, from 16 sites; whereas in 2008 records came from 104 locations, mostly in mid- and east Berkshire, with a minimum of 85 birds from 33 sites in May, and 63 birds reported from 32 sites in August.

Hobbies usually arrive in Britain in mid- to late April. Between 1974 and 1994 the earliest arrival dates in Berkshire ranged from 9th April to 4th May, with the average date being 26th April. Between 1995 and 2012, the earliest arrival dates ranged from 1st April to 24th April, with the average date being 13th April, almost two weeks earlier than the average for the previous 20 years. Many of the spring records relate to passage birds, and in some years there have been relatively large gatherings (more than 10 birds) over gravel pits, *e.g.* up to 13 at Horton in May 2000, 15 at Wraysbury in May 2002, 20 at Woolhampton in May 2008 and 22 at Moatlands pit, Theale in May 2009. Breeding occurs relatively late in the year compared with other falcon species, with eggs being laid in June and the young fledging in mid-August, coinciding with peak numbers of prey species. After the breeding season Hobbies disperse widely but are frequently seen around gravel pits hunting hirundines, dragonflies and high-flying insects, especially during August and early September. Between 1974 and 1994, the latest departures were from 10th September to 17th October, with the average date being 27th September. Between 1995 and 2012 the latest dates were from 3rd October to 4th November, with the average last date being 15th October, over two weeks later than the average for the previous 20 years.

There is one recovery involving a Hobby ringed in Berkshire, a bird ringed as a nestling in east Berkshire in August 1976 being recovered the following June in Belgium. There have been three recoveries of Hobbies in Berkshire: a nestling ringed in Surrey in August 1946 found dead in Finchampstead in September 1946; a nestling ringed just over the border in Buckinghamshire in July 1986, shot in Slough in June 1989; and a nestling ringed in Oxfordshire in August 2010 found dead in Newbury in September 2011.

Prior to the 20th century, Lamb (1880) regarded the Hobby as rare, and Clarke Kennedy (1868) recorded it as a regular summer visitor, but never in great numbers. He also gives mid-April for its arrival and October for its departure. Noble (1906) includes records for several of the areas where the Hobby is still seen today and, as is regrettably still the case, felt it necessary not to disclose a site where it had recently bred, the species being regularly shot at that time.

*Sponsored by Patrick Crowley*

## Gyr Falcon   Sch. 1

*Falco rusticolus*

*Rare vagrant, two records, probably of one bird*

The Gyr Falcon is a rare vagrant to Berkshire and has been recorded on just two occasions, although both probably relate to a single individual. One was seen over the Downs at Aldworth on 12th December 1970 and one was seen crossing fields, mobbed by crows, at Binfield on 24th January 1971.

*Sponsored by Mark Chapman*

## Peregrine Falcon   Green   Sch. 1

*Falco peregrinus*

*Scarce resident, winter visitor and passage migrant.*

The status of the Peregrine in Berkshire reflects its fortunes nationally. Formerly very rare, it now occurs throughout the year and breeds in small numbers. The population of the Peregrine in Britain has undergone dramatic change since the onset of the Second World War, when the birds were considered to pose a threat to the military use of homing pigeons. Large numbers were killed, reducing the English population by 1944 by nearly 50%. Before a full recovery could be made, numbers were to crash from 1956 to 1966 due to the effects of organochlorine pesticides (*1968–72 BTO Atlas*). With a ban on organochlorine insecticides and reduction in persecution, Peregrine numbers have steadily increased since the 1970s and their range extended from the residual populations in the north and west (*1988–91 BTO Atlas*). They now breed around much of the coast and at many inland sites (Banks, Coombs and Crick, 2003).

In Berkshire, Noble (1906) records Peregrines as having been seen in winter, spring and autumn in most years and cites some 11 records for the period from 1866 to 1904, with locations ranging from Hungerford to Billingbear. Similarly, for much of the 20th century, the Peregrine was an occasional visitor to Berkshire, averaging one sighting a year although not occurring annually. Nearly all sightings were of single birds and most were seen only for one day, although there is some evidence that birds may hunt the same area for a few days or weeks. A small proportion of records have been of escaped birds with jesses.

Towards the end of the 20th century, a number of sites became established wintering areas, and birds were being recorded for much of the year at Queen Mother Reservoir and in the Theale area. The 1998/99 county report records up to six Peregrines wintering and up to four present in the summer months. Although pairs were present in earlier years, the first recorded breeding attempt was on a pylon in central Berkshire in 2006, the male of the pair bearing jesses. Although the first attempt was unsuccessful (the nest collapsed), pairs of Peregrines were seen in subsequent years using pylons in the area. By 2010, pairs had also been recorded during the breeding season at Queen Mother Reservoir, on high buildings in Bracknell and Reading, with single birds in Slough and Newbury. The first confirmed successful breeding was on a tower at Queen Mother Reservoir in 2010, when at least one chick fledged.

During the 1990s Peregrines first bred at Didcot power station in Oxfordshire, which may be the source of many of the sightings on the Berkshire Downs and perhaps

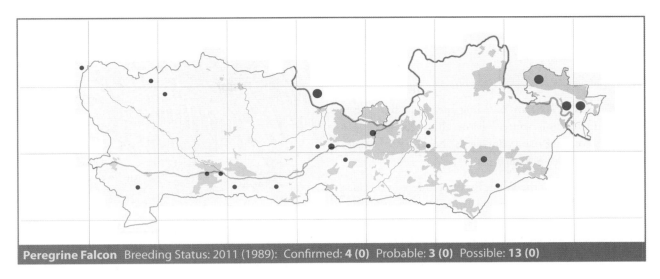

**Peregrine Falcon**  Breeding Status: 2011 (1989):  Confirmed: **4 (0)**  Probable: **3 (0)**  Possible: **13 (0)**

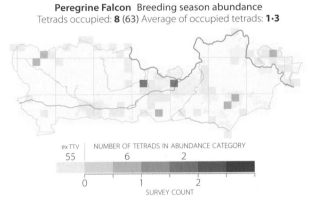

**Peregrine Falcon**  Breeding season abundance
Tetrads occupied: **8 (63)** Average of occupied tetrads: **1·3**

| ex TTV | NUMBER OF TETRADS IN ABUNDANCE CATEGORY | |
|---|---|---|
| 55 | 6 | 2 |

0          1          2
SURVEY COUNT

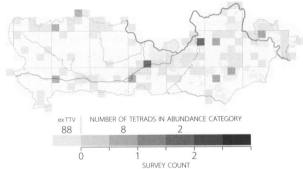

**Peregrine Falcon**  Winter abundance
Tetrads occupied: **10 (98)** Average of occupied tetrads: **1·2**

| ex TTV | NUMBER OF TETRADS IN ABUNDANCE CATEGORY | |
|---|---|---|
| 88 | 8 | 2 |

0          1          2
SURVEY COUNT

also of the birds which colonized sites in central and west Berkshire in between 2000 and 2010.

Whilst the town centre sites are already in the public domain, to protect the birds from possible persecution, the breeding tetrads of some others have been have been mapped elsewhere in their 10 km square. The tetrad analysis shows Peregrine in 63 tetrads in the breeding season, focused around the main town sites, Theale and Queen Mother Reservoir. The winter records show sightings to be twice as numerous and more widespread, with more records on the Berkshire Downs and at wetland sites throughout the county. The extent to which this reflects an influx of winter visitors or greater use of downland and wetland for hunting is unclear.

*Sponsored by Year 3 Cheam School*

Peregrine, Queen Mother Reservoir  *Michaael McKee*

# Water Rail

*Rallus aquaticus*

*Uncommon winter visitor, rare in summer*

The Water Rail is a rare breeding species in Berkshire and an uncommon winter visitor although, given its extremely secretive habits during the breeding season, it may well be under-recorded.

It would appear that the Water Rail has suffered a decline in Berkshire during the last two centuries, primarily due to lowland drainage schemes and a change in farming practices, especially the loss of traditional water meadows and cress beds. This decline does not appear to have been offset by the creation of wetland habitats associated with gravel extraction. Prior to 1900 Lamb (1880) regarded the Water Rail as common in 1814, Clark Kennedy (1868) refers to nests taken at Eton, and Noble (1906) to several nests near Reading and in Windsor Great Park, which would indicate that the species was formerly more widespread. None of these authors suggest that it was common in summer, however, Noble noting that it was numerous only in winter.

Whilst it is often thought of as a breeding bird of extensive reedbeds, the Water Rail is equally at home in any overgrown wetland, especially in the winter. This has

allowed the species to begin to utilise the more neglected margins of gravel pits. The Breeding Distribution map shows that Water Rails in the breeding season are closely tied to the occurrence of reedbeds and marshes along the main river valleys, especially the Kennet, resulting in a westerly bias in distribution in the county. Breeding was confirmed in five tetrads in the 2007–11 Atlas Survey compared to just one in the 1987–89 Atlas Survey, but overall there is a good deal of consistency in the distribution of this species between surveys with records from 22 tetrads in both. The skulking habits of this species and its liking for dense cover make confirming breeding difficult. The most consistent breeding site for this species in the county is Thatcham Reedbeds, the largest area of reeds in Berkshire, where

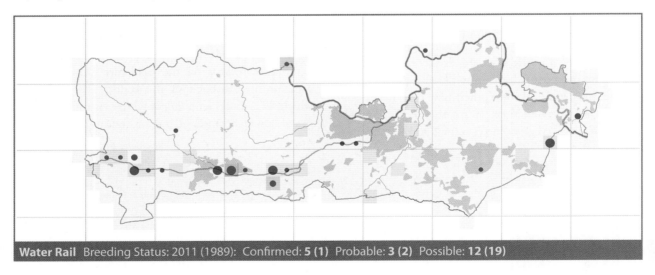

**Water Rail** Breeding Status: 2011 (1989): Confirmed: **5 (1)** Probable: **3 (2)** Possible: **12 (19)**

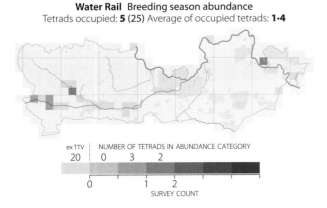

**Water Rail** Breeding season abundance
Tetrads occupied: **5 (25)** Average of occupied tetrads: **1·4**

| ex TTV | NUMBER OF TETRADS IN ABUNDANCE CATEGORY | | |
|---|---|---|---|
| 20 | 0 | 3 | 2 |

0          1          2
SURVEY COUNT

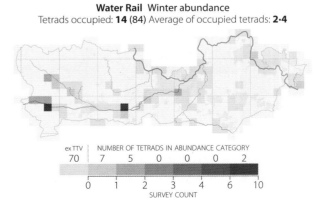

**Water Rail** Winter abundance
Tetrads occupied: **14 (84)** Average of occupied tetrads: **2·4**

| ex TTV | NUMBER OF TETRADS IN ABUNDANCE CATEGORY | | | | | |
|---|---|---|---|---|---|---|
| 70 | 7 | 5 | 0 | 0 | 0 | 2 |

0      1      2      3      4      6      10
SURVEY COUNT

Water Rail probably breeds annually. Between 2000 and 2012 breeding has been confirmed at Thatcham Reedbeds in five years, and also at Brimpton Gravel Pit, Kintbury Cressbeds (twice), Thames Valley Park and at Great Meadow Pond in Windsor Great Park.

Winter records are now typically received from about 30 locations in Berkshire each year, usually from river valleys, especially the Kennet, gravel pits and other wetland sites. As the Winter Map indicates, the distribution in winter, unlike in the breeding season, is more evenly spread across the county. The highest counts in the county were

of an estimated 12 birds on three occasions, at Slough Sewage Farm on 11th December 1943, Hosehill Lake on 27th November 2001 and Dorney Wetlands on 5th December 2010.

National ringing information indicates that the wintering population includes immigrants from continental Europe and this may explain the higher number of winter records. The only Berkshire recovery was of a bird ringed at Lake Druzno, Zolwiniec, Poland in July 1978 and recovered at Sonning in February 1979.

*Sponsored by Hugh Wilson*

# Spotted Crake

Amber  Sch. 1

*Porzana porzana*

*Rare passage migrant*

The Spotted Crake is one of Britain's most elusive breeding birds, preferring wetland sites with a dense cover of tangled vegetation. It is primarily a trans-Saharan migrant, and, although certainly under-recorded, the species appears to be a rare passage migrant in Berkshire. There are a number of records from the winter, which is inconsistent with the species' status in England (Brown and Grice, 2005), and which casts doubt on a number of records previously published for the county.

In the late 19th century the Spotted Crake declined as a breeding species in Britain, possibly in part due to land drainage. There are no published reports for Berkshire after 1889 until one was seen at Slough Sewage Farm in November and December 1938, a gap of some 50 years. There were two further records in the following 25 years, one at Slough Sewage Farm in September 1945 and one, somewhat bizarrely, found dead outside the Museum in the centre of Reading on 12th September 1963.

The number of Spotted Crakes reported in Berkshire changed in 1966. Until that year there had been just three records in 75 years, but it was reported almost annually, with birds recorded in 20 of the 30 winters from 1966/67 to 1995/96. While an increase in observer cover from the 1960s may have contributed to this increase, and 12 of the records for the county have been from old-style sewage farms, almost all of which have since been modernised, it also seems significant that there has been a notable absence of winter records since the mid-1980s, with only autumn passage records since 1985. There were no records after 1991 until one at Thatcham Marsh on 21st August 1994. After two records in 1997 and one in 1999, there have been four between 2000 and 2011, with a seven year gap between one at Great Meadow Pond in September 2004 and

one at the Thatcham Nature Discovery Centre on 3rd September 2011.

Figure 60 sets out the pattern of records that have appeared in county reports, including the winter records, which must now be regarded as doubtful, but excludes a number of records which have recently been re-assessed and rejected by the Berkshire Records Committee. The records in the figure include the only 20th century report of two birds together, at Reading Sewage Farm in January 1976.

The earliest autumn arrival was one at Lavell's Lake on 7th August 1999. Of the 30 records in Figure 60, 18 were first observed between 26th August and 14th October. There is only one spring record, a bird heard calling briefly at Thatcham Marsh early on 6th May 1990. Most of the Spotted Crakes recorded in Berkshire since 1938 have been seen or heard for only one day, but there have been five records of birds remaining at a site for a month or more. The sites most frequented in recent decades have been Thatcham Marsh and Lavell's Lake, the latter accounting for three of the seven records between 1997 and 2011.

In the early part of the 19th century, Spotted Crakes are likely to have bred on a fairly regular basis in the Kennet Valley. Lamb (1880) records that a female was shot at Kintbury in March 1810, and Clark Kennedy (1868) notes that birds usually arrive at the end of March or beginning of April and leave in October. According to Noble (1906) birds were often flushed in the breeding season at Thatcham Marsh and records of individuals being caught in Berkshire were numerous. In total, there are ten published records involving at least 11 birds for the 30 years from 1860 to 1889, including a pair taken near Eton in about 1865.

*Sponsored by John Swallow*

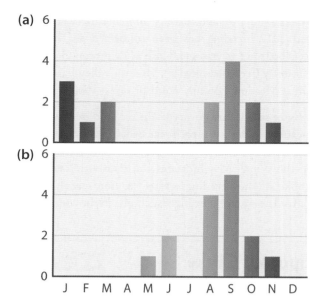

**Figure 60: Spotted Crake: all birds recorded by month of arrival.** (a) 1964/65–1983/84; (b) 1994/95–2010/11.

# Sora Rail

*Porzana carolina*

*Rare vagrant, one record*

Berkshire has the distinction of being the first county in Britain to record this rare vagrant from North America, when one was shot by a Mr Eyre on the banks of the Kennet near Newbury in October 1865. It was exhibited by Professor Newton at a meeting of the Zoological Society in February 1866 under its then common name of Carolina Crake (Noble, 1906).

*Sponsored by Brian Clews*

# Baillon's Crake

*Porzana pusilla*

*Rare vagrant, recorded on one occasion*

Baillon's Crake is a rare vagrant to Britain, its normal breeding range stretching from southern Europe across Asia to Australasia. Berkshire's only confirmed record was one seen at Thatcham Marsh on 23rd February 1972 for just long enough to enable sufficient details to be obtained to allow specific identification. Clark Kennedy (1868) was informed that one had been shot near Newbury several years before 1868, but was unable to obtain further details and the record remains unsubstantiated.

*Sponsored by Renton Righelato*

216

# Corncrake

Red   Sch. 1

*Crex crex*

*Former summer visitor, now a rare passage migrant*

In common with so many parts of Britain, the Corncrake was once a widespread summer visitor to Berkshire, but probably became extinct as a breeding species in the county in about 1950, its disappearance reflecting a major decline throughout north-west Europe. The continued decline of the species lead to conservation projects and specific management work by the RSPB since 1983, which has lead to a 2·5 fold increase in breeding population in 15 years in Scotland. A small population has also been re-introduced at Nene Washes, Cambridgeshire. The species is now only recorded in Berkshire as a rare passage migrant.

In the 19th century the Corncrake was a common summer visitor to Berkshire and was described by Clark Kennedy (1868) as "very numerous after the end of April". Summering birds were regular in the Thames Valley meadows and departed at the end of September, occasionally later (Noble, 1906). The earliest published county record is of a female brought alive to Dr Lamb in July 1793 which "laid an egg on my hand" (Lamb, 1880).

Corncrakes were still being quite widely reported during the 1930s, with records from the Downs around Combe and Aldworth, from river valley meadows at Hamstead Marshall, Aldermaston, Bradfield, Wargrave and Remenham, and from Greenham Common. By 1938, however, passage records outweighed summering records, with reports in August and September from Slough Sewage Farm in 1938, 1942 and 1944, two shot at Fifield in September 1948, and one found dead under telegraph wires at Cookham in August 1947. In 1949, one was heard again at Wargrave in April, and in August a party of six birds was seen in a barley field at Combe. Figure 61 demonstrates the decline in records in the county since 1931, the slight increase in the 1970s coinciding with a general upturn in records in central and southern England at the time (*1968–72 BTO Atlas*).

There are a few later records which might be indicative of summering birds. Single calling birds were recorded at Inkpen at the end of June 1969, and at Lowbury Hill on 27th May 1973. There have been just three records in Berkshire since 1980. There was one at Theale Gravel Pits on 24th July 1983 and then a break of 22 years before the next, in June 2005, when one was heard in a field near Grazeley. The latest bird was one believed to have been calling every night from 6th to 27th June 2008 at Hurst, but despite much effort few reliable sightings were possible due to the height of the crop.

It is also likely that a number of calling birds will not have been reported to the county's ornithological societies, one such instance being of one, probably two, calling from farmland at Shurlock Row in May and June in about 1976, eventually reported by a farmer in July 1992.

Figure 62 shows the monthly distribution of records in Berkshire from 1950 to 2010, the extreme dates for arrival and departure being 20th April in 1978 at Theale Gravel Pits and 26th October in 1977 at Hawthorn Hill. There have been three winter records: Clark Kennedy (1868) reported that one was picked up in poor condition at Eton on 25th December 1865, Noble (1906) shot one in November some time before 1905, and one is reported to have been flushed near Combe on 18th January 1932.

*Sponsored by Crex Group*

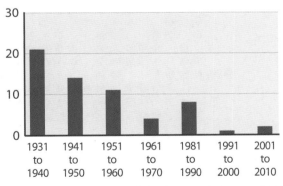

**Figure 61: Corncrake: all birds recorded 1931–2010, by decade.**

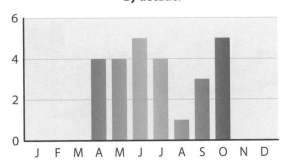

**Figure 62: Corncrake: all birds recorded 1950–2010, by month of arrival.**

# Moorhen

## Gallinula chloropus

*Common and widespread resident and winter visitor*

The Moorhen is common and widespread in Berkshire and occurs throughout the year on almost any stretch of water, no matter how small or overgrown. On larger bodies of water it is restricted to the margins, where its poor swimming ability is less of a handicap in the presence either of predators or aggressive competitors such as the Coot.

Moorhen populations in England are likely to have suffered during the 19th century from the draining of marshes and water meadows and the loss of many village and farm ponds, even the smallest of which may have held one or two pairs. However, the 2007–11 Breeding Distribution Map confirms that the Moorhen is widespread in Berkshire and catholic in its choice of habitat, being recorded from 74% (290) of all tetrads, despite many of these being quite unsuitable for almost any other water bird. This represents a small reduction in range compared to the 1987–89 Atlas Survey when 80% of tetrads in Berkshire were occupied. Reasons for this reduction in range are not clear, though it has been suggested that predation by American mink (*Mustela*

*vison*), which is now quite widespread in Berkshire, may impact particularly upon Moorhens. However, a study of the impact of mink on water birds in the Upper Thames (Ferreras & Macdonald, 1996) concluded that although some negative effects were seen, Moorhens seem well adapted to withstand mink predation. This conclusion is supported by the slight increase seen in the UK population from 1989–2009 as revealed by the CBC and BBS.

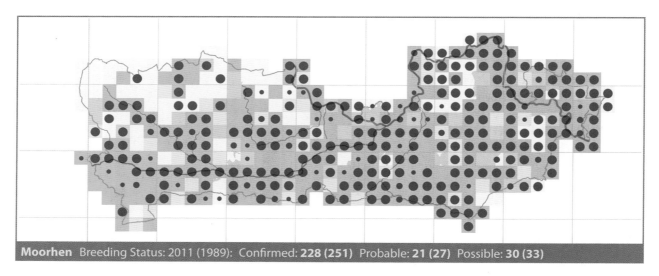

**Moorhen** Breeding Status: 2011 (1989): Confirmed: **228 (251)** Probable: **21 (27)** Possible: **30 (33)**

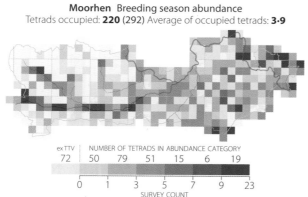

**Moorhen** Breeding season abundance
Tetrads occupied: **220 (292)** Average of occupied tetrads: **3·9**

| exTTV | NUMBER OF TETRADS IN ABUNDANCE CATEGORY | | | | | |
|---|---|---|---|---|---|---|
| 72 | 50 | 79 | 51 | 15 | 6 | 19 |

0    1    3    5    7    9    23
SURVEY COUNT

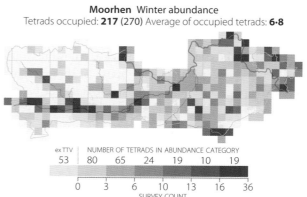

**Moorhen** Winter abundance
Tetrads occupied: **217 (270)** Average of occupied tetrads: **6·8**

| exTTV | NUMBER OF TETRADS IN ABUNDANCE CATEGORY | | | | | |
|---|---|---|---|---|---|---|
| 53 | 80 | 65 | 24 | 19 | 10 | 19 |

0    3    6    10    13    16    36
SURVEY COUNT

Moorhens can be very secretive when breeding, but once the young have hatched and begin to accompany the adults on feeding trips, their presence is usually obvious. This, plus the fact that the Moorhen has a long breeding season with often two and sometimes three broods, means that it is unlikely that the species was under-recorded during the 2007–11 Atlas Survey. Another factor may be that the latter part of the 2007–11 survey coincided with the onset of a prolonged dry period which persisted until the spring of 2012, possibly resulting in a number of smaller transient waterbodies away from the main rivers drying up.

The 2007–11 Winter Map shows a similar but slightly reduced distribution (recorded in 270 tetrads) to that in the breeding season. In both seasons the main gaps in distribution in Berkshire are in Northern regions of West Berkshire, including the Downs. The Winter Map indicates that the highest density of Moorhens in Berkshire at this time of year occurs in the river valleys where the local population may be joined by continental birds. Sizeable flocks may occur, with birds often being seen grazing on pastures beside rivers and gravel pits. Winter survey data from WeBS counts are not considered to monitor Moorhen populations very well due to the restricted coverage, but the data indicate a static winter population since 1995/96 winter until a drop off in winters of 2009/10 and 2010/11, believed to be due to reduced survival during these hard winters. The highest count recorded in Berkshire was an estimated 2,000 at Reading Sewage Farm on 20th February 1927. The highest count in recent years was about 150 at Donnington Lake, Newbury on 8th January 1984, and the only counts above 100 since 1996 were of 100+ at Theale GP on 17th August 1999 and 107 on Jubilee River on 2nd September 2005. Leucistic birds were reported from Purley in 1980 and Slough Sewage Farm in 1984.

There are two ringing recoveries of Moorhen in Berkshire which provide evidence of movement between southern England and the Low Countries. A bird ringed in the Netherlands in August 1966 was recovered at Swallowfield in March 1968, and one ringed at Denford Mill in January 1979 was recovered in Belgium in December 1980.

*Sponsored by Renee Grayer*

Moorhen, Dinton Pastures *Tony Harden*

# Coot

*Fulica atra*

*Common resident and winter visitor*

In Berkshire, the Coot is a common resident and winter visitor, which often forms large flocks outside the breeding season on lakes, gravel pits and larger rivers. It is a strong, though chiefly nocturnal, flier and despite the infrequency with which it takes to the air, birds spending the winter in southern England may come from as far afield as Latvia and Estonia, while the local breeding population may move south and west in winter.

The increase in the extent of open water due to gravel extraction in Berkshire has had a considerable impact upon the Coot population, especially in winter when the birds favour such productive and usually ice-free sites. The larger areas of open water in Berkshire, however, tend to support relatively few breeding pairs of Coot, primarily because many have steep or poorly vegetated banks which lack the fringing vegetation favoured by the species for nesting sites.

After a period of steady increase in both the breeding and wintering numbers of Coot in Great Britain in the second half of the twentieth century, the population has been fairly stable since 2000. The Tetrad Surveys show little change in the breeding season distribution of Coot over the 20 years after the late 1980s in Berkshire. It breeds throughout Berkshire where there are areas of open water with well vegetated edges. The Coot has a much more restricted breeding distribution than the almost ubiquitous Moorhen, the tetrads in which it was recorded correlating well with the distribution of rivers, reedbed, marshes as well as areas of open water. During the breeding season the Coot is ferociously territorial and fights between pairs, often involving all four birds,

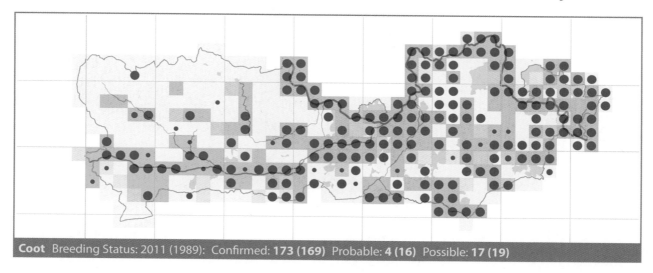

**Coot** Breeding Status: 2011 (1989): Confirmed: **173 (169)** Probable: **4 (16)** Possible: **17 (19)**

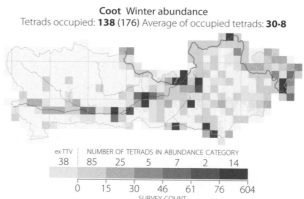

**Coot** Breeding season abundance
Tetrads occupied: **158 (202)** Average of occupied tetrads: **13·0**

| exTTV | NUMBER OF TETRADS IN ABUNDANCE CATEGORY | | | | | |
|---|---|---|---|---|---|---|
| 44 | 90 | 27 | 15 | 9 | 5 | 12 |

0    6    12    19    25    32    258
SURVEY COUNT

**Coot** Winter abundance
Tetrads occupied: **138 (176)** Average of occupied tetrads: **30·8**

| exTTV | NUMBER OF TETRADS IN ABUNDANCE CATEGORY | | | | | |
|---|---|---|---|---|---|---|
| 38 | 85 | 25 | 5 | 7 | 2 | 14 |

0    15    30    46    61    76    604
SURVEY COUNT

are one of the characteristic waterside sights of March and April.

The breeding cycle of this species is longer than that of the Moorhen and only rarely is there more than a single brood in a season. The breeding success of individual pairs is highly variable, perhaps due to the unpredictable abundance of aquatic invertebrates which are an important component of their diet, though some young are usually reared. This, together with the species' long breeding season, means that it is unlikely that the species was under-recorded during the Tetrad Survey.

Coots tend to form large flocks in the winter. Although the winter population as recorded by the TTV surveys is only approximately twice that in the breeding season (the winter count being 3,662, the breeding season 1,747), they are less dispersed, with WeBS counts indicating large numbers concentrated on a few major sites (Figure 63). Winter influxes are possibly linked to hard weather on the continent. The highest counts recorded have been at Dinton Pastures, where numbers reached 1,500 in December 1981 and at Wraysbury Gravel Pits, where there were 1,490 in December 2010. In 1989, the population of Coot on waters counted by observers during January was estimated to total some 2,500, comparable to the 3,662 counted in the late winter

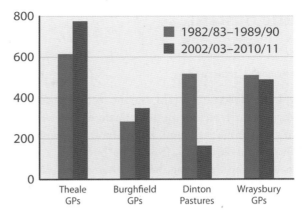

**Figure 63: Coot: average of winter maxima at selected sites.** Data from WeBS for sites reporting more than 400 birds.

tetrad surveys in 2007–11. The winter population in Great Britain of 180,000 (Musgrove et al., 2011) is approximately three times larger than that of breeding adults and includes immigrants from north-west Europe. However there have only been three ringing recoveries of Coot in Berkshire, all recovered less than 100 km from the ringing sites. The most distant involved a bird ringed as an adult at Rye Meads, Hertfordshire in December 1973 which was recovered in July 1984 at Maidenhead.

*Sponsored by Blackwater Valley Countryside Trust*

# Crane

Amber

## *Grus grus*

*Rare vagrant, eight records involving 24 birds*

Before the turn of the century the Crane had only been recorded in Berkshire on two occasions, both on the same day in 1987. During a hard weather movement of other species, two birds were seen at separate localities in the Slough area on 11th January 1987. A brown-headed juvenile was seen to land and feed for about 15 minutes on the Dorney Common side of Slough Sewage Farm before being disturbed and flying off westwards towards Bray. Quite independently, an adult was observed flying over Langley from Buckinghamshire into Berkshire at the same time.

In the last ten years there have been an increased number of sightings, all involving birds in flight. A single bird was seen to circle over Theale on 14th January 2002, followed by two birds flying south between East and West Ilsley on 7th April in the same year. In 2003 a party of nine was observed flying from the south west on the edge of Berkshire airspace north of Slough on 2nd March, which coincided with an influx of continental birds into Britain. More recently two birds were seen circling high

west of Maidenhead on 11th May 2010, while single birds were reported over Three Mile Cross on 27th February 2011 and over Cookham on 6th April 2011. On 5th April 2012 three were seen passing through the county, firstly at Moor Green Lakes, then at Pingewood, Earley and finally flying northeast into Oxfordshire. The recent sightings have yet to be reviewed by the Berkshire Records Committee.

*Sponsored by Bob Lyle*

# Little Bustard

*Tetrax tetrax*

*Rare vagrant, recorded once*

The Little Bustard is a rare vagrant to Berkshire with a single county record, an adult male of the western, nominate subspecies found injured on the Downs near Compton on 28th July 1958. The bird had a badly damaged wing and later died. Although its plumage suggested that it was an adult male, a histological examination revealed bisexual characteristics (Lewis, 1958). The skin was preserved and was kept for many years at the Institute for Animal Health at Compton.

The nearest breeding population to Britain is in central France, but this has been in decline for many years, which is reflected in the scarcity of recent records in Britain.

*Sponsored by Jenny Williams*

# Great Bustard

*Otis tarda*

*A former resident, absent for over two centuries, but with recent records from a re-introduction project.*

The former status of the Great Bustard in Berkshire was aptly described by Noble (1906) who wrote "there is little doubt that this magnificent bird was at one time resident and bred on the open Downs of Berkshire, but it has long since passed away and the records left behind are meagre in the extreme." Just two detailed records remain. Lamb (1880) recalls that Great Bustards were sometimes seen on the Lambourn Downs before they were enclosed, and refers specifically to them being seen in March 1802. There is also a report, which first appeared in The Zoologist for 1856, of a young male found with a broken leg near Hungerford on 3rd January that year. When it was later dissected it was considered to be about 18 months old (Noble, 1906).

Since 2004 there has been a project to reintroduce Great Bustards on Salisbury Plain in Wiltshire, with these birds breeding successfully in the wild for the first time in 2012. Some of the birds have wandered further afield, and in 2011 a Great Bustard seen flying north-east over Queen Mother Reservoir on 17th November was probably from the project. The following year, one was present on the Downs from 7th to 12th June, carrying a wing tag from the project, which identified the bird as a first-summer female. It was reported as having returned to the release site the following day. These sightings raise the prospect of the return of this spectacular bird as a county resident if this project succeeds.

*Sponsored by Ken White*

# Stone Curlew

Amber   Sch. 1

*Burhinus oedicnemus*

*Scarce and localised summer visitor*

The Stone Curlew is a summer visitor to restricted areas in England and is a very localised breeding species in Berkshire. The county is the centre of the third largest concentration of the species in England away from the principal populations in the Brecks of East Anglia and Salisbury Plain. The local population has benefited from intense conservation action since the early 1990s.

Stone Curlew appear to have been widely dispersed in Berkshire before the 20th century; Clark Kennedy (1868) refers to birds killed near Newbury and seen near Reading, and Palmer (1886) includes a reference to one shot at Snelsmore Common in about 1870. These locations support Noble's (1906) statement that the species is partial to open heaths and waste lands. His only breeding record, however, is for the Downs near Aldworth in June 1890.

Despite a decline in numbers since the 19th century, the Stone Curlew was still a widespread breeding bird on suitable terrain in the county up to the Second World War, when the relatively bare ground or close-cropped turf which it favours for nesting was plentiful on the Downs. Annual reports of the OOS in the 1930s showed that there were fair numbers breeding regularly on the Berkshire Downs, part of which is now in Oxfordshire. An investigation into its status in 1931 recorded three, possibly four, pairs at one site on the Berkshire Downs and two pairs at another. In south-west Berkshire, near the Hampshire border, there were eight nests in 1930. Counts were made regularly of the post-breeding flocks which tend to gather from August until late October, often at traditional sites, and these showed that flocks of 30 or 40 were not uncommon, and on one occasion in September 1932 over 100 were recorded.

During and after the Second World War, extensive ploughing for crops severely reduced the species' favoured habitat. The decimation of the rabbit population as a result of myxomatosis in the 1950s, which led an increase in vegetation growth, was also an adverse factor. A decline in the number of Stone Curlews in Berkshire was the inevitable result. By the 1980s it was clear that conservation measures were urgently needed if the Stone Curlew was to continue to breed in the county. An RSPB project for the protection of the species was initiated in East Anglia in 1985 and soon showed a 37% improvement in breeding success there (Green, 1988). Nests were located and the co-operation of farmers and landowners obtained to protect eggs and chicks during farming activities. Advice has been given so that

potential breeding sites are created. Since the project was extended to Berkshire in 1991 it has helped to stabilise the breeding population in the county, and since 2000 the number of pairs has increased.

The 1987–89 Tetrad Survey confirmed breeding in only five tetrads in Berkshire, with possible or probable breeding in eight more, a contraction of range compared with the distribution given in the *1968–72 BTO Atlas*, Stone Curlews even then being absent from most of the apparently suitable downland areas in the county. However the 2007–11 survey proved breeding in seven tetrads, with possible breeding in two more. As the species is especially vulnerable to disturbance the maps have not been published.

Stone Curlews can be difficult to find, especially after eggs have been laid, as they are relatively inactive by day and well camouflaged. Even after dusk, when most of the feeding takes place, they do not necessarily betray their presence by calling. A county-wide search for nesting sites organised by the RSPB has been carried out annually since 1990. Although three breeding pairs with four nest sites were found in 1990, only two clutches are known to have hatched successfully. The RSPB project began the following year, when six pairs and two unpaired birds were located and five young fledged. In the early years the number of breeding pairs has varied from three to five, although in most years non-breeding pairs and single adults are also located (RSPB, 1995). By 2005 to 2010 numbers had increased with between seven and 12 pairs located, although breeding success is often poor. For example, in 2008 seven pairs only successfully reared two young.

Autumn gatherings on the Downs can be quite large, with, for example, 26 in mid-September 2002, 21 in late September 2005 and 29 in October 2006. Information on the arrival and departure dates in the county reports is sparse, with earliest and latest dates of 3rd April and 12th October, both in 2010.

There are few records of Stone Curlew in Berkshire away from the Downs. These include one calling at night over Old Windsor on 31st July 1961, two calling at night over Maidenhead on 14th October in the same year, one flying north at Old Windsor on 7th April 1962, one flying over Reading Sewage Farm on 9th October 1977, and one at Theale Gravel Pits in May 1994. Records since 2000 include single birds at Pingewood Gravel Pit in April 2004, at Englefield in April 2007, at Cookham Rise in May 2007, and at Colnbrook on 29th March 2013.

Habitat loss is widely accepted as being the main cause of the decline in the Stone Curlew population, but the species has adapted to some extent and the majority now nest on arable land (*1988–91 BTO Atlas*). The birds usually arrive from late March and soon select nesting territories, often in spring-sown crops where the ground is still fairly bare. Subsequent farming operations, such as rolling or spraying, are liable to destroy eggs or chicks and there is a danger of birds deserting if the crop grows quickly. Other factors, such as predation, especially by crows and foxes, and human disturbance from recreation also affect breeding success, and egg-collecting unfortunately still occurs. Although replacement clutches may be laid, it is increasingly difficult for the birds to find suitable areas of bare ground for nesting as the season advances.

There has been one recovery of a Stone Curlew ringed in Berkshire, a bird which was ringed as a nestling in 1991 later being found shot in France. Colour ringing has shown that there is movement between the different regional populations in Britain. A bird from Norfolk was sighted in 1995, and one from Wiltshire in 2003.

*In memory of Ian Bell*

Stone Curlew, Berkshire Downs *Jerry O'Brien*

# Black-winged Stilt

**Sch. 1**

*Himantopus himantopus*

*Rare vagrant, two or three records involving six or eight birds*

There have been just three Berkshire records of Black-winged Stilt, although these involve a total of eight birds. A party of four was at Reading Sewage Farm from 17th to 21st May 1922. These birds were considered to have been two males, one female and an immature. During their stay they paid visits to the River Thames between Reading and Sonning. In 1945 there were two at Ham Sewage Farm on 17th May and two at Slough Sewage Farm on 22nd June. Although there is a month between the two records, it is possible that the same birds were involved. In that year, there were several records of Black-winged Stilts in Britain and breeding took place at a Northampton sewage farm.

It is uncertain whether "one killed at Shiplake, Oxfordshire, prior to 1849" (Aplin, 1889) used the Berkshire bank of the Thames.

*Sponsored by Dick Haydon*

# Avocet

**Amber** **Sch. 1**

*Recurvirostra avosetta*

*Rare passage migrant*

The Avocet remains a rare passage migrant in Berkshire, despite a steady increase in the British breeding population since the 1940s (*1968–72 BTO Atlas, 1988–91 BTO Atlas*), an increase in the extent of suitable habitat, and better observer coverage. The maps show the distribution of passage records during the 2007–11 Berkshire Atlas survey, with records from gravel pits, the Jubilee River and Queen Mother Reservoir.

The first 20th century record involved a single bird at Reading Sewage Farm on 10th May 1936. After a further isolated record of one at Burghfield Gravel Pits on 4th May 1951, there were more frequent records from 1969, with one at Ham Sewage Farm on 16th September 1969, one at Reading Sewage Farm on 6th December 1970, and two at Twyford Gravel Pits from 24th April to 1st May 1976.

A further increase in the frequency of sightings took place in the early 1980s, coinciding with the increase in the number of Avocets wintering in Suffolk (*1981–84 BTO Winter Atlas*). Records came from Theale Gravel Pits with one on 5th June 1980, three on 7th May and again on 25th May 1981 and a party of 14 on 27th March 1983 (although this record was never formally submitted for publication in the county report). There was also one at Dinton Pastures on 13th March 1984. There was then a gap of five years without records until singles were seen at Queen Mother Reservoir on 1st December 1989, Racecourse Gravel Pit, Newbury on 17th November 1991, Theale Gravel Pits on 11th March 1992, Thatcham Gravel Pits on 20th April 1992 and Eversley Gravel Pits on 26th April 1992.

Since the mid-nineties there have been records in every year except 2005 and 2006, although normally no more

**Avocet** Spring migration occurrence
Tetrads used: **8** Average of used tetrads: **3·3**

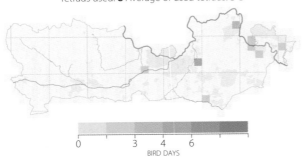

0   3   4   6
BIRD DAYS

**Avocet** Autumn migration occurrence
Tetrads used: **3** Average of used tetrads: **6·3**

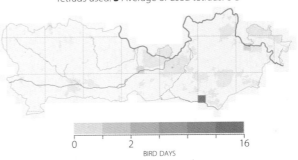

0   2   16
BIRD DAYS

225

than three in any year and generally of one or two birds passing through during the spring period. Larger counts involved groups of six seen over Horton Gravel Pits on 2nd March 1995, nine on the island in Moatlands Gravel Pit on 26th April 1999, and seven at Horton in March 2012. Late autumn has also produced a few records of single birds and, exceptionally, three at Field Farm Gravel Pit, Theale on 11th September 2000 and a party of nine at Queen Mother Reservoir on 29th November 2003. This increased frequency of sightings is consistent with the continuing rise in the number of Avocets wintering on the estuaries of southern England, where total numbers, which include birds that breed in England along with substantial numbers that breed in other western European countries, are now estimated to exceed 7,500 and the national index is now at its highest ever level (Eaton et al., 2011).

Figure 64 shows the monthly pattern of records since the first 20th century record in 1936, and Figure 65 the decadal totals. There have been records involving a further 18 birds in the three years 2010 to 2012.

Prior to 1900, there is just one county record, a party of six shot "near Sonning" in 1794 (Lamb, 1880).

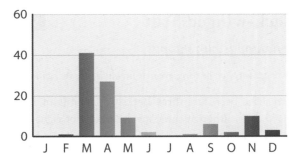

**Figure 64: Avocet: all birds recorded 1930–2012, by month of arrival.**

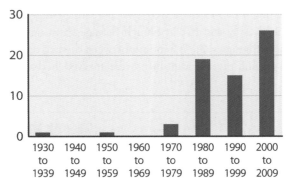

**Figure 65: Avocet: all birds recorded 1930–2009, by decade.**

*Sponsored by Ismael Hazari*

# Oystercatcher

Amber

*Haematopus ostralegus*

*Regular and increasing passage migrant, scarce breeder and occasional winter visitor.*

Oystercatchers are predominantly coastal birds, breeding on rocky, sandy and estuarine shores and nearby grassland around the whole of the UK. Part of the British breeding population moves south in the winter and large numbers of birds from the Icelandic and NW European populations winter in British estuaries (*Migration Atlas*). Oystercatchers started to breed in inland areas in Scotland in the nineteenth century and over the last century small numbers have adopted inland sites progressively further south in England. In recent years, there has been a decline in the numbers of Oystercatchers breeding in Scotland, but a steady increase in England: BBS data show a 50% increase between 1995 and 2009.

Prior to 1946, the Oystercatcher was a rare vagrant in Berkshire. One was recorded at Burghfield in January 1794 (Lamb, 1880), and Clark Kennedy (1868) reports that birds had occasionally been shot along the Thames in the nineteenth century. It was one of the few waders not to be reported from Reading Sewage Farm in the 1920s and 1930s. Although the extent of suitable

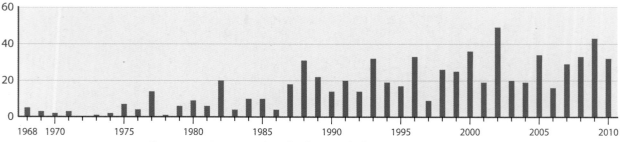

**Figure 66: Oystercatcher: birds recorded per year 1968–2010.**

226

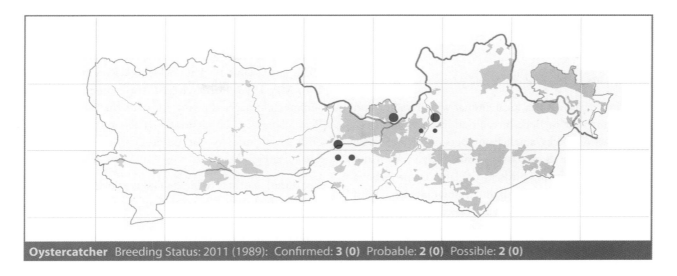

**Oystercatcher** Breeding Status: 2011 (1989): Confirmed: **3 (0)** Probable: **2 (0)** Possible: **2 (0)**

**Oystercatcher** Breeding season abundance
Tetrads occupied: **4 (31)** Average of occupied tetrads: **1·8**

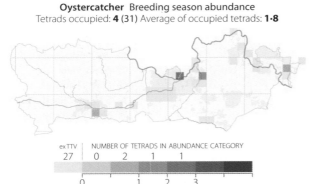

| ex TTV | NUMBER OF TETRADS IN ABUNDANCE CATEGORY | | | |
|---|---|---|---|---|
| 27 | 0 | 2 | 1 | 1 |

0      1      2      3
SURVEY COUNT

**Oystercatcher** Winter abundance
Tetrads occupied: **0 (7)** Average of occupied tetrads: **0**

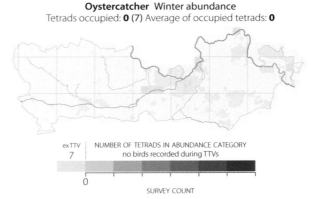

| ex TTV | NUMBER OF TETRADS IN ABUNDANCE CATEGORY |
|---|---|
| 7 | no birds recorded during TTVs |

0
SURVEY COUNT

habitat for passage waders increased as a result of gravel extraction between 1946 and 1967, the period only produced a further 13 records, all of single birds apart from a small party heard at night over Earley in 1960.

From the 1970s, Oystercatchers have been observed more frequently, in both spring and autumn passage periods, at Queen Mother Reservoir and many of the gravel pits. Figure 66 shows the number of birds recorded at all sites from 1968 to 2008; given the high degree of mobility between sites, it is likely that the Figure overstates the numbers of birds involved. From 2001, when a pair remained at Hosehill from May to August, birds were present most summers and in 2010, breeding was recorded in Berkshire for the first time, on gravel pits at Theale and Twyford. Chicks were reared successfully in 2010 and 2011, although flooding in 2012 destroyed breeding attempts at two sites. With the growth of the inland breeding population, we can anticipate hearing and seeing this charismatic wader at increasing numbers of gravel pits in the county through much of the year.

*Sponsored by Duncan Spence*

Oystercatcher,
Queen Mother Reservoir
*Michael McKee*

# Golden Plover

*Pluvialis apricaria*

*Common but local winter visitor and passage migrant*

The Golden Plover is a local annual winter visitor and passage migrant in Berkshire. In addition to the large regular winter flocks, smaller numbers of birds are now recorded most years on passage, principally in April and September. Wintering birds in England are probably a mixture of British bred birds and immigrants from both the Icelandic and Scandinavian breeding populations (*Migration Atlas*).

Most birds arrive in Berkshire during October and November, followed in some mild winters by a large December influx, as in 2001 when numbers reached about 5,000 at Lower Farm, Thatcham. Most birds have left by the end of March or early April, though a flock of 60 was recorded at Brimpton Gravel Pits on 4th May 1981, and a lame bird at Tickleback Row from 7th to 10th May 1993. In March and April some birds are in summer plumage, allowing those of the northern race *P. a. albifrons* to be identified. A few records of single birds in July and August are probably unrelated to the late autumn influx.

The duration of stay of Golden Plover flocks in Berkshire is dependent upon the severity of the winter. Although flocks tend to remain at a chosen site throughout the winter if the weather conditions are favourable, hard frosts which prevent access to food may force them to disperse or move away from the county. As the winter map shows, whilst wintering birds have a clear preference

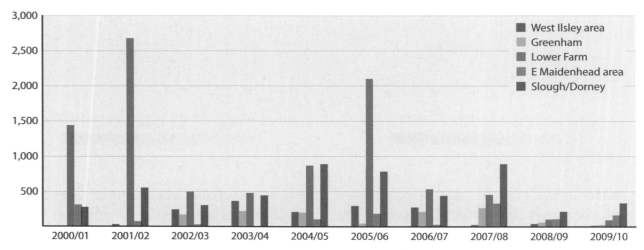

**Figure 67: Golden Plover: Maximum counts at main wintering sites.** Average of monthly maxima October–February.

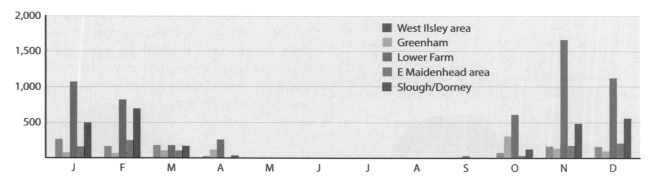

**Figure 68: Golden Plover: average monthly maxima for the main wintering sites, 2000/01 to 2009/10.**

for arable land in the Kennet Valley and to a lesser extent alongside the Thames, they are also observed regularly on the Downs. As many downland sightings have been in April and September, it seems likely that in Berkshire this habitat is used more frequently at times of passage than for wintering.

The average of the highest reported counts for each month over the period from 2000/01 to 2009/10 for the main Berkshire wintering and passage areas is shown in Figure 67. Whereas between the 1970s and the 1990s most of the main sites were in mid- and west Berkshire, since 2000, Dorney Wetlands and the area between Reading and Maidenhead have often held large flocks. Since 2007, Lower Farm, Thatcham, which had held the largest numbers of Golden Plover in the county in the preceding ten years, appears to have become less attractive.

As well as the larger wintering flocks, there are scattered records of Golden Plovers from elsewhere in Berkshire. These are mainly of passage birds, often flight records, from such places as gravel pits, reservoirs and sewage farms, significantly those areas to which birdwatchers are attracted. Some movements appear to result from the onset of severe weather and often involve association with Lapwings.

**Golden Plover** Winter abundance
Tetrads occupied: **21** (118) Average of occupied tetrads: **94·5**

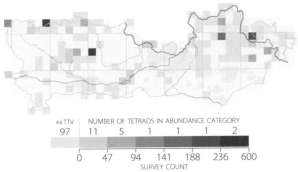

| exTTV | NUMBER OF TETRADS IN ABUNDANCE CATEGORY | | | | | |
|---|---|---|---|---|---|---|
| 97 | 11 | 5 | 1 | 1 | 1 | 2 |

0    47    94    141    188    236    600
SURVEY COUNT

Golden Plovers have probably always passed through and wintered in some numbers in Berkshire. Hewett (1911), writing about the Downs around Compton in 1861, states that Golden Plovers sometime return in late August but most arrive "in large wings" in November and remain until February, although they "are sometimes seen in April in pairs". Clark Kennedy (1868) records them as a "regular winter visitor to open marshy ground and the banks of the Thames" and notes that "200–300 may be occasionally observed feeding on the fallow lands near Datchet and Slough".

*Sponsored by John Dellow*

# Grey Plover

Amber

*Pluvialis squatarola*

*Uncommon but regular passage migrant*

The Grey Plover is an uncommon but regular passage migrant in very small numbers in Berkshire. The first county record was from Reading Sewage Farm on 21st September 1924, (an adult and an immature), followed by records of single birds at this site in 1926 and 1928. Modernisation of the sewage farm in the early 1930s put an end to the records, the next sighting in the county not being for another 20 years, when two were at Ham Sewage Farm in 1948.

Grey Plover, with Turnstone and Bar-tailed Godwit, Queen Mother Reservoir, 3rd May 2012 *Michael McKee*

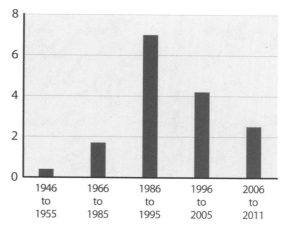

**Figure 69: Grey Plover: birds recorded per year.**
Period averages.

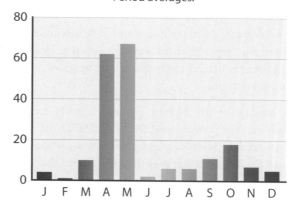

**Figure 70: Grey Plover: all birds recorded 1924–2011, by month of arrival.**

Since 1948, there was an increase in records until the mid-1990s, since when they have declined a little, as shown in Figure 69. Although the increase in the number of records of Grey Plover coincide with the increase in the extent of gravel pits in Berkshire, it is likely that greater observer cover has also been a factor as many records have been of over-flying birds. Most records are of birds on spring passage. Nearly 20% of records between 1924 and 2011 were in April and over 40% in May. A smaller passage occurs in autumn, with numbers between 1924 and 2011 peaking in October, which accounts for just over 10% of records. The small number of winter records are believed mainly to involve juvenile birds on migration (*1981–84 BTO Winter Atlas*).

Sightings of Grey Plovers have been annual since 1983, except in 2000, with the highest annual total of 12 in 2002. A high proportion of records, some 90%, are of one or two birds. The largest groups recorded were of five birds in May 1984, May 2002 and April 2004. Instances of birds staying for longer than one day are uncommon, the longest being for about a week at Queen Mother Reservoir in November 1988 and September 1990.

*Sponsored by Stanley Roach*

# Sociable Plover

## *Chettusia gregaria*

*Rare vagrant, one record*

There is one record of Sociable Plover for Berkshire, a male in summer plumage at Brimpton Gravel Pits on 10th April 1991. Although the bird had not been visible on the ground, it was seen when a small helicopter flushed it with a flock of some 80 Lapwings.

This species has suffered a dramatic decline in recent decades within its main breeding area, Kazakhstan and south-east Russia, so it is unlikely that any recurrence of this remarkable record will occur.

*Sponsored by David Chopping*

# Lapwing

## Vanellus vanellus

*Common but declining resident, passage migrant and winter visitor*

The Lapwing is a common resident in Berkshire, whose numbers are increased considerably by the influx of passage birds, especially during winter when large numbers move to escape from harsh weather in other areas. Although still a widespread breeder, numbers in Berkshire have decreased over the last few decades, a trend which applies to the whole of southern England. Changes in land use and farming practice are thought to have been responsible for the observed halving of the UK population between 1985 and 1995, which has been followed by a continuing slow decline. In 2009 Lapwing was added to the UK Red List of birds of conservation concern.

Breeding commences in early April, the preferred nesting habitat being short grassland, ploughed fields and other waste areas where ground cover is sparse. One unusual habitat used for breeding in Berkshire is plantations of young Christmas trees on the Yattendon Estate. The Tetrad Surveys show that Lapwings breed in most parts of the county, and the breeding distribution correlates quite well with the distribution of arable land

DA.Trelwell.

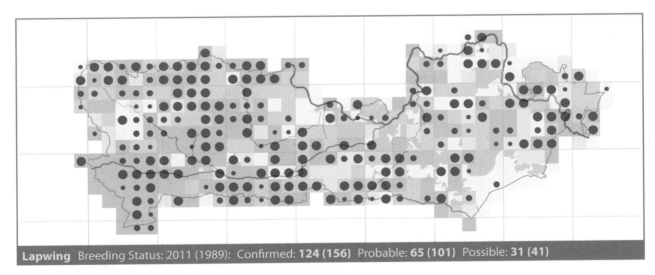

**Lapwing**  Breeding Status: 2011 (1989):  Confirmed: **124 (156)**  Probable: **65 (101)**  Possible: **31 (41)**

**Lapwing**  Breeding season abundance
Tetrads occupied: **161 (246)** Average of occupied tetrads: **8·8**

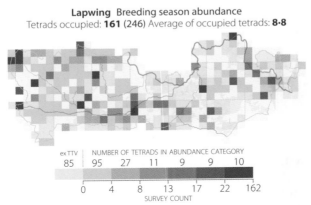

| ex TTV | NUMBER OF TETRADS IN ABUNDANCE CATEGORY | | | | | |
|---|---|---|---|---|---|---|
| 85 | 95 | 27 | 11 | 9 | 9 | 10 |

| 0 | 4 | 8 | 13 | 17 | 22 | 162 |
SURVEY COUNT

**Lapwing**  Winter abundance
Tetrads occupied: **91 (203)** Average of occupied tetrads: **73·9**

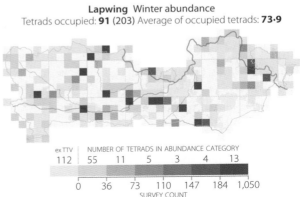

| ex TTV | NUMBER OF TETRADS IN ABUNDANCE CATEGORY | | | | | |
|---|---|---|---|---|---|---|
| 112 | 55 | 11 | 5 | 3 | 4 | 13 |

| 0 | 36 | 73 | 110 | 147 | 184 | 1,050 |
SURVEY COUNT

and with the river valleys, where gravel workings and landfill sites are also used. The 2007–11 survey shows a 22% reduction in the number of tetrads in which breeding was confirmed compared to twenty years earlier, which probably understates the decline in breeding pairs.

Studies have demonstrated that conversion from spring to autumn cereals has involved the extensive loss of the best nesting habitat, as Lapwings avoid nesting in the partly emerged winter sown crop (Shrubb, 1990). Since this conversion was largely complete in Berkshire by the mid-1980s, it is likely that other factors have been driving the continued decline. Losses have been greatest in the populated central and east Berkshire where disturbance and hence increased vulnerability to predators may be a factor.

Large flocks may be encountered at any time from June to March, but tend to reach peak numbers in mid-winter. The *1981–84 BTO Winter Atlas* states that the main immigration from north-west Europe occurs in November and December. The Winter Distribution map from the 2007–11 Berkshire Atlas indicates that the west of the county supports more Lapwings in winter.

In very cold weather there is often considerable passage in a south or south-westerly direction, with consequent reports of large flocks. This occurred in the winter of 1978/79 when, along with the first snow at the end of December, 4,150 flew south over Maidenhead in two hours and 11,000 flew south over Wraysbury, both on 31st December. During mild spells in winter flocks may build up to over 1,000 at, for example, Dorney Wetlands, Woodlands Park, Maidenhead, the Lea Farm-Hurst area and on suitable farmland across the county. Occasionally larger flocks assemble, such as an estimated 5,500–6,000 by the Kennet near Reading and 6,000 at Hurst in January 1993. Only one flock over 1,500 birds has been recorded between 2000 and 2010, which may reflect the reduction in the European population, which has shown similar trends to those in the UK, or less harsh winter conditions.

Ringing of chicks in the 1920s and 1930s established that local breeding birds wintered outside the county, with recoveries in France and Spain. Since the first overseas recovery in 1922, six have been recovered in France and four in Spain. The variable pattern of movement to and from continental Europe is well illustrated by two birds ringed on the same day at Pingewood in October 1981. One was recovered on 3rd December 1981 on the west coast of France, and the other at Alsonmedi, Hungary, on 27th March 1986. Another ringed in Berkshire in September 1956 was recovered in Katowice, Poland in April 1960.

The ring of a bird ringed as a nestling in southern Norway in May 1955 was found at Bucklebury in January 2004, though no details of the finding circumstances are known.

*Sponsored by Rachel Powell*

# Little Ringed Plover    Green    Sch. 1
## *Charadrius dubius*

*Uncommon summer visitor and passage migrant*

The Little Ringed Plover is an uncommon summer visitor and passage migrant to Berkshire, breeding regularly at a small number of sites, predominantly gravel workings. Numbers are increasing slowly, but breeding is largely dependent upon gravel extraction to provide suitable nest sites. It is a protected species in Schedule 1 of the Wildlife & Countryside Act, 1981; the co-operation of many site operators in affording protection is gratefully acknowledged. After breeding, it migrates to sub-saharan Africa to winter, returning early in spring.

The species was first recorded in Berkshire in 1943, when one was seen at Ham Sewage Farm on 8th July. This was followed by a second sighting on 19th July 1944. Little Ringed Plovers had first nested in Britain at Tring Reservoir, Hertfordshire, in 1938, and breeding was first confirmed in Berkshire at Ham Sewage Farm in 1947, although the nest was subsequently destroyed. Pairs were seen at both Ham and Slough Sewage Farms

in 1948, but breeding was not confirmed. Successful breeding then occurred at a gravel pit near Reading in 1949 and in subsequent years. Passage numbers were

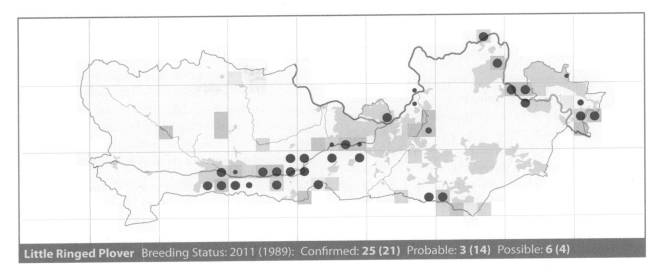

also increasing at this time, with a peak count of 14 at Ham Sewage Farm in autumn 1949. An account of the spread of the Little Ringed Plover was written by Kenneth Allsop, a member of the MTNHS, in 1949. Entitled "Adventure Lit Their Star", the account was written as a novel with place names disguised.

Subsequent censuses organised by the BTO revealed 19 pairs in Berkshire, with six confirmed breeding and four probably breeding, in the summer of 1973. In 1984, there was a total of 54 adults at 11 sites, with breeding confirmed at seven of these. A further BTO survey in 2007 showed a continuing increase in the national population

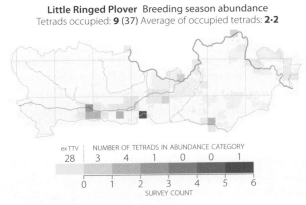

**Little Ringed Plover**  Breeding season abundance
Tetrads occupied: **9 (37)** Average of occupied tetrads: **2·2**

| exTTV | NUMBER OF TETRADS IN ABUNDANCE CATEGORY | | | | | |
|---|---|---|---|---|---|---|
| 28 | 3 | 4 | 1 | 0 | 0 | 1 |

0   1   2   3   4   5   6
SURVEY COUNT

Little Ringed Plover  *Jerry O'Brien*

to approximately 1,115 pairs, mostly at inland sites in England, though the Berkshire population appears not to have changed significantly (Conway *et al.*, 2008).

The Tetrad Surveys carried out in 1987–89 and in 2008–11 showed similar numbers of occupied tetrads, with breeding confirmed in 24 tetrads in the more recent survey and 21 in the earlier period. This is probably a good indication of the true status and distribution of Little Ringed Plover in the county, since it makes its presence known by its display flight and call, and is fairly easy to observe in the open habitat which it frequents. Although some observations during the Tetrad Surveys are likely to relate to transient birds, and some breeding sites are known to overlap two or three tetrads, it is estimated that the Little Ringed Plover breeds in most years at 15–20 different sites across the county.

The gravel extraction industry within the county creates the ideal nesting habitat for the Little Ringed Plover and, as expected, the Tetrad Surveys show a very strong correlation between the distribution of breeding sites and current gravel workings, most of which are concentrated in the river valleys of the Loddon, Colne, Kennet and Thames. The Little Ringed Plover can just as readily utilise other dry sites which provide an open vista and, as a consequence, has been found breeding at localities such as at Slough Sewage Farm, on landfill sites and Greenham Common. Gravel pits and similar sites are often used as a breeding area for only one or two years, during which time the vegetation regenerates and the site gradually becomes less suitable for nesting. It tolerates the activities of a working gravel pit and human disturbance remarkably well, and breeds successfully in such areas despite the risk of nests being destroyed accidentally. As suitable habitat is created, it is frequently occupied in the first succeeding season, suggesting that habitat availability limits the Berkshire population. For example, seven pairs bred at the Jubilee River in the first year of workings on the flood relief scheme in 1997, though numbers have fallen as the area has become vegetated. Thus the breeding population in Berkshire outside a small number of managed nature reserves depends on the repeated creation of new habitat.

On passage, the Little Ringed Plover often appears in small numbers in Berkshire feeding mainly along the margins of gravel pits on shingle, sand or mud, and on the open beds and settling ponds of sewage farms. Occasionally larger numbers of between ten and 40 birds may concentrate at suitable feeding areas, particularly in autumn when juveniles are present. There were over 40 at Reading Sewage Farm in July 1984, and at least 22 at Berry's Lane Gravel Pit in June 2011.

The first spring arrivals in the county have been recorded in mid-March but are more typical later in the month, with the majority of the birds arriving in April. Autumn departure occurs from mid-August to the end of September, with latest departures occurring in early October. There is an exceptional winter record of a bird which was present at Reading Sewage Farm from 20th January to the end of March 1974.

The future success of Little Ringed Plover as a breeding species in Berkshire depends chiefly upon the continued creation of bare gravel areas to provide nesting sites, whether this is by continued gravel extraction or the maintenance of suitable areas at nature reserves by appropriate management.

*Sponsored by Theale Area Bird Group*

# Ringed Plover

*Charadrius hiaticula*

*Uncommon passage migrant and scarce summer visitor*

The Ringed Plover was formerly only a scarce passage migrant through Berkshire, but now regularly breeds in small numbers, and is more regular on passage. The *1968–72 BTO Atlas* showed that this species breeds mostly in coastal areas, but after the mid-1950s there was an increasing tendency for it to nest inland, particularly in northern Britain. The first breeding record for Berkshire was of a pair at Wraysbury Gravel Pits in 1971, and breeding probably occurred at Datchet in 1973 during the construction of the Queen Mother Reservoir. This was followed by a breeding record in central Berkshire at Theale Gravel Pits in 1975 and breeding has been confirmed at this site each year since 1977.

After 1977, the county reports showed a slow but steady increase in the number of breeding Ringed Plover in Berkshire. During the 1987–89 Tetrad Survey breeding was confirmed in ten tetrads, with probable breeding

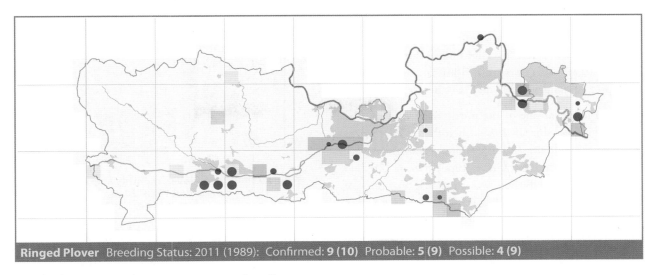

**Ringed Plover** Breeding Status: 2011 (1989): Confirmed: **9 (10)** Probable: **5 (9)** Possible: **4 (9)**

in a further nine. In the 2007–11 survey, breeding was confirmed in eight tetrads (four of which relate to one site, Greenham Common) with probable breeding in a further five. There has been no discernible trend in numbers of Ringed Plover recorded in the County bird report over the period between the two surveys (1988–2008), in either the breeding season or during migration. In contrast, a BTO survey in 2007 (Burton and Conway, 2008) recorded a 76% decline in inland breeding Ringed Plovers in England compared with an earlier survey in 1984. The same survey reported no breeding Ringed Plover in Berkshire in 2007, whilst the county report shows three confirmed sites.

Ringed Plover prefer a breeding habitat of bare gravel, thus the distribution of breeding sites shows a strong correlation with gravel extraction and landfill activities in the county. Unlike the Little Ringed Plover, which appears to require a minimum area of virtually bare gravel, the Ringed Plover can utilise a sparsely vegetated gravel area with scattered plant cover. The establishment of Greenham Common as a nature reserve, with areas managed to maintain sparsely vegetated stony ground, has provided a further breeding habitat. Occasionally arable fields with spring-sown crops are also used. At present, where breeding sites are shared with Little Ringed Plover, there are no signs of strong competition, probably because numbers have not reached high densities. The Ringed Plover returns in early February to early March, some four to six weeks ahead of the Little Ringed Plover.

Breeding success is low, with probably less than a third of attempts leading to fledged young, due to predation, disturbance and flooding. Many breeding sites are ephemeral and become overgrown or are developed, causing Ringed Plover to move to other areas, often within the same gravel pit complex. Future breeding success will depend largely upon the continuing availability of suitable areas created during the course of

**Ringed Plover** Breeding season abundance
Tetrads occupied: **3 (28)** Average of occupied tetrads: **1·3**

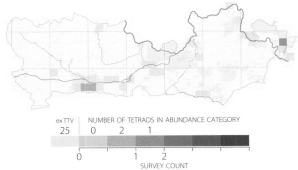

| exTTV | NUMBER OF TETRADS IN ABUNDANCE CATEGORY | | |
|---|---|---|---|
| 25 | 0 | 2 | 1 |

gravel extraction, or as a result of positive conservation measures being taken to maintain such habitat.

Ringed Plover breeding in the southern part of the British Isles appear to undertake a relatively short migration to wintering grounds on the coast of France and N Spain (*Migration Atlas*). A bird ringed as a chick in July 1980 in Berkshire was recovered in Finistere, France, in December 1980, and another ringed in May 1997 recovered in Charente Maritime on the west coast of France in October of the same year.

Ringed Plover are frequently recorded in Berkshire during spring and autumn passage, with peak numbers in spring in March, April and early May and a smaller peak in autumn in late July and August, with a few into September and October (Figure 71). From 1900 to the 1960s, the highest counts at the two favoured sites, Reading and Slough Sewage Farms, were 21 in September 1923 and 19 in May 1941 respectively. Although passage is now more widely distributed across the county, occasional concentrations do occur; for example there were 32 at Wraysbury Gravel Pits on 6th August 1971 and 40–50 at Slough Sewage Farm on May 27th 1998.

There are few winter records of Ringed Plover for Berkshire. Since 1977 there have been two: a single bird at Summerleaze Gravel Pits on 1st January 1979 (during a hard weather movement involving many species), and up to three birds at Queen Mother Reservoir on 24th December 1983. One at Eversley Gravel Pits from 22nd January 1994, with two from 30th January and one there on 25th January 1997 may have been early arrivals.

Ringed Plovers of one of the northern races were first observed in Berkshire in 1988, when there were records of up to three adults and a juvenile at Slough Sewage Farm and Summerleaze Gravel Pits between 21st and 31st August; in 2008 there was an exceptional flock of 19 northern race birds at Horton Gravel Pits on 25th May. According to *BWP III*, birds of these races breed to the north of the British Isles and winter as far south as west Africa.

Prior to 1900, the Ringed Plover was described both as a regular passage migrant (Clark Kennedy, 1868), and

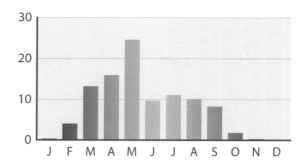

**Figure 71: Ringed Plover: monthly average of birds recorded 1988–2010.**
Data not available for 1989, 1991, 1992, 1997, 1999.

an occasional visitor (Noble, 1906), with the earliest specific record coming somewhat surprisingly from the Ilsley Downs where one was shot in April 1810 (Lamb, 1880).

*Sponsored by Bob & Margaret Walker*

# Killdeer

*Charadrius vociferus*

*Rare vagrant, one record*

The only county record of this American wader is of one at Holyport Gravel Pit from 25th February to 4th March 1984.

*Sponsored by Graeme Stewart*

# Kentish Plover    Sch. 1

*Charadrius alexandrinus*

*Rare vagrant, recorded six times*

There have been five spring records and one autumn record of Kentish Plovers in Berkshire, all involving single birds. Three of these have been from Reading Sewage Farm, on 14th April 1935, 5th April 1936 and 26th to 27th April 1978. The bird seen in 1936 was considered to be a female. The only autumn record was one at Brimpton Gravel Pits on 30th August 1975 which was with three juvenile Little Ringed Plovers. A male was seen at Theale Gravel Pits on 5th May 1981 and one was with two Ringed Plovers at Eversley Gravel Pits on 11th April 1986.

*Sponsored by Ken White 'BOC Spring Raptormania 2012'*

# Dotterel

*Charadrius morinellus*

*Rare passage migrant*

The Dotterel is a rare passage migrant in Berkshire with just two definite 20th century records: one at Bury Down on 15th October 1975 and one found on the Ridgeway on the county border near Aldworth on 12th May 1990. In addition, the ROC report for 1965 recounts that a horse-rider described three birds thought to be Dotterel in a ploughed field near Theale.

Since the turn of the new century, however, there have been eight records involving at least 12 birds: one at Bury Down on 17th May 2004 (which stayed until the 18th), a 'trip' of three birds in a bean field at Burnthouse Farm, Pingewood on 30th April 2005 (the first confirmed record involving more than one bird since 1886 and away from the Downs since 1885), a single bird on the Downs on 20th April 2007, five or six birds between 25th April and 2nd May 2008, including a trip of four on Bury Down on 26th April, one on 28th August 2009 at West Ilsley and another there from 27th to 29th April 2013. It is possible that the Dotterel remains under-recorded in Berkshire, since relatively few birdwatchers visit downland sites when the species is on passage. This is in contrast to the patrolling of the Downs by shooters in the 19th century.

Dotterel apparently occurred with some regularity on passage in Berkshire prior to the middle of the 19th century. Although many older observations would have been on downland which may now be in Oxfordshire, this species is noted by Hewett (1895–1911), writing in 1861, as arriving in the Compton area in April and returning in the middle of August, when they were generally in 'trips' of 12 to 16, although he had seen at least 60 together on one occasion. By the 1880s, a decline appears to have set in, Palmer (1886) noting that they were once a regular spring and autumn migrant on the Ilsley Downs. Whether such passage records ceased abruptly or gradually declined is not known. Palmer (1886) provides the only specific records of this species in the 19th century, a pair shot at Greenham Common some time in 1885, and six killed near Compton in 1886.

*Sponsored by Jerry O'Brien*

# Whimbrel

*Numenius phaeopus*

*Uncommon passage migrant*

The Whimbrel occurs in Berkshire as a spring and autumn passage migrant in varying numbers. Most records of birds on the ground are from gravel pits or other waterbodies, and in the past from sewage farms. However, as many records are of over-flying birds, frequently at night, it is not possible to accurately determine the number of birds passing through the county. For the purpose of this account, a bird or birds heard calling at night have been treated as a count of one, and where monthly totals are referred to, these are minima.

The only specific records of Whimbrel prior to 1926 are of "one shot at Sunning (Sonning) in January 1794" (Lamb, 1880), and "two shot on the banks of the Blackwater in the autumn of 1892" (Noble, 1906). The species was otherwise known only as an over-flying migrant with the apt local name of "May-bird" (Noble, 1906), and was noted by 19th century commentators as not easy to shoot.

Observations at Reading Sewage Farm and improved observer skills produced a succession of records from 1926, with nine in the 20 years from 1926 to 1945.

From 1946 to 2010, there were only five years with no records, and Whimbrel have been recorded every year since 1961, apart from 1978. A growing familiarity with the call of the species amongst observers has helped to increase the number of records, but its status in Berkshire as a passage bird does not appear to have changed significantly in the 20th century. The number of records has, however, varied considerably between years, for example, there were 17 records in 1988 involving at least 110 birds, but only three records in 1995 each involving single birds. The minimum number of Whimbrel seen in

**Whimbrel** Spring migration occurrence
Tetrads used: **21** Average of used tetrads: **8·2**

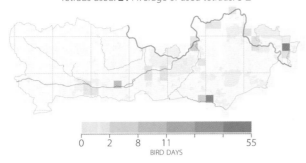

0  2  8  11          55
BIRD DAYS

**Whimbrel** Autumn migration occurrence
Tetrads used: **10** Average of used tetrads: **11·9**

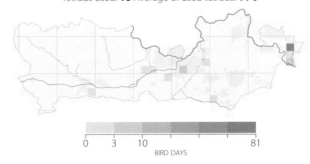

0  3  10          81
BIRD DAYS

Berkshire each month between 1923 and 2010 are shown in Figure 72. The total of 110 in 1988 is the highest annual, the next highest being 54 in 2008.

Main spring passage is from mid-April, the earliest record being on 7th April 1979. The highest count during April has been of 15 birds over Slough on the 27th in 1946. The volume of passage increases towards the end of April and reaches a peak in early May, although the proportion of April records has been greater since the mid-1990s, possibly indicating earlier northward migration. Records fall away rapidly after 22nd May, with only six subsequently, on 24th May in 1974 and 2006, on 26th May 1991, on 27th May in 1952 and 1996, and on 30th May 1937. The peak counts in May have been of about 60 over Newbury on the 10th in 1988, the largest flock seen in Berkshire, 30 over Maidenhead on the 8th in 1993 and 28 at Moor Green Lakes, Eversley on 8th May 2010.

The four June records were from Reading Sewage Farm on the 4th in 1979, from the Lambourn Downs on the 9th in 1963, over Holyport on 26th June 1979 and at Eversley Gravel Pits on 30th June 2003. The first two of these records appear to relate to late spring stragglers, while the latter two may have involved early returning birds. Apart from a record for 2nd July, passage has not been recorded before 8th July, with a maximum count for the month of 17 over Slough Sewage Farm on the 22nd in 1988. As Figure 72 indicates, autumn passage tends to be lighter than the spring. This pattern is reflected in the Migration Maps. Peak autumn counts occur in August, numbers normally being well short of the number observed in May. Numbers of birds in the figure reflect exceptional passage on 1st August 2009, when two flocks of 55 and five were recorded at Queen Mother Reservoir. The next largest flock in August was 32 over Ascot in 1969. Passage then dwindles steadily throughout early September, with only four records after the 12th (on the 26th in 2009 and on the 29th in 1949, 1997 and 2007). The two October records involved a single bird at Theale on the 1st in 1979 and an exceptional record of one on the 20th at Lower Farm Gravel Pit, Newbury in 2007. A bird at Dinton Pastures from 17th to 19th April 1985 is the longest

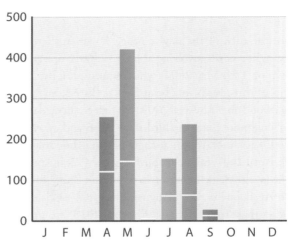

**Figure 72: Whimbrel: all birds recorded 1923–2010, by month of arrival.** Columns – birds; white line – records.

stay recorded, indicating how swiftly this species passes through the county.

The only winter record, apart from the one shot at Sonning in 1794 (Lamb, 1880) which was claimed to be of this species, was of one at Greenham Common on 2nd January 1979 for which a full description does not appear to have been made available, leaving its acceptability in doubt. Even on the coast, the Whimbrel is scarce in winter in Great Britain, with a total of probably less than 30 in any one year (*1981–84 BTO Winter Atlas*).

*Sponsored by Andrew Taylor*

Whimbrel, Berkshire Downs *Jerry O'Brien*

# Curlew

*Numenius arquata*

*Uncommon passage migrant and rare breeding summer visitor and winter visitor*

The Curlew is an uncommon but regular passage migrant through Berkshire that breeds locally in very small numbers, and a few occur irregularly in winter. In Britain its preferred habitats are wet meadows, upland areas and deep estuarine mud, and it is not surprising, therefore, that it does not feature prominently in the county. In Berkshire it is most often encountered on the Downs or at wetland sites, but passage birds are sometimes seen in other parts of the county.

The Tetrad Survey maps show a small breeding population on the Downs. This is a relatively recent phenomenon. The one confirmed breeding record in the 1987–89 Atlas survey was from a site in a border tetrad that was actually in Oxfordshire, and in most springs since, displaying birds have been noted nearby north of Aldworth, Compton and East Ilsley, but breeding has been only been confirmed from the Berkshire side of the county boundary in this area in 1994 and 1996, and it possibly occurred in 1997 and 2002. A second area has also become established as a regular summering site on

the Downs at Lambourn, where breeding was confirmed in 1996, 1997 and 2008. There were also summering birds at Woolley Down for a few years in the early 2000s. Most of the remaining breeding season records in the tetrad surveys almost certainly relate to passage birds.

The number and pattern of records away from the small summering population on the Downs varies considerably from year to year, with a wide variation in the number seen in any one year. For example, there were only ten in 1978 but 125 in 1990. Figure 73 shows the average number of sightings for each month during the period from 1978 to 2010, excluding summering birds. Spring passage seems to mainly occur in March and April

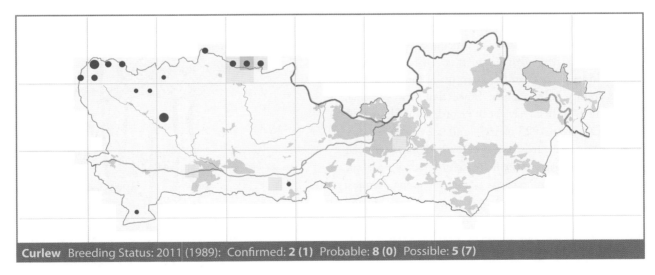

**Curlew** Breeding Status: 2011 (1989): Confirmed: **2 (1)** Probable: **8 (0)** Possible: **5 (7)**

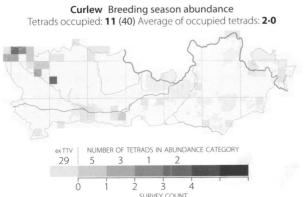

**Curlew** Breeding season abundance
Tetrads occupied: **11 (40)** Average of occupied tetrads: **2·0**

| exTTV | NUMBER OF TETRADS IN ABUNDANCE CATEGORY | | | |
|---|---|---|---|---|
| 29 | 5 | 3 | 1 | 2 |

0    1    2    3    4
SURVEY COUNT

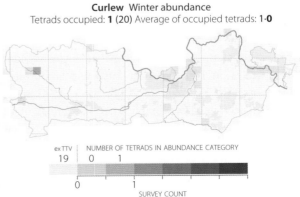

**Curlew** Winter abundance
Tetrads occupied: **1 (20)** Average of occupied tetrads: **1·0**

| exTTV | NUMBER OF TETRADS IN ABUNDANCE CATEGORY | |
|---|---|---|
| 19 | 0 | 1 |

0              1
SURVEY COUNT

239

(with more in March in recent years), and return passage seems to start in June, peaking in August. There seem to be few late autumn birds, but sometimes arrivals in December and January. The December total is enhanced by an unusual record of 10 together at Holyport on 6th December 1996. Birds seldom remain for more than a day, although one or two were at Borough Marsh, Wargrave between 28th January and 12th March 2009, and up to three were there from the 12th to the 21st January 2011.

Counts of 10 or more are unusual. The highest count since 1974 was 22 at Farnborough Down on 28th March 2002. There were 12 at Wraysbury in August 1979, 15 at Dinton Pastures in August 1984, 16 over Dinton Pastures in May 1989, 16 over Holyport on the late date of 30th October 1989, and 14 (parties of ten and four) over Queen Mother Reservoir in April 1994.

Prior to 1900, the Curlew was regarded as a rare visitor to Berkshire (Noble, 1906) or occasional passage migrant (Clark Kennedy, 1868), with dated records of

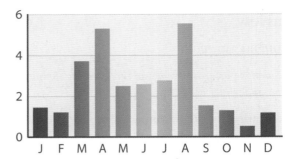

**Figure 73: Curlew: monthly average of birds recorded 1978–2010.**

birds shot confined to the winter months, at Pangbourne in February 1795, Newbury in February 1811 (Lamb, 1880), and Halfway in January 1881 (Palmer, 1886). Crows were observed taking the eggs of a pair attempting to breed on the Berkshire side of the Blackwater in 1944, and a nest with eggs was discovered at Broadmoor in June 1952, indicating that the Blackwater valley may have been a breeding site before substantial development occurred during the 20th century.

*Sponsored by Andrew and Ginny Taylor*

# Black-tailed Godwit Red Sch. 1

## *Limosa limosa*

*Scarce passage migrant*

The Black-tailed Godwit is a scarce passage migrant in Berkshire, the first county record being one at Reading Sewage Farm from 7th August to 14th September 1923, a longer stay than has been usual for the species in the county subsequently. Since that first sighting, Black-tailed Godwits have been recorded in all but 18 of the 72 years from 1923 to 1994 and in every year since. The increase in records is undoubtedly due to increased observer coverage, and the increase in flooded gravel pit habitat (where most records occur) in recent decades. As the Migration Maps, derived from records during the years of the 2007–11 Atlas survey, show, passage is often noted in the valleys of the Kennet, Loddon and Blackwater, or the waterbodies in east Berkshire.

Figure 74 shows an analysis of Black-tailed Godwit records up to 2011 by month of arrival. The bulk of spring passage occurs between early March and mid-April, although there are early records of singles at Moor Green Lakes on 13th February 1993 and at Borough Marsh on 13th February in 2008. Since 2000, more have been seen in May. Notably there was a flock of 12 at Pingewood Gravel Pits on 1st May 2004, and 10 flew over Lea Farm on 4th May 2001. The latest were three in winter plumage at Moatlands Gravel Pit, Theale on the 23rd May 2000.

Return passage usually occurs from July. Since 1994 the number of June records has increased with occurrences in seven years up to 2012. There was an exceptional record of a party of seven birds at Theale Gravel Pits on 27th June 1984, a further group of six at Horton Gravel Pits on 10th June 1999, and a party of 14 at Moor Green Lakes on the early date of 1st

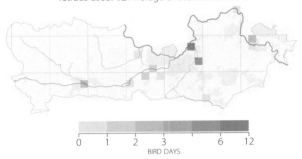

**Black-tailed Godwit** Spring migration occurrence
Tetrads used: **12** Average of used tetrads: **2·8**

0   1   2   3   6   12
BIRD DAYS

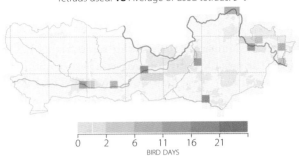

**Black-tailed Godwit** Autumn migration occurrence
Tetrads used: **18** Average of used tetrads: **9·1**

0   2   6   11   16   21
BIRD DAYS

July 2003. Passage continues through August with birds appearing that month in every year since 2000, except 2003. September records are sporadic but a surprising 28 were seen at Moor Green Lakes on 2nd September 2007. A long staying bird was at Lavell's Lake from 16th September to 22nd October 2001. There is also a record of a Black-tailed Godwit which lingered in the Theale and Burghfield Gravel Pits area and was observed on many dates from 16th September to 15th December 1984. October records are still infrequent, but unusually, birds appeared briefly in November in 2002, 2003 and 2008. Just two records of single birds have occurred in December, both at Moor Green Lakes, in 2002 and 2004.

Birds of the subspecies *islandica* which breed in Iceland have occasionally been recorded since three were identified at Eton Wick on 7th July 2000, and another four at the same site just two days later. Later records of this subspecies, which may constitute a large part of the birds passing through, include three at Slough Sewage Farm on 12th July 2005.

*Sponsored by Carol Long*

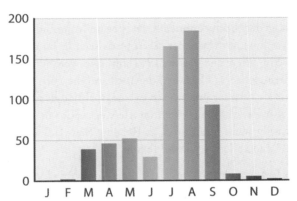

**Figure 74: Black-tailed Godwit: all birds recorded 1923–2011, by month of arrival.**

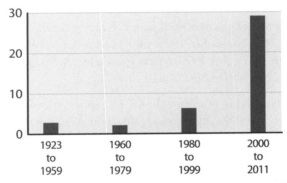

**Figure 75: Black-tailed Godwit: average number of birds recorded per year.**

# Bar-tailed Godwit

*Limosa lapponica*

*Scarce passage migrant*

The Bar-tailed Godwit is an annual spring and autumn passage migrant in Berkshire in small numbers. Most records are from gravel pits or Queen Mother Reservoir. Apart from an isolated report of one shot "near Reading" in 1802 (Lamb, 1880), records for this species, as for Black-tailed Godwit, began in 1923 with the discovery by ornithologists of Reading Sewage Farm. After two were seen there in September that year, from one to three birds were observed in 11 of the 27 years from 1923 to 1949, first at Reading Sewage Farm and from the 1930s at Slough Sewage Farm. The increase in observer coverage from the 1950s, and the steady growth in the

241

number of gravel pits in the county, led to an increase in the number of sightings, with records in most years from 1950 to the present time.

Figure 76 summarises the monthly totals from 1923 to 2011. The earliest passage records have been of one flying north-west over Wraysbury Reservoir (into Berkshire) on 18th January 1985; one at Ham Sewage Farm from 2nd February to 12th March 1950, one at Theale Gravel Pits on 18th February 1990, two at Reading Sewage Farm on 21st March 1969 and one at Queen Mother Reservoir on 23rd March 2000. Otherwise, spring passage has been confined to the period from 2nd April to 1st June. Of the other seven birds seen in June, four were in 1947, one was in 1951 and two were in 1977, all being observed between the 19th and the 24th. Most birds are seen for only one or two days, although stays of up to a week have occurred on a few occasions in spring but only twice in autumn, at Reading Sewage Farm in 1923 and at Theale Gravel Pits in 1988.

The return passage of Bar-tailed Godwits does not normally occur through Berkshire before 5th August, there being only two earlier records, on 15th July 1970 and 30th July 1944, and in some years autumn migration is finished by the end of August. The latest records are of single birds seen at Reading Sewage Farm on 24th November 1925, over Horton Gravel Pits on 24th November 1973, and at Queen Mother Reservoir on 22nd November 2008.

The monthly numbers shown in Figure 76 include a party of 100+ flying south-east over Windsor Great Park on 28th August 1978. Other large parties, of above 20, include 43 seen flying south-west over Crowthorne on 10th September 1992, 54 flying over Woodley on

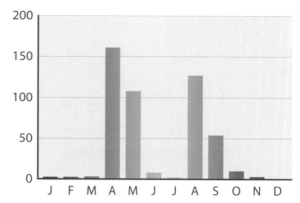

Figure 76: Bar-tailed Godwit: all records 1923–2011, by month of arrival. Includes records of 100+ in August 1978, 43 in September 1992, 54 in April 2007, 33 in May 2011.

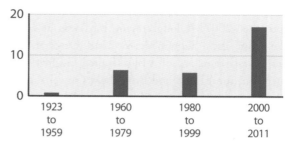

Figure 77: Bar-tailed Godwit: average number of birds recorded per year.

29th April 2007, and a flock of 33 over Queen Mother Reservoir on 1st May 2011. The records suggest that birdwatchers are more confident about their identification skills than they used to be, as the increase in numbers in recent years is due largely to identification of overflying parties, and there is little evidence of any major change in numbers of this long distance migrating species nationally (Holt et al., 2012).

*Sponsored by Margaret Chopping*

# Turnstone

Amber

*Arenaria interpres*

*Scarce passage migrant and rare winter visitor*

The Turnstone is a scarce, but now annual, passage migrant and rare winter visitor to Berkshire. The discovery of Reading Sewage Farm by ornithologists in 1922 produced the first county record of Turnstone, one being seen there on 30th August that year. Although regularly watched in successive years, the next sighting there was not until 1932, when there were both spring and autumn records, two on 2nd May, one in August, and parties of seven on 3rd September and eight on 13th September, counts that have yet to be exceeded.

Until 1949, all sightings were from these old-style sewage farms. The growth of gravel pits during the

1950s and 1960s then provided an increasing amount of alternative habitat, but this did not result in any significant increase in the number of records. Until 1969 Turnstones were seen on average only once every two

years, and annual totals did not exceed two until five were recorded in 1967.

Figure 78 shows the monthly totals of Turnstone in Berkshire since 1922. There was some increase in the frequency of records during the 1970s, with five records in 1970 and sightings in seven of the years in that decade, but from 1980 numbers increased dramatically. Whilst some of this increase is likely to be a reflection of an increase in the number of observers and in available habitat (including the Queen Mother Reservoir from 1982), there appears to have been a real increase in the volume of overland migration. From 1985 to 1994 there was an average of nine Turnstones a year, compared to an average of three for the preceding ten years, an average that has been maintained through to 2011. Records have been annual since 1977.

Until recently, the highest annual totals had been 11 in 1932 and ten in 1980, but after 14 in 1992 there was a total of 24 birds in 1993 (including parties of six at Theale Gravel Pits on 8th May and five at Eversley Gravel Pits on 14th May), and in 2003 up to 26 birds were reported.

Spring passage begins in April when the earliest arrival dates in recent years have been 16th April in 1996, and 18th April in 2003. Peak passage occurs in May, with numbers declining towards the end of the month and continuing into June in only three years, on the 1st and 3rd in 1935 and on the 1st in 1987, when there were three birds at Summerleaze Gravel Pit, and one at Eversley Gravel Pits on 5th June 1992.

Autumn passage begins in mid-July, the earliest date being the 13th at Slough Sewage Farm in 1985, rising to a peak in the first half of August. Late birds continue on passage in a few years until the end of August, and there

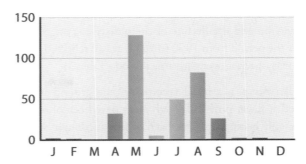

**Figure 78: Turnstone: all birds recorded 1922–2011, by month of arrival.**

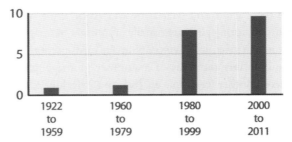

**Figure 79: Turnstone: average number of birds recorded per year.**

have been 12 September records, the latest of which were at Queen Mother Reservoir on the 25th in 1992 and 1997. The only later records are of single birds at Queen Mother Reservoir from 18th to 19th October 1987, at Burghfield Gravel Pits on 26th October 1986, at Ham Sewage Farm on 20th November 1949, and at Queen Mother Reservoir on 21st November 2003.

There have been just three mid-winter records during hard weather, one at Queen Mother Reservoir in January and early February 1987, one at Horton Gravel Pits and at Queen Mother Reservoir in February 1989, and one at Widbrook Common in January 2003.

*Sponsored by Bob & Margaret Walker*

# Knot

## Calidris canutus

*Scarce passage migrant and winter visitor*

The Knot is a winter visitor to the UK, where it feeds in large numbers on mud and sand flats in large coastal estuaries. The great majority of the UK wintering population is of the *islandica* race, which migrates via Iceland to and from its breeding areas in Greenland and the Canadian high arctic. Some first winter birds remain to summer in the UK (*Migration Atlas*). In Berkshire, though scarce, it can occur throughout the year, with a higher frequency during the spring and autumn migrations.

The first 20th century record of Knot was from Slough Sewage Farm where five birds were seen from 15th to 21st April 1939. There had been no records from

Reading Sewage Farm in the 1920s and 1930s, when so many other wader species were recorded there. The first gravel pit record is of an immature shot at Aldermaston Gravel Pit in October 1949, but the next ten records from 1943 to 1958 were again from sewage farms.

The increase in gravel pits, construction of Queen Mother Reservoir, and the decline of the old-style sewage farms over the period from 1950 to 2011, are all reflected in the records of Knot over the same period (Table 2).

In Berkshire, nearly all records on the ground involve three or fewer birds, although most have been of singles. The only exceptions have been of five at Slough Sewage Farm in April 1939, and five or six at this site in February 1959. Most Knot in Berkshire are seen for just one day, the only stay to exceed six days being the five birds at Slough Sewage Farm from 15th to 21st April 1939, and one there from 2nd March to 2nd April 1944. Where recorded, spring birds are usually in summer plumage, and in autumn juvenile or winter plumage birds predominate. The only July record is of a summer plumage adult at Queen Mother Reservoir on 28th and 29th July 2008.

There are several records of over-flying parties of Knot in the autumn migration period, all from the eastern end of the county: about 100 at Wraysbury Gravel Pits in August 1968, 24 flying south over Wraysbury Reservoir in August 1973 which crossed into Berkshire, and three records from Queen Mother Reservoir. These involved 15 flying west in September 1993; 90, mostly juveniles and accompanied by 17 Bar-tailed Godwits, on 17th August 2007; and 33 on 7th September 2008. The totals of Knot since 1939 shown in Table 2 and Figure 80 exclude the over-flying parties recorded above.

|  | Sewage farms | Gravel pits | Queen Mother Reservoir | Other sites |
|---|---|---|---|---|
| 1939–1959 | 16 | 1 | – | 0 |
| 1960–1979 | 13 | 10 | – | 0 |
| 1980–1999 | 2 | 13 | 11 | 2 |
| 2000–2011 | 0 | 6 | 8 | 0 |

**Table 2: Knot: habitat used 1939–2011.**

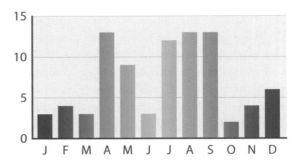

**Figure 80: Knot: all birds recorded 1939–2011, by month of arrival.**

Early records point to the Knot having always been a rare over-flying migrant in Berkshire. Two were reported shot near Reading in 1795 (Lamb, 1880), and one shot in winter near Cookham in 1865 (Clark Kennedy, 1868).

*Sponsored by John Westmacott*

Knot, Queen Mother Reservoir, 15th August 2011 *Michael McKee*

# Ruff

*Calidris pugnax*

*Scarce passage migrant and rare winter visitor*

First recorded in Berkshire in the 20th century in 1922, the Ruff is an uncommon passage migrant and winter visitor which has been reported annually in the county since 1932, initially from sewage farms and more recently from gravel pits and reservoirs. There has been a marked reduction in the number of records since the 1970s, and in the numbers seen together at any one time. In the past, the frequent long duration of stays by overwintering birds from October to March makes a detailed analysis of records difficult, and it is not easy to distinguish between departing winter birds and passage in spring. There have been few winter records in recent years.

After only four records for January and February in the 20 years to 1954, Ruff were observed during the winter months in 33 of the 59 years from 1955 to 2013. The number of birds seen exceeded ten in 12 of these years, with peak counts of 22 at Wraysbury Gravel Pits in January 1972 and 24 in February 1981, and peak counts of 29 at Slough Sewage Farm in 1960. Notably, Ruff were recorded in January and February in all but five years between 1971 and 1994 but in only six years since then, in 1996, 1997, 2002, 2009, 2012 and 2013. Most of these records were short-staying individuals, but the 2009 record was a female present between 5th and 15th January at Eversley Gravel Pits. Ruffs thus appear no longer to be a wintering species in the county, but a visitor in small numbers occasionally moving through in response to hard weather elsewhere.

Spring passage appears mostly to occur through both March and April. At this time, parties of from 20 to 24 birds were seen in both months at the old-style sewage farms during the 1950s, but since 1960 this peak was only exceeded in 1976, when numbers reached 48 at Wraysbury Gravel Pits in March and 40 at Reading Sewage Farm in April (the highest recorded numbers for Berkshire). Until 1988, few Ruff were recorded in May, with just five records of single birds from 1970 to 1987. From 1988 to 2000, there were May records in all years but 1995, with 15 at Slough Sewage Farm on 1st May 1990. From 2001 to 2011, however, there were May records in only four years, in 2004, 2005, 2009 and 2012. There appear to have been only three June records since 1922, in 1940, 1989 and 1992. This pattern is reflected in the Migration Maps, derived from records received during the years of the 2007–11 Atlas Survey, which show fewer spring than autumn records.

Return passage takes place from early July, usually in ones and twos, followed by heavier passage in August and September. The largest autumn parties recorded since 1977 have been just five birds, at Slough Sewage Farm in both August 1984 and 1986, six birds in flight low over Queen Mother Reservoir on 9th September 1996, and eight birds in flight at Moatlands Gravel Pit, Theale on 28th August 2005. This is well below the September peaks of the 1970s, when up to 20 birds were seen on two or three occasions. Passage records quickly give way to sporadic records of small parties which can occur at any time from October to December. Although parties of ten or more were occasionally reported prior to the mid-1970s in late autumn and early winter, and an exceptional count of about 30 at Slough Sewage Farm on 20th December 1958, the highest counts since have been of 13 together at Borough Marsh on 3rd December 2011, and eight at Queen Mother Reservoir in November 1988, increasing to nine in December that year.

The steady decline in records in Berkshire since the 1970s does not match the trend from national WeBS counts,

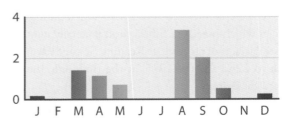

**Figure 81: Ruff: monthly average of birds recorded 2000–2009.**

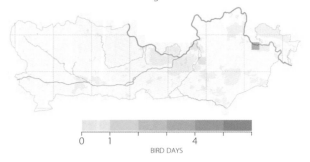

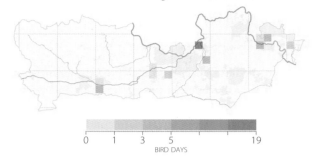

which are largely derived from counts at coastal locations, and which showed an increase from the late 1980s to the early 2000s (Holt *et al.*, 2012). It does though match the pattern in Buckinghamshire, though this can probably be attributed to the loss of suitable habitat at the species' favoured site in the county, Willen Lakes (Ferguson, 2013). In Berkshire the years between 2006 and 2009 saw very low numbers, with just three or four records involving four or five birds in each year. There has been an apparent increase since, with records of 11 and about 16 birds in 2010 and 2011 respectively, the latter including the record of 13 at Borough Marsh referred to above.

Males (ruffs) are thought to precede females (reeves) during spring passage, with the former moving through in late March and females after the second week of April (*1981–84 BTO Winter Atlas*). The records for Berkshire tended to support this, although the lower numbers in recent years show a more mixed picture, and there are earlier records of both sexes together in spring, with reports of reeves from about the end of the first week of March as well as of ruffs into late April and May. At Reading Sewage Farm, two ruffs in full breeding plumage were observed displaying to a reeve on 27th April 1932, and at this site in 1933 two ruffs (one in full breeding plumage) and two reeves were seen together on 23rd April. In 1935, three ruffs in breeding plumage and a reeve were seen there as early as 31st March.

Ruff, Lea Farm *Michael McKee*

There are, however, no records of attempted breeding in Berkshire. In autumn, both sexes appear to occur on passage at the same time, when juvenile birds are also occasionally noted.

Prior to 1922, the Ruff appears to have been a rare vagrant to Berkshire, with a reeve killed near Cookham in the 1860s being the only record (Clark Kennedy, 1868).

*Sponsored by John and Katherine Walker*

# Sharp-tailed Sandpiper

## *Calidris acuminata*

*Rare vagrant, recorded once*

The only Berkshire record of Sharp-tailed Sandpiper, a species which breeds in Siberia and normally winters in Australasia, is of an adult at Reading Sewage Farm from 17th to 22nd August 1975, at the time only the 13th record for Britain.

*In memory of John Field*

# Broad-billed Sandpiper

## *Calidris falcinellus*

*Rare vagrant, recorded once*

The only Berkshire record of Broad-billed Sandpiper, a wader which breeds from north Scandinavia to Siberia and normally winters in south Asia and Australia, is of one seen at Ham Sewage Farm on 19th September 1956.

*Sponsored by Colin Wilson*

---

# Curlew Sandpiper
Green

## *Calidris ferruginea*

*Uncommon passage migrant*

Curlew Sandpipers are passage migrants in the UK, between their breeding grounds in the Siberian arctic and wintering grounds in Africa. In Berkshire, it is a scarce passage migrant, which occurs in variable numbers. The first county record was from Reading Sewage Farm in 1922, with four there on 25th August, seven on 2nd September and falling numbers until 1st October, when the last bird was seen. The species was then recorded there every year until 1928, suggesting that it had probably been regular at the site prior to its discovery by ornithologists in 1922. In 1924, there was a party of 14 on 21st September.

From 1932 until 1945, nearly all records were from Slough Sewage Farm, Reading Sewage Farm having been modernised. During this period, some large parties were observed, the highest count being of about 20 at Slough Sewage Farm on 13th and 16th September 1936. There have been fewer records since 1960, an average of two birds per year over the subsequent 50 years. The only counts to exceed four birds have been of 13 at Reading Sewage Farm in August 1969, of eight there in September 1969, of five juveniles at Slough Sewage Farm in September 1988, and five there in September 2001. The preponderance of August and September records can be seen from Figure 82, which excludes a small flock of an unspecified number of birds in September 1926. Arrivals of Curlew Sandpipers in Berkshire often coincide with records of Little Stints.

Apart from two at Reading Sewage Farm on 3rd April 1927, two at Theale Gravel Pits in May 1990, and two at Eversley Gravel Pits on 29th May 1997, all spring records of Curlew Sandpiper have been of single birds, the last being a late record on 6th June 2009 at Midgham Gravel Pits.

The steady reduction in the number of old-style sewage farms appears to have played a major part in the decline

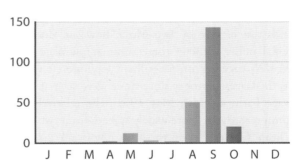

**Figure 82: Curlew Sandpiper: all birds recorded 1922–2011, by month of arrival.**

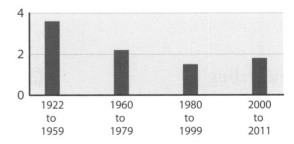

**Figure 83: Curlew Sandpiper: average number of birds recorded per year.**

in records of the species in the county after the 1950s (Figure 83). The only counts of more than two birds not at sewage farms have been of four juveniles at Thatcham on 23rd August 1981, four at Borough Marsh on 7th September 2007, and three at Eversley Gravel Pits on 23rd September 2007.

*Sponsored by Chloe Crossman*

247

# Temminck's Stint

Red | Sch. 1

## Calidris temminckii

*Scarce passage migrant, predominantly in spring*

In England, Temminck's Stints are scarce passage migrants between their Scandinavian breeding grounds and wintering grounds in southern Europe and north Africa. In Berkshire it is scarce, with most records occurring in spring. The first Temminck's Stint was not recorded in the county until one at Reading Sewage Farm on 26th May 1935. Sewage farms accounted for the next three sightings, in 1936, 1940 and 1948, with the first gravel pit record, and first record of two birds, at Burghfield in 1949. In the following 61 years from 1950 to 2010, there have been a further 46 records involving 63 birds, divided between sightings at sewage farms and gravel pits, with the latter habitat predominating since 1980. The number of birds seen each month is shown in Figure 84.

The only March record occurred at Ham Sewage Farm on the 18th in 1948. Most records occur in mid-May, with 32 of these (63%) occurring from 12th to 20th May. The latest spring record was of one at Eversley Gravel Pits from 31st May to 1st June 1991. Most records are of one or two birds; however, during a national influx in 2004 three summer plumage birds were seen together on Greenham Common on 12th May, the largest number since three were seen at Ham Sewage Farm on 16th May 1951. The relatively few autumn records are more widely spread, from two birds at Theale Gravel Pits on the 19th July in 1972 to one bird at Reading Sewage Farm on the 12th October in 1974.

*Sponsored by Patrick Crowley*

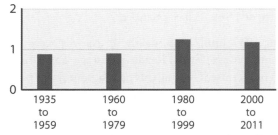

**Figure 84: Temminck's Stint: all birds recorded 1935–2010, by month of arrival.**

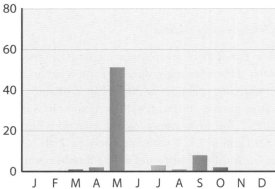

**Figure 85: Temminck's Stint: average number of birds recorded per year.**

---

# Sanderling

Green

## Calidris alba

*Scarce but increasing passage migrant*

The Sanderling breeds in the high arctic and is a common passage migrant and winter visitor on sandy coasts in the UK. Inland it is a scarce passage migrant, which has occurred increasingly frequently in Berkshire in recent years with the increase in gravel pits and the construction of the Queen Mother Reservoir.

The first 20th century record was from Reading Sewage Farm, with a sighting of three on 16th May 1933, a full ten years after this site began to be watched for passage waders. There were further records of 19 birds at either

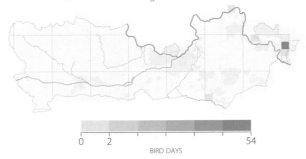

**Sanderling** Spring migration occurrence
Tetrads used: **5** Average of used tetrads: **12·2**

0  2  54
BIRD DAYS

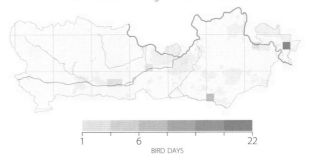

**Sanderling** Autumn migration occurrence
Tetrads used: **6** Average of used tetrads: **5·5**

1  6  22
BIRD DAYS

Reading or Slough Sewage Farms from 1934 to 1944, followed by the first gravel pit record at Burghfield in May 1950. The opening of Queen Mother Reservoir in 1976 resulted in many more Berkshire records and provided 87% of all records of Sanderling in the first decade of the 21st century, the remainder being found on gravel pits across the county. This pattern of occurrence is reflected in the Migration Maps, based on records received during passage between 2008 and 2011.

May is the peak month for Sanderling passage in Berkshire (Figure 86), accounting for 60% of all records. Since 1980 there has been an increasing number of June records, with the latest on 18th June 1990, and an increasing number of July records, of which the earliest was on the 16th at Queen Mother Reservoir in 2008. There have been only seven winter records since 1933, including three birds at Queen Mother Reservoir on 1st December 2010.

Most records have been of one to three birds, with four together at Slough Sewage Farm in May 1934 and at Ham Sewage Farm in May 1950. All higher counts have been at Queen Mother Reservoir. In 1988, numbers there built up to a maximum of 13 in May when the water level was low, and 10 were recorded together there in May 1995, June 1997 and again in May 2007.

There are only two records of Sanderling for Berkshire before 1933. Strangely both are for winter, a pair reported shot at Wokingham in February 1795 (Lamb,

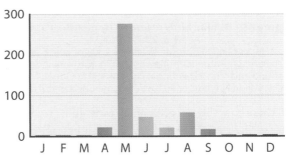

**Figure 86: Sanderling: all birds recorded 1933–2011, by month of arrival.**

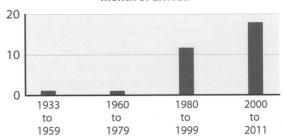

**Figure 87: Sanderling: average number of birds recorded per year.**

1880) and a single bird shot on the banks of the Thames near Surley Hall, near Windsor, in the winter of 1866 (Clark Kennedy, 1868). The fact that the 1795 record refers to a pair, and that Sanderling have only been recorded in February on one occasion since, casts some doubt on the identification of these birds.

*In memory of Gordon Langsbury*

---

# Dunlin
Red

*Calidris alpina*

*Passage migrant and winter visitor*

The Dunlin is a passage migrant and winter visitor in the UK. Birds of the race *C. a. schinzii* breed in Iceland and the north of the UK and pass through the UK to winter in West Africa, whilst birds of the nominate race, *C. a. alpina*, which breed in Fennoscandia and Siberia, winter around the coasts of Western Europe, including the UK.

Dunlin occur regularly in Berkshire, both in winter and on passage, and have been recorded every year since the

first annual county report in 1915. In the 19th century, it was observed along the banks of rivers such as the Thames (Clark Kennedy, 1868), and in the 20th century it regularly occurred at old-style sewage farms, gravel pits and Queen Mother Reservoir, demonstrating the ability to utilise a wider range of wetland habitats than most other waders.

A typical year for records of this species involves isolated sightings of from one to three birds during January and February, and an increase in the frequency of sightings during March. Further increases then occur in April and May, often including small parties of up to ten birds,

249

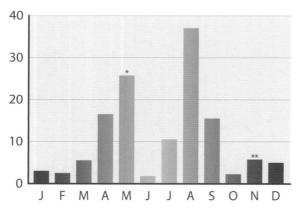

**Figure 88: Dunlin: birds recorded by month of arrival.**
Average 2008–2011.
*Flocks of 40 at Burghfield in May 2008 of which an unspecified number identified as Dunlin, the remainder not identified and **an exceptional flock of 160 at Queen Mother Reservoir in November 2010 are not included in the data.

**Dunlin** Spring migration occurrence
Tetrads used: **20** Average of used tetrads: **10·3**

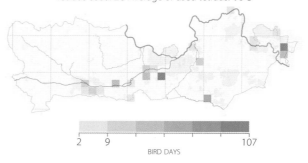

BIRD DAYS

**Dunlin** Autumn migration occurrence
Tetrads used: **19** Average of used tetrads: **15·2**

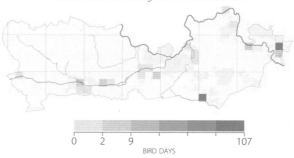

BIRD DAYS

**Dunlin** Winter abundance
Tetrads occupied: **0** (21) Average of occupied tetrads: **0**

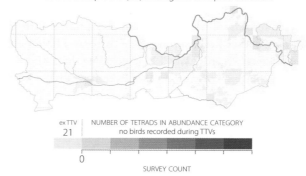

ex TTV  NUMBER OF TETRADS IN ABUNDANCE CATEGORY
21  no birds recorded during TTVs

SURVEY COUNT

and there may be an occasional early June record to bring spring passage to a close. Autumn passage begins in July and the number of records increases thereafter into August, when again parties of up to ten birds often occur. There is then a decline during September and occasional records, usually of from one to three birds, occur through October, November and December. Figure 88 shows the records for the four years 2008–11, excluding an exceptional flock in November 2010 referred to below, which reflect this pattern.

In addition to the regular occurrence of small numbers of Dunlin, both on passage and in winter, much larger parties are occasionally seen, the largest being a passing flock of 160 at Queen Mother Reservoir in November 2010. A flock of up to 110 birds was also present during the construction of the reservoir in December 1974, with the flock then decreasing until the site was flooded the following April.

During the four years of the recent Atlas surveys, Dunlin were recorded in 28 tetrads where gravel pits and other wet areas are located throughout the county, with the greatest numbers at Queen Mother Reservoir, and in a similar number of tetrads in spring and autumn (see maps).

The races of Dunlin are difficult to separate in the field and are not usually identified in the county reports, though a small number of birds recorded in the summer months have been assigned to the races *C. a. schinzii* and *arctica*.

*Sponsored by Louise Hayward*

# Purple Sandpiper

Amber | Sch. 1

*Calidris maritima*

*Rare vagrant, five records*

The first Berkshire record of Purple Sandpiper, which normally occurs on rocky coasts in Britain in winter, was a single bird at Thatcham Gravel Pits on 7th November 1983. The second was of another single bird, a juvenile, which spent three hours at Queen Mother Reservoir on 24th September 2001. There have been three further records there, on 20th September 2002, on 26th December 2006 and on 8th November 2011.

*Sponsored by Bill Nicoll*

# Little Stint

Green

*Calidris minuta*

*Scarce passage migrant, principally in autumn*

The Little Stint is a passage migrant in the UK, moving between its arctic breeding grounds and African wintering grounds. It is a regular, if scarce, passage migrant in Berkshire, with the majority of records occurring in autumn. The first Berkshire record was of a small party of from two to six at Reading Sewage Farm between 1st and 9th September 1922. The old-style sewage farms were to provide excellent passage habitat for this diminutive wader for the next 40 years, first at Reading and later at Slough. During this period, the highest count was a party of at least 20 birds at Slough Sewage Farm on 11th September 1936, which increased to a maximum of 25 on 18th and 25th September. The only other counts to exceed eight birds were of 15 at the same site in August 1961 and 42 there on 27th September 1996 (see below).

Although Slough Sewage Farm, the only remaining old-style sewage farm with open settling beds, continues to produce many of the sightings of Little Stints, many records now come from gravel pits and Queen Mother Reservoir. There have been only nine years from 1946 to 2012 in which Little Stints have not been recorded in Berkshire, the last occasion being in 2005. There has been no systematic trend in occurrence over the last 50 years (Figure 89): up to 24 birds have been recorded annually since 1996, with an average of 6.1 per year, similar to the average since 1960 of 6.3.

Spring passage is unusual, accounting for 8% of the birds. Birds have been recorded in about half the springs for which data are available, including eight in March 1938 (the highest ever in spring). The 28 spring records, involving 43 birds, have occurred over a wide

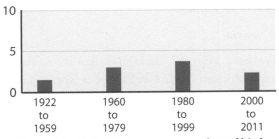

**Figure 89: Little Stint: average number of birds recorded per year.** The exceptional 1996 year, in which at least 107 birds were recorded, is excluded.

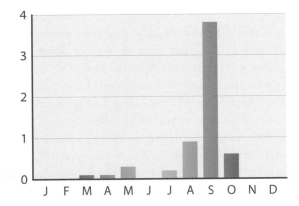

**Figure 90: Little Stint: average number of birds recorded by month of arrival.** Average 1922–2011. The exceptional 1996 year, in which at least 107 birds were recorded, is excluded.

range of dates from the earliest on 3rd March in 1982 at Theale Gravel Pits, to the latest on 9th June in 2001, at Pingewood Gravel Pits.

The predominance of sightings in autumn is clearly shown in Figure 90. Autumn arrival dates have ranged from 21st July in 2009 to 24th November in 2000, and a bird from an exceptional influx in 1996 lingered at Queen Mother Reservoir to the 29th November. Peak passage is spread over several weeks from the end of August to the end of September. Although almost annual in autumn, there is considerable variation in the numbers seen; for example, there were at least 26 birds in 1990 followed by nine in 1991, and at least 109 in 1996 followed by none in 1997. The remarkable influx in 1996, part of an exceptional influx into western Europe, began on 14th September and peaked with 25 at Queen Mother Reservoir on 26th September and 40 at Slough Sewage Farm on 27th, with some birds remaining at these and several gravel pit sites into October.

*Sponsored by Nancy Roach*

# Least Sandpiper

*Calidris minutilla*

*Rare vagrant, one record*

The only Berkshire record of this diminutive American wader is of one at Brimpton Gravel Pits on 11th October 1975, at the time only the 19th record for Britain. Typical of many of the new world waders, the bird allowed the observer to approach to within two feet and obtain a photographic record.

*Sponsored by Rosie Hall, WSP Environment & Energy*

# Pectoral Sandpiper

*Calidris melanotos*

*Rare vagrant*

There have been 17 Berkshire records of Pectoral Sandpiper up to August 2013, one in spring and the remainder in autumn. The first county record was of one at Slough Sewage Farm on 1st August 1944 (at that time part of Buckinghamshire). Appropriately for an American migrant, the bird was found and identified by a sergeant in the US forces stationed in Britain.

Although the number of sightings of Pectoral Sandpiper in southern England steadily increased through the 1950s and 1960s, there were no further sightings in Berkshire until four records in the early 1970s, when there were single birds at Ham Sewage Farm from 16th to 22nd September 1970, Reading Sewage Farm from 19th to 28th September 1970, Ham Sewage Farm from 30th August to 7th September 1973, and Reading Sewage Farm from 26th to 30th September 1975. The occurrence of two in the county at the same time in 1970 coincided with a national influx of around 50 birds.

After an isolated record of a juvenile at Burghfield Gravel Pits from 20th to 27th October 1979, there were

four further records in the 1980s, with single birds at Summerleaze Gravel Pits on 25th July 1985, at Slough Sewage Farm on 4th September 1988, and again there from 28th September to 9th October 1988 (both juveniles). The following year one was at Theale Gravel Pits from 13th to 15th May 1989, the only spring record. There was a juvenile at Slough Sewage Farm from 2nd to 4th September 1994, and another there from 6th to 13th October 1996. A juvenile was reported from two sites in the east of the county in 2003, at Eversley Gravel Pits

252

from 1st to 7th November then at Dorney Wetlands and Slough Sewage Farm on 12th and 13th November, the sightings being thought to relate to the same bird. In 2004 one was at Pingewood Gravel Pits from 26th August to 3rd September. In September 2011 there was a bird at Crookham Common, and there were single birds at Eton Wick on 18th September 2012 and 4th August 2013.

*Sponsored by Roger Murfitt*

## Wilson's Phalarope

*Phalaropus tricolor*

*Rare vagrant, two records*

The only Berkshire records of this elegant New World wader are of a juvenile at Beenham Gravel Pit from 9th to 10th September 1979, which was one of an influx of 16 birds into Britain at that time, and a first-year bird at Dinton Pastures on 30th August 1987.

*Sponsored by Colin Wilson*

## Red-necked Phalarope `Red` `Sch. 1`

*Phalaropus lobatus*

*Rare vagrant, five records involving seven birds*

The Red-necked Phalarope is a rare vagrant to Berkshire which has been recorded on five occasions, involving seven birds. The first county record was an adult female in winter plumage found dead near Newbury on 18th October 1932. This was quickly followed by a second record of one at Reading Sewage Farm on 25th September 1933, and there were unconfirmed reports that it may have remained there into October. Three were seen together at Slough Sewage Farm on 12th October 1940, two remaining until the 13th October, one having been shot.

After a gap of nearly 60 years, the next record was not until 4th May 2000, when a moulting adult was

at Eversley Gravel Pits for about an hour. This was followed by a juvenile seen on 3rd and 4th September 2001 at Queen Mother Reservoir.

*Sponsored by Renton Righelato*

## Grey Phalarope

*Phalaropus fulicarius*

*Rare vagrant*

The Grey Phalarope is a scarce autumn and winter vagrant to Berkshire and usually occurs in the county after severe gales. There have been 29 records involving 34 birds, 22 of which have occurred since 1900, and seven have occurred on Queen Mother Reservoir. All the autumn records have occurred between 2nd September and 22nd November.

One killed at Shinfield in March 1794 (Lamb, 1880) is the earliest claimed county record, but the date, if correct, is surprising, as spring records in Britain are unusual. All 19th century records are of birds which were shot, with the exception of one on the Thames near Maidenhead in autumn 1867 which escaped despite being struck with an oar! (Clark Kennedy, 1868). Singles were shot on the Thames at Windsor in December 1851 and between Whitchurch and Pangbourne on 19th September 1866 (Clark Kennedy, 1868), and two were shot near Newbury on 27th September 1866 (Noble, 1906). The 1866 records were both part of a large 'wreck' of Grey Phalaropes over England that year. One was shot at Oare on 20th October 1869 and others at Wargrave on 24th October 1870 (Noble, 1906), at Newbury on 10th November 1870 (Herbert, 1872), between Tilehurst and Reading on 16th October 1891, and two near Mortimer on 24th October 1891 (Noble, 1906).

The first 20th century record is of two at Reading Sewage Farm on 2nd September 1922, followed by another there from 11th to 17th October 1935, and one at Slough Sewage Farm on 23rd September that year. There were two records in 1950, single birds at Ham Sewage Farm from 17th to 21st September and at Ascot Place on 18th September. One was seen over Virginia Water on 6th October 1951, and Slough Sewage Farm produced records of single birds in consecutive years on 3rd October 1957 and on 22nd November 1958. There was then a considerable period before the next record, one at Theale Gravel Pits on 13th November 1983.

The great storm of the night of 15th October 1987 produced records of two at Queen Mother Reservoir on 16th October, with one remaining until 19th October, two at Dinton Pastures also on 16th October, and one at Twyford Gravel Pits on 18th October. On the morning of 18th November 1990, one was seen briefly at Theale Gravel Pits and then later that day at Burghfield Gravel Pits. In 1996 a single individual was found feeding in open water at Queen Mother Reservoir on 9th November. The next record of this species was at Theale Main Gravel Pit, with the bird staying from 29th September to 30th September 1999.

In the present century, there have been six records. In November 2003, one was found at Queen Mother Reservoir on 15th, remaining until the 20th; in November 2005, one at Queen Mother Reservoir on 2nd November 2005, remaining until the 5th; and a second at Lower Farm Gravel Pit, Thatcham on 3rd November, though this individual remained for one day only. A juvenile bird moulting into first winter plumage was recorded on 2nd September 2008 at Queen Mother Reservoir, equalling the previous earliest autumn arrival date for this species set in 1922. Another juvenile bird was noted on 15th November 2009 at Moatlands Gravel Pit, Theale. This flighty bird remained for a short time only during the morning. A longer staying juvenile was recorded in 2011 at Queen Mother Reservoir, remaining from 12th September until the evening of the 15th September.

*Sponsored by Neil Bucknell*

# Common Sandpiper

*Actitus hypoleucos*

*Common passage migrant and rare summer and winter visitor, has bred*

The Common Sandpiper is one of the commonest and most widespread of the migrant waders that occur in Berkshire and can be found at gravel pits, reservoirs and along rivers and streams throughout migration periods. This is reflected in the records from which the Migration Maps are derived.

In some years, the first Common Sandpipers to arrive in Berkshire can appear in March, the earliest since 1946 being at Eversley Gravel Pit on the 13th in 2008, but spring passage is generally from early April to the end of May, peaking during the middle of that period. Common Sandpipers are usually observed in ones and twos, or groups of up to four at this time, but larger numbers occur in some years, the highest count in spring being 25 at Burghfield Gravel Pits on 21st May 1948.

**Common Sandpiper** Spring migration occurrence
Tetrads used: **53** Average of used tetrads: **12·2**

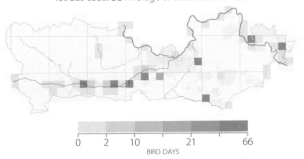

0   2   10   21   66
BIRD DAYS

**Common Sandpiper** Autumn migration occurrence
Tetrads used: **44** Average of used tetrads: **47·0**

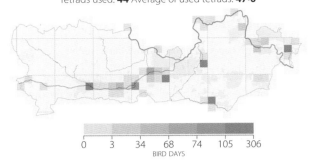

0   3   34   68   74   105   306
BIRD DAYS

**Common Sandpiper** Breeding season abundance
Tetrads occupied: **5** (68) Average of occupied tetrads: **1·8**

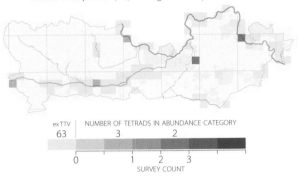

| ex TTV | NUMBER OF TETRADS IN ABUNDANCE CATEGORY | |
| 63 | 3 | 2 |

0   1   2   3
SURVEY COUNT

**Common Sandpiper** Winter abundance
Tetrads occupied: **0** (8) Average of occupied tetrads: **0**

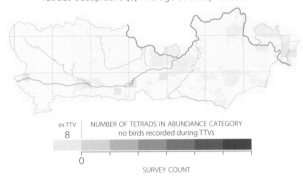

| ex TTV | NUMBER OF TETRADS IN ABUNDANCE CATEGORY |
| 8 | no birds recorded during TTVs |

0
SURVEY COUNT

In 1934 a pair was seen with three fledged young near Sonning. As the record appears in the county report under Oxfordshire, the birds presumably bred on that side of the Thames. Since then there have been two runs of summer records of Common Sandpiper in Berkshire, the first in the period from 1948 to 1957. During this period attempted breeding was considered possible at Burghfield Gravel Pits in 1949, 1950, 1951 and 1952, and birds summered at Aldermaston Gravel Pits from 1953 to 1957. Confirmation of breeding was obtained at the latter site when two chicks were seen on 20th July 1955, one of which was caught and estimated to be about seven to ten days old. It is likely that an adult and four flying young seen at this site on 1st August 1953 had also bred there. After isolated records of birds apparently summering at Dinton Pastures in 1981 and 1982, there was a second run of records from 1991, with birds summering at Queen Mother Reservoir in 1991 and 1992, and then there was successful breeding at a site in mid-Berkshire between 1994 and 1997, where young birds were seen. However, since 1998, there have been no reports of summering or breeding birds in the county.

Autumn passage extends from early July to the end of September, with a few stragglers occurring in October and occasionally into November. Peak passage is during August and early September, when counts of ten to 15 birds have been made. Most of the highest counts have come at this time from old-style sewage farms, and these include peaks of up to 30 at Ham in August 1944, 32

there in autumn 1947 and about 50, again at this site, on 9th August 1950 (the highest county total). Gravel pits can also attract high numbers, the highest count being an estimated total at all the gravel pits in the Theale area of 35 in early August 1989.

Southern England is on the northern edge of the wintering range of the Common Sandpiper (*1981–84 BTO Winter Atlas*), and this is reflected in the small number of winter records for Berkshire, although the Winter Map shows that birds were located in eight tetrads spread across the county, mainly along the Kennet Valley in the west and around the reservoirs in the east. The 38 winters from 1948/49 to 1985/86 produced winter records during the period from November to February in only ten years. However, milder winters since 1985/86 resulted in records in eight of the ten winters from 1986/87 to 1995/96, and there have been annual winter records since, mainly of single birds, with Padworth Gravel Pit hosting a regular wintering bird from 1999/2000 to 2008/09.

*Sponsored by Andrew Taylor*

Common Sandpiper, Dinton Pastures *Tony Harden*

# Green Sandpiper

Amber  Sch. 1

*Tringa ochropus*

*Uncommon passage migrant and winter visitor*

The Green Sandpiper is seen in Berkshire in every month of the year, although there is notable passage in both spring and autumn (see Migration Maps). Most records are from well-watched gravel pit and sewage farm sites, but any river valley site can produce sightings, especially in winter.

Winter sightings from November to February are usually of just one or two birds at a site, as shown in the winter abundance map, but occasionally three or four occur, and at favoured sites up to six may be recorded. Higher concentrations in winter are rare, with seven at Stanford Dingley in February 1983, at Horton Gravel Pits in February 1994, and at Padworth Lane Gravel Pits in November 2006, and counts from Slough Sewage Farm which peaked at 11 in November 2003, being the only records in excess of six since 1974.

Sightings are widely spread along the county's river valleys in winter wherever suitable marshy or waterside habitat is available, a pattern reflected in the Winter Map, which showed them to be present in 47 tetrads across the county during the period of the survey. At this time of year, Green Sandpipers are known to be more elusive and may be found in ditches and streams making their location more difficult, so some may be overlooked. One on farmland near Thatcham on 17th January 1989 was unusual, but provides an indication of the range of habitat which can be exploited at this time of year.

As illustrated by the Migration Maps, of the waders regularly encountered on migration in Berkshire, only Common Sandpipers are usually recorded from more sites. Spring passage is usually noted in March and April, peaking in April, when Green Sandpipers can be seen regularly at gravel pits and sewage farms, often in small, loose groups of up to five birds. Higher concentrations are uncommon, and peak counts of ten at Slough Sewage Farm on 22nd April 1989, and nine at Woolhampton Gravel Pits on 24th March 2002, were exceptional counts for Berkshire.

Green Sandpiper records in Berkshire are generally at their lowest during May, with only occasional birds, but numbers start to increase slowly in June, when return migration begins, and continue to increase through July. There was an exceptional count of 30 at Lower Farm Gravel Pit on 26th June 2009. High July counts include seven in the Theale Gravel Pits area in 1989, nine at Slough Sewage Farm on 30th June 1993 and nine at Padworth Lane on 19th July 2007. Autumn passage

**Green Sandpiper** Spring migration occurrence
Tetrads used: **47** Average of used tetrads: **15·8**

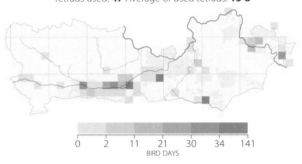

| 0 | 2 | 11 | 21 | 30 | 34 | 141 |

BIRD DAYS

**Green Sandpiper** Autumn migration occurrence
Tetrads used: **46** Average of used tetrads: **48·7**

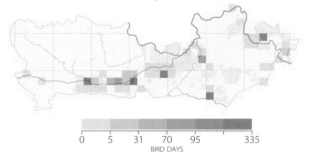

| 0 | 5 | 31 | 70 | 95 | 335 |

BIRD DAYS

**Green Sandpiper** Winter abundance
Tetrads occupied: **10** (47) Average of occupied tetrads: **1·2**

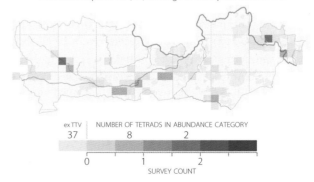

| ex TTV | NUMBER OF TETRADS IN ABUNDANCE CATEGORY | |
|---|---|---|
| 37 | 8 | 2 |

| 0 | 1 | 2 |

SURVEY COUNT

then continues until the end of October, with the highest numbers being recorded during August and September. Again, there are many records from gravel pits and the few remaining sewage farms. The highest counts for the year occur at these locations in autumn. Since 1974 the highest counts have been 20 at Thatcham Gravel Pits in September 1981, 20 at Theale Gravel Pits in August 1994, 18 at Twyford Gravel Pits in 1990, 18 at Beenham Gravel Pit in September 1979, and 18 at Slough Sewage Farm in August 2002.

In spite of these relatively high counts in recent years, they fall well below those prior to the 1960s, when autumn passage numbers at some sewage farms could exceed 30 birds. For example, there was a maximum of about 40 at Ham Sewage Farm in both August 1949 and August 1952, about 30 there in August 1950, and at Reading Sewage Farm there were at least 50 or 60 in autumn 1925.

There have only been six ringing recoveries of Green Sandpiper of birds ringed overseas in Britain. A bird seen regularly at Moor Green Lakes outside the breeding season since 2010, apparently wearing a red ring, was photographed on 30th July 2013. The image was good enough for the ring number to be read. It was, in fact, a discoloured ring applied to the bird at Castricum in the Netherlands in July 2010, making this the second UK recovery of a bird ringed at this site.

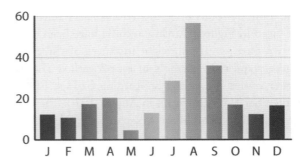

**Figure 90: Green Sandpiper: number of birds recorded per month.** Averages of the years 1990, 2000 and 2010, for which the totals recorded were 250, 244 and 243 respectively. Mobility between sites may have resulted in some overestimation of the numbers of birds involved.

Prior to the 20th century, the Green Sandpiper was a regular visitor in small numbers in Berkshire. Lamb (1880) describes them as frequent on the banks of the Kennet up to 1814, and Clark Kennedy (1868) as occasionally seen on passage and in winter.

*Sponsored by Friends Of Lavell's Lake*

# Spotted Redshank     Amber

## Tringa erythropus

*Scarce passage migrant*

The Spotted Redshank is a scarce passage migrant in Berkshire. The first county record is of two at Reading Sewage Farm in September 1922, which was followed by records in ten of the 27 years from 1923 to 1949, all at old-style sewage farms except for an immature bird at early gravel workings at Aldermaston in October 1935. In the 50 years from 1950 to 1999 Spotted Redshanks were seen in all but three years, and since 2000 they have been recorded in 10 of the 12 years to 2011, although generally there have been records of one or two birds in any given year. The number seen annually has never been high and has only exceeded six birds in 1940 (8), 1965 (12), 1966 (9), 1968 (12), 1970 (12), 1974 (10), 1987 (7), 1999 (7) and 2001 (6). Records have declined in recent decades, with a total of only 19 birds recorded in the 12 years between 2000 and 2011.

Spring passage through Berkshire is light, with records of only 44 birds from 1922 to 2011, the earliest date being on 5th March in 1940 at Slough Sewage Farm, and the latest on 23rd May 1954 at Ham Sewage Farm. Six birds have been seen in June, one at Ham Sewage Farm from the 16th to the 17th in 1957, one there on the 17th in 1974, three at Wraysbury Gravel Pits on 21st June 1974 and one bird in summer plumage at Queen Mother Reservoir on 27th June 1995. The distribution of

August records shows a pronounced peak in the second half of the month, with 84 of the 102 records occurring after the 15th. Moderate passage continues through September into early October, with an exceptionally late record of one on 8th November 2010 at Queen Mother Reservoir.

Inland winter records of Spotted Redshank are rare (*1981–84 BTO Winter Atlas*). There have been six such records involving seven birds in Berkshire, one at Slough Sewage Farm on 1st December 1940, one at Reading Sewage Farm on 3rd December 1950, one at Cockmarsh on 4th December 1992, one at Queen Mother Reservoir on 20th December 1988, one heard over Leighton Park on 5th January 1968, and two birds at Thatcham Marsh on 31st January 1976.

The monthly totals of Spotted Redshanks since 1922 are given in Figure 91. Most records have been of one or two birds, with only eight instances of three birds together and two instances of four together. The only higher counts are of five at Reading Sewage Farm in September 1965 and again in August 1970. The fall in records since 1979 is likely to be partly, if not largely, due to the decline in suitable wetland habitat, most notably at sewage farms.

Most of the Berkshire records of Spotted Redshank have been of birds in non-breeding plumage, but three flying over Wraysbury on 21st June 1974, the bird at Queen Mother Reservoir on 27th June 1995, and two together at Wigmore Lane Gravel Pit on 27th April 1996 were in summer plumage. The number of passage birds in autumn is swollen by juvenile birds, and since 1987 a small number of juveniles have been observed in July, August and September.

*Sponsored by Dot Lincoln*

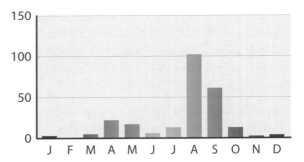

**Figure 91: Spotted Redshank: all birds recorded 1922–2011, by month of arrival.**

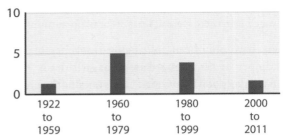

**Figure 92: Spotted Redshank: average number of birds recorded per year.**

# Greenshank

*Tringa nebularia*

*Uncommon passage migrant*

The Greenshank is a regular passage migrant in small numbers in Berkshire. In the 19th century it was considered to be uncommon in the county (Clark Kennedy, 1868), but was occasionally obtained during the spring and autumn. Clark Kennedy's few examples of specific records include the rather unusual instance of "one killed on Ascot Heath". Records in the 20th century have been from wetland habitats in the river valleys, the first from near Aldermaston in May 1916, then Reading Sewage Farm (from 1922) and later Slough Sewage Farm (from 1935), with only isolated records from other sites until 1944, when records from Ham Sewage Farm commenced. Since the 1970s, Greenshanks have been recorded annually, mainly from gravel pits, Slough Sewage Farm and Queen Mother Reservoir.

The Migration Maps reflect the typical distribution of records during the spring and autumn, with records from most of the river valleys and waterbodies in the county in both seasons.

Spring passage occurs mainly from mid-April to mid-May, with only a few earlier or later records. There have been ten March sightings since recording on a systematic basis began in 1915 until 2013, the first being one at Reading Sewage Farm on 17th March 1936, and the earliest being one at Crookham/Greenham Common on 2nd March 2004. All have been records of single birds, except two together at Slough Sewage Farm on 5th

March 1945, two over Pingewood Gravel Pits on 28th March 2004 and two seen at Dorney Wetlands on 21st March 2010. Numbers of Greenshanks in spring are less than in autumn, although in some years spring passage can be well marked, as in 1978 when there were seven together at Reading Sewage Farm on 8th May, in 1990 when numbers reached 13 at Slough Sewage Farm on 1st May, and in 2000 when nine birds were at Lea Farm Gravel Pit, Hurst on the 4th and 5th May and eight birds were recorded at Tickleback Row on the 5th May.

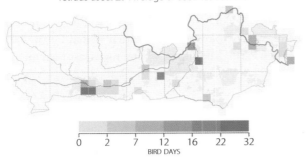

**Greenshank** Spring migration occurrence
Tetrads used: **27** Average of used tetrads: **9·0**

0 2 7 12 16 22 32
BIRD DAYS

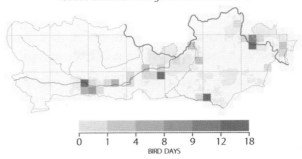

**Greenshank** Autumn migration occurrence
Tetrads used: **25** Average of used tetrads: **5·4**

0 1 4 8 9 12 18
BIRD DAYS

June records have been rather more frequent than might be expected. From 1915 to 1987 there were just eight sightings involving 11 birds, all of which were of single birds except for two together from 1st to 4th June 1948, and three together on 8th June 1940. From 1988 to 1993 June records were annual, and they have occurred in all but five (1994, 1996, 1999, 2002 and 2007) of the 19 years thereafter. Most occurred before mid-month, but there have been at least ten records from the second half of the month up to 2012, including three recorded in flight over Dorney Wetlands on the 30th June 2003.

Though some of the later June dates may consist of early autumn migration, this usually only commences in July. In the 16 years from 1974 to 1989 there was a surprising consistency in the start of autumn passage, with arrivals between 1st and 7th July in about half of those years, most frequently around 5th July. Similar patterns have been noted in recent years, with passage volume increasing throughout July and into August, when parties of from six to eight birds are not uncommon. In 1992, immediately after a severe thunderstorm, an exceptional party of 34 birds was seen briefly at Theale Gravel Pits on 21st July. Autumn passage continues throughout September and into early October, occasionally later. Most are records of single birds, but there were five at Theale Gravel Pits on 26th October 1990. November records include a juvenile at Bottom Lane Floods and

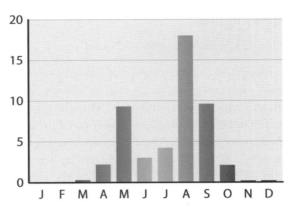

**Figure 93: Greenshank: number of birds recorded per month.** Average 2000–2009.

Wigmore Lane Gravel Pit, Theale from 4th October to 1st November 1998, a bird at Lower Farm Gravel Pit on 2nd and 3rd November 2005, and a late bird at Theale Gravel Pits on 24th to 26th November 1990.

Not unexpectedly, there have been few winter records of Greenshank, although these include the two earliest county records, one shot at Sonning in December 1801, and one shot at Newbury in January 1811 (Lamb, 1880). Since 1915, there have been 11 winter records of the species in December, January or February, all involving just one record in each winter, in 1972, 1983, 1985, 1989, 1992, 1996, 2000, 2002, 2004, 2007 and 2011.

*Sponsored by Sarah and Ken White*

# Lesser Yellowlegs

*Tringa flavipes*

*Rare vagrant, two records*

The Lesser Yellowlegs is a rare vagrant to Berkshire from America for which there have been two acceptable records, both in the 1950s. In 1952, a wader seen well at Ham Sewage Farm on 17th August appeared to be this species, but the record was initially placed in square brackets in the county report, possibly because of the rarity of the species in Britain at the time. However, the occurrence of a second record the following year, when a Lesser Yellowlegs was present at the same site

from 6th September to 22nd November 1953, led to reconsideration of the 1952 record and its full acceptance. Another sighting at Ham Sewage Farm on 1st August 1969 was not submitted to the British Birds Records Committee, so must be regarded as unsubstantiated.

The long-staying bird at Ham in 1953 was photographed both on 27th September and 25th October (reproduced in the MTNHS Report), and by the later date the comparative absence of speckling on the upperparts was very obvious. It was seen also at Langley Sewage Farm on 21st November and often visited Perry Oaks Sewage Farm, Middlesex, where it was last seen on 9th December (Veysey, 1953).

*Sponsored by Dick Haydon*

# Marsh Sandpiper

*Tringa stagnatilis*

*Rare vagrant, with one unconfirmed record*

The only possible county record of this rare vagrant to Britain concerns a sandpiper seen at Slough Sewage Farm on 19th, 21st and 22nd May 1940, which was felt, from the description provided, almost certainly to have been this species. It was placed in square brackets by the then editor of county reports, Bernard Tucker, as the published description does lack some of the clinching features of Marsh Sandpiper.

*Sponsored by Peter Hickman*

# Wood Sandpiper

Amber Sch. 1

*Tringa glareola*

*Scarce passage migrant*

The Wood Sandpiper was first recorded in the county at Reading Sewage Farm on 22nd August 1922. Wood Sandpipers were then seen in seven of the next 19 years and have since been recorded annually since 1942, with considerable variations in the numbers seen from year to year. Annual figures range from as high as 24 in 1970 (the county maximum) to as low as just one in 1982. The average number of birds recorded annually has fallen from a peak of around 10 in the 1960s and 1970s, despite the increase in observer coverage, to an average of under five per year, due at least in part to the loss of the old style sewage farm habitat. Passage tends to be heaviest in autumn. During the migration periods during the 2007–11 Atlas Survey, only autumn records were received, so only an autumn Migration Map has been included in this account.

Figure 94 shows the monthly totals of Wood Sandpiper in Berkshire since 1922. There have only been four records for the first half of April since 1922, the earliest being two at Theale Gravel Pits on 8th and 9th April 1959. Most of the spring passage occurs in the second half of May, particularly since 1980. Early June records are unusual,

**Wood Sandpiper** Autumn migration occurrence
Tetrads used: **6** Average of used tetrads: **4·0**

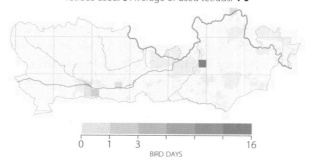

0   1   3   16
BIRD DAYS

with just six reports of birds being seen in the first half of the month, the latest being at Dinton Pastures from 14th to 15th June 1990. Most spring records have been of one or two birds, with the highest counts being of four at Ham Sewage Farm in May 1956, four at Pingewood Gravel Pit on 11th May 2005 and seven at Theale Gravel Pits on 30th May 1981. Individual birds may linger at a site for a few days, occasionally for up to a week.

There have been six records in the second half of June, the earliest being of two birds at Silwood on 23rd June 1957, presumably marking the onset of the autumn migration. Passage increases throughout July and reaches a peak in August, before declining through September. There have been 13 sightings since 1922 in the second half of September and only seven records of birds which apparently arrived in the county in October, all since 1960, the latest date recorded being 25th October 1964.

Determining the number of birds seen in autumn is complicated by the long duration of their stay in some years. For example, in 1970, which was a particularly good year for the species, Wood Sandpipers were present at Reading Sewage Farm daily from 11th August to 4th September, with the number on any day ranging from two to 16. The count of 16 on 21st and 22nd August is

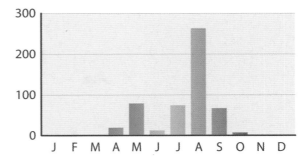

**Figure 94: Wood Sandpiper: all birds recorded 1922–2011, by month of arrival.**

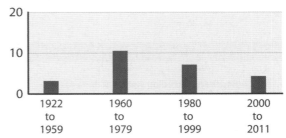

**Figure 95: Wood Sandpiper: average number of birds recorded per year.**

the highest for the species in Berkshire, followed by 13 together at Slough Sewage Farm on 14th August 1961. No other count has exceeded ten birds.

*Sponsored by Ken White 'BOC Spring Raptormania 2011'*

# Redshank

Amber

*Tringa totanus*

*Frequent passage migrant and scarce summer visitor*

The Redshank is frequently seen on passage in Berkshire but, in common with many southern English counties, has only a tenuous hold as a breeding species.

During the 2007–11 Atlas Survey, coverage of suitable breeding sites for Redshank was good and birds were found in 42 tetrads, down from 49 tetrads in the 1987–89 Atlas Survey. In just over 20% of these they were confirmed to have bred, and breeding probably occurred in about one third of the remainder, with possible breeding in a similar proportion of tetrads. Sadly this represents a decline in the Redshank as a breeding species in the county, consistent with its status nationally which shows a continuing decline, particularly along waterways and on wet meadows.

Breeding is thinly spread across the county in suitable riparian or gravel pit locations. A number of traditional sites, mainly around gravel pits along the river valleys of the Thames and Kennet continue to attract breeding birds, while the development of reserves under active management, such as at Eversley, Greenham Common and Lea Farm should provide the habitat which

hopefully will enable Redshanks to continue breeding at such sites.

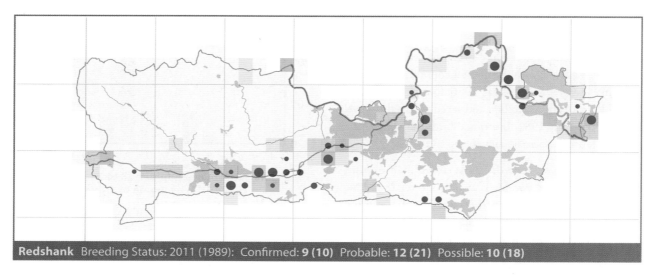

**Redshank** Breeding Status: 2011 (1989): Confirmed: **9 (10)** Probable: **12 (21)** Possible: **10 (18)**

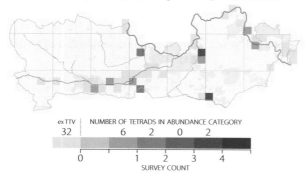

**Redshank** Breeding season abundance
Tetrads occupied: **10 (42)** Average of occupied tetrads: **1·8**

| exTTV | NUMBER OF TETRADS IN ABUNDANCE CATEGORY | | | |
|---|---|---|---|---|
| 32 | 6 | 2 | 0 | 2 |

0   1   2   3   4
SURVEY COUNT

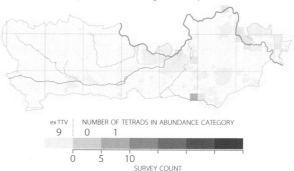

**Redshank** Winter abundance
Tetrads occupied: **1 (10)** Average of occupied tetrads: **10·0**

| exTTV | NUMBER OF TETRADS IN ABUNDANCE CATEGORY | |
|---|---|---|
| 9 | 0 | 1 |

0   5   10
SURVEY COUNT

Redshank used to be recorded throughout the year in Berkshire with reports typically from about 15 different sites, but, while the number of potential sites remains about the same, the number of records has declined noticeably since the 1980s. Peak spring passage is from March to May, although passage numbers are obscured by the presence of summering birds, but at no sites do numbers reach double figures. For example in 2007 peak counts at two of the main sites, Eversley Gravel Pits and Greenham Common, were seven in April and May and eight in June, with lower numbers at other sites across the county. Unlike some other waders, there is little discernible autumn passage, the number of birds falling sharply after June, with now only occasional reports of birds, typically singletons, during the winter months,

some months having no records at all. This is in stark contrast with counts from the 1970s and 1980s when, for example, there were 23 at Reading Sewage Farm in December 1974 and 18 at Queen Mother Reservoir in January 1989. The 2007–11 Atlas Winter Map shows that Redshank were found in only ten tetrads, all in the eastern half of the county, with no records from any of the breeding areas along the Kennet Valley in the west.

There has been one recovery of a Redshank ringed in Berkshire, a juvenile ringed at Burghfield in July 1985 being recovered at Twyford Gravel Pits in May 1990.

Historically, the Redshank was regarded as a rare straggler to Berkshire (Noble, 1906). Lamb (1880) records one shot on the Loddon in 1799 and Clark Kennedy (1868)

Redshank, Queen Mother Reservoir *Marek Walford*

refs to several shot at Wraysbury in 1854. Records after 1900 increased with the discovery of Reading Sewage Farm by ornithologists in 1922, one pair being found nesting in 1923. By 1925 the species was a common breeder at this site, with 25 birds counted on 14th June 1932. By 1934, breeding was being reported from at least two sites in the Kennet Valley, and in that year over 100 were counted at Reading Sewage Farm in April/May and about 20 at Slough Sewage Farm. In 1948 there were about 70 at Ham Sewage Farm on 20th March.

*Sponsored by Moor Green Lakes Group*

# Jack Snipe

`Amber`

## *Lymnocryptes minimus*

*Uncommon localised winter visitor and passage migrant*

The Jack Snipe is a localised winter visitor to Berkshire, which in good years is reported from some ten to 15 different locations in the county. Typical wintering habitats include the old-style sewage farms, gravel pits and less well-visited wet or marshy areas. The secretive nature of the species and its reluctance to take flight until closely approached makes it difficult to observe, and it is very likely that it has been heavily under-recorded.

Figure 96 shows the number of birds observed each month from 1974 to 2011. There is an element of guesswork in the analysis, as it can be difficult to determine whether more than one record from a site in a month (or winter) relate to the same bird or birds.

The earliest autumn arrival date was one on 8th September in 1978 at Burghfield Gravel Pits, and most wintering birds begin to arrive in October. Post-winter departure appears to start soon after the end of February although birds are occasionally observed in late April, with the latest record being one at Manor Farm Sewage Works, Reading on the 30th in 1975, pointing to some limited spring passage through the county. There has only been one summer record, a single bird at Reading Sewage Farm on 27th June 1927.

Most records of Jack Snipe have been of one or two individuals, but at suitable marshy and undisturbed sites much larger numbers can occur. In the period from 1921 to 1927, a total of 37 birds were taken during shoots of Freeman's Marsh between October and February, the highest tally being 15 in the winter of 1923/24. At Slough Sewage Farm, 44 birds were flushed on 20th November 1943, nearly all of which were considered to be different birds. The following year at this site, a marked influx of birds resulted in a count of 20 on the 21st December. Subsequent counts did not exceeded 16 birds at any one site until 2001, when there were 19 at Horton Gravel Pits on 27th November and 20 there on 6th December. This site has produced most of the substantial counts in recent years, with 16 there on 3rd December 1998 and 11th January 2005. There were also 15 there in December 1999 and there have three counts of up to this figure at

Slough Sewage Farm in January 1945, at Holyport in February 1977 and at Theale Gravel Pits in March 1984.

In the 19th century, the Jack Snipe was noted by Clark Kennedy (1868) as a regular winter visitor to Berkshire, usually from October to February. Its status then was probably very much as it is now, although it seems likely that there has been a reduction in numbers resulting from the loss in the 20th century of much of the county's marshy habitat which was favoured by the species during winter.

*Sponsored by Daniel Peacock*

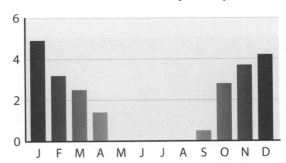

**Figure 96: Jack Snipe: number of birds recorded per month.** Average 1974–2011.

Winter abundance
Tetrads occupied: **2** (30) Average of occupied tetrads: **1·0**

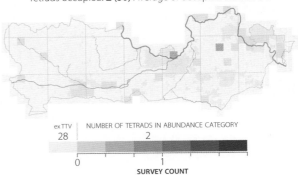

| exTTV | NUMBER OF TETRADS IN ABUNDANCE CATEGORY |
|---|---|
| 28 | 2 |

0          1
SURVEY COUNT

# Woodcock

*Scolopax rusticola*

*Uncommon localised and declining breeding bird and winter visitor*

The Woodcock is an uncommon resident and winter visitor to Berkshire. Unusually for a wader, the Woodcock nests in woodland and feeds in wetter areas. It is also crepuscular which makes census work rather difficult.

The 2007–11 Tetrad Survey has shown a marked contraction in the breeding range of the species in Berkshire since the 1987–89 survey. By the late 1980s, *Population Trends* noted that the Woodcock had already shown a decline nationally in the previous two decades, indicated by its CBC index. It is thought that this may reflect the decline in woodland cover in southern England where most census plots are located. This followed an apparent increase nationally since the 19th century which was probably due to a reduction in pressure from shooting. As far as Berkshire is concerned, the same historical picture emerges. Both Clark Kennedy (1868) and Noble (1906) regarded the species as an autumn migrant and winter visitor, with few remaining to breed.

The Woodcock's territorial display flight ('roding') in the breeding season is likely to have contributed to the registration of probable breeding in some 20% of tetrads in the 1987–89 survey and the presence of downy young was noted in a total of 17 tetrads. It was then present in many wooded areas of the south, west and east of the county indicating (as did the *1968–72 BTO Atlas*) that the Woodcock then occurred widely in Berkshire in areas of suitable habitat. In the latest survey, its range has retreated largely to the heathland areas along the southern boundary of the county and the heathland fragments remaining elsewhere, and breeding was proved in only one tetrad. This reflects the national picture emerging from the results of the BTO Atlas survey between 2007 and 2011, with a contraction of its range in much of England and a considerable reduction in the number of confirmed breeding records.

The Woodcock is known to be a winter visitor to Britain, particularly from Scandinavia, and evidence that continental birds occur in Berkshire was provided when an adult ringed in Windsor Forest in February 1959 was shot near Leningrad the following May. More recently, birds ringed in Belgium, Norway and Finland

Woodcock, *Tony Harden*

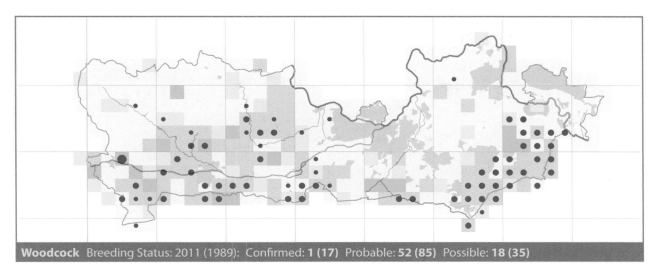

**Woodcock** Breeding Status: 2011 (1989): Confirmed: **1 (17)** Probable: **52 (85)** Possible: **18 (35)**

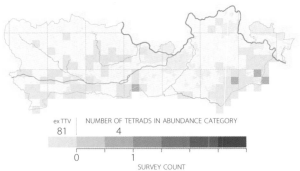

**Woodcock** Breeding season abundance
Tetrads occupied: **4 (85)** Average of occupied tetrads: **1·0**

| ex TTV | NUMBER OF TETRADS IN ABUNDANCE CATEGORY |
|--------|------------------------------------------|
| 81 | 4 |

0          1
SURVEY COUNT

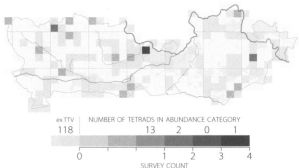

**Woodcock** Winter abundance
Tetrads occupied: **16 (134)** Average of occupied tetrads: **1·3**

| ex TTV | NUMBER OF TETRADS IN ABUNDANCE CATEGORY | | | |
|--------|-----|----|---|---|
| 118 | 13 | 2 | 0 | 1 |

0          1     2     3     4
SURVEY COUNT

have been recovered in Berkshire. In cold weather, occasional records are received from river valleys and gravel pits, and in very cold winters several Woodcock may be found together, at least six being located at a Wraysbury lake in 1987. The Winter Tetrad Map shows that its winter distribution is wider than its current breeding distribution and that recorded in the 1987–89

Tetrad breeding survey, with birds occurring in winter at gravel pit and river valley sites as well. Numbers vary considerably from winter to winter, but hard weather can result in influxes of (presumably) continental birds. One such influx occurred in the winter of 2010/11 and is reflected in the Winter Tetrad map.

*Sponsored by Blackwater Valley Countryside Trust*

# Snipe

Amber

## *Gallinago gallinago*

*Widespread winter visitor in suitable habitat, formerly bred.*

The Snipe is a winter visitor to Berkshire, which used to breed. The dependence of the species on tussocky wet pasture for breeding, a habitat which has largely disappeared in Berkshire, accounts for its decline and disappearance as a breeding species.

No breeding was confirmed in the four summers of the 2007–11 Tetrad Survey. The two tetrads where probable breeding and 13 where possible breeding was recorded almost certainly relate to lingering wintering or passage birds, no confirmed breeding records having been reported since the 1987–89 Tetrad Survey. Then, although birds were recorded in 14% of the tetrads

265

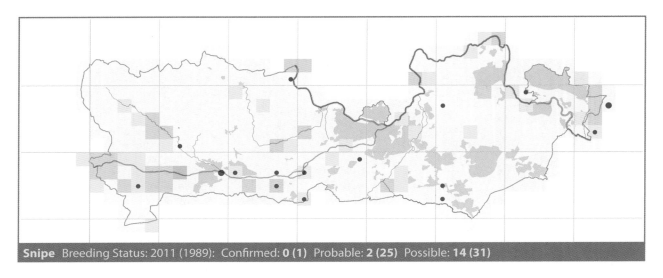

**Snipe** Breeding Status: 2011 (1989): Confirmed: **0 (1)** Probable: **2 (25)** Possible: **14 (31)**

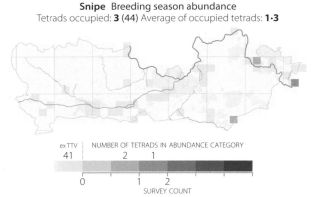

**Snipe** Breeding season abundance
Tetrads occupied: **3 (44)** Average of occupied tetrads: **1·3**

| exTTV | NUMBER OF TETRADS IN ABUNDANCE CATEGORY | | |
|---|---|---|---|
| 41 | 2 | 1 | |

0          1          2
SURVEY COUNT

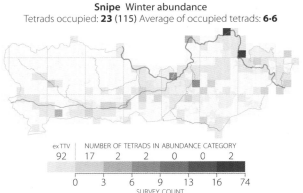

**Snipe** Winter abundance
Tetrads occupied: **23 (115)** Average of occupied tetrads: **6·6**

| exTTV | NUMBER OF TETRADS IN ABUNDANCE CATEGORY | | | | | |
|---|---|---|---|---|---|---|
| 92 | 17 | 2 | 2 | 0 | 0 | 2 |

0      3      6      9     13    16    74
SURVEY COUNT

during the survey, breeding was only confirmed in one. Snipe are, however, a difficult species to prove breeding, and the fact that displaying males were recorded in no fewer than 14 tetrads suggests that the number of birds actually breeding in the late 1980s may have been greater than the survey statistics might indicate. Nevertheless, the 1987–89 Tetrad Survey results showed a marked and rapid decline in the breeding population of Snipe in Berkshire since the *1968–72 BTO Atlas*, when breeding was confirmed in 16 of the 10 km squares covering the present county boundary.

Snipe have been particularly affected by the scale of changes in grassland management in Britain (O'Connor and Shrubb, 1986). The main impact on the breeding population has been from drainage and the resultant increase in stocking densities, leading to trampling of nests and young. In Berkshire today most wet pastures formerly suitable for breeding Snipe have been drained. This reflects the status of the species nationally and in much of western Europe, with a decline of 62% recorded between UK national surveys of wet meadows in 1982 and 2002 (Wilson *et al.*, 2005).

The current status of the Snipe as a breeding bird in Berkshire is very different from that in the 19th century, evidence of which is provided by Clark Kennedy

(1868) who refers to eggs being procured from various commons around Reading and along the Surrey border. It was clearly also common as a breeding bird in the 1920s and 1930s, since there are numerous breeding records included in the county reports from the Thames and Kennet valleys and elsewhere, including reference to several pairs at Calcot in 1929 and five pairs breeding at Slough Sewage Farm in 1935.

The distribution shown by the winter tetrad map indicates that the species is still widely encountered in suitable habitat in the river valleys of Berkshire, with groups of birds regularly occurring around the less disturbed lakes, gravel pits, reservoirs and wet meadows, and occasionally away from wet areas on farmland. Since 1974, the county report has recorded gatherings of 50 or more at the following locations during the period from September to March (maximum counts being shown in brackets): Jealott's Hill (300), Manor Farm (255), Aldermaston Soke (135), Dorney Wetlands/Jubilee River (121), Horton and Wraysbury Gravel Pits (100), Theale Gravel Pits (100), Englemere Pond (100), Old Slade Sewage Farm (80), Greenham Common (75), Holyport (70), Brimpton, Bray, Eversley, Pingewood, Woolhampton and Twyford Gravel Pits, Chamberhouse Marsh, Freeman's Marsh, Hamstead Marshall, Padworth Common, Purley and Slough

Sewage Farm. Counts in excess of 100 have though not been frequent in recent years, with only the wetland created by the construction of the Jubilee River flood relief project producing counts in excess of 100 since 2000.

The relative abundance of the species at this time of year is due to a combination of immigration from the east and a general movement south of the British breeding population. Evidence of the former is provided by winter recoveries in Berkshire of birds ringed in Germany in May, and southern Sweden in August. Berkshire also produced a very early ringing recovery of Snipe, a bird ringed at Aldermaston on 26th May 1912 being recovered later that year on 7th November at Stanford Dingley.

*Sponsored by John Mead*

# Great Snipe

## Gallinago media

*Rare vagrant, five records*

There are five records of Great Snipe for Berkshire, three between 1860 and 1880 and two in the 1950s. Not unexpectedly, the earliest county records are of birds which were shot, with one near Cookham about 1860 (Clark Kennedy, 1868), and another near Hungerford in October 1874 (Noble, 1906). The first sight record is of a bird seen by Noble which was flushed twice during a snipe shoot in 1880 at Hennerton and which he considered to be of this species.

The decline in snipe shooting after the turn of the century is probably largely responsible for the gap in records after 1880, there being no further sightings until one at Ham Sewage Farm on 10th September 1950 which provided good views. This was followed quickly by another bird, this time at Slough Sewage Farm, on 29th September 1956. A report of two birds there a few days earlier on 17th September was never substantiated.

Despite the increase in observer coverage at potentially suitable sites since the 1950s, there have been no further confirmed sightings. The nearest breeding populations to Britain are in Poland and Norway, and it is on the IUCN's Red List of threatened species as a result of a rapid decline in its global population.

*Sponsored by Renton Righelato*

# Black-winged Pratincole

## Glareola nordmanni

*Rare vagrant, one record*

The Black-winged Pratincole is a rare vagrant to Britain whose breeding range extends from central Asia to south-east Europe. The only Berkshire record is of an adult at Reading Sewage Farm from 5th August to 9th August 1976. It spent its time roosting at the nearby Smallmead Gravel Pit, or hunting for insects over the fields between there and the few remaining sewage sludge beds. This was, at the time, only the 15th record of this species in Britain. The record is also noteworthy as the stimulus for one of the more infamous clashes between twitchers and a landowner. A farmer, upset at unauthorised access onto his land by those looking for the bird, took the law into his own hands and sprayed his unwelcome visitors with his muckspreader to persuade them to leave!

*Sponsored by Peter Standley*

# Pomarine Skua

Green

*Stercorarius pomarinus*

*Rare vagrant, six records involving 18 birds*

The Pomarine Skua is a rare vagrant to Berkshire, with seven records from within the current county boundary. The first record was of "a male killed in a wood near Newbury on or about 25th October 1877" (Noble, 1906). Noble records that the bird was discovered by a Mr Wallis in a taxidermist's shop in Newbury where it had been sent to be made into a fan! On dissection it proved to be a male in very poor condition.

In 1972 a dark morph adult was at Wraysbury Reservoir (now Surrey, but partly Berkshire at the time) from 26th November to 7th December; on the first date it was seen to kill and eat a Black-headed Gull. The next record was not until 1985, when a juvenile was seen at the Queen Mother Reservoir gull roost on 23rd November 1985 and again early the following morning. This bird occurred during a year of exceptional numbers along the east coast during the autumn. It followed a record of another juvenile on 7th October from nearby Wraysbury Reservoir.

There was then a gap of eleven years before another record, this time a dark morph juvenile at Queen Mother Reservoir on 14th November 1996. This was followed by a possible Pomarine Skua which was seen briefly at Theale Main Pit on 30th November 1999. In 2003 an unprecedented flock of 13 (a rare spring inland record) circled Queen Mother Reservoir on the evening of the 25th April before heading off north (Heard, 2006).

The last records are of two sightings at Queen Mother Reservoir in 2007: a dark morph juvenile on 10th November and a paler intermediate morph which stayed from 20th to 22nd November; like the 1972 bird, the latter was seen feeding on a Black-headed Gull. These records occurred during an influx with at least eight other inland records in England around the same time.

*Sponsored by David Fuller*

# Arctic Skua

Red

*Stercorarius parasiticus*

*Rare vagrant, principally in autumn*

The Arctic Skua is a rare passage migrant in Berkshire, which usually occurs over open water sites. There is a regular inland passage of Arctic Skuas in very small numbers during autumn (*1981–84 BTO Winter Atlas*) and the majority of the county records fit this pattern.

The first record of Arctic Skua for Berkshire in the 20th century was of one in very weak condition at Reading Sewage Farm on 17th October 1934. It was caught and fed in captivity but eventually died on 10th November. There were no other records until one over Ham Sewage Farm on 29th September 1960. Subsequently, from 1968 to 1990, there were a further 12 records involving 13 birds. This increase is likely to be due largely to a combination of the increase in the number of skilled observers since the 1950s, an increase in the number of gravel pits, and particularly the building of the Queen Mother Reservoir. These open water sites have produced records of 22 out of the 23 birds seen between 1977 and 2012, and Queen Mother Reservoir has produced all such records after 1990. The incidence of records since 1960 is shown in Figure 97 and their monthly distribution is shown in Figure 98.

Spring records are very rare, with only three single birds being reported, a pale morph soaring over Windsor Forest, which drifted to the north-east over High Standing Hill, on 24th May 1984, one flying north over Queen Mother Reservoir on 27th May 2007, another, at the same site, heading north-east on 31st May 2011, and a dark-morph adult seen over Swinley Forest on the unusual date of 24th June 1972. Extreme dates for autumn passage are 29th July 1968 over Ham Sewage Farm and one which was at Queen Mother Reservoir until 20th October 2003.

Until recently the only record involving more than one bird was of two flying west over Brimpton Gravel Pits on 30th September 1978, but now the largest recorded flock was of five birds (two adults and three juveniles) flying south-east over Queen Mother Reservoir on 23rd September 2004 and, subsequently, three adult birds were at the same site on 14th August 2007. All but three records have been of birds only seen in flight. Of the exceptions, the first was an immature picked up after dark in Tilehurst on 13th September 1976 and released at the coast some days later after regaining its strength, the second was also an immature bird which lingered at Theale Gravel Pits from 6th to 17th September 1985, and the other was the pale morph juvenile which arrived at Queen Mother Reservoir on 18th October 2003 and departed on the 20th.

There is only one record from the 19th century, the rather vague reference to one being killed "near

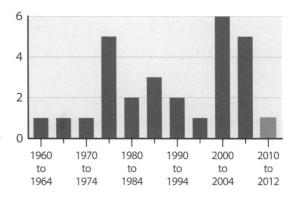

**Figure 97: Arctic Skua: all birds recorded 1960–2012.**
Periods are five years except for 2010–2012.

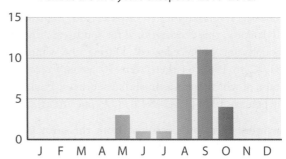

**Figure 98: Arctic Skua: all birds recorded 1960–2012, by month of arrival.**

Broadmoor about 1877" (Noble, 1906). Although one shot near Newbury in 1883 has been previously attributed to Berkshire, the bird was killed at Ashmansworth in Hampshire.

*Sponsored by Michael McKee*

# Long-tailed Skua

Green

*Stercorarius longicaudus*

*Rare vagrant, eight records*

The first county record of Long-tailed Skua was a juvenile seen initially on Wraysbury Reservoir in Surrey on 30th August 1978, which was subsequently observed to depart southwards over Wraysbury Gravel Pits.

Since 2000, there have been a further seven records, all at Queen Mother Reservoir. A dark morph juvenile was recorded on 17th August 2003. This was followed by an intermediate morph juvenile which arrived on 9th September 2006 and stayed for a remarkable nine days until 17th September (Heard, 2012). Another intermediate morph made a fleeting visit on 21st August 2007, and then a dark morph juvenile lingered for twenty minutes on 24th September 2008. In 2012 there were

two records: a light morph juvenile flew over on 17th September and, later the same month, an intermediate morph juvenile was present for a few minutes on 23rd. The first Spring record occurred in 2013 when a full adult was present on the evening of 24th of May.

*Sponsored by Rebecca Blamey, WSP Environment & Energy*

# Great Skua

Amber

*Stercorarius skua*

*Rare vagrant, nine records involving 11 birds*

The Great Skua is a rare vagrant to Berkshire which has been recorded on just nine occasions. It was first recorded in 1980, when there were two: one moving west low over Theale Gravel Pits on 6th January, and another at the same site on 28th September, which left to the west after being mobbed by gulls. Surprisingly, there was another winter record in 1984, when one was observed harassing a large gull flock at Holyport on 7th January. Two of the three birds recorded prior to October 1987 were seen in early January; this is exceptional for south-east England, although not unprecedented. During the winters of 1981/82 to 1983/84 there were 30 January records in Britain, of which one was inland in southeast England in early January 1983 (*1981–84 BTO Winter Atlas*).

A number of records resulted from the great gale of the night of 15th October 1987. The following day there were sightings of two Great Skuas flying south over Queen Mother Reservoir and of three flying south over Wraysbury Reservoir towards Berkshire. On 17th October, there was a further sighting of one at Queen Mother Reservoir, and another bird, which was found at Tilehurst, was taken to Dinton Pastures for release.

A probable Great Skua was seen flying past Eversley Gravel Pits on 3rd July 1999. Summer records are unusual, although a small number of Great Skuas do move along the south coast during June and July.

A juvenile first recorded at Queen Mother Reservoir on 22nd September 2004 was subsequently found dead on 27th September, probably from starvation. This was a year of widely-publicized breeding failures at Great Skua colonies, and consequently juveniles were scarce that autumn (Heard, 2008).

*Sponsored by Andrew Taylor*

# Puffin

Amber

*Fratercula arctica*

*Rare vagrant*

Although the Puffin is a rare vagrant in Berkshire, it is the most frequently recorded auk in the county, sometimes in somewhat bizarre circumstances. As Puffins leave their British coastal breeding colonies in August and do not approach land again until spring (*1981–84 BTO Winter Atlas*), it is somewhat surprising that the species should have occurred more frequently in Berkshire than both Guillemot or Little Auk which winter closer to land.

Twelve of the 20th century records of Puffin in Berkshire have been in autumn, from August to November, the exceptions being one found in a garden in Shinfield on about 10th February 1917, a female found at Sandhurst on 16th March 1933 and an immature found on Datchet Golf Course on 19th December 1945. The monthly distribution of records is summarised in Figure 99. All but one have been found away from open water, usually being discovered exhausted after adverse weather, and a number have been picked up either for attempted rehabilitation or to be taken to the coast to be released. The only bird to be found on open water was an immature on Queen Mother Reservoir on 21st August 1978, which was found dead two days later.

The first autumn record was one at Langley on 19th November 1910 (Fraser, 1954), and the second was an immature bird found in a ditch at Ascot on 1st November 1911, which died three days later (Collings, 1911). The other records relate to one picked up exhausted near Reading in late September 1925, one picked up near Combe on 5th November 1934, and one picked up at Theale on 22nd October 1935, which was ringed at Reading

Museum and released onto the Thames on the 25th. An immature was picked up alive at a roadside in Woodley on 26th September 1945 and was taken to Sonning Eye Gravel Pits, Oxfordshire where it remained until at least the 28th. Another immature was found on a farm at Sindlesham on 6th October 1955 and was taken to Reading Museum where it died on the 11th. There was an exceptional series of three records in October 1958: an immature at Bucklebury on the 9th which was taken and released at Keyhaven, Hampshire; one at Thatcham Marsh on the 17th which lived until 15th November, and one of unspecified age at White Waltham Aerodrome on the 21st, which was released at Portsmouth. Since then there have been just three records, one "waddling down a road" in Bradfield early in October 1971, whose photograph appeared in the Evening Post on the 13th, the 1978 record at Queen Mother Reservoir, and one found by a postman in the road at Inkpen on 18th November 1996, which was taken to a wildlife hospital in Sussex where it died.

The decline in records (ten in the 34 years from 1925 to 1958 but only three since then) is surprising in view of

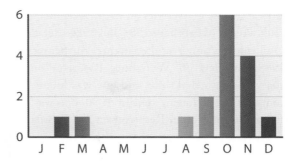

**Figure 99: Puffin: all birds recorded 1910–2012, by month of arrival.**

the increase in the number of observers and in the area of open water in Berkshire since 1959.

There are two 19th Century records of Puffin in Berkshire. One was caught in Northbrook Street, Newbury, on 16th March 1810 and was kept alive on small fish for fifteen days (Lamb, 1880). One seen in a taxidermist's shop in Newbury on 17th December 1877 had apparently been knocked down by a whip as it rose from a ditch! (Noble, 1906).

*Sponsored by Amy McKee*

# Razorbill

*Alca torda*

*Rare vagrant, one record*

There is just one record of Razorbill for Berkshire, a bird seen on the Thames at Old Windsor on 13th October 1948, although according to a ferryman it had been there for a week. Close views of the bird were obtained from a boat and when diving it was noted to jump slightly out of the water. The bird was last seen on 16th October.

*Sponsored by Andrew Taylor*

# Little Auk

*Alle alle*

*Rare vagrant*

The Little Auk is a rare winter vagrant to Berkshire, which has been recorded on 15 occasions since 1807. Lamb (1880) records one that spent most of the day in early November 1807 diving in a mill stream at Newbury and bringing up minnows in the manner of a Little Grebe. In the tradition of the time it was then shot and found to be a male, its stomach containing five minnows. It is assumed that a reference by Clark Kennedy (1868) to 'one near Newbury' relates to this bird. Noble (1906) notes that one was shot at Shinfield in January 1895.

The next three records are all of dead or injured birds. One was reported in *The Field* for 9th December 1926 as

having been found injured on the road between Henley and Maidenhead. Another was found at Curridge, near Newbury, on 10th February 1950, and one which subsequently died was found moribund in a puddle at Whitley Wood on 26th March 1975.

The first 20th century record of an apparently healthy bird was one seen swimming and diving for a few minutes at Theale Gravel Pits on 24th December 1978. The auk 'wrecks' of February 1983 and 1986 (detailed in the Guillemot account) resulted in three further records. In 1983, one flew off Wraysbury Reservoir on 9th February and into Berkshire, and one was found dead at Compton the following day. In 1986, one was seen briefly on Queen Mother Reservoir on 2nd February. A further wreck in 1995 resulted in three more records, one on the Thames at Bourne End on 2nd November, one on Queen Mother Reservoir on 3rd November, and one found dead near Holyport on 5th November.

The next two records were remarkable, but for different reasons; in 1999 an adult was found in a fishpond in Wildridings, Bracknell on 10th November and was taken to a local vet, and eventually released at the coast the following day. The next occasion was in 2007 when, after heavy passage along the east coast of Britain, a group of eight appeared at Queen Mother Reservoir on 14th November. Not only was this the first multiple sighting of this species in Berkshire, it is also considered to be the second-largest inland group encountered (after nine flew over Derbyshire in 1995). All flew off east after a few minutes. One at Queen Mother Reservoir the following day constituted the 15th record for Berkshire.

*Sponsored by Peter Hickman*

---

# Guillemot Amber

## *Uria aalge*

### Rare vagrant, seven records

The Guillemot is a rare vagrant to Berkshire, with all but one of the seven records having occurred during national or local auk 'wrecks', first in 1983 and then in 1986. The exception, and the first county record, was of one picked up dead near Newbury on 13th February 1904, this bird having been previously seen alive (Noble, 1906).

Nearly 80 years were to pass before the next records in 1983, when three birds reached Berkshire as part of a massive 'wreck' of some 10,000 auks which took place from 5th February, primarily along the east coast of Britain (*1981–84 BTO Winter Atlas*). One bird was picked up alive at Finchampstead on 19th February, a bridled morph bird was seen on Queen Mother Reservoir the same day, and a third, presumably different, bird was first reported on the Thames at Maidenhead on 26th February.

Remarkably for such a rare vagrant to Berkshire, exactly three years later another 'wreck' resulted in a further three records. One was seen on Queen Mother Reservoir

on 16th and 17th February 1986, a bird of the bridled morph was found in a garden at Woodley on 27th February 1986, which was taken first to Dinton Pastures Country Park and then to the coast for release, and a third bird was present for a few days from 2nd March 1986 on Queen Mother Reservoir. The 1986 records coincided with reports of at least 90 Guillemots, and perhaps as many as 126, in the London area over a period of 18 days from 13th February. The birds had been wintering in the Thames Estuary and appear to have been driven up river by unrelenting, cold, easterly winds in the coldest February nationally since 1947 (Hastings, 1986).

*Sponsored by David Tudor*

---

# Little Tern Amber Sch. 1

## *Sternula albifrons*

### Scarce passage migrant

Prior to 1946, the Little Tern was a scarce vagrant to Berkshire, although it is now more regular and is recorded in most years. From 1900 to 1945 there were just three records, one on the Thames between Caversham and Sonning on 13th May 1918, a party of five at Reading Sewage Farm on 3rd May 1933, and one at Slough Sewage Farm in August 1939.

A growth in both number of observers and flooded

gravel pits from 1946 produced records in 17 of the 34 years from 1946 to 1979, and in 25 of the following 32 years from 1980 to 2011. Little Terns were seen with increasing frequency from 1980, following an increase of about 40% in the British breeding population between 1969–70 and 1985–87 (Stroud and Glue, 1991). Records have, though, diminished in recent years.

Figure 100 shows the monthly totals of Little Terns in Berkshire from 1918 to 2011. The earliest date for spring passage is 15th April 2003 at Dinton Pastures, and passage typically continues through May and into early June. From 1980, there were an increasing number of June records, particularly on the 17th and 18th of the month, when 14 of the 21 birds recorded in June were seen, including an exceptional party of nine birds on 18th June 1983 at Dinton Pastures.

Return passage has been recorded from 14th July, and most records are from the end of July to 13th August. There have been just three records later in August, and three September records from 5th to 20th September, when there were two at Theale Gravel Pits in 1980. Most records have involved from one to three birds, but there have been 15 records of three or more, as shown in Figure 101, only one of which has been since 1995.

The years in which the highest number of Little Terns have been recorded on passage in Berkshire were: 1950, with 14 birds reported; 1980, with 15 birds; and 1983, with 18 birds.

Birds were recorded in both spring and autumn in all three years. In no other year has the number of birds recorded exceeded eight. Although most records have been of one or two birds, 40% of the birds recorded have been in parties of three or more birds (Figure 101).

Records have come from flooded gravel pit sites, reservoirs and from the Thames. Passage has occasionally been in association with Black Terns, and on only six occasions have apparently the same birds been seen on successive days, the longest staying bird lingering at Horton Gravel Pits from 8th to 11th September 1980. Autumn passage includes a proportion of immature birds, and two adults and three juveniles seen at Theale Gravel Pits on 31st July 1962 may have been a family party.

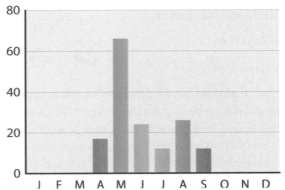

**Figure 100:** Little Tern: all birds recorded 1918–2011, by month of arrival.

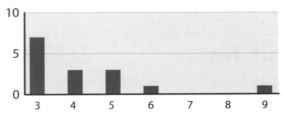

**Figure 101:** Little Tern: numbers of parties of three or more birds 1918–2011.

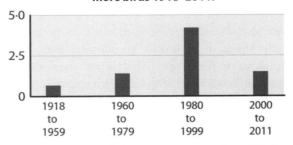

**Figure 102:** Little Tern: average number of birds recorded per year.

Prior to 1900, there were only occasional records of Little Terns in Berkshire. Clark Kennedy (1868) records that one was shot near Windsor in July 1867, another was killed at Cookham Grove a few years earlier and others were obtained near Eton. Noble (1906) states that there is mention of one in the Wellington College Natural Science Report for 1867, and that the landlord of the Swan at Pangbourne had one in his possession which had been killed in the district, presumably on the Thames.

*Sponsored by David White*

# Caspian Tern

*Hydroprogne caspia*

*Rare vagrant, one record*

The only Berkshire record of Caspian Tern, whose closest breeding sites to Britain are in the Baltic Sea, was of an adult in summer plumage which spent much of 12th August 1979 at Theale Gravel Pits.

*Sponsored by Graeme Stewart*

# Whiskered Tern

*Chlidonias hybrida*

*Rare vagrant, one record*

The only Berkshire record of this species, whose breeding range extends no further north in western Europe than central France, was one at Moor Green Lakes on 21st, 24th and 27th May 2005. The bird, a second summer bird, could be distinguished by a missing tail feather, and was also seen at Fleet Pond, Hampshire and Staines Reservoir, Surrey.

*Sponsored by Bruce Archer*

---

# Black Tern

Amber  Sch. 1

*Chlidonias niger*

*Uncommon passage migrant*

The Black Tern is an annual passage migrant in moderate numbers through Berkshire, with passage being more pronounced in some years, particularly in periods of easterly winds. It is usually encountered over larger waterbodies or along rivers. This pattern seems to have changed little since the 18th and 19th centuries. Lamb (1880) noted that one was shot at Maiden Erleigh in September 1794, and there were a succession of isolated 19th century records including one obtained near Maidenhead in May 1866 (Clark Kennedy, 1868). Noble (1906) reported that Black Terns were "a not uncommon spring and autumn visitor". Most of these early records appear to be of birds following the course of rivers.

The discovery of Reading Sewage Farm by ornithologists in 1922 produced records of small numbers of Black Tern from 1926 to 1928, and again from 1931, and the first significant count when 17 were seen on 3rd May 1933. Following records from Reading Sewage Farm, birds were then observed at Slough Sewage Farm. From 1946 onwards, records came increasingly from the river valley gravel pits, although there have also been records from Windsor Great Park and Virginia Water. There have been annual county records of Black Terns since

1926, with the exception only of 1929, 1930, 1937, 1941 to 1943 and 1963.

The actual number of Black Terns passing through the county is difficult to establish. Large parties can be difficult to count, and observers can rarely be certain whether birds seen on successive days are the same or different birds on continuing passage. Even during a particular day numbers can fluctuate from hour to hour. During a continuous watch of Burghfield Gravel Pits throughout the afternoon and evening of 15th May 1950, a succession of parties of 26, five, six and 12 birds were observed. All parties departed the site except the

**Black Tern** Spring migration occurrence
Tetrads used: **17** Average of used tetrads: **11·8**

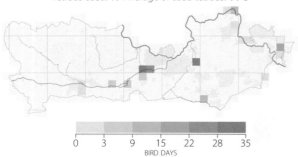

0   3   9   15   22   28   35
BIRD DAYS

**Black Tern** Autumn migration occurrence
Tetrads used: **10** Average of used tetrads: **34·7**

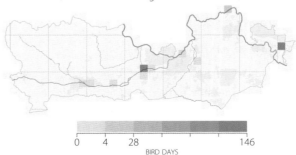

0   4   28   146
BIRD DAYS

last, which settled on a small gravel islet, probably to roost. There are other instances which point to birds roosting overnight, and of birds arriving and departing during the day. In this account, it has been assumed that records on successive days relate to the same birds unless there is evidence to the contrary, and the figures given are therefore probably an underestimate of the true number of birds involved.

Figure 103 shows the estimated monthly totals of Black Terns, and Figure 104 the average number of birds recorded per year for each decade since 1946. Generally autumn records account for just over half the records, but proportions vary over the period. May accounts for 86% of spring records and August and September for 92% of autumn records. Numbers vary considerably from year to year, with the occasional occurrence of large parties of birds either in spring or autumn. As an indication of the annual fluctuations which can occur, about 100 birds were recorded in 1950 but only seven in 1951, and 82 in 1991 were followed by an annual total of over 300 in 1992. The smallest annual total in the 1970s was five in 1972, whereas in the 1980s it was 21 in 1985. Fluctuations since the mid-1990s have been more modest, but totals have still ranged between 20 (2007) and 149 (2000).

Within the year, spring passage is more concentrated than in autumn. In only 19 of the 50 years up to 1995 was spring passage first recorded in April, although April passage occurred in 11 of the 16 years from 1996 to 2011. The earliest record is of four birds at Theale Gravel Pits on 14 April 1980. In only two years since 1995 have more than ten birds been seen in April, and the total of 42 in April 1984 has not been exceeded.

The number of passage Black Terns increases rapidly from the beginning of May, making this the peak month for the species in Berkshire. There have been records in May every year since 1973. Four of the five highest totals for any month of the year have been in May, with at least 106 in 1950, 107 in 1990, 91 in 1993 and 144 in 2000. By the end of May, spring passage is largely over and has only extended into June in 14 of the 66 years up to 2011, the latest date being on the 16th. In 1973, 1985 and 1988, however, small parties of from two to eight birds were reported between 27th June and 1st July, presumably representing early autumn passage, and a single bird was reported at Eversley Gravel Pits on 26 June 2009.

Autumn passage traditionally peaked in August, when a proportion of birds in immature plumage are reported. Passage volume then decreased throughout September, but there has been a different trend since 1994 with larger numbers being recorded in September in nine years out of 17. Passage has extended into October in only 14 of the 66 years, with the latest date being on the

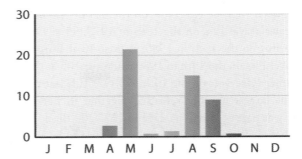

**Figure 103: Black Tern: birds recorded per month.**
Average 1946–2005

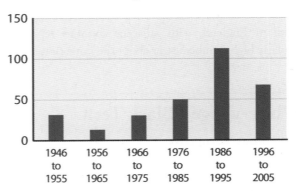

**Figure 104: Black Tern: average number of birds recorded per year.**

24th in 1967. The only later record is of a single bird seen at Theale Gravel Pits on 11th November 1984.

A notable feature of Black Tern passage in Berkshire is the often sudden appearance of large parties of birds. With the exception of 56 at Theale Gravel Pits on 25th September 2011 and 42 at Queen Mother Reservoir on 2nd September 2004, the largest concentrations recorded have all been in August and, remarkably, mainly on the 19th of that month. There were about 70 at Burghfield Gravel Pits on the 5th in 1954, 41 at Queen Mother Reservoir on the 5th in 1999, 54

Black Tern, Woolhampton GPs *Jerry O'Brien*

275

at Queen Mother Reservoir on the 6th in 2009, 60 at Theale Gravel Pits on the 19th in 1978, 55 at Dinton Pastures on the 19th in 1986, at least 40 at Burghfield Gravel Pits on the 19th in 1989, and over 105 at Queen Mother Reservoir on the 19th in 1992. This last record is the largest number recorded together in Berkshire, and was part of a total passage of 167–200 Black Terns at that site that day. Flocks in spring tend to be smaller than in the autumn, with 55–60 at Theale Gravel Pits on 28th May 1990 being the highest count. In some years such concentrations are clearly part of a much wider movement of Black Terns on a broad front through southern England, with adjacent counties reporting similarly high numbers at or about the same time.

A study of autumn tern passage at Theale Gravel Pits in 1967 showed a bias towards arrivals during easterly winds. On other occasions, heavy passage has been noted at times of low cloud and rain. It seems likely, therefore, that prevailing weather conditions play a significant part in determining the extent to which over-flying birds will visit gravel pits and other stretches of open water whilst on passage. Where the directions in which birds were flying has been noted, this has pointed to birds passing from west to east in spring and in the opposite direction in autumn. Birds leaving Theale Gravel Pits in autumn are frequently seen to head westwards up the Kennet Valley.

*Sponsored by Dick Haydon*

# White-winged Black Tern

*Chlidonias leucopterus*

*Rare passage migrant, recorded nine times*

The White-winged Black Tern is a rare visitor to Berkshire and has been recorded on nine occasions. The difficulty of distinguishing this species from Black Tern in autumn may be one reason for the absence of county records until a juvenile was identified at Theale Gravel Pits on 14th September 1948.

Subsequent records, which involve eight or possibly nine birds, coincide with an increase in the level of observer coverage since the 1960s, but do not appear to be related to the growth in the number of gravel pits, since all records have come from those at Theale, and there have been none since three records in the early 1990s. There were single adults there on 27th October 1968 and 27th August 1979, and a juvenile was seen for four to five minutes during a heavy passage of Black Tern on 7th September 1980.

In 1992 there were three, or possibly four birds, an adult and a first-summer bird on 18th May, and possibly a different sub-adult the following day, and one from 10th to 11th August. The May records coincided with a major influx of the species into Britain. In 1993, one was seen on 21st May and in 1994 a moulting adult was seen from 11th to 13th August.

*Sponsored by Brian Hackett*

# Sandwich Tern      Amber

*Sterna sandvicensis*

*Uncommon passage migrant, principally in autumn*

The Sandwich Tern is now an annual passage migrant in Berkshire, with most records occurring in autumn, although prior to 1951 there had only been two records for the county: a party of eight birds spent much of the 10th April 1895 on the Thames at Marlow (Noble, 1906), and a single bird was seen at Reading Sewage Farm on 6th June 1927.

The species remained a rare vagrant to Berkshire until 1965, with just five birds in 1951, one in 1955 and 1959, and two in 1960, all at Burghfield and Theale Gravel Pits.

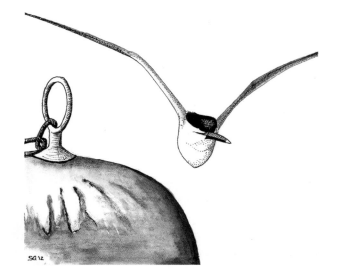

**Sandwich Tern** Spring migration occurrence
Tetrads used: **8** Average of used tetrads: **2·3**

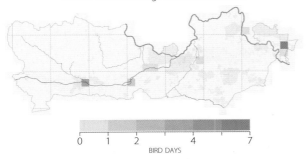

**Sandwich Tern** Autumn migration occurrence
Tetrads used: **5** Average of used tetrads: **9·6**

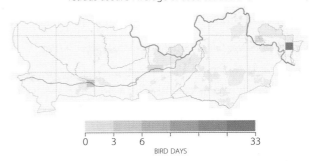

There were then three records involving five birds in 1965. During the period from August to October 1967, extensive observations were made of tern passage at Theale Gravel Pits which produced a total of six records involving 21 Sandwich Terns. The study showed that in spite of few previous records, Sandwich Tern passage was likely to be regular through the Kennet Valley, and that most records occurred during periods when there were easterly winds or conditions were calm (Lucas and Standley, 1967). Sandwich Terns have been recorded annually in Berkshire since then, and there was an increase both in the number of records and the frequency with which large parties of this species have been observed, but between 2003 and 2012 there has only been one year when more than 15 birds have been recorded in the autumn. It is likely that prevailing weather conditions partly account for the wide annual variations in the number of passage birds observed since 1967. For example, after 32 birds were seen in 1974, including parties of ten and 14 at Burghfield Gravel Pits, only one was recorded in both 1975 and 1976. The fact that Sandwich Terns are very short stayers in Berkshire also increases the likelihood of annual variations in recorded observations.

Figure 105 shows an analysis of the sightings of the 851 Sandwich Terns seen in Berkshire from 1950 to 2011. In spring, there has been only one report of more than four birds together. Higher numbers begin to occur in July, when up to four birds have been seen together, and increase throughout August when parties of up to nine have been observed. The two largest counts have occurred when autumn passage peaks in September: an exceptional party of about 80 birds on 10th September 1989 noisily approaching Twyford Gravel Pits from the south, and 29 at Theale Gravel Pits on 21st September 1980. In addition, there were 13 at Theale Gravel Pits in 1985 and 13 near Windsor Great Park in 1987. The only other high autumn count was of 11 at Queen Mother Reservoir on 13th October 1990.

Passage dates have ranged from one on 25th March 2013 to a party of three on 17th October 1987 following the great storm that year. In the autumn, numbers are supplemented by a proportion of immature birds. Where direction of flight has been noted in the autumn, this

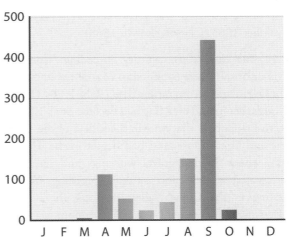

**Figure 105: Sandwich Tern: all birds recorded 1950–2011, by month of arrival.**

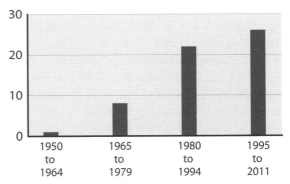

**Figure 106: Sandwich Tern: average number of birds recorded per year.**

has been predominantly west or south-west, pointing to passage through the county along the Thames and Kennet Valleys. Some records indicate passage on a broader front, for example 13 being seen over Windsor Great Park in September 1987, four over Tilehurst in August 2003, and three over Earley in July 1981. This last record is of further interest as the only sighting of night passage, the birds being lit from below against a clear sky, and the party comprising an adult and two noisily calling juveniles. Many sightings of Sandwich Tern in Berkshire have been of over-flying birds, sometimes in association with other terns. Observations at Theale in autumn 1967 suggested that Sandwich and Black Terns were most likely to occur together on passage.

*Sponsored by Andrew Taylor*

# Common Tern

Amber

*Sterna hirundo*

*Common passage migrant and regular summer visitor*

The Common Tern is a frequent passage migrant and relatively recent coloniser as a breeding species in Berkshire. The Common Tern appears always to have been a regular passage migrant through Berkshire and was regarded as such by Clark Kennedy (1868) and Noble (1906), who noted that small flocks sometimes occurred. A late bird was killed at Boveney Lock in November 1865 (Clark Kennedy, 1868).

Before the mid-20th century, breeding Common Terns in Britain were confined to coastal habitats, only occurring inland on migration. The *1968–72 BTO Atlas* indicates that inland breeding had become established in eastern England, at that time in the valleys of the Trent, Nene and Great Ouse, and had begun in the Thames Basin, where flooded gravel workings and reservoirs had created a new and suitable breeding habitat. Breeding in the Colne Valley, then on the borders of Buckinghamshire and Greater London, was first confirmed when the LNHS carried out a Tetrad Survey at the same time as fieldwork for the *1968–72 BTO Atlas* (Montier, 1977). Breeding occurred just outside Berkshire at Henley Road Gravel Pit, Oxfordshire, from 1969, and at Old Slade Nature Reserve, now in Berkshire, from 1968 (Lack & Ferguson, 1993). Two pairs attempted to breed at Wraysbury Gravel Pits in 1971 but were unsuccessful and one pair bred successfully at Theale Gravel Pits in 1972, adults being seen with four young on 2nd August. More regular breeding occurred from 1974 at Wraysbury, and from 1980 at Theale Gravel Pits. In 1980, breeding probably also took place at Twyford Gravel Pits and, by 1984, 27 pairs were recorded breeding at five sites in Berkshire.

The breeding distribution of Common Terns in Berkshire is closely associated with sizeable expanses of open water with the major colonies occurring in three main areas: the flooded gravel pits in the valleys of the Thames, Kennet and Loddon around Reading and westwards up the Kennet valley, similar habitats near Marlow and the open waters at the eastern extremity of the county, with another regular breeding site at Eversley Gravel Pits. The breeding range has expanded between the two Berkshire Atlas Surveys from 16 tetrads with confirmed breeding in the 1987–89 survey to 27 in the 2007–11 survey. The number of breeding pairs fluctuates. In 1989 the county's breeding population was described in the county report as healthy, with 16 pairs nesting at the Hosehill Lake (Theale), 18 pairs and 15 juveniles counted at Dinton Pastures, and breeding also

occurring at Summerleaze Gravel Pit near Maidenhead, Queen Mother Reservoir and Wraysbury Gravel Pits. Numbers continued to grow until 2001, when there was a sharp drop in the number of breeding pairs recorded. This was particularly noticeable at the county's main colony at Theale gravel pits where 70–76 pairs bred in 2000, whereas only 37 pairs bred in 2002 and almost none in 2005. The reduction in numbers has been reflected at other colonies across the county. Numbers have started to build again from this low point, but by 2012 were not back to the previous levels, and the breeding population is now distributed across a number of smaller colonies. Tern breeding numbers have been badly hit by predation, normally by fox or mink, and the colonisation of Berkshire by Black-headed Gulls from around 2000 onwards has seen the gulls taking over former tern colonies. The situation has not been helped by unusually heavy or prolonged rainfall over a number of summers which has resulted in nests being flooded. The provision of nesting rafts at some sites has helped reduce the risk from fox predation and flooding.

Feeding terns have been recorded from many of the lakes and rivers around the county. When feeding young, parent Common Terns often cover considerable distances between nesting and fishing areas. In June, July and August, adults are frequently seen over-flying urban areas of south Reading, sometimes carrying small fish. In 1988, numerous observations revealed a regular flight path, taking in Dinton Pastures, Woodley, Whiteknights Park, Whitley, Rose Kiln Lane, the Kennet and Avon Canal and possibly Burghfield Gravel Pits. These fishing excursions would appear to involve a round trip of up to 12 miles.

As well as now being well-established as a breeding bird in suitable habitats in Berkshire, the Common Tern is also frequently recorded as a passage migrant over gravel pits and along the Thames. The first birds arrive from late March onwards, with earliest dates of 17th March 2010 on the Jubilee River and 24th March 2005 at Eversley Gravel Pits. The main spring passage normally begins in the second week of April; migrant numbers

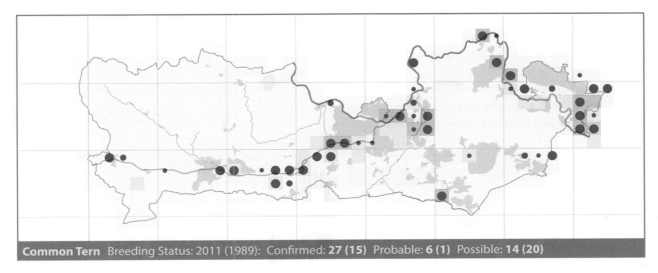

**Common Tern** Breeding Status: 2011 (1989): Confirmed: **27 (15)** Probable: **6 (1)** Possible: **14 (20)**

vary considerably, with good years like 1989 producing flocks of over 50, usually at Theale Gravel Pits, while in poor years the largest concentrations may number less than ten. The highest spring counts since 1946 have been 240 at Moatlands Gravel Pit, Theale in May 2005 and 130, again at Moatlands Gravel Pit in May 2002. Return migration occurs from July; in most years the majority of birds have normally departed by the end of August, although migration continues into October. There have been three November records since 1946, at Virginia Water on 2nd November 1963, Theale Gravel Pits on 18th November 1975, and a bird that stayed at Hosehill Lake, Theale from 18th October to 13th November 2002.

The usual passage dates may be modified by exceptional weather conditions. The great gale of October 1987, for example, brought a spate of late records in the second

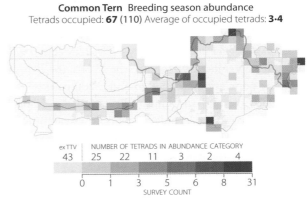

**Common Tern** Breeding season abundance
Tetrads occupied: **67** (110) Average of occupied tetrads: **3·4**

| exTTV | NUMBER OF TETRADS IN ABUNDANCE CATEGORY | | | | | |
|---|---|---|---|---|---|---|
| 43 | 25 | 22 | 11 | 3 | 2 | 4 |

| 0 | 1 | 3 | 5 | 6 | 8 | 31 |
|---|---|---|---|---|---|---|

SURVEY COUNT

half of October, from Wraysbury and Queen Mother Reservoir in the east, from Moatlands Gravel Pit, Theale in central Berkshire, and from Thatcham Gravel Pits in west Berkshire.

Common Tern, Lea Farm *Alex Berryman*

Ringing recoveries have indicated that there may be an interchange between English inland breeding colonies. Two birds ringed as juveniles in the Lea Valley, Hertfordshire have been recovered in Berkshire in subsequent years, and one ringed as a juvenile at Yeoveney Gravel Pit in 1985 was recovered in Hertfordshire in 1991. There has also been one recovery of a bird ringed as a juvenile in June 1984, again at Yeoveney Gravel Pit, from the species' wintering area in Ghana the following May. A colour-ringing scheme was started in 2011, ringing Common Tern nestlings at Lea Farm pit at Dinton Pastures, Theale and Eversley Gravel Pits.

*Sponsored by Angela Houghton*

---

# Roseate Tern

`Red` `Sch. 1`

## *Sterna dougallii*

*Rare vagrant*

The Roseate Tern is a rare, but recently more frequent, vagrant to Berkshire. The first acceptable record was one on the Thames at Pangbourne on 6th September 1967. This was followed by further records of single birds, all at Theale Gravel Pits, on 8th May 1971, 22nd June 1973 and 9th September 1984. Since the 1960s, the British breeding population declined to under 200 pairs by the late 1980s (Stroud and Glue, 1991), and the Seabird 2000 survey estimated only 52 pairs in Great Britain, although the Irish population had recovered somewhat to over 700 (Mitchell *et al.*, 2004). It is possible that the latter population is the source of a recent increase in sightings, with singles at Queen Mother Reservoir, and several sites nearby, during 9th–13th May 2011 and another there on 9th May 2012. In 2013 three birds passed through Queen Mother Reservoir, with two on

22nd May (the first sighting of two together) and then another on 10th June. The other west London reservoirs have shown a similar increase in sightings and, indeed, some of the recent birds at Queen Mother Reservoir were also seen nearby at Staines Reservoirs in Surrey. These records await consideration by the Berkshire Records Committee.

*Sponsored by David Fuller*

---

# Arctic Tern

`Amber`

## *Sterna paradisaea*

*Uncommon passage migrant*

The Arctic Tern is an uncommon passage migrant through Berkshire, usually in small numbers. Most birds move quickly through the county, particularly in the spring, and are seen only occasionally for more than a day. The difficulty involved in separating Arctic and Common Terns on passage probably accounts for the scarcity of Arctic Tern records prior to 1947. Up until this time there were just three records for the county, one obtained near Maidenhead in May 1866 (Clark Kennedy, 1868), one killed near Windsor before 1900 (Noble, 1906), and one at Slough Sewage Farm on 24th August 1941. Both Clark Kennedy and Noble described the species as an occasional visitor, however.

Improved identification knowledge from 1947 revealed the Arctic Tern to be an annual passage migrant in small numbers through the newly created and increasing number of stretches of open water resulting from gravel extraction. From 1947 to 1953, there were 14 records

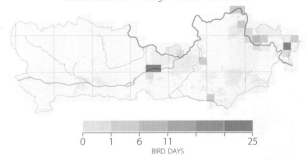

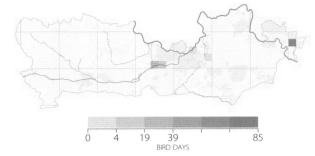

involving at least 32 birds and, since the 1950s, the species has been reported annually, usually up to ten birds but occasionally in larger numbers. The monthly averages shown in Figure 108 for the period from 1991 to 2011 reflect that the bulk of records are on spring passage, but there have been a few years with much higher (1995, 2005, 2008) and much lower (2000, 2001) numbers, some associated with weather events. These variations may also be influenced by the difficulty that can still be experienced in clearly separating Arctic from Common Terns, notwithstanding the apparent increasing confidence of observers. In the 2002 County Report the Berkshire Records Committee encouraged observers still to submit records where identification was not definite.

Peak passage in spring occurs during a comparatively short period from late April to early May, but in autumn is more protracted with both adults and juveniles being seen from the end of July to the beginning of October. This pattern is consistent with the breeding cycle of British-breeding birds, which return in May and produce fledged young from July onwards (*1988–91 BTO Atlas*).

The earliest arrivals have been on 6th and 9th April 2003 at Moatlands Pit, Theale, and 10th April 1991 at Theale Gravel Pits. Passage has been recorded to the end of May in a few years, and there are June records for 1947, 1974, 1986 and 1997; these late spring or early summer records often involve individuals in second-summer type plumage (*e.g.* singles on 23rd May 2000, 20th July 2007 and 12th June 2013). The latest departures involve a bird on the Kennet in 1982 which remained from 26th October to 2nd November, and a first-winter bird which circled the pontoons at Queen Mother Reservoir on 7th November 2011.

Most county records are of one to three birds, but larger parties occur when appropriate weather conditions prevail, particularly in spring. The first such occasion was in 1947 when, after south-westerly gales, there were 13 terns, all apparently Arctic, at Ham Sewage Farm on 26th April, with further Arctic Terns among 14 birds at Theale Gravel Pits the same day. In 1978, there was a large fall of about 150 terns in heavy rain and low cloud at Theale Gravel Pits on 2nd May, of which a high percentage

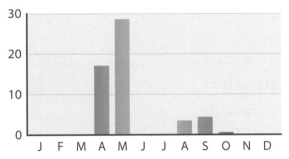

**Figure 107: Arctic Tern: birds recorded per year from 1991–2011.** The 1991 figure represents a minimum estimate of the exceptional passage in April and May.

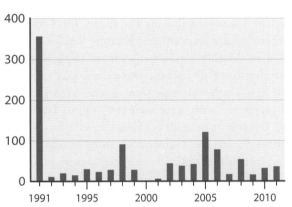

**Figure 108: Arctic Tern: birds recorded by month of arrival.** Average 1991–2011.

were Arctic. About 100 terns seen shortly afterwards at Burghfield Gravel Pits were mainly Arctic. An even larger number was observed at Theale Gravel Pits in similar conditions and at the same time of year in 1991: during a spell of generally dull, cold and wet weather there were parties of 49, 26 and 20+ terns on 30th April, a minimum of 85 on 3rd May, about 40 on 5th May, and some 70 there on 6th May, most considered to be Arctic Terns. The total number of Arctic Terns involved in this movement over the seven days appears to have been at least 245 and was part of a wider inland movement across southern England at that time. There were further substantial counts in early May in 1998 (at least 68 birds at Theale Main Gravel Pit on 1st May during Northeast winds), and 2005 (about 60 at Moatlands and Main Gravel Pits at Theale on 4th May and 36 at Dinton Pastures on 5th May).

*Sponsored by John Newport*

# Sabine's Gull

*Xema sabini*

*Rare vagrant*

The Sabine's Gull was first recorded in Berkshire following the great gale of the night of the 15th–16th October 1987. A low pressure area, the cause of the storm, deepened and intensified over the Bay of Biscay, an area frequented by Sabine's Gulls in autumn, before moving very rapidly across south-east England.

On 16th October, following the storm, there were up to three adults and three immature Sabine's Gulls at Queen Mother Reservoir, with up to three adults remaining there for two or three days. Elsewhere, an adult flew south-west over Grazeley on 17th October, and immature birds were seen at Dinton Pastures on 17th October and at Burghfield Gravel Pits on 18th October. From 21st October, up to three adults were found in fields just outside the then county boundary at Colnbrook, and it is probable that an adult from this group was seen at Queen Mother Reservoir on 22nd and at Horton Gravel Pits on 25th, 27th and 28th October. In addition, an immature bird was seen at Queen Mother Reservoir on 24th October. A minimum of 12 birds were therefore seen within Berkshire following

the storm, six adults and six immatures. Much larger numbers were observed to the east in the London area.

Since then, this species has only been recorded twice, both at Queen Mother Reservoir: an adult in summer plumage on 5th August 1994, and a moulting adult on 29th September 1999. Most sightings in the London area have been in September or October, so the 1994 record is unusual (County Report 1994–95). One on the unusual date of 27th August 2013 awaits consideration by the Berkshire Records Committee.

*Sponsored by Berkshire Bird Bulletin*

# Kittiwake   Amber

*Rissa tridactyla*

*Scarce spring migrant and winter visitor*

The Kittiwake is primarily a scarce spring and winter visitor to Berkshire, most frequently occurring after stormy weather, but it also occurs occasionally in small numbers in summer and autumn. The pattern of records for Kittiwake is more complex than for any of the other gulls recorded in the county. Although most birds occur after storms, they rarely do so in autumn, and records for September and October have virtually ceased since 1979. While the bulk of sightings have been of single birds, a number of relatively large flocks were recorded during the 1980s and early 1990s, and more recently in 2005 and 2007.

Early Kittiwake records differ from those of other gulls in Berkshire in that there was no increase in the number of published records after 1900, there being four from 1865 to 1904 and three from 1905 to 1944. Single birds were killed near Eton in 1865 and at Newbury in January 1872, and one was caught with a rod and line on the Thames near Mapledurham in January 1901 (Noble, 1906). Clark Kennedy (1868) saw one

near Datchet in March 1867 and claims, but without supporting details, that "small flocks are occasionally seen at Pangbourne". The next record was not until one was found dead in Windsor Great Park in March 1937.

After two records in 1939, including an immature bird at Slough Sewage Farm in August, which represented the first autumn record, there were a small number of sightings of single birds from 1946, two together in February 1957, and a small party of up to four birds on the Thames at Windsor from 26th February to 8th March 1959. This was one of only eight county records of birds staying longer than four days. The number of birds seen annually remained low, at from one to four, until 1980; eight in 1968 and five in 1979 being the only exceptions.

After 1980, both the number of records and the number of birds seen each year increased significantly as shown in Figure 109. In total, up to 1994, 89 of the 110 county records of Kittiwake were of single birds, but since 1980 a number of larger parties have been observed. Twenty-six were seen on 24th April 1985 (part of a large inland movement at that time), and on 25th March 1986 there were parties of 28 and 14 at Enborne, and a flock of over 60 flying south-west over Holyport. On 26th March 1992, 27 flew west near Windsor.

In 1993, all previous county records were eclipsed when an unprecedented number of at least 642 Kittiwakes moved south over Queen Mother Reservoir during the afternoon of 25th January; this was the minimum counted as coverage was not continuous that day (Heard, 1997). This movement followed records of large numbers of Kittiwakes on the east coast. Kittiwakes have been seen every year from 1995, except in 2000, still generally as single birds or very small groups, but a flock of 85 adult and first year birds was present for a short time at Queen Mother Reservoir on 4th April 2005, and at least 40 birds passed through the same site on 9th November 2007.

Even before the high count in January 1993, the bulk of Kittiwake recorded in Berkshire had occurred from January to April (Figure 110). Where details of the age of birds is known, the percentage of adults has generally been very high from January to June. Since 1995 this has

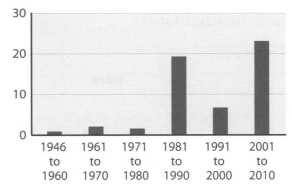

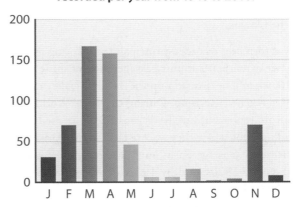

**Figure 109: Kittiwake: average number of birds recorded per year from 1946 to 2010.**

**Figure 110: Kittiwake: all birds recorded 1981–2010, by month of arrival.** A fall of 642 at Queen Mother Reservoir in January 1993 is excluded.

also been the case from July to December, but previously there was some evidence of a higher percentage of immature birds in these months. This may partly reflect poor productivity in north Atlantic breeding colonies following over-exploitation of sandeel fisheries and a decline in food resources attributed to warming seas (Frederiksen et al., 2004).

*Sponsored by Dot Lincoln*

# Bonaparte's Gull

## Chroicocephalus philadelphia

*Rare vagrant – one record*

Berkshire's only record of this small North American Gull was of an adult in full summer plumage at Theale Gravel Pits on 26th April 2013. It was first seen on the Main Pit, and later relocated by the same observer at Hosehill Lake. Although the record is subject to validation by the British Birds Rarities Committee at the time of publication, the record of this distinctive species was from an experienced observer. Unlike many North American vagrants, which are mostly recorded in autumn, Bonaparte's Gulls occur in Britain throughout the year, although most of the 180 British records up to 2011 have been from western or coastal counties.

*Sponsored by Cathy McEwan*

# Black-headed Gull

Amber

*Chroicocephalus ridibundus*

*Abundant winter visitor and passage migrant, now breeding in increasing numbers*

The Black-headed Gull was the commonest gull in Berkshire during the 19th century and remains so today with records from both urban and rural habitats. It now occurs throughout the year, but is commonest and most widespread in winter. The Winter Map indicates that it is most numerous in river valleys and around flooded gravel pits, but substantial numbers also occur in winter on the Downs.

It was formerly recorded principally as a spring and, to a lesser extent, an autumn passage migrant until about 1910, when its expansion up the Thames Valley during winter reached Reading. During the First World War there are reports of hundreds roosting on the ledges of Reading Gaol, where they were fed by German prisoners. At Reading Sewage Farm, numbers reached about 70 in the early 1920s, and by 1932 there were reports of hundreds there in December, with numbers decreasing until the species' departure in April. It was thought that these birds may have either roosted at Sonning Eye Gravel Pit on the Oxfordshire side of the Thames

or used this site as a temporary halt before moving eastwards to roost at Staines Reservoir. Roosting at Burghfield Gravel Pits was noted from 1952 and this and other pits have been used for this purpose in many years since, although perhaps not until the 1970s on a regular basis.

Post-breeding flocks start building up from July onwards. The first reported count to reach 1,000 birds was from Ham Sewage Farm in February 1944, and gatherings of this size were reported on a number of occasions thereafter, although it was not until 1972 that higher numbers were reported, with 2,247 at Reading Sewage Farm in February that year and about 2,500 gathering to roost at Theale Gravel Pits on 5th March.

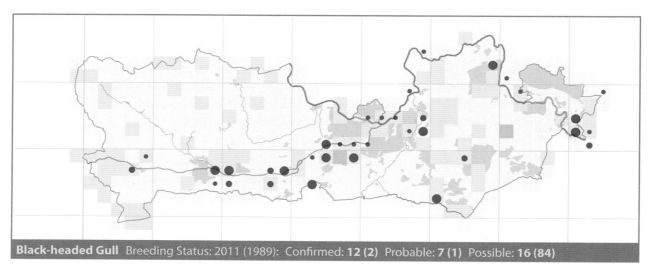

**Black-headed Gull** Breeding Status: 2011 (1989): Confirmed: **12 (2)** Probable: **7 (1)** Possible: **16 (84)**

**Black-headed Gull** Breeding season abundance
Tetrads occupied: **101 (164)** Average of occupied tetrads: **10·6**

**Black-headed Gull** Winter abundance
Tetrads occupied: **250 (307)** Average of occupied tetrads: **82·1**

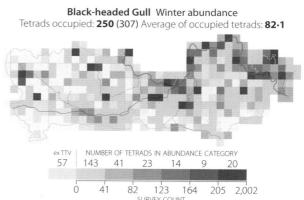

| exTTV | NUMBER OF TETRADS IN ABUNDANCE CATEGORY | | | | | |
|---|---|---|---|---|---|---|
| 63 | 61 | 11 | 9 | 7 | 4 | 9 |

| 0 | 5 | 10 | 15 | 21 | 26 | 202 |
SURVEY COUNT

| exTTV | NUMBER OF TETRADS IN ABUNDANCE CATEGORY | | | | | |
|---|---|---|---|---|---|---|
| 57 | 143 | 41 | 23 | 14 | 9 | 20 |

| 0 | 41 | 82 | 123 | 164 | 205 | 2,002 |
SURVEY COUNT

More recently, even higher numbers have been observed with an estimated total of 6,200 coming in to roost at Queen Mother Reservoir in December 1983, and a further estimated 4,500 on nearby Wraysbury Reservoir in Surrey. In 1991, 3,000–4,000 Black-headed Gulls were regularly roosting at Theale Gravel Pits in January, with an estimated peak of 6,000–8,000 on the 26th and the 27th. Numbers have continued to increase since then with a maximum of 50,000 at Queen Mother Reservoir in 1995 and 25,000 in 2001. The roost at Moatlands Gravel Pit, Theale regularly holds numbers of up to 10,000 birds, with a peak of 17,000 in 2008. The winter map shows that numbers are lower in west Berkshire.

Passage occurs during March and April and can be quite marked. In 1964, after 270 were seen at Ham on 3rd April there was an influx of over 1,000 birds on 4th but only about 30 were there on the 6th. Heavy passage involving hundreds of birds was also observed at Theale Gravel Pits on 9th March 1980. Large flocks are occasionally reported in March, the largest being 12,500 in the Theale area and 1,100+ on fields near Hurst, both in 2006. After April, numbers in the county decline rapidly.

Black-headed Gulls now breed in increasing numbers in Berkshire. The first report of apparent summering was at Reading Sewage Farm in 1926, when a bird present throughout May was joined by another on 7th June. The next instance of summering was not until about 1945, when there is an uncorroborated record of a pair of gulls (probably Black-headed Gulls) nesting at Aldermaston Gravel Pits. This was followed in 1949 by the discovery of four nests at Slough Sewage Farm, all of which were subsequently robbed. A pair attempted to breed at Ham Sewage Farm in 1956 where eggs were laid, but no young were reported. The first apparent record of successful breeding is in 1981 when a pair nested at Theale Gravel Pits and raised one chick, though it is not certain whether the chick fledged successfully.

During the 1987–89 Atlas Survey, an occupied nest was found at Burghfield and fledged young were seen at Winkfield. A pair were seen nest-building at Theale in 1994, but the next definite breeding record was in 1998 when two pairs nested at Moatlands Gravel Pit, Theale, with one pair raising two young. This increased to seven pairs in 1999, and there have been breeding records in increasing numbers at a number of sites every year since then. During the 2007–11 Atlas Survey, Black-headed Gulls were recorded breeding in 12 tetrads, with the main sites at Theale, Lea Farm/Lavell's Lake, Moor Green Lakes, Lower Farm and Eversley. Probable or possible breeding was recorded in a further 23 tetrads with other summer sightings, possibly foraging birds from the breeding sites, immature birds or early

| Country | Ringed overseas, reported in Berkshire | Ringed in Berkshire, reported from overseas |
|---|---|---|
| Belgium | 4 | 0 |
| Channel Islands | 0 | 2 |
| Denmark | 4 | 1 |
| Estonia | 1 | 1 |
| Finland | 6 | 1 |
| France | 1 | 5 |
| Germany | 1 | 1 |
| Latvia | 1 | 0 |
| Lithuania | 7 | 0 |
| Poland | 7 | 0 |
| Russia | 2 | 0 |
| Spain | 1 | 0 |
| Sweden | 1 | 1 |
| The Netherlands | 1 | 3 |

**Table 3**: **Ringing recoveries of Black-headed Gulls.**

returning autumn birds. On sites where Black-headed Gulls share the breeding grounds with Common Terns, the gull colonies are now significantly larger than the tern colonies, in some cases resulting in the site being abandoned by the terns.

An understanding of the origins of the Black-headed Gulls in Berkshire can be gained from ringing recoveries and sightings of colour-ringed or dye-marked gulls. Table 3 shows the source of overseas-ringed birds recorded in Berkshire and overseas records of birds ringed in Berkshire, for both summer and winter. Winter flocks include birds from the continent and the ringing data shows a clear pattern of movement from the east. The furthest distances travelled by Black-headed Gulls recorded by the ringing recoveries in Berkshire are 2,149 km (Leningrad) and 1,936 km (Estonia). A bird ringed in Latvia as an adult in April 2012 was seen on a number of dates between 27th October 2012 and 30th March 2013 on the Thames at Datchet. Ringing records also show movement within Britain and Ireland, with records involving 30 counties. The movement is again predominately east-west with the majority of the records involving birds from Gloucestershire and Dyfed.

The Reading & Basingstoke Ringing group carries out a programme of ringing gull chicks at Moor Green Lakes, Hosehill Lake (Theale) and Lea Farm using both metal BTO rings and colour rings. Hosehill Lake is registered as a BTO RAS (Registering Adults for Survival) project, with the data being used to monitor survival rates. Since starting work in 2009 it has produced a remarkable number of control records, and in 2011 provided 941 out of 1,819 records of re-trapped or recovered birds in Britain and Ireland – 51% of the total.

Birds in immature plumage have been observed in all months and there have been a wide range of dates recorded for adult summer plumage, some as early as the end of December. Plumage variations have also been noted on a number of occasions. Albino, or partial albino birds with nearly all white plumage, have been observed at a number of sites, most recently at Moatlands Gravel Pit, Theale in March 2005 and Dinton Pastures in 2012. Leucistic (cream-coloured) birds have been mainly observed at Queen Mother Reservoir with a series of sightings involving one or two birds from 2005 to 2008. Melanistic (rather than oiled) birds are much less common than the previous two variants with a possible seen in January 1988 and one in 1995, both at Queen Mother Reservoir.

*Sponsored by Reading and Basingstoke Ringing*

# Little Gull

Amber | Sch. 1

*Hydrocoloeus minutus*

*Scarce passage and winter visitor*

The Little Gull is a scarce annual passage migrant, particularly in periods of easterly winds, and scarce winter visitor to Berkshire, although numbers have increased in recent years. It typically occurs over larger water bodies in the county.

The first county record, a single bird at Reading Sewage Farm from 4th to 13th October 1923, was followed in 1924 by a party of three birds there from 21st to 22nd September and in 1925 by a single bird in September. There were then records for September and October 1932, September 1933 and September 1934, after which this site was modernized. In contrast, the existence from the mid-1930s of similar habitat at Slough Sewage Farm failed to produce any indications of passage, the first record being one found dead there on 4th February 1950, the first in winter.

The next series of records came from Ham Sewage Farm in the 1950s. One was seen there in September 1951, followed by an adult from 2nd to 12th August 1953. In 1954, an adult in full summer plumage was present from 28th July until 7th September, during which time it moulted into winter plumage. The speed with which this bird moulted its head feathers was particularly rapid, from almost full summer plumage on 29th July to near winter by 8th August (Veysey, 1954). There were further records of prolonged stays at Ham Sewage Farm of adults, perhaps the same bird, from 12th July to 12th September 1955, from 13th July to 22nd September 1956, and from 21st July to 3rd August 1957. Records then ceased from this site until an immature was seen in November 1963.

The frequency of sightings increased from 1960 as the number of observers rose and more areas of open water were created by gravel extraction. Except for 1977, there have been annual records of Little Gulls in Berkshire since 1967, and the growth in county records has followed the national picture which showed a marked

**Little Gull** Spring migration occurrence
Tetrads used: **14** Average of used tetrads: **8·6**

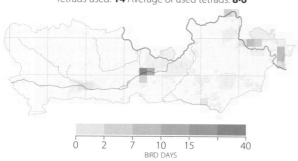

0   2   7   10  15   40
BIRD DAYS

**Little Gull** Autumn migration occurrence
Tetrads used: **7** Average of used tetrads: **5·1**

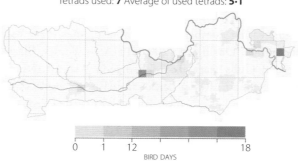

0   1   12   18
BIRD DAYS

increase in passage from the mid-1950s (*1981–84 BTO Winter Atlas*). This trend continued until the end of the 20th century, after which the number of county sightings increased remarkably. Although the number of records varies from year to year, the average number of birds seen each year increased from an average of about 15 birds per year in the 1990s to something closer to 50 since 2000 (Figure 111).

Since 1970, Little Gulls have been recorded in Berkshire in every month of the year, although the species remains scarce in winter and mid-summer. In recent years spring passage has tended to start earlier, with the first birds passing through in March, peaking in April (a month which accounts for around half of the yearly sightings) and continuing into May (Figure 112). The flock of nine birds which flew eastwards across Queen Mother Reservoir on 22nd February 2006 was exceptional and is probably the earliest ever record of passage in the county. Return passage generally starts in August and continues through September and October, but is not as heavy as the spring passage.

Most Little Gulls have been seen for no longer than one or sometimes two days, but in 1975 an adult was seen at Wraysbury Gravel Pits in July, August and September. In 1987 extreme weather conditions resulted in one bird being seen at Queen Mother Reservoir on many dates from 16th January well into February, and a juvenile which arrived at Moatlands Gravel Pit on 28th August 2005 remained until 12th September.

The bulk of county records have been of one to two birds and, although there was an early record of three birds together in 1924, this number was not exceeded until 1974 when there were parties of six, at both Theale Gravel Pits in May and at Wraysbury Gravel Pits in August. In 1984, a year of previously unprecedented passage in Berkshire involving at least 28 birds, there were parties in May of ten (all adults) at Brimpton Gravel Pits and 16 (including 11 adults) at Theale Gravel Pits. In 1987, a party of at least ten birds was seen in October at Queen Mother Reservoir after the great storm on 15th October. Recent years have seen flock sizes increasing. In 2003 a total of 89 birds passed through the county in April, including 46 in one day on the 16th April at Queen Mother Reservoir, one flock numbering 23. There was another heavy passage of Little Gulls through the county in the spring of 2005, which featured the largest ever recorded flock of 33 birds (all but four being adults) which flew east-southeast over Queen Mother Reservoir on 22nd April.

*Sponsored by Chris Robinson*

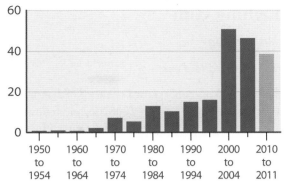

**Figure 111:  Little Gull: average number of birds recorded per year 1950–2011.**

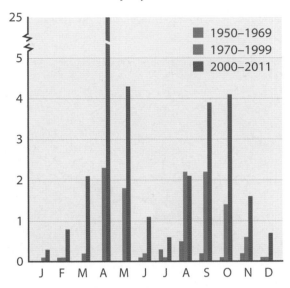

**Figure 112:  Little Gull: average number of birds recorded per month.**

Little Gull, Hosehill Lake  *Michael McKee*

# Laughing Gull

*Larus atricilla*

*Rare vagrant, recorded once*

Berkshire's first and only record of this North American gull occurred in the winter of 2005/06, and followed an influx of the species into Britain following Hurricane Wilma in October. It was seen first by a visitor from Bristol at Green Park, Reading on 2nd December 2005, and was then seen at a number of sites south of Reading and west to Theale Gravel Pits. It frequented Reading Gate Retail Park, where it fed on fast food scraps with other gulls. A winter plumage adult on arrival, it had come into adult plumage by March 2006 and was last seen at Theale Gravel Pits on the 29th.

*Sponsored by Zoe Greenwood*

Laughing Gull Reading, 12th February 2006 (top); the same individual 19th March 2006 (bottom)  *Michael McKee*

# Mediterranean Gull

**Amber** **Sch. 1**

*Larus melanocephalus*

*Scarce visitor*

The Mediterranean Gull is a scarce, but now regular visitor to Berkshire. Until recently it was mainly a winter visitor to the county; birds are now recorded in the summer months too and breeding has been attempted.

An adult at Queen Mother Reservoir on 22nd February 1981 was the first record for Berkshire. The species has been expanding its range across Europe over the last 50 years and, in the UK, the breeding population has increased significantly since the turn of the century, with the number of breeding pairs increasing from 100 to around 700 pairs between 2000 and 2010, mostly on the south and south-east coast. This coincided with a significant rise in Berkshire records over the same period, as shown in Figure 113. It is possible that at least some of the Mediterranean Gulls seen in the county now come from the expanding UK breeding population. Birds of all ages are recorded, with approximately half of the records being of adult birds.

Birds are now recorded in all months of the year. Figure 114 illustrates the change in the pattern of records since 2000. Before then, it was a bird primarily found among wintering gull flocks, with peak counts

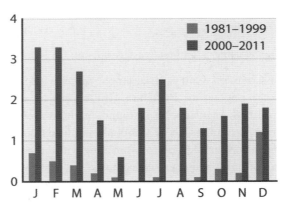

**Figure 114: Mediterranean Gull: average number of birds recorded 1981–2011, by month of arrival.**

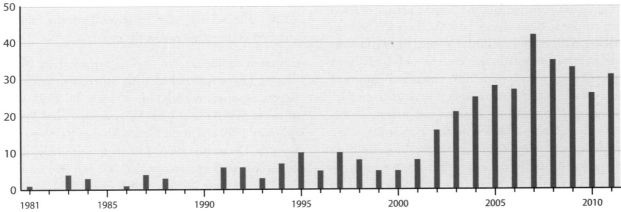

**Figure 113: Mediterranean Gull: birds recorded per year 1981–2011.**

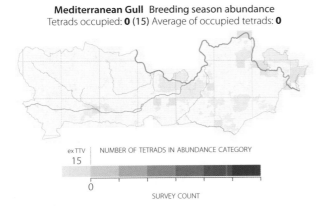

**Mediterranean Gull** Breeding season abundance
Tetrads occupied: **0** (15) Average of occupied tetrads: **0**

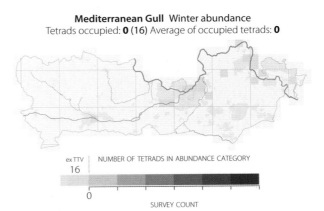

**Mediterranean Gull** Winter abundance
Tetrads occupied: **0** (16) Average of occupied tetrads: **0**

ex TTV   NUMBER OF TETRADS IN ABUNDANCE CATEGORY
15

0
SURVEY COUNT

ex TTV   NUMBER OF TETRADS IN ABUNDANCE CATEGORY
16

0
SURVEY COUNT

in mid-winter. In recent years the months with fewest records have been April and May when birds are mainly at their breeding sites. Records start to increase in June and July when post-breeding dispersal starts and juvenile birds are sometimes recorded, with the earliest record of a juvenile being on 5th July 2011 at Queen Mother Reservoir.

Records have come from sites across the county, mainly rubbish tips, gravel pits and reservoirs, with the majority of records from the middle or east of the county where gulls congregate, most notably Queen Mother Reservoir, which hosted the largest count of five birds on 5th July 2011, consisting of one moulting summer plumage adult, one first-summer bird, one second-summer bird and two juveniles.

There has been a single record of a breeding attempt: a bird paired with a Black-headed Gull at Hosehill Lake, Theale in 2013. Hybrids with Black-headed Gull have been observed on a couple of occasions: an adult at Queen Mother Reservoir on 30th January 2006 and another adult there on 5th February 2012.

*Sponsored by Carole White*

# Common Gull

Amber

*Larus canus*

*Common winter visitor and passage migrant*

The Common Gull is a common winter visitor and passage migrant to Berkshire. The species is widely distributed, regularly being found on mown or well grazed grassland, such as school playing fields, airfields or farmland, in addition to associating with other gulls at rubbish tips and open-water roosts.

The county reports show that the pattern of records within the year remained fairly consistent over the period between 1945 and the mid-1990s. In most years, one or two birds were noted during June with evidence of light passage during July and August, usually of fewer than ten birds. Since the mid-1990s, there has been an increase in the number of birds recorded throughout the year. Summer records have increased with birds being reported every month from 2006 onwards; numbers of birds occurring during these months have also increased, with up to 15 birds being recorded each month, mainly first-summer birds, but with the occasional adult. Juveniles start to arrive during August. Most birds do not appear to stay in the area and it is often not until October that larger parties occur and are reported on a regular basis. This reflects the national picture, with

the first migrants reaching Britain in July and arrivals continuing until late October (*1981–84 BTO Winter Atlas*). The winter map indicates that the highest numbers occur in the east of the county.

Common Gulls are far less numerous than Black-headed Gulls with which they often associate. The largest reported concentrations prior to 1991 were of about 600 birds at both Wraysbury Gravel Pits in February 1974 and at the Queen Mother Reservoir gull roost in December 1983, and there were only about 20 records of flocks of between 200 and 500 birds in the 45 years from 1951 to 1994. From 1991 to 1994, however, counts of 800 birds or more were recorded on

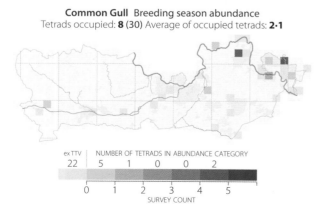

**Common Gull** Breeding season abundance
Tetrads occupied: **8 (30)** Average of occupied tetrads: **2·1**

| ex TTV | NUMBER OF TETRADS IN ABUNDANCE CATEGORY | | | | |
|---|---|---|---|---|---|
| 22 | 5 | 1 | 0 | 0 | 2 |

0   1   2   3   4   5
SURVEY COUNT

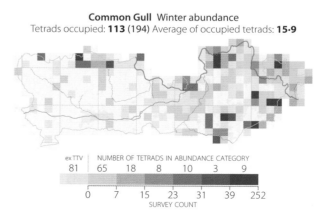

**Common Gull** Winter abundance
Tetrads occupied: **113 (194)** Average of occupied tetrads: **15·9**

| ex TTV | NUMBER OF TETRADS IN ABUNDANCE CATEGORY | | | | | |
|---|---|---|---|---|---|---|
| 81 | 65 | 18 | 8 | 10 | 3 | 9 |

0   7   15   23   31   39   252
SURVEY COUNT

four occasions, and in early 1994 there were two counts of over 1,000. Of an estimated 5,000–8,000 gulls at Bisham on 16th January 1994, some 60% were Common Gulls and some 40% were Black-headed Gulls, and at least 1,129 were counted at Cockmarsh in March 1994. Since 1996 flocks of over 400 have been recorded every winter. The highest counts since 1994 were 1,600 on 9th January 2003 at Remenham, and 1,070 in January 2010 at Moatlands Gravel Pit, Theale.

Common Gulls return to their nest sites in February and early March, but their return passage is not complete until April (*1968–72 BTO Atlas*). Numbers within the county are much diminished by April and in most years there are only a few reports, usually of no more than five birds, during April and May. However smaller movements also occur into April, with 32 birds over Queen Mother Reservoir on 23rd April 2004, 37 at the Jubilee River on 8th April 2005, and 150 birds at Remenham on 2nd April 2007. Movement was noted on a exceptional scale on 3rd April 1953 when an estimated 500–600 birds were seen spiralling to a great height above Burghfield Gravel Pits before drifting away to the north-west. In 1948, one bird remained at Burghfield Gravel Pits until found dead on the 11th June. Observations of a school playing field at Wokingham over a number of years prior to 1994 showed that the main period of departure was during the first week of April, the latest being on the 20th.

At the beginning of the 20th century, Common Gulls were reported by Noble (1906) as "frequently seen in spring and autumn, more especially in spring". Although no mention is made of wintering birds these clearly did occur as Noble notes that a Common Gull was killed at Sulhamstead on 8th February 1902. Early records from Reading Sewage Farm also include birds in winter, the first record from this site being three immatures in October 1922, and there were about 12 birds there in January 1927. Although there were 30 at Windsor in December 1929, the first flocks of any size were not reported until the winter of 1943/44 when numbers reached 280 at Eton in January and February.

*Sponsored by Iain Oldcorn*

# Ring-billed Gull

*Larus delawarensis*

*Rare vagrant, ten records*

The Ring-billed Gull is an American species which is a rare vagrant to Berkshire, with 10 acceptable records. All records have, with one exception, been of single birds recorded on one or two occasions. The first record for the county was a first-year bird at the Smallmead Rubbish Tip on 26th March 1984, which was followed a few days later on 2nd April by the discovery of an adult at the same site. This was followed by a moulting second-winter bird on the Berkshire part of Virginia Water on 14th February 1989, another second-winter bird at Cockmarsh on 26th September and 26th October 1994, and an adult at Queen Mother Reservoir on 27th November 1994. An adult was recorded at Cockmarsh on 5th and 25th October 1995, a first-winter bird was seen for 20 minutes at Eversley Gravel Pits on 25th January 1997 before it flew off west, and an adult was seen (and videoed) at Pingewood Gravel Pits on 19th February 2001.

On 1st April 2004, a second-winter bird was recorded in the gull roost at Queen Mother Reservoir. It was subsequently relocated, now in second-summer plumage, at Little Marlow Gravel Pit, just over the border in Buckinghamshire, where it was observed on several occasions between 16th July and 6th August. During this time it was also seen on three occasions in the gull roost

at Queen Mother Reservoir, on 21st, 24th and 27th July. In the following year (2005) an adult was recorded in the pre-roost gathering at Little Marlow Gravel Pit and was seen to leave the site heading south-east, presumably entering Berkshire over Cockmarsh. However it was not seen at the Queen Mother Reservoir gull roost. This was a different, smaller bird to the one seen in 2004.

Nationally, there is a pronounced spring passage of Ring-billed Gulls through western Britain, with a peak in late March (*1981–84 BTO Winter Atlas*), and seven of the Berkshire records may relate to this migratory movement.

*Sponsored by David White*

# Lesser Black-backed Gull

*Larus fuscus*

*Common passage migrant and winter visitor that has bred in recent years.*

The Lesser Black-backed Gull is a common passage migrant and winter visitor to Berkshire which has also bred in the county in recent years. Nationally, there has been a significant change in the migratory pattern of Lesser Black-backed Gulls since the mid-20th century. The species was formerly a complete migrant with only the occasional bird remaining in Britain in winter. In contrast, large numbers now winter in Britain, mainly in the south and largely inland. Migrants of the British and Scandinavian races reach southern Britain in October and passage continues for another three months (*1981–84 BTO Winter Atlas*). Peak numbers occur in Berkshire during the autumn passage, and this species is now usually the most numerous of the large gull species found in the gull roosts in Berkshire (except at Queen Mother Reservoir). The wintering population in the lower Kennet valley, at Theale and Burghfield gravel pits, is of international importance as it comprises more than 1% of the world population, as measured by the 2003/04 to 2005/06 Winter Gull Roost Survey undertaken by the BTO (Burton *et al.*, 2013). It was

the second largest concentration of the species in the UK found in the survey, although in subsequent years numbers at the roost have declined somewhat, but increased at Eversley Gravel Pits.

Until 1934 the Lesser Black-backed Gull appears to have been a scarce visitor to Berkshire. Early records include one shot at Wash Common in 1884 (Palmer, 1888), and an adult taken at Upper Mapledurham Lock on 30th April 1898 (Noble, 1906), the fact that both were shot being an indication of how scarce the species was at that time.

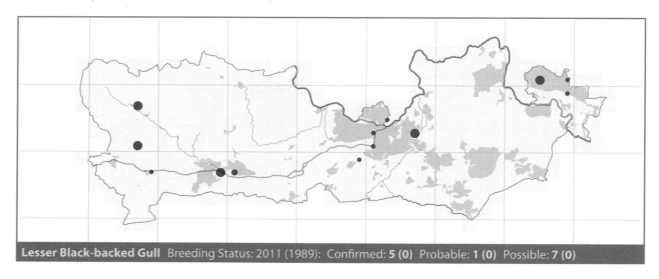

**Lesser Black-backed Gull** Breeding Status: 2011 (1989): Confirmed: **5 (0)** Probable: **1 (0)** Possible: **7 (0)**

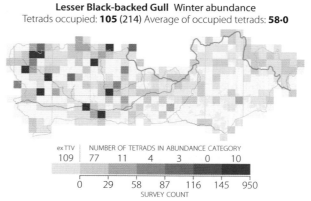

**Lesser Black-backed Gull** Breeding season abundance
Tetrads occupied: **52 (121)** Average of occupied tetrads: **16·1**

| ex TTV | AVERAGE OF COUNTS IN OCCUPIED TETRADS | | | | | |
|---|---|---|---|---|---|---|
| 69 | 41 | 4 | 1 | 1 | 0 | 5 |

0   8   16   24   32   40   260
SURVEY COUNT

**Lesser Black-backed Gull** Winter abundance
Tetrads occupied: **105 (214)** Average of occupied tetrads: **58·0**

| ex TTV | NUMBER OF TETRADS IN ABUNDANCE CATEGORY | | | | | |
|---|---|---|---|---|---|---|
| 109 | 77 | 11 | 4 | 3 | 0 | 10 |

0   29   58   87   116   145   950
SURVEY COUNT

The first appearance of the species in county reports is of two records of single birds in August and September 1934 at Old Windsor, to be followed quickly in 1935 by four records involving eight birds at Reading Sewage Farm in April and May and sightings at a further four locations in east Berkshire. After an isolated record of a bird at Reading Sewage Farm in January 1936, there were occasional winter records in Berkshire from 1942 and more regular records from 1949, although the number of birds seen was not high.

The first passage flock of any size was of about 100 birds in August 1955. There were 200 seen as early as July in 1958, but the first year of significant numbers in autumn and winter was 1960, with a maximum count of 400+ at Widbrook Common in October and winter flocks of 107 and 64. Numbers have increased over the years, with peak counts in the 1970s of 1,100 at the Theale gull roost in October 1979 and 900+ at Reading Sewage Farm in September 1971. By the 1990s numbers had increased further, with the highest count being 11,000 at Theale on 4th October 1994. This county record was broken again at Theale in September 2003 when a series of high counts at the roost peaked at 22,000 birds on the 23rd.

Prior to 1993, winter counts from November to February were lower than in the autumn, only rarely reaching 200 and not exceeding 50 in some years. The exceptions were records from the Theale gull roost of 900 in February 1980 and 1,000 in January 1991. From 1993 onwards, however, winter numbers have increased with numbers at roost sites peaking in the thousands; the maximum counts have been at the roost at Theale

Main Pit (7,500 in November 2008), and at Moatlands Gravel Pit with 6,800 in January 2004, 7,000+ in January 2005 and 7,000 in November 2008. Most congregations of Lesser Black-backed Gulls have been at rubbish tips or at roosts on flooded gravel pits in association with other gull species. In a study carried out during 2003 and 2004, Lesser Black-backed Gull was found to be the commonest gull species on landfill sites in the county during the autumn, occurring on nine of the 13 sites monitored. Since then the number of landfill sites where gulls can feed have been closed, which is likely to affect the numbers and distribution of gulls (Cropper, 2006). Since 1993 there have been increasing numbers reported feeding on the Downs during the autumn and winter months, normally in flocks of several hundred, with numbers exceeding 1,000 in January 2004 (1,000+ at Compton Downs), August 2005 (1,200+ at Bury Down) and December 2007 (1,000 at Sheepdrove Farm). Flocks of birds returning from feeding by day on farmland can often be seen in autumn and winter flying back to their overnight roost sites.

Numbers decline after February but returning passage birds can swell numbers in March and April and there were peak counts of 800+ at Wraysbury Gravel Pits in March 1974 and 600+ at Moatlands Gravel Pit in March 2002. Most birds depart during the second half of April and, prior to 1994, records for May and June were few and normally involved less than ten birds. A party of 96 on the Compton Downs on 17th June 1994 was well above normal for that month. Since 1994, increased numbers of immature and non-breeders over the summer have become a regular feature.

Breeding was first confirmed in 2005, when an adult and a chick were observed on a factory roof near Slough. Between 2008 and 2011 breeding was confirmed in five tetrads. This follows a pattern of Lesser Black-backed Gulls spreading inland as a breeding bird in Britain using urban nesting sites, despite an overall decline in numbers of 32% between 2000 and 2011 (Eaton *et al.*, 2012), linked to declines at traditional coastal breeding sites.

Birds of the Scandinavian race (*L. f. intermedius*), which have darker mantles than British Lesser Black-backed Gulls, reach Britain in autumn and have been recorded on a number of occasions in Berkshire since the first report of one at Slough Sewage Farm in September 1938. Most of the birds in a flock of Lesser Black-backed Gulls at Reading Sewage Farm in October 1976 were considered to be of the Scandinavian race, and there was an influx of Lesser Black-backed Gulls in August 1997, most of which were of this race. The only other records are of three at Twyford in August 2000, a few in the roost at Langley in October 2003 and one possible record at Lower Farm in September 2009.

The absence of records in a particular year is likely to be a consequence of under-recording, rather than the fact that all passage birds were of the British race.

There have also been two reports of Baltic Gull (*L. f. fuscus*) – four birds showing these characteristics at Cockmarsh in October 1994 and another at Slough Sewage Farm in August 1997; however, the field identification of this form is problematic and the BBRC does not consider it to be safely diagnosable from intermedius in the field (Kehoe, 2006).

A number of ringing recoveries and reports of colour ringed birds give a clue to the origins of some of the birds that come to Berkshire. Most of the birds ringed in the UK have come from Gloucestershire, Avon or Suffolk. There have been recoveries of four birds ringed overseas – two from the Channel Islands and one each from Germany, The Netherlands and Norway – with a further three colour-ringed birds seen in Berkshire also having been recorded in Spain or Portugal.

*Sponsored by Gordon Newport*

---

# Herring Gull

`Red`

## *Larus argentatus*

*Common passage migrant and winter visitor which now breeds*

The Herring Gull is a common passage migrant and winter visitor which also now breeds in Berkshire. It was the only large gull reported in some numbers prior to 1920. Noble (1906) records it as "often seen in stormy weather flying high over the county". Lower flying birds were still being shot late in the 19th century, a "fine example of a second year bird" being taken at South Hill Park, Bracknell in August 1889 (Noble, 1906).

After an immature bird was recorded at Reading Sewage Farm in May 1923, there were several reports from this site in subsequent years, and by 1932 the species was regarded as an irregular winter visitor to this site, usually one to four birds. The first indication of any substantial passage movement was of 16 birds at Ilsley in April 1924, and the first year of significant winter numbers was in 1934 when there were up to 50 birds at Reading Sewage Farm. By 1938, Herring Gulls had been reported in every month of the year, not just from sewage farms, but from other sites such as Great Meadow Pond in Windsor Great Park and the newly created gravel pits, seven birds at Theale Gravel Pits in January 1937 being one of the earliest records from this site. The first large flock to be recorded was of about 500 birds flying north-west over Combe in November 1938.

Up to the end of the 20th century, Herring Gull were reported only infrequently during the summer months, but changes became apparent in 2001 when 11 were on the Jubilee River on 7th June and about 80 seen following the plough at East Shefford on 15th July. The trend continued in 2002 when 342 immature birds were counted at Pingewood Gravel Pits on 14th May and a similar group of 54 immature birds was at Tickleback Row on 29th May. With a number of adult birds now being seen during the summer months, particularly around some town centres, it was suspected that breeding was taking place. This was finally confirmed in 2005, when three broods were located on a factory roof-top in the Slough Industrial Estate on 28th June. Now, the sight and sound of Herring Gulls has become increasingly familiar in some Berkshire towns, and

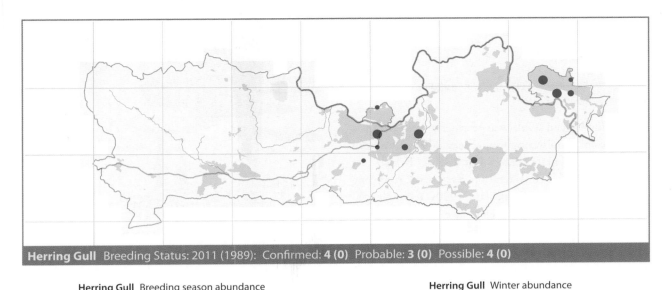

**Herring Gull** Breeding Status: 2011 (1989): Confirmed: **4 (0)** Probable: **3 (0)** Possible: **4 (0)**

**Herring Gull** Breeding season abundance
Tetrads occupied: **34 (80)** Average of occupied tetrads: **10·5**

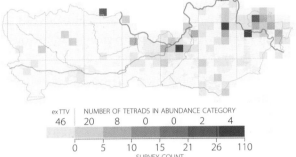

| ex TTV | NUMBER OF TETRADS IN ABUNDANCE CATEGORY | | | | | |
|---|---|---|---|---|---|---|
| 46 | 20 | 8 | 0 | 0 | 2 | 4 |

0    5    10    15    21    26    110
SURVEY COUNT

**Herring Gull** Winter abundance
Tetrads occupied: **81 (154)** Average of occupied tetrads: **41·8**

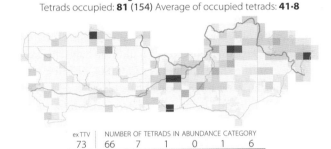

| ex TTV | NUMBER OF TETRADS IN ABUNDANCE CATEGORY | | | | | |
|---|---|---|---|---|---|---|
| 73 | 66 | 7 | 1 | 0 | 1 | 6 |

0    20    41    62    83    104    1,004
SURVEY COUNT

further breeding sites have been identified. The 2007–11 Atlas Survey confirmed that breeding was taking place in at least four locations around Reading and Slough, and breeding was probable at a further three sites.

Due to familiarity, Herring Gulls are almost certainly under-recorded, but the indications are that numbers in the county increase from as early as July, with local birds being joined by birds from outside the county, and many of the reports of Herring Gulls involve birds moving between daytime feeding areas and night-time roosts.

Winter flocks and roosts in Berkshire occur at various sites on a relatively small scale, primarily in the eastern half of the county where it is more numerous, in contrast to the Lesser Black-backed Gull which is more numerous in the more agricultural western half (see Winter Map). Roost sites include gravel pits and other open water sites like Queen Mother Reservoir, where in December 1983 at least 1,500 Herring Gulls were using the site, with a further 2,250+ on nearby Wraysbury Reservoir; estimates have become more difficult in recent years as increasing numbers arrive after dark (perhaps as a result of mandatory bird scaring activity during the daytime at rubbish tips). Apart from those roosting counts, there were only five other reports of more than 500 birds from 1962 to 1994, although a count of about 3,000 in the

Burghfield Gravel Pits area in November 1975 remains the county maximum. Counts of over 500 birds still occur, most recently at Cold Harbour on 29th August 2009, where about 800 were recorded. Some of the largest more recent winter gatherings have now been seen to comprise mainly birds of the Scandinavian race (*L. a. argentatus*), such as the flock of 800+ at Colnbrook on 14th January 2001, and that of 1,000+ at Dinton Pastures Country Park on 9th December 2004. These birds generally start arriving in early September and are thought to be almost as abundant as the native race (*L. a. argenteus*) by late autumn; the same conclusion has been reached in Surrey, with further evidence from the recovery of ringed birds in Arctic Norway and Russia (Wheatley, J. 2007). By late February winter visiting birds have normally left the county, but this is difficult to assess due to under-recording and the recently increased summer population. There has been one recovery of an overseas-ringed bird in Berkshire, one ringed in the Murmansk region of Arctic Russia in July 1960 that was shot at Wraysbury in December 1962.

There have been a number of county reports of individual Herring Gulls with leucistic plumage, their similarity in appearance at a distance to Glaucous or Iceland Gulls raising the possibility of confusion with those species.

*Sponsored by Gordon Newport*

295

# Yellow-legged Gull

## Larus michahellis

*Uncommon but increasingly reported autumn passage migrant and winter visitor*

The Yellow-legged Gull was formerly considered a subspecies of the Herring Gull. Since 2005 it has been regarded as a separate species on the BOU British List after many years of consideration. Systematic recording by observers was sporadic until the 1990s. Yellow-legged Gulls from the Mediterranean have been increasing northwards along the Channel coast of France and into south-east England since the 1970s (*1981–84 BTO Winter Atlas*) and this together with increased observer awareness has been reflected in the steady increase in the number of county records since the first in June 1974 .

The pattern of records prior to the mid-1990s probably reflects the fact that observers would not have checked Herring Gulls to find Yellow-legged Gulls. The first was a subadult at Wraysbury Gravel Pits on 17th and 23rd June 1974, followed by another there on 24th October 1976. Two adults were found during cold weather in December 1981 (one of them photographed), and there were subsequent records in every year except 1983 and 1985. At first there might only be a few records each year, but as more observers started noting Yellow-legged Gulls, an annual pattern of records emerged. In the years from 2003 to 2012 there have been records from between 15 and 25 sites, mostly gravel pits or reservoirs, but some too from other sites which attract gulls, for example five were among other gulls at Cow Down, West Ilsley on 16th August 2009.

There is a clear influx during the summer, with the highest numbers being from the east of the county. The date of arrival varies from year to year, but it can be unclear if occasional records in late May are the last of the winter birds or the first returning autumn birds. In most years numbers at the principal sites build up in June or July, peaking in July or August and then numbers decline during the autumn. This influx is largely confined to the eastern end of the county, with by far the highest counts from a few sites, particularly Queen Mother Reservoir, where the highest count of 86 was recorded on 19th July 2005, and the second highest count of 85 on 24th July 2010. There have also been high counts from nearby sites, with up to 60 at Colnbrook and up to 58 at Horton. A similar pattern emerges from nearby sites in Surrey (Wheatley, 2007).

Records, usually of one or two, are received from suitable sites throughout the county from June through the autumn and winter, but less frequently in west Berkshire, and diminish after February, with few in April and May. There are occasional records of counts in double figures outside the substantial passage through the east of the county in late summer. This pattern is reflected in both the Breeding Season and Winter Abundance Maps, the former showing late departing winter birds and the onset of the autumn passage. Numbers in winter even at Queen Mother Reservoir are seldom in double figures. There were though 80 there on 13th August 2012 and 40 on 20th July 2012.

As more attention has been paid to the species, it has been noted that they are more readily found earlier in winter when their "cleaner" appearance can make them easier to pick out among more "streaky-headed" winter Herring Gulls. As juveniles do not show this difference, they may be overlooked.

*Sponsored by Rachel and John Westmacott*

**Yellow-legged Gull** Breeding season abundance
Tetrads occupied: **0** (21) Average of occupied tetrads: **0**

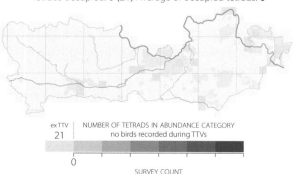

| ex TTV | NUMBER OF TETRADS IN ABUNDANCE CATEGORY |
|---|---|
| 21 | no birds recorded during TTVs |

0

SURVEY COUNT

**Yellow-legged Gull** Winter abundance
Tetrads occupied: **4** (31) Average of occupied tetrads: **1·3**

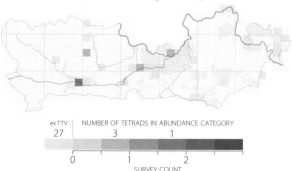

| ex TTV | NUMBER OF TETRADS IN ABUNDANCE CATEGORY | |
|---|---|---|
| 27 | 3 | 1 |

0          1          2

SURVEY COUNT

# Caspian Gull

*Larus cachinnans*

*Scarce winter visitor*

When taxonomists examined the status of the larger grey-backed gulls formerly all regarded as subspecies of Herring Gull *L. argentatus* with the assistance of DNA analysis in the early 2000s , they concluded that the yellow-legged birds of eastern Europe and northern Asia were a separate species to the Yellow-legged Gulls of Atlantic France, the Iberian peninsula and the Mediterranean (Sangster *et al.*, 2007). Even before the split was confirmed, increasing knowledge of the characteristics of these birds meant that from the 1990s records started to be received from a number of sites in Britain.

The first gull identified as a Caspian Gull in Berkshire was a near-adult at Colnbrook rubbish-tip on 13th September 1998 and then nearby at Queen Mother Reservoir on 1st October, followed by adults at Bray Gravel Pits and Wraysbury Gravel Pits in November and December of that year, and another near-adult at Wraysbury in January 1999. The number of records grew as familiarity with the identification points spread. Between 2003 and 2008 there were between eight and 40 records each year. Most records are from Queen Mother Reservoir and the surrounding area or the gravel pits to the south of Reading, and are of one or two birds, a pattern reflected in the Winter Atlas map. As the individuals are often intensively studied, individuals identified from plumage, injury or other distinctive marks have been seen on a number of occasions and the number of records annually includes re-sightings of such birds. Notably a gull with a Polish colour ring was present at Queen Mother Reservoir and Colnbrook between 22nd October 2007 and 31st January 2008. The highest count was five at Queen Mother Reservoir on 27th November 2004 during a late autumn influx also noted in Surrey and south Oxfordshire.

Although most records are from the winter period from August to February, there are a few records of birds lingering or occurring later in spring, including one at Moatlands Gravel Pit, Theale on 14th May 2005, and another at Queen Mother Reservoir on 20th May 2008. The earliest autumn records have all been from Queen Mother Reservoir where July records have occurred in four years up to 2012, including the earliest record, a first-summer, on 11th July in 2007.

Due to the evolving nature of Caspian Gull identification, the recognition of different age-groups has changed with time. Interestingly, like Yellow-legged Gull, the first to be identified in the county was a subadult (perhaps because these plumages may stand out, even though proving their identification can be more difficult). Most subsequent records were of adult types, until a first-winter was recognized in January 2002, and first- and second-winter birds now make up the majority of sightings. A juvenile at Queen Mother Reservoir on 16th and 17th August 2005 remains the only sighting of a bird in this easily-overlooked plumage.

*Sponsored by Paul Bright-Thomas*

Caspian Gull, Queen Mother Reservoir, 19th August 2011
*Michael McKee*

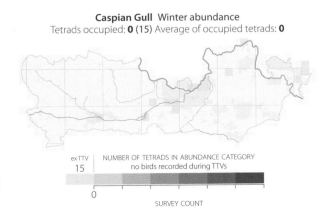

**Caspian Gull** Winter abundance
Tetrads occupied: **0** (15) Average of occupied tetrads: **0**

ex TTV | NUMBER OF TETRADS IN ABUNDANCE CATEGORY
15 | no birds recorded during TTVs

0

SURVEY COUNT

# Iceland Gull

*Larus glaucoides*

*Rare winter visitor*

The Iceland Gull is a rare winter visitor to Berkshire. Problems of distinguishing this species from Glaucous Gulls, hybrid Glaucous × Herring Gulls, or Herring Gulls showing some degree of albinism, means that the small number of fully acceptable records is likely to be an underestimate of the frequency of occurrence of Iceland Gulls in the county.

The first Berkshire record of an Iceland Gull was of one seen at Slough Sewage Farm on 6th April 1940 and there were only a further seven sightings until the late 1990s, five of which have been seen from 14th to 20th February. In 1976, an adult was seen at Holyport on 13th November and 18th December, and in 1979 there was one at Wraysbury Gravel Pits on 18th February. In 1984 there were two records, a second-year bird in the area of Reading Sewage Farm and Burghfield Gravel Pits on 14th February, and a first-year bird in the same area from 20th February to 14th March. Two birds were seen again in 1986, an adult on 11th February and an immature on 18th February, followed in 1987 by a first-winter bird on 17th January and two birds on 24th February 1994, all at Queen Mother Reservoir.

From 1998 onwards, Iceland Gull has been recorded annually in the county, mainly at the Queen Mother Reservoir gull roost, but with records in 2001, 2002 and 2004 at Smallmead Gravel Pit, Reading, and at Colebrook Lake in 2005. What is thought to have been the same bird appeared in the Queen Mother Reservoir gull roost for seven winters from 1998. In common with other gull species, Iceland Gull will move away from the roost site to feed; this has resulted in what appears to be the same bird being reported from several different locations, both around the county and outside it, particularly from Buckinghamshire.

The records from Berkshire fit the national pattern for wintering Iceland Gull, which mostly arrive at the end of December or January in the south, with most leaving by mid-March (*1981–84 BTO Winter Atlas*). The earliest arrival date was in 2007 when an adult was seen at Queen Mother Reservoir on 9th November, although birds have lingered into April in five years from 1998 to 2013, the latest date being 28th April 2004. Since records increased in the late 1990s, most years see one or two birds staying throughout the winter, but three birds were recorded doing so in 1998 and 2000 and four in 2005. The presence of two birds in 1984 coincided with a large influx of over 300 Iceland Gulls into the north and west of Britain, with many areas having record numbers. Similarly the record number in 2005 reflects increased numbers elsewhere in the country.

The North American race of Iceland Gull, known as Kumlien's Gull *L. g. kumlieni*, has been recorded on three occasions: a subadult at Langley, showed very well in fields by Parlaunt Lane on 29th March 2001; it later flew off south-west and was relocated in the gull-roost at Queen Mother Reservoir. In 2004 an adult was seen at Lower Farm Gravel Pit on 2nd March and possibly the same bird was present at Pingewood Gravel Pits the following day. Plumage features, and the age and date of the records, may indicate the same bird was seen in 2001 and 2004. An adult at Queen Mother Reservoir on 15th February 2007 was much paler on the primaries and clearly a different bird. These records fit the national pattern for peak occurrences in the late winter or early spring, but surprisingly the unprecedented influx into Britain of Kumlien's Gulls during the winter of 2012 (Fray *et al.*, 2012) produced no Berkshire records.

The conclusive identification of a Kumlien's Gull is beset by a number of problems. Not all Kumlien's Gulls are separable from nominate Iceland Gulls, particularly in the more subtle and less well-known immature plumages. Herring Gulls which are leucistic or partly albinistic or of the northern race which show much more white in the

**Iceland Gull** Winter abundance
Tetrads occupied: **0** (4) Average of occupied tetrads: **0**

ex TTV | NUMBER OF TETRADS IN ABUNDANCE CATEGORY
4 | no birds recorded during TTVs

0

SURVEY COUNT

tips of the primaries may also cause problems, as might some hybrid gulls. Two adult Glaucous × Herring Gull hybrids that have been observed in the county bore a superficial resemblance to adult Kumlien's Gull (Heard, 1989).

*Sponsored by Roger Stansfield*

# Glaucous Gull Amber

## *Larus hyperboreus*

*Rare winter visitor*

The Glaucous Gull is a rare winter visitor to Berkshire which was not recorded until an immature bird was seen at Ham Sewage Farm from 17th March to 15th April 1951. After an isolated record of a second winter bird in February 1958, sightings became almost annual from 1969/70, with records in 17 of the 25 winters to 1993/94, including two series of records each of seven consecutive winters from 1973/74 to 1979/80 and from 1984/85 to 1990/91. However, there have been records in only 10 of the 18 winters from 1994/95 to 2011/12, including three consecutive winters with no records from 2008/09 to 2010/11. The high proportion of apparent first-winter birds means that the regularity of occurrence is not wholly due to the same birds returning in subsequent years, although this species has a tendency to return to the same wintering sites over several years (*1981–84 BTO Winter Atlas*).

The number of birds present in any winter is difficult to establish with certainty because of the frequent movement of gulls to and from roosts, so records from different parts of the county might refer to the same individual. When account is taken of the likelihood of one bird accounting for more than one record, there is a surprising consistency in the number of birds reported each winter, with probably just one bird in 20 of the 32 winters for which there are reports, two in a further six winters and three or four birds in the remaining six winters. Figure 115 shows the records of Glaucous Gulls in Berkshire broken down by month of arrival and the age of the birds involved.

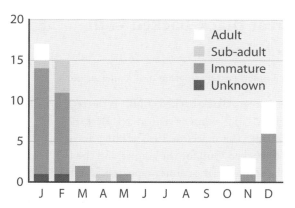

**Figure 115: Glaucous Gull: all birds recorded 1951–2011, by month of arrival**

The earliest arrival date of Glaucous Gull in Berkshire was an adult at Holyport on 16th October 1978, a day ahead of another adult in Windsor Great Park on 17th October 1971. The latest arrival and departure dates involved a first summer bird that was observed at Queen Mother Reservoir from 2nd to 4th May 2007. Adult birds predominate in October and November, and from January to March most records are of first-winter or immature birds. Most sightings have been of single birds, even in winters when it appears that more than one bird

Glaucous Gull, Woodley, 14th February 2011  *Michael McKee*

has been present. Since 1995 there has been an increase in the number of records of birds thought to have spent long periods (up to one month) at the same site. There are only three county records west of Theale Gravel Pits, and the majority of observations are connected with the regular gull roost at Queen Mother Reservoir.

There have a number of records of hybrid Glaucous × Herring Gulls in Berkshire, details of which appear in the *Summary of records of hybrids in Berkshire* (*page 482*). The county report for 1986–87 includes an article on the identification of these birds (Heard. 1989). A significant proportion of the mostly resident Icelandic breeding population of large gulls is of hybrid Glaucous × Herring Gull stock (*1981–84 BTO Winter Atlas*), and

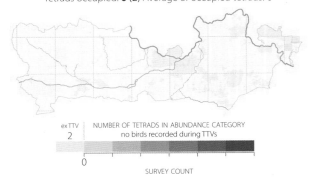

**Glaucous Gull** Winter abundance
Tetrads occupied: **0** (2) Average of occupied tetrads: **0**

| ex TTV | NUMBER OF TETRADS IN ABUNDANCE CATEGORY no birds recorded during TTVs |
|---|---|
| 2 | |
| 0 | SURVEY COUNT |

the birds seen in Berkshire may be from that population.

*Sponsored by Andrew Taylor*

# Great Black-backed Gull Amber

## *Larus marinus*

*Uncommon passage migrant and winter visitor.*

The Great Black-backed Gull is a regular passage migrant and winter visitor to Berkshire in small numbers. There are no 19th century records of Great Black-backed Gull for the county and the first reference to the species in the county reports was of four observed at Reading Sewage Farm on 5th January 1935. This was quickly followed by one at Slough Sewage Farm in 1936 and one on the Thames at Eton in 1937. There were then reports of one or two birds in 1938, 1944, 1945, 1946 and 1947, including three records during April. Since 1950 sightings have been annual.

Quite why records of Great Black-backed Gulls should have started suddenly in 1935 is unclear, although it does mirror the increase in the number of Lesser Black-backed Gulls in Berkshire. Since many Great Black-backed Gulls show a marked tendency to return to the same wintering areas from year to year (*1981–84 BTO Winter Atlas*), birds could be expected to return in subsequent years.

By 1963, Great Black-backed Gulls had been recorded in Berkshire in every month of the year, in May as early as 1950, in June by 1960 and in July in 1963. Since then, there have been an increasing number of records for the months of August to April, but records for May and June remain uncommon.

The monthly distribution pattern of Great Black-backed Gull records in Berkshire today is very similar to that shown in Figure 116, a typical year involving the passage of occasional birds from August to October, and the presence of larger wintering numbers from November until their dispersal in March. As with some

other gull species, it is difficult to distinguish between passage movements and roosting flights, but five flying north over Thatcham in March 1962, one flying west over West Woodhay Down on 5th July 1975, 11 in a field at Enborne on 3rd May 1989, and five following a plough at Beedon on 5th September 1989 point to the occurrence of passage through the county.

Although there are occasional records from farmland, most Great Black-backed Gulls are seen in association with other gulls at rubbish tips, infill sites and at the Queen Mother Reservoir gull roost. Most reports are of fewer than five birds, although parties of up to 20 or 30 are now not infrequent. The first record to exceed ten birds was of 40 at Ham Sewage Farm in January 1958. Counts of 100+ became regular during the 1980s

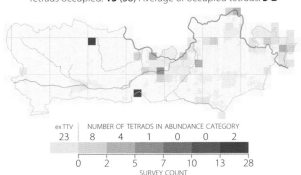

**Great Black-backed Gull** Winter abundance
Tetrads occupied: **15** (38) Average of occupied tetrads: **5·2**

| ex TTV | NUMBER OF TETRADS IN ABUNDANCE CATEGORY | | | | | |
|---|---|---|---|---|---|---|
| 23 | 8 | 4 | 1 | 0 | 0 | 2 |
| | 0 | 2 | 5 | 7 | 10 | 13 | 28 |
| | | | SURVEY COUNT | | | |

and 1990s, with 150+ going to roost at Queen Mother Reservoir in December 1983, 180 at Wraysbury Gravel Pits in January 1985, 120 at Burghfield Gravel Pits in December 1989, an estimated 200 at Theale Gravel Pits in January 1991, at least 120 there in December 1994 and 150 in December 1996.

Until 2004 the area around Smallmead landfill site attracted sizeable flocks of loafing Great Black-backed Gulls, the largest being 140 at Green Park in December 2001, but with the cessation of tipping at this site, numbers decreased rapidly. At the same time, numbers at Queen Mother Reservoir began to increase, setting new county records with 255 in December 2005, an estimated 500 present in December 2007, and there were 350 there in January 2008. Away from Smallmead and Queen Mother Reservoir the only other 21st century record of 100 or more was 151 at Hurst landfill in February 2004.

Despite the large increase in winter numbers this species remains scarce during May to July, with most records consisting of immature birds. The easterly bias within the county remains, probably more marked in

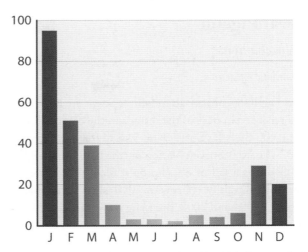

**Figure 116: Great Black-backed Gull: all birds recorded 1935–64.** After 1964 recording was too incomplete for inclusion; although numbers have increased, there is no indication of a change in the pattern of seasonal occurrence.

recent years, with fewer birds associating with central Berkshire gravel pit sites and only low counts coming from the west of the county.

*Sponsored by Gordon Newport*

# Pallas's Sandgrouse

## *Syrrhaptes paradoxus*

*Rare, irruptive vagrant*

As is the case for many other parts of Britain, Pallas's Sandgrouse has only occurred in Berkshire as a result of the great invasion in the spring of 1888 and the smaller invasion of 1908. Apart from such irruptions, which have not recurred since, it is a very rare vagrant to Britain, with only seven records after 1950, and none since 1990.

The only detailed account of local sightings, following the arrival of birds all along the east coast in the spring of 1888, is by Noble (1906). His information came from Mr Aplin and relates to two birds seen near Newbury and two at Peasemore in 1888, and to a flock of about 30 birds flying over the Compton Downs early in January 1889, one of which was recovered when it apparently hit telegraph wires (an early date for a bird being killed in such a way). There were reports from elsewhere in Britain of breeding attempts, and apparently a number of birds survived for a considerable time in Britain, as there was a report in *The Field* for 19th October 1889 of three birds being seen on 15th October on a sandy railway bank between Twyford and Reading.

The smaller, but still considerable, influx of 1908 was confined mainly to south-east England, East Anglia,

Yorkshire and Cheshire. In that year, there was a single Berkshire record of a bird which was picked up "near the River Kennet" on 6th June (Partridge, 1908). Finally, there was a report in *The Field* for 5th June 1915 of two seen on the Berkshire Downs about a month earlier. As the birds were only seen from a moving car, apparently without the use of binoculars, the possibility of mis-identification cannot be ruled out. It is unclear whether the record relates to the Berkshire or Oxfordshire side of the present county boundary. There were evidently no other records for Britain in 1915.

*Sponsored by County Ornithological Services*

# Feral Pigeon

## Columba livia

*Abundant resident*

The Feral Pigeon, an abundant resident in Berkshire, was recorded in 61% of the tetrads in the county during the 1987–89 Atlas Survey, and 51% of the tetrads in the 2007–11 Atlas Survey. Nationally the BBS trend 1995–2009 shows a fall of 8% (Eaton *et al.*, 2011) while the Berkshire Bird Index (Crowley, 2010) shows little change between 1994 and 2008. Breeding was either confirmed, or evidence of possible breeding was obtained, in 37% of the tetrads in the 1987–89 Atlas Survey, but in only 21% of the tetrads in 2007–11. The figures may reflect a real reduction in numbers. It is likely that this species is under-recorded: the Birds of Berkshire Annual Reports contain very few records for Feral Pigeon. Moreover, it is hard to obtain an accurate estimate of the population because of the difficulty of separating feral and semi-domesticated birds and the fact that many thousands of young birds, especially young homing pigeons, join the population every year (Brown and Grice, 2005). The breeding season and winter abundance maps both show a strong correlation with built-up areas in Berkshire. While there are some outlying breeding records, which probably relate to farm buildings, abundance both in summer and winter remains greatest in the towns.

Feral pigeons successfully exploit the nest sites and abundant food sources provided by man in towns and cities, but the increase in oilseed rape and higher cereal yields has provided more food in the countryside too. They are also very productive breeders, raising up to six broods a year, and young birds are able to breed when only six or seven months old. The main factor limiting

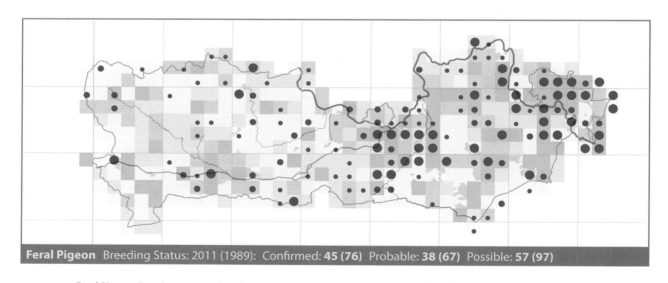

**Feral Pigeon**  Breeding Status: 2011 (1989):  Confirmed: **45 (76)**  Probable: **38 (67)**  Possible: **57 (97)**

**Feral Pigeon**  Breeding season abundance
Tetrads occupied: **126 (199)** Average of occupied tetrads: **14·5**

**Feral Pigeon**  Winter abundance
Tetrads occupied: **144 (211)** Average of occupied tetrads: **23·5**

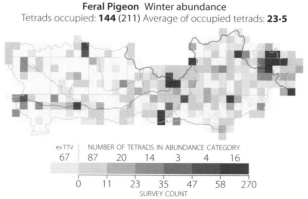

| exTTV | NUMBER OF TETRADS IN ABUNDANCE CATEGORY | | | | | |
|---|---|---|---|---|---|---|
| 73 | 76 | 15 | 7 | 8 | 6 | 14 |

| 0 | 7 | 14 | 21 | 29 | 36 | 110 |
SURVEY COUNT

| exTTV | NUMBER OF TETRADS IN ABUNDANCE CATEGORY | | | | | |
|---|---|---|---|---|---|---|
| 67 | 87 | 20 | 14 | 3 | 4 | 16 |

| 0 | 11 | 23 | 35 | 47 | 58 | 270 |
SURVEY COUNT

population is the availability of nest sites (Brown and Grice, 2005). The reduction in traditional farm buildings still used for agriculture, and efforts to control what is regarded as a problem species in towns may account for any decline.

Although some 25% of rural Feral Pigeons, and more than 25% of urban ones, continue to breed in the winter, sizeable flocks form at this time of year when they descend on stubble fields. Counts of 300–500 birds are not unusual and particularly large gatherings were reported from Arborfield Hall Farm in November 1996 (900 birds); Widbrook Common/Summerleaze in October 2004 (550 birds); Woodlands Park in November 2006 (two flocks totalling 950 birds on bean stubble).

There would appear to be no significant threats to the Feral Pigeon in Berkshire whilst their natural predators are few, and the opportunities for scavenging are likely to remain. It would, however, be desirable to encourage better recording of this species in order to understand its status in the county more fully.

*Sponsored by Renee Grayer*

# Stock Dove Amber

## *Columba oenas*

*Common resident and winter visitor*

The Stock Dove is a widespread resident in Berkshire, and during the 1987–89 Atlas Survey it was recorded as present in the breeding season in 79% of the tetrads, with breeding probable or confirmed in 60%. By the time of the 2007–11 Atlas Survey, Stock Dove had increased its breeding distribution, with some breeding evidence in 91% of the tetrads, and breeding was probable or confirmed in 66%. Nationally there has been a substantial increase of 83% in the breeding population between 1970 and 2009. A surprisingly large proportion of the European population of Stock Doves (44%) is resident in Britain (Hagemeijer and Blair, 1997).

Stock Doves nest in holes in trees and old buildings and feed on seeds in farmland. Their favoured breeding habitat in Berkshire is therefore rural parkland and wooded farmland with old trees. Despite this, some arable areas, such as parts of the Downs, produced some of the higher densities in the results of the Breeding Season timed surveys in the 2007–11 Atlas, and birds are present in many built-up areas where they nest in town parks. In winter, the *1981–84 BTO Winter Atlas* states that Stock Doves are most numerous in areas of mixed farming, and are relatively scarce where land-use is predominantly arable or grassland. Notwithstanding this, the Winter Map shows some arable areas with good numbers in Berkshire.

After the breeding season, there is some influx from continental populations and Stock Doves are sometimes seen in large flocks. In Berkshire counts of 500 or more birds have been reported in a number of years, and a flock of 1,500 at Cold Harbour on 29th September 2001 was the largest ever recorded in Berkshire. The highest count in west Berkshire was 900 at Warren Down in 2004. Such large counts are generally made between late summer and early spring although flocking can continue into May. Stock Doves normally feed on weed seeds and grain from October to December and on fallow land or winter stubble from January to March. Although it might have been expected that the substantial shift to winter cereals since the 1970s would have reduced the scope for winter-feeding, the large winter flocks seem to indicate there being little problem with food availability. In east Berkshire, small parties can be found frequently in coniferous woodland feeding on conifer seeds.

There was a dramatic decline in Stock Dove numbers in central southern England in the 1950s and 1960s, coinciding with the use of organochlorine chemicals in seed-dressings, which caused reduced breeding productivity. This was exacerbated by the loss of the elm *Ulmus* spp. and many kilometres of hedgerow with mature trees, resulting in a reduction of suitable nest sites (O'Connor and Mead, 1984). Increases since 1970, after organochlorine pesticides were banned, have substantially restored populations, although numbers are still thought to be below those of the 1950s (Brown and Grice, 2005).

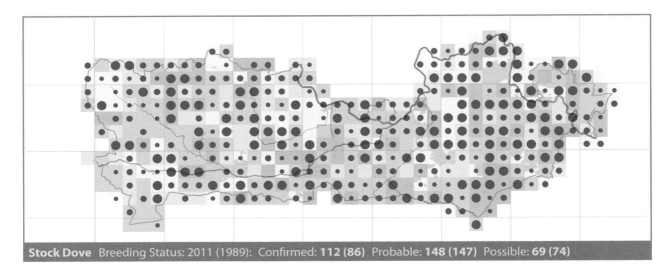

**Stock Dove** Breeding Status: 2011 (1989): Confirmed: **112 (86)** Probable: **148 (147)** Possible: **69 (74)**

**Stock Dove** Breeding season abundance
Tetrads occupied: **238 (357)** Average of occupied tetrads: **3·9**

| ex TTV | NUMBER OF TETRADS IN ABUNDANCE CATEGORY | | | | | |
|---|---|---|---|---|---|---|
| 119 | 55 | 90 | 47 | 18 | 14 | 14 |

0    1    3    5    7    9    39
SURVEY COUNT

**Stock Dove** Winter abundance
Tetrads occupied: **164 (259)** Average of occupied tetrads: **8·8**

| ex TTV | NUMBER OF TETRADS IN ABUNDANCE CATEGORY | | | | | |
|---|---|---|---|---|---|---|
| 95 | 112 | 19 | 12 | 7 | 5 | 9 |

0    4    8    13    17    22    402
SURVEY COUNT

The Stock Dove was described by Lamb (1880) as 'common' in Berkshire before 1814, and as 'still common' in 1906 (Noble, 1906). Palmer (1886) makes the interesting observation that the species had been breeding in a rabbit burrow at Enborne for some years. The Stock Dove was selected for special study in Berkshire in 1939 to determine its distribution and nest sites. In addition to traditional hole-nesting in trees, pollarded willows and buildings, it was found using rabbit-warrens in tree-less downland country, in forks of dark, close-foliaged trees such as Yew *Taxus baccata*, and in old nests of Rooks and Magpies. At this time flocks were reported as seen mostly from July to May with the largest being of 200 birds (Morley, 1940).

*Sponsored by Rose & John Beeston*

Stock Dove, Charvil  *Dave Rimes www.lookatthebirds.co.uk*

# Woodpigeon

*Columba palumbus*

*Abundant resident and winter visitor*

The Woodpigeon is an abundant resident in Berkshire, with numbers augmented in winter by immigration from northern and eastern populations. It is one of our most widespread and numerous birds, recorded throughout the county both in the breeding season and during the winter, occupying virtually all habitats in both rural and urban areas. In the 1987–89 Atlas survey, probable plus confirmed breeding was recorded in 95% of the tetrads and in the 2007–11 survey the figure was almost identical at 94%. The Winter and Breeding Season Abundance Maps both show the greatest abundance of birds to be in the arable areas of the county, particularly the downland of the northwest.

Nationally there has been a steady increase in Woodpigeon numbers, rising by 169% between 1967 and 2010 (Baillie *et al.*, 2013). This is probably linked to the increase of arable farming and, in particular, the amount of oilseed rape which has been grown since 1970 (Inglis *et al.*, 1997). The Berkshire Bird Index showed a doubling in the population between 1994 and 2008 (Crowley, 2010), a higher growth rate than shown

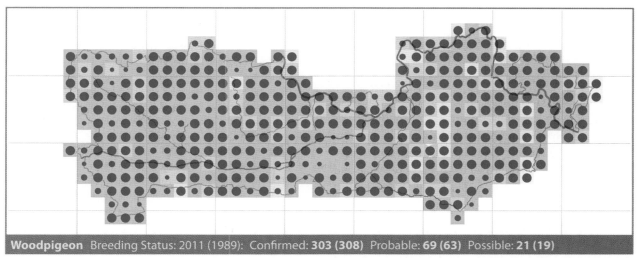

Woodpigeon  Breeding Status: 2011 (1989):  Confirmed: **303 (308)**  Probable: **69 (63)**  Possible: **21 (19)**

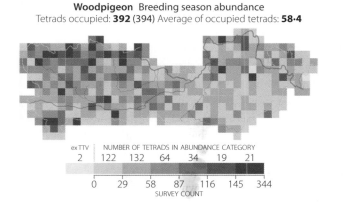

**Woodpigeon**  Breeding season abundance
Tetrads occupied: **392 (394)** Average of occupied tetrads: **58·4**

| ex TTV | NUMBER OF TETRADS IN ABUNDANCE CATEGORY | | | | | |
|---|---|---|---|---|---|---|
| 2 | 122 | 132 | 64 | 34 | 19 | 21 |

| 0 | 29 | 58 | 87 | 116 | 145 | 344 |
|---|---|---|---|---|---|---|

SURVEY COUNT

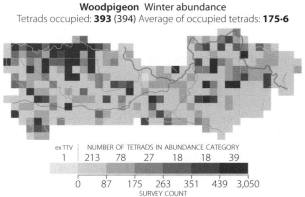

**Woodpigeon**  Winter abundance
Tetrads occupied: **393 (394)** Average of occupied tetrads: **175·6**

| ex TTV | NUMBER OF TETRADS IN ABUNDANCE CATEGORY | | | | | |
|---|---|---|---|---|---|---|
| 1 | 213 | 78 | 27 | 18 | 18 | 39 |

| 0 | 87 | 175 | 263 | 351 | 439 | 3,050 |
|---|---|---|---|---|---|---|

SURVEY COUNT

by the national (40%) and regional (33%) measures for the period.

Woodpigeons in Britain are largely sedentary, though some birds disperse in their first two winters (Murton and Ridpath 1962; Haynes *et al.*, 2003). They also move in response to severe weather conditions and to find food, gathering in large foraging flocks in winter. Some of the largest counts in Berkshire include 5,500 flying south from Queen Mother Reservoir in November 1995; 4,000+ going to roost in Windsor Great Park in December 2006; 3,000+ at Compton Downs in November 2007; and a passage of at least 6,110 birds recorded moving south through the county in a broad front in November 2005. Most observations of large numbers relate to birds moving between feeding and roosting areas. However, Woodpigeons from northern Europe winter in Iberia and southern France, accounting for the regular spring and autumn passage observed in southern and eastern England (Brown and Grice, 2005). Some British birds apparently also move south-west out of the country: the only overseas recovery of a Woodpigeon ringed in Berkshire being a bird ringed at Cookham in July 1955 which was recovered in Finistere, western France, the following December.

Widely regarded as a pest, the Woodpigeon may be shot throughout the year. BASC's National Shooting Survey for the seasons 1980/81–1987/88 indicated that its members alone shoot between 2·0 and 4·4 million birds annually; the total bag could be twice this figure (Harradine and Reynolds, 1997).

*Sponsored by Ricki Bull*

# Collared Dove Green

## *Streptopelia decaocto*

*Widespread and common resident*

The Collared Dove is now a widespread and familiar resident in Berkshire. The species' arrival in Britain and subsequent colonisation has been well documented (*Population Trends*), and it was in 1960, eight years after its initial appearance in Britain, that the first individual was reported in the county at Widbrook Common. Breeding was finally confirmed in 1964, when four nests were found in Forbury Gardens, Reading.

By the time of the 1987–89 Atlas Survey the Collared Dove had become widely distributed over most of Berkshire, with breeding recorded as confirmed or probable in 86% of the county tetrads. By comparison, the 2008–11 Breeding Distribution Map shows only 72% of tetrads with confirmed or probable breeding and this apparent decline is also evident in the Berkshire Bird Index, which records a statistically significant reduction of 39% during the period 1994–2008. This contrasts with the national picture where the BBS trend 1995–2009 shows a 25% increase. The Collared Dove, like all the common pigeon and dove species, suffers from being under-recorded and it would be useful to obtain more data in order to check whether this reflects a real difference between Berkshire and the country as a whole.

Perhaps surprisingly, in view of their spectacular range expansion, established Collared Doves are believed to be highly sedentary with their winter distribution closely matching that of the breeding season (*1981–84 BTO Winter Atlas*). A comparison of the Berkshire Winter Map with the Breeding Season Abundance Map certainly shows this to be the case in Berkshire, with Collared Doves

recorded in 84% of the tetrads in winter and showing a very similar pattern of abundance to the breeding season.

The Breeding Season Abundance and Winter Maps both show a close association with the built environment, including towns, villages, suburbs and isolated farmsteads. The dynamic expansion of the species has been due largely to its ability to exploit man-made feeding opportunities, ranging from spilled grain from agricultural operations to food provided on bird-tables. Moreover, like its close relatives, it has a prolonged and prolific breeding season. One pair on a northwest Oxfordshire farm laid nine clutches in a single season (Robertson, 1990), and birds commonly begin laying new clutches while still feeding dependent young (Brown and Grice, 2005).

Collared Dove *Ken White*

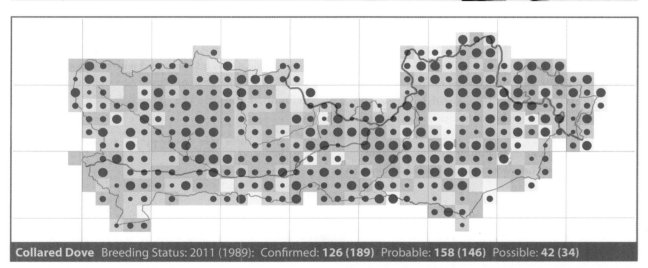

**Collared Dove** Breeding Status: 2011 (1989): Confirmed: **126 (189)** Probable: **158 (146)** Possible: **42 (34)**

**Collared Dove** Breeding season abundance
Tetrads occupied: **304 (351)** Average of occupied tetrads: **5·3**

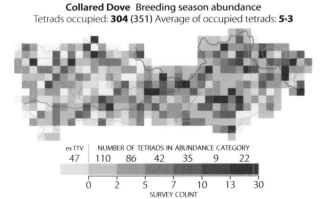

| exTTV | NUMBER OF TETRADS IN ABUNDANCE CATEGORY | | | | | |
|---|---|---|---|---|---|---|
| 47 | 110 | 86 | 42 | 35 | 9 | 22 |

0　　2　　5　　7　　10　　13　　30
SURVEY COUNT

**Collared Dove** Winter abundance
Tetrads occupied: **280 (331)** Average of occupied tetrads: **6·1**

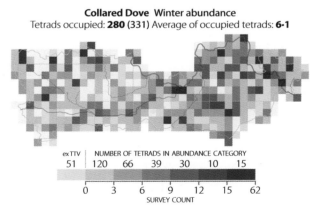

| exTTV | NUMBER OF TETRADS IN ABUNDANCE CATEGORY | | | | | |
|---|---|---|---|---|---|---|
| 51 | 120 | 66 | 39 | 30 | 10 | 15 |

0　　3　　6　　9　　12　　15　　62
SURVEY COUNT

In autumn, when populations are at their maximum, Collared Doves become more gregarious and flocks gather in favoured feeding areas. High counts in Berkshire have included 450 in Windsor Great Park in 1975, 300 at Shinfield in 1983, and 400 at West End, Bracknell in 2000. However, it seems that the large flocks which used to be reported are no longer encountered, with one of 172 at Pinkneys Green in 2003 being the latest count in three figures.

*Sponsored by Renee Grayer*

307

# Turtle Dove

*Streptopelia turtur*

*Uncommon summer visitor*

During the 1987–89 Atlas Survey, Turtle Doves were recorded in 58% of the tetrads in the county, with confirmed breeding in 10% and they were described as a 'common but localised' summer visitor. However, in the 2007–11 Atlas Survey, they were recorded in just 12% of tetrads and confirmed as having bred in only three of them. Turtle Dove would seem to be on the verge of extinction as a breeding species in Berkshire. This also reflects the national trend, as the CBC has indicted that Turtle Doves have declined by 70% between 1995 and 2009, and they are red-listed and a UK BAP (Biodiversity Action Plan) species.

The Turtle Dove is a rather inconspicuous summer visitor to Berkshire. It breeds mainly in areas of scrub, copses and tall hedgerows, requires open weedy or arable areas in which to feed, and is most strongly associated with dry, warm conditions (Brown and Grice, 2005). The 1987–89 Atlas Survey showed the greatest concentration of breeding Turtle Doves in Berkshire to be in the mid-west of the county, north of Newbury. However this is no longer the case, with very few records from this area. The only confirmed breeding is now from the Brimpton and Woolhampton Gravel Pits area and from the Hampshire border area near Bramshill. There is also a concentration of probable breeding records west of Windsor.

Whilst Turtle Dove numbers showed a national increase from 1962 to the mid-1970s, since then there has been a catastrophic decline. The factors which are most likely to be affecting the population in Britain include a reduction of seeds available due to crop spraying with selective herbicides, drought in their wintering area in the Sahel, and hunting during spring migration in south-west Europe. The reduction in availability of weed seeds may be particularly significant: a study between 1958 and 1962 showed the bulk of their food to be weed seeds, especially fumitory and chickweed (Murton *et al.*, 1964). More recent work has found that, in the absence of weeds, their food is now dominated by cultivated seeds (grains and oilseed rape) and that birds may travel considerable distances to find food. This may explain why Turtle Doves now have a shorter breeding season and produce half the number of clutches, only raising a single brood compared with two or three in the 1960s. This change alone could account for the decline in numbers (Browne and Aebischer, 2004).

**Turtle Dove** Breeding season abundance
Tetrads occupied: **11** (59) Average of occupied tetrads: **1·4**

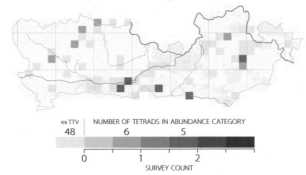

| exTTV | NUMBER OF TETRADS IN ABUNDANCE CATEGORY | |
|---|---|---|
| 48 | 6 | 5 |

0          1          2
SURVEY COUNT

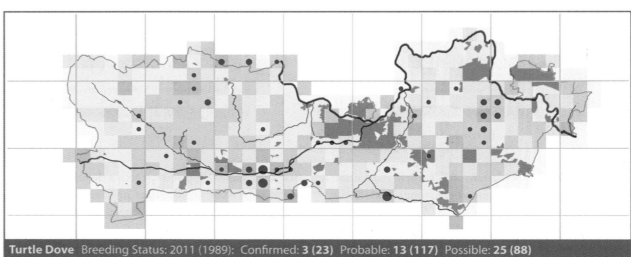

**Turtle Dove** Breeding Status: 2011 (1989): Confirmed: **3 (23)** Probable: **13 (117)** Possible: **25 (88)**

Turtle Doves normally arrive in Berkshire in the second half of April, with the earliest date during the period from 1974 to 2007 being 12th April 2007. Departure normally occurs in August and September, with the latest date during the same period being 9th October 1980. Prior to departure, sizeable flocks used to be observed, the largest since 1974 being of 63 birds at Brimpton Gravel Pits in August 1976. The largest post-breeding flock recorded in Berkshire since the first edition of this book in 1996 was a group of 13 birds at Brimpton Gravel Pits on 20 August 2003.

There have been three overseas recoveries of Turtle Doves ringed in Berkshire, and these have come from western France, northern Spain and Portugal, all recovered shot, their location reflecting the south-westerly direction in which birds migrate from Britain.

*Sponsored by Berks, Bucks and Oxford Wildlife Trust*

Turtle Dove, Woolhampton Gravel Pits *Jerry O'Brien*

# Ring-necked Parakeet

*Psittacula krameri*

*Increasingly common but localised resident*

The Ring-necked Parakeet is a long-living, exotic addition to the British avifauna, having been introduced from Southern Asia and sub-Saharan Africa in 1969, and becoming recognised as a fully naturalised British species in 1983. Within Berkshire its distribution continues to be concentrated in the east, although the number of tetrads in which it has been noted in the 2007–11 Atlas Survey, 115, has risen eightfold since the 1987–89 Atlas Survey, and by 2011 its range had extended westwards to the Remenham, Twyford and Wokingham districts, as shown on the Winter Map. This area lies at the westernmost edge of the main part of the species' disjointed range in south-east England, which includes much of Greater London, and is the most northerly breeding parrot population in the world. In Britain they seem to show a strong preference for riverside woodland with tall poplar *Populus* spp.

Ring-necked Parakeets were first recorded in Berkshire in February 1971 when one was seen at Earley. During the 1980s the Wraysbury area became the species' stronghold in Berkshire, and it produces most of the highest counts. There were 450 birds together there

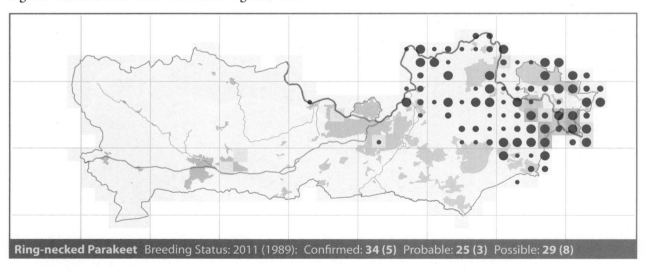

Ring-necked Parakeet  Breeding Status: 2011 (1989):  Confirmed: **34 (5)**  Probable: **25 (3)**  Possible: **29 (8)**

**Ring-necked Parakeet**  Breeding season abundance
Tetrads occupied: **81** (114) Average of occupied tetrads: **5·1**

**Ring-necked Parakeet**  Winter abundance
Tetrads occupied: **82** (115) Average of occupied tetrads: **8·0**

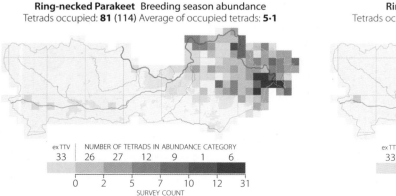

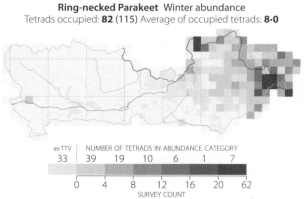

| ex TTV | NUMBER OF TETRADS IN ABUNDANCE CATEGORY | | | | | |
|---|---|---|---|---|---|---|
| 33 | 26 | 27 | 12 | 9 | 1 | 6 |

| 0 | 2 | 5 | 7 | 10 | 12 | 31 |
SURVEY COUNT

| ex TTV | NUMBER OF TETRADS IN ABUNDANCE CATEGORY | | | | | |
|---|---|---|---|---|---|---|
| 33 | 39 | 19 | 10 | 6 | 1 | 7 |

| 0 | 4 | 8 | 12 | 16 | 20 | 62 |
SURVEY COUNT

on 24th September 1993, possibly on their way to Shepperton, Surrey, where a major roost was present for some time, 1,400 at Hythe End, Wraysbury on 22nd December 2007 and 845 there on 27th December 2011. Elsewhere in the east of the county parties of 20 to 70 in flight, particularly at dusk, are not unusual. While counts of over 100 are still unusual away from the Wraysbury area, there were 227 at Bray on August 20th 2003, a total of 275 were seen flying over Queen Mother Reservoir on 28th August 2006, and since the winter of 2011/12 an overnight roost of between 400 and 500 has been established near Slough Sewage Treatment Works.

Comparison between the breeding distribution maps in the two tetrad Atlas surveys shows the steady westward expansion of the species' range in the county. The 2007–11 Atlas Survey found breeding evidence in no fewer than 88 tetrads, compared to 16 in 1987–89. Increasing numbers of records, usually of single birds, have come from further west, even as far as Hungerford, suggesting the likelihood of continued range expansion. It also seems to have been relatively unaffected by several hard winters, and numbers continue to increase.

When not shrieking loudly, this bird can be remarkably unobtrusive and, perhaps because they tend to occupy areas that are otherwise of little interest to birdwatchers, there are surprisingly few breeding season observations in the county reports. A hole-nesting species, it usually uses the vacated nest cavities of Great Spotted or Green Woodpeckers. This has earned the Parakeet a reputation for out-competing other birds, such as Starlings and Nuthatches for the use of such sites, especially as the parakeets commence setting up territories very early in the year, often by January, and can still be present beyond the end of May. However, recent studies have failed to prove any link between parakeet breeding behaviour and populations of other species (Strubbe and Matthysen, 2011; Newsom *et al.*, 2011).

Food sources reported have varied from fruits, buds, berries, and chestnuts, but from the late 1990s, there have been increasing numbers of records of the birds using garden feeders.

Other *Psittacula* parakeet species have occasionally been found at liberty in Berkshire and care should be taken to ensure that birds seen, particularly away from their usual areas, are in fact Ring-necked Parakeets. Slaty-headed Parakeets *P. himalayana* have occurred in Windsor Forest, and Alexandrine Parakeet *P. eupatria* is similar to Ring-necked and has also established feral populations outside its native range; it can be distinguished by its larger size, heavier bill and a maroon patch on the shoulder.

*Sponsored by Bracknell Forest Natural History Society*

Ring-necked Parakeet, Odney Island, Cookham  *Michael Vogel*

# Cuckoo

*Cuculus canorus*

*Common, but decreasing, summer visitor*

The Cuckoo is a widespread summer visitor, but it may not be described as 'common' for much longer: its UK breeding population is judged to be in rapid decline and numbers as recorded by the CBC have fallen nationally by 61% between 1970 and 2009. The decline has been particularly marked in the south and east of Britain. In Berkshire, a very similar trend has been demonstrated through the Berkshire Bird Index (Crowley, 2010), with a 57% fall in numbers between 2000 and 2008. The Cuckoo is therefore now red-listed and a priority species in the UK Biodiversity Action Plan. It is, as yet, unclear what the main drivers are of this population decline and the causes are under investigation. It could be linked to food supply, as Cuckoos feed mainly on caterpillars; it could be associated with reduction in breeding success or factors associated with migration and wintering grounds in Africa, as a number of other sub-Saharan migrants are also in decline.

The 1987–89 Tetrad map showed Cuckoos present over most of the county, with the exception of urban areas, and a total of 84% of tetrads in which breeding evidence was recorded, compared with 52% in 2008–11. The new Breeding Distribution Map shows, in addition to gaps in coverage over urban areas, a large area of the Berkshire Downs in the north west of the county without records. The Breeding Season Abundance Map indicates that parts of the Kennet valley hold most Cuckoos in the county. The species is rather difficult to prove breeding so the probable and confirmed breeding records taken together may provide the best indication of its true breeding distribution in the county. Comparison of the number of tetrads showing probable plus confirmed

breeding also shows a decline: in the 1987–89 Tetrad Map it was 44% while in the 2007–11 Atlas Breeding Distribution Map it had fallen to only 13%. The overall abundance is also low at only 1·31 per occupied tetrad.

The Cuckoo generally arrives in Berkshire during the second week of April with spring passage continuing to be evident at gravel pit sites until the second half of May. A small number of arrivals in March have been recorded, notably early dates being 19th in 1811 near Hungerford (Lamb, 1880), 15th in 1885 at Welford (Palmer, 1886) and more recently 20th at Windsor Great Park in 1994.

**Cuckoo** Breeding season abundance
Tetrads occupied: **84** (232) Average of occupied tetrads: **1·3**

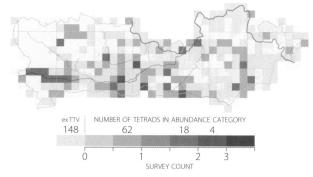

| ex TTV | NUMBER OF TETRADS IN ABUNDANCE CATEGORY | | |
|---|---|---|---|
| 148 | 62 | 18 | 4 |

SURVEY COUNT

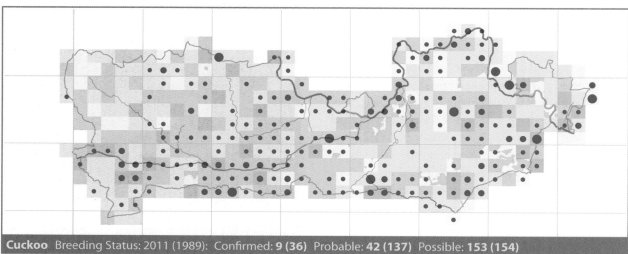

**Cuckoo** Breeding Status: 2011 (1989): Confirmed: **9 (36)** Probable: **42 (137)** Possible: **153 (154)**

No obvious trend towards earlier arrival is apparent, indeed Clark Kennedy (1868) gives 10th April as the average arrival date and it is still much the same today. An influx of 10–12 birds was reported at Thatcham Marsh on 14th April 1988, one of the highest spring concentrations recorded in Berkshire.

Adult birds have seldom been noted after July, one on 11th September 1984 at Dinton Pastures was very late. Most birds encountered during August and September are juveniles, with single birds often being seen at gravel pits and sewage farms. Apart from an exceptional straggler on 31st October 1982 at Dinton Pastures, the latest Cuckoos in Berkshire from 1974 to 2008 were recorded on dates ranging from 4th August to 29th September, with most falling in the second half of August. There was a congregation of young birds in August 1934 at Reading Sewage Farm, which reached a peak of 14 on the 6th and the 8th.

Until 2011, a Berkshire-ringed Cuckoo provided the only information about UK Cuckoos migrating to Africa: a nestling ringed in a Pied Wagtail's nest in Eton in June 1928 was shot by bow-and-arrow in Cameroon, West Africa in January 1930. Another Berkshire bird, ringed at Leighton Park School, Reading in July 1937, was recovered in August that year in Belgium.

A new BTO project, which commenced in spring 2011 has sought to find out more about Cuckoo migration routes and strategies by fitting birds with satellite tags.

By this means, it has now been established that cuckoos leave the UK earlier than was previously thought: in the first three years most left by the end of June. They have also taken very different routes to Africa. It had been thought all birds went via Italy, as indeed some have, but others have taken a westerly route via Spain. In 2012, these suffered heavy losses as a result of adverse weather. The scheme may reveal more on the factors influencing the population changes that have occurred in recent decades.

Cuckoos are the UK's only obligate brood parasite, laying their eggs in nests of other species. Data from the Nest Record Scheme between 1939 and 1982 showed there were five main host species accounting for 90% of the nests recorded: Reed Warbler, Meadow Pipit, Dunnock, Robin and Pied Wagtail, although the last two species are now used less than in Victorian times (Brown and Grice, 2005). They are divided into several host-specific races with female birds laying eggs which mimic those of their host. Thus a bird raised from a Meadow Pipit's nest will itself lay eggs mimicking a Meadow Pipit (Davies, 2000). In Berkshire the most common hosts are likely to be Dunnock and Reed Warbler, although there is little direct evidence as most confirmed breeding reports are of fledgling birds. There was an exceptional record of a Spotted Flycatcher acting as host from Leighton Park, Reading in 1928.

*Sponsored by Hayley Douthwaite*

Cuckoo, Caesar's Camp  *Jerry O'Brien*

# Barn Owl

*Tyto alba*

*Uncommon and localised resident*

The Barn Owl, which had been in decline throughout Britain for the past century and within Berkshire had become a scarce breeding resident, has shown a welcome recovery since the 1980s.

It was described as very common in the county prior to 1814 (Lamb, 1880), but even by the beginning of the 20th century was reported to be decreasing, although still common (Noble, 1906). A survey by Blaker (1934) showed that there was a concentration of Barn Owls in south-east England. A limited survey was undertaken in Berkshire in 1933 which found nests near Warfield and Winkfield, a pair at Englefield Park and one bird at Remenham. Subsequently, Radford (1966) commented that "the Barn Owl is now much decreased in numbers". There was a marked decrease in 1963 and 1964, possibly due to the severe winter of 1962/63, and this decrease continued subsequently, with just 14 single birds being recorded in 1977, most in the west of the county.

The systematic reduction of permanent pasture and hedgerows in many areas during the latter half of the twentieth century led to a drastic reduction in the vole population on which the Barn Owl depends. The replacement of old barns, and the removal of old buildings and old trees, reduced the availability of suitable nesting sites. In addition, many birds are killed by collision with vehicles while hunting on road verges, since they are often a productive hunting habitat. All of these factors undoubtedly reduced the species and even eliminated it from many areas where it was formerly common. Moreover, the most northerly breeding population of the Barn Owl in the world occurs in Britain, and it is therefore likely to be particularly vulnerable to any small but unfavourable climatic shift. Shawyer (1987) attributed the decline of the Barn Owl in Britain primarily to the long-term deterioration in

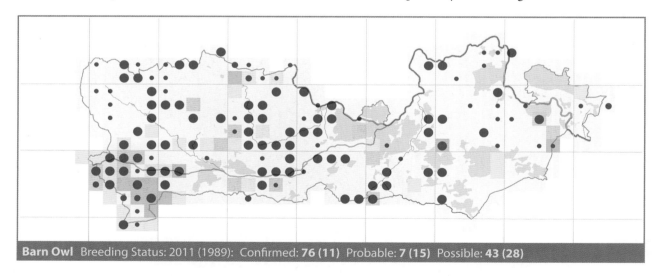

**Barn Owl** Breeding Status: 2011 (1989): Confirmed: **76 (11)** Probable: **7 (15)** Possible: **43 (28)**

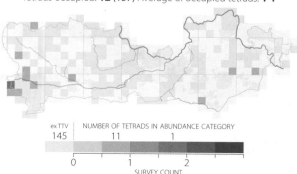

**Barn Owl** Breeding season abundance
Tetrads occupied: **12 (157)** Average of occupied tetrads: **1·1**

| exTTV | NUMBER OF TETRADS IN ABUNDANCE CATEGORY | |
|---|---|---|
| 145 | 11 | 1 |

0          1          2
SURVEY COUNT

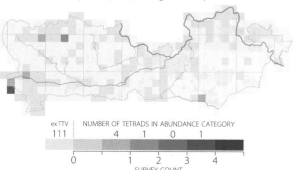

**Barn Owl** Winter abundance
Tetrads occupied: **6 (117)** Average of occupied tetrads: **1·7**

| exTTV | NUMBER OF TETRADS IN ABUNDANCE CATEGORY | | | |
|---|---|---|---|---|
| 111 | 4 | 1 | 0 | 1 |

0      1      2      3      4
SURVEY COUNT

the winter climate together with the loss of habitat. It is possible that the species benefitted from the warmer winters which prevailed during the 1990s and 2000s.

Over the five year period from 1982 to 1987, the Hawk and Owl Trust conducted a national survey of the Barn Owl. The results for Berkshire showed that the population was some 38 pairs, representing a decrease of 68% over the preceding 50 years. Although it is easier to find than other nocturnal birds, as it often hunts well before dusk, it is likely that its numbers were underestimated. Its distribution within the county was concentrated in the south-west where suitable habitat for feeding and breeding was still to be found.

Towards the end of the twentieth century, large numbers of captive-bred Barn Owls were being released into the wild in Britain, though few survived to breed (Green and Ramsden, 2001). Between 1984 and 1988, 13 pairs were released at widely differing locations in Berkshire. Of these, three disappeared immediately, and ten became established at the release site and continued to rear at least one brood of young. Fifteen birds were released in the Hurst, Arborfield, and Farley Hill areas in 1988, with two more birds in 1989. During the 1987–89 Tetrad Survey, the Barn Owl was recorded in 54 tetrads in the county, though was only proved to have bred in 11 of these. Since 1993, the Hawk and Owl Trust and others have run Barn Owl nest-box schemes, after which Barn Owls have bred successfully in the Thames, Loddon, Kennet and Pang Valleys. By 2011 at least 120 Barn Owl boxes had been put up in Berkshire, and breeding was confirmed in 21 of them that year.

The distribution in the 2007–11 Atlas survey reflects the provision of nest boxes, and shows a dramatic increase in numbers over the survey in 1987–89, with 157 tetrads occupied. The increase in confirmed breeding (76 tetrads compared to 11 in 1987–89) was proportionately much higher than in the 1987–89 survey, which may partly be attributed to the ease of confirming when birds breed in nest boxes. Whilst Barn Owls show very high site fidelity (Taylor, 1994), there may have been movement between tetrads over the four year survey period; moreover, some tetrads held more than one breeding pair; hence the tetrad survey does not itself provide a precise measure of breeding pairs. Taking these factors into account, it seems likely that the Berkshire population in 2011 was 60–100 breeding pairs.

Provision of nest boxes has greatly enhanced ringing of the species: in the four years 2007–10, an average of 55 owlets and five full-grown Barn Owls were ringed each year. The recovery data are consistent with the pattern of juvenile dispersal described in the *Migration Atlas* (*Migration Atlas*), which shows a median distance of natal dispersal of 12 km. Whilst most of the 86 recoveries of birds ringed or recovered in Berkshire more than 5 km from the ringing site have been local, there have been five recoveries of birds that have travelled much further. A nestling ringed in Berkshire, was recovered in Retford, Nottinghamshire (215 km) and another in Huddersfield, W Yorkshire (252 km). Birds ringed as nestlings in Devon (209 km), N Yorkshire (305 km) and Shropshire (111 km) were killed by cars in Berkshire.

A specimen, thought to be of the dark-breasted northern and central European race *T. a. guttata*, which had been obtained at Coley Park was brought to Reading Museum on 21st November 1915 (Wallis, 1916). A recent re-examination of the specimen (Righelato, 2012) against new criteria (French, 2009) suggests that this bird might best be regarded as an intergrade towards the *guttata* end of the *alba-guttata* spectrum. Both typical *guttata* and intergrades are rare in the UK, particularly so far inland and we can only speculate on its origin.

*Sponsored by Ollie Stares*

# Little Owl

## *Athene noctua*

*Widespread but declining resident*

The Little Owl is a widespread and locally common resident in Berkshire. It prefers farmland, especially where there are plenty of mature hedgerow trees, and other areas with scattered mature trees, such as parkland and old orchards. Pollarded willows *Salix* spp. are often favoured, although oak *Quercus* spp. trees are also often used as nest sites.

Little Owls are more diurnal than other British owls, hunting at dawn and dusk, and occasionally calling during the day. However, they are not conspicuous and

may go unnoticed by observers unfamiliar with the call. Once a territory has been found, it is fairly easy to relocate the bird on subsequent visits, since Little Owls tend to use the same perches, often near the nest. Breeding is most often confirmed once the young have hatched, and over half of confirmed breeding records related to a nest with young or to the presence of recently fledged young.

The distribution shows a good correlation with those parts of Berkshire which have areas of open farmland with mature trees as well as parkland, such as around Windsor Great Park. There is a marked absence of records from densely wooded areas, especially in the south-east of the county, and it is thinly distributed on the Downs. Reflecting its sedentary nature, summer and winter distributions are similar.

The Tetrad Surveys show a significant decline in the distribution of Little Owl, from 58% of tetrads occupied in 1987–89 to 36% in the 2007–11 survey. Although the proportion of occupied tetrads in which breeding was confirmed was higher in the recent survey, the combined number in which breeding was either probable or confirmed was 77, compared with 127 in 1987–89. The decline of approximately 40% in tetrad occupancy observed in Berkshire between 1989 and 2011 reflects

a national decline in abundance of approximately half over the period based on the results of the BTO's CBC/BBS annual surveys. The reasons for the decline in the UK are unclear, though there is evidence from elsewhere in Europe that both winter survival and reduced productivity may contribute (Birdlife International, 2004).

In suitable habitat there may be several pairs in a tetrad. In mid-Berkshire, one farm of less than 18 hectares held five pairs in 1985. Using a conservative assumption of 1–3 pairs per occupied tetrad (those in which any of three categories of breeding were recorded), the Berkshire population would be 165–495 pairs.

Little Owls were introduced into various parts of Britain during the late 19th century and have since spread into most of England and Wales. In Berkshire, a pair were seen at the beginning of 1907 in Windsor Forest (Witherby and Ticehurst, 1908), and two adults with fledged young were seen near Windsor in the early summer of 1910 (Van de Weyer, 1911). Nationally, numbers peaked during the 1950s, then decreased markedly in south-east England after 1955, possibly due to pesticides (*1968–72 BTO Atlas*).

*Sponsored by Ruth Angus*

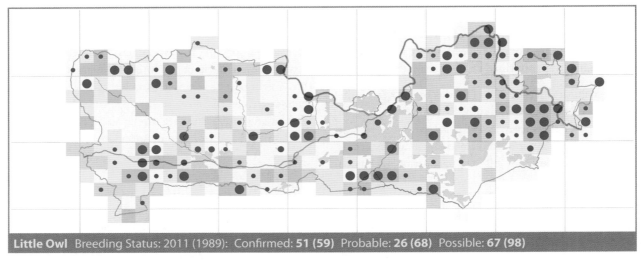

**Little Owl** Breeding Status: 2011 (1989): Confirmed: **51 (59)** Probable: **26 (68)** Possible: **67 (98)**

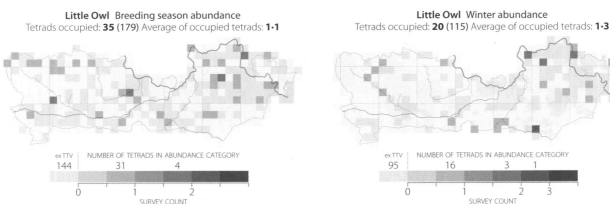

**Little Owl** Breeding season abundance
Tetrads occupied: **35 (179)** Average of occupied tetrads: **1·1**

| ex TTV | NUMBER OF TETRADS IN ABUNDANCE CATEGORY | |
|---|---|---|
| 144 | 31 | 4 |

0          1          2
SURVEY COUNT

**Little Owl** Winter abundance
Tetrads occupied: **20 (115)** Average of occupied tetrads: **1·3**

| ex TTV | NUMBER OF TETRADS IN ABUNDANCE CATEGORY | | |
|---|---|---|---|
| 95 | 16 | 3 | 1 |

0          1          2          3
SURVEY COUNT

# Tawny Owl

*Strix aluco*

*Widespread resident*

The Tawny Owl is a widespread resident in Berkshire, mainly in woodland habitats, but also in parks, gardens, churchyards and other areas containing mature trees. It prefers broadleaved and mixed woodland, but is also found in coniferous plantations. Tawny Owls are also found in urban areas which have mature trees and suitable habitat for hunting.

Tawny Owls are mainly nocturnal, but their distinctive hooting and "ke-wick" calls can be heard over long distances, making it easy to locate a breeding territory. Fledged owlets are very noisy at night, but make a variety of calls which may be unfamiliar to observers. Accurate surveying of Tawny Owls therefore requires several visits to likely areas after dark, especially early in the year. The relatively low rate of confirmed breeding in the atlas surveys is likely to be a reflection of the level of coverage at the optimum time of year to prove breeding.

The Tetrad Survey maps show a wide distribution over most of the county and indicate that Tawny Owls are the most widespread of Berkshire's owls. Tawny Owls remain territorial throughout the winter, which

is reflected in the maps for both recording seasons. The distribution reflects the Tawny Owl's preference for woodland habitat. There are few records from urban areas where the only suitable habitat is likely to be parks and large gardens. Predominantly arable areas generally have fewer records, though the 2007–11 survey recorded more occupied tetrads on the Downs, where quite small copses are used.

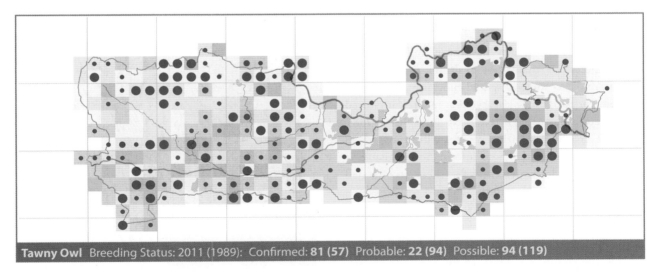

**Tawny Owl** Breeding Status: 2011 (1989): Confirmed: **81 (57)** Probable: **22 (94)** Possible: **94 (119)**

**Tawny Owl** Breeding season abundance
Tetrads occupied: **28 (232)** Average of occupied tetrads: **1·1**

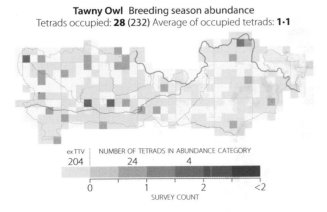

| ex TTV | NUMBER OF TETRADS IN ABUNDANCE CATEGORY | |
|---|---|---|
| 204 | 24 | 4 |

0    1    2    <2
SURVEY COUNT

**Tawny Owl** Winter abundance
Tetrads occupied: **21 (202)** Average of occupied tetrads: **1·1**

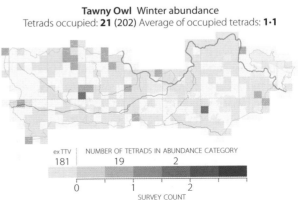

| ex TTV | NUMBER OF TETRADS IN ABUNDANCE CATEGORY | |
|---|---|---|
| 181 | 19 | 2 |

0    1    2
SURVEY COUNT

Tawny Owls were recorded in 69% of the tetrads in the 1987–89 Atlas survey and 55% in the 2007–11 survey. Over the same period the UK population, as measured by the CBC and BBS, has decreased approximately 30%, though a BTO national survey carried out in 2005 indicated little change from a previous survey in 1989 (Freeman *et al.*, 2007). The distribution of the Tawny Owl in Berkshire in the latest survey, on a 10 km square basis, is very similar to that recorded during the *1968–72* and *1988–91 BTO Atlases*.

As with Little and Barn Owls, the proportion of occupied tetrads in which breeding was confirmed in the 2007–11 survey (37%) was substantially higher than in 1987–89 (21%), reflecting perhaps a greater (although still inconsistent) nocturnal survey effort. In suitable woodland, quite high densities of Tawny Owls can be found, with winter tetrad population estimates, based on calling birds, of 10 or more in three tetrads. However, because of inconsistent nocturnal surveying, abundance shown in the tetrad atlas maps is likely to be a considerable underestimate.

All 24 Berkshire ringing recoveries have been within Berkshire or its adjoining counties, reflecting that this is highly sedentary species, rarely moving more than a few kilometres from its natal site (*Migration Atlas*).

Tawny Owls were persecuted during the 19th century, but the population increased in many areas of Britain during the first half of the 20th century and has since stabilised. Local declines are likely to occur due to habitat loss with the spread of urban areas or the felling of mature trees.

*Sponsored by Dick Haydon*

# Long-eared Owl

Green

## *Asio otus*

*Rare resident and occasional winter visitor*

The Long-eared Owl is a rare and localised resident in Berkshire, with numbers occasionally augmented by wintering birds from Europe. Most records have come from the Downs although there have been records from other parts of the county, chiefly in winter.

The Long-eared Owl may have been under-recorded during successive Atlas Surveys, since it is notoriously difficult to detect unless a special effort is made to carry out fieldwork early in the year and at night. Long-eared Owls were confirmed to have bred during the *1968–72 BTO Atlas* in two 10 km squares which now lie on the Oxfordshire border. The information available is insufficient to determine whether these records fall within the post–1974 county boundary of Berkshire, however. During the 1987–89 Atlas Survey, Long-eared Owls were recorded in just three tetrads, all being of possible breeding only. Breeding was confirmed just outside the county boundary in the 2007–11 survey, with the birds often hunting in Berkshire. Because of the sensitivity of this species, no breeding maps are shown.

Long-eared Owls have bred sporadically in Berkshire, mainly in isolated coniferous woods and copses in the downland areas in the north-west of the county, where breeding was proved in 1976, 1977, 1982, 1991 and 2001, with birds present in 1978 and 1980, although no more than a single pair appears to have been involved in each year. There were also probable breeding records in the north-east of the county, and a nest and three young were found in east Berkshire in July 1992.

There appears to have been an upturn in fortunes for this species in the county during the 21st century, both as a breeding and wintering species; in 2002 two pairs bred, and in 2005 three pairs with young were located. In addition, a pair breeding just over the county boundary was often seen entering Berkshire. A regular winter roost appears to have become established in the west of the county where up to four birds were located in 2004, six in January 2005, 13 in December 2005, up to 15 in January 2006, 12 in 2007 and 14 in 2008.

Since 1974, there have been winter records from mid- and east Berkshire in 1977, from 1979 to 1984, in 1987 and 1989, from 1991 to 1995, 2000, 2005/06 and 2009, presumably of migrant birds. In 1979 at least three birds were present and the 2005/06 record concerned a roost, initially, of three birds.

In Britain as a whole, there has been a substantial decline in the population of Long-eared Owls in the 20th century. It is thought that competition from Tawny Owls may have been partly responsible for this decline, since it coincided with an increase in the Tawny Owl population (*1968–72 BTO Atlas*). There is no clear evidence of conflict between the two species in Berkshire.

Prior to 1900, Clark Kennedy (1868) refers to the presence of Long-eared Owls in Windsor Forest and to breeding near Winkfield, and Noble (1906) mentions that a nest had been found in Windsor Forest. This indicates that they were more widely distributed in the 19th century than they are today.

*Sponsored by John Macphee*

# Short-eared Owl Amber

## *Asio flammeus*

*Scarce winter visitor and passage migrant, has bred.*

The Short-eared Owl is predominantly a winter visitor and passage migrant to Berkshire in small but fluctuating numbers. The areas where wintering birds can usually be found are the stretches of downland between Lambourn and Aldworth and in the Combe area, the quieter parts of the Kennet Valley, near Kintbury and some of the larger gravel workings. Since the mid-1970s, two potential wintering areas for the species in mid-Berkshire have been lost to development: the area around Reading Sewage Farm and at the former airfield at Woodley. It is a very rare breeder in the south of England on open plain and downland.

The Short-eared Owl is a highly mobile, nomadic species, and from late August to November a large but variable number of birds arrive in Britain from the continent (*1981–84 BTO Winter Atlas*). In Berkshire, it has been recorded in most years since 1931, and annually since 1969, although there were none in the winters of 1994/95, 1996/97 or 2000/01.

There are difficulties in determining the number of passage and wintering birds in Berkshire because of the fragmented nature of observer coverage on the Downs and the possibility of birds moving between sites. It is clear, however, that there is considerable variation in the numbers of Short-eared Owls considered to remain for the winter from year to year (Figure 117).

There have been three August records of Short-eared Owl, one seen at West Ilsley on 16th August 2008, one at Enborne on 26th August 1988 and two birds at West Ilsley on 28th August 1960. September arrivals, although unusual, have been recorded in half of the years since 1990. The main autumn passage is in October and November, when birds may be seen at many sites across the county. The favoured wintering sites since 1990 have been on the Downs, with few birds recorded elsewhere, even in the peak 2007/08 winter in which 22 birds were recorded on the Downs. By contrast, in the two good winters for Short-eared Owls in 1978/79 and 1988/89, there were more present in the river valleys than on the Downs. In the winter of 1978/79, although up to three birds arrived on the Downs in October, there was only one sighting of a single bird after 5th November. This contrasts with a total of at least seven birds

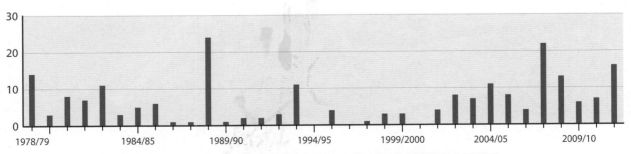

**Figure 117: Short-eared Owl: winter maxima from 1978/79–2011/12.**

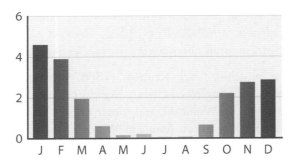

**Figure 118: Short-eared Owl: birds recorded by month of arrival.** Average 1992–2011.

wintering until February at Wraysbury Gravel Pits, Woodley Airfield and Reading Sewage Farm. In 1988/89, although at least three birds wintered on the Downs, there were up to eight birds from late November through December in the Kintbury area, and apparently a further eight on the North Standen Estate, Hungerford. One of the more unusual records for Short-eared Owl occurred during the invasion of the winter of 1988/89, when one roosted overnight in a garden at Wokingham, where it was seen and photographed on a rose trellis on the morning of 9th November 1988.

In 'good' years, several birds may congregate at sites where there is a ready supply of food. The largest number seen together was 14 at the Bury Down/Cow Down roost on 23rd January 2008, and a party of 14 had been seen on the Berkshire/Hampshire border near Combe early in 1939, although it is not clear whether all the birds were seen together in Berkshire.

Birds frequently stay on the wintering sites into March, though March records are usually a mixture of lingering wintering birds and those on return passage. In April passage birds predominate.

Between 1947 and 1999 there had been only five summer records of Short-eared Owl, in May, June and July. Since then there have been five records comprising six birds; apart from one at Eversley from 12th to 14th May 2006, all birds have been seen at locations on the Downs between 7th and 22nd May and on 24th July. Whether these relate to birds on passage or to summering or breeding birds is uncertain. Although Short-eared Owls have bred in a number of counties in south-east England, the nearest in north Hampshire (1988–91 BTO Breeding Atlas), they had not been proved to breed in Berkshire until 2010, when a recently fledged bird was observed with an adult at a site in the west of the county. In 1979, a young bird still showing some down was brought to a Tilehurst animal

Short-eared Owl, Berkshire Downs  *Dave Rimes www.lookatthebirds.co.uk*

refuge in July. Unfortunately, details were not taken of where this bird was found so it is not known whether it had come from Berkshire.

The only analysis of Short-eared Owl pellets recorded is from the Lowbury Hill area where six to seven birds wintered in 1956/57. Their pellets were found to contain a high proportion of bird remains, chiefly thrushes. A bird at Ham on 18th September 1952 was seen descending to attack Sand Martins going to roost.

Wintering Short-eared Owls were clearly common in Berkshire long before their presence was ever reported by ornithologists. At the end of the 18th century they were already common around Newbury, and in November 1795 one was kept alive for many weeks on mice and raw meat in a chicken coop (Lamb, 1880). Clark Kennedy (1868) comments that they were occasionally procured in Windsor Forest and in many other localities, and

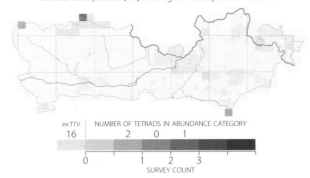

**Short-eared Owl** Winter abundance
Tetrads occupied: **3** (19) Average of occupied tetrads: **1·7**

| ex TTV | NUMBER OF TETRADS IN ABUNDANCE CATEGORY | | |
|---|---|---|---|
| 16 | 2 | 0 | 1 |

SURVEY COUNT 0 1 2 3

Noble (1906) refers to them as occurring in some numbers in winter, usually being seen about the end of October. The only count of birds is provided by Palmer (1886), eight at Welford in 1825.

*Sponsored by Samantha Timms*

# Tengmalm's Owl

## *Aegolius funereus*

*Rare vagrant, one record*

Although Tengmalm's Owl is widely distributed across north and central Europe and Asia, from the Pyrenees to eastern Siberia, it is a very rare vagrant to Britain. The only two records for Berkshire come from Clark Kennedy (1868). He refers to a female being "brought to a Mr Hasell, the bird-stuffer of Windsor" in the summer of 1864 to be preserved, having reportedly been shot in Windsor Forest by one of the gamekeepers. He then refers, without supporting details, to "another being killed a few years previously in the same park and also preserved". Clark Kennedy commented that Mr Hasell is "well acquainted with the species and the above statement may be depended upon".

*Sponsored by Terrence Hemmett*

# Nightjar

## *Caprimulgus europaeus*

*Uncommon summer visitor*

The Nightjar is a localised summer visitor to Berkshire. The species' preferred habitat is dry, well-drained and open areas such as heathland and woodland clearings. Its numbers decreased between the end of the 19th century and the late 1980s, especially between the early 1960s and the early 1980s. The cause of the decline is unclear, but habitat loss and disturbance have been put forward as possible reasons. Since the 1980s, national surveys have shown a welcome, almost two-fold, increase in the population.

The heathland areas favoured by Nightjars in Berkshire usually border areas of mature woodland and typically have scattered trees such as pine *Pinus* spp. and birch *Betula* spp. If left unchecked, this habitat will eventually become dense woodland which is unsuitable for breeding Nightjars. This has already occurred in a few areas, particularly in the south-west of the county, but where the growth is regularly thinned the species can persist, such as at Snelsmore Common which is managed to provide open spaces and provides ideal habitat for Nightjars. The national trend for Nightjars to occupy new forestry plantations, perhaps as a response to the loss of heathland, is apparent in Berkshire, with birds being found in central southern and south-eastern Berkshire, where coniferous plantations have been established on areas which were formerly heathland, and where the clear-felling and replanting cycle provides a supply of suitable habitat.

Nightjars are amongst the latest of the summer visitors to arrive in Britain and one of the earliest to depart. The first birds usually arrive in Berkshire around the second week in May, although there is an exceptionally early record from Windsor Great Park of one being seen on 4th April 1966. Most birds have usually departed by the end of August, with occasional records well into September. The one overseas recovery of a Nightjar ringed in Berkshire is noteworthy in that it involved a bird ringed as a juvenile at Snelsmore Common in July 1934 being recovered at Valencia, Spain, in December 1935. Local ringing studies have shown that Nightjars are extremely faithful to their breeding sites, with birds not only returning to the same territories year after year, but also often nesting on, or very close to, the spot where they bred the previous year.

The first attempt at determining the population of Nightjars in the county was made in 1934 (Walford, 1934), and found the highest breeding density to be along the Bagshot Beds from east Berkshire to near Newbury. There were fewer birds around Newbury and Bradfield, but an estimated 33 singing males were counted in an area of about eight square miles around Windsor Forest and Bracknell. At this time, birds were also breeding on the Downs and between Wargrave and Maidenhead, areas that are no longer occupied.

Nightjar, south Berkshire *Tim Ball, Reading and Basingstoke Ringing*

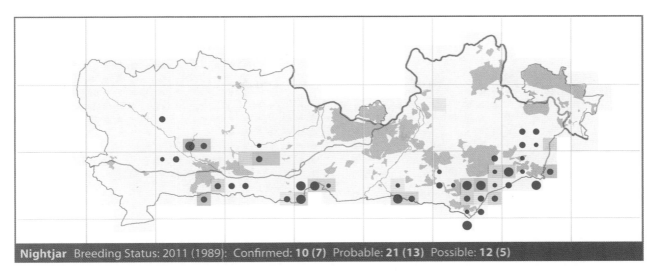

**Nightjar** Breeding Status: 2011 (1989): Confirmed: **10 (7)** Probable: **21 (13)** Possible: **12 (5)**

Although there have been many studies of Berkshire's Nightjars in recent years, it is difficult to make direct comparisons between them due to differences in methodology, the period during which surveys were conducted and the intensity of observer coverage. The BTO survey of 1981 produced 35 singing males in Berkshire at 14 different sites. A repeat of the survey in 1992 located 48 singing males. The latest BTO survey, in 2004, found a total of 73 singing males at 15 sites, including 33 in the Swinley Forest area. The two-fold increase in numbers of singing birds in Berkshire since 1981 is consistent with the national trend observed in the surveys. Despite this, the distribution of Nightjars, as shown in the tetrad maps, has changed little between the Atlas surveys of 1987–89 and 2007–11.

Accounts of the species prior to 1900 lack precise information on the extent to which Nightjars were present in Berkshire, although Lamb (1880) describes it as very frequent about Reading and Newbury in 1814.

**Nightjar** Breeding season abundance
Tetrads occupied: **0** (44) Average of occupied tetrads: **0**

| ex TTV | NUMBER OF TETRADS IN ABUNDANCE CATEGORY |
|---|---|
| 44 | no birds recorded during TTVs |

SURVEY COUNT

The welcome recovery of the Nightjar in Berkshire probably owes much to measures that have been taken to protect heathland, and to the transient suitable habitat created by coniferous forestry. Many of the areas of suitable habitat are though vulnerable to human disturbance.

*Sponsored by Rebecca Couzens*

# Swift

*Apus apus*

*Common summer visitor*

The Swift is a widespread summer visitor to Berkshire but, as there are no known natural nest sites in the county, the entire breeding population utilises man-made structures. A range of buildings are used, including church towers, old houses, and old farm buildings such as wooden barns with cavities under the roof. Swifts will utilise almost any structure which provides cavities and has sufficient elevation and a good flight path directly to the nest entrance, although many modern buildings provide few suitable nest sites. The Swift is a colonial breeder and the largest recorded colony was at West Mills, Newbury which reached a peak of 350 birds in July 1984.

The Tetrad Surveys show that the Swift is widely distributed throughout Berkshire, with confirmed breeding corresponding fairly well with the distribution of towns and villages. Obtaining confirmation of

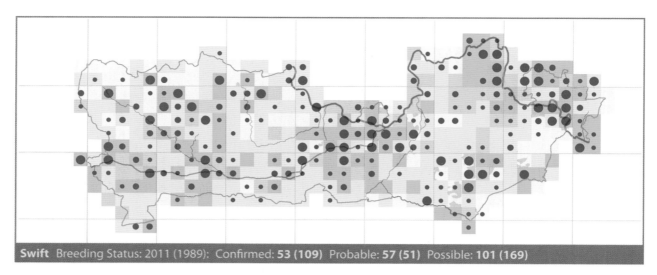

**Swift** Breeding Status: 2011 (1989): Confirmed: **53 (109)** Probable: **57 (51)** Possible: **101 (169)**

breeding mostly depended upon observing the adult birds entering or leaving their nest holes, which is much easier to see than observing eggs or young. In both surveys, a rather large proportion (approx. 50%) of the records were of possible breeding and were based chiefly on the repeated observation of Swifts during the breeding season in what appeared to be suitable habitat. Since Swifts readily travel many miles to feed, breeding is unlikely to be as widespread as the Tetrad Survey map indicates, and possible and probable breeding records should be treated with caution. The tetrad surveys show a substantial decline in the number of tetrads where breeding was confirmed, from 28% of tetrads in the 1987–89, to 13% in the 2007–11 survey. Over the same period national BBS data show a decrease in abundance of around one third, and in 2009, the Swift was added to the Amber List of Species of Conservation Concern (Eaton *et al.*, 2009).

It is likely that the regeneration of urban areas, involving the replacement or renovation of old buildings which once provided nesting sites, has had an adverse effect on numbers. Changes in the wider environment, such as the extensive use of insecticides and changes in agricultural practice, have reduced the insect population which provides the Swifts' sole food source. In recent years, mitigation measures have been developed whereby new artificial nesting cavities for Swifts can be installed in new buildings to compensate for the loss of older breeding sites.

Between 2001 and 2011 the first arrival dates of the Swift in Berkshire have varied from 31st March to 20th April (median 15th April), significantly ($p < 0.05$) earlier than during the decade from 1975 to 1984, when the arrival dates were between 20th April and 6th May (median 24th April). At the end of summer the latest departing birds have been recorded between 31st August and 14th October. The vast majority of local birds have left by mid-August, and it is likely that later records relate

**Swift** Breeding season abundance
Tetrads occupied: **232 (335)** Average of occupied tetrads: **10·7**

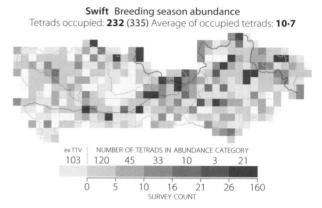

| ex TTV | NUMBER OF TETRADS IN ABUNDANCE CATEGORY | | | | | |
|---|---|---|---|---|---|---|
| 103 | 120 | 45 | 33 | 10 | 3 | 21 |

| 0 | 5 | 10 | 16 | 21 | 26 | 160 |
|---|---|---|---|---|---|---|
SURVEY COUNT

to birds on passage from further north. Large passage movements are recorded regularly in Berkshire in spring and autumn. The largest count in spring since 1974 was made at Wraysbury Gravel Pits on 10th May 1983, when a minimum of 5,000 birds moved through in two hours. Spring passage counts of 1,000–1,500 were reported most years in the Wraysbury area in the 1980s and 1990s. In the autumn, large numbers of returning birds are less frequently recorded, but at least 4,000 were observed in the Smallmead Farm and Burghfield Gravel Pits area on 11th July 1993. In more recent years, the highest count was of 2,000 over Queen Mother Reservoir in a thunderstorm on 7th July 2008. Counts of 500–1,000 have been recorded most years on spring passage in May over the gravel pits to the west of Reading.

The latest record of Swift for Berkshire was one at Maidenhead on 9th November 1988, evidently a juvenile which failed to depart on migration and remained through October. Apart from this record, the latest migrating bird since 1974 appears to have been one over Finchampstead Ridges on 27th October 1990.

Evidence of the longevity of the Swift is provided by the recovery of one in Kent on 8th May 1932 which had been ringed as an adult at Theale in May 1922, making it at least 11 years old. Coincidentally, a bird ringed on the same day at Theale in May 1922 was recovered eight years later at the same site when it was killed, remarkably, in an aerial collision with another Swift.

We have no historic quantitative data on Swift populations, but Clark Kennedy (1868) commented on the decline of the Swift in Berkshire and Oxfordshire in the 19th century; noting that "The Swift is numerous in the vicinity of Windsor, but has sadly decreased in numbers in many places throughout the two counties where it used to be common. A few pairs remain to breed every year…"

*Sponsored by Thames Valley Environmental Records Centre*

---

# Alpine Swift

## *Apus melba*

*Rare vagrant, six records*

The Alpine Swift is an annual vagrant to Britain, which has reached Berkshire on just five occasions. The Berkshire records have been in Spring and early summer. One was seen over the lake at Silwood on 7th June 1955. Another was seen frequently over Wraysbury Gravel Pits from 9th May to at least 25th May 1983. Berkshire shared in the national influx of this species in 2006 with a bird at Maidenhead and Summerleaze Gravel Pits (15–18th April), and another seen briefly at Greenham Common on 23rd April. In 2010, one was seen in the Wargrave area on 20th March.

*Sponsored by Brian Clews*

---

# Kingfisher  Amber  Sch. 1

## *Alcedo atthis*

*Uncommon resident*

The Kingfisher is an uncommon but regularly encountered resident in suitable habitats in Berkshire. Its numbers can decline dramatically after severe winter weather but recover well after one or two mild winters.

The Kingfisher is confined to still or slow-moving water, from which it can catch its staple diet of small fish and, not unexpectedly, both Tetrad Surveys showed its distribution in Berkshire to match closely the distribution of such habitat. There are some differences between the results of the 1987–89 and 2007–11 surveys. In the former the main concentration of confirmed breeding records came from the Kennet Valley downstream as far as Woolhampton, and there was a second, but rather more fragmented, concentration of confirmed and probable breeding records along the Thames from Winter Hill to Wraysbury Gravel Pits. In the latter there were more along the Thames. This indicates, perhaps, the level of coverage in each survey, the western part of the Kennet being particularly well covered in 1987–89, whereas coverage in parts of central Berkshire was better in 2007–11. Overall there was an increase in the number of tetrads in which breeding was proved, but fewer with possible or probable breeding recorded. Kingfishers are a difficult species to prove breeding, one of the principal difficulties arising from the fact that the nesting tunnel can sometimes be 250 metres or more away from the water used for fishing (*BWP IV*). Noble (1906) records one "in a wood quite a mile from water".

At a local level, the River Pang only produced one confirmed and one probable breeding record in both surveys, neither of which related to the Stanford Dingley or Tidmarsh areas where the species was once resident. This may be due to the fact that the river was in the process of drying-up during both surveys. Nationally, the Waterways Bird Survey and Waterways Breeding Bird Surveys indicated a slight increase between 1989 and 2009.

A survey was undertaken by BOC and NDOC in 2005. It was carried out on a 1 km square basis, and disclosed a breeding population of between 78 and 84 pairs (Robinson, 2009). Earlier surveys included one of breeding Kingfishers along the Thames undertaken in 1934 and 1935 which revealed a density of about one pair every 3·2 km. Three pairs were counted between Whitchurch and Mapledurham in 1974 (one pair every 1·4 km) and five pairs were counted between Remenham and Medmenham in 1979 (one pair every 1·1 km).

Along the River Loddon, five pairs were located between Charvil and Arborfield in 1981 (one pair every 2·1 km).

The winter distribution of Kingfishers in Berkshire is similar to that during the breeding season, except that additional localities are occupied. Some of these localities, such as suburban lakes, lack suitable banks for nesting, but are otherwise acceptable, while others are occupied simply as a consequence of the increased population after the breeding season. Support for this comes from an analysis of the monthly counts made in the east of the county during 1989, and the 2005 survey which showed that more sites were occupied by more birds during September to March than during the early summer months. This may though reflect the fact that birds are less conspicuous while young are in the nest. The 2007–11 Winter Map broadly reflects the distribution shown by the summer abundance map, although there is an indication that the species is less numerous along the Kennet Valley than along the Thames and its tributaries in the area around Reading at this time of year. A winter count carried out between Fobney Lock, Reading and Moatlands Gravel Pit, Theale, revealed 13 birds in 1980.

The Kingfisher is particularly vulnerable to frozen wintry conditions. It was nearly exterminated in Berkshire by the extensive freeze-up during 1962/63, yet by 1966 had made a full recovery in the Reading area. The county

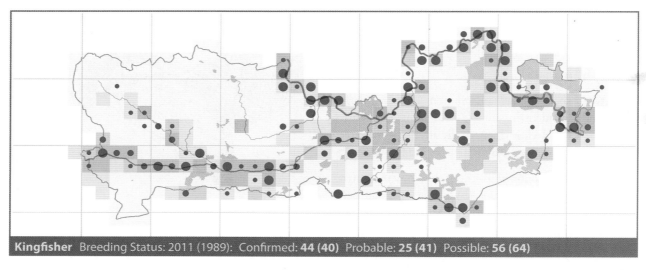

**Kingfisher** Breeding Status: 2011 (1989): Confirmed: **44** (40) Probable: **25** (41) Possible: **56** (64)

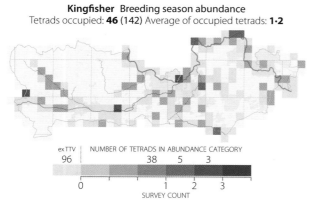

**Kingfisher** Breeding season abundance
Tetrads occupied: **46** (142) Average of occupied tetrads: **1·2**

| exTTV | NUMBER OF TETRADS IN ABUNDANCE CATEGORY | | |
|---|---|---|---|
| 96 | 38 | 5 | 3 |

0        1        2        3
SURVEY COUNT

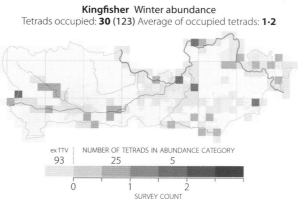

**Kingfisher** Winter abundance
Tetrads occupied: **30** (123) Average of occupied tetrads: **1·2**

| exTTV | NUMBER OF TETRADS IN ABUNDANCE CATEGORY | |
|---|---|---|
| 93 | 25 | 5 |

0        1        2
SURVEY COUNT

reports suggest, albeit sketchily, that numbers were not affected much by the cold winter of 1978/79, but that a decline may have followed that of 1981/82.

Ringing recoveries have shown that Kingfishers seldom travel more than 10 km, unless forced to do so by severe weather. Two notable recoveries are one ringed at Theale Gravel Pits on 18th August 1989 being recovered at Sennybridge, Powys on 8th September 1989, and one ringed as a nestling in Wokingham on 7th July 1927 being recovered at Dagenham on 1st August 1928.

*Sponsored by Ken and Sarah White*

# Roller

## *Coracias garrulus*

*Rare vagrant, one record*

A Roller shot at Eton on 28th May 1927 constitutes the only Berkshire record of this rare vagrant to Britain, whose usual summer breeding range in Europe extends no closer to Britain than southern France.

*Sponsored by Hazel Clews*

# Hoopoe Sch. 1

## *Upupa epops*

*Scarce passage migrant*

The Hoopoe is a scarce visitor to Berkshire, for which the average number of records has remained fairly consistent at between one and two per year since 1946, although they have declined since the mid-2000s. The considerable increase in the number of observers over this period has not led to an increase in the number of sightings, probably in part due to the Hoopoe's preference for the lawns of private gardens which are not usually visited regularly by birdwatchers. Its striking appearance makes it possible to accept many of these garden records even when the bird has not been seen by an experienced observer.

In the forty years from 1906, there were only four reports of Hoopoe in Berkshire, one in Hungerford Park in April 1924, one in a Brimpton garden in late May 1926, one shot by a keeper "in mistake for a Jay" on the county boundary near Newbury in July 1936, and one at Bearwood in May 1944. Since 1948, Hoopoes have been more frequent. They only went unrecorded in

seven of the 47 years from 1948 to 1994, but there has been some decline since (Figure 119), with no records in eight of the 18 years from 1995 to 2012, the last being one seen on a byway near Oare on 6 April 2008. There was a secondhand report of one at Combe on 27th March 2012 from a shepherd.

The predominance of April and May records (Figure 120) fits the pattern for southern England (*1968–72 BTO Atlas*) and was particularly marked in the period from 1976 to 1985, when all sixteen records fell in the period from 13th April to 30th May. The first of only three March arrivals was on about 20th March 1948 at Caversham, the bird staying for a few days, with a gap of 42 years until 25th March 1990 when one was recorded at Crowthorne. One was reported in a Reading garden on 29th March 2005, and almost certainly the same bird was observed over a period of three days from 29th to 31st March 2005 in the gardens of the former Courage Brewery site at Worton Grange, less than a mile away.

Although there have been nine records in June and July since 1946, none of the birds were seen in circumstances which indicate summering. The five June records are spread throughout the month and include three from gardens or parks. Whilst most birds seen in April and May rarely stay for more than a day, this is not the case for later records. Of the four July records, one was seen over two weeks in the Walbury Hill area in July 1949, and one was present for over a week in the Bucklebury to Stanford Dingley area in 1967. Two of the August arrivals occurred at Woodley, in 1957 and 1962, while the third involved a tail-less bird present at Twyford Gravel Pits in 2000 from 24th August to 9th September; it had re-grown its tail and been seen by an estimated 1,000 observers during its 17 day stay, much of which was spent feeding in an area of well grazed grassland adjacent to a gravel pit. The latest of just four September records was from the 23rd to the 26th in 1957 at Theale Gravel Pits. The only October records are of one at Sandhurst on the 21st in 1992, one at Whiteknights Park, Reading on the 13th or 14th in 1993, one in 2002 at Lower Earley on 23 and 24th, and one at Englefield on the 3rd in 2006.

Winter reports are of one at Cookham from 4th to 9th December 1961 and one in a derelict garden at Maidenhead from 21st to 28th November 1990. For the first time, a Hoopoe wintered in Berkshire in 1995/96

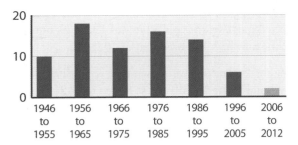

**Figure 119: Hoopoe: all birds recorded 1946–2012.** 78 birds have been recorded since 1946.

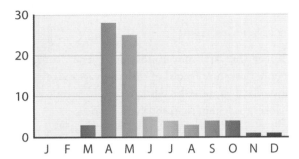

**Figure 120: Hoopoe: all birds recorded 1946–2012, by month of arrival.**

when there was one at Eversley Gravel Pits from 28th September to 18th October and again from mid-December to 25th February 1996. One at Arborfield from 6th November to about 8th December 1995 was presumably the same bird. This was a remarkable stay so far north of usual wintering grounds and the longest ever for Berkshire.

The maximum number of birds seen in any one year has been four in 1980 and again in 1992. The only records of two birds together were at Upper Basildon in the last two weeks of May 1959 and at Streatley for about a week from 14th April 1980.

Berkshire has apparently always enjoyed a scattering of records of this eye-catching species. Lamb (1880) reports that one was caught near Reading in the spring of 1790 which was kept alive, chiefly on meal worms, at a bakers in the town. Clark Kennedy (1868) and Noble (1906) record some ten or 11 occurrences during the 19th century. Their reports are mostly of birds killed and come from all parts of the county, including from Newbury in April 1866, East Ilsley in August 1877, Wellington College in June 1864 and Cookham in the 1860s. One caught at Eton about 1861–62 was kept alive for two years and became quite tame and would "come to the call of its master" (Clark Kennedy, 1868).

*Sponsored by Courage Brewery*

328

# Wryneck

**Red** **Sch. 1**

*Jynx torquilla*

*Scarce passage migrant, former common summer visitor*

The Wryneck is now only a scarce passage migrant in Berkshire, although it was formerly a common summer visitor. Since breeding ceased in 1956, most records have been in the migration periods (Figure 121), with only one June record since 1966.

Wrynecks have been recorded in Berkshire in August or September in 28 of the 46 years from 1967 to 2012. Apart from one on 10th August 1984 and one on 4th October 1976, all autumn records have been between 19th August and 28th September. The single July record in this period was of one seen at Hungerford at the end of the month in 1987. It is possible that the majority of these passage migrants are of Scandinavian origin as a bird ringed as a nestling in Norway has been recovered in Reading (Brucker *et al.*, 1992).

There has been a scattering of spring records, with one in April and eight in May between 1980 and 2012. A singing male at Wishmoor Bottom on 26th May 2001 remained until 3rd June, which was the first instance of a bird holding territory within the county since 1956. It was probably the only territorial male recorded in England that year as no records appeared in the British Birds, Rare Breeding Birds report for 2001.

The earliest reported arrival is on 28th February 1919, but as this comes only from a report in *The Field* of that year it needs to be treated with some caution. The earliest date otherwise was a bird seen at Pinkneys Green, Maidenhead on 24th March 1956. The latest departure date is of one seen in Windsor Great Park from 15th to 25th October 1956. The highest number of records in any year since 1957 is five, in the autumn of 1976.

Records have become scarcer in recent years (Figure 122), with birds recorded in only three years between 2004 and 2012. One was seen at Queen Mother Reservoir on 28th August 2008, one at Brimpton on 31st August 2010, and in 2012 there was one at Riseley on 19th May and one at Lavell's Lake, Dinton Pastures on 29th August. One was seen and photographed at Greenham Common on 23rd September 2013.

At the end of the 18th century, Wrynecks were reported by Lamb (1880) as common about Reading, although rare around Newbury, and by Noble (1906) as fairly common as a spring migrant at the start of the 20th century. County reports from 1915 to 1954 contain numerous reports of breeding from several parts of the county, but apart from those from Inkpen in 1935 and Bucklebury Common from 1945 to 1949, most records are either from the Reading area, particularly in the early 1950s, or the general area of Maidenhead and Cookham, where there were eight to ten pairs in 1945. There was evidence of birds returning to the same area in subsequent years, as one ringed as a juvenile at Eton in June 1926 was reported from Maidenhead in June 1928.

When the status of the Wryneck was reviewed in the 1931 county report for Oxfordshire, Berkshire and Buckinghamshire, it appeared that the species was then regular or fairly frequent only in south-east Oxfordshire, south Buckinghamshire and north-east Berkshire. There were also signs of diminishing numbers in the Reading area where Wrynecks had been comparatively common from 1915 to 1920. The 1945 county report systematic list includes an account by E. Giles on the status of the Wryneck in north-east Berkshire and south Buckinghamshire from 1930 to 1945, an area which he estimated had held about 30 pairs in most years. He attributed this density to the presence of many old orchards in what had once been a fruit-growing area until it became more profitable to sell the land for property development. Nearly all nest sites were in orchards larger than a quarter of an acre.

A number of reasons for the decline of the Wryneck in Britain have been suggested (*1988–91 BTO Atlas*). At the local level, loss of habitat resulting from the destruction of old orchards was one factor, but the occupation of remaining suitable nest holes by Great Tits and Starlings appears to have been another. Up to 1945, Wrynecks in the Cookham Dean area were being helped to breed by three local ornithologists who actively encouraged breeding in their gardens by preventing Wrynecks from being evicted from their nesting sites by Great Tits. The departure of those three ornithologists and some further loss of old orchards to development appear to have played a significant part in the final extinction of this small local population. There were still seven summering records from the Maidenhead area in

1950, but only two by 1954 and one in 1955, followed by an isolated record of a pair breeding in east Berkshire in 1956, the last occasion on which this occurred in the county.

In west Berkshire although there had been two breeding pairs in the Bucklebury area in 1945, these had disappeared by 1950, and the last record from the area is of one in summer 1954. A similar rapid final decline was noted in the Reading area where from 1951 to 1953. Wrynecks bred in nest boxes in Caversham, with three in use in 1953. A further pair bred in Reading itself in 1952 and breeding was reported in Tilehurst in 1954 and 1955. A check of potential breeding locations in the Reading area in 1954 produced just two breeding sites and nine further areas where birds were calling. Two years later, in 1956, there were no records at all for the Reading area. In Berkshire as a whole, the number of summering birds or breeding pairs declined from 15 in 1954, to five in 1955, to one in 1956, with none at all in 1957.

*Sponsored by Richard Harwood*

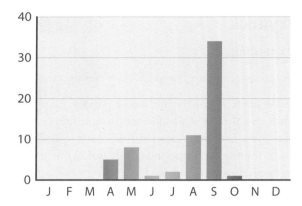

**Figure 121: Wryneck: all birds recorded 1957–2012, by month of arrival.**

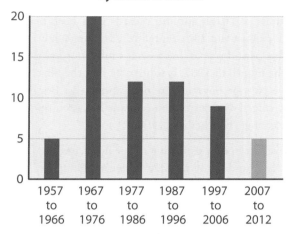

**Figure 122: Wryneck: all birds recorded 1957–2012.**
62 birds have been recorded since 1957.

# Green Woodpecker

Amber

*Picus viridis*

*Common resident*

The Green Woodpecker is a common resident in Berkshire, found in open mature woodland, parkland, heathland, farmland and gardens with plenty of mature broadleaved trees. It prefers more open habitat than the other woodpeckers since it often feeds on the ground and, as a consequence, its numbers can be affected by severe winters.

It is widely distributed throughout the county, being found in most areas other than the more open downland and some urban areas. The 2007–11 Atlas Survey showed it present in 89% of all tetrads during the summer and 86% during the winter, a small increase on the 1987–89 survey in which 77% of tetrads were occupied, perhaps reflecting the twofold increase in abundance recorded nationally over the period by the CBC and BBS.

Given that the Green Woodpecker feeds in more open habitats, it might be expected that it would be

more widespread in such areas than the Great Spotted Woodpecker, but this does not seem to be the case (the Great Spotted Woodpecker was present in 98% of tetrads during the summer and 93% in the winter). For such a large and often noisy bird, it is surprisingly difficult to confirm breeding, which probably explains why it was confirmed as breeding in only 40% of tetrads in the county in the 2007–11 Atlas Survey and 33% in 1987–89. In contrast, the Great Spotted Woodpecker, was confirmed as breeding in 70% of the tetrads in the county.

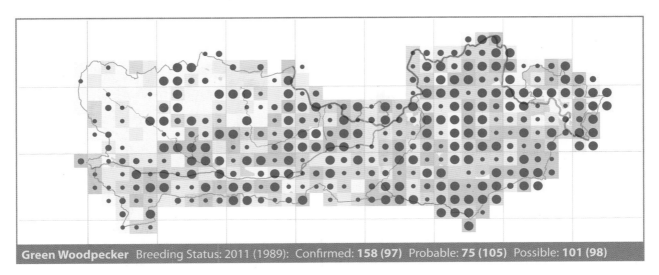

**Green Woodpecker** Breeding Status: 2011 (1989): Confirmed: **158 (97)** Probable: **75 (105)** Possible: **101 (98)**

**Green Woodpecker** Breeding season abundance
Tetrads occupied: **294 (352)** Average of occupied tetrads: **2·5**

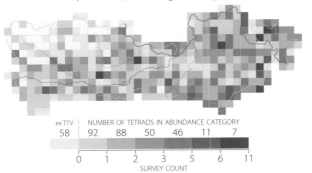

| exTTV | NUMBER OF TETRADS IN ABUNDANCE CATEGORY | | | | | |
|---|---|---|---|---|---|---|
| 58 | 92 | 88 | 50 | 46 | 11 | 7 |

0  1  2  3  5  6  11
SURVEY COUNT

**Green Woodpecker** Winter abundance
Tetrads occupied: **269 (338)** Average of occupied tetrads: **2·1**

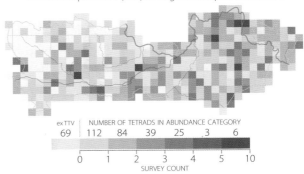

| exTTV | NUMBER OF TETRADS IN ABUNDANCE CATEGORY | | | | | |
|---|---|---|---|---|---|---|
| 69 | 112 | 84 | 39 | 25 | 3 | 6 |

0  1  2  3  4  5  10
SURVEY COUNT

The Green Woodpecker is a rather sedentary species, although immature birds may disperse locally into more open grassland after the breeding season. This is borne out by the abundance maps, which show similar distributions in the winter and the breeding season. Although the population is known to be reduced during hard winters, recovering in subsequent years, there is insufficient information from local records to confirm that his has been the case in Berkshire.

Prior to 1900, both Clark Kennedy (1868) and Noble (1906) described the Green Woodpecker as the commonest woodpecker in Berkshire.

*Sponsored by Charlotte Pollecutt-Gray*

Green Woodpecker, Bracknell *David Lowther*

# Great Spotted Woodpecker   Green

*Dendrocopos major*

*Common resident*

The Great Spotted Woodpecker is a common resident in Berkshire, found in all wooded areas, although preferring mixed woodland. It also occurs in hedgerows, parks and gardens, and is a regular visitor to bird tables throughout the year, with reported numbers peaking in early summer when juvenile birds are taught to use peanut feeders by their parents.

The 2007–11 Atlas Survey shows a wide distribution of the Great Spotted Woodpecker across the county, with only a few downland areas in the north-west of the county having no records. It is the most widespread of the three woodpeckers in Berkshire, with evidence of breeding in 95% of all tetrads and breeding confirmed in 70%, compared with 90% and 47% respectively in the 1987–89 Atlas Survey. This small increase in distribution does not reflect the substantial increase in abundance recorded nationally (a rise of 139% in the UK population between 1995 and 2010 recorded by the BBS) and in the Berkshire Bird Index (87% increase between 1994 and 2008).

The Great Spotted Woodpecker is highly vocal, so it is unlikely to have been overlooked in many tetrads during surveys, and it is the easiest of the woodpeckers to confirm breeding, since it often nests around three to five metres from the ground and the young tend to be noisy.

The abundance maps show the Great Spotted Woodpecker's preference for woodland habitat, especially broadleaved and mixed woodland, which is widespread in Berkshire. There is a slight bias towards the southern and eastern parts of the county, where there are more woodlands, with relatively fewer records from the downland and grassland areas in the west of the county, and urban and other areas which have little woodland. Even though Great Spotted Woodpeckers often nest in quite small woods, they appear to require a reasonable area of trees nearby in which to search for food. The species is fairly sedentary as indicated by the similarity of the summer and winter abundance maps.

Outside the breeding season, Great Spotted Woodpeckers tend to remain in the same areas, although they do sometimes wander, as indicated by the number of birds which have been caught in mist-nets in reedbed and willow scrub habitat at Thatcham and Brimpton Gravel Pits after the breeding season. Ringing recoveries have all been local, 18 within Berkshire and five involving neighbouring counties. However, in 'irruption' years

birds from northern European populations appear on the east coast in autumn and it is possible that a few of these may reach Berkshire.

The Great Spotted Woodpecker appears to have been much less common in Berkshire during the 19th century than it is today. Clark Kennedy (1868) describes it as not very numerous and notes that the occurrence of one in a small garden in central Reading for several successive Sundays in the early 1860s prompted a letter to *The Zoologist*. Palmer (1886) describes it as rather rare.

*Sponsored by Dick Haydon*

Great Spotted Woodpecker, Lavell's Lake  *Marek Walford*

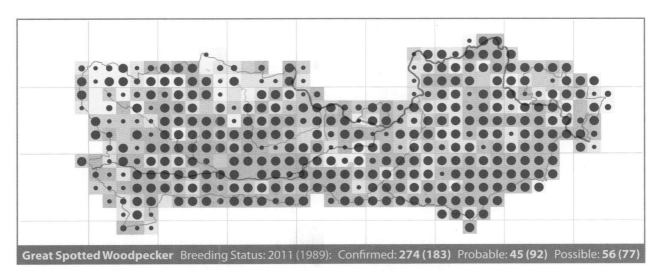

**Great Spotted Woodpecker** Breeding Status: 2011 (1989): Confirmed: **274 (183)** Probable: **45 (92)** Possible: **56 (77)**

**Great Spotted Woodpecker** Breeding season abundance
Tetrads occupied: **336 (385)** Average of occupied tetrads: **3·2**

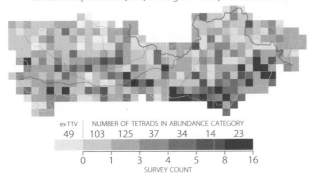

| exTTV | NUMBER OF TETRADS IN ABUNDANCE CATEGORY | | | | | |
|---|---|---|---|---|---|---|
| 49 | 103 | 125 | 37 | 34 | 14 | 23 |

0  1  3  4  5  8  16
SURVEY COUNT

**Great Spotted Woodpecker** Winter abundance
Tetrads occupied: **322 (368)** Average of occupied tetrads: **3·0**

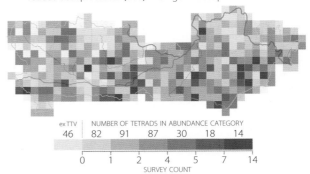

| exTTV | NUMBER OF TETRADS IN ABUNDANCE CATEGORY | | | | | |
|---|---|---|---|---|---|---|
| 46 | 82 | 91 | 87 | 30 | 18 | 14 |

0  1  2  4  5  7  14
SURVEY COUNT

# Lesser Spotted Woodpecker  `Red`

## *Dendrocopos minor*

*Uncommon resident*

The Lesser Spotted Woodpecker is resident in Berkshire, but is uncommon and is now very thinly spread across the county. It prefers open broadleaved woodland, especially damp woodlands of oak *Quercus* spp., hornbeam *Carpinus betulus*, willow *Salix* spp., alder *Alnus glutinosa* and poplar *Populus* spp. It also occurs in scattered trees, such as those found in hedgerows, parkland, old orchards and along river banks, but tends to avoid conifers. It often occurs in similar woodland habitat to Great Spotted Woodpecker, but it is a shy bird and may easily be overlooked.

Lesser Spotted Woodpeckers have declined markedly in Berkshire in recent years, as they have across the UK. In the 2007–11 Atlas Survey, breeding evidence was recorded 36 tetrads (9%), compared with 116 (30%) in the 1987–89 survey. Almost all the tetrads in which Lesser Spotted Woodpeckers were recorded contained broadleaved or mixed woodland, and there is a concentration of records in the Windsor Great Park

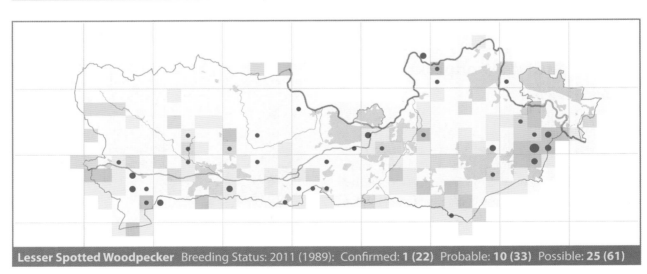

**Lesser Spotted Woodpecker** Breeding Status: 2011 (1989): Confirmed: **1 (22)** Probable: **10 (33)** Possible: **25 (61)**

**Lesser Spotted Woodpecker** Breeding season abundance
Tetrads occupied: **5 (46)** Average of occupied tetrads: **1·4**

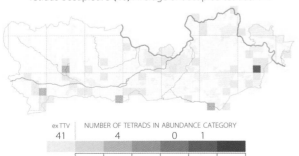

| ex TTV | NUMBER OF TETRADS IN ABUNDANCE CATEGORY | | |
|--------|-----|---|---|
| 41 | 4 | 0 | 1 |

0       1       2       3
SURVEY COUNT

**Lesser Spotted Woodpecker** Winter abundance
Tetrads occupied: **8 (51)** Average of occupied tetrads: **1·0**

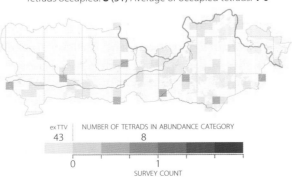

| ex TTV | NUMBER OF TETRADS IN ABUNDANCE CATEGORY |
|--------|-----|
| 43 | 8 |

0       1
SURVEY COUNT

area, which has an abundance of mature, open woodland and parkland. Similarly, there is a bias towards the south-east and south-west of the county, with a notable absence from the north-west, but generally corresponding to the availability of suitable habitat.

Since the species is resident and fairly sedentary it might be expected that most of the probable and possible breeding records related to breeding birds. However, it was confirmed as breeding in only one out of 46 tetrads in which it was recorded during the breeding season in the 2007–11 survey. It is unclear why the confirmation rate has declined. It may reflect the difficulty of detecting breeding evidence of a bird that usually nests around two to eight metres from the ground, higher than other woodpeckers; however, by comparison it was confirmed as breeding in 22 tetrads in 1987–89.

CBC and BBS data show the Lesser Spotted Woodpecker to have been in steep decline nationally since 1980. The reasons for its decline are not clear, but competition with and predation by Great Spotted Woodpeckers (whose population is increasing), and reductions in small-diameter dead wood suitable for foraging, are likely causes, while large-scale changes in woodland (such as loss of mature broadleaved woodland, losses of non-woodland trees such as elms, and woodland fragmentation) may also be important. There is no reason to believe that the decline of this species has been reversed in recent years.

Outside the breeding season Lesser Spotted Woodpeckers tend to remain in the same areas, as indicated by the abundance maps. They can be quite mobile, sometimes associating with foraging flocks of tits. The dispersal after breeding sometimes takes them into non-arboreal habitat and, in the past, juvenile birds have been caught in mist-nets in reedbed and willow scrub habitat at Brimpton Gravel Pits in late summer and autumn. In recent years however, ringing records of Lesser Spotted Woodpecker have all but disappeared, with only one record in Berkshire since 2006.

*Sponsored by Berks, Bucks and Oxford Wildlife Trust*

# Golden Oriole Sch. 1

## *Oriolus oriolus*

### *Rare passage migrant*

The Golden Oriole is a rare passage migrant in Berkshire. Its strictly arboreal nature makes it difficult to observe, however, and perhaps influences the frequency with which it is recorded. The earliest authenticated 20th century record was of a bird found dead beside a greenhouse in late May or early June 1937, apparently near Newbury, which was sent to *The Field* for identification on 11th June. Although there are three earlier records, these are less well substantiated and appear doubtful. They involved one seen in Englefield Park by the son of the person submitting the record on the early date of 15th April 1925, one reported by an inexperienced observer between Bagshot and Reading on 26th May 1929, and one reported in *The Field* as seen in Berkshire on 23rd September 1936 which may not have been seen within the present county boundary.

After 1950 the frequency of sightings of Golden Orioles in Berkshire increased, coinciding with an increase in its population nationally and its establishment as a regular, albeit rare, breeding species in Britain (*1968–72 BTO Atlas*). However since the 1980s records have decreased, again reflecting a reversal in the fortunes of the species nationally. A male was seen well in Windsor Great Park on 20th September 1956, spending most of the day in high Beech *Fagus sylvatica* trees and calling constantly. The following year there was a well-documented autumn

passage record involving a male and a female seen in a garden at Ascot on the rather late date of 4th October 1957. There was then a gap of 14 years before the next record, a male seen at Ashley Hill on 13th May 1971.

The number of Berkshire records of Golden Oriole increased in the 1980s, with one being seen in an orchard to the west of Newbury on 11th and 13th May 1981, an immature male being seen briefly in osiers

*Salix* spp. at Theale Gravel Pits on 23rd May 1983, and one being heard at dawn in Windsor Great Park on 12th May 1990 during a sponsored bird race. A pair was at Rapley on 29th and 30th May 1992, and on 19th May 2002 a male was at Clayfield Copse, Caversham for sufficient time to be seen by a number of observers. A record of a female or juvenile at Wraysbury on 2nd July 2013 awaits consideration by the Berkshire Records Committee. In view of the elusive nature of the species and the ease with which it can be overlooked, even when summering, these few records doubtless represent only a proportion of the true number of Golden Orioles which have reached Berkshire.

Prior to the 20th century there only appear to be two documented records. Clark Kennedy (1868) only knew of one record, a bird at Billingbear some years before 1868 which had drawn attention to itself by its distinctive call. The observer crawled into a dense thicket of Ash *Fraxinus excelsior* to obtain views of the bird, an early example of birdwatching rather than resorting to the gun. Noble (1906) cites a further record of two birds at Enborne in 1870.

*Sponsored by Brian Bennett*

# Red-backed Shrike `Red` `Sch. 1`

## *Lanius collurio*

*Former summer visitor, now a rare passage migrant*

The Red-backed Shrike was formerly a common breeding species in Berkshire, but since the early 1960s has become a rare passage migrant. The dramatic decline of the species in Britain, from a relatively common and widespread breeding bird to an occasional passage migrant, is well documented (*e.g. 1968–72 BTO Atlas*) and this account provides a summary of its demise within Berkshire.

The Red-backed Shrike was evidently a widespread breeding species in the county during the 19th century, being noted by Clark Kennedy (1868) as "numerous over every part of Berkshire" and "breeds abundantly", and by Noble (1906) as "fairly common and breeds in many parts of the county". During the 1930s and 1940s it was still widespread, breeding in urban Reading and Maidenhead, in gardens and parks, in railway cuttings, on the outskirts of towns, at gravel pits and sewage farms, on the Downs and on heaths and commons. On occasion, two or three pairs would nest in the same area, sometimes as close as 200 metres apart. Because of the variation in observer coverage between years it is not possible from the published records to be certain of the overall size of the Red-backed Shrike population in Berkshire during this period. A special report on the status of the species appeared in the 1937 county report, however, and provided an estimate of six to eight pairs around Maidenhead, and records from a further five areas, but not including the Reading area, giving a total of from 11 to 13 pairs.

The population appears to have suffered a significant decline during the 1940s, since by the end of the decade there were records of only three to five pairs in the county. Records from urban Reading helped to produce

a peak count of six pairs in Berkshire in 1950, after which the number of breeding pairs declined further. The last breeding records for west Berkshire came from Aldermaston and Bucklebury Common in 1951, and for east Berkshire from Langley in 1955. The statement in the county report for 1953 that Red-backed Shrikes bred "in many districts in east Berkshire" is incorrect, since this was based on the MTNHS Report for that year which related to the whole of the Society's area, and included Buckinghamshire where a few pairs continued to breed.

The last known breeding record of the Red-backed Shrike in Berkshire was at Shinfield where adults and at least three young were seen on 6th and 8th August 1957. There was also a claim of a second pair breeding in the

Caversham area that year but, although a male was present on 31st May, confirmation that breeding had occurred was not obtained. Two subsequent breeding records which appear in county reports are both erroneous. A report of adults and young at Sunningdale in 1960 involved a site just over the county boundary in Surrey (E .E. Green *pers. comm.*), and the statement in the 1965 county report that Red-backed Shrikes "bred in two areas in Berkshire" is apparently an incorrect transcription of a comment in the MTNHS Report for that year that birds "bred in two areas in Buckinghamshire". Red-backed Shrikes did breed successfully close to the Berkshire boundary some years after 1957, however: in south Buckinghamshire in 1970 (Lack and Ferguson, 1993), in north Hampshire at Silchester in 1968 (Clark and Eyre, 1993), and in south Oxfordshire in 1963 (Brucker *et al.*, 1992).

After the last breeding record in 1957, Red-backed Shrikes occurred in Berkshire as summer visitors for a few years. In 1958 there was a male at Reading on 2nd July and a female or first-year male at Aldworth on 28th August. There was a female in Windsor Forest on 13th May 1959 and a male near Lowbury Hill on 7th June 1960. A juvenile at South Fawley on 14th September 1958 was presumably on passage. There were then three records in 1961: a male at Colthrop on 16th May, a singing male at Hermitage from 21st to 28th May, and a female at Hartshill Gravel Pit on 2nd July.

The next record was not until a passage male was seen at Sulham on 20th August 1968, followed by a male at Mortimer Common in May 1969. One seen in Windsor Great Park in May 1969 was in the Surrey section of the park. The next Berkshire records involved five sightings in just two years: a male apparently summering on the Downs near Lambourn from at least 30th June to 18th July 1973 and constituting the last summer record for Berkshire; a passage female at Hungerford on 14th August 1973; a male at Caversham on 2nd May 1974 and a female at Reading Sewage Farm on 12th September 1974. A record of a bird at Earley on the 18th April 1974 is no longer considered reliable, the previous earliest date being 2nd May 1950.

Since 1975 there have been just seven records: a male in Reading on 26th May 1975; a male at Woolhampton on 17th May 1978; a juvenile at Wraysbury Gravel Pits on 19th September 1986; an adult female at Wigmore Lane Gravel Pit, Theale on 18th July 1999; a juvenile at Slough Sewage Farm from 21st to 24th August 2002, an adult female on Greenham Common from 3rd to 6th August 2003 and a juvenile at the same site from 20th–28th September 2013.

The reasons for the decline in the Red-backed Shrike in Britain are unclear, although it seems unlikely that in Berkshire habitat loss is entirely to blame, since much of its favoured habitat in the areas in which it formerly bred remains today.

*Sponsored by Bill Stacey*

# Great Grey Shrike

*Lanius excubitor*

*Scarce winter visitor*

The Great Grey Shrike is a scarce but regular winter visitor to Berkshire. Birds normally arrive about the second week of October and are strongly territorial, defending a large area where they may spend the entire winter. The species' favoured wintering habitat is heathland or other open areas with isolated bushes, and individuals often return to the same area for several winters in succession (*1981–84 BTO Winter Atlas*).

The first 20th century record was one at Cookham Dean Common in January and March 1934. This was followed by one which was killed at Newbury on 10th July 1940. After 1945 the frequency of records increased significantly and Great Grey Shrikes were seen in 46 of the 65 winters from 1947/48 to 2012/13. Apart from the three winters from 1973/74 to 1975/76 when there were above average numbers, there has been little change in the frequency with which Great Grey Shrikes have

been recorded over this period. A breakdown of the records from 1947/48 to 2012/13 by month of arrival is given in Figure 123, but it should be borne in mind that some apparently new 'arrivals' after November may be due to the movement of birds between territories.

The number of Berkshire's over-wintering Great Grey Shrikes has only exceeded two in four of the winters since 1947/48. Six were recorded in 1973/74 followed by an unprecedented nine in both 1974/75 and 1975/76, giving a total for these three consecutive years of 24. There were also three birds in 2011. The cause of the influx of birds in October and November 1973 is unclear, although the species' tendency to return to the same territory in succeeding years is likely to account, at least in part, for the high numbers in the following years.

Between 1975/76 and 1994/95 the number of wintering birds fell back to an average of one a year, with no records at all during 1981/82, 1982/83 and from 1984/85 to 1987/88, and thereafter there have records in just 12 of the 17 years to 2013. Many of the records are from Wishmoor Bottom, which may possibly be the same individual returning in consecutive years. Another regular returnee was a single bird seen at Freeman's Marsh for four consecutive winters from 1972/73. Figure 124 shows the number of birds in each winter from 1991/92 to 2012/13.

The earliest autumn arrival date recorded in Berkshire was a bird seen at Reading Sewage Farm on 4th October 1970, ten days ahead of the next earliest date of 8th October in 2008. A number of the birds seen in the county have stayed for a considerable period of time and Table 4 provides a summary of the durations of stay for all birds recorded between the winters of 1947/48 and 2012/13. Most of the short-staying birds occurred in October or between February and April and were apparently on passage. Some light passage certainly appears to take place in April, since the only occasions on which two birds have been seen together in the 20th century have been in that month, at Crowthorne on 3rd April 1976 and at Aldermaston on 7th April 1953, in both cases a male and a female bird. The two latest post-winter departure dates recorded have been one at Dinton Pastures on 21st April 1974, and one at Wishmoor Bottom on 29th April 2000.

Great Grey Shrikes recorded in Berkshire have been seen chasing Meadow Pipits and Lesser Redpolls, and others have been seen to catch small rodents. A male shot at Wasing in mistake for a Jay in March 1957 had the head of a bumble bee *Bombus* sp. and some beetles *Coleoptera* in its stomach, in addition to rodent *Rodentia* remains. More unusually, the stomach of one shot at Newbury in December 1810 is reported to have contained a few fish scales (Lamb, 1880), although it seems that these were more likely to have been the wing cases of beetles. There has been only one record of vocalization, a bird calling at Wishmoor Bottom in early 2009.

Prior to the 20th century most records of Great Grey Shrike in Berkshire were of birds which had been shot. Lamb (1880) noted three such cases, a male by the Thames near Reading on 28th November 1792, a female near Aldermaston on 6th January 1795 and a female near the Kennet at Newbury on 20th December 1810. Clark Kennedy (1868) reported several shot from 1853 to 1866, and one seen several times at Billingbear. Noble (1906) added further records for the years 1872

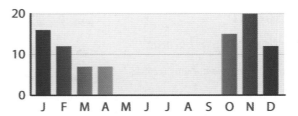

**Figure 123: Great Grey Shrike: all birds recorded 1947/48–2012/13, by month of arrival.**

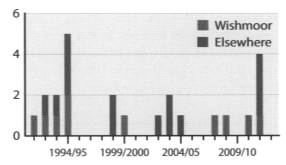

**Figure 124: Great Grey Shrike: birds recorded in winter from 1991/92–2012/13.**
Birds recorded from November to February.

| Number of days | | | Number of months | | | Not recorded |
|---|---|---|---|---|---|---|
| 1–4 | 5–14 | 15–30 | 1–2 | 2–3 | >3 | |
| 46 | 10 | 6 | 8 | 10 | 8 | 1 |

**Table 4: Great Grey Shrike: Duration of recorded stay 1947/48–2012/13.**

to 1897, including two shot at Bucklebury in 1878 and two shot by the Blackwater in 1891. This small number of early records was spread widely across the county, from Hungerford in the west to Windsor in the east, although in contrast to their occurrence in Berkshire today a number were procured or seen close to rivers or streams.

*Sponsored by Michael McKee*

# Woodchat Shrike

*Lanius senator*

*Rare vagrant, two records*

The Woodchat Shrike is a summer visitor to Mediterranean Europe, and a rare vagrant to Berkshire. Apart from a specimen in the British Museum which is labelled "Reading - Theo Fisher Esq", about which there are no other particulars (Noble, 1906), the remaining two county records are of single birds seen in 1989 and 1991. The first of these records was a female close to the railway line at Theale on 22nd May 1989, and the second was of another female which was seen for 50 minutes, also on the side of the railway line, near Hamstead Marshall Lock on 19th May 1991.

*In memory of Lew R Lewis*

# Chough

Amber | Sch. 1

*Pyrrhocorax pyrrhocorax*

*Rare vagrant, one dubious record*

The Chough is possibly a rare vagrant to Berkshire, but the sole record may well relate to a bird of captive origin. Herbert (1871) states that he had one in his collection, said to have been killed near Newbury on 13th August 1868, which he saw "in the flesh". Weight is added to the possibility that the bird was an escapee by Palmer (1886), who noted that the species is sometimes kept in captivity and gave a local example: "Major Thurlow has a tame one on the lawn at Shaw-house".

*Sponsored by Heidi Bailey*

# Magpie

Green

*Pica pica*

*Abundant resident*

The Magpie is a common resident throughout most of Berkshire, occurring in a wide variety of habitats in rural, suburban and urban areas where there are hedgerows, bushes or trees available for it to build its nest. There is little information available on the size of its population in the county, although the conspicuous nature of the Magpie may give a false impression of numbers in comparison with other, less noticeable, species.

The Tetrad Surveys showed the Magpie to be widely distributed throughout Berkshire, being recorded in most tetrads in both 1987–89 and 2007–11. There was however a decline of about 6% in the number of tetrads where breeding was confirmed, with a notable reduction in the westernmost part of the county, where breeding confirmation was sparser in 1987–89. It remains, though, widely recorded from most habitats, including built-up areas. The high proportion of tetrads in which breeding was confirmed indicates the relative ease with which its bulky nest can be found and noisy family parties seen.

Over the period from 1966 to 1988, information from the CBC indicates that the number of Magpies in Britain increased by a factor of 1·92 in farmland and by 3·31 in woodland (*Population Trends*). However subsequent CBC and BBS results indicate that the rise tailed off in the early 1990s, and there was a slight decline of about 7% from 1999 to 2009, consistent with the reduction in breeding confirmation in the 2007–11 survey.

Both the Breeding Season and Winter abundance maps show the highest counts to be in the east of the county. This reflects the pattern disclosed by records in the County Reports. As the numbers of Magpies increased into the 1980s, counts of 20 or more became more frequent. In subsequent years, the highest counts have tended all to be from the east or centre of the county. Some sites seem to produce high counts more frequently, particularly in winter, notably South Hill Park, Bracknell, where 80 were counted on 15th January 2002, the area around Whiteknights Park and Earley, with maxima of 70 in January 1997 and December 2010, and Slough Sewage Farm, where there were at least 60 on 11th July 1998, an unusual date for so large a count. The area around the Jubilee River also attracts substantial numbers, with notable counts along the river in 2007 of 123 on 28th February and 101 on 3rd March.

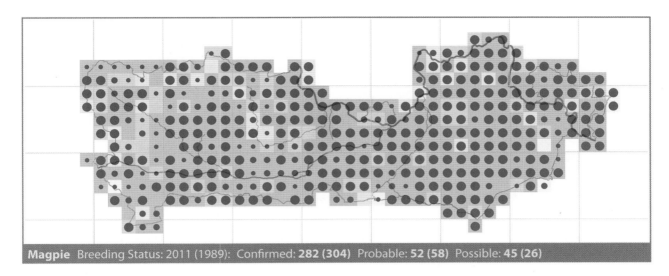

**Magpie** Breeding Status: 2011 (1989): Confirmed: **282 (304)** Probable: **52 (58)** Possible: **45 (26)**

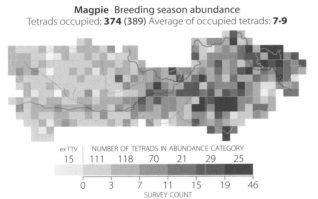

**Magpie** Breeding season abundance
Tetrads occupied: **374 (389)** Average of occupied tetrads: **7·9**

| ex TTV | NUMBER OF TETRADS IN ABUNDANCE CATEGORY | | | | | |
|---|---|---|---|---|---|---|
| 15 | 111 | 118 | 70 | 21 | 29 | 25 |

0   3   7   11   15   19   46
SURVEY COUNT

**Magpie** Winter abundance
Tetrads occupied: **383 (392)** Average of occupied tetrads: **10·5**

| ex TTV | NUMBER OF TETRADS IN ABUNDANCE CATEGORY | | | | | |
|---|---|---|---|---|---|---|
| 9 | 142 | 96 | 59 | 43 | 15 | 28 |

0   5   10   15   21   26   50
SURVEY COUNT

The highest counts from the west of the county have been 20–30 at Thatcham Sewage Farm in July 1986, and 30 at Brimpton Gravel Pits in February 2000.

At the end of the 19th century, the Magpie was evidently uncommon in Berkshire (*Historical Atlas*), and Noble (1906) noted that they had ceased to breed in the area to the north of Maidenhead. This indicates that there had been a decline in its population during the nineteenth century since Lamb (1880), writing in 1814, described it as "very frequent", and Hewett (1911), writing in the early 1860s, recalled seeing 20 Magpies together in the autumn near East Ilsley and refers to an old saying that "when Magpies collect a wedding will take place".

*Sponsored by Des Sussex*

# Jay

*Garrulus glandarius*

*Common resident and winter visitor*

The Jay is a common resident in Berkshire whose numbers are sometimes augmented by an influx of wintering birds from continental Europe. It is found in both broadleaved and coniferous woodland as well as in gardens and parks, although it shows a preference for habitats which contain a proportion of oak *Quercus* spp. trees, the acorns of which provide an important food source. Jays readily visit gardens in suburban areas in search of food and often predate nesting garden birds. They are usually seen singly or in pairs, or family parties.

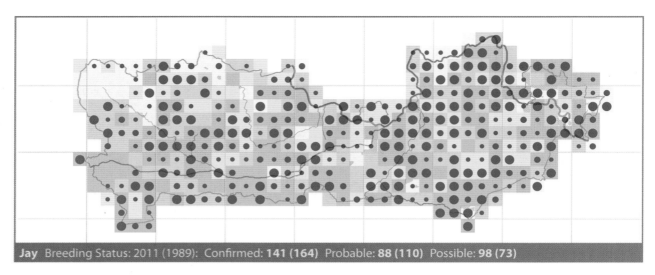

**Jay** Breeding Status: 2011 (1989): Confirmed: **141 (164)** Probable: **88 (110)** Possible: **98 (73)**

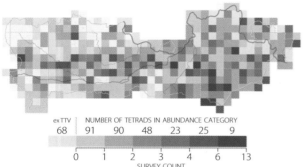

**Jay** Breeding season abundance
Tetrads occupied: **286 (354)** Average of occupied tetrads: **2·5**

| ex TTV | NUMBER OF TETRADS IN ABUNDANCE CATEGORY | | | | | |
|--------|----|----|----|----|----|---|
| 68 | 91 | 90 | 48 | 23 | 25 | 9 |

0 1 2 3 4 6 13
SURVEY COUNT

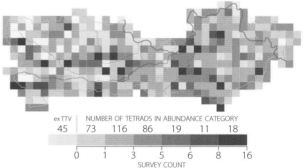

**Jay** Winter abundance
Tetrads occupied: **323 (368)** Average of occupied tetrads: **3·4**

| ex TTV | NUMBER OF TETRADS IN ABUNDANCE CATEGORY | | | | | |
|--------|----|-----|----|----|----|----|
| 45 | 73 | 116 | 86 | 19 | 11 | 18 |

0 1 3 5 6 8 16
SURVEY COUNT

The Tetrad Surveys showed the Jay to have a widespread distribution throughout Berkshire, breeding evidence being recorded in over 89% of the tetrads, and confirmed to have bred in some 42% of these in the 1987–89 survey, but rather fewer, 83% and 36% respectively in the 2007–11 survey. There also appears to be something of a shift in distribution, with more confirmed breeding in the east of Berkshire and fewer in the south west, although this may reflect the levels of fieldwork in these areas in the two surveys. In both surveys it was absent or thinly distributed only in the areas of downland in the north-west of the county where suitable habitat is restricted. In the Breeding Season TTV survey in 2007–11 there are records from most tetrads in the south west, , despite the lack of breeding evidence in them.

The Winter Map shows a similar pattern of distribution, with fewer Jays being found on the higher ground in the county in winter. The species was recorded in more tetrads, and the average count was 36% higher too, perhaps indicating an influx of birds for the winter

The resident population of Jays in Britain is occasionally augmented in autumn by immigrants from the continent, probably in response to a failure of the acorn crop (*1981–84 BTO Winter Atlas*). One such invasion occurred in 1983 and is documented by John and Roskell (1985). Within Berkshire, there were records

during this invasion of eight birds at Lower Denford on 6th October, 14 at Great Shefford on 23rd October, and 20 at Dinton Pastures through September and October. A further 20 birds were counted in a period of 30 minutes at Brimpton on 2nd October as they flew from one copse to another foraging for acorns. In 1986 further movements were noted, with 40 birds flying westward at Fifield on 20th September and 11 flying in a westerly direction at Twyford three days later. Movements of Jays have also been recorded in Berkshire in other years, with an apparent increase in records in the autumn indicating a possible arrival of wintering birds, although in some years, such as 2006, this does not produce any counts into double figures. Since 2000 the highest count was 22 in Swinley Forest on 22nd October 2010.

Ringing data though does not disclose details of any long distance movements. These reflect the generally sedentary nature of the species in Berkshire, with only seven out of 37 ringing recoveries disclosing movements into or out of the county, and all bar one (which involved a movement to Kent) involving adjoining counties.

The Jay was also regarded as a common resident in Berkshire in the 19th century (Clark Kennedy, 1868), and Noble (1906) perceptively considered it to be an autumn passage migrant.

*Sponsored by Renton Righelato*

# Nutcracker

## Nucifraga caryocatactes

*Rare vagrant, three records in one irruption*

The Nutcracker is a rare vagrant to Berkshire, recorded only during the famous 'irruption' of 1968. Occasional vagrants reach Britain, normally averaging just one record a year, but in 1968 there was an unprecedented invasion in which at least 315 Nutcrackers were recorded in the period from 6th August to October, some staying until autumn 1969 (*1968–72 BTO Atlas*). During this period there were three records involving four birds in Berkshire. The first of these records involved a bird at Crowthorne on 24th August 1968, details of which were obtained after following up a report in the local press. The second record was of a bird found dead in the south-west corner of Windsor Great Park on 10th September and which was presented to Reading Museum. The third record was of two birds seen well at Sots Hole, just north of Pangbourne, on 3rd October. These birds, like the others involved in the irruption, were of the slender-billed race *N. c. macrorhynchos*, the race which occurs across Siberia from the Urals east to the Pacific Ocean.

*Sponsored by Peter Hickman*

# Jackdaw

Green

## Corvus monedula

*Widespread and abundant resident*

The Jackdaw is a widespread and familiar resident in Berkshire, occurring in urban areas as well as in most rural habitats and parkland. It breeds wherever there are adequate food supplies and suitable nesting cavities. It would appear that the status of the species in the county has changed little since Clark Kennedy (1868) referred to it as common and Noble (1906) as abundant. Its sharp calls are familiar in most built-up areas of the county, and flocks of Jackdaws, often with Rooks, are frequently seen out of the breeding season.

During the 2007–11 Atlas Survey, breeding evidence of Jackdaws was recorded in 95% of the tetrads in Berkshire and breeding was confirmed in 72%, an increase from 92% and 57% respectively recorded in the 1987–89 survey, and with a higher confirmation rate in the eastern half of the county. There seems little correlation between the species' distribution and that of any particular habitat type, perhaps indicating its adaptability to a range of conditions. Jackdaws remain absent from, or are infrequent in, some tetrads in urban or suburban areas, particularly around the larger towns in the county. This may reflect the lack of traditional chimney stacks,

a favoured nesting site, in modern suburban housing. Jackdaws are also effectively absent from the area to the south-east of Bracknell where coniferous woodland and heathland predominate, but have populated more areas of open farmland on the Downs. The winter abundance map shows the distribution to be broadly similar to the breeding distribution.

The population of Jackdaws in Britain has increased since the early 1970s (*Population Trends*) driven by reduced nest failure rate, (Henderson & Hart. 1993). Jackdaws flock together, often in association with Rooks, on stubble or pasture or at rubbish tips where there is a good supply of food. These flocks are often numbered in thousands particularly at some traditional roost sites. Wraysbury

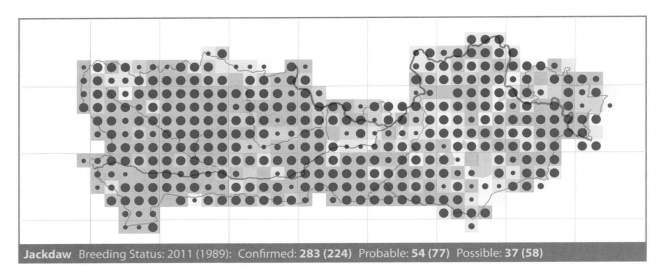

**Jackdaw** Breeding Status: 2011 (1989): Confirmed: **283 (224)** Probable: **54 (77)** Possible: **37 (58)**

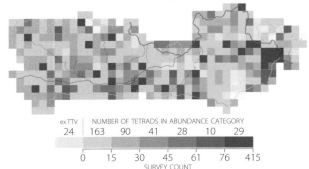

**Jackdaw** Breeding season abundance
Tetrads occupied: **361 (385)** Average of occupied tetrads: **30·5**

| ex TTV | NUMBER OF TETRADS IN ABUNDANCE CATEGORY | | | | | |
|---|---|---|---|---|---|---|
| 24 | 163 | 90 | 41 | 28 | 10 | 29 |

| 0 | 15 | 30 | 45 | 61 | 76 | 415 |

SURVEY COUNT

**Jackdaw** Winter abundance
Tetrads occupied: **356 (379)** Average of occupied tetrads: **49·6**

| ex TTV | NUMBER OF TETRADS IN ABUNDANCE CATEGORY | | | | | |
|---|---|---|---|---|---|---|
| 23 | 161 | 69 | 60 | 19 | 17 | 30 |

| 0 | 24 | 49 | 74 | 99 | 124 | 1,050 |

SURVEY COUNT

Gravel Pits is one such location, with 4,800 recorded in February 1994 and at least 4,000 in December 1988. Baynes and Bowdown Woods is another regular site with at least 8,000 in January 1990 and over 5,000 in January 1992. Jackdaws frequently establish regular roosting flight-lines, and in addition to the sites in Table 5, several more are just over boundaries with adjacent counties. Examples include the two evening flight-paths, at right angles to each other over Maidenhead and Cookham, where half the Jackdaws head for the Little Marlow Gravel Pit roost to the north, and half fly east across the Thames to a roost near Hedgerley, both roosts being in Buckinghamshire. A small group heard overhead at Cookham six hours after nightfall on 6th November 2007 was presumably still making this journey.

Jackdaws are hole- or cavity-nesting birds, and larger nest boxes are often used. Examples include a Kestrel box at Hell Corner Farm, Inkpen in 2009, and Barn Owl boxes at Lavell's Lake and at Sheepdrove Farm, Lambourn in 2010. At the last site two young were reared in a Tawny Owl box which had fallen to the ground in 2008. It is not known if it was occupied before it fell.

There have been occasional reports of Jackdaws exhibiting unusual plumage variations. One bird, which was entirely light silver-grey (the colour which

| Year | Highest Count | Place | Date |
|---|---|---|---|
| 1996 | 1,130 | Sunnymeads Gravel Pit | 4th January |
| 1997 | 600 | Lambourn Woodland | December |
| 1998 | 1,000 | Drift Road | 8th December |
| 1999 | 3,000 | Shefford Woodlands | 15th July |
| 2000 | 350 | Englefield | 6th August |
| 2001 | 1,000 | Bucklebury | 28th December |
| 2002 | 2,500 | Binfield | 24th January |
| 2003 | 5,000 | Thatcham | 25th January |
| 2004 | 2,000 | Hurst Tip | 21st September |
| 2005 | 1,900 | Binfield | 15th March |
| 2006 | 5,000 | Greenham Common | 29th October |
| 2007 | 1,000 | Binfield | 4th January |
| 2008 | 2,000 | Windsor Marina | 7th July |
| 2009 | 500 | Binfield | 3rd December |
| 2010 | 2,500 | Wraysbury | 30th November |
| 2011 | 500 | Winkfield | 5th May |
| 2012 | 500 | Binfield | 29th January |

**Table 5**: **Jackdaw: counts 1996–2012**

is normally confined to the nape), was seen in Reading in July 1974, and a leucistic individual was reported at Burghfield Gravel Pits on 10th September 1989.

Two aberrant birds, with extensive fawn brown feathering on head and upper body and wings, were at Wargrave on 28th October 2010. A breeding adult, showing features typical of Eastern Race (Nordic), was at Windsor Great Park, on 12th May 2005, and present until at least 2008.

*Sponsored by Jean Newport*

# Rook

Green

*Corvus frugilegus*

*Abundant resident*

The Rook is one of the familiar sights, and sounds, across the county, and is an abundant resident of farmland and rural areas where highly visible nesting colonies ensure that it is not easily overlooked.

During both the 1987–89 and 2007–11 Atlas Surveys, Rooks were found to be widely distributed across the county and were confirmed to have bred in some 56% and 52% respectively of the tetrads. In Berkshire, the species' preferred habitat is mixed farmland with small woods. The only parts of the county where it remains largely absent are the extensive coniferous woodland and heathland area in the south-east, and some urban and suburban areas. There also appears to have been a loss of breeding Rooks in the far east of the county between the two surveys. Nationally, surveys in 1975 and 1996 and the results of both CBC and BBS indicated a long-term increase between the 1970s and 2000, but a 10% decline in England during the first decade of the 21st century (Baillie *et al.*, 2013).

The Berkshire results of the BTO's national survey of rookeries in 1975 (Wilson, 1977) showed a similar

distribution to that established by the 1987–89 Atlas Survey, save that in the latter it appeared that the Rook was more widely distributed in the west of the county. The largest rookery recorded in the 1975 BTO survey was one of 282 nests at East Garston and there were ten rookeries of 100 or more nests. Half of the rookeries contained fewer than 16 nests and occasionally comprised just two or three nests in a single tree.

Following the 1987–89 Atlas Survey, a study of rookeries in west Berkshire was carried out by the NDOC (Webb, 1991), which revealed that there had been a significant change in their distribution since the 1975 BTO survey. In addition to an overall drop of 9% in the number of nests,

Rook *Gordon Langsbury*

from 5,181 to 4,727, major changes in the distribution of nests between 10 km squares was noted. Whilst some 10 km squares experienced falls of up to 45%, others increased by up to 500%. The factors advanced by Webb (1991) to account for this shift in the population included the loss of mature trees during severe gales in the years preceding the survey, and the effect of Dutch Elm disease. In 1975 some 30% of the Rook nests in west Berkshire were in elm *Ulmus* spp. trees, even though they comprised only 8% of all trees in the county (Osborne, 1982). As an example of the scale of the change at a local level, the large rookery at East Garston which contained 282 nests in 1975 held just 33 in 1991.

Another, less comprehensive, count of rookeries across the county was conducted between 2005 and 2007. A total of 123 rookeries were located; 56 in West Berkshire, 40 in Mid-Berkshire, and 27 in East Berkshire. Whilst not being as complete as previous surveys, only six were found to contain over 100 nests and only 24 had 50 or more. However, consistent with the 1975 survey, nearly half the rookeries comprised 16 or fewer nests, and a rookery of 300 nests in the Chieveley area had reduced to just over 100.

During both the breeding season and winter higher numbers tend to be found in west Berkshire as indicated by the abundance maps. From as early as July, Rooks can form substantial post-breeding flocks, often involving several hundred, or even thousands, of birds. Most of these groups are found in open farmland but sometimes also at rubbish tips, an example being 2,000 at Smallmead tip, Reading in December 1992. Rooks often associate with other corvids, notably Jackdaws, often in quite large gatherings, affording some of the most spectacular birdwatching sights available in the county. This behaviour commences when fledged young of both species are taken out onto farmland to be taught to forage. The highest counts of such groups tend to occur in July and in recent years include flocks near Moss End (800 in 2002, 600 in 2003 and 3,000 in 2007), and in the Pinkneys Green/Cookham area (580 in 2008). But by far the largest flocks have occurred in mid-winter, with 8,000 at Greenham Common in January 2004, 10,000 at Thatcham in December 2001, and an outstanding 15,000 estimated at Crookham Common in January 2007. Some summer counts indicate the presence of numbers of Carrion Crows too, but separating them from juvenile Rooks which lack the distinctive grey facial patch of the adults poses problems at a distance.

*Sponsored by Ian & Kay Fewtrell-Smith*

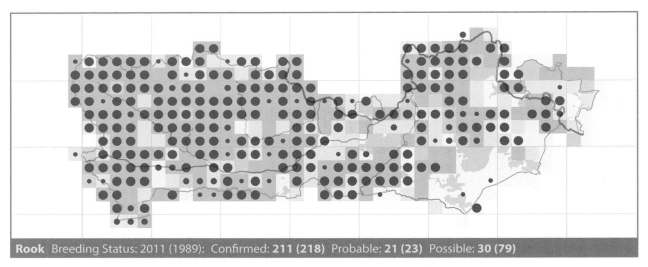

**Rook** Breeding Status: 2011 (1989): Confirmed: **211 (218)** Probable: **21 (23)** Possible: **30 (79)**

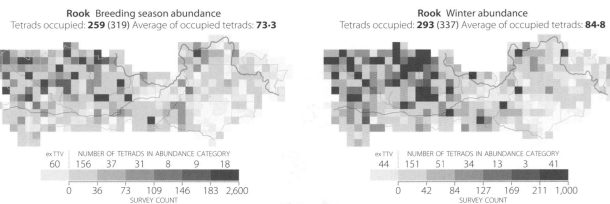

**Rook** Breeding season abundance
Tetrads occupied: **259 (319)** Average of occupied tetrads: **73·3**

| exTTV | NUMBER OF TETRADS IN ABUNDANCE CATEGORY | | | | | |
|---|---|---|---|---|---|---|
| 60 | 156 | 37 | 31 | 8 | 9 | 18 |

| 0 | 36 | 73 | 109 | 146 | 183 | 2,600 |
SURVEY COUNT

**Rook** Winter abundance
Tetrads occupied: **293 (337)** Average of occupied tetrads: **84·8**

| exTTV | NUMBER OF TETRADS IN ABUNDANCE CATEGORY | | | | | |
|---|---|---|---|---|---|---|
| 44 | 151 | 51 | 34 | 13 | 3 | 41 |

| 0 | 42 | 84 | 127 | 169 | 211 | 1,000 |
SURVEY COUNT

# Carrion Crow

*Corvus corone*

*Abundant resident*

The Carrion Crow is a familiar and abundant resident. It breeds wherever suitable nesting trees are available in both broadleaved and coniferous woodland, on farmland, heathland and in urban and suburban areas, and is distributed over the whole county. During the 1987–89 Atlas Survey breeding evidence was recorded in 92% of tetrads and confirmed in 67%, which increased to 96% and 77% during the 2007–11 Atlas Survey.

Adult Carrion Crows are normally resident and remain within their territory throughout the winter. When the young fledge, family parties of from four to six birds may be seen into early autumn before the juveniles disperse, and often congregate to form large flocks. Between 1995 and 2011 flocks of 200 or more were recorded in most years. The higher counts tend to be from the east of the county, with highest counts of 600 at Binfield in March 2005 and between 500 and 550 at Burchetts Green in the winter of 2001/2. This pattern is reflected in the abundance maps and is in contrast to Rooks, which were more numerous in the west.

The CBC and BBS index shows that the population of Carrion Crows more than doubled during the period from 1965 to 2011, accompanied by an increase in breeding success rates (Baillie *et al.*, 2011). Although the Carrion Crow continues to be viewed by some as a pest species and is still persecuted, it continues to thrive, particularly in suburban areas where it is perhaps less threatened. This may help to explain the distribution shown by the abundance maps which indicate that Carrion Crows become increasingly numerous towards the eastern end of the county, corresponding with the areas of greater urbanisation. They have been recorded taking a wide variety of food items in Berkshire, often foraging on

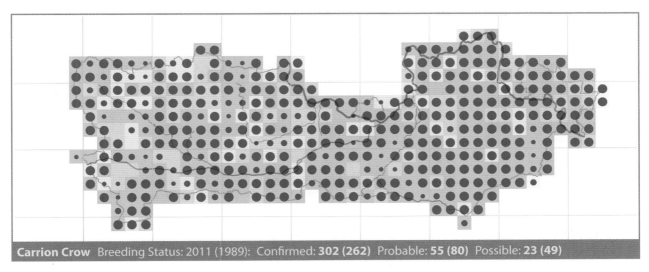

**Carrion Crow** Breeding Status: 2011 (1989): Confirmed: **302 (262)** Probable: **55 (80)** Possible: **23 (49)**

**Carrion Crow** Breeding season abundance
Tetrads occupied: **384** (393) Average of occupied tetrads: **15·2**

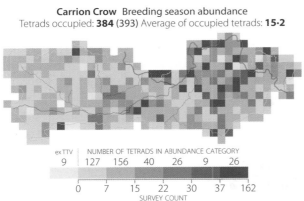

| exTTV | NUMBER OF TETRADS IN ABUNDANCE CATEGORY | | | | | |
|---|---|---|---|---|---|---|
| 9 | 127 | 156 | 40 | 26 | 9 | 26 |

0 7 15 22 30 37 162
SURVEY COUNT

**Carrion Crow** Winter abundance
Tetrads occupied: **391** (393) Average of occupied tetrads: **21·8**

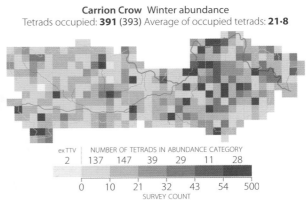

| exTTV | NUMBER OF TETRADS IN ABUNDANCE CATEGORY | | | | | |
|---|---|---|---|---|---|---|
| 2 | 137 | 147 | 39 | 29 | 11 | 28 |

0 10 21 32 43 54 500
SURVEY COUNT

rubbish tips. Their habit of taking eggs and young birds has made them unpopular with gamekeepers. They are also the birds most likely to be seen harrying Buzzards and Red Kites, even outside the breeding season.

Historical information on the status of the Carrion Crow suggests that it was formerly much scarcer than at present. The *Historical Atlas* classified the species as uncommon, and Noble (1906) stated that it was "very local", only ever having found one nest in his area, although it was apparently commoner to the west and north-west of the county. He blamed keepering for the elimination of the species in the Windsor area.

Individual birds with extensive white patches on the wings are often reported, and a distinctive leucistic individual was first noted in January 2002 near Aldworth. This bird had chocolate brown body feathers, and fawn-coloured wings and tail, and was seen on several occasions until 2010.

*Sponsored by Mr S Graham*

# Hooded Crow Green

*Corvus cornix*

*Rare winter visitor, none since 1980*

The Hooded Crow replaces the Carrion Cow in Highland Scotland, Ireland and the Isle of Man. Until 2003 it was regarded as a form or race of the Carrion Crow, and is still regarded as such elsewhere in Europe, where the two species or races tend to occupy adjacent areas with zones of hybridization between, as is the case in Scotland. In Berkshire it has been a rare winter visitor, but has not been recorded since 1980.

Prior to 1900, Hooded Crows appear to have been regular winter visitors to the downland areas of Berkshire, Lamb (1880) noting, in 1814, that they "are not often seen unless on the Downs", and Noble (1906) commenting that he had seen many on the hills near Compton and that a few are killed most years near Newbury. Specific early records away from the Downs are few, but there are records of birds seen or killed at Park Place, Maidenhead Thicket and Windsor (Noble, 1906). A specimen in the Reading Museum which bears a label "Hambleden, Berkshire" was presumably procured in Buckinghamshire if the location is correctly stated.

The first records of Hooded Crow to be included in the county reports were of one near Aldworth on the late date of 24th May 1920 and one at Reading Sewage Farm in October 1927. A small influx then occurred during the winter of 1934/35 with "some" seen near Combe in November, one or two in the Ascot/Windsor Great Park area in December, two shot near Combe in February, and a freshly dead specimen on a keeper's gibbet at West Ilsley on 9th May 1935. The number of birds seen each decade from winter 1940/41 is shown in Figure 125, and records are analysed by month of arrival in Figure 126.

The earliest recorded arrival date of Hooded Crow in Berkshire was a bird seen in Windsor Great Park on 30th August 1951, although whether it was actually in Berkshire or in Surrey was not specified. This was

significantly earlier than the next earliest date of 18th October in 1952. Most records have been of single birds which have been seen for up to about a month, although there have been four records of birds wintering in the county: one at Widbrook Common from 6th November 1960 to 12th January 1961; one at Woodley Rubbish Tip, Reading from 18th December 1966 to 10th April 1967; one at Smallmead Rubbish Tip from 4th December 1970 to 10th April 1971, and one at the same site from 13th December 1975 to 14th February 1976. No more than three birds have been recorded in any winter other than that of 1934/35 when there were at least five. Apart from an unspecified number near Combe in November 1934, the most seen together has been two, this number having been recorded on five occasions from 1934 to 1980. Although most Hooded Crows recorded in Berkshire prior to 1900 were seen on the Downs, such sightings have been in the minority in the 20th century, with ten of the 25 birds recorded from 1941 to 1980 being recorded from rubbish tips and sewage farms and only three from downland sites.

The most recent record of Hooded Crow in Berkshire was one seen in Reading on 18th November 1980. It is not clear why records should then have suddenly ceased, particularly as birds had been seen in seven of the nine winters from 1969/70 to 1977/78, and a northward retreat of the range of Hooded Crows into Highland Scotland occurred largely in the first half of the 20th century, before records ceased in Berkshire. However, it is possible that a number of the records during the 1970s related to birds returning to the same area in successive years. The distinctive plumage of the birds makes it unlikely many have been overlooked.

*Sponsored by William Brown*

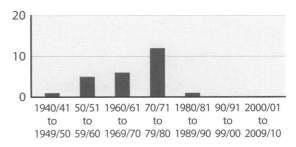

**Figure 125: Hooded Crow: all birds recorded 1940/41–2009/10.**

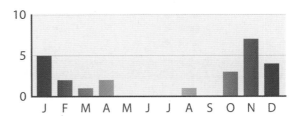

**Figure 126: Hooded Crow: All birds recorded 1940/41–2009/10, by month of arrival.**

# Raven

Green

*Corvus corax*

*Increasing visitor and recently re-established breeding resident*

Until the beginning of the 21st century, the Raven remained a rare vagrant to Berkshire, having become extinct in the county in the 19th century. It had occurred on only a few occasions since the 1950s, despite the increase in the number of observers. In recent years the number of records has increased considerably, and the species has now begun to breed again after an absence of 148 years.

The first 20th century record was from Berkshire Golf Course, Ascot on 27th March 1931, which may have been an escapee, but one seen at West Ilsley on 17th April 1934, and another at Quarry Wood, Cookham Dean on 5th February 1937 appear to have involved genuinely wild birds. These sightings followed the increase in the Raven population in Britain that took place from 1914 (*1968–72 BTO Atlas*). There were singles at Greenham Common from 22nd to 23rd February 1951 and on 18th January 1954, then two were seen flying over the Berkshire Downs near the Fairmile on 24th January 1970, which are assumed to have entered the county. The next record was not until 1983, when one was at Wraysbury on 13th March, and one or two flying south into Berkshire at Churn, Oxfordshire on 20th February 1985. There was then another gap of nearly ten years until two sightings in Windsor Great Park in August 1994, two on the 20th and one on the 29th. After three records in 1996, records have been annual since 1998 and have increased considerably in recent years, rising to 25 in 2003, 51 in 2007, 137 in 2009 and 186 in 2010.

Counts have increased too. Twenty five were found roosting together in Beech trees near Lambourn on the 1st November 2011, and 37 were at Combe Gibbet on the 13th October 2012.

Although most records from the 20th century were in the winter, records have been received in recent years all year round, with most from the west and eastern ends of the county. These appear to reflect the pattern of spread of Ravens into adjoining counties. In Wiltshire at least one pair was confirmed to have bred in 1994, the first since the 1880s (Turner *et al.*, 1995) heralding the re-colonisation of the county. Breeding was confirmed in eight tetrads in the Wiltshire Atlas survey between 1995 and 2000 (Wiltshire Ornithological Society, 2007), and in 2000 breeding was first noted just over the Hampshire border at Highclere. Breeding also commenced in the

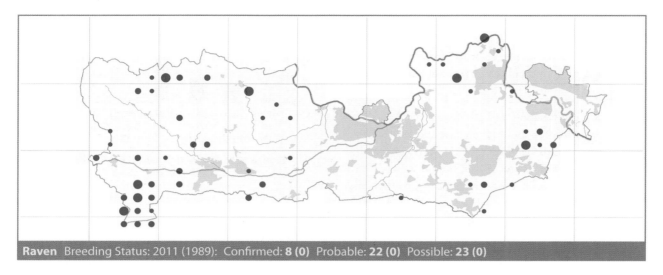

**Raven** Breeding Status: 2011 (1989): Confirmed: **8 (0)** Probable: **22 (0)** Possible: **23 (0)**

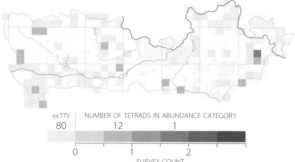

**Raven** Breeding season abundance
Tetrads occupied: **13** (93) Average of occupied tetrads: **1·1**

| ex TTV | NUMBER OF TETRADS IN ABUNDANCE CATEGORY | |
|---|---|---|
| 80 | 12 | 1 |

0    1    2
SURVEY COUNT

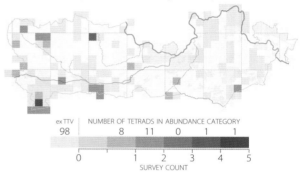

**Raven** Winter abundance
Tetrads occupied: **21** (119) Average of occupied tetrads: **1·9**

| ex TTV | NUMBER OF TETRADS IN ABUNDANCE CATEGORY | | | | |
|---|---|---|---|---|---|
| 98 | 8 | 11 | 0 | 1 | 1 |

0    1    2    3    4    5
SURVEY COUNT

Chilterns in Buckinghamshire, with breeding noted at ten sites in 2009.

The first indication of possible breeding in Berkshire since the 19th century was a pair starting to build a nest at Hamstead Park in 2003, but there was no evidence of hatching or rearing of young. In March 2004, one of two birds near Farnborough Down was seen to be carrying what could have been nest material. In 2006, the first successful breeding may have occurred in the west of the county, as a possible family party of five was seen on June 15th at a site where a pair had been seen regularly beforehand. Similar evidence occurred again in the following year at the same location. Confirmation of breeding was obtained for the first time after 148 years in 2009, with two nests in the Windsor and Maidenhead areas. During the period of the 2007–11 Atlas survey breeding was eventually proved in eight tetrads in the county.

Ravens had not bred in Berkshire since the middle of the 19th century. They reputedly bred in Windsor Great Park in about 1848 (Clark Kennedy, 1868), and certainly bred in Hamstead Park regularly until the last bird of the pair was killed in 1860 (Summers-Smith, 1951), by coincidence the same site from which the first evidence of breeding since was obtained.

*Sponsored by Claire, Ian, Raven, and Dorrian*

Raven, Combe *Jerry O'Brien*

# Goldcrest

Green

*Regulus regulus*

*Common resident and winter visitor*

The Goldcrest is a common and widespread resident in Berkshire, typically found in coniferous habitats, both natural and man-made. This appears always to have been the case, as Noble (1906) described the species as "plentiful" in the county at the end of the 19th century. It is equally at home in tall heathland pines, coniferous plantations and the ornamental conifers of suburban parks and gardens. In years when the population is high, for example following a succession of mild winters, deciduous woodlands are also utilised as breeding habitat. In winter, numbers are sometimes augmented by wintering birds from the north of Britain or continental Europe.

The 2007–11 Atlas Survey showed that the breeding distribution of the Goldcrest was very similar to that in the 1987–89 Atlas Survey, breeding evidence being recorded in 319 tetrads in 2007–11 compared to 317 in 1987–89. It is widely distributed across the county, although is largely absent from the Downs in the north-west where there are few coniferous woodlands. Some indication of the abundance of this species as a breeding bird is given by a survey in 2005 of four blocks of

woodland in south east Berkshire, which found a total of 525 singing males.

Although the breeding population of the Goldcrest in Berkshire is believed to be resident and therefore susceptible to hard winters, the species exhibits a remarkable ability to recover both steadily and quickly following a crash in numbers. For example, the population was reduced by about 90% during the severe winter of 1962/63, yet had increased to its former level by 1975 (*Population Trends*). Outside the breeding season, Goldcrests are often found in loose feeding flocks in association with other species, especially tits, although there have been counts of flocks

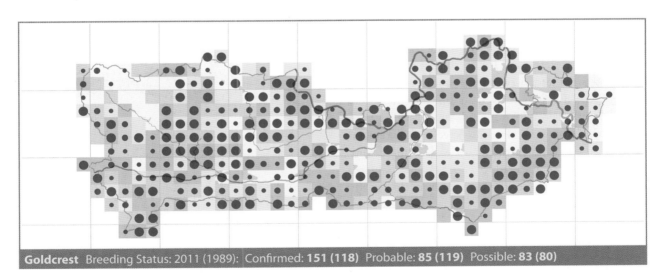

**Goldcrest** Breeding Status: 2011 (1989): Confirmed: **151 (118)** Probable: **85 (119)** Possible: **83 (80)**

**Goldcrest** Breeding season abundance
Tetrads occupied: **202 (331)** Average of occupied tetrads: **4·0**

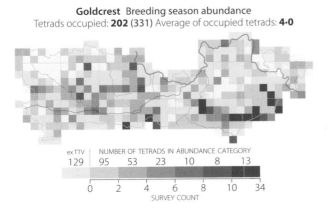

| ex TTV | NUMBER OF TETRADS IN ABUNDANCE CATEGORY | | | | | |
|---|---|---|---|---|---|---|
| 129 | 95 | 53 | 23 | 10 | 8 | 13 |

0   2   4   6   8   10   34
SURVEY COUNT

**Goldcrest** Winter abundance
Tetrads occupied: **245 (334)** Average of occupied tetrads: **4·3**

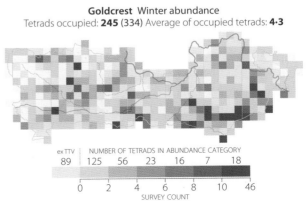

| ex TTV | NUMBER OF TETRADS IN ABUNDANCE CATEGORY | | | | | |
|---|---|---|---|---|---|---|
| 89 | 125 | 56 | 23 | 16 | 7 | 18 |

0   2   4   6   8   10   46
SURVEY COUNT

of Goldcrests alone. The largest of these was 100+ at Caesar's Camp, Swinley Forest, in December 2004. There have also been reports of flocks of about 50, at Ascot in December 1990, and again at Caesar's Camp in January 2008. The Winter Map indicates that the distribution of the Goldcrest in Berkshire during the winter is very similar to the summer, with high densities in the coniferous woodland in the south east, and the distribution further west showing higher numbers in tetrads with more coniferous woodland.

Passage occurs in both spring and autumn, although is only occasionally evident. In 1990, near Kintbury, 14 were ringed from 9th to 22nd March when normally only a few birds would be present. Similarly, in autumn that year there was an arrival of Goldcrests at Thatcham Marsh in October, where 20 were ringed on the 14th,

and a November influx at Bagnor Cress Beds where there were 15–20 on the 11th.

Ringing recoveries indicate that there may be an influx of Goldcrests into Berkshire from the north-west in winter. One ringed on Bardsey Island off the Welsh coast and two ringed on Copeland Island, Northern Ireland have been recovered in Berkshire in winter, and one ringed at Denford Mill on 16th March 1990 was recovered sixteen days later at Port Erin on the Isle of Man. A further movement to the Isle of Man involved a bird ringed at Wellington College, Crowthorne, in November 2007, which was re-caught on Calf of Man in April 2008. Movement to and from the Continent is indicated by the recovery in March 2000 in Belgium of a juvenile ringed in September 1999 at Brimpton.

*Sponsored by Clare and Mike Workman*

# Firecrest

Amber   Sch. 1

## *Regulus ignicapilla*

*Scarce visitor in all seasons*

The Firecrest is a scarce passage migrant, winter and summer visitor to Berkshire. Most records are from mixed or coniferous woodland in the east of the county, and the number of records has increased in recent years reflecting an increase nationally.

In the 2007–11 Atlas Survey, breeding evidence was recorded for 39 tetrads (11 with confirmed breeding) compared to 20 tetrads (two with confirmed breeding) in the 1987–89 Atlas Survey. Its breeding range has extended since 1987–89 into mid- and west Berkshire, though the stronghold for this species still remains coniferous woodland in the south east of the county. The winter map shows a reduced distribution compared to the breeding season with records from 20 tetrads, mainly in east Berkshire.

The first records from the county in spring or summer were in 1972, just a year after breeding was proved in Buckinghamshire (Lack & Ferguson, 1993), when two were seen at Thatcham Marsh on 28th May, and one was seen in a garden in Mortimer on 22nd July. In east Berkshire, singing males were first reported from Windsor Forest in 1974, and since then they have regularly summered or bred in this area. Up until 2001 the highest annual totals of singing males were 16 in 1983 and 13 in 1979. However, our knowledge of the breeding status of the species in Berkshire was transformed from 2001 when intensive fieldwork in the woodlands of east Berkshire found 43 singing males or pairs. The survey work has shown that Berkshire is a stronghold of this species in the UK with, for example,

over a quarter of the known UK breeding population found in the county annually from 2002 to 2004, and numbers reaching a peak of 92 territories in 2010. Numbers of males holding territory since 2001 are shown in Figure 127.

The only earlier evidence of breeding in Berkshire came from the Crowthorne area where a small colony existed, probably continuously, from 1976 until 1990. A nest was found in 1979 and provided the first evidence of Firecrests having bred in the county. In 2001 breeding was confirmed at five sites and the observation of fledged juveniles being fed was the first proof of successful breeding in the county. Between 2001 and 2010 breeding has been confirmed in all but two years.

The first 20th century winter record of Firecrest for Berkshire was in 1958, when one was seen with Goldcrests

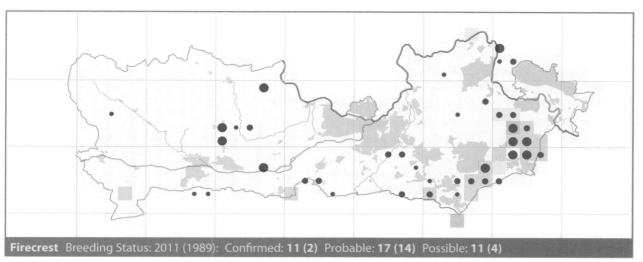

**Firecrest** Breeding Status: 2011 (1989): Confirmed: **11 (2)** Probable: **17 (14)** Possible: **11 (4)**

**Firecrest** Breeding season abundance
Tetrads occupied: **14 (41)** Average of occupied tetrads: **2·4**

**Firecrest** Winter abundance
Tetrads occupied: **2 (20)** Average of occupied tetrads: **2·0**

| exTTV | NUMBER OF TETRADS IN ABUNDANCE CATEGORY | | | | |
|---|---|---|---|---|---|
| 27 | 6 | 2 | 3 | 1 | 2 |

0   1   2   3   4   6
SURVEY COUNT

| exTTV | NUMBER OF TETRADS IN ABUNDANCE CATEGORY | | |
|---|---|---|---|
| 18 | 1 | 0 | 1 |

0   1   2   3
SURVEY COUNT

Firecrest, Swinley Forest  *Jerry O'Brien*

353

at Barkham Common on 12th January and again on 30th January. This was quickly followed by two records in 1960, at Bulmershe in March and south of Lowbury Hill on the Berkshire Downs in October. Following another record from Barkham in January 1962, single birds were seen in Berkshire in 1967 and 1968, and a male was caught and ringed at Thatcham Marsh in November 1970. Winter records have been annual since 1974. Firecrests first appear to have over-wintered in Berkshire in 1974/75, when a single bird was seen in the Wraysbury Gravel Pits area between December and March. There were no further records of overwintering until 1984/85, but wintering was then recorded in 1985/86, 1987/88 and in every winter from 1989/90 to 1993/94, probably in response to a run of milder winters. Until 1990/91 no more than two birds had been recorded wintering, but in November and December 1990 four were seen together at Burghfield Gravel Pits, and there were four further birds at three other sites. Gravel pits have been the most frequently reported sites for wintering birds, but are also most frequently visited by birdwatchers. More recently overwintering was demonstrated by ringing recaptures at two sites in east Berkshire in 2004/05, and was presumed on Finchampstead Ridges in 2006/07. A ringed bird was seen to overwinter at Dinton Pastures in 2010/11.

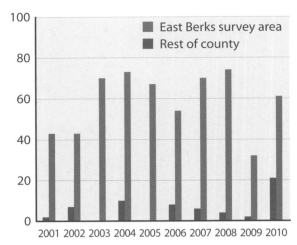

**Figure 127: Firecrest: Breeding numbers since intensive fieldwork began in 2001.**

The earliest county record of Firecrest is of two procured near Eton in about 1865 (Clark Kennedy, 1880). The claim that the species bred close to Frogmore House in Home Park in 1863 by the same author is now regarded as an unreliable record, in the absence of supporting information for what would have been an exceptional record at that time. A record of five birds at Combe in March 1973 is also now considered unreliable for similar reasons.

*Sponsored by Abigail Stares*

# Penduline Tit

*Remiz pendulinus*

*Rare vagrant, one record*

The range of the Penduline Tit has extended into north-west Europe in recent decades, but it remains a rare visitor to Britain. The sole Berkshire record is of an adult female trapped and ringed at Brimpton Gravel Pits on 1st October 1988. This constituted the nineteenth British record and was only the second to be caught and ringed. It had not been seen or heard before it was trapped.

*Sponsored by Rachel Westmacott*

# Blue Tit

*Cyanistes caeruleus*

*Abundant resident*

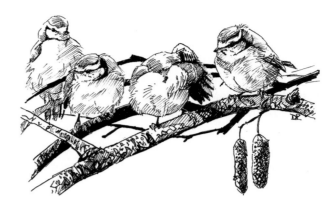

The Blue Tit is an abundant resident in Berkshire and is found in most of the county's habitats, including deciduous, mixed and coniferous woodland, heathland scrub, farmland, and parks and gardens. It will readily take up nest boxes in summer and visits garden feeding stations in winter, and is one of the most familiar of the county's garden birds.

In the 2007–11 Atlas Survey, the Blue Tit was present in all tetrads in the county and confirmed as breeding in 98% of them, marginally more than the 95% recorded in the 1987–89 survey. In 2012, Blue Tits overtook Blackbirds as the third most prominent species in the 33-year old national Big Garden Birdwatch, having increased by 21% in this survey since it commenced, whilst the State of the UK's Birds report for 2011 indicates an increase of 29% in the previous 40 years.

Breeding normally starts early in the third week of April, with most pairs laying within two weeks of each other, their breeding season timed to coincide with the peak emergence of caterpillars. An early nest with young was found during the 1987–89 Tetrad Survey at Kiln Green

on 18th April 1989, reflecting the mild winter and spring that year.

On occasion, unlikely nest sites are used, such as on an external speaker at the Bounty Pub, Cockmarsh in 2009 and, at Cookham Dean in 2010, young were heard from inside a wooden fence post, the only access being a 1·5 cm bolt hole. Another pair, at Odney, nested inside a car tyre on a children's swing and would continue feeding the brood whilst the swing was in use. Bat boxes, an 'End of Motorway' sign, and a Sand Martin bank have also been utilized.

In winter, the Blue Tit forms roaming flocks in association with other tits and small passerines. Within

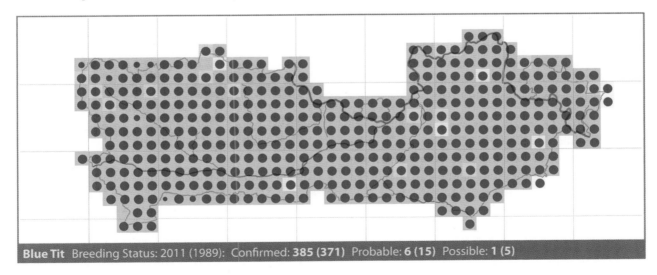

**Blue Tit** Breeding Status: 2011 (1989): Confirmed: **385 (371)** Probable: **6 (15)** Possible: **1 (5)**

**Blue Tit** Breeding season abundance
Tetrads occupied: **391 (394)** Average of occupied tetrads: **16·3**

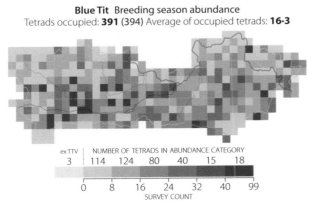

| exTTV | NUMBER OF TETRADS IN ABUNDANCE CATEGORY | | | | | |
|---|---|---|---|---|---|---|
| 3 | 114 | 124 | 80 | 40 | 15 | 18 |

0    8    16    24    32    40    99
SURVEY COUNT

**Blue Tit** Winter abundance
Tetrads occupied: **393 (394)** Average of occupied tetrads: **22·4**

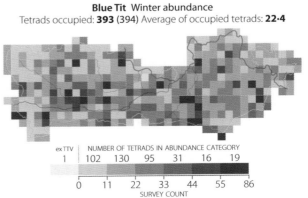

| exTTV | NUMBER OF TETRADS IN ABUNDANCE CATEGORY | | | | | |
|---|---|---|---|---|---|---|
| 1 | 102 | 130 | 95 | 31 | 16 | 19 |

0    11    22    33    44    55    86
SURVEY COUNT

these foraging parties numbers may exceed 200, as on 12th October 1981 when 252 were counted in a mixed flock of tits and finches at Dinton Pastures. Approximately 100 were seen in winter 2002 in the Tilehurst area, whilst an evening roost of up to 87 individuals was located at Legoland, Windsor on 1st April 2010. The Winter Map shows a patchy but widespread distribution with highest numbers around the main built-up areas in the county, probably a reflection of the large numbers which are attracted to garden feeding stations particularly in suburban and urban areas at this time of year.

Occasionally, birds with odd features have been reported. A leucistic bird, looking yellow and white in flight, was feeding with other Blue Tits at Bray Gravel Pits in September 1989. A bird with melanistic flanks and belly was seen in a Hurley garden in 2010. An individual in South Ascot on 2nd February 1998 had an extended upper mandible about the length of the bird's head. This was almost identical to similarly-deformed bird which visited a Cookham garden between 2001 and 2004, always feeding from the side of the beak. Another, with an upturned bill three times normal length, was noted to be using a stick to aid feeding in a Cox Green garden on 11th March 2006 and again in 2007.

Large numbers are processed during ringing studies in Berkshire and this has confirmed that the Blue Tit is a sedentary species, the vast majority of recoveries being close to the ringing site. The longest confirmed distance travelled involved a bird originally caught on 25th September 1994 at Kintbury, which was re-trapped 260 km away at Immingham, Humberside, on 18th January 1996.

*Sponsored by Renee Grayer*

## Great Tit

*Parus major*

*Abundant resident*

A common and widespread resident in Berkshire, the Great Tit mainly favours broadleaved woodland, but is also found in a wide variety of other habitats, including suburban and urban areas, wherever suitable food sources and nesting cavities can be found. It readily uses nest boxes (even Little Owl and Tawny Owl boxes), and comes to garden feeding stations particularly during the winter. Unusual nest sites have included a rolled up carpet at Sheepdrove on 4th July 2010.

In the 2007–11 Atlas Survey, the species was confirmed to have bred in 96% of all tetrads, with no particular pattern to the handful of tetrads where only 'possible' or 'probable' breeding status was established. This represented an increase from the 89% of tetrads in which breeding was confirmed in the 1987–89 survey, consistent with the results of the CBC and BBS national monitoring schemes, which have shown an increase of about 60% in the intervening period.

In winter, parties of 30 or 40 may be found with feeding flocks of Blue Tits and other small passerines. The largest flock recorded in Berkshire was 175 at Warren Row in a mixed flock of tits during January 1988. Both the breeding season and winter abundance maps indicate that Great Tits are more numerous in wooded and suburban areas and less so in areas of open downland, as is the case with the Blue Tit. The survey counts indicate the Great Tit to be almost as abundant as the Blue Tit and the county population is estimated to be approximately 35,000 territories (Appendix IV).

Ringing studies carried out in Berkshire have shown that the Great Tit is essentially a sedentary species, with the bulk of those ringed being recovered within nine kilometres. Notable exceptions concern two birds ringed at Hurley on 5th March 1981, both of which were recovered 155 km away in Dover, one on 25th October and one on 2nd November in the same year. Another individual, a female, ringed in Oaken Copse on 16th May 1980 travelled 160 km before being caught at Castle Bytham, Lincs, on 19th May 1998, whilst the furthest-travelled was yet another female from Oaken Copse ringed on 26th February 1994, and subsequently trapped at Newbourne Springs, Suffolk, 205 km away, on 22nd April the same year.

Birds exhibiting plumage aberrations occur on occasion, such as a leucistic bird seen in Windsor Great Park in March 1991 which was mostly pale yellow, and a

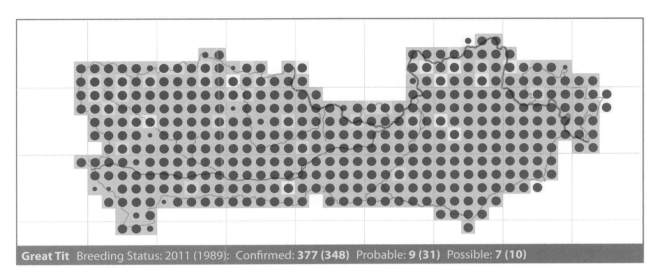

**Great Tit** Breeding Status: 2011 (1989): Confirmed: **377 (348)** Probable: **9 (31)** Possible: **7 (10)**

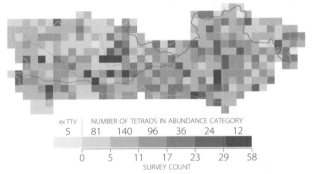

**Great Tit** Breeding season abundance
Tetrads occupied: **389 (394)** Average of occupied tetrads: **11·9**

| ex TTV | NUMBER OF TETRADS IN ABUNDANCE CATEGORY | | | | | |
|---|---|---|---|---|---|---|
| 5 | 81 | 140 | 96 | 36 | 24 | 12 |

| 0 | 5 | 11 | 17 | 23 | 29 | 58 |
SURVEY COUNT

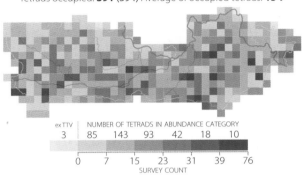

**Great Tit** Winter abundance
Tetrads occupied: **391 (394)** Average of occupied tetrads: **15·7**

| ex TTV | NUMBER OF TETRADS IN ABUNDANCE CATEGORY | | | | | |
|---|---|---|---|---|---|---|
| 3 | 85 | 143 | 93 | 42 | 18 | 10 |

| 0 | 7 | 15 | 23 | 31 | 39 | 76 |
SURVEY COUNT

melanistic individual in a garden in Hurst on 27th December 2008, with possibly the same individual noted feeding on sunflower hearts there on 6th July 2009. A bird with a long, curved upper mandible was present in a Maidens Green garden on 11th January 2008.

The abundance of Great Tits in Berkshire has evidently not changed noticeably since the 19th century, with Clark Kennedy (1868) stating that the species was one of the commonest residents, and Noble (1906) remarking that it was commoner than either the Blue or the Coal Tit.

*Sponsored by Barry Williams*

# Coal Tit

*Periparus ater*

*Common resident*

The Coal Tit is a widespread and common resident in Berkshire, which is particularly associated with coniferous trees, resulting in noticeable concentrations in the south-west and south-east, where mixed and coniferous woodlands predominate. Breeding evidence for the species was recorded in 75% of the tetrads in the county during the 1987–89 Atlas Survey, and from 73% in the 2007–11 Atlas Survey. Unsurprisingly, the Coal Tit was found less frequently in the relatively less wooded downland in the north. However, the Coal Tit was widespread elsewhere, demonstrating its ability to exploit even urban areas where it breeds in parks, large gardens and churchyards. The survey counts suggest it to be considerably less abundant than Great and Blue Tits.

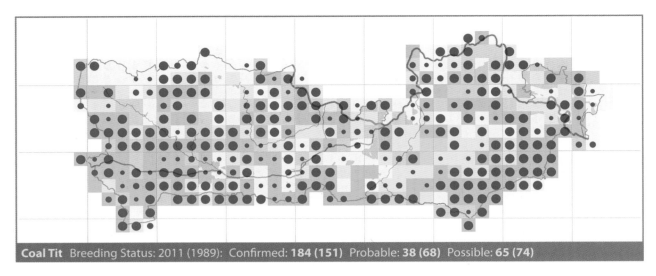

**Coal Tit** Breeding Status: 2011 (1989): Confirmed: **184 (151)** Probable: **38 (68)** Possible: **65 (74)**

**Coal Tit** Breeding season abundance
Tetrads occupied: **196 (305)** Average of occupied tetrads: **4·8**

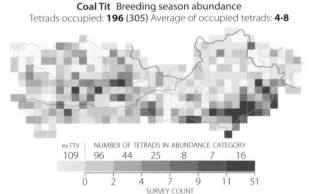

| ex TTV | NUMBER OF TETRADS IN ABUNDANCE CATEGORY | | | | | |
|---|---|---|---|---|---|---|
| 109 | 96 | 44 | 25 | 8 | 7 | 16 |

0  2  4  7  9  11  51
SURVEY COUNT

**Coal Tit** Winter abundance
Tetrads occupied: **217 (315)** Average of occupied tetrads: **4·6**

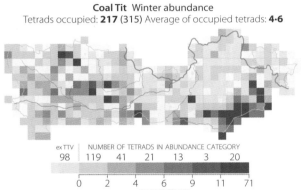

| ex TTV | NUMBER OF TETRADS IN ABUNDANCE CATEGORY | | | | | |
|---|---|---|---|---|---|---|
| 98 | 119 | 41 | 21 | 13 | 3 | 20 |

0  2  4  6  9  11  71
SURVEY COUNT

In Berkshire the Coal Tit normally commences breeding in early to mid-April, at which time it is mainly insectivorous. In winter it switches to a mixture of seeds and insects, although in some Pine *Pinus* spp. woods it may remain exclusively insectivorous. A variety of nest sites have been reported, including garden nest boxes, holes in brickwork and, in woodland, at ground level in a decaying fallen branch. A comprehensive survey undertaken across the East Berkshire heaths and forests in 2007 discovered 544 territories, just prior to the commencement of the 2007–11 Atlas Survey.

The CBC/BBS shows that the British population of Coal Tits has increased slightly since a period of relative stability from 1970s to the 1990s, which followed a period of increase, attributed to the increase in the extent of conifer afforestation in the early and mid-20th century. The summer and winter abundance maps show that the highest densities are in the south of the county, and the Bucklebury-Ashampstead area, matching the distribution of mixed and coniferous woodland. The removal of coniferous stands from many woodlands may have a negative impact on its population in the future.

The similarity between summer and winter distributions is largely to be expected as the species is essentially sedentary. In some years, however, the local population may be swollen by irruptions from the continent, triggered by high population densities and poor seed crops (Cramp *et al.*, 1960; Perrins & Owen, 1958). This may explain some substantial winter counts, including a flock of 80 at Mortimer on 29th January 1997, another of 40–50 on Beech mast in Swinley Forest on 16th December 2000, and flocks of approximately 100 reported at Upper Star Post, Wishmoor, on 12th December 2004 and Swinley Park on 26th December 2006.

Ringing activity attracts significantly fewer Coal Tits than Blue Tits and Great Tits; nonetheless, by 2010, typically 280 Coal Tits were being caught each year. There have however been only a few recoveries from outside the county, and none from further afield than Kent.

*Sponsored by John Claridge*

# Willow Tit

*Poecile montanus*

*Uncommon localised resident*

The Willow Tit is an uncommon localised resident in Berkshire and the least widespread of the five true tit species. It is uncommon and local in the west of the county and all but extinct in the east. The species' preferred habitat is damp, mixed woodland with trees of varying age that provide a succession of rotten stumps or boughs where it excavates its nest chambers. This habitat is most commonly found in the west of Berkshire, and more particularly the Kennet Valley and the south-west downland of the county; this matches the distribution pattern of earlier, and to some extent current, records.

In line with the national trend there has been a rapid decline since the 1987–89 Tetrad Survey. The national population monitoring schemes (the CBC and its replacement, the BBS) indicate a decline of 90% between 1967 and 2009 (Baillie *et al.*, 2012). In the 2007–11 surveys, breeding evidence for Willow Tits was recorded in 17 tetrads and they were confirmed to have bred in only five, down from 124 and 52 twenty years earlier. The reason for the rapid decline is unclear, but may be linked to changes in woodland structure and management (Baillie *et al.*, 2012).

The *1968–72 BTO Atlas* showed confirmed breeding in all but one 10 km square (SU 48) in Berkshire. The 1987–89 Tetrad Atlas showed an apparent retreat from east Berkshire, but the contraction in range now shown by the 2007–11 survey is dramatic, with the species having disappeared from the east and centre of the county, and breeding only being confirmed from the

far southwest, except for an isolated tetrad in the Pang valley. It has largely disappeared from the Kennet Valley, formerly regarded as a stronghold of the species.

The Winter Map shows a similar distribution to the summer map reflecting the Willow Tit's sedentary nature. There is some evidence of post breeding dispersal from local ringing studies, which have shown that some Willow Tits move locally, usually less than 10 km, including from exposed locations on downland to more sheltered lowland areas in winter. Annual ringing totals for west Berkshire show a rapid decline, with double figure totals up to 1992 falling to single figures since 1999, although a colour-ringing scheme started recently in 2010 has augmented these. The oldest bird recovered was 4 years 3 months old (Newbury Ringing Group).

The first reference to the Willow Tit in Berkshire, after it was recognised as a separate species from the Marsh

Willow Tit, Combe Wood *Jerry O'Brien*

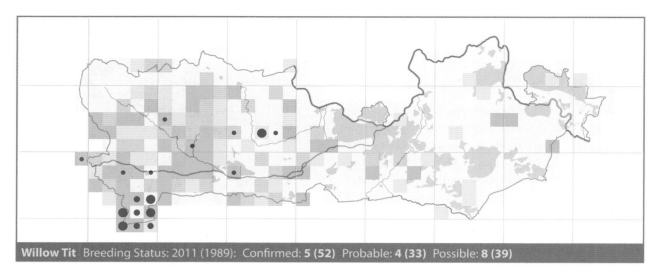

**Willow Tit** Breeding Status: 2011 (1989): Confirmed: **5 (52)** Probable: **4 (33)** Possible: **8 (39)**

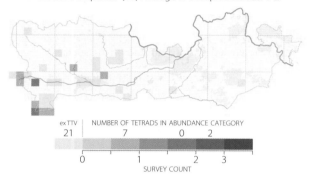

**Willow Tit** Breeding season abundance
Tetrads occupied: **9 (30)** Average of occupied tetrads: **1·2**

| ex TTV | NUMBER OF TETRADS IN ABUNDANCE CATEGORY | | |
| --- | --- | --- | --- |
| 21 | 7 | 0 | 2 |

0     1     2     3
SURVEY COUNT

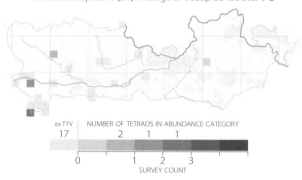

**Willow Tit** Winter abundance
Tetrads occupied: **4 (21)** Average of occupied tetrads: **1·8**

| ex TTV | NUMBER OF TETRADS IN ABUNDANCE CATEGORY | | |
| --- | --- | --- | --- |
| 17 | 2 | 1 | 1 |

0     1     2     3
SURVEY COUNT

Tit in 1897, is of a bird which was considered to be almost certainly this species at Maidenhead Thicket in 1926. This was followed by one at Inkpen Beacon on 20th December 1928, and one seen in the same area, near Combe, in the winter of 1931/32. The species was present in Windsor Great Park in 1934 and was reported from five sites in 1935. The first published breeding record, somewhat unusually, was of one nesting in a Walnut tree *Juglans* spp. at Cookham Dean in 1938.

*Sponsored by John Lerpiniere*

# Marsh Tit

`Red`

*Poecile palustris*

*Locally common resident*

The Marsh Tit is a locally common resident in Berkshire, and more widespread than its close relative the Willow Tit. Its preferred habitat is oak *Quercus* spp. and Beech *Fagus sylvatica* woodland with a high, closed canopy, although it often occurs in mature broadleaved or mixed woodland or plantations where Alder *Alnus glutinosa*, Ash *Fraxinus excelsior* or birch *Betula* spp. predominate. Marsh Tits are also occasionally found in mature coniferous woodlands, including plantations, and in mature, overgrown hedgerows and borders with standard trees.

Marsh Tits were recorded in 39% of the tetrads in the county during the 2007–11 Tetrad Survey and were confirmed to have bred in 45% of those. There has been a moderate decline in the range since the 1987–89 Tetrad Survey, particularly in the east of the county. In the 2007–11 Tetrad Survey breeding was confirmed in many tetrads where the Marsh Tit was not found or confirmed in 1987–89, despite an overall contraction

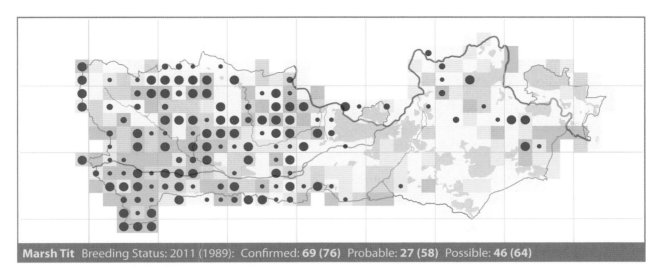

**Marsh Tit** Breeding Status: 2011 (1989): Confirmed: **69 (76)** Probable: **27 (58)** Possible: **46 (64)**

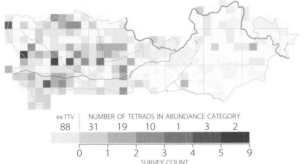

**Marsh Tit** Breeding season abundance
Tetrads occupied: **66** (154) Average of occupied tetrads: **2·0**

| exTTV | NUMBER OF TETRADS IN ABUNDANCE CATEGORY | | | | | |
|---|---|---|---|---|---|---|
| 88 | 31 | 19 | 10 | 1 | 3 | 2 |

0   1   2   3   4   5   9
SURVEY COUNT

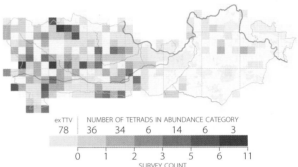

**Marsh Tit** Winter abundance
Tetrads occupied: **99** (177) Average of occupied tetrads: **2·5**

| exTTV | NUMBER OF TETRADS IN ABUNDANCE CATEGORY | | | | | |
|---|---|---|---|---|---|---|
| 78 | 36 | 34 | 6 | 14 | 6 | 3 |

0   1   2   3   5   6   11
SURVEY COUNT

in range. Although considerably more abundant, it shows the same west and south-west bias as Willow Tit. The contraction in range reflects the national trend. The species is in the "Red List" of birds of conservation concern in the UK (Eaton *et al.*, 2009), having declined by more than 50% since the 1960s. Although most of the apparently unoccupied tetrads correspond either to extensive arable farms, downland or urban areas, the Marsh Tit occurs most frequently in the west of the county where its favoured habitats predominate. However, since it is a rather sedentary species which occurs in relatively low densities, it can be overlooked and may have gone unrecorded in some of the tetrads where it was present. The scarcity of Marsh Tits in east Berkshire was evident as early as the middle of the 19th century when Clark Kennedy (1868) considered it thinly distributed, even allowing for the fact that the Willow Tit was not recognised as a separate species at that time. Woodland management and the increasing deer population that reduce woodland under-storey may be a contributory factor to its overall decline in the county.

Little information is available on the population density of Marsh Tits in Berkshire but a survey carried out in the Warren Row area in 1985 located 10 to 20 pairs. Based on the 2007–11 abundance surveys, Berkshire was estimated to hold around 600 territories in total (Appendix IV).

The winter map has a similar, though somewhat wider, distribution to that of the summer map and reflects the sedentary nature of the species. This is reflected in the results of local ringing studies, the furthest distance from which any bird ringed in the county has been recovered being 11 km.

The number of Marsh Tits ringed in Berkshire each year has been relatively low, possibly reflecting the location of ringing sites rather than the size of the population. At feeding stations operated by the Newbury Ringing Group in the Winterbourne Valley, Snelsmore Common and Greenham Common few birds were trapped, even during hard winters when they might have been expected to move out of nearby woodland. Formerly regular in small numbers, the species' visits to feeding stations have declined in the last few years. Those that occur usually arrive in the autumn and many are first-winter birds indicating post breeding dispersal. The oldest bird recovered is 5 years 10 months. The infrequency of visits to the feeding stations later in the winter may be a reflection of the species' early breeding season, with pairs forming and territories being established as early as February.

*Sponsored by John Lerpiniere*

# Bearded Tit

Amber   Sch. 1

## *Panurus biarmicus*

*Scarce winter visitor and rare summer visitor*

The Bearded Tit is a scarce winter and rare summer visitor to Berkshire. It has very specific habitat requirements closely linked to *Phragmites* reed beds. These requirements and the susceptibility of the species to severe winters, means that its range in this country is limited. The British breeding population has a generally eastern and coastal bias and is thought to comprise only some 700 pairs. The occurrence of the species in an inland county such as Berkshire is therefore unusual.

The Bearded Tit's preferred habitat of *Phragmites* reed bed is found in isolated areas along the Kennet Valley. The frequency with which the species has occurred in Berkshire in the past has been influenced by the route of the railway following the course of the River Kennet. Before steam engines were replaced in the 1960s sparks often set fire to the adjacent reed beds and this, together with some management for shooting, protected the habitat as its use for thatching declined. The reedbeds that remain are found mainly in areas where the railway or the river has isolated them from adjacent agricultural land and development. Gravel extraction has led to the destruction of some important areas of *Phragmites*, but elsewhere it has created suitable conditions for reed beds to develop. These can be transient, either being destroyed by redevelopment or lost through succession to scrub. Some areas of reed bed remain either on private land where access is restricted, or on nature reserves where they are maintained and are afforded a degree of sustainability and protection.

Bearded Tits were resident species in Berkshire at the beginning of the 19th century and said to "frequent the banks of the Kennet between Reading and Newbury and undoubtedly breed about Newbury" (Lamb, 1880).

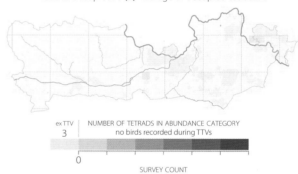

**Bearded Tit** Winter abundance
Tetrads occupied: **0** (3) Average of occupied tetrads: **0**

ex TTV   NUMBER OF TETRADS IN ABUNDANCE CATEGORY
3   no birds recorded during TTVs

0

SURVEY COUNT

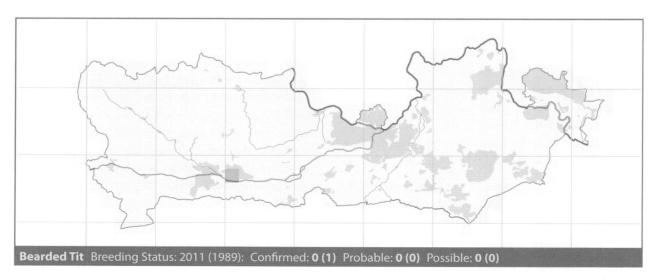

**Bearded Tit** Breeding Status: 2011 (1989): Confirmed: **0 (1)** Probable: **0 (0)** Possible: **0 (0)**

Clark Kennedy (1868) considered the species to be fairly numerous along the reedy banks of the Thames, but Noble (1906) stated that it was no longer found in the Thames Valley. The species seems to have died out in Berkshire sometime in the late 19th century, probably as a result of drainage and cultivation.

The first 20th century record was of one near Theale on 30th August 1916 (Summers-Smith, 1951). The next record was when four birds were at Thatcham Marsh in March 1961, followed by two there in March 1964. In 1965, three were ringed at nearby Newbury Sewage Farm in January, and up to four were present at Thatcham Marsh from January to March. Several individuals could be found, each winter, between November and April at Thatcham Marsh from 1965/66 to 1974/75, when records ceased due to the loss of habitat in the roosting area, until 10–12 birds were seen on 19th October 1980. In the period 1985/86 to 1988/89 there was a run of records at Thatcham Marsh, mostly in winter. In the 1995/96 winter, up to 10 were seen here in October and November, and at least five in January. Since then no sustained presence has been reported from this area.

Elsewhere in Berkshire, there was an influx of Bearded Tits in 1972, with eight in Windsor Great Park in October, eight at Bray Gravel Pits in November, and at least 13 at Reading Sewage Farm in November. A smaller influx occurred in the winter of 1973/74, with two at Reading Sewage Farm in October, six at Twyford Gravel Pits in November and four there in February 1974. Singles were seen at Brimpton Gravel Pits in October 1976 and May 1990, three were at Reading Sewage Farm in October 1976, three were at Wraysbury Gravel Pits in March 1978 and one in December 1975, at least six were at Theale Gravel Pits in October 1980 and one there in March 1983, and one was at Summerleaze Gravel Pits on 13th December 1992. No other records then occurred until 20th March 1999 when one was at Great Meadow Pond, Windsor. Since the 1990s the trend for irregular occurrences of Bearded Tit has continued. Most arrivals are from October through to March, in *Phragmites* habitat, usually newish regeneration, such as vegetation fringing gravel workings, lakes and ponds. Many of the traditional reed beds have degenerated and have little of the fresh growth the species is known to need. Some visits are fleeting but occasionally an individual or more stays for weeks over a winter period. In 2003/04, a male wintered in the Burghfield Mill Gravel Pits area; two were at Freeman's Marsh, Hungerford on 6th November 2008, up to three were at Dorney Wetlands in December 2010 and January 2011; and between one and three were present at Dinton Pastures between October and December 2011.

A pair of Bearded Tits present at a site in east Berkshire from 3rd April to 15 May 1975 was seen displaying and carrying nesting material; breeding was not confirmed however. The first confirmed breeding record for the species in Berkshire in the 20th century came from Thatcham Marsh, when an adult and juveniles were seen on 3rd June 1986. Subsequently, a pair bred successfully at this site in 1987 and summered in 1988. During the 2007–11 Atlas Survey two sites recorded Bearded Tit in suitable habitat outside the breeding season but no breeding activity was reported.

A number of Bearded Tits were ringed at Thatcham Marsh from 1965 to 1975 when the ringing area was destroyed by gravel workings. During this period birds which had been ringed at Minsmere in Suffolk, Sittingbourne in Kent, Weymouth in Dorset, and Bradwell-on-Sea in Essex were trapped, as well as 54 un-ringed birds. Since then the only individual ringed in Berkshire was in 1990 when one was ringed at Brimpton Gravel Pits on 20th May. It was last seen on the 27th May and two days later it was trapped at Rutland Water, Leicestershire; the only Berkshire-ringed bird recovered outside the county.

*Sponsored by Sandy Studd*

# Short-toed Lark

## *Calandrella brachydactyla*

*Rare vagrant, one record*

The only Berkshire record of Short-toed Lark, whose normal breeding range is the arid zones from southern Europe to central Asia, is of one found with a small flock of Skylarks at Slough Sewage Farm from 3rd to 13th January 1987. This sighting was the first January record of Short-toed Lark in Britain, most of the 20 or so records each year being of birds on the south or east coast during the spring or autumn migration.

*Sponsored by Duncan Spence*

# Woodlark

Amber  Sch. 1

*Lullula arborea*

*Scarce in summer and winter*

The Woodlark is a localised, scarce breeding species in Berkshire, which is mainly restricted to a few suitable areas of heathland and felled forest during the breeding season. After breeding, birds are harder to locate on their summering areas and some appear to disperse, sometimes being found in other areas away from breeding habitat.

The 2007–11 Atlas Survey shows that breeding is no longer confined to the southern edge of the county, adjoining the heaths of Surrey and Hampshire, and is now to be found in other suitable heathland areas, mainly further west in the county, most notably at Greenham and Snelsmore Commons. Breeding evidence was reported from 34 tetrads, with breeding confirmed in 14 and probable in a further nine. This is a considerable increase on the occupancy found in the 1987–89 Atlas Survey, when it was reported from only 11 tetrads. This is consistent with the trend in Britain as a whole, national surveys showing an increase of 88% in Woodlark numbers between 1997 and 2006 (Conway *et al.*, 2009).

The Winter Map suggests that most Berkshire Woodlarks winter in their breeding areas, with records from 31 tetrads mainly coinciding with breeding areas, but some may disperse further afield. In the past, there have been occasional records of winter flocks in Berkshire, such as 60 at Silwood in January 1951, and in some years there are a small number of passage records, chiefly from well-watched gravel pits, but such winter records are uncommon.

EL

In the 19th century, and at the beginning of the 20th century, the Woodlark was regarded as rare and extremely localised (*Historical Atlas*, Noble, 1906). The species increased in Berkshire through the first half of the 20th century, and Alexander (1952) indicates that by 1950 it was breeding widely in Berkshire. By 1960, there was a marked decrease which was not reversed until the early 1990s. It was recorded almost every year from the heathland areas along the southern edge of the county, although breeding was not always proven since nesting birds and nests are notoriously difficult to find. Breeding was confirmed in 19 years during the period from 1945 to 1985, although the species was recorded every year with the exceptions of 1964 and 1966. The Woodlark was recorded breeding regularly in Windsor Great Park up to about 1960, an area which it has since deserted. Breeding also

Woodlark, Greenham Common  *Marek Walford*

364

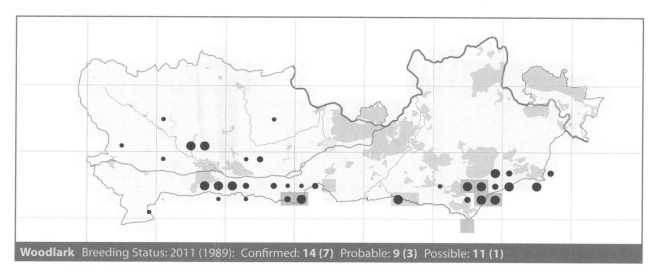

**Woodlark** Breeding Status: 2011 (1989): Confirmed: **14 (7)** Probable: **9 (3)** Possible: **11 (1)**

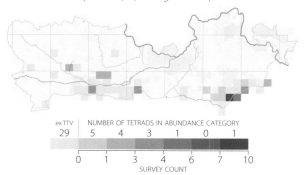

**Woodlark** Breeding season abundance
Tetrads occupied: **14 (43)** Average of occupied tetrads: **3·0**

| exTTV | NUMBER OF TETRADS IN ABUNDANCE CATEGORY | | | | | |
|---|---|---|---|---|---|---|
| 29 | 5 | 4 | 3 | 1 | 0 | 1 |

0    1    3    4    6    7    10
SURVEY COUNT

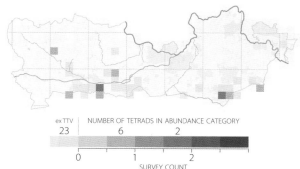

**Woodlark** Winter abundance
Tetrads occupied: **8 (31)** Average of occupied tetrads: **1·3**

| exTTV | NUMBER OF TETRADS IN ABUNDANCE CATEGORY | | |
|---|---|---|---|
| 23 | 6 | 2 | |

0         1         2
SURVEY COUNT

occurred in the Mortimer and Padworth area up to about 1963 and again from about 1985. This decline in the Woodlark population in Berkshire at this time paralleled the national decline summarised by Sitters (1986), although numbers do fluctuate in response to severe winter weather and the availability of suitable habitat. Southern Britain is at the northern edge of the breeding range of the Woodlark in Europe and hence its population here is likely to be sensitive to adverse weather.

Some of the fluctuations in local populations are probably due to the temporary creation of suitable habitat such as occurs in the early stages of growth of conifer plantations. Although these become progressively less attractive to Woodlark as they mature, areas which are clear-felled and left to regenerate, or are replanted in later years may again temporarily provide suitable conditions for re-colonisation. In the Crowthorne and Sandhurst area they bred regularly on rides between the conifer plantations.

*Sponsored by Sarah and Ken White*

# Skylark

*Alauda arvensis*

*Common resident, passage migrant and winter visitor*

The Skylark is a common and familiar resident throughout the open areas of Berkshire, its sustained singing ensuring that its presence over open arable land is not easily overlooked during the breeding season. It is also a passage migrant and winter visitor, occurring in considerable numbers in some years.

In the 1987–89 Atlas Survey it was shown to be widespread and numerous, with breeding evidence

EL

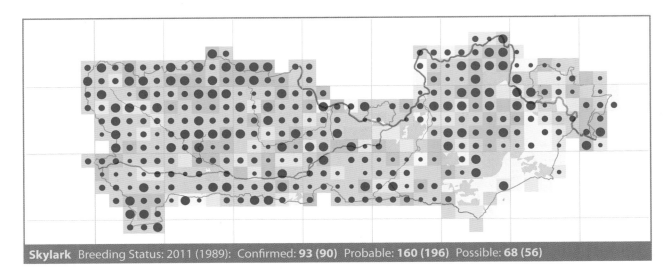

**Skylark** Breeding Status: 2011 (1989): Confirmed: **93 (90)** Probable: **160 (196)** Possible: **68 (56)**

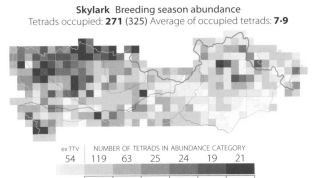

**Skylark** Breeding season abundance
Tetrads occupied: **271 (325)** Average of occupied tetrads: **7·9**

| ex TTV | NUMBER OF TETRADS IN ABUNDANCE CATEGORY | | | | | |
|---|---|---|---|---|---|---|
| 54 | 119 | 63 | 25 | 24 | 19 | 21 |

| 0 | 3 | 7 | 11 | 15 | 19 | 66 |
|---|---|---|---|---|---|---|

SURVEY COUNT

**Skylark** Winter abundance
Tetrads occupied: **194 (277)** Average of occupied tetrads: **15·4**

| ex TTV | NUMBER OF TETRADS IN ABUNDANCE CATEGORY | | | | | |
|---|---|---|---|---|---|---|
| 83 | 105 | 38 | 19 | 9 | 3 | 20 |

| 0 | 7 | 15 | 23 | 30 | 38 | 214 |
|---|---|---|---|---|---|---|

SURVEY COUNT

recorded in 87% of tetrads, breeding being confirmed or probable in 73%. The 2007–11 Atlas Survey shows a reduction in its range, with breeding evidence recorded in 81% of tetrads, and breeding confirmed or probable in 64%. While, in some cases, this decline is due to change of land use and loss of suitable habitat, it almost certainly indicates an overall reduction in numbers, particularly in the east of the county. Monitoring of Skylarks by the CBC nationally showed a steep decline from the mid-1970s until the mid-1980s, mainly attributed to changes in farming practice, with the spread of more intensive methods and the change from spring to autumn sowing of cereal crops. Subsequently the species has continued to decline in the UK, albeit at a slower rate, a 30% decline in abundance being recorded in the period between the 1987–89 and 2007–11 Atlas surveys by the CBC and BBS annual surveys.

The distribution maps illustrates the Skylark's preference for areas of open fields. Although rarely found in urban areas, the species will tolerate some human activity to the extent of nesting on the scrubby margins of working gravel pits.

Skylarks occur throughout Berkshire in winter, although not as widely as during the summer, being found in 70% of tetrads. Winter numbers are augmented by immigrants from north-east Europe, and sizeable flocks occur widely on farmland, downland, heaths and other open areas where they can find the short vegetation or bare ground suitable for feeding. Migrating birds can often be heard flying over on fine autumn days. Flocks of over 100 occur in most winters, particularly on the Downs and other areas in the west of the county, and smaller flocks are commonly noted during autumn migration from late September to November, but rarely in spring. Some larger gatherings are still recorded, most recently in the winter of 2010/11 when the largest single flock was of 500 birds at Bucklebury in December 2010. In some years huge flocks have gathered during severe weather conditions. For example, from December 1978 to January 1979, 4,000 were at Wraysbury Gravel Pits, 3,000 at Summerleaze Gravel Pits, 2,500 per hour at Marlow crossing into Berkshire and 3,000 at Cookham Rise.

It seems that Skylarks were numerous in Berkshire in the 19th Century. Hewett (1911), writing in 1861, commented on immense flocks on the Downs and thousands being caught and sent to London, and Noble (1906) noted that "a man shot dozens while standing in a small garden" during a winter flock movement.

*Sponsored by Dick Haydon*

# Shore Lark

*Eremophila alpestris*

*Rare winter vagrant, two records*

The Shore Lark is a rare winter vagrant to Berkshire and has been recorded on just two occasions. The first involved a bird which stayed for four days at Theale Gravel Pits from 18th to 21st December 1973 and associated with a party of Linnets. This record coincided with a period when there was an increase in records throughout Britain (*1981–84 BTO Winter Atlas*). After a gap of over 24 years, the next record was a bird that was present in fields adjacent to Eversley Gravel Pits from 10th to 12th April 1998. A bird reported as being seen at "Wraysbury" from 22nd December 1971 was in fact located, and stayed, on Wraysbury Reservoir and, as far as is known, was not seen to enter Berkshire (C. Heard *in litt.*).

*Sponsored by Bill Nicoll*

# Sand Martin

*Riparia riparia*

*Locally common summer visitor and passage migrant*

The Sand Martin is a locally common summer visitor to Berkshire and also occurs in considerable numbers on passage. Its natural nesting site is in steep sand banks, usually alongside rivers or streams, where it excavates a burrow. Because of the slow-flowing nature of most of Berkshire's rivers there are few steep riverbanks cut by erosion and hence few natural nest sites for Sand Martins. Moreover, some river banks are occupied by moored boats during summer months. The species is an opportunistic nester, however, and is quick to exploit man-made habitats, such as the temporary steep faces which are created during gravel extraction and sand quarrying, and artificial banks such as those created at Hosehill Lake, Theale, Lea Farm, and Lavell's Lake. It often occurs away from breeding areas when feeding, on migration and during post-breeding dispersal.

The Tetrad Surveys show that the breeding distribution of Sand Martins in Berkshire remains very strongly correlated with the major river systems, where suitable banks and gravel workings are to be found. Although breeding was confirmed in more tetrads in the recent survey than in 1987–89, there is little evidence of a significant change in breeding distribution. The Sand Martin is a localised breeding bird in the county compared to the Swallow and House Martin, which are to be found over almost the entire county.

Nesting colonies away from watercourses, such as sand quarries or other man-made sites, are transient. Many

sites holding large colonies in the 1980s, such as Long Lane Pit, Hermitage, (370 pairs in 1980), Wraysbury Gravel Pits, (217 nests in 1977), and Field Farm Gravel Pit (250 nest holes in 1988), have been replaced with others, but colonies have become noticeably smaller. Since 2000, several suitable sites have been abandoned. Now there are few colonies approaching 100; a bank with a colony at Woolhampton Gravel Pits that had 147 nest holes in 2006 has subsequently been levelled. Birds have also bred in a compacted soil pile near Poyle for several years. As long ago as 1895, birds were observed flying into pipes of the bridge over Sonning Cutting (Anon, 1895), and still today, and drainage pipe entrances in other riverside walls and bridges are being increasingly occupied.

The Sand Martin is one of the earliest summer migrants to return to Britain. The earliest arrivals since 1996 have ranged from 7th March to 21st March, with the majority of birds arriving by mid-April. Exceptionally early birds have been one at Wraysbury Gravel Pits on 25th February

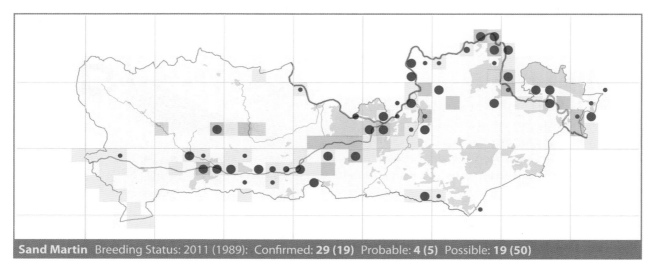

**Sand Martin**  Breeding Status: 2011 (1989):  Confirmed: **29 (19)**  Probable: **4 (5)**  Possible: **19 (50)**

1993, and two at Summerleaze Gravel Pits, Maidenhead on 27th February 2008. Few recent spring passage counts have approached the 1,500 at Burghfield Gravel Pits in April 1994, but an estimated 500 were at Theale Gravel Pits in April 2000 and April 2009. Autumn departures have been noted from 11th September to 30th October, latest dates after 2004 being remarkably consistent, being between 3rd and 6th of October, but the majority of birds leave their colonies by early September. Some dispersal commences as early as July, when juveniles from the first brood and some adults begin to leave their breeding colonies, 500 being noted at Queen Mother Reservoir on

**Sand Martin**  Breeding season abundance
Tetrads occupied: **26 (79)** Average of occupied tetrads: **7·3**

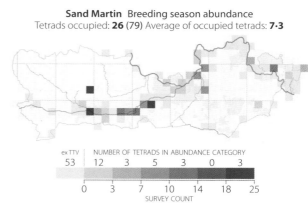

| ex TTV | NUMBER OF TETRADS IN ABUNDANCE CATEGORY | | | | | |
|---|---|---|---|---|---|---|
| 53 | 12 | 3 | 5 | 3 | 0 | 3 |

0    3    7    10    14    18    25
SURVEY COUNT

Sand Martin, Queen Mother Reservoir  *Michael McKee*

9th July 2008. However, most birds disperse in August and early September when large autumn gatherings can be seen over gravel pits or roosting in reedbeds. There were 4,000 at Woodley Airfield on 1st August 1977, but the size of the largest flocks in recent autumns have all been far smaller, the highest being about 500 at Cookham in September 2000, and at Theale Gravel Pits in August 2010 and September 2011.

Two ringing recoveries give an indication of the speed of the autumn passage: one ringed at Willington, Cheshire on 15th July 1965 was recovered near Newbury three days later, and one ringed at Brimpton on 9th July 1989 was recovered at Jorgeau, Loiret, western France five days later, a distance of some 457 km SSE. Out of 55 recoveries of Berkshire-ringed birds, 11 have been in France, and one each in south-west Spain and Morocco.

The British population of Sand Martin suffered a decline in 1968 and 1969, and again in 1983 and 1984 and, although numbers have recovered somewhat since, they are still below their pre–1968 levels (Bird Life International, 2004). The *1968–72 BTO Atlas* attributes the earlier decline to drought, reducing food supply in the Sahel region of Africa where the Sand Martin winters. There are no counts of the Sand Martin population in Berkshire, although the 1987–89 Tetrad Survey fieldwork did not show any breeding on the Thames west of Reading where it used to occur in the early 1970s. It is likely that the population of the species in Berkshire in future will be influenced by both conditions in its wintering quarters, and the availability of nesting sites, which is largely reliant upon the continuation of gravel and sand extraction.

*Sponsored by Rose-Ann Movsovic*

# Swallow　　Amber

## *Hirundo rustica*

*Abundant summer visitor and passage migrant*

The Swallow is a common and widespread summer visitor to Berkshire that breeds in rural areas throughout the county, using a wide range of man-made structures (such as farm buildings, sheds, small stables and horse shelters) as nesting sites. It is also common on passage, often occurring in considerable numbers. Obtaining confirmation of breeding is therefore relatively easy, and made even easier by the fact that the breeding season is prolonged, with second broods often being raised.

The 2007–11 Tetrad Survey recorded breeding evidence in 86% of the tetrads in the county, a little lower than in the 1987–89 survey (94%), though breeding was confirmed in two thirds of all tetrads in both surveys. It was only absent from the centres of urban development and some of the larger tracts of woodland and heathland in the south-east of the county, which have few suitable nest sites. Elsewhere, over downland, farmland and mixed woodland areas, the Swallow is a familiar breeding bird.

Nationally, Swallow abundance measured by the CBC/BBS has shown a 50% increase between 1989 and 2011, although the population in the arable areas of the east has not shown this increase (Evans and Robinson, 2004). In Berkshire it continues to be an abundant breeding species, with the Berkshire Bird Index showing a significant increase between 1994 and 2008, though there may be local declines with loss of nesting or feeding habitat.

County records up to 1994 showed that the first arrival dates were usually from 21st March to 10th April, the 13th March being historically the earliest. But in seven

of the subsequent 15 years, the first arrival has been between 16th and 20th March and in remaining years, none were later than March 30th. The earliest date was one at Kintbury on 12th March 2011. The main spring arrival is usually during the first half of May, but birds often occur in distinct waves separated by several days or even weeks if inclement weather further south interrupts their migration. There are rarely spring gatherings above 300 or 400, but some years produce records of substantial flocks during the spring migration, such as in 2002 when 1,150 were estimated at Theale on 13th May, and in 2004 when several large groups could be found including 1,000 at Theale on 29th April.

After the breeding season, large numbers of adults and juveniles gather together in late August or September, often at communal roosts. Such gatherings include 1,000 roosting in maize at Sonning in September 2004, and 5,000 at Greenham Common on 17th September 1981.

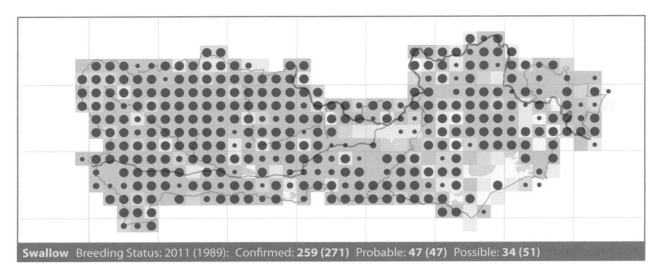

**Swallow** Breeding Status: 2011 (1989): Confirmed: **259 (271)** Probable: **47 (47)** Possible: **34 (51)**

In September 2007, an estimated 2,000 Swallows per hour were seen passing over Theale Gravel Pits for several hours during the morning of the 23rd. The last departure dates recorded since 1974 have ranged from 18th October to 24th November, the latter being a juvenile bird at Thatcham Marsh in 1994. Berkshire produced an early long-distance ringing recovery of Swallow, when one ringed near Windsor in August 1921 was recovered the following January in Cape Province, South Africa, and a second bird ringed in the county was recovered in Transvaal in 1967.

*Sponsored by John Swallow*

**Swallow** Breeding season abundance
Tetrads occupied: **328 (368)** Average of occupied tetrads: **7·8**

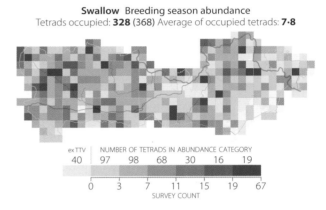

| exTTV | NUMBER OF TETRADS IN ABUNDANCE CATEGORY | | | | | |
|---|---|---|---|---|---|---|
| 40 | 97 | 98 | 68 | 30 | 16 | 19 |

| | 0 | 3 | 7 | 11 | 15 | 19 | 67 |
|---|---|---|---|---|---|---|---|

SURVEY COUNT

# House Martin Amber

## *Delichon urbica*

*Common and widespread summer visitor*

The House Martin is a common and widespread summer visitor to Berkshire which has a very close association with man during its breeding season, nesting on suitable buildings and structures such as bridges in both rural and urban areas. It also occurs in considerable numbers in the county on passage.

The species suffered a substantial contraction of its range in Berkshire between the two Atlas Surveys, with breeding confirmed in 47% of tetrads in the 2007–11 survey, compared to 82% in 1987–89. This is despite the ease with which the species can be recorded, especially when young are being fed in the nest. The House Martin has an extended breeding season, raising two or three broods, and is often seen feeding young in the nest as late as September. A steady decline in breeding success began shortly after the 1987–89 Atlas Survey, the largest colony, at Greenham Common Airfield, reducing from 400 nests annually to 20–30 just prior to the demolition of the aircraft hangars. Other substantial colonies also declined or disappeared, with observers reporting the cessation of breeding at

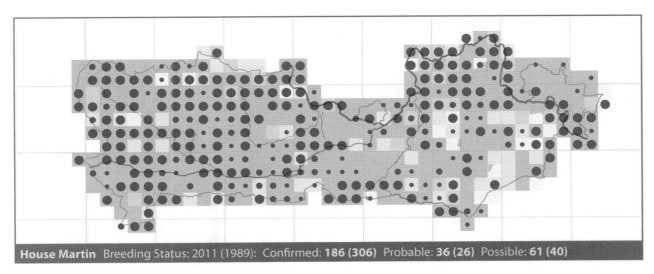

**House Martin** Breeding Status: 2011 (1989): Confirmed: **186 (306)** Probable: **36 (26)** Possible: **61 (40)**

several traditional sites. By 2005 the largest colony reported was of 74 at Jealott's Hill. Comparison of the breeding distribution in the two Atlas Surveys shows the species to have been lost from many urban areas in the centre and east of the county. The local decline reflects the national picture. Although the trend disclosed by the CBC and BBS varies between the regions, the species is regarded as being in probable rapid decline in England.

The first spring arrivals are normally in early or mid-April, but the earliest records have come from Lea Farm on 10th March 2013, Horton Gravel Pits on 13th March 1977, and 14th March 2009 at Moor Green Lakes. Autumn departure dates however have remained typically from 20th October to early November, the latest bird to date being at Dinton Pastures on 10th December 2006. The spring passage normally peaks in mid-May, whilst in autumn large numbers gather from mid-August to the end of September. Recent maximum spring counts include 750 at Brimpton in May 2007, and 1,150 at Theale in May 2003. Theale Gravel Pits regularly produce

**House Martin** Breeding season abundance
Tetrads occupied: **218 (324)** Average of occupied tetrads: **8·8**

| ex TTV | NUMBER OF TETRADS IN ABUNDANCE CATEGORY | | | | | |
|---|---|---|---|---|---|---|
| 106 | 98 | 43 | 33 | 19 | 14 | 11 |

| 0 | 4 | 8 | 13 | 17 | 22 | 90 |
|---|---|---|---|---|---|---|

SURVEY COUNT

substantial autumn counts too, with 1,000 recorded in August 2006 and September 2010, whilst passage of 1,000 per hour was noted there in September 2007.

Despite being a trans-saharan migrant, the longest movement of any bird ringed or recovered in Berkshire involved a bird ringed in Sussex in September 1975, which was recovered in Berkshire in May 1976.

*Sponsored by Renee Grayer*

# Red-rumped Swallow

## *Cecropis daurica*

*Rare vagrant, three records*

The Red-rumped Swallow is a rare vagrant to Britain, with about ten records a year. Its normal range extends from southern Europe across central Asia to the Far East. In Berkshire it has been recorded on just three occasions. The first record was of a bird which was seen well whilst flying with other hirundines over Theale Gravel Pits on 2nd May 1992, and the second was of one briefly at Bray Gravel Pits, on 5th May 1996. Another was seen well by many observers between 8th and 11th May 1999 at Hosehill Lake, Theale, since when there have only been unconfirmed reports.

*Sponsored by Ken White 'BOC Autumn Raptormania 2011'*

# Cetti's Warbler

*Cettia cetti*

*Scarce, localised resident*

The Cetti's Warbler is a scarce breeding resident of reedbeds and damp scrub, and is a fairly recent addition to Britain's list of breeding birds, being first recorded in 1961 and confirmed to be breeding in 1972. The first Berkshire record was in October 1971, when a bird was ringed at Thatcham Marsh. It remained until the following May and was often heard singing. Singing males were then recorded in 1973 and 1976, and the first probable breeding record was of a female with a brood patch which was ringed in June 1978. Cetti's Warblers were not regularly present during the breeding season until the early 1980s, and it was 1985 before breeding was confirmed, when a nest with young was found.

Since the 1987–89 Atlas Survey (when Cetti's Warbler was found in eight tetrads in Berkshire during the breeding season, with breeding confirmed or probable in only two tetrads) the species has continued to slowly colonise Berkshire's river valleys where there is suitable habitat. In the 2007–11 Atlas Survey it was recorded during the breeding season in 54 tetrads (with breeding confirmed in 13 and probable in 17 more). Although

it is a shy and skulking species, the Cetti's Warbler is quite vocal, particularly in the early mornings and, since the song is loud and distinctive, it is unlikely that many birds are overlooked during surveys. Obtaining proof of breeding is, however, difficult due to its skulking habits and the densely vegetated habitat that it favours. It is therefore likely that breeding actually occurred in more tetrads than the surveys indicate.

The Cetti's Warbler's preferred breeding habitat in Berkshire seems to be *Phragmites* reedbeds, interspersed or bordered by dense areas of Willow *Salix* spp., Alder

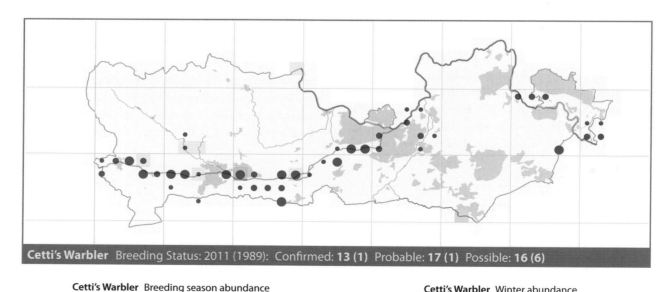

**Cetti's Warbler** Breeding Status: 2011 (1989): Confirmed: **13 (1)** Probable: **17 (1)** Possible: **16 (6)**

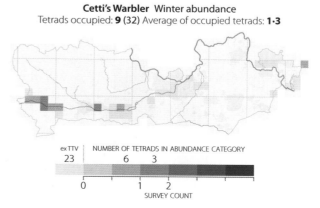

**Cetti's Warbler** Breeding season abundance
Tetrads occupied: **20 (54)** Average of occupied tetrads: **2·6**

| exTTV | NUMBER OF TETRADS IN ABUNDANCE CATEGORY | | | | | |
|---|---|---|---|---|---|---|
| 34 | 10 | 5 | 1 | 2 | 0 | 2 |

| 0 | 1 | 2 | 3 | 5 | 6 | 12 |
SURVEY COUNT

**Cetti's Warbler** Winter abundance
Tetrads occupied: **9 (32)** Average of occupied tetrads: **1·3**

| exTTV | NUMBER OF TETRADS IN ABUNDANCE CATEGORY | |
|---|---|---|
| 23 | 6 | 3 |

| 0 | 1 | 2 |
SURVEY COUNT

*Alnus glutinosa* carr or other scrub. The birds tend to spend most of their time in or on the periphery of the scrub or in bushes, only occasionally going deep into the reedbeds. While the majority of records come from the Kennet Valley, at sites like Thatcham Marshes and Woolhampton Gravel Pits, it has also now moved into other areas, such as Dinton Pastures on the River Loddon, and some sites close to the Thames in the east of the county, such as Dorney Wetlands and Windsor Great Park.

The bird recorded at Thatcham Marsh in 1971, which appears as a possible breeding record in the *1968–72 BTO Atlas*, was the only inland record at the time; all other records being on the south-east coast. Since then, there has been a steady colonisation of suitable habitats in England, particularly to the west and especially in Dorset, but breeding records have come from as far as north of the Humber, and even further west as far as Cornwall and Wales (Baillie *et al.*, 2011). As the species is mainly insectivorous, it is particularly vulnerable to prolonged cold weather, following which numbers often decline, especially where the species has expanded into areas away from the relatively mild climate of coastal areas. This may explain the relatively slow build up of the breeding population in Berkshire, where winters are not generally as mild as on the coast or further west. After the UK population was estimated to have fallen by over one third between 1984 and 1986, it then rose steeply until, by 2009, there were estimated to be at least 2,257 singing males in the UK (Holling & RBBP, 2011).

Post-breeding dispersal usually takes place in late July and August, although its presence during the winter in much the same areas as in the breeding season suggests that it does not generally venture far. Ten of the twelve recoveries of ringed birds have involved movement within Berkshire, Hampshire or Wiltshire. There have, though, been two movements of more than 100 km. A bird ringed in Suffolk in October 2007 was re-trapped the following March in Windsor Great Park, and one ringed at Thatcham Marsh in August 2000 was re-trapped the following October at Newport, Gwent.

*Sponsored by Martin Gostling*

Cetti's Warbler, Eton Wick  *Dave Rimes www.lookatthebirds.co.uk*

# Long-tailed Tit

*Aegithalos caudatus*

*Widespread and common resident*

The Long-tailed Tit is a widespread and common resident in Berkshire, occurring in scrub or hedgerows containing thorny shrubs or in woodland. It has become an increasingly frequent visitor to gardens.

During the 2007–11 Tetrad Survey it was recorded in most tetrads throughout the county both in the breeding season and the winter. The number of tetrads in which breeding was confirmed increased from 287 in the 1987–89 survey to 331 in the latest survey. The high proportion of proven breeding records in both surveys probably reflects the ease with which recently fledged young can be found. The apparent increase in the range in Berkshire reflects growth in the national population, which has increased by about 60% as measured by the CBC and BBS in the intervening period.

Between the two surveys Long-tailed Tits appear to have moved into areas where they were apparently absent or sparsely distributed during the first Tetrad Survey, such as parts of the Downs in the north-west of the county and in some of the most heavily developed tetrads in Maidenhead and Slough, although the few

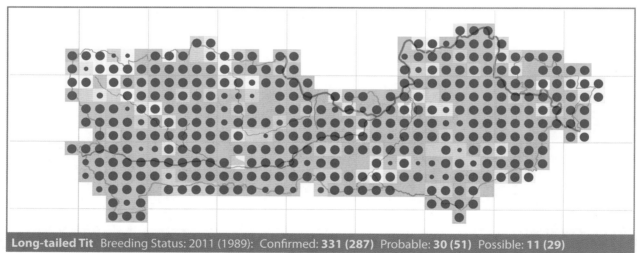

**Long-tailed Tit** Breeding Status: 2011 (1989): Confirmed: **331 (287)** Probable: **30 (51)** Possible: **11 (29)**

**Long-tailed Tit** Breeding season abundance
Tetrads occupied: **309 (383)** Average of occupied tetrads: **5·8**

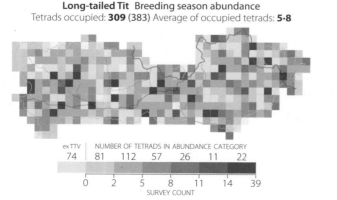

| exTTV | NUMBER OF TETRADS IN ABUNDANCE CATEGORY | | | | | |
|---|---|---|---|---|---|---|
| 74 | 81 | 112 | 57 | 26 | 11 | 22 |

0    2    5    8    11    14    39
SURVEY COUNT

**Long-tailed Tit** Winter abundance
Tetrads occupied: **358 (384)** Average of occupied tetrads: **11·9**

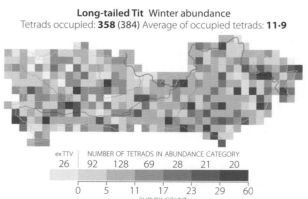

| exTTV | NUMBER OF TETRADS IN ABUNDANCE CATEGORY | | | | | |
|---|---|---|---|---|---|---|
| 26 | 92 | 128 | 69 | 28 | 21 | 20 |

0    5    11    17    23    29    60
SURVEY COUNT

gaps in the range that remain are still in the north-west. The abundance maps do though indicate that the species is now quite evenly distributed through the county.

Local ringing returns have provided evidence that birds tend to be sedentary, most recoveries being within a few kilometres of the location at which the individual was ringed. This is further supported by the similarity between the distribution as shown in the breeding season and winter abundance maps. There has though been a ringing record showing a substantial movement, involving a bird ringed at Dinton Pastures in July 2010 being found dead in Birmingham the following February. There has been one record of a bird showing the characteristics of the white-headed northern European race *A. c. caudatus* which was trapped and ringed at Fence Wood near Newbury on 1st October 1973.

Out of the breeding season flocks often form, the species regularly associating with other small garden birds in mixed flocks. There have been a few counts of 100 or more: a flock of 100 was counted at Dinton Pastures on 10th November 1991, there were 150 in four flocks at Burghfield Gravel Pits on 13th November 2003, 100 at Eversley Gravel Pits on 1st January 2005 and 103 at Thatcham Marsh on 12th October 2007. There have been two exceptional early records of early nest building on 25th January 2010 at Burghfield Gravel Pits, and on 2nd February 2008 at Marsh Benham, and a February record of young being fed on the 28th at Cox Green in 2004.

The status of the Long-tailed Tit in Berkshire appears to have changed little since the 19th century when it was evidently common, Lamb (1880) referring to flocks of 40–50 in autumn in about 1810.

*Sponsored by Kintbury Wildlife Group*

Long-tailed Tit *Brian Winter*

# Pallas's Warbler

*Phylloscopus proregulus*

*Rare vagrant, one record*

Berkshire's only record of this asiatic warbler was a long staying individual at Moor Green Lakes, which was first seen on 3rd January 2013, and which remained until 18th April, frequently in full song towards the end of its stay. Mostly seen along the River Blackwater, it was sometimes found over the county boundary in Hampshire during this period. Originally identified as a Yellow-browed Warbler, which would also have been an exceptional record at this time of year, it was confirmed as Pallas's from subsequent better views.

*Sponsored by Ian Paine*

Pallas's Warbler, Moor Green Lakes *Josie Hewitt*

# Yellow-browed Warbler

*Phylloscopus inornatus*

*Rare vagrant, mainly autumn*

The Yellow-browed Warbler is a rare vagrant to Berkshire which was first recorded in a garden at Thatcham between 6th December 1986 and 17th January 1987. The duration of its stay appeared to be due largely to an ample supply of Woolly Aphids *Eriosoma lanigerum* on an apple tree in the garden on which it was seen to feed regularly. There was then a gap of over 16 years until the next bird was recorded at Theale Main Gravel Pit on 30th October 2003, during an autumn when good numbers of this species occurred in south-east England. After a further four years, one was found on the patio of a Bracknell garden on 19 October 2007; it may have struck a window but, after being photographed, it subsequently flew off. Another autumn record followed on 7th November 2009, when one was seen and heard calling alongside the Heron Lakes complex at Wraysbury Gravel Pits and, most recently, one was seen at Ascot Heath on 20th October 2012. This last record awaits consideration by the Berkshire Records Committee.

*Sponsored by Robert Godden*

# Western Bonelli's Warbler

*Phylloscopus bonelli*

*Rare vagrant, one record, subject to review*

The only record of a Bonelli's Warbler, whose breeding range extends around the Mediterranean Sea and into France, relates to a bird seen in a mixed party of warblers near Smallmead Gravel Pits on 23rd August 1975. At the time the two species of Bonelli's Warbler (Eastern and Western) were treated as one. Following the split of the species all earlier records have been attributed to the western species, whose usual range is much closer to Britain, unless there is evidence to the contrary. The record is currently under review by the British Birds Rarities Committee, so it may not stand as a confirmed record of this species.

*In memory of Terry Finnigan*

# Wood Warbler Red

*Phylloscopus sibilatrix*

*Now rare summer visitor and scarce migrant*

During the 1987–89 Atlas Survey breeding evidence for Wood Warbler was recorded in 42 tetrads, with breeding confirmed in four, but in the 2007–11 Atlas Survey, it was recorded in only 16 tetrads, with no confirmed breeding records, and only one record of probable breeding, at Snelsmore Common in 2009. Singing birds were recorded as possible breeders in a further nine tetrads, but, as Wood Warblers frequently sing while on migration, it is likely that these records were of passage birds. The last confirmed breeding was in 1999 when a pair raised a single chick to fledging near the Oval Pond, Padworth.

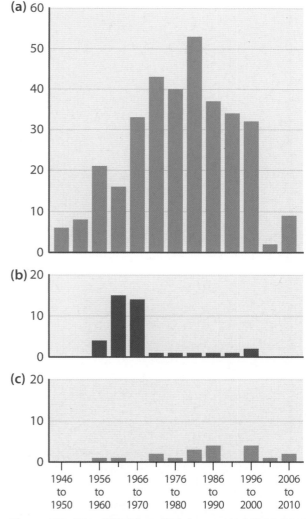

**Figure 128: Wood Warbler: all birds recorded 1946–2010.**
(a) singing males; (b) breeding pairs; (c) autumn records

A summary of the records of Wood Warbler in county reports is presented in Figure 128. This shows that the number of breeding birds peaked during the 1960s.

This was followed by a marked decline with no more than a single pair breeding in any one year, and no records of breeding in most years since 1970. Since the late 1990s the situation has worsened as the number of passage birds has also noticeably decreased, consistent with the national status of the species, which has shown a rapid decline since 1994 (Baillie *et al.*, 2012).

The reason for the disappearance of the Berkshire breeding population of Wood Warblers does not appear to be habitat loss, as suitable areas of mature broadleaved woodland with a sparse understorey, favoured by the species, still exist. It is, though, one of a number of species whose wintering range is the savannah forest zone of West Africa, and whose breeding populations has declined since the 1970s. The species' decline has been widespread over lowland England, and it has also ceased to breed in Oxfordshire (Brucker *et al.*, 1992).

The first arrivals of Wood Warblers on passage are usually in late April, the earliest date since 1974 being 14th April 1982 at Bucklebury Common. The arrival of the species in spring is normally readily detected when the bird delivers its characteristic trilling descending song which carries far through woodland. There have been relatively few autumn records, although it probably remains largely undetected on return passage. Most autumn sightings are during August, although a late bird was trapped and ringed on 10th September 1978 at Wraysbury Gravel Pits. The number of reported passage birds has fluctuated over the years, but since 2000, no year has produced more than six records, with several years in which only a single record was received, and none in 2002.

Wood Warbler, Snelsmore Common *Jerry O'Brien*

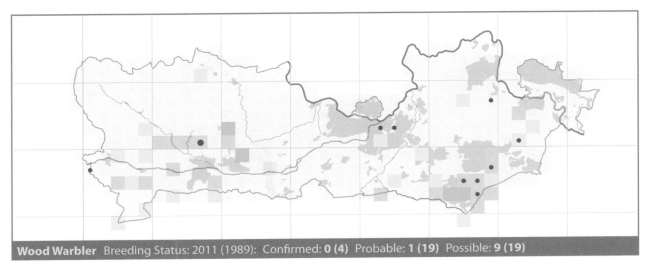

**Wood Warbler** Breeding Status: 2011 (1989): Confirmed: **0 (4)** Probable: **1 (19)** Possible: **9 (19)**

In the 19th century, the Wood Warbler was noted by Noble (1906) to be a "regular migrant, not very abundant, but a pair or two may be looked for in most woods with large trees, especially beech". The species appears to have bred more widely and at a greater density in the 1930s. In 1933 breeding occurred near Bradfield and there were about four pairs in a two hectare site near Burchett's Green. In 1935, there were about eight nests in Quarry Wood, the Beech *Fagus sylvatica* woodland habitat referred to by Noble.

*Sponsored by Mark Whitaker*

**Wood Warbler** Breeding season abundance
Tetrads occupied: **0 (16)** Average of occupied tetrads: **0**

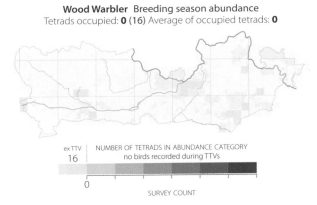

| exTTV | NUMBER OF TETRADS IN ABUNDANCE CATEGORY |
|---|---|
| 16 | no birds recorded during TTVs |

SURVEY COUNT

# Chiffchaff

Green

*Phylloscopus collybita*

*Common summer visitor and increasing winter visitor*

The Chiffchaff is one of the commonest of Berkshire's summer visitors and is an increasing winter visitor. It is typically found breeding in woodlands and parks, but will also nest in mature hedgerows with standard trees. The 2007–11 Atlas Survey showed the species to be abundant across the county during the breeding season, present in 98% of tetrads, with breeding confirmed or probable in 78%, similar to the status in the 1987–89 Atlas Survey when breeding was confirmed or probable in 83%.

With more Chiffchaffs spending the winter in the county it has become increasingly difficult to differentiate between wintering birds and early spring arrivals, particularly as wintering birds are sometimes heard singing in January and February. Chiffchaffs are among the earliest of the spring migrants to arrive in Berkshire, usually in mid-March, and make their presence known by singing loudly, even in damp, blustery weather. Peak passage usually occurs in the first half of April, but in recent years arrivals have tended to be earlier, sometimes

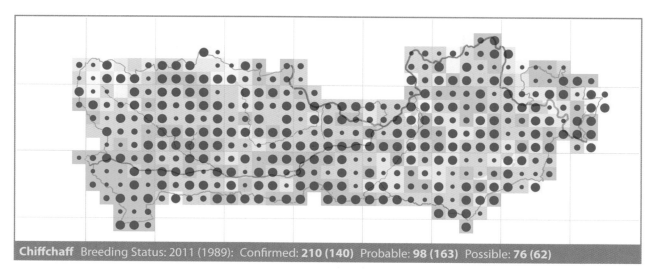

**Chiffchaff** Breeding Status: 2011 (1989): Confirmed: **210 (140)** Probable: **98 (163)** Possible: **76 (62)**

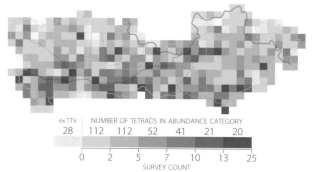

**Chiffchaff** Breeding season abundance
Tetrads occupied: **358 (386)** Average of occupied tetrads: **5·3**

| ex TTV | NUMBER OF TETRADS IN ABUNDANCE CATEGORY | | | | | |
|---|---|---|---|---|---|---|
| 28 | 112 | 112 | 52 | 41 | 21 | 20 |

0    2    5    7    10    13    25
SURVEY COUNT

**Chiffchaff** Winter abundance
Tetrads occupied: **20 (81)** Average of occupied tetrads: **1·3**

| ex TTV | NUMBER OF TETRADS IN ABUNDANCE CATEGORY | | | |
|---|---|---|---|---|
| 61 | 17 | 2 | 0 | 1 |

0    1    2    3    4
SURVEY COUNT

arriving before the end of February. Autumn passage occurs from late August to late October. Parties of Chiffchaffs are sometimes seen during both spring and autumn passage, often at sites such as Wraysbury Gravel Pits and Thatcham Marsh, and also in places such as gardens, where they do not normally breed.

The Winter Map illustrates how numerous and widespread a wintering bird this species has become, with records from 20% of tetrads, mostly in river valleys and other low lying areas. This represents a considerable increase compared to an average of about eight winter records a year in the 1970s and 1980s. The departure of summer visiting birds in October appears to overlap the early arrival of wintering birds which makes it difficult to distinguish between the two populations. During the winter months most records consist of one or two birds, but larger gatherings are not unknown, usually along ditches, streams and rivers or at sewage works; at least eight were seen together at Sandhurst Sewage Treatment Works during January and February 2009. As the Winter Abundance Map shows, it was quite widely recorded from the river valleys of Berkshire in winter during the 2007–11 Atlas Survey.

Since 1974, there have been almost annual winter records of Chiffchaffs showing the characteristics of either the Scandinavian race *P. c. abietinus*, or the Siberian race *P. c. tristis* (Siberian Chiffchaff). In some cases the identification has been based mainly on plumage features, but where the birds have been heard to call or sing a more accurate identification may be possible. Heard (2012) discussed the identification of *P. c. tristis* and its status in Berkshire. He concluded that five definite *tristis* Chiffchaffs had been seen in the county up to 2008, and that this eastern vagrant may well occur annually.

There have been nine overseas recoveries of Chiffchaffs ringed in Berkshire, three each from France and Spain, two from Morocco and one from Senegal. The last was a bird ringed at Denford Mill in July 1992 and recovered the following November in the Djoudj National Park, Senegal, a distance of over 4,100 km. There is another noteworthy recovery of a bird ringed at Denford on the early date of 21st March 1990, which was recovered one week later at Bovey Tracey, Devon, indicating that early arrivals in the spring do not necessarily move further north.

*Sponsored by Gordon & Sue Thornton*

# Willow Warbler

*Phylloscopus trochilus*

*Common summer visitor and passage migrant*

Whilst the Willow Warbler remains fairly common and widespread as a summer visitor and passage migrant, in Berkshire it is declining as a breeding species.

In the 1987–89 Atlas Survey Willow Warblers were shown to be breeding over almost the entire county, with breeding evidence in 96% of all tetrads and confirmation of breeding in 49%. Twenty years later, the 2007–11 Atlas Survey recorded breeding evidence in only 67% of tetrads, with breeding confirmed in 15%. The Breeding Map shows widespread losses, most marked in the east of the county, consistent with the situation nationally where there have been significant reductions in southern England and Wales, particularly during the 1980s and early 1990s, although populations in the North and Scotland have remained fairly stable (Baillie *et al.*, 2012).

Willow Warblers breed in a wide range of habitats provided there are a few bushes and ground cover available for nesting. The abundance map shows that the preferred areas in Berkshire are the higher land of the Downs, and tetrads which contain heath and coniferous woodland, where the forestry cycle provides suitable open scrubby areas.

Between 1974 and 1994 the first arrivals were recorded between 16th March and 5th April, but since 1995, with the exception of 2007 (when the first arrivals were unusually late on April 13th) all the first arrival dates have been in a very small window between the 20th and 29th of March. Unlike that of several other warbler species, the earliest arrival date appears not to have changed between the 1980s and the first decade of the 21st century (see Table ii, *page 50*). Spring passage movement was observed as occurring in two waves in

1973 at Sulham Woods, when 26 birds were counted from 12th to 16th April, followed by 50 birds from 24th to 26th April. Observations at three different sites in west Berkshire showed that in spring newly arrived birds occupy territory quickly, and the population builds up in about 12 to 14 days from the arrival of the first bird to the maximum breeding population. Counts carried out at Bucklebury and Lower Commons indicated that late snowfall in April might cause temporary desertion of heathland habitat (Lewis, 1981).

The return passage peaks in August, with latest departure dates from 16th September to 9th November, most last dates being in the last week of September.

**Willow Warbler** Breeding season abundance
Tetrads occupied: **174 (294)** Average of occupied tetrads: **3·0**

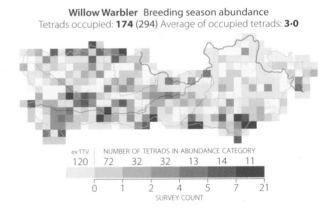

| exTTV | NUMBER OF TETRADS IN ABUNDANCE CATEGORY | | | | | |
|---|---|---|---|---|---|---|
| 120 | 72 | 32 | 32 | 13 | 14 | 11 |

0     1     2     4     5     7     21
SURVEY COUNT

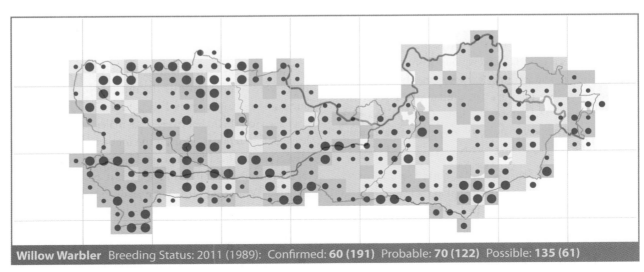

**Willow Warbler** Breeding Status: 2011 (1989): Confirmed: **60 (191)** Probable: **70 (122)** Possible: **135 (61)**

The latest record of 9th November was at Wraysbury Gravel Pits in 1989. In August 1983, a total of 214 birds were caught and ringed at Wraysbury Gravel Pits, including 65 birds in one day. There have been two recoveries of Berkshire-ringed birds from each of France and Spain.

The only winter records of Willow Warbler in Berkshire were of two on 25th January 1986 at Purley, followed by one there on 8th February and one at Summerleaze Gravel Pits from 13th to 22nd December 1992.

*Sponsored by Renee Grayer*

# Blackcap

## Sylvia atricapilla

*Common summer migrant, and increasing winter visitor*

The Blackcap is a common passage migrant and widespread summer visitor in Berkshire, and is now a regular winter visitor to areas across the county. Most of the winter visitors are thought to come from Central Europe.

The spring passage occurs from late March but the presence of over-wintering birds obscures earliest arrival dates. In 1990/91 up to six birds wintered at Boulter's Lock from December 1990 to 8th March 1991, and song was heard on two dates in January and in February. This suggest that over-wintering birds can start to sing before they leave their wintering areas, and singing males in early to mid-March may therefore be over-wintering birds rather than passage migrants. Spring passage continues throughout April and into May when breeding begins.

Summering Blackcaps were recorded in almost all tetrads in the county during the 2007–11 Atlas Survey, with breeding proven or probable in 89%, somewhat higher than in the 1987–89 survey (82%). The Berkshire Bird Index showed an increase of 114% in the Blackcap population between 1994 and 2008, consistent with the national trend of steady growth since the late 1970s, with CBS/BBS surveys indicating a doubling of the UK population between 1990 and 2010 (Baillie *et al.*, 2011).

The breeding season abundance map shows Blackcaps to be fairly evenly distributed across the county, found wherever there is suitable habitat, which includes deciduous woodlands, hedgerows, parks and gardens. Adult males are especially conspicuous in the breeding season when in the vicinity of their nest. The Blackcap's favoured breeding habitats are similar to those of the less numerous and more skulking Garden Warbler, and where both species are found together they usually occur in mutually exclusive territories.

Blackcap breeding density can be quite high: a survey carried out at Theale and Burghfield Gravel Pits in 1996 located 37 singing males. Berkshire may hold approximately 15,000 territories, based on the 2007–11 surveys (Appendix IV), equivalent to an average of 40 territories per occupied tetrad.

Post-breeding dispersal occurs from the end of July and continues through August and September, with a few birds remaining into October. In areas of suitable habitat, considerable numbers can occur in autumn. At Wraysbury Gravel Pits in 1995, for example, 112 birds were ringed in July and 52 in August. The number of Blackcaps ringed at this site in July has steadily increased, as there were only 44 in 1990. In 1993, heavy passage occurred in early September when 25 birds were ringed at Thatcham Marsh on the 8th.

Prior to 1960, Blackcaps occurred in Berkshire only rarely in winter, the first records being of a female found dead at Hungerford on 23rd January 1923, and a male at Wokingham from 30th November to 4th December in 1938. After a late bird at Barkham on 19th November 1958, there was one at Twyford in January and a female at a bird table at Inkpen, both in 1961. Wintering Blackcaps then became regular in small but increasing numbers and in 1978/79, when a BTO survey was carried out, 39 birds were located in the county in spite of severe weather in December. The survey prompted a study of a small wintering population at The Warren, Caversham in 1978/79. A total of 10 birds were recorded at this site during November 1978 and most remained until February 1979. The last bird was seen on 19th February and males were found to leave before females. During the following summer this area was occupied by at least 11 singing males which arrived from 7th April and were last recorded on 8th August. Wintering birds were again present from 21st November. The precise number involved at any site is difficult to establish however, since ringing studies have shown repeated sightings may not actually be of the same bird. In a garden at Pangbourne in December

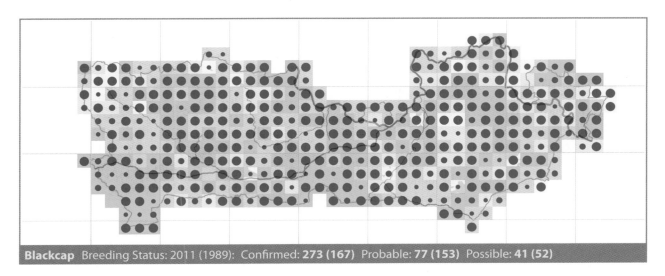

**Blackcap** Breeding Status: 2011 (1989): Confirmed: **273 (167)** Probable: **77 (153)** Possible: **41 (52)**

**Blackcap** Breeding season abundance
Tetrads occupied: **348** (392) Average of occupied tetrads: **6·0**

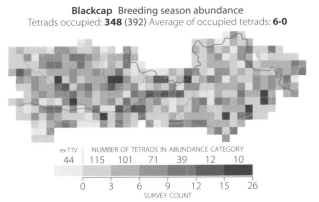

| ex TTV | NUMBER OF TETRADS IN ABUNDANCE CATEGORY | | | | | |
|---|---|---|---|---|---|---|
| 44 | 115 | 101 | 71 | 39 | 12 | 10 |

0    3    6    9    12    15    26
SURVEY COUNT

**Blackcap** Winter abundance
Tetrads occupied: **25** (137) Average of occupied tetrads: **1·2**

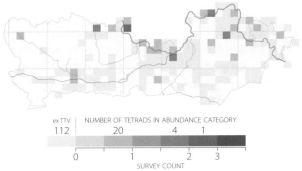

| ex TTV | NUMBER OF TETRADS IN ABUNDANCE CATEGORY | | |
|---|---|---|---|
| 112 | 20 | 4 | 1 |

0        1        2        3
SURVEY COUNT

1994, three males were caught on the 18th, three females on the 22nd, three further males on the 25th and a further three on the 30th. The pattern of records also points to the arrival of new birds throughout the winter, particularly in February. In the 2007–11 Atlas Survey over 26% of Berkshire tetrads held wintering Blackcaps, while wintering Blackcaps were reported from over 16% of Berkshire gardens covered by the BTO Garden BirdWatch in December 2010. The winter abundance map indicates that wintering Blackaps seem to favour more urban areas, though this may reflect the relative ease of observation in gardens where they visit feeders and bird tables.

Most recoveries of birds ringed in Berkshire reflect the wintering and migratory habits of the summer breeding populations. There have been ten recoveries from Morocco, six from Algeria, seven from Spain and four from France. The Newbury Ringing Group has also had a number of recoveries of Berkshire Blackcaps migrating south, including records from Morocco, Tunisia and Senegal. Interestingly, having regard to the movement from Germany into Britain in winter, there have been two recoveries in September, one each in Belgium and Germany, of birds which had travelled east from the UK. There has also been a recovery in the winter months of a bird ringed on the continent; one ringed at Castricum,

Netherlands in September 1989 being recovered in November 1991 in Reading.

*Sponsored by Christopher Wardell*

Blackcap *Dave Bartlett*

383

# Garden Warbler

*Sylvia borin*

*Common summer visitor and passage migrant*

The Garden Warbler remains a widespread passage migrant and summer visitor in Berkshire, but it does seem currently to be declining across the county. It occurs in dense scrub, along woodland edges and in deciduous woodland, and can often be found inhabiting the same areas as the more numerous and widespread Blackcap. The two species are both often located by their song, but can be difficult to distinguish. This may mean that the less common Garden Warbler is overlooked, even in a comprehensive survey, and so any survey may understate the species' distribution. Nevertheless during the 2007–11 Atlas Survey breeding was confirmed or probable in 34% of the tetrads in the county, compared to 52% in the 1987–89 Atlas Survey. The species seems to have disappeared from some areas, particularly in the west and the north of the county. It is a less numerous bird than the Blackcap, with the Berkshire population estimated from data derived from the 2007–11 Atlas survey as about a tenth at approximately 1,500 territories (Appendix IV).

In the most recent Atlas Survey, in tetrads where the Garden Warbler was recorded, breeding was confirmed in only 26% of them and recorded as probably breeding in a further 34%, broadly comparable figures to those from the earlier Atlas Survey (28% and 43% respectively). This low rate of confirmation is undoubtedly partly due to the skulking nature of the species and its frequent choice of dense scrub and Bramble *Rubus fruticosus* for nesting. Obtaining confirmation of breeding is further hampered by the fact that males sing considerably less frequently once breeding has commenced. There are concentrations of confirmed breeding records in areas where there is dense scrub: in the Thames, Kennet,

Loddon and Colne Valleys, along with other areas not far from bodies of water (such as Wraysbury and Theale Gravel Pits), although by no means exclusively. For example, a survey of Swinley Forest in 2006 revealed 31 territories.

Garden Warblers occur regularly on passage from mid-April, with first arrival dates from 1974 to 2011 ranging from 1st April to early May, apart from an exceptionally early individual at Caversham on 23rd March 1975.

*Sponsored by Andrew Bolton*

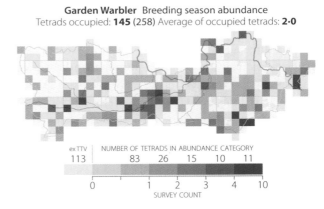

**Garden Warbler** Breeding season abundance
Tetrads occupied: **145** (258) Average of occupied tetrads: **2·0**

| ex TTV | NUMBER OF TETRADS IN ABUNDANCE CATEGORY | | | | |
|---|---|---|---|---|---|
| 113 | 83 | 26 | 15 | 10 | 11 |

| 0 | 1 | 2 | 3 | 4 | 10 |
SURVEY COUNT

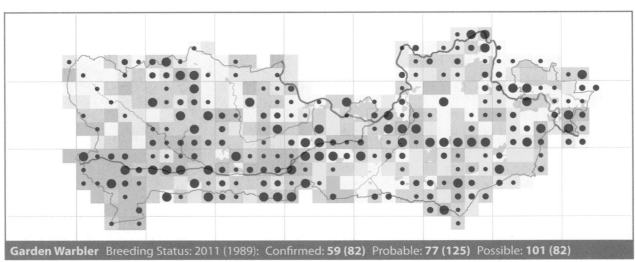

**Garden Warbler** Breeding Status: 2011 (1989): Confirmed: **59** (82) Probable: **77** (125) Possible: **101** (82)

# Lesser Whitethroat Green

*Sylvia curruca*

*Common summer visitor and passage migrant*

The Lesser Whitethroat is a locally common passage migrant and summer visitor in Berkshire. The *1968–72 BTO Atlas* noted that it has a preference for hedgerows that contain isolated trees which the males use as song posts. Like the Whitethroat, it occurs widely in scrub but is generally a much shyer bird, tending to remain in cover, its secretive habits making it appear to be scarcer than it actually is. Breeding pairs can be very difficult to locate and, since birds pair quickly after arrival in April, and males seldom sing after the eggs have been laid in early May, there is only a short period of time when their presence is easily detected.

Lesser Whitethroats were recorded in 50% of the tetrads in Berkshire during the 2007–11 Tetrad Survey and showed a wide distribution across the county, with concentrations in the Kennet, lower Loddon, lower Colne Valleys and on the Compton Downs. This represents a decline in the number of tetrads where any category of breeding was recorded since the 1987–89 Tetrad Survey, and the number of tetrads in which breeding was either proved or from which probable breeding evidence was obtained declined from 138 to 58. Lesser Whitethroat populations nationally appear to fluctuate markedly from year to year, with no long-term decline or increase discernible between the 1960s and the 1980s (*Population Trends*), but BBS data from 1995 to 2010 indicated a decline of 27% in south east England.

The tetrad surveys indicate that the species is normally either under-recorded or overlooked. For example, during the years of the 1987–89 Tetrad Survey, there were only reports for some 16 to 24 sites submitted by observers for publication in the county report, compared with 207 tetrads with records during the survey. Sites such as Dinton Pastures, Eversley, Theale, Burghfield and particularly Wraysbury Gravel Pits often produce records of between three and 10 breeding pairs or singing males. However the Atlas surveys indicate that generally the species is thinly distributed across the county, with no areas producing large concentrations or counts.

Passage through Berkshire occurs on a wide front, but with concentrations in the river valleys. From 1974 to 2011, the first arrivals were recorded between 9th April and 3rd May, and the latest dates ranged between 26th August and 2nd October. Unlike the Whitethroat, there is no evidence of advance of first arrival dates (Table ii, *page 50*). Small flocks or groups are sometimes reported

**Lesser Whitethroat** Breeding season abundance
Tetrads occupied: **44 (198)** Average of occupied tetrads: **1·3**

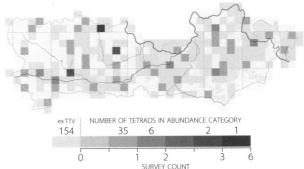

| exTTV | NUMBER OF TETRADS IN ABUNDANCE CATEGORY | | | |
|---|---|---|---|---|
| 154 | 35 | 6 | 2 | 1 |

0    1    2    3    6
SURVEY COUNT

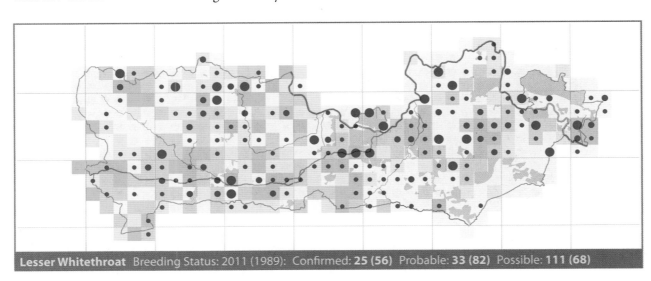

**Lesser Whitethroat** Breeding Status: 2011 (1989): Confirmed: **25 (56)** Probable: **33 (82)** Possible: **111 (68)**

on passage in the autumn and there was an exceptional count of 17 together at Wargrave on 15th August 1978. In the autumn of 1976, 48 different birds were ringed at Burghfield Gravel Pits, and in July and August 1995 some 87 were ringed at Wraysbury Gravel Pits.

The migration pattern is different from that of the Whitethroat, birds migrating in a south-easterly direction to winter in Sudan and Ethiopia. The overseas recoveries of birds ringed in Berkshire reflect this, with single birds recovered in Belgium, Italy, Israel and Lebanon.

The *Historical Atlas* indicates that the Lesser Whitethroat was uncommon in Berkshire in the late 19th Century, but Noble (1906) indicated that it was as numerous as the Whitethroat in his area west of Maidenhead.

*Sponsored by Karen Tucker*

# Whitethroat Amber

## *Sylvia communis*

*Common summer visitor and passage migrant*

The Whitethroat is a common passage migrant and summer visitor in Berkshire, being found in any part of the county that contains scrub, whether on farmland, heathland, downland or waste ground, along woodland edges, or in hedgerows or unkempt gardens. It is double-brooded and the male performs his display flight throughout the season. A breeding pair will perch in the open and scold actively when the nest site is approached, helping to confirm territories and breeding.

Breeding evidence was recorded in 92% of tetrads and was confirmed in 68% of the tetrads in which the species was recorded during the 2007–11 Tetrad Survey, an increase from 83% and 46% respectively over the 1987–89 survey. The gaps in the species' distribution in Berkshire mostly correspond to built-up areas, and the coniferous forests and heathland areas of the south east of the county, though some unexplained absences occur. These results reflect a recovery in the national population in the intervening period which is indicated by an increase in the national index level derived from CBC and BBS of about 60%. This is part of a long term recovery from the dramatic crash in numbers of Whitethroats in Britain, which was first noted in 1969

**Whitethroat** Breeding season abundance
Tetrads occupied: **277** (363) Average of occupied tetrads: **4·6**

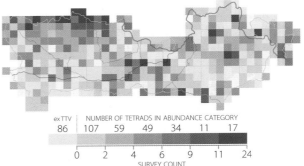

| exTTV | NUMBER OF TETRADS IN ABUNDANCE CATEGORY | | | | | |
|---|---|---|---|---|---|---|
| 86 | 107 | 59 | 49 | 34 | 11 | 17 |

0    2    4    6    9    11    24
SURVEY COUNT

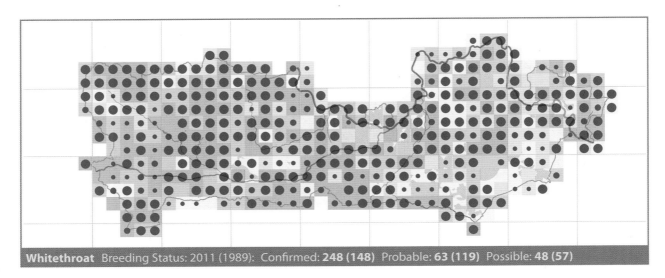

**Whitethroat** Breeding Status: 2011 (1989): Confirmed: **248** (148) Probable: **63** (119) Possible: **48** (57)

and has been attributed primarily to drought conditions in the Sahel in Africa where the species winters. The results of the CBC indicated that by 1974 numbers were only one sixth of those in 1968 (*Population Trends*). Despite this recovery, the species still has an amber conservation status.

Since 1974, the first spring arrivals in Berkshire have been between 31st March and 22nd April and have advanced significantly over the period 1980 to 2009 (Table ii, *page 50*). Significant numbers can be found after the main arrivals such as counts of singing birds of 36 at Wraysbury Gravel Pits on 21st April 2010, and 29 at Greenham Common on 25th April 2011. There were estimated to be 50 at the Eversley Gravel Pit complex on 19th June 2009. The latest autumn departures have ranged from 19th August to 29th October. Unlike many other warbler species, there is a paucity of interesting ringing recoveries, with only one record of a bird ringed in Berkshire being recovered overseas, in France.

*Sponsored by Jim and Joan Walling*

# Dartford Warbler

Amber  Sch. 1

## Sylvia undata

*Scarce, localized resident*

The Dartford Warbler is a scarce breeding resident of heathland which was first confirmed as breeding in the county in 1991, prior to which it was recorded mainly as an occasional autumn vagrant. Berkshire lies at the northern edge of the main breeding range of the species in Britain, where its dependence upon lowland heath with mature Gorse *Ulex europaeus* and Heather *Calluna vulgaris* restricts its range, and as a resident species it is severely affected by hard winters. The opportunity for some re-colonisation is created by autumn dispersal of birds, usually in October, from areas where breeding has taken place, as indicated by the Winter Tetrad Map and other recent records from parts of the county outside their known breeding range.

The first 20th century record was of a male seen in bracken near Great Meadow Pond in Windsor Great Park on 25th October 1936, and this was followed by one at Pinkneys Green on 31st October 1937. In 1944, a male and two females were seen at an unspecified site on the Berkshire side of the border with Hampshire on 11th July, the first acceptable summer record for the county. Just prior to the crash in the population of the species during the severe winters of 1961/62 and 1962/63, a female or immature bird was seen on the Berkshire side of Surrey Hill on 12th October 1960.

Subsequent county records reflect the species' recovery after its population crash in the early 1960s. In 1973, there was one at Greenham Common from December until 24th February the following year, and there were further records from this site on 2nd January 1975, and from 30th November 1975 to 29th December when two were seen. This was followed by one which was associating with a Stonechat and feeding in thistles *Cirsium* spp. at Hurley on 14th and 20th November 1976.

Post-breeding dispersal in the 1980s led to colonisation of a heathland site in east Berkshire. In 1986, Dartford

Warblers were recorded at two sites in the east of the county, being present at one from 26th October to 2nd November and being seen on 20th December at the other. A bird returned to one of the sites from 22nd November to 17th December 1988 and breeding was confirmed there in 1991. Although a first brood was apparently lost following a fire, two, or possibly three, juveniles were seen on 27th June. In 1994, there were two singing males at this site and one pair bred. At the second site occupied in 1986, a female was seen in 1990 and a singing male was heard in 1993. A party of five birds seen there in August 1989 were presumed to have bred outside Berkshire.

The 2007–11 Atlas Survey shows an encouraging increase in the number of breeding records, with breeding confirmed in 11 tetrads, all at sites along the

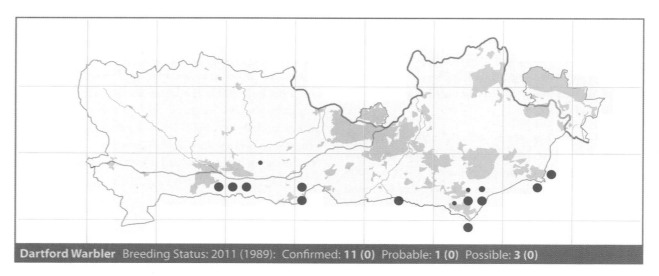

**Dartford Warbler** Breeding Status: 2011 (1989): Confirmed: **11 (0)** Probable: **1 (0)** Possible: **3 (0)**

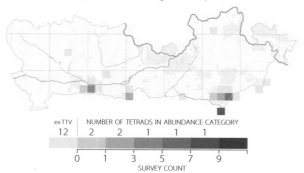

**Dartford Warbler** Breeding season abundance
Tetrads occupied: **7 (19)** Average of occupied tetrads: **3·7**

| ex TTV | NUMBER OF TETRADS IN ABUNDANCE CATEGORY | | | | |
|---|---|---|---|---|---|
| 12 | 2 | 2 | 1 | 1 | 1 |

0   1   3   5   7   9
SURVEY COUNT

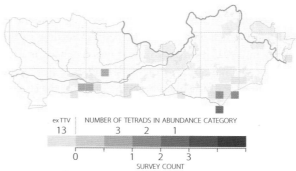

**Dartford Warbler** Winter abundance
Tetrads occupied: **6 (19)** Average of occupied tetrads: **1·7**

| ex TTV | NUMBER OF TETRADS IN ABUNDANCE CATEGORY | | |
|---|---|---|---|
| 13 | 3 | 2 | 1 |

0   1   2   3
SURVEY COUNT

southern edge of the county, bordering Surrey and Hampshire. With the growth of the population in these neighbouring counties, suitable heathland habitat nearby in Berkshire has been colonised. Dartford Warblers have established two main strongholds in the county over recent years, on the Thames Basin Heaths in east Berkshire, where surveys in 2007 found 22 occupied territories (a similar survey in 2003 found around 30 territories), and at Greenham Common, where eight territories were identified in the same year. Whether this increase will be maintained will depend on continued availability of suitable habitat and, importantly, on sufficiently mild winters. Nationally, the UK population was estimated at 3,214 territories in 2006, representing an increase of 70% since 1994, with the main areas of range expansion being in southwest England and Wales (Wotton *et al.*, 2009). Recent harsher winters will certainly have had an adverse impact on populations. A cold spell early in 2009 reduced the number of territories reported from the Thames Basin Heaths (which include the east Berkshire population) and the Weald from 271 to 50, and only five territories were reported from Berkshire (Holling *et al.*, 2011). In addition, one of UK's worst heathland fires occurred in this area in May 2011 and will have undoubtedly affected Dartford Warbler territories.

Away from heathland, mainly outside of the breeding season, birds have been occasionally recorded at sites around the county, quite commonly in association with Stonechats, as was the case with the 1976 bird at Hurley. Most recently birds have been recorded from such diverse sites as Bray Field Farm in November

Dartford Warbler, Wildmoor Heath *David Lowther*

2004, Bury Down in January 2007, and Colnbrook from October to December 2009.

There is no conclusive evidence that the species bred in Berkshire prior to 1991. A reference by Clark Kennedy (1886) to birds breeding "in the vicinity of Sunninghill" almost certainly refers to Chobham Common in Surrey, and his reference to a nest found and the adults shot at Frogmore in 1866 apparently relates to Yateley Common which is in Hampshire. Noble (1906) refers to one which passed through the hands of a taxidermist at Henley in 1888 having been obtained in Berkshire, but it is possible that the bird may not have been obtained from within the current county boundary. The first county record therefore appears to be of one seen at Maidenhead Thicket prior to 1906 (Noble, 1906) which was undated but which may well have been a short-distance migrant. A record of three pairs at Yateley Common in 1924 is also attributable to Hampshire.

*Sponsored by Mike Brown*

# Grasshopper Warbler   `Red`

## *Locustella naevia*

*Scarce summer visitor and uncommon passage migrant*

The Grasshopper Warbler is a scarce summer visitor to Berkshire. Clark Kennedy (1868) and Noble (1906) both considered it to be an uncommon or local summer visitor to the county in the 19th century. From the 1930s to the 1970s the species was considerably more numerous than at present, but it has since suffered a large decline, both nationally and in Berkshire.

The Berkshire breeding range of Grasshopper Warbler had already declined from being recorded in all of the 10 km squares that include at least part of the county in the 1969–72 BTO Atlas to just seven in the 1987–89 Atlas Survey. Its range has since reduced still further, there being confirmed breeding in only two tetrads during the 2007–11 Atlas Survey, both in the west of the county. Even if 'probable breeding' records are included in the comparison, the reduction is from 12 tetrads in the earlier survey to seven in the recent one. The number of tetrads in which possible breeding was recorded increased, although most of these records refer to singing birds in April that were likely to have been on passage. It is, however, possible that Grasshopper Warblers are under-recorded as they can be difficult to detect and, despite the fact that their reeling song can carry for over a kilometre, small areas of habitat that may be occupied are easy to overlook.

The majority of the tetrads occupied by Grasshopper Warblers are in river valleys, particularly the Kennet, corresponding with the species' favoured habitat of marshes and reedbeds. In the early 1970s, reeling was reported from 10–20 localities each year, with over half being to the west of Theale, involving some 20–30 birds each year. When the breeding population was highest during the 1970s, many birds were found to be breeding in Berkshire in young conifer plantations (see below). Since such areas are only suitable for breeding when the trees are less than three metres high, this represents a rather transient habitat.

There was a significant population of Grasshopper Warblers on Forestry Commission land at Sulham during the late 1960s, and the changing fortunes of the species were documented by Karpowicz (1975). Grasshopper Warblers appeared in 1966, following the planting of young Corsican Pines *Pinus nigra* in 1965. Ten singing males were present in April 1968 within an area of some 32 hectares, some of which remained to breed successfully. Numbers reached a peak in 1970 when 11 adults were singing in May. As the conifers grew, numbers declined to only two pairs in 1973, and by 1978, and probably earlier, breeding had ceased. For several years, recordings of reeling Grasshopper Warblers were made by university researchers at Wraysbury, where the habitat occupied was scattered hawthorn bushes in rank grassland. The highest number of birds heard here was a minimum of 12 on 29th April 1995.

Passage migrants in Berkshire are much more evident in spring than in autumn with singing birds which do not stay to breed being recorded in small numbers in most years. Other sites used by migrants have included Lowbury Hill and even Whiteknights Lake in suburban Reading, where for several years in the 1970s individuals could be heard at dusk in a very small thicket. Between 1974 and 2011, the earliest arrivals were on

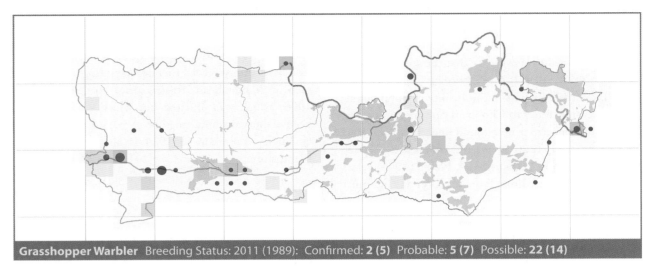

**Grasshopper Warbler** Breeding Status: 2011 (1989): Confirmed: **2 (5)** Probable: **5 (7)** Possible: **22 (14)**

dates ranging from 4th April to 26th April. A small number of Grasshopper Warblers have been recorded in August and September but due to their secretive nature it is likely that many birds pass unnoticed. Autumn migrants exceptionally sing, an example being one at Hurley on 17th August 1975. Karpowicz (1975) suggested that most of the birds breeding at Sulham vacated their breeding ground by the end of July. Since 1974, the latest departure dates were on 27th September in 1997 at Brimpton Gravel Pits and in 2007 at Wraysbury.

Nationally, breeding bird surveys have shown wide fluctuations in abundance since 1994 after a period of rapid decline, but numbers are showing a shallow increase amounting to 23% between 1994 and 2009 (Eaton *et al.*, 2011). There is no shortage of apparently suitable habitat in Berkshire, and hopefully the trend will continue and the county will share in the growth of the population.

There has been only one ringing recovery of a Grasshopper Warbler in Berkshire, a bird ringed at Cholsey, Oxfordshire on 29th June 1981 being recovered at Thatcham Marsh on 4th July 1982.

*Sponsored by Carol Long*

**Grasshopper Warbler** Breeding season abundance
Tetrads occupied: **1 (45)** Average of occupied tetrads: **1·0**

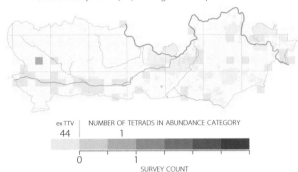

| ex TTV | NUMBER OF TETRADS IN ABUNDANCE CATEGORY |
| --- | --- |
| 44 | 1 |

0    1
SURVEY COUNT

# Savi's Warbler

*Locustella luscinioides*

*Rare vagrant, one record*

There has been only one record of Savi's Warbler in Berkshire, a bird which was trapped and ringed at Hambridge Lake, Newbury on 6th May 1968. The species, which is widespread but local across much of Europe and temperate Asia, became extinct as a British breeding bird in the mid-19th century, but there was an increase in records in the 1960s and 1970s, following which they have declined again.

*Sponsored by Andrew Kitching*

390

# Icterine Warbler

## Hippolais icterina

*Rare vagrant, three records*

The Icterine Warbler is a rare vagrant to Britain, normally occurring as a summer visitor to north and central Europe. There have been only three acceptable records in Berkshire. The first two of these occurred during August, one at Theale Gravel Pits on 18th August 1963, and one at Burghfield Gravel Pits on 9th August 1970. During the 1987–89 Tetrad Survey a singing male was present at Denford on 2nd June 1989 but was not seen subsequently. Numbers have declined by about 40% in their European breeding range since the early 1980s, which may explain the lack of subsequent records.

Due to the difficulty in identifying Icterine and Melodious Warblers in the field, there are five records of *Hippolais* warblers in Berkshire which cannot be ascribed safely to one species or the other. Two of these records involved single birds at Burghfield Gravel Pits on 24th August 1974 and 6th August 1975, and the descriptions suggest that they were probably Icterine Warblers. The other records relate to one seen by several observers at Englefield Park on 20th August 1967, which could be viewed no closer than the top of a tall poplar *Populus* spp. tree, one at Upper Woolhampton on 1st August 1977, and one at Thatcham Marsh on 12th August and 24th August 1986.

*Sponsored by Angela Simmons, WSP Environment & Energy*

# Melodious Warbler

## Hippolais polyglotta

*Rare vagrant, one record*

There has been only one acceptable record for Berkshire of Melodious Warbler, whose normal breeding range extends north to central France, being one at Burghfield Gravel Pits from 28th to 31st July 1972. Although July is early for an autumn arrival to Britain, the bird arrived during a heavy passage of other warbler species and its short stay enabled it to be seen by a number of observers.

*Sponsored by Simon Clews*

# Aquatic Warbler

*Acrocephalus paludicola*

*Rare vagrant, five records*

The Aquatic Warbler is a rare vagrant to Berkshire, with just five records. It was not until the late 1950s that it was shown that some juvenile Sedge Warblers could exhibit a pale central stripe to the crown, a characteristic which was previously believed to be a diagnostic feature of the Aquatic Warbler. In the light of this, the early records of Aquatic Warbler for Berkshire have been re-examined and those from Slough Sewage Farm on 14th September 1942, Windsor Great Park on 14th September 1958 and Ham Island Sewage Farm on 29th August 1959 are now considered to be unacceptable.

The first acceptable record for the county was one seen at Slough Sewage Farm on 6th, 9th and 10th August 1944. This bird was distinctly more colourful than accompanying Sedge Warblers and the description provided ruled out any possibility of confusion. The subsequent records were of a bird seen well at Ham Island Sewage Farm on 13th September 1959, one at Theale Gravel Pits on 2nd August 1961, one near Reading Sewage Farm on 28th August 1972 (which was part of an invasion of 58 Aquatic Warblers into Britain that year that started on 12th August) and, most recently, one caught and ringed at Lower Denford on 28th August 1991.

The species has a limited breeding range in eastern Europe, although it occurs regularly in north-

west Europe on migration. Numbers have declined considerably since the 1980s, and it is considered Europe's most threatened migratory passerine (Fraser, 2013), so the prospect of further records is uncertain.

*Sponsored by Renton Righelato*

# Sedge Warbler

*Acrocephalus schoenobaenus*

*Locally common breeding summer migrant*

The Sedge Warbler is a locally common summer visitor to Berkshire which favours the drier margins of wetlands, particularly areas with low, dense vegetation such as willow *Salix* spp. and other scrub, although they will often nest in drier habitats including young plantations, and farmland crops such as rape (*1968–72 BTO Atlas*).

Although Sedge Warblers are more catholic in their choice of habitat than Reed Warblers, the Atlas Surveys show that their distribution in Berkshire is very closely associated with river valleys and gravel pit complexes, particularly those which support *Phragmites* reedbeds. Sedge Warblers were present in 28% of the tetrads in Berkshire in the 2007–11 Atlas Survey, but were only confirmed to have bred in 30% of these. There seems to

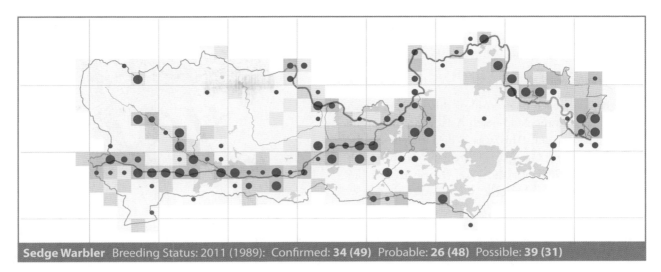

**Sedge Warbler** Breeding Status: 2011 (1989): Confirmed: **34 (49)** Probable: **26 (48)** Possible: **39 (31)**

be a significant contraction in range when these results are compared to those of the 1987–89 survey, with the number of tetrads with any category of breeding evidence declining from 128 to 99, notwithstanding the national population levels monitored by the CBC and BBS showing no significant change. In Berkshire there seems to have been a retreat from marginal areas away from the river valleys in the intervening period. This proportion of confirmed breeding records was lower than for Reed Warbler in both surveys, and may reflect the Sedge Warbler's less conspicuous behaviour when young leave the nest.

A decline had been noted up to the 1980s nationally. That decline was believed to be due to drought conditions in the species' wintering quarters in Africa (*Population Trends*). The number of birds breeding at Thatcham Marsh has shown a serious decline, from approximately 400 pairs in 1969 to about 120 pairs in 1986 and a high count of only 20+ in 2008, although some of this decline is due to changes in the habitat referred to in the Reed Warbler account below.

The spring arrival of Sedge Warblers is usually about a week ahead of the Reed Warbler, with the earliest date since 1974 being 23rd March 2004. The median earliest arrival date for the 2000s was 1st April, seven days earlier than for the 1980s (Table ii, *page 50*). Ringing studies at Thatcham Marsh have shown that local breeding birds often arrive from the first week of April, and that juveniles are present from mid-June onwards. Occasional reports of a second brood being raised include one from 1995 at Moatlands Gravel Pits. Most of the adult birds which breed in Berkshire have departed by early August, although passage birds have been recorded into October in 15 of the 19 years to 2012, with the latest being on 26th October in 1991 at Theale Gravel Pits. Passage birds in autumn regularly stop-over in reedbeds with abundant willow scrub to build up fat reserves prior to onward migration, and

**Sedge Warbler** Breeding season abundance
Tetrads occupied: **57 (112)** Average of occupied tetrads: **4·5**

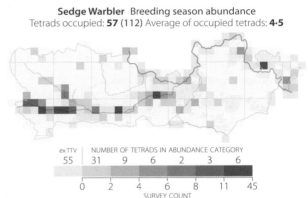

| exTTV | NUMBER OF TETRADS IN ABUNDANCE CATEGORY | | | | | |
|---|---|---|---|---|---|---|
| 55 | 31 | 9 | 6 | 2 | 3 | 6 |

0    2    4    6    8    11    45
SURVEY COUNT

local ringing studies have shown that some double their weight before departing.

There have been three recoveries in Africa of birds ringed in Berkshire: one ringed at Thatcham Marsh in 1980 was controlled at Lac Aougoundou Hopti, Mali in 1982, a distance of 3,970 kilometres, and two birds ringed at Hungerford Marsh and Denford Mill in summer 1991 were recovered in the following winter in the Djoudj National Park, Senegal, more than 4,100 km away, the furthest travelled of any Sedge Warbler ringed in Berkshire. Two birds ringed in Wraysbury have been re-trapped in the Iberian peninsula, firstly one on 3rd May 2003, found in Spain the following year on 17th April (1,089 km), and another on 26th April 2006 which turned up in Portugal on 16th August 2010 (1,665 km). Autumn recoveries here have included several birds ringed in Ireland, and spring recoveries have included two birds from Belgium and three from Spain between 1994 and 2010.

Historically, Noble (1906) described the Sedge Warbler as "very numerous, especially along the Thames, near ponds and reservoirs and even occasionally far from water". In contrast, the *Historical Atlas* classified it as uncommon.

*Sponsored by Renee Grayer*

# Paddyfield Warbler

*Acrocephalus agricola*

*Rare vagrant, one record*

There has only been one record of this warbler, which breeds in east Europe and north Asia, wintering in the Indian subcontinent. This was a bird caught by the Newbury Ringing Group at Thatcham Marsh on 7th September 1997. It was the 42nd British record, but only the second inland record.

*Sponsored by Newbury Ringing Group*

# Marsh Warbler

Red Sch. 1

*Acrocephalus palustris*

*Rare passage migrant and summer visitor*

The Marsh Warbler is a rare passage migrant and summer visitor to Berkshire. Since 1950 there have been seven records of Marsh Warbler in Berkshire. A singing male was at Thatcham Marsh on 23rd June 1963 and, in 1974, breeding may have occurred at Burghfield Gravel Pits, with two adults and a juvenile bird being seen on 8th August and an adult observed collecting food on 10th August. On 9th July 1979 an adult was again seen at Burghfield Gravel Pits, and singing males were reported from Dinton Pastures on 10th and 11th June 1989, and Thatcham Marsh from 25th to at least 28th May 1993. In 1995 at least one was seen and heard at Bray Gravel Pits from 12th June to 8th July, with possibly a second bird present on 25th June. There was one at Theale Gravel Pits from 11th June to at least 12th June 1997.

The species formerly bred sporadically in the county. There were six breeding records in Berkshire in the first half of the 20th century, the first being of a nest containing two eggs and the egg of a Cuckoo which was found in a dense Nettle *Urtica dioica* bed near Magna Carta Island on 14th June 1909, with a second nest at the same site which contained four eggs and one Cuckoo's egg on 30th June that year (Kerr, 1909). In 1918, two nests were found, one with three eggs near Pangbourne on 27th May, an exceptionally early date, and another with eggs near Wargrave on 6th July. Breeding was next recorded in 1923 from an island in the Kennet Valley, where a nest was found and where breeding had apparently also occurred in the three preceding years. The next breeding record was in 1943 at another Kennet Valley site, the precise details of which were not provided. A hide was erected to observe the birds at this nest which was found on 19th June with one egg. On 20th June the female, after

sitting for 25 minutes, mounted the edge of the nest and gave a loud burst of song. Following this, the male flew up and perched nearby singing strongly; there was then some display and coition took place (Allen, 1946).

Although the Marsh Warbler has declined almost to the point of extinction as a breeding species in southern England, small numbers continued to reach Berkshire until the 1990s. The ability to distinguish the two species on song became less clear-cut with the recognition in the 1960s that some Reed Warblers possess a particularly highly developed, mimetic and musical song, which can approach the quality and range of the song of the Marsh Warbler. At least two-thirds of the song of a Reed Warbler at Burghfield Gravel Pits on 28th April 1966 comprised rich mimicry, including phrases of Goldfinch, Swallow and House Sparrow, as well as a range of other calls including the Blackbird's alarm note, the remainder being the more typical song of a Reed Warbler.

*Sponsored by Paul Cropper*

# Reed Warbler

*Acrocephalus scirpaceus*

*Localised summer visitor and passage migrant*

The Reed Warbler is a localised summer visitor to Berkshire and is closely associated with one particular plant, the Common Reed *Phragmites australis*, whether in reedbeds or as vegetation fringing gravel pits or rivers. This association is confirmed by the results of both Atlas Surveys, which show that the species' distribution closely follows the river valleys in the west of the county. There were fewer records from the Loddon Valley, except where it joins the Thames just east of Reading. The Kennet Valley west of Reading is of particular importance for Reed Warblers, as it contains several reed beds, the largest being Thatcham Marsh, and another important area is the lower Colne valley at the eastern end of the county. It is the most frequently recorded species whose nests are parasitised by Cuckoos in Berkshire.

The Reed Warbler is usually a colonial nester and a vocal bird on its territory, so there is little difficulty in obtaining evidence of possible or probable breeding. Reed Warblers were located in 28% of the tetrads in Berkshire during the 2007–11 Atlas Survey and were confirmed to be breeding in 47% of them. There has been an expansion in the breeding distribution of the species in the county since the 1987–89 survey, with more tetrads along the Thames and Blackwater producing breeding evidence, and an increase in tetrads with breeding evidence from 73 to 106.

Although this is consistent with the national trend from CBC and BBS data, which show a moderate increase in the UK population as a whole during the 1990s and 2000s, the number of Reed Warblers at some sites in Berkshire has declined over the same period, in particular at Thatcham Marsh, probably due to the degeneration of the reedbeds. There were estimated to be about 400

pairs at Thatcham Marsh in 1969, but this was down to about 150 pairs in 1986 and reported to be below 100 singing males in each annual report between 1994 and 2011. Other areas of reeds were lost with the restoration and reopening of the Kennet and Avon Canal in 1990. Many parts of the canal in west Berkshire were overgrown and had good areas of *Phragmites*, which

**Reed Warbler** Breeding season abundance
Tetrads occupied: **63** (110) Average of occupied tetrads: **4·2**

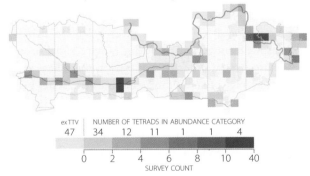

| exTTV | NUMBER OF TETRADS IN ABUNDANCE CATEGORY | | | | | |
|---|---|---|---|---|---|---|
| 47 | 34 | 12 | 11 | 1 | 1 | 4 |

0　　2　　4　　6　　8　　10　　40
SURVEY COUNT

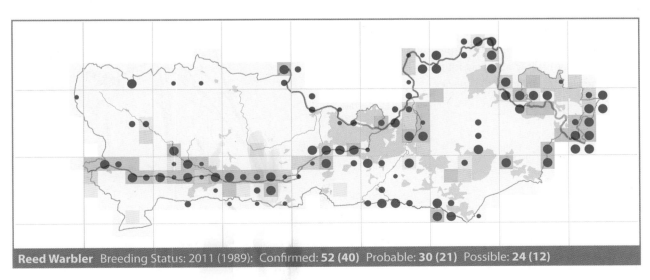

**Reed Warbler** Breeding Status: 2011 (1989): Confirmed: **52 (40)** Probable: **30 (21)** Possible: **24 (12)**

were removed. These adverse developments have been offset by the spread of gravel workings along the Kennet Valley and elsewhere in the county. Reed Warblers colonise such areas as they mature and reeds start to grow around the edges, and the birds do not appear to be affected by recreational activities. The species also seems to be spreading in fringing vegetation along the Thames and Jubilee rivers.

Spring passage is primarily in late April and May, though continues well into June. The first arrivals recorded from 1974 to 1994 were between 12th April and 7th May and, from 1994 to 2011, between 31st March and 24th April. Median first arrival dates advanced six days between the 1980s and the 2000s (Table ii, *page 50*). Ringing studies from Thatcham Marsh showed that the first juveniles usually fledge by mid-July and most breeding adults have left by mid-August, although from 1994 to 2011 fledged juveniles were ringed or recorded being fed by adults between 4th June and 24th August. Young birds and a few late breeders stay much later, and numbers are augmented by passage migrants through September and the first week of October. The latest departure date recorded is of one at Thatcham Marsh on 29th October 2001.

Ringing results have confirmed that there is a passage of birds from further north in Britain through the reedbeds in Berkshire in both spring and autumn. The autumn passage is more marked, probably reflecting the higher numbers in the population following the breeding season. There have been a number of foreign recoveries of birds ringed in Berkshire, from France, Portugal and Africa, three from Morocco, one from Western Sahara and one from Ghana. The latter recovery is the farthest south of any Reed Warbler ringed in Britain and involved a bird trapped at Thatcham Marsh in August 1969, which was found dead in Asrema, Ghana, the following December. Birds ringed as far away as Senegal have been re-trapped in Berkshire too. In 1999 a male was caught in Brimpton Gravel Pit where it had been originally ringed as a juvenile 10 years earlier (two years less than the longevity record for this species).

Prior to 1900, Noble (1906) noted that the Reed Warbler was a common species of reedbeds, but had declined late in the previous 20 years. The *Historical Atlas* indicates it was uncommon late in the 19th century in Berkshire.

*Sponsored by Gordon Newport*

# Great Reed Warbler

*Acrocephalus arundinaceus*

*Rare vagrant, three records*

The Great Reed Warbler is a rare vagrant to Britain, and despite having a wide breeding range across Europe, temperate Asia and north-west Africa, there have only been an average of about four records a year. It has been recorded on just three occasions in Berkshire. The first two records came from Thatcham Marsh, with the first there from 1st to 2nd June 1960, and the second ten years later, when a bird was caught and ringed there on 30th May 1970. The only stay of any duration occurred in 1990, when a male was present at Great Meadow Pond in Windsor Great Park from 22nd May to 16th June, during which time it sang frequently. This bird was trapped during its stay and was found to be at the top end of the weight range for the species.

*Sponsored by Val Tarr*

# Waxwing

*Bombycilla garrulus*

*Irregular and scarce winter visitor*

The Waxwing is a scarce winter visitor to Berkshire, occurring most frequently when large numbers reach Britain. Between 1943 and 1964, there were no significant arrivals, and relatively few individuals. This changed dramatically in the winter of 1965/66 when an unprecedented irruption of Waxwings into Britain, involving several thousand birds, resulted in around 150–200 birds being located in the county. Subsequent irruptions have occurred during the winters of 1970/71, 1988/89, 1995/96, 2004/05, 2010/11 and 2012/13.

The typical pattern in irruption years is one of arrivals in Berkshire in November/December, numbers peaking in February and the last birds leaving in April or early May (Figure 130). The 1965/66 arrival commenced with 16 birds on 21st November, increasing in January to about 22 in the Reading area and up to ten at Windsor, with still more in February, when there were up to 24 in the Reading area and good numbers in east Berkshire, including a flock of at least 100 at Old Windsor on 19th February 1966, the largest count ever recorded in Berkshire at that point. Similar numbers reached Berkshire during the winter of 1970/71 with four records involving 14 birds in November and December in Bracknell, slowly increasing to a peak of 46 on 27th March in Maidenhead. The final birds were recorded on 23rd April 1971. With other smaller parties the minimum number involved in this influx appears to have been about 108. A still smaller influx occurred during the winter of 1988/89 when, in January, there were five at Woolhampton and up to ten at Cippenham, where smaller numbers were seen until six on 13th April. This was followed by another influx in 1992, commencing with one at Twyford in January and 11 in Bracknell in March and April, with eight still present on 3rd May. This constituted only the third May record, after a single at Leighton Park in 1925 and two at Hungerford in early May 1946. The irruption of 1996 was the second largest to that point, and included a flock of up to 75 at Bracknell from 18th February until 21st March. Six other sites contributed 59 other individuals.

In years without major influxes, most records occur in the months from February to April.

There has been a higher frequency of irruptions since the beginning of the 21st century (Figure 131). Without doubt, the winter of 2004/05 produced the highest numbers arriving in the county, in a winter when records came from nearly 2,000 locations across the UK, (including one Scottish flock of 1,800 birds). Allowing for the difficulty of estimating numbers of roving parties

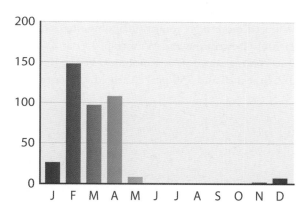

**Figure 129: Waxwing: sum of monthly totals in 19 non-irruption years between 1989/90 and 2012/13.**
Nineteen years with maximum counts of fewer than 50 in December to March are included. In 11 years there were no records and in three years only one bird was recorded. In non-irruption years from 1943/44–1988/89, with 50 of the 84 records in February.

**Waxwing** Winter abundance
Tetrads occupied: **1** (103) Average of occupied tetrads: **3·0**

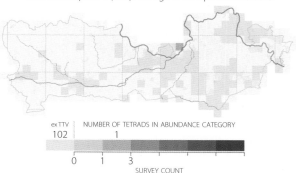

| ex TTV | NUMBER OF TETRADS IN ABUNDANCE CATEGORY |
|--------|------------------------------------------|
| 102 | 1 |

0   1   3

SURVEY COUNT

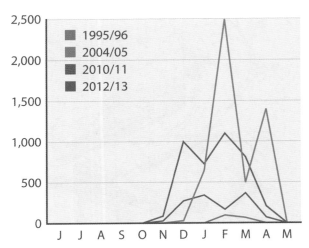

**Figure 130: Waxwing: monthly counts during four invasion years between 1989/90 and 2012/13.**

of this species, it is possible no fewer than 2,500 birds were present in Berkshire at the peak in February 2005. This included flocks, equalling or exceeding the previous highest count, at Sandhurst (100), Windsor (100), Ascot (100), Wokingham (120), Thatcham (148) and Slough (150), with still larger groups at Bracknell (270), and Maidenhead, where an amazing 300 could be observed.

Six years later, another significant arrival in 2010/11, contributed more high counts, including flocks of 100 at each of Crowthorne and Winnersh, 114 at Datchet, 120 at Wokingham, 130 at Sandhurst, 170 in Reading, 200 at Bracknell and 250 near Warfield. Other records

of smaller parties came from no fewer than 59 other locations, leading to a potential overall total of around 1,000 birds. The winter of 2012/13 produced further notable counts, with 27 birds across two sites in November 2012, some 270 individuals across nine locations in December 2012, and around 340 birds across ten sites by January 2013.

Generally, Waxwings tend to utilize sites not regularly observed, particularly modern housing estates and commercial developments where berry-bearing Rowan (*Sorbus aucuparia*), *Cotoneaster* spp. and similar plants have been grown. Perhaps for this reason, Bracknell has featured regularly in Waxwing years, although more recent invasions have been characterized by a greater spread of locations visited, as evidenced by the Winter Map, the survey period for which included the 2010/11 influx, and which shows records from 103 tetrads. Waxwings have also been noted taking other food: a party at Bracknell in January 1971 fed on fallen apples, whilst a party of eight birds, again in Bracknell, was feeding actively on insects they were finding on the trunk and branches of a large tree on 3rd May 1991.

For some time, the earliest arrival date for Waxwing in Berkshire was at Holyport on 12th November 1981, but the first five birds noted in the 2011 invasion were detected on 6th November at Forest Park, Bracknell. The 2001 invasion was notable as only having records during April, possibly of birds which had overwintered

Waxwing, Dorney Wetlands  *Michael McKee*

elsewhere, stopping to feed during their return journey to their breeding grounds.

There have been three ringing recoveries of Waxwing in Berkshire, which involved a bird ringed at Farnham, Surrey on 1st December 1965 and caught and released at Cookham Rise on 2nd March 1966, a female seen in Bracknell on 29th March 1992 had been ringed in Mannofield, Aberdeen as a first-winter bird on 30th November 1991, and a female ringed in Inverurie, Grampian, on 31st October 2004 that was found dead in Wokingham on 13th February 2005.

The earliest records of Waxwing in Berkshire occurred during the irruption of 1866/67 when birds were shot, or shot at, in the Hermitage area in November 1866 and January 1867 (Noble, 1906). There were then isolated records of single birds shot near Hermitage in 1868, near Wellington College in 1883 and at Binfield in February 1895, and two seen at Maidenhead Thicket on 3rd April 1905 (Noble, 1906). From then until 1944, county reports contain only three further records: a male at Binfield in February 1917, one at Leighton Park, Reading in May 1925, and what appears to have been a male and female at Inkpen in March 1936.

*Sponsored by Doug Wilson*

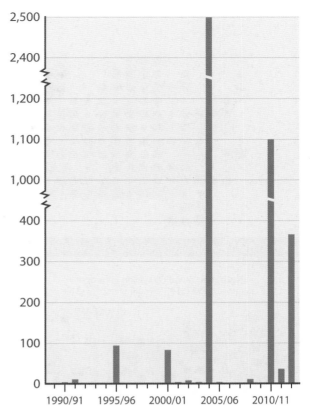

**Figure 131:  Waxwing: peak month counts 1989/9–2012/13.**

# Nuthatch Green

## *Sitta europaea*

*Widespread resident*

The Nuthatch is a widespread resident in Berkshire, occurring in broadleaved or mixed woodland, open parkland, hedgerows with mature trees, and even gardens, sometimes in the centre of towns, such as Forbury Gardens in Reading. It is also found in coniferous woodland in the south-east of the county. Nuthatches have taken to visiting garden feeding stations, often visiting peanut and sunflower seed feeders. One was observed at Brimpton in December 1990 pecking at apples hanging on a tree when the ground was snow covered.

The 2007–11 Tetrad Survey recorded breeding evidence in 323 of the tetrads in the county and breeding was confirmed in 230. Although the former represents a modest increase in range since the 1987–89 survey, the latter is a substantial increase compared to the 164 tetrads in the previous survey, indicating a substantial increase in the breeding population. This would be consistent with the national trends as disclosed by the results of the BBS, which disclose an increase of 48% for south east England between 1995 and 2010. The species was conspicuously absent only from some of the

relatively treeless areas of downland in the north-west of the county and some urban areas.

The breeding season and winter abundance maps show similar distributions, reflecting the sedentary nature of the species. This is also reflected in the ringing recoveries, with 17 of the 19 records being re-trapped in the county, two in adjoining counties and two recoveries of birds ringed in adjoining counties.

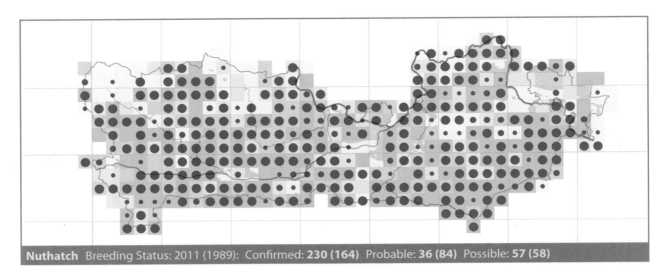

**Nuthatch** Breeding Status: 2011 (1989): Confirmed: **230 (164)** Probable: **36 (84)** Possible: **57 (58)**

**Nuthatch** Breeding season abundance
Tetrads occupied: **238 (334)** Average of occupied tetrads: **3·4**

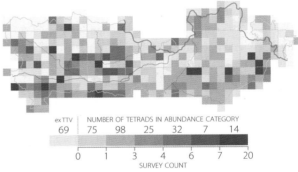

| ex TTV | NUMBER OF TETRADS IN ABUNDANCE CATEGORY | | | | | |
|---|---|---|---|---|---|---|
| 96 | 69 | 86 | 41 | 11 | 20 | 11 |

0    1    3    5    6    8    20
SURVEY COUNT

**Nuthatch** Winter abundance
Tetrads occupied: **251 (320)** Average of occupied tetrads: **3·1**

| ex TTV | NUMBER OF TETRADS IN ABUNDANCE CATEGORY | | | | | |
|---|---|---|---|---|---|---|
| 69 | 75 | 98 | 25 | 32 | 7 | 14 |

0    1    3    4    6    7    20
SURVEY COUNT

Although Nuthatches often associate with other small birds, particularly tits, in winter foraging flocks, they seldom form flocks with others of their species, and counts in double figures are unusual. The highest count recorded was 20 at Windsor Great Park on 7th February 1999. Nuthatches tend to be widely but thinly distributed in the breeding season. In 2007, a count in the extensive area of Swinley Park, Swinley Forest and Windsor Great Park found 68 territories.

During the 19th century, Nuthatches do not appear to have been particularly common in Berkshire. Clark Kennedy (1868) remarks that, although generally dispersed, it is not very common, and Noble (1906) described the species as local, but common, in parkland, with a considerable increase from 1880. It is also classed as uncommon in the *Historical Atlas*.

*Sponsored by Thames Valley Environmental Records Centre*

# Treecreeper

Green

*Certhia familiaris*

*Common resident*

The Treecreeper is a widespread resident in Berkshire, found principally in broadleaved and mixed woodland, although it is present throughout most of the mature coniferous woodland to the east of Bracknell.

During the two Tetrad Surveys, Treecreepers were confirmed to breed in almost the same number of tetrads (149 in 1987–89, and 150 in 2007–11), although the number of tetrads with probable and possible breeding reduced. The breeding distribution shows a strong correlation with the distribution of the species'

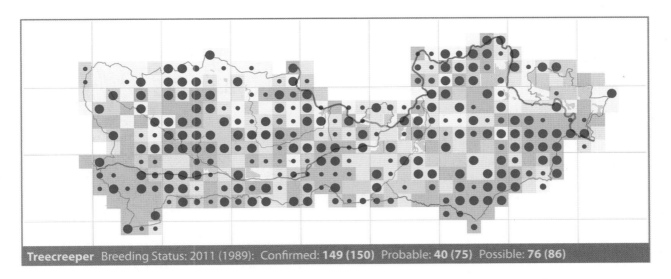

**Treecreeper** Breeding Status: 2011 (1989): Confirmed: **149 (150)** Probable: **40 (75)** Possible: **76 (86)**

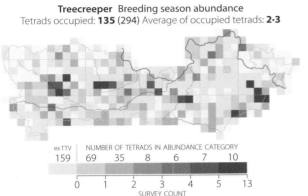

**Treecreeper** Breeding season abundance
Tetrads occupied: **135 (294)** Average of occupied tetrads: **2·3**

| exTTV | NUMBER OF TETRADS IN ABUNDANCE CATEGORY | | | | | |
|---|---|---|---|---|---|---|
| 159 | 69 | 35 | 8 | 6 | 7 | 10 |

0   1   2   3   4   5   13
SURVEY COUNT

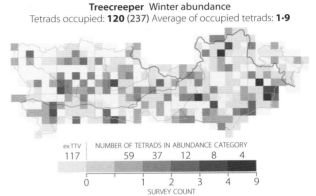

**Treecreeper** Winter abundance
Tetrads occupied: **120 (237)** Average of occupied tetrads: **1·9**

| exTTV | NUMBER OF TETRADS IN ABUNDANCE CATEGORY | | | | |
|---|---|---|---|---|---|
| 117 | 59 | 37 | 12 | 8 | 4 |

0   1   2   3   4   9
SURVEY COUNT

favoured woodland habitats, although there were records from urbanised areas with mature trees, such as in Wokingham, Maidenhead, Windsor and Slough. In one such area Treecreepers were recorded nesting between stacked fence panels. As would be expected, it was mostly absent from the largely treeless areas of the Downs in the north-west of the county, and showed a remarkably similar distribution to that of the Nuthatch, although the latter species, whose numbers have been increasing, now occupies more tetrads. This reflects the similarity in the habitat requirements of the two species. An apparent decline in the south-west of the county may reflect a higher level of coverage in the 1987–89 survey rather than any intervening decline.

The Treecreeper is a sedentary species, and its winter distribution in Berkshire is similar to its distribution during the breeding season, as demonstrated by the abundance maps. The species is particularly affected by hard weather which prevents it from obtaining food if freezing rain or fog coats tree trunks with ice (*Population Trends*), but there has been little weather of this nature in recent decades.

*Sponsored by Lesley Staves*

Treecreeper, Swinley Forest *David Lowther*

401

# Wren

*Troglodytes troglodytes*

*Abundant resident and winter visitor*

The Wren is an abundant and widespread breeding resident in Berkshire, which was recorded in every tetrad in the county during both the 1987–89 and 2007–11 Tetrad Surveys, and was confirmed to be breeding in at least 75% on both occasions. It is evidently a very adaptable species, being recorded in a wide variety of habitats throughout the county, not only in its more favoured habitats of woodland, waterside vegetation and farmland hedgerows, but also in urban gardens.

Wrens have a fairly long breeding season, from April into July, and in optimum habitats two broods are reared and males are often polygamous. This long and active breeding season may account for the high proportion of confirmed breeding records during the Tetrad Surveys. It is likely that failure to confirm breeding was due to insufficient observer time in the field rather than failure to breed. Estimates based on the timed counts in the 2007–11 Atlas survey indicate that Berkshire has a population of about 76,000 pairs (Appendix IV), making it the most numerous breeding bird in the county, along with the Woodpigeon.

Distribution and abundance in winter was similar to summer, with 99% of tetrads occupied in the 2007–11 Tetrad Survey. There were no obvious associations between habitat and abundance, suggesting that Wrens are flexible in their choice of wintering habitat.

Locally bred Wrens are considered to be fairly sedentary in southern Britain, the usual post-breeding dispersal involving only local movements. During the winter,

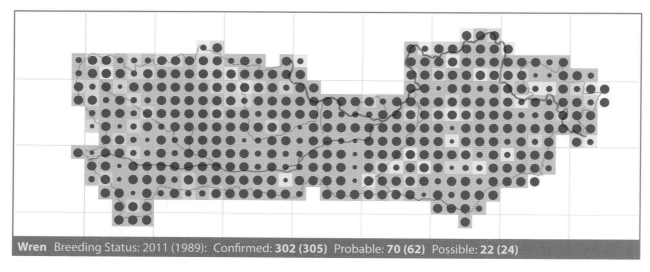

**Wren** Breeding Status: 2011 (1989): Confirmed: **302 (305)** Probable: **70 (62)** Possible: **22 (24)**

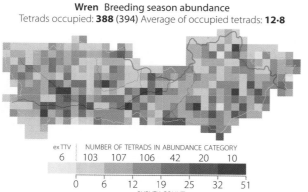

**Wren** Breeding season abundance
Tetrads occupied: **388 (394)** Average of occupied tetrads: **12·8**

| exTTV | NUMBER OF TETRADS IN ABUNDANCE CATEGORY | | | | | |
|---|---|---|---|---|---|---|
| 6 | 103 | 107 | 106 | 42 | 20 | 10 |

0   6   12   19   25   32   51
SURVEY COUNT

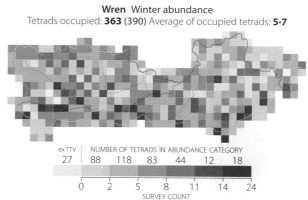

**Wren** Winter abundance
Tetrads occupied: **363 (390)** Average of occupied tetrads: **5·7**

| exTTV | NUMBER OF TETRADS IN ABUNDANCE CATEGORY | | | | | |
|---|---|---|---|---|---|---|
| 27 | 88 | 118 | 83 | 44 | 12 | 18 |

0   2   5   8   11   14   24
SURVEY COUNT

however, there is believed to be an influx of birds from further north and possibly from the continent (*Migration Atlas*). In Berkshire the local winter movement of birds, often into reedbeds, is usually random in direction and mainly involves distances of less than 25 km (Hawthorn and Mead, 1975). Studies at Thatcham Marsh have showed that movements occur from August to December in the autumn, and from February to April in spring (Hawthorn *et al.*, 1971, Hawthorn, 1975). These studies revealed a high level of wintering site fidelity, with 40% of Wrens caught in one winter re-trapped the next.

An unusual ringing record for Berkshire is of a Wren ringed at St. Albans Head, Dorset on 20th October 1988 and caught and released at Bagnor, 105 km north-east ten days later, a movement in the opposite direction from the expected autumn migration south. The furthest movement recorded for any bird ringed or recovered in Berkshire was a Wren found at Great Shefford on 28th July 1988, which had been ringed near Clacton-on-Sea, 188 km away, about nine months earlier. The longevity record for a Berkshire Wren is held by a first year bird ringed at Thatcham on 24th September 2000 and found freshly dead in the same place on 9th October 2005.

It is known that Wrens are vulnerable to severe winters, when numbers can decline rapidly after even fairly short periods of freezing weather. Following the harsh winter of 1962/63, the Wren population crashed both nationally and in Berkshire but quickly recovered thereafter. National surveys (CBC/BBS) showed a similarly rapid recovery after a reduction of 20–25% following the cold winters of the early 1980s and that the UK population had increased by 44% over the period 1970–2009. The Berkshire Bird Index (Crowley, 2010) measured a significant increase over the 1994–2008 period.

*Sponsored by Newbury District Ornithological Club*

# Starling

Red

*Sturnus vulgaris*

*Common resident and winter visitor*

The Starling is a common, formerly abundant resident and winter visitor to Berkshire, occurring widely throughout the county at all times of the year and in a variety of habitats. It has been in sharp decline throughout northern Europe (BirdLife International, 2004), and in Britain a marked decline started in the late 1960s and has continued since, so that the breeding population in the United Kingdom in 2009 is thought to have declined by between 82 and 90 percent from 1966, and by between 41 and 48 percent since 1995. The results of the two Berkshire Tetrad Atlas surveys appear to confirm this decline locally.

During the 1987–89 Tetrad Survey it was one of the most widespread species recorded, with breeding evidence reported in 388 (99%) of the tetrads in Berkshire and was absent only from four tetrads. Breeding was confirmed in 364 (94%) of tetrads, amongst the highest for any species recorded during the survey. In the 2007–11 survey, the number of tetrads with confirmed breeding had fallen to 273, with substantial areas where no breeding evidence was found, both on the Downs, in west Berkshire and the heaths of the south-east of the county. The breeding season abundance map indicates that what was once one of the county's most abundant birds produced an average count of less than 20 individuals in the tetrads in which it was encountered.

During the winter, the Starling population in Berkshire is augmented by large numbers of birds from the continent. The results of the *1981–84 BTO Winter Atlas*

survey indicated that the highest numbers tend to occur to the east of the county. After the breeding season and during the winter Starlings form large roosts, although these are only occasionally reported by observers and published records do not present a complete picture. However such information that has been published does point to a dramatic decrease in the county's winter population. Radford (1966) notes that a known roost site near Farnborough on the Downs was estimated to hold "millions" of birds in 1958, but that such large roost sites tended to move from year to year, and town centre roosts used to occur regularly in Reading and elsewhere.

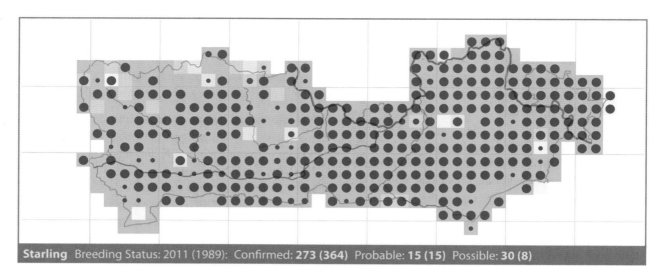

**Starling** Breeding Status: 2011 (1989): Confirmed: **273 (364)** Probable: **15 (15)** Possible: **30 (8)**

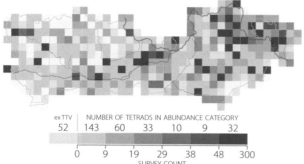

**Starling** Breeding season abundance
Tetrads occupied: **287 (339)** Average of occupied tetrads: **19·5**

| exTTV | NUMBER OF TETRADS IN ABUNDANCE CATEGORY | | | | | |
|---|---|---|---|---|---|---|
| 52 | 143 | 60 | 33 | 10 | 9 | 32 |

0    9    19    29    38    48    300
SURVEY COUNT

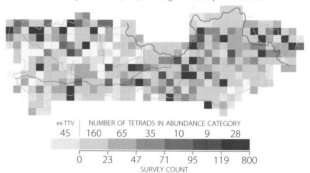

**Starling** Winter abundance
Tetrads occupied: **307 (352)** Average of occupied tetrads: **47·7**

| exTTV | NUMBER OF TETRADS IN ABUNDANCE CATEGORY | | | | | |
|---|---|---|---|---|---|---|
| 45 | 160 | 65 | 35 | 10 | 9 | 28 |

0    23    47    71    95    119    800
SURVEY COUNT

There have been no reports or counts of urban roosts of thousands of birds since the 1970s, and the last record of over 20,000 birds was in 1978 when a large roost at Sandford built up from May to early September and was estimated to hold some 100,000 individuals.

Most reports of roosts in the county in the 1980s and 1990s estimated the number of birds involved to be between 5,000 and 10,000, examples being 5,000 at a post-breeding roost at Brimpton in July 1991, 10,000 at Thatcham Marsh in October 1991 and 5,000 at Southcote in October 1992. In the 21st century there have only been three counts of 10,000 or more birds: 12,000 at Thatcham in January 2000, 10,000 at Brimpton in November 2004 and 10,000 in Newbury in March 2013. Even if the numbers are a small fraction of those in the 1950s, the tendency for roosts to move over the years remains evident from published records. There appears to have been a winter roost in the Kennet valley for most years since the mid-1990s, but in some years the highest counts have been from Theale Gravel Pits, Brimpton Gravel Pits, Thatcham Marsh or Lower Farm Gravel Pit, Newbury. However in the latter part of the first decade of the 21st century such counts were less frequent. Substantial flocks (now numbering hundreds rather than thousands) still occur on the Downs, as is evident in the Winter Map which shows highest counts from this area.

| Country of recovery | Number | Month(s) when ringed | Month(s) when recovered |
|---|---|---|---|
| Belgium | 3 | January | October, November |
| Netherlands | 5 | November-January | February, April, May, October |
| Germany | 9 | November-February | March-July |
| Poland | 1 | January | March |
| Sweden | 1 | March | April |
| Finland | 1 | January | April |
| Belarus | 1 | February | May |
| Russia | 4 | January, February, December | April, June, September |
| In North Sea | 2 | December, January | November, October |
| In Baltic Sea | 1 | February | March |

**Table 6: Overseas recoveries of Starlings ringed in Berkshire from 1911[1].** Recoveries reported by BTO up to July 2013.

Early ringing studies which were carried out at Bradfield in 1911 and 1912 produced four overseas recoveries, from Finland, Poland, Germany and the Netherlands. The bird found dead in Finland was, at the time, the first British recovery over such a distance. Table 6 shows a summary of overseas recoveries of Starlings ringed in Berkshire, and provides an indication of the source of winter visitors and their route across Europe. There has also been one Berkshire recovery of a bird ringed in Denmark. It is perhaps indicative of the decline of the bird in northern Europe that most of these records date from before the 1980s. Also noteworthy is a recovery from Scotland of a bird ringed at Jealott's Hill in May 1981 being recovered at Drumnadrochit, Highland Region the following January, an apparently anomalous northern movement in winter. The most bizarre recovery involved a bird ringed in Reading in 1923 which was found in 1927 on a railway engine running between Torquay and London.

At the beginning of the 19th century Starlings were described by Lamb (1880) as "common and in vast flocks about the meadows; in the winter inhabiting dovecotes", and they continued to be regarded as common by both Clark Kennedy (1868) and Noble (1906).

*Sponsored by Sarah and Ken White*

# Rose-coloured Starling

*Pastor roseus*

*Rare vagrant, three records*

The Rose-coloured Starling is a rare vagrant to Britain from its breeding range in central Asia, Anatolia and south-east Europe, and has occurred on just three occasions in Berkshire, all of which have been adult birds. Two of these records were in the 19th century: a male shot in September 1810 whilst feeding amongst cows in "Newbury Common fields", its stomach containing some undigested beetles (Lamb, 1880); and one picked up in an exhausted condition near Three-legged Cross, Newbury in 1875 or 1876 (Palmer, 1886), although further details are lacking.

The only 20th century record was of an adult which was present at Purley from 14th to 16th July 1975. This bird was first seen coming to a Cherry *Prunus* spp. tree in a small front garden. It was associating with a

flock of Starlings, Blackbirds and Mistle Thrushes that were feeding on the half-ripe cherries. Active and aggressive, the Rose-coloured Starling fed all day until it was last seen at about 19.00 hours on 16th July.

*Sponsored by Val Tarr*

# Dipper

`Green`

*Cinclus cinclus*

*Scarce vagrant*

In Britain, the Dipper is largely resident in areas with shallow, fast-flowing stretches of water in which it breeds. It finds these conditions in some years as close to Berkshire as west Wiltshire and west Oxfordshire, and it is not surprising that, given its distribution and particular habitat requirements, all the 20th and 21st century records in Berkshire have been from the Kennet and its tributaries from Aldermaston westwards, with the exception of one seen in flight along the Thames at Bourne End on 30th September 1989.

Since the first 20th century record of one at Marsh Benham on 29th September 1951, there were records of Dipper in Berkshire in 12 of the 39 years up to 1989, a surprising number in view of the sedentary nature of this

species. Two were seen on 11th May 1960 at Hamstead Marshall and one was seen at Bagnor in June 1965, the first summer record since 1899. To considerable local surprise, a pair bred on the Kennet and Avon Canal at Aldermaston in 1976, with adults and young being seen in May and June. At this time water levels were very low higher up the Kennet, which may have induced birds to move downstream. One was seen near Hungerford on

30th March 1977, close to the Wiltshire boundary, and breeding occurred there the following year when after several sightings of adults, two juveniles were seen in July and August 1979 which may have been from a Berkshire nest site.

Breeding was proved most recently in the county the next year, 1980, when although a dead adult was found at Bagnor in April, an adult and a fully fledged juvenile were seen there on 5th May. A singing male with a female were at Marsh Benham from 25th February to 3rd March 1981. A run of six years with summer records of Dipper then came to an end, a pattern of records which coincided with an expansion noted in Oxfordshire from 1970 which peaked in 1978 and declined after 1984 (Brucker et al., 1992). After a gap of five years without records, a Dipper was seen at Woolhampton in February 1986, and in 1987 there was a record from Great Shefford on 30th June and 6th July. This was the first record from the upper Lambourn Valley but there was no evidence of breeding then or subsequently. After the Thames record referred to above, there have been only two records, both in winter (Figure 132). One was at Easton on the Lambourn on 30th January 2004, and the most recent record was a long staying

**Figure 132: Dipper: all birds recorded 1951–2012, by month.** Since 1990, there have only two records (pale blue), one of a bird at Welford from December 2010 to January 2011

individual at Welford from 23rd December 2010 to 30th January 2011.

The first county record is of one taken at Newbury Mill in 1803 (Lamb, 1880). Noble (1906) stated that several had been taken in the county, although many of these records may refer to streams in areas which are now in Oxfordshire. Noble also refers to "one recently reported from the Holybrook at Reading Sewage Farm" but provides no further detail. The only breeding record was the remarkable occurrence in the summer of 1899 of a pair which nested in a hole in the masonry of the weir at Mapledurham and successfully reared young (Noble, 1906).

*Sponsored by Gerry Studd*

# Ring Ouzel Red

*Turdus torquatus*

*Scarce passage migrant*

The Ring Ouzel is an almost annual passage migrant in Berkshire in small numbers in both spring and autumn although, in more recent years, the majority of records have been from the spring period. Sightings come from locations across the county, with the majority from downland sites in the west.

The first 20th century record was not until 1933 when one was seen near Combe in early May. There was then another period without records until a male and two females were seen at Eversley on the extremely early date of 21st February 1945 (Allen, 1945). There was a male at Thurle Down, Streatley in April 1945 and, after two records in 1950, there were then reports of Ring Ouzels in 48 of the 56 years from 1956 to 2012, despite a decline nationally in the 1950s, and from the 1990s. Between 1995 and 2012, the only years that Ring Ouzels were not recorded in Berkshire were 1996, 2000 and 2001. Figure 133 shows the number of Ring Ouzels recorded, by month of arrival, from 1951 to 2010. There has been an increase in the number of Berkshire records since the beginning of the 21st century, particularly in the spring (Figure 134), despite the decline of the UK

breeding population (Sim et al., 2010). It is possible that increased observer coverage and knowledge of the species accounts for this increase.

The earliest spring passage record was one near Windsor on 11th March 1950, and the latest was one in a Finchampstead garden from the 2nd to 4th June 2005. The occurrence of passage birds in the county appears to have become later since the 1960s, with the majority of sightings coming during April. Most sightings have been of single birds, with occasionally two or three birds together, although sometimes larger parties have been recorded. A group of nine (six males and three females) at Inkpen Hill on 26th April 2003 was exceptional.

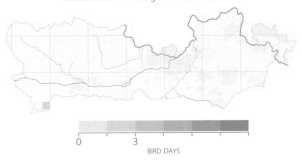

**Ring Ouzel** Spring migration occurrence
Tetrads used: **1** Average of used tetrads: **3·0**

0    3
BIRD DAYS

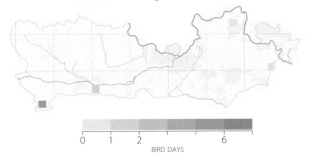

**Ring Ouzel** Autumn migration occurrence
Tetrads used: **4** Average of used tetrads: **2·5**

0    1    2         6
BIRD DAYS

Most records have been of birds which apparently stayed for no longer than a day, although a group compromising both male and female birds (maximum of three males and one female) lingered at Streatley Warren from the 9th to 17th April 2007.

The four September records were of a particularly early bird at Bucklebury Common on the 1st September 1972, one at Swinley on 20th September 1968, a female at Cannon Court, Maidenhead on 16th September 2011 and one, thought to have hit a window, found dead by a cat at Frogmill, Hurley on 29th September 2007. Until around the turn of the last century, passage in October was seen to occur mainly in the first half of the month, with only five of the 49 birds recorded having been reported after the 15th of the month. However, since 2000, there have been more birds reported from the second half of the month, an indication that the breeding season may be extending or moving later in the year. The latest departure involved a bird calling in flight when flying to the south west over Wishmoor on 22nd November 1995.

By far the largest party was one of at least 30 which came in to roost in Windsor Great Park on 5th October 1966. They were present early the following morning,

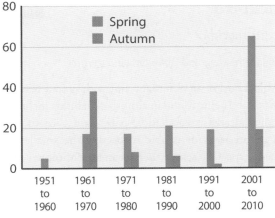

**Figure 133: Ring Ouzel: all birds recorded 1951–2010, by month of arrival.** Including a single party of 30 in October 1966.

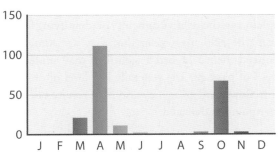

**Figure 134: Ring Ouzel: all birds recorded 1951–2010.** Spring, green; autumn, brown.

Ring Ouzel, Pinkneys Green *Jerry O'Brien*

407

but did not return to roost that evening. This was part of a large influx of birds into south-east England at the time which, for example, produced the highest count ever recorded in Sussex, 200 on the 9th October (James, 1996). A possible family party of six birds (one male, one female and four first winter birds) was reported from Walbury Hill on 4th October 2010.

Of the 276 birds seen in Berkshire between 1950 and 2011, 145 were males and 46 females, with the remainder unspecified or unsexed first winter birds (including the single flock of 30). This apparent discrepancy is difficult to explain, but the relative difficulty of identifying female birds in the field may mean that they are sometimes overlooked, hence reported sightings may understate the level of passage. The generally low level of observer cover in downland areas may also have resulted in some passage going undetected.

Ring Ouzels appear always to have passed intermittently through Berkshire in small numbers. Lamb (1880) states that four were shot near Reading and Newbury before 1814. Clark Kennedy (1868) regarded the species as a "rare passing visitor", citing a record of a male shot at Cookham Dean in spring 1867, and commenting that the Rev F. O. Morris had seen one or two during his occupancy of the vicarage at East Garston, which would have been in about 1826–27. Noble (1906) knew of a number of birds which had been taken in Berkshire, including one killed at Winkfield in January 1894. In the absence of any supporting detail, this winter record needs to be treated with some reservation. Noble (1906) was also informed that a pair had started to build a nest at Farley Hill in 1899, but had not completed the process. Although there were a number of scattered breeding records from lowland England up to the end of the 19th century, the absence of any details and the second-hand nature of the record leaves its reliability in doubt.

*Sponsored by Carol White*

# Blackbird

## *Turdus merula*

### *Abundant resident and common winter visitor*

The Blackbird is an abundant and widespread resident in Berkshire, being found in almost all habitats including agricultural areas, woodlands, parks and gardens, and even urban areas. It is able to occupy the smallest of gardens, especially where there is an area of mown grass and surrounding shrubs, and is one of the commonest species to be found in the more developed parts of the county.

During the 2007–11 Atlas Survey, Blackbirds were found in every tetrad during the breeding season, and they were recorded from all but one tetrad in the 1987–89 Survey. They were confirmed to be breeding in 94% of tetrads in the 2007–11 Survey, and were probably breeding in a further 5%, compared with 93% and 6% respectively in 1987–89. During the winter surveys they were reported in all but one tetrad. The Blackbird is one of the most numerous birds in Berkshire, with the county population estimated from the results of the timed counts in the 2007–11 Atlas Survey to be around 48,000 (Appendix IV). Perhaps because it is such a commonplace and familiar species little information on the species appears in county reports, unless albino or partially albino birds are seen.

There is occasionally a noticeable increase in Blackbird numbers, especially in late autumn when many congregate to feed on fallen apples. Studies by Snow

(1966) indicate that the species is fairly sedentary in the south of Britain, but is a partial migrant in the north. The number of birds wintering in southern counties, such as Berkshire, is therefore swollen by birds from the north, and these may be further supplemented by birds from the continent which regularly move into Britain to escape from harsh winter weather. A survey which was carried out throughout the winter of 1981/82 along the escarpment at Walbury Hill in west Berkshire showed an influx of birds in the autumn, followed by an exodus during snowy weather in January and a return of a smaller number of birds in April and May (Lewis *in litt.*). Small flocks occasionally occur in winter: there were 60 at Freeman's Marsh on 5th November 2007, 52 at Dinton Pastures in November 1981, 40 at Waltham St Lawrence and at Winterbourne, both on 11th

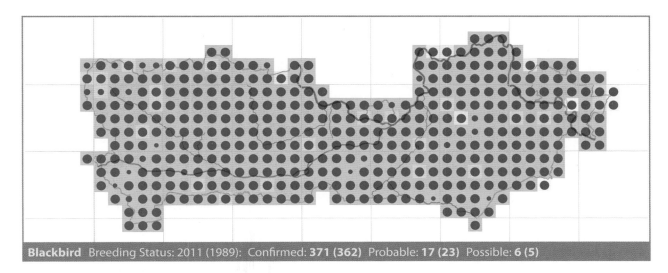

**Blackbird** Breeding Status: 2011 (1989): Confirmed: **371 (362)** Probable: **17 (23)** Possible: **6 (5)**

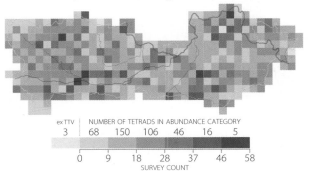

**Blackbird** Breeding season abundance
Tetrads occupied: **391 (394)** Average of occupied tetrads: **18·7**

| ex TTV | NUMBER OF TETRADS IN ABUNDANCE CATEGORY | | | | | |
|---|---|---|---|---|---|---|
| 3 | 68 | 150 | 106 | 46 | 16 | 5 |

| 0 | 9 | 18 | 28 | 37 | 46 | 58 |

SURVEY COUNT

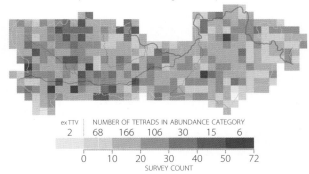

**Blackbird** Winter abundance
Tetrads occupied: **391 (393)** Average of occupied tetrads: **20·0**

| ex TTV | NUMBER OF TETRADS IN ABUNDANCE CATEGORY | | | | | |
|---|---|---|---|---|---|---|
| 2 | 68 | 166 | 106 | 30 | 15 | 6 |

| 0 | 10 | 20 | 30 | 40 | 50 | 72 |

SURVEY COUNT

December 2008, and several counts of over 30 in January and December 2010. In bad weather migrant Blackbirds often swell garden populations: at such times, gatherings of 10 or more are sometimes reported: for example 15 were in a Maidenhead garden on 6th December 1999; 14 were in a Twyford garden on 1st January 2006; and 15 were in adjacent Newbury gardens on 8th January 2006.

Recoveries of birds which were ringed in Berkshire and recovered abroad or vice versa provide an indication of the source of some of the winter visitors. A summary of the overseas recoveries is given in Tables 7 and 8.

Nationally the fortunes of Blackbirds have fluctuated since the 1960s, a decline in the 1970s and 1980s being followed by a partial recovery (Baillie *et al.*, 2012), but it has always been one of the nation's commonest and most familiar birds. Locally the Blackbird remains one of the commonest birds in the county and seems likely to continue to thrive in rural, suburban and urban areas.

*Sponsored by Renee Grayer*

| Country of recovery | Number | Month(s) when ringed | Month(s) when recovered |
|---|---|---|---|
| Belgium | 2 | December, March | October, February |
| Denmark | 3 | January, November | February, May |
| Finland | 2 | March, December | April, June |
| France | 2 | November, March | April, December |
| Germany | 6 | October–March | January, March, April, August |
| Ireland | 1 | March | November |
| Netherlands | 2 | December | February |
| Sweden | 3 | February, December | April, July, August |

**Table 7: Blackbird: overseas ringing recoveries of birds ringed in Berkshire 1909–2010.**

| Country of ringing | No | Month(s) when recovered | Month(s) when ringed |
|---|---|---|---|
| Belgium | 1 | March | July |
| Germany | 1 | February | October |
| Netherlands | 3 | February, February, April | July, October |
| Sweden | 2 | November, February | July, September |

**Table 8: Blackbird: recoveries in Berkshire of birds ringed in Europe**

# Black-throated Thrush

## *Turdus atrogularis*

*Rare vagrant, one record*

The only Berkshire record of this thrush from north and central Asia was a male bird, first seen in a garden in the Woodlands Park estate, Cox Green, Maidenhead on 27th December 1998. It remained throughout January, but was not then seen until 3rd March. It was last seen on 31st March 1999.

*Sponsored by Brian Pavey*

Black-throated Thrush, Maidenhead *Michael McKee*

# Fieldfare

`Red`  `Sch. 1`

## *Turdus pilaris*

*Common winter visitor which has bred*

The Fieldfare is a gregarious species which often occurs in large numbers in Berkshire during the autumn and winter. It is found throughout the county, primarily on grassland but also on winter stubble, ploughed fields, recreation areas and occasionally in parks and gardens. Fieldfares can also be found feeding in hedgerows and orchards. The first birds to arrive in Berkshire usually do so in early October, but there have been 14 September records since 1930, the earliest of which was on 1st September 1991 at Brimpton. The largest flocks seen in recent years were 2,000 at Windsor Great Park in November 1975, 7,000 at Bucklebury in January 1979, 2,500–3,000 on the Compton Downs in December 1990, and 2,000 at Sheepdrove Farm, Lambourn in December 2010.

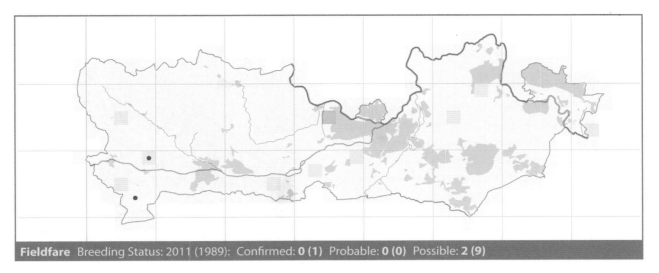

**Fieldfare** Breeding Status: 2011 (1989): Confirmed: **0 (1)** Probable: **0 (0)** Possible: **2 (9)**

The winter map shows that the Fieldfare is widely distributed throughout Berkshire, although numbers vary from year to year depending on the severity of the winter and on the availability of food. Although it frequently associates with Redwings, it is more numerous in open country, the winter map showing greater abundance on the Downs in the north-west and other predominantly arable areas. By contrast, Redwings are more widely distributed and tend to visit gardens more regularly than Fieldfares, which only tend to do so during hard weather. The relative numbers of the two species vary from year to year, although the population estimates based on the 2007–11 surveys (Appendix IV) indicate similar levels of average abundance.

The breeding range of the Fieldfare has been expanding westward in Europe in recent years, and the species first bred in Britain in 1967 in Orkney. Since the *1968–72 BTO Atlas*, summer records in Britain have spread south, although it is thought that the British breeding population is less than 25 pairs (*1988–91 BTO Atlas*). Sporadic observations since 1968 of Fieldfare during the summer months in south-east England culminated in the species being proved to breed in Berkshire in 1988 during the 1987–89 Tetrad Survey.

Confirmation that Fieldfares had bred in Berkshire was first obtained on 25th June 1988 when four fledged young, moving together as a group, were seen in Sulham Wood. Breeding may have also occurred the following year when there was a series of sightings at Tilehurst, within two miles of Sulham Wood. On 24th July one was observed in a garden feeding on Rowan *Sorbus aucuparia* berries and had probably been in the area for a week. Several further sightings were made up to 14th August, when four birds were seen. By 17th August there were eight birds visiting the gardens, after which sightings ceased.

In view of the breeding record in 1988, any birds seen during the summer period from May to September are potentially summering birds and hence of great interest.

**Fieldfare** Winter abundance
Tetrads occupied: **289** (366) Average of occupied tetrads: **55·2**

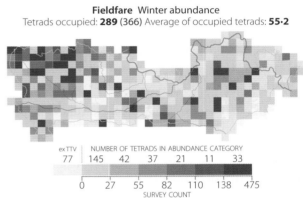

| exTTV | NUMBER OF TETRADS IN ABUNDANCE CATEGORY | | | | | |
|---|---|---|---|---|---|---|
| 77 | 145 | 42 | 37 | 21 | 11 | 33 |

0   27   55   82   110   138   475
SURVEY COUNT

A review of the records of Fieldfare in Berkshire during this summer period from 1930 to 2010 shows that in total 25 birds have been recorded in May. Of these, 20 occurred in the first half of the month and five in the second half, one on the 17th, three on the 19th and one on the 23rd. August records, in addition to those in 1988/89 mentioned above, have comprised six birds at Cheapside on 22nd August 1968, one at Theale Gravel Pits on 4th August 1992, followed by two at the same site on 6th August 1992, and five at Stoke Park golf course, Slough on 17th August 2010. These August records may be indicative of summering, though there has been no evidence of breeding. An analysis of breeding records of Fieldfare in the UK from 1974–2006 by Holling (2009) showed that breeding numbers vary from year to year (maximum of 13 pairs down to none in 1999) with no apparent pattern and no site fidelity, so it is perhaps not too surprising that there has been no firm evidence of breeding in Berkshire since 1988.

There have been five overseas recoveries of Fieldfares ringed in Berkshire, three autumn or winter recoveries from France, one from the Nordland province in Norway in June and one from Varmland in Sweden. A Fieldfare ringed in its first year in August 1993 in Sweden was found dead in Bracknell, Berkshire in February 1994.

*Sponsored by Dr Jay Maxwell*

# Song Thrush

*Turdus philomelos*

*Common resident and winter visitor*

The Song Thrush is an abundant and widespread resident in Berkshire, found in a variety of habitats including farmland with hedgerows, woodland, scrub, parks, suburban gardens and sometimes urban areas. It is also a winter visitor to the county from elsewhere in Britain and from continental Europe.

During the summer phases of the 2007–11 Atlas Survey, breeding evidence of the Song Thrush was recorded in six more tetrads in the county compared to the 1987–89 survey, with breeding confirmed in 61% of these, down from 76% during the 1987–89 Atlas survey. Nationally there was a long-term decline that began in the mid-1970s until the mid-1990s, with a partial recovery indicated by an increase of about 20% up to 2011 shown by the BBS.

An indication of the comparable fortunes of this species and of the Blackbird is provided by comparing the equivalent average counts for both species. The *Historical Atlas* notes that numbers of Blackbirds and Song Thrushes were probably comparable in the 19th century. By the time the 2007–11 Tetrad Atlas

survey was undertaken, Song Thrushes were between four to five times less numerous than Blackbirds in Berkshire (Appendix IV).

The Winter Atlas map indicated presence in about 95% of tetrads, with similar abundance on average to that in the breeding season.

Some emigration of Song Thrushes out of Britain to the south-west takes place in winter, especially in hard weather. There have been five overseas recoveries in winter of birds ringed in Berkshire, three in France,

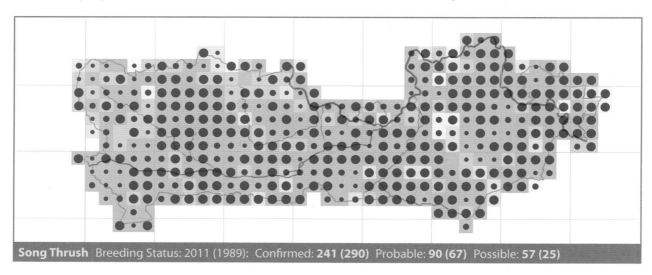

**Song Thrush** Breeding Status: 2011 (1989): Confirmed: **241 (290)** Probable: **90 (67)** Possible: **57 (25)**

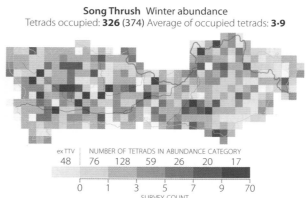

**Song Thrush** Breeding season abundance
Tetrads occupied: **363 (392)** Average of occupied tetrads: **4·4**

| exTTV | NUMBER OF TETRADS IN ABUNDANCE CATEGORY | | | | | |
|---|---|---|---|---|---|---|
| 29 | 124 | 95 | 73 | 30 | 21 | 20 |

0   2   4   6   8   10   22
SURVEY COUNT

**Song Thrush** Winter abundance
Tetrads occupied: **326 (374)** Average of occupied tetrads: **3·9**

| exTTV | NUMBER OF TETRADS IN ABUNDANCE CATEGORY | | | | | |
|---|---|---|---|---|---|---|
| 48 | 76 | 128 | 59 | 26 | 20 | 17 |

0   1   3   5   7   9   70
SURVEY COUNT

one from Jersey and one from Spain. One of the French recoveries and the Jersey record were in the hard winters of 1961/62 and 1962/63. There is also some immigration of birds from northern Europe, evidence for which is provided by records of one ringed at Thatcham Marsh on 3rd April 1988 being recovered in late April 1990 in Luneburg, north Germany, and another bird ringed at Wraysbury on 28th September 2002, which was recovered on 26th April 2004, also at Luneburg.

The widespread decline resulted in the species, once considered one of our commonest garden birds, being included in the RSPB's first Red List of species of high conservation concern in the mid-1990s (RSPB, 1996). In the light of the recovery in numbers between 1999 and 2009, the species was removed from that category. In Berkshire, it is unclear from the results of the two Tetrad Atlas surveys whether this recovery is yet evident in the county.

*Sponsored by Ron Bryant*

# Redwing

*Turdus iliacus*

*Common winter visitor*

The Redwing is a common winter visitor to Berkshire. The *1981–84 BTO Winter Atlas* notes that it is highly nomadic in winter, moving in response to weather conditions and the availability of food. In Berkshire, this is reflected by fluctuations in numbers both during and between winters.

Although Redwings occur widely on farmland with Fieldfares in mild weather, in cold weather they often move to woodland, unlike Fieldfares (*1981–84 BTO Winter Atlas*). They also visit urban and suburban areas more frequently than Fieldfares, especially in hard weather. The Winter Maps for the two species show that in much of the open downland area of north-west Berkshire, Fieldfares are more numerous than Redwing, whereas no discernible pattern emerges for Redwings, with tetrads with higher counts distributed throughout the county. The highest counts have been of birds on passage, notably in autumn, 2,500 were counted over Summerleaze Gravel Pits on 10th October 1989, and 1,200–1,300 over West Woodhay Down on 22nd October 1991, and in spring, when over 1,000 were seen at Wokingham on 10th February 2005. Otherwise, counts seldom exceed more than a few hundred, a count of 800 reported from the Hungerford and Kintbury area in November 1976 being noteworthy.

The first arrivals in autumn usually occur in late September or early October and are often detected as they migrate overhead in darkness by hearing their characteristic "zeet" note. The earliest records are one at Burghfield Common on 13th September 1994, five at Bracknell on 14th September 1979, and one at Winnersh on the same date in 2002. The latest spring departures are usually in April, but there have been three May records. A bird was seen on 1st and 2nd May 1951 at Ascot, and was heard in full song on the 1st, and two were seen at Rapley on 1st May 1978. Another was

**Redwing** Winter abundance
Tetrads occupied: **332** (382) Average of occupied tetrads: **30·6**

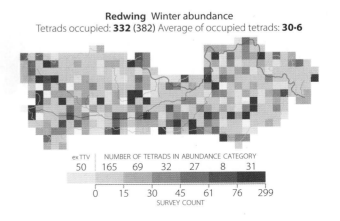

| exTTV | NUMBER OF TETRADS IN ABUNDANCE CATEGORY | | | | | |
|---|---|---|---|---|---|---|
| 50 | 165 | 69 | 32 | 27 | 8 | 31 |

0    15    30    45    61    76    299
SURVEY COUNT

seen at Brimpton on 20th May 1991 singing strongly early in the morning from the top of an apple tree, and again in the evening from a neighbouring garden. There is an unusual record of an apparently summering adult bird ringed at Wraysbury Gravel Pits on 26 June 2004.

There have been three overseas ringing recoveries involving Redwings travelling to and from Berkshire.

Birds ringed in the Telemark province of Norway and Estonia have been recorded in Berkshire, and one ringed at Wraysbury in October 1988 was recovered at Moustier, Lot-et-Garonne, France in February 1992.

*Sponsored by Andrew Taylor*

# Mistle Thrush Amber

*Turdus viscivorus*

*Widespread resident*

The Mistle Thrush remains a common and widespread resident in Berkshire, although in decline across the county. It can be encountered in almost all the county's habitats, and its distinctive song is one of the first to be heard as spring approaches, often well before New Year.

Mistle Thrushes are readily detected during the breeding season as they tend to be noisy when defending their nest and young, and in the 1987–89 Atlas Survey breeding evidence was recorded in 96% of the tetrads in the county, with breeding confirmed in 71%. The 2007–11 Atlas Survey showed a similarly wide distribution, but the number of tetrads in which breeding evidence was found had fallen to 87% of tetrads, and breeding was confirmed in only 47%. This is reflected in the Berkshire Bird Index, which recorded a significant decline between 1994 and 2008. Nationally the Mistle Thrush has been in decline since the 1970s (Eaton *et al.*, 2011) and BBS data show a fall of 40% in abundance between 1989 and 2010.

After breeding, family parties tend to stay together as groups, and sometimes larger flocks form, possibly augmented by an influx of continental birds in late summer and early autumn. In 1981, a large flock of 120–130 birds was seen in Windsor Great Park on 30th November. However, records of larger flocks have all but disappeared since the early 1990s, and the last count above 100 was of 108 birds at Swallowfield Park on 8th August 1992. No flock larger than 50 has been recorded since 2001, when 70 were seen at West Woodhay on 26th July 2001 and, more commonly, the largest flocks are in the order of 20–30 birds. Unlike the other thrush species, there have been no ringing recoveries involving birds ringed or recovered in Berkshire which have exceeded 100 km, presumably reflecting the sedentary nature of Berkshire's Mistle Thrushes.

Although Noble (1906) commented that the Mistle Thrush was exceedingly shy, it occurs quite frequently in Berkshire in urban and suburban areas. Males can be heard on mild or sunny days as early as November singing in Reading town centre, defending their winter feeding territories which they hold into the spring, when some exceptionally early breeding can occur. Most notable was a pair in Greyfriars churchyard, Reading which was seen to be sitting on eggs on 13th January 1997 and another clutch on 11th February the same year.

*Sponsored by Peter Newbound*

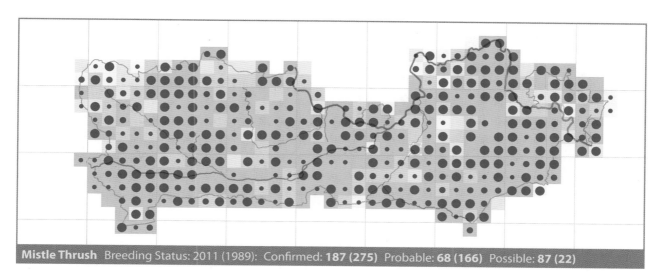

**Mistle Thrush** Breeding Status: 2011 (1989): Confirmed: **187 (275)** Probable: **68 (166)** Possible: **87 (22)**

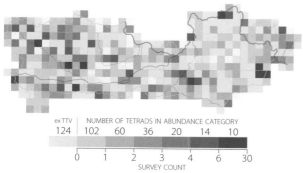

**Mistle Thrush** Breeding season abundance
Tetrads occupied: **242 (366)** Average of occupied tetrads: **2·5**

| exTTV | NUMBER OF TETRADS IN ABUNDANCE CATEGORY | | | | | |
|---|---|---|---|---|---|---|
| 124 | 102 | 60 | 36 | 20 | 14 | 10 |

0 1 2 3 4 6 30
SURVEY COUNT

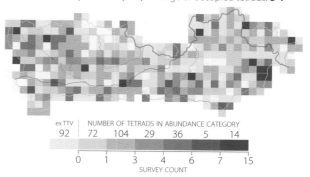

**Mistle Thrush** Winter abundance
Tetrads occupied: **260 (352)** Average of occupied tetrads: **3·1**

| exTTV | NUMBER OF TETRADS IN ABUNDANCE CATEGORY | | | | | |
|---|---|---|---|---|---|---|
| 92 | 72 | 104 | 29 | 36 | 5 | 14 |

0 1 3 4 6 7 15
SURVEY COUNT

# Spotted Flycatcher

Red

*Muscicapa striata*

*Uncommon summer visitor and passage migrant*

The Spotted Flycatcher is a declining, formerly widespread summer visitor to Berkshire, found most frequently in the west of the county. Its preferred habitats are broadleaved woodlands, parks and gardens, but it is occasionally found in other habitats such as coniferous woodlands when suitable nest sites are available.

The results of the 2007–11 Tetrad Survey highlighted the decline of the species in Berkshire. Whereas breeding evidence was found for Spotted Flycatchers in 71% of the tetrads in Berkshire during the 1987–89 Tetrad Survey, and they were confirmed to be breeding in over half of these, in the latest survey breeding

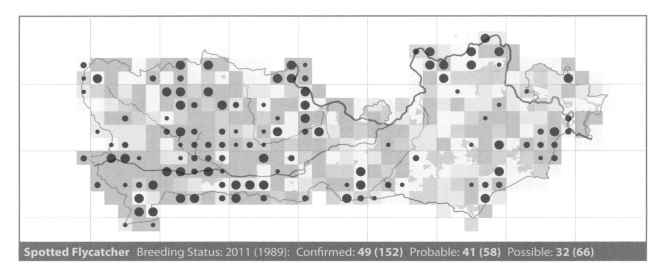

**Spotted Flycatcher** Breeding Status: 2011 (1989): Confirmed: **49 (152)** Probable: **41 (58)** Possible: **32 (66)**

evidence was recorded in just over a third of tetrads, and breeding confirmed in 40% of these. The species' habit of repeatedly sallying from an exposed perch to catch flying insects means that its presence is readily detected, and family parties are fairly conspicuous once the young have left the nest, so it is unlikely that birds were missed in the later survey on any substantial scale. Once widespread, Spotted Flycatchers have largely retreated to areas along the Thames and Kennet, wooded areas on the edges of the Downs, and the coniferous woodlands of the south east of the county. Counts undertaken in the Swinley Forest, Swinley Park and surrounding areas of Windsor Great Park and Ascot in some years since 2000 have revealed between 20 and 44 territories.

Although Spotted Flycatcher numbers fluctuate from year to year, the underlying trend is that the population in Britain has declined by about 90% since the early 1960s. The precise reasons for the decline are unclear but seem most likely to be linked to habitat and climate changes in the wintering area in Africa. There was little information available to quantify the decline in Berkshire until the results of the 2007–11 Tetrad Survey, however. The reporting rate in the county report has not shown the trend, but this almost certainly reflects the higher recording rate as the species has become scarcer, whereas in the 1980s, when birds were still frequently encountered in suburban areas of the towns in the county, many observers almost certainly did not consider their observations merited submission.

The earliest spring arrival dates for Spotted Flycatcher in Berkshire between 1974 and 2011 have varied from 2nd April to 16th May, but few birds are normally seen before mid-May. Unlike some summer visitors, there has been no tendency for arrivals to occur earlier in more recent years. There are two records of birds having been recorded in March, one of which was seen at Combe on the exceptionally early date of the 5th in 1934.

**Spotted Flycatcher** Breeding season abundance
Tetrads occupied: **44 (151)** Average of occupied tetrads: **1·8**

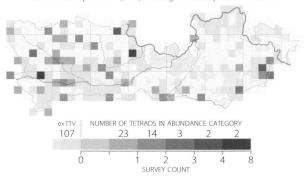

| ex TTV | NUMBER OF TETRADS IN ABUNDANCE CATEGORY | | | | |
|--------|------|------|------|------|------|
| 107 | 23 | 14 | 3 | 2 | 2 |

| 0 | 1 | 2 | 3 | 4 | 8 |
SURVEY COUNT

Good views were obtained of this bird and it would appear that it was the earliest ever to have been recorded in Britain. The other March record was from Eton Wick on 26th March 1944. Latest dates since 1974 have varied from 2nd September to 13th October (although normally in the last two weeks of September), and it is during late summer or in autumn that the highest counts are usually made. Counts of 25 at Woolhampton on 14th August 1991, and at least 25 at Waltham St Lawrence on 27th August 1993 have been the largest number seen together in Berkshire in recent decades.

There have been two overseas ringing recoveries of Spotted Flycatcher from Berkshire, a 1953 recovery in France, and a nestling ringed at Brimpton in June 1976 which was recovered in its winter quarters in Congo (Brazzaville) in equatorial Africa in the second half of September that year.

The *Historical Atlas* indicates that the Spotted Flycatcher was uncommon in Berkshire at the end of the 19th century, although Noble (1906) states that the species was abundant at the turn of the century.

*Sponsored by Sean Swallow*

# Robin

*Erithacus rubecula*

*Abundant resident*

The Robin continues to be a common and widespread resident in Berkshire. Although historically a woodland species, the Robin has proved so adaptable to the ways of man that it can flourish in a wide range of habitats. Robins were recorded in every tetrad and confirmed to be breeding or probably breeding in 99% of the tetrads in the county in the 2007–11 Atlas Survey, an increase of 3% over the 1987–89 survey. The few tetrads where it was not confirmed as breeding were scattered, mostly along the northern edge of the county, particularly on the Downs where breeding sites are likely to be more limited. Winter distribution of the Robin is very similar to that in the breeding season, with slightly lower abundance recorded in the north west of the county.

The *1988–91 BTO Atlas* indicates that there are considerable differences in the breeding density of Robins in different parts of the British Isles. The Berkshire Bird Index (Crowley, 2010) indicates a significant increase (75%) in abundance between 1994 and 2008, consistent with national CBC/BBS trend over the same period (+33%). Along with the

Woodpigeon and Wren, the Robin is one of the most numerous species in Berkshire, with an estimated total of around 70,000 territories based on the 2007–11 atlas abundance survey (Appendix IV).

Some female and juvenile Robins leave their breeding areas in late summer but normally return to breed 'within sight of their birthplace' (*Migration Atlas*). Some post-breeding movements are further, a bird ringed at Reading on 15th July 1954 was found at Sittingbourne, Kent 118 km away on 11th January 1955, and a nestling

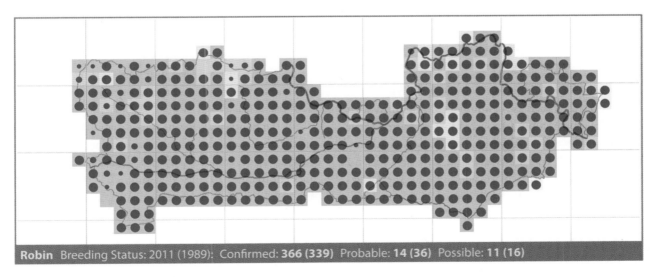

Robin  Breeding Status: 2011 (1989):  Confirmed: **366 (339)**  Probable: **14 (36)**  Possible: **11 (16)**

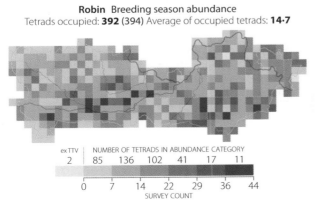

**Robin**  Breeding season abundance
Tetrads occupied: **392** (394) Average of occupied tetrads: **14·7**

| exTTV | NUMBER OF TETRADS IN ABUNDANCE CATEGORY | | | | | |
|---|---|---|---|---|---|---|
| 2 | 85 | 136 | 102 | 41 | 17 | 11 |

0    7    14    22    29    36    44
SURVEY COUNT

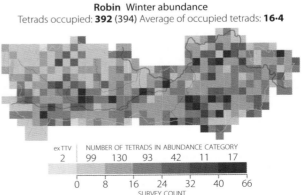

**Robin**  Winter abundance
Tetrads occupied: **392** (394) Average of occupied tetrads: **16·4**

| exTTV | NUMBER OF TETRADS IN ABUNDANCE CATEGORY | | | | | |
|---|---|---|---|---|---|---|
| 2 | 99 | 130 | 93 | 42 | 11 | 17 |

0    8    16    24    32    40    66
SURVEY COUNT

ringed on 23rd May 1990 near Hungerford was caught by a ringer on 4th August 1990 at Beachy Head, Eastbourne, a journey of 144 km in just 2 months and 12 days. Over a longer period of time, one ringed at Walbury Hill in March 1988 was reported at Hayle, Cornwall on 29th September 1990 having moved a distance of 304 km. The only overseas recovery involved one ringed as a juvenile in Bradfield in May 1912, which was recovered at Voorne, Zuid Holland, Netherlands in November 1914, 361 km away, the longest distance travelled by a Robin ringed in Berkshire. A Robin ringed

in Charente-Maritime, France in September 2001 was eaten by a cat in Windsor in March 2003, 662 km away.

With periodic fluctuation following periods of hard winter weather, the population of Robin in Britain has grown significantly in the last 50 years. Although agricultural operations have affected some of the habitats favoured by the species, it has adapted well to co-exist with man and seems likely to continue to flourish as one of the commonest and most widespread species in Berkshire.

*Sponsored by Sherrards Garden Services*

---

# Nightingale Amber

## *Luscinia megarhynchos*

*Uncommon and local passage migrant and summer visitor.*

The Nightingale is an uncommon passage migrant and summer visitor to Berkshire which underwent a general decline in numbers during the middle of the 20th century, and although it has increased numerically in the county in recent years, its range is much reduced.

The Atlas surveys of 1987–89 and 2007–11 revealed that the Nightingale was largely confined to river valleys, indicating a strong preference for damp areas such as mature gravel pits, with smaller numbers in scrub areas on heathland and in woodland. The number of tetrads in which breeding evidence was recorded fell from 79 in the earlier survey to 34 in 2007–11, and woodlands with suitable scrubby areas had virtually been abandoned.

BTO surveys carried out in 1976, 1980, 1999 and 2012 revealed a steady increase in numbers of singing males in Berkshire, but in a progressively more restricted range, reflecting the Atlas surveys. The survey conducted in 1976, which was unusually hot and dry, was not considered to be a particularly good year for the species, but the follow-up 1980 survey counted 91 singing males. The total had risen to 111 in 1999 and 166 in 2012, despite the number of occupied tetrads falling from 83 in 1989 to 46 in 2011 and only 24 in 2012.

The BTO survey in 2012 confirmed that in Berkshire the Nightingale is now virtually confined to the Kennet Valley, with small populations at Greenham Common and Dinton Pastures. The Theale and Burghfield gravel pits complex has emerged as a very important site for the species, not just in Berkshire, but also in the country as a whole. Unfortunately, this area is under threat from development, so local surveys were carried out by the Theale Area Bird Conservation Group in 1998, 2005 and 2007, which provided vital information on the importance of the area for the species; in 1998, 59 singing males were located, with 57 in 2005 and 2007,

but this figure had increased to an outstanding 109 in 2012 (Figure 135).

Nationally, the Nightingale is on the UK's Amber list of conservation concern, but the recent downward population trend indicates that the species now warrants Red-list status (Holt *et al.*, 2012). Between 1980 and 1999 Berkshire was one of only a handful of counties in Britain where the population had increased, whilst neighbouring counties suffered drastic declines: 78% in Oxfordshire, 79% in Wiltshire, 70% in Hampshire and 86% in Buckinghamshire (Wilson *et al.*, 2002). Much research is going on at present to determine the reasons for the decline.

Little information is available on the passage of Nightingales through Berkshire, although it would appear to be regular. The furthest distance covered by a

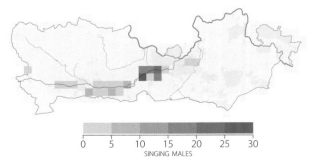

0   5   10   15   20   25   30
SINGING MALES

**Figure 135:  Nightingale: BTO survey, 2012.**

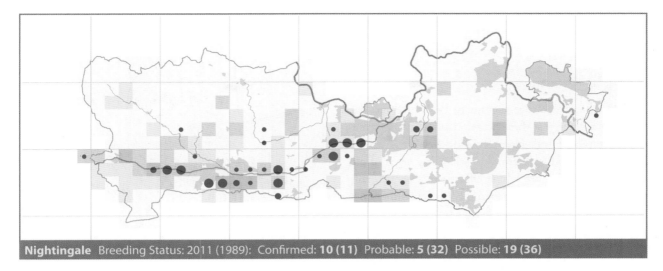

**Nightingale** Breeding Status: 2011 (1989):  Confirmed: **10 (11)** Probable: **5 (32)** Possible: **19 (36)**

bird ringed in the county, and the only overseas recovery, relate to one trapped at Aldermaston in June 1979 which was recovered in Les Landes, south-west France in April 1981. Birds have been re-trapped annually at a site near Aldermaston over a period of four consecutive years, indicating high breeding site fidelity. A male which was ringed at a site in west Berkshire was re-trapped over a period of six years.

In recent decades there has been a tendency for Nightingales to arrive earlier in spring, and since the beginning of the 21st century first arrivals are regularly appearing in the first week of April, and in 2010 one arrived at Searles Farm Lane, Burghfield Gravel Pits on 28th March, the earliest-ever record. An analysis of earliest arrival dates in 1980/89 and 2000/10 showed a significant eight day advance over the 20 year period (Table ii, *page 50*). Most birds depart by August, with the latest date since 1974 being one at Theale Gravel Pits on 8th September 1991.

**Nightingale** Breeding season abundance
Tetrads occupied: **16** (46) Average of occupied tetrads: **2·1**

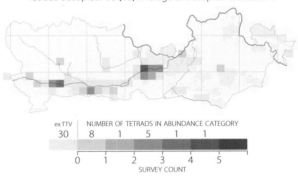

| ex TTV | NUMBER OF TETRADS IN ABUNDANCE CATEGORY | | | | |
|---|---|---|---|---|---|
| 30 | 8 | 1 | 5 | 1 | 1 |

| 0 | 1 | 2 | 3 | 4 | 5 |
|---|---|---|---|---|---|

SURVEY COUNT

The *Historical Atlas* indicates that Nightingales were regarded as common in Berkshire in the 19th century, although Noble (1906) noted that numbers varied considerably from year to year.

*Sponsored by Pat Martin*

Nightingale, Searles Lane Gravel Pit  *Jerry O'Brien*

419

# Bluethroat

*Luscinia svecica*

*Rare vagrant, three records*

The Bluethroat is a rare vagrant to Berkshire and has been recorded on just three occasions, all in the autumn. The first record was from Reading Sewage Farm in 1972 at a time when there were still a few areas of old style sewage beds onto which effluent was occasionally pumped. It was first located on 17th September in a small patch of Reed *Phragmites australis* in the middle of one of these beds and, perhaps because it could not easily be approached and was consequently undisturbed, remained until 24th September, being seen fairly frequently throughout its stay. The second record was of one seen at Whitley near Reading on 2nd October 1978 which was first located by its call. The most recent was

a male of the white-spotted race seen at Woolhampton Gravel Pits on 9th April 2009.

*Sponsored by Ken Moore*

# Pied Flycatcher

*Ficedula hypoleuca*

*Scarce passage migrant and rare summer visitor, has bred*

The Pied Flycatcher is a widespread but scarce annual passage migrant and rare summer visitor to Berkshire. Birds are often found by chance, as with many other migrant species, and it is likely that many are overlooked. Passage birds occur throughout the county, and 203 birds were recorded between 1943 and 2012, no less than 49 of which (24%) were observed in the relatively small area of Leighton and Whiteknights Parks in Reading.

The Pied Flycatcher was regarded as a rare summer visitor in Berkshire at the end of the 19th century (Noble, 1906), and remained so for a further 40 years, with the only records being from Streatley in April 1924, in Hungerford Park in May the same year, at Leighton Park School in 1925, at Slough in April 1931, at Eton from 15th May to 3rd June the same year, at Kintbury in April 1932 and a pair at Leighton Park on 26th July 1943. In contrast, there were records from all but four of the years from 1947 to 1967 and annually thereafter to 2006. The increase in records coincided with the expansion of the Pied Flycatcher after 1940 (*1968–72 BTO Atlas*) and improved observer coverage. Since 2006 it has only been recorded in four of the seven years to 2013, perhaps reflecting the national decline in the species in its breeding areas in the UK (Baillie *et al.*, 2012).

The distribution of passage records from 1947 to 2012 is shown in Figure 136. The earliest spring arrival date

recorded was on 2nd April in 1998 at Whiteknights Park, and the latest spring passage record was on 16th May in 1959 at Earley. The majority (68%) of spring records are of males, with most of the females arriving two or three weeks later. Nearly all sightings in spring have been of single birds, but there are five records of two birds together, and two records of three birds together, at Baynes Reserve on 22nd April 1983 and at Hungerford on 17th April 1984. In most years there have been fewer than five spring records, though heavy passage for three consecutive years from 1983 to 1985 produced exceptionally high counts of 11, ten and 17 birds. Pied Flycatchers are usually seen for just one day and only occasionally stay for two to three days. The only birds recorded as staying longer were all males and were from 11th to 15th May 1952 at Windsor Great Park, 19th to 23rd April 1970 at Whiteknights Park, from 13th to 17th May 1990 at Ascot, and from 12th to 14th April 1999 at Whiteknights Park. Some males on spring passage in Britain retain a considerable amount of brown plumage and there been have four records of such birds in Berkshire, one in 1983, two in 1985 and one in 1989.

The only birds to be reported in summer from 1906 to 1972 were one at Eton from 15th May to 3rd June 1931 and a male and a female at Leighton Park on 26th July 1943 which may have been early passage birds. From 1972 to 1991, there were more frequent records of Pied Flycatcher in summer in Berkshire. After five records between 1972 and 1982 of birds present at various sites between 20th May and the end of July, including males apparently holding territories at Oare Common in 1976 and at Woolhampton in 1978, a male was heard singing near Cold Ash from mid-May to 6th June 1985 and built a nest in a nest box. A female may also have been present but no eggs were laid. In 1991, a pair bred in a nest-box west of Newbury, laying nine eggs which hatched in mid-May, although unfortunately the young died on about 5th June after late frosts. These records follow an increase in the frequency of breeding in south-east England in the 1980s (*1988–91 BTO Atlas*), and, as with the first successful breeding of the species in Oxfordshire in 1989, the use of nest-boxes appears important to such success (Brucker *et al.*, 1992).

Return passage begins in late July or early August: a single male at West Woodhay on 30th July 2003 was the earliest returning bird, unless the male and female at Leighton Park on 26th July 1943 were on passage, rather than summering. Fewer birds are seen in autumn than in spring, the highest annual total being just five in 1968, 1989, 1992 and 2004, although passage is spread over a longer period. The latest departures both occurred in 1966, at Barkham Common on 1st October and in Windsor Great Park from 1st to 2nd October. A small number of immature birds have been noted in autumn, but the similarity in plumage of adult males, females and immatures at this time of year means that in many cases they cannot be differentiated; for this reason, Figure 136 only shows the total number of birds seen in the autumn period. Most autumn records are of single birds seen

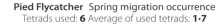

**Pied Flycatcher** Spring migration occurrence
Tetrads used: **6** Average of used tetrads: **1·7**

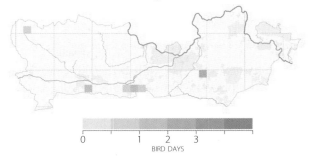

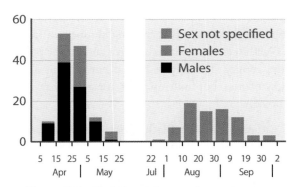

**Figure 136: Pied Flycatcher: spring and autumn passage.** All birds recorded from 1951–2010 in 10 day arrival intervals.

only for a day or occasionally for up to three days. The only longer stay appears to have been from 6th to 13th September 1972 at Leighton Park. There have been four autumn records of two birds together, and three were seen at Leighton Park in September 1971 and at Theale Gravel Pits in September 1989.

The first published record of a Pied Flycatcher in Berkshire, and the only one mentioned by Lamb (1880), is of a mutilated male bird brought to him in September 1795. Clark Kennedy (1868) considered it a rare visitor, noting that one was procured near Reading in about 1858. In the period from 1860 to about 1905 a number of breeding records were claimed. The first was of a nest and eggs being taken near Eton in 1860 which was apparently well authenticated at the time (Clark Kennedy, 1868), and Noble (1906) records that he was shown eggs taken from a nest at Hennerton in about 1880, and that a nest was found at Park Place in 1901. The 1880 and 1901 records must be regarded as doubtful as there is no reference to the birds having been seen and the eggs and nest site of the species are similar to those of the Redstart, a pair of which bred in a nest box at Park Place in 1895 (Noble, 1906). A pair was reliably reported nesting in a pollarded elm *Ulmus* sp. on the Bath Road near Reading in June 1897, and a pair also spent a few summers at Englefield Park just prior to 1905 where they were suspected to have bred (Noble, 1906).

*Sponsored by Terry Peters*

# Black Redstart

*Phoenicurus ochruros*

*Scarce passage migrant and rare summer visitor*

Although common and widespread in continental Europe, the Black Redstart is a rare breeding species in the UK, though commonly recorded on passage in the south and east of the country. In Berkshire, it is recorded in small numbers each year, principally as a passage migrant, although there have been occasional records of birds breeding and over-wintering. Despite being recorded in slowly increasing numbers in Britain, the Black Redstart remains a scarce and erratic breeder in the county. There have been records from a wide variety of sites, but built-up areas are strongly favoured for breeding.

The earliest record of a Black Redstart in Berkshire was of one at Formosa in 1861 (Clark Kennedy, 1868), which was presumably a winter record as the bird was seen in a snowstorm. The next records were in 1937, when one was seen in a Reading garden on 4th April, and one at Leighton Park School on 26th October. The first record of breeding in the county was at Windsor Castle in 1964, where singing males had been heard occasionally since 1958. Breeding was next reported in Maidenhead in 1973 when four young fledged, in Bracknell in 1974 when three young fledged, and in Reading in 1982 when three young fledged. At an industrial site near Aldermaston, two pairs each raising two broods were recorded in 1987, two pairs bred successfully in 1999 and three in 2002. Breeding was confirmed in Newbury in 1993; and again in central Reading in 1994, 2002 and 2010. Singing males were heard in most of the intervening years at Reading with a maximum of five singing males in 1997, though since 2004 not more than one pair has been located, and there have been few records at Aldermaston since 2002. With an average of only 44 pairs breeding in the UK in the period from 2005 to 2009 (Holling *et al.*, 2012), the small number of pairs in Berkshire is a significant fraction of the national population.

Three of the nest sites used by Black Redstarts in Berkshire have been described. The site chosen in Reading in 1982 was in a pallet of bricks, and one of the nests built at Aldermaston in 1987 was inside a small garage with permanently open doors. This nest consisted of a bulky moss outer structure with a hair-lined inner cup and was placed on top of a brick pillar inside the garage just below roof level, and about three metres above ground level. It was refurbished and used to raise the second brood a month later. A similar site was used in Bracknell in 1974, when the top of a two metre high brick pillar in an open fronted cycle shed was used. The fledging date of the first of the two broods at Aldermaston in 1987 was estimated from several observations to be about 8th June and the second brood fledged on 20th July. The first brood at the other site at Aldermaston in 1987 fledged on 29th June. The male of one of these pairs was almost indistinguishable from the female, indicating that it was in its first summer.

It is probable that some breeding pairs are overlooked, as they are unobtrusive small birds which most frequently occupy busy towns and industrial sites. Even allowing for this fact, the Black Redstart remains an erratic breeding species in Berkshire and town centre redevelopment may be removing suitable breeding habitat.

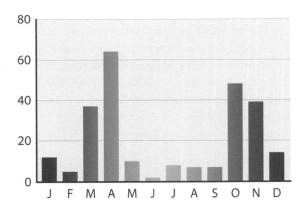

**Figure 137: Black Redstart: all birds recorded 1946–2011, by month, excluding summering birds.**

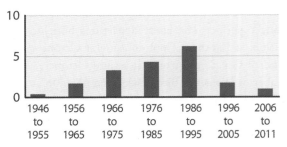

**Figure 138: Black Redstart: average number of birds recorded per year 1946–2011, excluding summering records.**

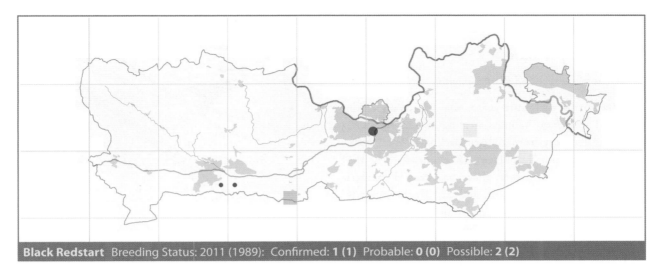

**Black Redstart** Breeding Status: 2011 (1989): Confirmed: **1 (1)** Probable: **0 (0)** Possible: **2 (2)**

Black Redstarts occur annually as a passage migrant in Berkshire in both spring and autumn at a variety of sites, including sewage farms, gravel pits, gardens and urban areas. Figure 137 shows the number of birds recorded in each month from 1946 to 2011, excluding summer birds at the breeding sites. Peak passage is in March/April and October/November, as observed at coastal sites (*Migration Atlas*). The extent to which the increase in the number recorded between the 1960s and the 1990s, as shown by Figure 138, includes locally bred birds is unknown; greater observer coverage may be the most significant factor.

As well as sporadic December and January records, Black Redstarts have over-wintered in the county on a number of occasions. The first was from Reading in the winter of 1951/52, subsequent records were from

**Black Redstart** Breeding season abundance
Tetrads occupied: **1 (9)** Average of occupied tetrads: **1·0**

| exTTV | NUMBER OF TETRADS IN ABUNDANCE CATEGORY |
|---|---|
| 8 | 1 |

0    1
SURVEY COUNT

Bracknell in 1974/75, Aldermaston in 1987/88, Slough Sewage Farm in 1993/94, 1994/95 and 1995/96 and at Warfield in 1994/95.

*Sponsored by Roger Stansfield*

Black Redstart, Queen Mother Reservoir  *Michael McKee*

# Redstart

*Phoenicurus phoenicurus*

Scarce summer visitor and passage migrant

The Redstart is a summer visitor that breeds in a wide variety of woodland habitats, nesting in holes in trees. Following recovery from a sharp decline in the 1960s, the UK population has shown slow growth over the last thirty years. However, there has been a marked retrenchment from the south and east to the uplands of the west and north of Great Britain (*1988–91 BTO Atlas*). In Berkshire, as a breeding species, it is in sharp decline, and is largely confined now to the forests of the south east of the county. It is more widely encountered as a passage migrant.

Overall, the numbers of tetrads in which breeding evidence was observed has fallen by nearly two thirds, between the 1987–89 and 2007–11 Atlas surveys. The latter failed to confirm breeding in the south west of the county, where only three tetrads had any evidence of breeding, whereas in 1987–89, ten tetrads had some breeding evidence, with breeding confirmed in two. No records of breeding were confirmed from the central region of Berkshire where the Redstart had bred sporadically in the past (*1968–72 BTO Atlas*).

The remaining stronghold for the Redstart is the coniferous and mixed woodland of the east Berkshire heaths. Prior to 1990, surveys in 1947, 1957, 1971 and 1979 in the east of the county showed between 19 and 21 territories. Figure 139 shows the results of surveys carried out in a number of years since 1990. The surveys have shown between 20 and 60 territories, but with a downward trend since 2005, coinciding with increased disturbance of much of its breeding area as a result of increased leisure use of the forests.

The favoured habitats in the south-east of the county are areas of mixed birch *Betula* spp., oak *Quercus* spp.

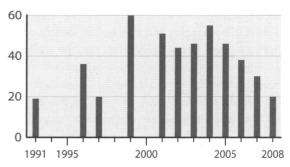

**Figure 139: Redstart: Territories on East Berkshire heaths 1993–2008.** Data from annual reports; no data available for 1992, 93, 96, 98.

**Redstart** Breeding season abundance
Tetrads occupied: **7 (45)** Average of occupied tetrads: **2·7**

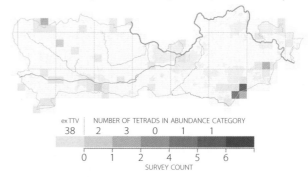

| ex TTV | NUMBER OF TETRADS IN ABUNDANCE CATEGORY | | | | |
|--------|---|---|---|---|---|
| 38 | 2 | 3 | 0 | 1 | 1 |

0   1   2   4   5   6
SURVEY COUNT

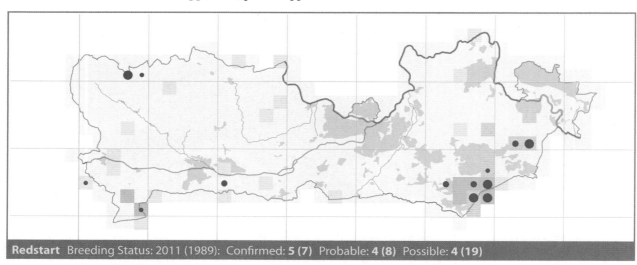

**Redstart** Breeding Status: 2011 (1989): Confirmed: **5 (7)** Probable: **4 (8)** Possible: **4 (19)**

and coniferous woodland. Nests have been found in holes in a variety of tree species, including pine *Pinus*, oak, birch and ash *Fraxinus*.

The Redstart was formerly much more widely distributed in summer in Berkshire than it is today. Noble (1906) mentions summer records for Englefield Park, Bucklebury and near Wargrave. In the 1920s and 1930s several pairs bred in Windsor Great Park, one pair in Aldermaston Park, four pairs in the grounds of Wellington College, and two pairs at Chavey Down. In 1938, there were about 15 pairs in about 80 hectares of Windsor Great Park.

On passage the Redstart is reported, usually singly, from all parts of the county, with an increased proportion of sightings in west Berkshire in autumn. The records disclosed by the breeding season abundance map largely relate to birds on passage. Perhaps because they may be more easily detected, they are often seen

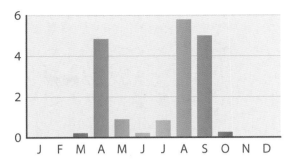

**Figure 140: Redstart: Average number of birds recorded per month outside the East Berkshire heath breeding area 1992–2011.**

in relatively open areas where there are scattered trees and hedgerows. Spring migration peaks in April, whilst autumn dispersal and migration extends from July to October (Figure 140). The earliest arrival date since 1974 was 28th March 1995 at Brimpton, and the latest autumn record was 17th October 1983 at Kintbury.

*Sponsored by Camberley Natural History Society*

# Whinchat

Amber

## Saxicola rubetra

*Passage migrant and rare summer visitor*

The Whinchat is a regular spring and autumn migrant in Berkshire, usually encountered perched on fences, crops or weeds in open areas. It has declined as a breeding bird in southern and eastern England throughout most of this century. In the 19th century the Whinchat bred "on many of the open heaths" (Noble, 1906), and in the period from 1925 to 1950 there were breeding records from Bradfield, Reading Sewage Farm, Sonning and Chavey Down. In 1927 there were up to five pairs at Slough Sewage Farm and in 1936 three to four pairs bred on Slough Trading Estate.

The *1968–72 BTO Atlas* showed the Whinchat to be restricted as a breeding species to four areas in Berkshire, near Hungerford, Lambourn, Streatley and Slough. Since then, the position has worsened, with no confirmation of breeding during the 1987–89 and 2007–11 Tetrad Surveys; the records of probable and possible breeding are likely to have related to passage birds. Since 1993, there have been just four summer records: a female was at Slough Sewage Farm on 28th June 1993, a male at Queen Mother Reservoir in June 1999, another bird was trapped and ringed in East Berks in June 2006, and a male was at Greenham Common on 30th June 2012.

The reasons for the decline in the Whinchat population in Berkshire are unclear. It is possible that changes in grassland management, the burning of railway banks and the cutting of roadside verges may have had an

effect (Gray, 1974). According to the *1968–72 BTO Atlas*, Whinchat favour breeding areas of tussocky grass with song posts about one metre high, conditions which are not difficult to find in Berkshire. Indeed, in the 1920s to 1940s, there were a number of breeding records from various sites in central and east Berkshire with this type of habitat. However, the disappearance of the Whinchat as a breeding bird in Berkshire is

**Whinchat** Spring migration occurrence
Tetrads used: **37** Average of used tetrads: **2·8**

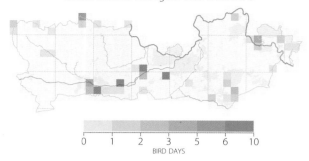

0    1    2    3    5    6    10
BIRD DAYS

**Whinchat** Autumn migration occurrence
Tetrads used: **44** Average of used tetrads: **6·3**

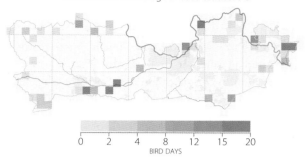

0    2    4    8    12    15    20
BIRD DAYS

in keeping with national trends, which show a 60% decline in abundance between 1994 and 2010 (BBS). The Whinchat has now disappeared as a breeding bird from large areas of lowland Britain, with a general retreat to higher terrain, such as moorlands.

Although no longer breeding, Whinchats are regular passage migrants in Berkshire, with small numbers being seen in spring and rather more in the autumn, when in some years passage can be heavy. Although passage migrants have been recorded from a range of sites, those which seem to have featured most prominently in county reports since 1974 include gravel pits, particularly Brimpton and Theale, downland, sewage farms, particularly Slough and Reading; and riverside farmland, such as at Purley, where growing crops of maize were frequented by Whinchats in autumn in the late 1970s and early 1980s. The fact that birds have been found in these locations is, however, more likely to reflect observer cover rather than habitat preference. The maps show the tetrads in which Whinchats were observed on spring and autumn passage during the years of the 2007–11 Atlas survey.

Spring passage tends to be less protracted than in the autumn, with the first arrivals usually being seen in mid- or late-April and few later than mid-May. An exceptionally early arrival was noted at Crookham Common on the 4th April 2007, when one of the two birds present was a singing male. In the autumn, passage tends to begin in July, with records continuing throughout August and September, and into October. Since 1974, there have been seven records in November, the latest being at Thatcham Marsh on 27th November 1976, and at Dorney Wetlands on 27th November 2001. The highest counts in the past were 23 at Welford on 8th October 1972 and 15–20 at Burghfield on 31st August 1984. On 21st and 22nd September 1980, there were 18 at Reading Sewage Farm, 17 at Sulham and 15 at Beenham and, in 1992, an estimated 112 birds were reported in August and September, with up to 16 at Slough Sewage Farm. Possibly indicative of the decline in numbers, the largest counts since then have been of seven birds at Greenham Common on 22nd August

2003, no more than four together even during an exceptional autumn passage in 2011, and nine together at Walbury Hill on 27th August 2012.

There has been only one ringing recovery of a Whinchat in Berkshire, a bird ringed at Burnfoot, Forest of Birse, Grampian in June 1984 being recovered on 1st September 1984 at Freeman's Marsh, Hungerford.

Although wintering Whinchats are rare in northern Europe (*BWP V*), a female was seen on five occasions between 11th January and 16th February 1975 at Thatcham Rubbish Tip and is believed to have wintered. There have been two other sightings of Whinchat in Berkshire during the winter, one at Reading on 4th March 1967, and one at Sandhurst on 4th December 1971, although it is not clear whether these were early and late migrants respectively, or wintering birds which were not seen subsequently or had been overlooked.

*Sponsored by Sarah White*

Whinchat, Queen Mother Reservoir *Michael McKee*

# Siberian Stonechat

*Saxicola maurus*

*Rare vagrant, one record*

Until 2011, Stonechats of the Asian form were treated as a subspecies of Common Stonechat *S. rubicola*. In that year, the taxonomic sub-committee of the BOU recommended that they be treated as a separate species (Sangster *et al.*, 2011), thereby adding a new species to the British List, as the species is a rare vagrant to Britain.

There has been one record of a Siberian Stonechat in Berkshire, a female which was trapped and ringed at Brimpton, where it was present from 31st October to 2nd November 1986.

*Sponsored by Ken Moore*

# Stonechat `Green`

*Saxicola torquatus*

*Uncommon winter visitor and passage migrant, and scarce resident or summer visitor*

The Stonechat is a scarce summer visitor to Berkshire and a passage migrant or winter visitor in larger numbers. It is typically found breeding on areas of heathland, but also occurs on commons and wasteland, particularly where Gorse *Ulex europaeus* is present, and in young coniferous plantations. On passage and in winter it also occurs at gravel pits, sewage farms and on farmland. Nationally the breeding population, which is sensitive to hard winter weather, fell through the latter half of the 20th century, then grew two- to three- fold from 1994 to 2007, during a period of generally mild winters, falling sharply following harder winter weather in 2009 and 2010. The population in Berkshire also seems to fluctuate in response to similar factors.

During the breeding season tetrad survey of the 2007–11 Atlas, Stonechats were recorded in 46 Berkshire tetrads, with breeding confirmed in 16, an increase of 60% compared to the 1987–89 survey. The distribution shows a strong correlation with the heathland in the south of the county. Although it can hold territory in small areas of suitable habitat, Stonechats are conspicuous and it is unlikely that many breeding pairs were overlooked: in 2008, 26 territories were located on the east Berkshire heaths and eight territories on Greenham Common. Subsequent cold winters may have reduced that number, the numbers of tetrads in which breeding was confirmed or recorded as probable each year falling from 10 in 2008 to six in 2011.

Breeding numbers had increased through the 20th century, though erratically: between 1946 and 1966, breeding was confirmed in only four years, with never more than three pairs involved. By the time of the 1987–89 tetrad survey, breeding was confirmed in 10 tetrads, though the highest number of pairs recorded breeding in any one year had been 14 in 1976, 12 of which were on the heaths in the east of the county. A survey of the east Berkshire heaths during the 1993 breeding season located 15–16 pairs of Stonechats, of which 13–14 pairs bred raising 35–38 young. A similar survey in 2007 located up to 26 pairs in the same area. Away from the heaths, there were two pairs in small areas of scrub on derelict industrial land at the Gillette Way Industrial Estate in Reading in 1986, one of which was seen carrying food during May. The 1987–89 tetrad survey produced a confirmed and a probable breeding record from south Reading. Much of this area has since been redeveloped as part of a regeneration plan, resulting in the clearance of much of the scrub.

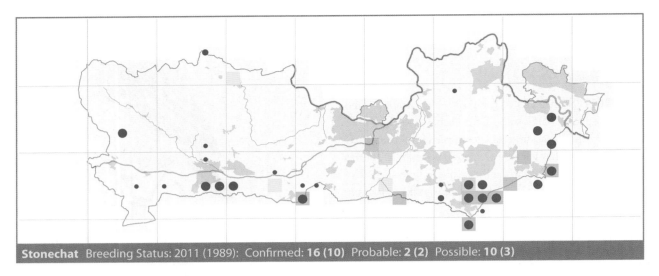

**Stonechat** Breeding Status: 2011 (1989): Confirmed: **16 (10)** Probable: **2 (2)** Possible: **10 (3)**

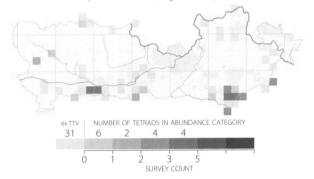

**Stonechat** Breeding season abundance
Tetrads occupied: **16 (47)** Average of occupied tetrads: **2·6**

| ex TTV | NUMBER OF TETRADS IN ABUNDANCE CATEGORY | | | |
|---|---|---|---|---|
| 31 | 6 | 2 | 4 | 4 |

0  1  2  3  5
SURVEY COUNT

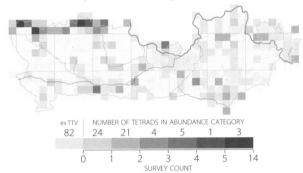

**Stonechat** Winter abundance
Tetrads occupied: **58 (140)** Average of occupied tetrads: **2·2**

| ex TTV | NUMBER OF TETRADS IN ABUNDANCE CATEGORY | | | | | |
|---|---|---|---|---|---|---|
| 82 | 24 | 21 | 4 | 5 | 1 | 3 |

0  1  2  3  4  5  14
SURVEY COUNT

No breeding evidence was reported from this area in the 2007–11 Atlas survey.

Wintering records increased in the 1970s, reaching a peak in 1976/77, when there were at least 20 birds in west Berkshire, including eight at Brimpton Gravel Pits, 20 in mid-Berkshire, and seven at Wraysbury Gravel Pits in the east. Records then declined, possibly as a result of a number of episodes of cold winter weather in the late 1970s and early 1980s. Although fluctuating from year to year, records tended to increase in the first decade of the 21st century. By the latter part of the decade, the peak numbers of birds wintering shown in annual reports had risen to between 90 and 100.

The results of the winter surveys undertaken as part of the 2007–11 Atlas project indicated that the winter population was threefold higher than in the breeding season, more dispersed and predominantly on the Downs in the north of Berkshire. The susceptibility of Stonechats to hard winters is shown clearly in the fall in abundance following the cold and snowy conditions in the winters of 2008/09 and 2009/10 (Figure 141).

Birds disperse from their winter quarters after February and an increasing number are then reported from traditional breeding areas. Figure 142 shows the total of records for each month published in annual reports

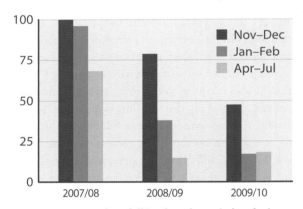

**Figure 141: Stonechat: fall in abundance in hard winters.**
After a series of relatively warm years, the winters of 2008/09 and 2009/10 had extended periods of freezing weather. Relative abundance was estimated from the tetrads surveyed in the seasons indicated, normalised to 100 for Nov–Dec 2007/08.

between 2001 and 2008. They show a decline in records as the winter progresses, then an increase in the early spring. Numbers are lowest at the end of the summer with post-breeding dispersal. A second influx occurs in autumn as wintering birds arrive. The extent to which the spring and autumn peaks represent passage birds is not clear, nor is it known whether part of the wintering population stays to breed. The only ringing evidence so far is the recovery at Finchampstead in March 1992 of a bird ringed in Strathclyde in August 1991, possibly indicating that wintering birds may be from breeding populations from northern Britain.

The *Historical Atlas* indicates that the Stonechat was uncommon in Berkshire in the 19th century, although Noble (1906) states that it was resident in many parts of the county. In contrast to the current pattern, it was then less common in winter than in summer. There were breeding or summering records in the 1930s and 1940s from Crookham Common, Bradfield, Burghfield, Twyford, Wellington College, Pinkneys Green, Eton and Slough Trading Estate. This represents a considerably wider summer distribution than is the case today.

*Sponsored by Berks, Bucks and Oxfordshire Wildlife Trust*

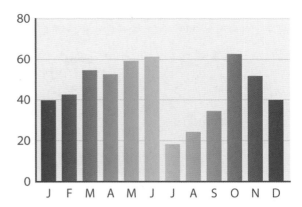

**Figure 142: Stonechat: average number of birds recorded per month 2001–2008.** During this period of mostly mild winters, the average monthly count rose from 33 to 63.

# Wheatear

Amber

*Oenanthe oenanthe*

*Common passage migrant and rare summer visitor*

The Wheatear is a common and widespread passage migrant through Berkshire, usually found in open country, typically on well-grazed or cultivated land before the crop has emerged or after it has been harvested, on tracks and rides, or on sparse shingle areas at gravel pits. There are occasional records from parks or even gardens, and in September 1974 one was observed on the roof of a building in Whiteknights Park.

Wheatears used to breed regularly on the Downs from Lambourn to Streatley, and in the Combe area, where an observer in 1935 noted that resident birds arrived about one week after the first migrants. The highest reported number of breeding birds was of six pairs at West Ilsley in 1936, although larger numbers bred in areas now in Oxfordshire to the north of Compton and Streatley. A decline in numbers had already been noted in the 1930s and 1940s, and this continued during the 1950s. They have only bred or summered sporadically in Berkshire since two pairs bred near at Streatley in 1947. A pair was feeding young at the nest at Slough Sewage Farm on 8th May 1955, the following year a male apparently held territory at Theale Gravel Pits for the first two weeks of May, and one was seen there on 16th June. A recently-fledged juvenile was seen on Combe Hill on 11th July 1959, and there were June records from the Lambourn Downs and at Combe in 1961. Two summers later, two pairs were thought to have bred at the former site, and one at the latter. A male was seen in the Olddean Common area on 28th June and 10th July 1971. In 1981, there were a number of records at Theale Gravel Pits from 11th June to 21st June, including both a male and a female, and a very recently-fledged juvenile was seen from 15th to 20th July. There were also two

records of birds exhibiting breeding behaviour: a male singing and a female entering rabbit holes in Windsor Great Park in May 1954, and a male displaying near West Ilsley from 10th to 17th May 1976.

Since the start of the 21st Century, evidence of possible breeding has been even more tenuous: a male was at Crookham Common from 4th to 7th June 2001, one near Eversley Gravel Pits on the 8th June the same year, and a female was at Dorney Wetlands on 16th June 2004. Such sightings may relate to birds passing through very late on spring passage. Of the records of Wheatear sightings during the 2007–11 Atlas Survey, all were considered to be passage birds, except for a pair displaying on the Oxfordshire side of the county boundary north of the Fairmile. The decline and disappearance of the Wheatear as a breeding species in Berkshire is consistent with the national picture, the species having retreated from much of southern and eastern England between the 19th century and the 1970s (*1967–72 BTO Atlas*).

Spring arrivals tend to be earlier on average than they were up to the 1970s, with birds recorded before 16th

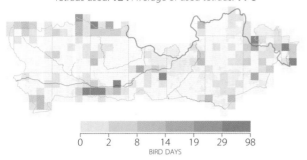

0  2  8  14  19  29  98
BIRD DAYS

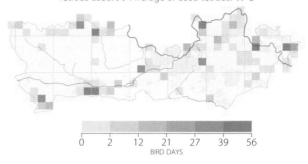

0  2  12  21  27  39  56
BIRD DAYS

March in 21 out of the 31 years up to 2011, compared with just 12 of the previous 44 years. However, there have been no records in the latter period to match the earliest recorded arrivals on 17th February 1954 at Windsor Great Park, 27th February 1960 at Woodley, and 1st March 1966 near Aldermaston.

In some years Wheatears pass through in waves, as in 1982, when the bulk of the spring passage was recorded between 27th March and 10th April, and again from 25th April to 9th May. A similar marked double peak occurred in 2003, in the fourth week of March and the fourth week of April. It is difficult to estimate exact numbers during passage, due to the mobility of the birds, when some linger, some move through more rapidly, and others replace them. Over the years the pattern of sightings has remained consistent, with most records being of single birds or small groups of two to five. There are occasional reports of ten or more, while a count of at least 20 was reported at Greenham Common on 28th April 2007, 24 were seen at Queen Mother Reservoir on 25th April 2010, 23 at Crookham Common on 7th April 2011, and 20 at Queen Mother Reservoir on 4th May 2012. The spring migrant map shows the distribution of birds recorded in March to June during the 2007–11 Atlas Survey period: records are widespread where there is open land, with greatest numbers seen around gravel pits and on the Downs.

Return passage has been noted from the middle of July to November, the earliest records being of single birds on 3rd July 1994 at Queen Mother Reservoir and on 9th July 1988 at Cookham Moor. As in spring, passage birds are seen in many parts of the county. Autumn records are most frequently of one to five birds, with counts no higher than this in years of poor passage. There have been some notable high counts, but none of more than 20 since 2000. A flock of 30 birds was on a railway line at Reading on 13th October 1967, when some were killed by a passing train. There were 50 birds at Greenham in August 1977, and 60 on 3rd September 1972; counts were in excess of 100 at Welford, on 30th September 1971, 8th October 1972, and 27th September 1973, with counts of 30 or 40 being made regularly. Since the turn of the century the

highest single count has been 20 at Wellbottom Down on 19th August 2001. The total numbers of Wheatears noted on return migration are generally lower than in spring, suggesting that some birds may have a different route or strategy on the return leg. The distribution shown by the autumn migrant map is broadly similar to that in the spring, though fewer tetrads were used.

The pattern of two peaks of records in spring fits the known migration patterns of the two races which move through Britain: the nominate race *O. o. oenanthe* moves northwards about two weeks before the Greenland race, *O. o. leucorhoa*. (*Migration Atlas*). Birds exhibiting the characteristics of the Greenland race, which are brighter and larger, have been reported mainly in spring from 16th April to 30th May. The Berkshire records in autumn are less frequent, but also consistent with the national pattern of migration for this race, which occurs later than the main European race, and have been between 19th September and 30th October. Falls of apparent Greenland Wheatears have been noted: about 20 birds on the Lambourn Downs on 27th April 1947; a party of about 20 birds at Lowbury Hill on 11th May 1979 contained at least 10 which appeared to be of the Greenland race; and a flock of 24 birds at Queen Mother reservoir on 25th April 2010 consisted of mostly Greenland-type birds.

There has only been one ringing recovery in Berkshire. A female, which had been ringed in Lincolnshire in August 1970, was recovered at an unknown Berkshire location in March 1972.

*Sponsored by Gordon Newport*

# Dunnock

*Prunella modularis*

*Widespread resident*

The Dunnock is a common and widespread resident which occurs throughout Berkshire. Little information on the population or breeding success of the species in the county appears in the published reports, but it is known to be present in most types of habitat where scrub or secondary growth is present. It is a pioneer species and colonises readily as soon as there is sufficient cover, even in derelict areas in the middle of towns. For this reason it can be found in urban, suburban and rural habitats throughout the county.

Dunnocks were found to be present in 99% of the tetrads in Berkshire during the 1987–89 and 2007–11 Tetrad Surveys and were confirmed to have bred in 69% of tetrads in both surveys, perhaps being overlooked in the few tetrads in which they were not recorded.

Dunnock ringing data confirm the generally sedentary nature of the species. Despite attempts made by the Newbury Ringing Group in the early 1970s to establish the origin of the Dunnocks which move into the reedbed areas of Thatcham Marsh in late summer, no significant data was obtained. There is one ringing recovery that is indicative of local movement of Dunnocks in winter. This involved a bird which was ringed at Enborne in late

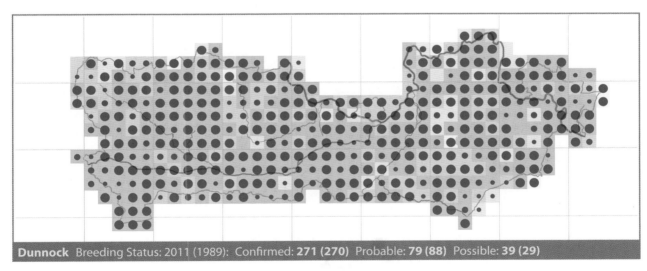

**Dunnock** Breeding Status: 2011 (1989): Confirmed: **271 (270)** Probable: **79 (88)** Possible: **39 (29)**

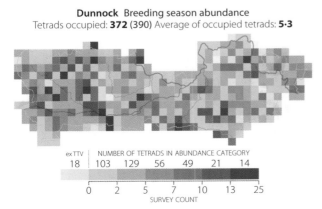

**Dunnock** Breeding season abundance
Tetrads occupied: **372 (390)** Average of occupied tetrads: **5·3**

| exTTV | NUMBER OF TETRADS IN ABUNDANCE CATEGORY | | | | | |
|---|---|---|---|---|---|---|
| 18 | 103 | 129 | 56 | 49 | 21 | 14 |

| 0 | 2 | 5 | 7 | 10 | 13 | 25 |
|---|---|---|---|---|---|---|

SURVEY COUNT

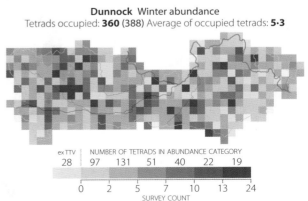

**Dunnock** Winter abundance
Tetrads occupied: **360 (388)** Average of occupied tetrads: **5·3**

| exTTV | NUMBER OF TETRADS IN ABUNDANCE CATEGORY | | | | | |
|---|---|---|---|---|---|---|
| 28 | 97 | 131 | 51 | 40 | 22 | 19 |

| 0 | 2 | 5 | 7 | 10 | 13 | 24 |
|---|---|---|---|---|---|---|

SURVEY COUNT

summer 1986, was controlled at a feeding station in the Winterbourne Valley during the first winter period of 1987, and was re-trapped back at Enborne later in the same winter. The similarity between the Breeding Season and Winter Abundance Maps from the 2007–11 Atlas Survey also indicate the sedentary nature of the species.

The longevity record for Berkshire is a bird killed by a cat on 29th June 1988 at Cookham Dean aged 7 years, 11 months and 2 days, having moved just 2 km from where it was first ringed as a first year bird.

The Dunnock is Amber listed as a species of conservation concern, due to a substantial decline in the UK breeding population during the period between 1969 and 1985. Since then, the population has grown slowly, with BBS showing an increase of 10% over the period 1994–2008 in South East England. In Berkshire since 2000 the Berkshire Bird Index has also shown a similar increase over the same period (Crowley, 2010).

*Sponsored by John Woodard*

# House Sparrow

`Red`

*Passer domesticus*

*Common, but declining resident*

The House Sparrow is a common resident in Berkshire, occurring wherever there is human habitation whether in the centre of towns or at isolated farms. It uses a wide range of cavities for breeding, and nests communally in parks and gardens. The decline of the species and its disappearance from areas where it used to be numerous, particularly city centres, throughout northern Europe has been the focus of much publicity and research in recent years (Summers-Smith, 2005). This trend

appears to be reflected in the results of the Atlas surveys and other records in Berkshire.

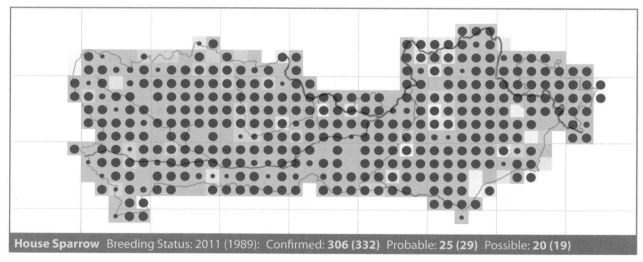

**House Sparrow** Breeding Status: 2011 (1989): Confirmed: **306 (332)** Probable: **25 (29)** Possible: **20 (19)**

**House Sparrow** Breeding season abundance
Tetrads occupied: **304 (359)** Average of occupied tetrads: **12·5**

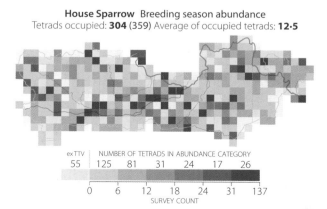

| exTTV | NUMBER OF TETRADS IN ABUNDANCE CATEGORY | | | | | |
|---|---|---|---|---|---|---|
| 55 | 125 | 81 | 31 | 24 | 17 | 26 |

0   6   12   18   24   31   137
SURVEY COUNT

**House Sparrow** Winter abundance
Tetrads occupied: **265 (332)** Average of occupied tetrads: **11·4**

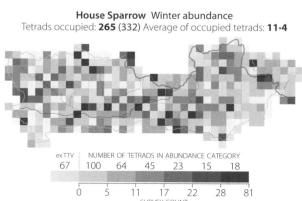

| exTTV | NUMBER OF TETRADS IN ABUNDANCE CATEGORY | | | | | |
|---|---|---|---|---|---|---|
| 67 | 100 | 64 | 45 | 23 | 15 | 18 |

0   5   11   17   22   28   81
SURVEY COUNT

Breeding evidence of the species was recorded in 380 (97%) of the tetrads in Berkshire during the 1987–89 Tetrad Survey, but only from 351 (89%) in the 2007–11 survey, but was confirmed to have bred in some 87% of these in both surveys. The species was absent from tetrads with heaths and coniferous woodland in the south east of Berkshire in both surveys, but many of the tetrads which lost House Sparrows between the two surveys were areas of arable cultivation or open areas of downland.

Wider studies have shown that the populations which have declined most have been those in the larger towns and cities, followed by rural areas with smallest declines in smaller settlements (Summers-Smith, 2005). A number of possible factors have been suggested, including the replacement or conversion of old-fashioned farm buildings which once provided access to food and nesting places, loss of mixed farming, the loss of urban derelict sites to redevelopment and regeneration, and greater prosperity resulting in higher standards of maintenance of housing and tidier gardens. All these factors apply in Berkshire. The results of the timed surveys in the 2007–11 project show an average count of only 11 to 12 birds in each two hour survey for a species that was once numerous in suitable habitat. By contrast, the *1981–84 BTO Winter Atlas*, which used different methodology based on 10 km squares, indicated that in two such squares, SU47 and SU67 (the latter comprising much of the central and eastern part of the Reading conurbation), a six hour count would produce between 200 and 400 birds. Although the Breeding Distribution map shows that House Sparrows are still present in tetrads comprising the centre of Reading and other larger towns, the Breeding Season Abundance and Winter Maps both show below average counts in most of such areas.

Nationally, results of the CBC and (from 1995) BBS show the population of House Sparrows in Britain to have declined by 71% between 1977 and 2009, but the rate of decline appears to have slowed later in the period, with a decline of only 18% between 1995 and 2009. Little information on the species appears in county reports until the mid-1990s. Two observers, in Bracknell and Cookham, have submitted details of the highest counts from their gardens in this period, both of which showed a decline from counts of 50 or more to only single figures. However the occasional substantial counts are recorded, such as 120 at Woodlands Park, Maidenhead on 22nd July 2010. Local ringing studies have shown that the species is generally sedentary, with most individuals never moving more than one or two kilometres. However, there has been one record involving a movement of some 113 km, a bird ringed in west Berkshire in February 1972 being recovered in Kent the following August.

Earlier writers about the birds of Berkshire prior to 1900 all describe the House Sparrow as a common resident.

*Sponsored by Mary Stacey*

---

# Tree Sparrow

## *Passer montanus*

*Previously resident, now scarce winter visitor*

The Tree Sparrow was a common and widespread resident in Berkshire until the 1980s, but since then it has disappeared as a breeding species and is now a scarce visitor in the county. The *1968–72 BTO Atlas* described the Tree Sparrow as quite common and widely distributed in Britain and it was proved to be breeding in all 10 km squares in Berkshire. By the time of the 1987–89 tetrad surveys, breeding was confirmed in only two thirds of 10 km squares and only 24 tetrads. The last year in which breeding was confirmed was 1996 at Beenham; there have been no records in the breeding season since 2002 and in the 2007–11 surveys it was only recorded in eight tetrads in the winter.

Tree Sparrows are most conspicuous in winter when they may form feeding flocks, often associating with finches and buntings on stubbles and game strips. They are largely sedentary; however, there is some evidence from ringing recoveries that birds wintering in

433

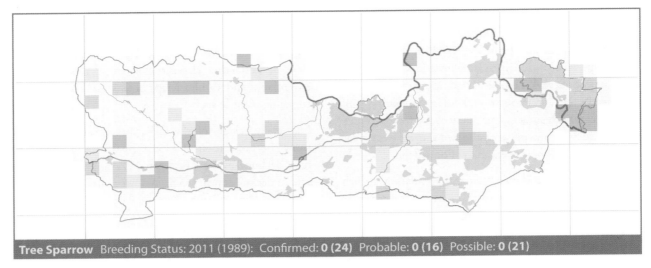

**Tree Sparrow** Breeding Status: 2011 (1989): Confirmed: **0 (24)** Probable: **0 (16)** Possible: **0 (21)**

Berkshire may have come from farther afield: one found dead in Reading on 11th July 1978 had been ringed in June 1976 in St. Albans, Hertfordshire and was the second Berkshire recovery of a bird ringed in that county. Another which was recovered near Wargrave in June 1977 had been ringed the previous December some 100 km away near Ringwood in Hampshire.

Winter counts of Tree Sparrows in Berkshire reflect the pattern of decline in the species' population nationally since the 1970s, with an apparent acceleration in the rate of decline since 1990. During the 1970s and 1980s winter counts of 100 or more Tree Sparrows were reported almost annually, for example at least 150 were seen at Ham Fields in January 1978, 100 at Maidenhead Sewage Farm during the winter of 1982/83 and about 120 at Slough Sewage Farm in the winter of 1990/91. From 1992 to 2012, the highest counts reported from any site were 15 at Slough Sewage Farm in 1992 and 17 at Remenham in the winter of 2010/11.

Tree Sparrow,
Jealott's Hill
*Dave Bartlett*

**Tree Sparrow** Winter abundance
Tetrads occupied: **1 (8)** Average of occupied tetrads: **1·0**

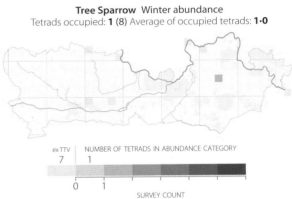

| ex TTV | NUMBER OF TETRADS IN ABUNDANCE CATEGORY | | |
|--------|------|------|------|
| 7 | 1 | | |

0    1
SURVEY COUNT

The reasons for the species' rapid decline and eastward retrenchment in Britain (*1988–91 BTO Atlas*) are not entirely clear. Britain lies on the western edge of the Tree Sparrow's range where its population may be more vulnerable. There was apparently a continuous decline from the turn of the 20th century until the 1950s, when numbers increased until the 1970s before declining

steeply after 1976 (*Population Trends*). The population collapse in Berkshire does not appear to be linked to habitat availability since there is no shortage of apparently suitable parks, large gardens or pollarded willows along rivers or canals, or on the Downs, where it formerly bred. Demographic evidence suggests that the reasons lie outside the breeding season (Baillie *et al.*, 2012) and winter food availability may be a factor. Programmes of winter feeding, coupled with nest box provision in Wiltshire and Oxfordshire, appear to have had some success and may be a model for future recovery projects in Berkshire.

At the beginning of the 19th century Lamb (1880), writing in 1814, knew of only two summer records of Tree Sparrow in Berkshire. According to the *Historical Atlas* the species was uncommon during the last quarter

of the 19th century, although Noble (1906) described it as "fairly common" but "local". There are few published records of Tree Sparrows in Berkshire from 1900 to 1930, but the species became more widely reported, and in some numbers, after 1931, perhaps due to increased observer coverage. In 1932 there were several reports of small breeding colonies and small winter flocks, and in December 1934 there were 400–500 on fields in Windsor Great Park. The next count to exceed 100 was of 250 at Slough Sewage Farm in September 1940, and this pattern of records of small breeding colonies, mostly in the centre and east of the county, and of wintering parties of around 100 birds, largely at sewage farms in east Berkshire, continued until the 1970s.

*In memory of Dave Callam*

# Yellow Wagtail Red

## *Motacilla flava*

*Passage migrant and uncommon summer visitor*

The Yellow Wagtail is a regular passage migrant and uncommon breeding summer visitor to Berkshire. Traditionally, the species' preferred habitats were considered to be wet meadows and marshland along river valleys, sewage works, and the fringes of water-bodies. However in recent decades a shift towards breeding on downland and cultivated land with low vegetation has been evident.

The 1987–89 Tetrad Survey revealed that changes had occurred since the *1968–72 BTO Atlas*, with no confirmed breeding records in the south-east corner of the county and more records from the downland areas in the north-west. This trend has continued, with almost all breeding evidence in the 2007–11 Tetrad Survey being from arable areas, particularly in the north-west of the county, and very few records from river valley or wetland sites. The largest recorded breeding concentration of Yellow Wagtails in Berkshire occurred at Ham Island Sewage Farm in 1959, (15 pairs) and at Theale Gravel Pits in 1963 (12 pairs). Another regular breeding site used to be Brimpton Gravel Pits, where birds probably bred annually from 1974 until the 1990s. Although such sites have now largely been abandoned, the increase in breeding on the Downs has resulted in little change in the numbers of tetrads in which breeding was recorded between the 1987–89 and 2007–11 Atlas surveys. These data may, however, mask a decline in the population as abundance was not measured in the earlier survey. The shift to arable land reflects the national pattern revealed by the BTO surveys. Between 1970 and 2008 the combined CBC/BBS index recorded a 77% decline, but the

Waterways Bird Survey/WBBS index, compiled from surveys which are only conducted along waterways, recorded a decline of 96% (Eaton *et al.*, 2009).

The first birds to arrive in Berkshire in spring usually do so during late March or early April, although the peak passage is in late April and early May. The earliest spring dates since 1974 have been 15th March 1994 and 19th March 2004. March arrivals have increased in recent years, with records in most years since 1994. An analysis of earliest arrival dates shows an eight day advance between the 1980s and the first decade of the 20th century (Table ii, *page 50*). In the autumn, most birds depart from late August to mid-September, although since 1974 there have been October records in all but three years, with a latest date of 15th November in 1991 at Queen Mother Reservoir, and an exceptional record of one at Wokingham Sewage Farm on 17th December 2003. Slough Sewage Farm has produced some of the highest passage counts, with 200 on 31st August 1949 and 18th April 1953, and 114 on 24th August 1983. Counts in more recent years have been lower, although autumn counts of from ten to 50 are often received from river valley sites. There was however an exceptional passage noted at Englefield in the autumn of 2001, with over 100 on the 14th and 23rd September, and a cumulative total of at least 370 birds

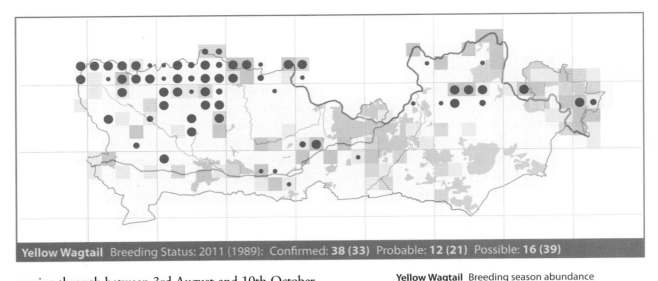

**Yellow Wagtail** Breeding Status: 2011 (1989):   Confirmed: **38 (33)**   Probable: **12 (21)**   Possible: **16 (39)**

passing through between 3rd August and 10th October (Crawford, 2007).

The British race of the Yellow Wagtail *M. f. flavissima* is one of a number of races of the species which shows extensive geographical variation in the head pattern and colour of males. The Blue-headed Wagtail *M. f. flava*, the race which occurs on the near continent, is the most regular of the other forms to occur in Berkshire, a few being recorded most years. This race has also bred in the county, usually with female *M. f. flavissima*, and such records have come from Ham Island Sewage Farm in 1963 and Summerleaze Gravel Pits in 1987. The Ashy-headed Wagtail *M. f. cinereocapilla* has been reported in Berkshire very occasionally on passage, and there has been one breeding record of a bird at Theale Gravel Pits in 1968 paired with a female *M. f. flavissima*. A male at Slough from 26th April to 10th May 1941 apparently resembled the Siberian race *M. f. beema*. It is now thought to be a so-called "Channel Wagtail", with characteristics indicating a hybrid between *M. f. flavissima* and *M. f. flava*. Individuals exhibiting traits of this form were present at Slough Sewage Farm in April 1980 and at Cold Harbour

**Yellow Wagtail** Breeding season abundance
Tetrads occupied: **23 (98)** Average of occupied tetrads: **2·1**

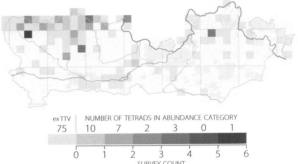

| ex TTV | NUMBER OF TETRADS IN ABUNDANCE CATEGORY | | | | |
|--------|------|------|------|------|------|
| 75 | 10 | 7 | 2 | 3 | 0 | 1 |

SURVEY COUNT

in both May 2001 and May 2003. A bird of the northern Scandinavian race *M. f. thunbergi* was at Queen Mother Reservoir on 30th May 2009.

In the 19th century, Herbert (1870) considered the Yellow Wagtail to be rare, although Noble regarded it to be a regular migrant. The form *M. f. flava* was recorded as rare by Herbert (1870) and Noble (1906) refers to one "seen by a Mr Walker on telegraph wires at Thatcham Marsh in May 1890".

Yellow Wagtail, Queen Mother Reservoir *Michael McKee*

The Yellow Wagtail is now a species of conservation concern in Berkshire. Previously its decline was linked to problems in its wintering areas in the Sahel zone in Africa. The change in habitat use, and abandonment of apparently suitable breeding areas previously used, indicates that there is more to be discovered about the factors driving its decline.

*Sponsored by Richard Crawford*

# Grey Wagtail Amber

## *Motacilla cinerea*

*Uncommon resident and winter visitor*

The Grey Wagtail is a rather uncommon resident in Berkshire, being found primarily near stretches of fast flowing water, rivers and streams, particularly near weirs, mill races, outflows from lakes and canal locks. It does not avoid built-up areas near water and can often be seen or heard in central Reading.

The breeding distribution shown by the Tetrad Surveys corresponds to these habitats, with the species mainly occurring on the rivers and the Kennet and Avon Canal in the west of the county, and being more thinly scattered on small streams in the east. Grey Wagtails are easily located due to the distinctive flight call and localised habitat and it is unlikely that the presence of birds was overlooked during either Atlas Survey. There does not seem to be any material change in the breeding distribution between the 1987–89 and 2007–11

surveys, except that fewer tetrads in the Lambourn Valley were occupied in 2007–11 compared to 1987–89. This may be attributable to the drought that occurred during the latter part of the survey period in the later atlas survey. Notwithstanding that breeding was only confirmed in 49% (in the 1987–89 survey) or 59% (in the 2007–11 survey) of the tetrads in which any breeding evidence was recorded, it is likely that many of the probable breeding records did in fact relate to successful pairs. The relatively

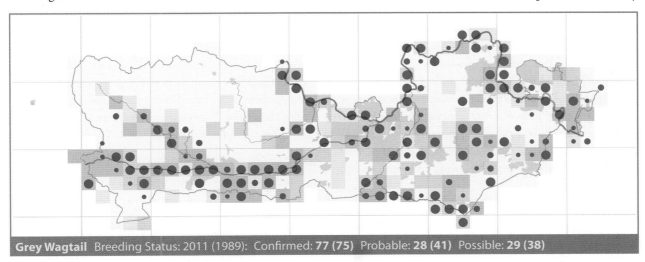

**Grey Wagtail** Breeding Status: 2011 (1989): Confirmed: **77 (75)** Probable: **28 (41)** Possible: **29 (38)**

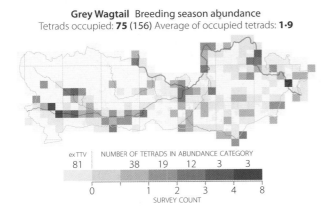

**Grey Wagtail** Breeding season abundance
Tetrads occupied: **75 (156)** Average of occupied tetrads: **1·9**

| ex TTV | NUMBER OF TETRADS IN ABUNDANCE CATEGORY | | | | |
|---|---|---|---|---|---|
| 81 | 38 | 19 | 12 | 3 | 3 |

0   1   2   3   4   8
SURVEY COUNT

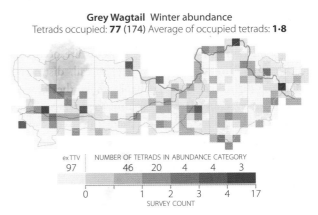

**Grey Wagtail** Winter abundance
Tetrads occupied: **77 (174)** Average of occupied tetrads: **1·8**

| ex TTV | NUMBER OF TETRADS IN ABUNDANCE CATEGORY | | | | |
|---|---|---|---|---|---|
| 97 | 46 | 20 | 4 | 4 | 3 |

0   1   2   3   4   17
SURVEY COUNT

Grey Wagtail, Arborfield *Dave Bartlett*

high number of probable breeding records may reflect birds moving between tetrads whilst searching for suitable nesting sites or feeding.

The winter and summer abundance maps show similar distributions for Grey Wagtails in Berkshire, with small numbers present along all the river valleys. Favoured sites during the winter include gravel pits, rivers and sewage farms, although wintering birds may not be the same birds that breed in the county, since ringing recoveries have shown that many Grey Wagtails from northern Britain move south to south-west through England and Ireland, and often into northern France, after the breeding season (Tyler, 1979). Evidence of such movement into Berkshire is provided by the recovery of a bird at Denford in December 1985, which had been ringed in Glen Almond, Tayside in May the previous year. The only other long-distance ringing recovery from Berkshire was noteworthy for apparently going against this general pattern of movement, a bird ringed in west Berkshire on 16th August 1969 being recovered on 9th

September in Suffolk the same year. Some winter records of Grey Wagtails in Britain involve continental birds, with ringing recoveries of Danish, Belgian and German birds from southern Britain. The largest winter count to have been made in Berkshire in recent years was 15 to 20 at Slough Sewage Farm on 8th January 1989.

The *Historical Atlas* notes that the Grey Wagtail occurred only occasionally in Berkshire in the late 19th century. It appears to have been exclusively a winter visitor to Berkshire until the first record of breeding at Padworth in 1898 (Noble, 1906). Since that time it has spread its range in lowland Britain, although this expansion has evidently been checked periodically by severe winters (*Population Trends*). A decline of over 25% between 1970 and 1990 resulted in the species being placed on the "Amber List" of species of conservation concern, but since then the UK population has recovered somewhat, being largely stable between 1987–89 and 2007–11.

*Sponsored by Colin Wilson*

## Pied Wagtail Green

*Motacilla alba*

*Common resident, passage migrant and winter visitor*

The Pied Wagtail (*M. a. yarrellii*) is a common resident, passage migrant and winter visitor to Berkshire, occurring in all areas. The sharp "chisick" flight call, distinctive bounding flight and obtrusive habits make the location of the Pied Wagtail relatively easy, but the nests are often hard to find. A wide range of habitats is used, usually with open stretches of level grass, often near water and frequently associated with human activity.

Pied Wagtails used to be a common farmyard breeding bird, and the *1968–72 BTO Atlas* indicated that there

had been a decline in areas where there was a marked change from mixed to arable farming, that change being also apparent from the fieldwork for the *1988–91 BTO Atlas*. This appears to be reflected in the distribution in Berkshire, with fewer confirmed breeding records from downland areas in the north, the south west, and between Reading and Newbury in the 2007–11 tetrad atlas survey compared to the results of the 1987–89 tetrad survey, and some apparent losses in the south east and east of the county. Pied Wagtails are common in urban areas, from industrial sites, gravel pits and sewage farms to gardens, and their ability to utilise a wide range of breeding habitats is reflected in their distribution, being found in over 80% of tetrads in summer during both the 1987–89 and 2007–11 surveys. CBC/BBS data show no significant change between 1989 and 2009 (though there is some indication of a more recent decline), and the Berkshire Bird Index covering the period 1994–2008 also indicated no significant change.

The winter distribution within Berkshire revealed by the Winter Map shows a similar pattern to that in the breeding season, with gaps in arable land in the west and heaths of the southeast. Pied Wagtails roost communally in warm and sheltered sites, particularly low bushes, reed beds and sewage works where large numbers may congregate. Roosts have been located throughout the county, with the number of birds involved ranging from tens to over a thousand. The largest counts are in winter and the two biggest roosts have occurred at Reading Sewage Farm,

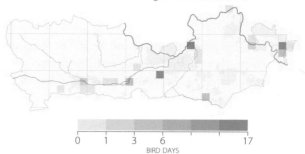

**White Wagtail** Spring migration occurrence
Tetrads used: **19** Average of used tetrads: **4·8**

BIRD DAYS
0   1   3   6   17

**Figure 143: White Wagtail: occurrence on spring migration.**

where there were an estimated 2,000 birds in the winter of 1972/73, and at Slough Sewage Farm, where the peak count was 3,529 birds in November 1981. The Reading roost was the subject of an extensive study between 1969 and 1973 by a group from Reading University (Broom *et al.*, 1976), which showed that the roost was used all year, although only a few locally-breeding birds used it in the summer. Over 4,000 birds were ringed and recoveries demonstrated that birds moved south in winter in Britain. Colour-ringing also showed that most of the birds fed within 12 km of the roost. Numbers recorded at roosts since the 1987–89 Atlas have been much lower, and in recent years highest counts have been around 200, usually at sewage treatment works or in Reading town centre,

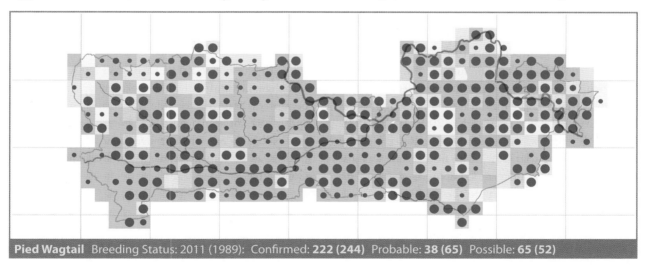

**Pied Wagtail**  Breeding Status: 2011 (1989):  Confirmed: **222 (244)**  Probable: **38 (65)**  Possible: **65 (52)**

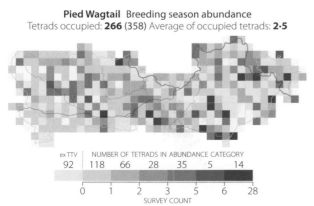

**Pied Wagtail** Breeding season abundance
Tetrads occupied: **266 (358)** Average of occupied tetrads: **2·5**

| exTTV | NUMBER OF TETRADS IN ABUNDANCE CATEGORY | | | | | |
|---|---|---|---|---|---|---|
| 92 | 118 | 66 | 28 | 35 | 5 | 14 |

SURVEY COUNT
0   1   2   3   5   6   28

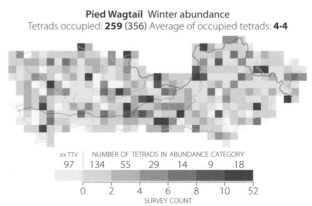

**Pied Wagtail** Winter abundance
Tetrads occupied: **259 (356)** Average of occupied tetrads: **4·4**

| exTTV | NUMBER OF TETRADS IN ABUNDANCE CATEGORY | | | | | |
|---|---|---|---|---|---|---|
| 97 | 134 | 55 | 29 | 14 | 9 | 18 |

SURVEY COUNT
0   2   4   6   8   10   52

but 422 were counted at Sandhurst Sewage Treatment Works in January 2003, showing that winter roosts are still important for the species.

The BTO *Migration Atlas* has shown that Pied Wagtails in southern Britain are largely sedentary, but with some immigration in winter and a degree of southerly migration. The winter population is boosted mainly by birds from northern Britain and by some from the continent. Illustrating this point, a bird ringed as a nestling in Grampian in June 1990 was trapped 684 km to the south at Hungerford Marsh four months later in October. Southerly movements begin in August and continue into November with a few southern British birds migrating to southern Spain and Portugal. Of note in a Berkshire context, a bird ringed in central Berkshire in March 1970 was recovered the following January in Loire Atlantique, west France, and another ringed at Englemere Pond in October 1994 was re-trapped in St Lo, Manche, France in January 1997.

In spring, varying numbers of the continental nominate race *M. a. alba*, the White Wagtail, occur in Berkshire. Most records of this form are in April, although they have occurred from late March to mid-May. There are few autumn records, possibly due to difficulties in separating such birds from juvenile Pied Wagtails. At a site in East Berkshire in 2008, a female White Wagtail was observed gathering food and feeding, firstly two, then one young. The race of the other parent was not confirmed.

*Pied Wagtail Sponsored by Graham Scholey*
*White Wagtail sponsored by Amy McKee*

# Richard's Pipit

## Anthus richardi

*Rare vagrant, seven records*

The Richard's Pipit is a rare vagrant to Berkshire which has been recorded on six occasions. This species is principally an autumn passage migrant in Britain, occurring regularly despite its usual breeding range being in east Asia, and its wintering area in south Asia.

The first record for the county was a bird located at Dorney Common, Buckinghamshire and Slough Sewage Farm from 7th to 24th October 1967. The second record was one at Crookham Common on 4th November 1973, which was seen and heard subsequently on 5th and 7th November. The third was found in long grass, at Wraysbury Gravel Pits, from 13th to 20th October 1988. The fourth record was at Queen Mother Reservoir from 28th April to 1st May 1995. The fifth record was just inside the county boundary at Compton Downs on 29th September and again on 5th October in 2002

On 12th November 2011 a Richard's Pipit was found at Cookham in a stubble field. Unfortunately, a subsequent organised shoot led to wide dispersal of birds locally and it was not seen again. The seventh record was one at Colnbrook on 7th October 2012. These last two records await consideration by the Berkshire Records Committee.

*Sponsored by Richard Capewell*

# Tawny Pipit

## Anthus campestris

*Rare vagrant, one record*

The Tawny Pipit is a rare vagrant to Berkshire and has been recorded on just one occasion, at Reading Sewage Farm on 26th September 1975. This bird arrived during an influx of Meadow Pipits. The record fits the pattern of sightings for Britain with most occurring during autumn from the end of August to mid-October. The normal breeding range lies further south and east in Europe.

*Sponsored by Richard Lewis*

# Olive-backed Pipit

*Anthus hodgsoni*

*Rare vagrant, one nationally famous record*

The Olive-backed Pipit is a rare vagrant to Britain and has been recorded just once in Berkshire. This record was however rather bizarre, in that it came from the small garden of a house in a built-up area of Bracknell. Even more remarkably, the bird was encouraged to continue to feed in the garden for the rest of the winter, the first ever record of this species over-wintering in Britain.

The bird was first noticed by the owners of the house, Dave and Maggie Parker, on 19th February 1984, and may have arrived in the area that day as it appeared to be in poor condition. It was attracted to wild bird seed put out nightly for local birds and was seen daily for 29 days until 18th March. When not feeding on the lawn, it perched in the pine trees in and around the garden where it could be recognised in silhouette by its tail-pumping habit. Because of the small size of the garden, the food was only a few yards from the house and the Parkers kindly allowed a succession of birdwatchers from all over the country to enter their home to view the bird at close range from the lounge window! It became the first Berkshire rarity to appear on television. The bird was seen on five further occasions between 18th March and 2nd April when it was seen to have a

damaged leg, probably having been attacked, perhaps by a cat. It was last seen on 15th April 1984, by which time an estimated 3,000 birdwatchers had availed themselves of a unique opportunity to see the 28th Olive-backed Pipit to be recorded in Britain.

*Sponsored by Rob Still*

# Tree Pipit Red

*Anthus trivialis*

*Locally common summer visitor and uncommon passage migrant*

The Tree Pipit is a locally common, but fast declining, summer visitor to suitable areas of Berkshire, utilising open spaces which have a scattering of tall trees, shrubs or even poles or pylons from which the males can make their distinctive display flights. Heathland, open woodland and scrubby areas are the favoured habitats in Berkshire, although recently-felled woodland areas are readily colonised provided some trees are left. A study carried out in Thetford in 1999 to 2005 showed that the species' exploitation of such areas may however be short-term (Burton, 2007), and that utilization of such habitat peaked at two to four years age of restock and then trailed off rapidly over the next three or four years.

The distribution of the Tree Pipit in Berkshire shown by the Tetrad Surveys indicates a preference for heathland with scattered trees. This includes Snelsmore Common, Bucklebury Common, Pamber Heath, and from Padworth to Inkpen Common in the west,

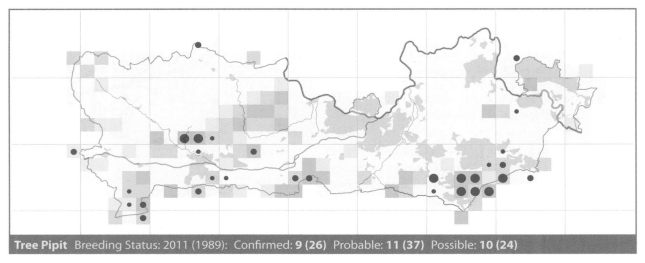

**Tree Pipit** Breeding Status: 2011 (1989): Confirmed: **9 (26)** Probable: **11 (37)** Possible: **10 (24)**

and the Crowthorne, Owlsmoor and Swinley Forest areas in the east. To this was added a substantial area of regenerated heathland following the closure of Greenham Common Airbase in 1993. Birds are readily recorded during the breeding season since they have a loud song and distinctive song flight. The song can be heard from mid-April through to the end of July. Obtaining confirmation of breeding, as with other pipits and wagtails, is straightforward when the young are being fed, since the adults perch conspicuously with bills full of food and call anxiously if disturbed. The 1987–89 Tetrad Survey indicated a possible reduction in the breeding distribution, as the range appeared to have contracted since the *1968–72 BTO Atlas*. Subsequent declines appear to have been substantial. Whilst a survey of heathland in south-east Berkshire in 1993 located 59 singing males, and there were over 110 territories in east Berkshire heathland in 2000, numbers of singing males in these areas have since fallen by approximately 50%. The 2007–11 Tetrad Survey recorded breeding evidence in just 30 tetrads compared with 87 in 1987–89, reflecting the national CBC/BBS national trend, which showed an approximately 80% decline in abundance over the same period. The causes of the decline, which led to the species being added to the Red List of Threatened Birds in the UK in 2009, are unclear.

**Tree Pipit** Breeding season abundance
Tetrads occupied: **16 (43)** Average of occupied tetrads: **3·8**

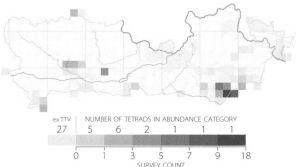

| ex TTV | NUMBER OF TETRADS IN ABUNDANCE CATEGORY | | | | | |
|---|---|---|---|---|---|---|
| 27 | 5 | 6 | 2 | 1 | 1 | 1 |

0    1    3    5    7    9    18
SURVEY COUNT

Since 1974, the first Tree Pipits to arrive in spring have occurred between 16th March and 16th April, whilst the latest autumn departure date was 15th October, in 2005. Passage migrants are noted annually in spring and autumn, a few at locations well away from their breeding sites, with occurrences in the late 2000s at sites including gravel pits, Thatcham Marsh, Colnbrook, Bagnor Cress Beds, the Downs, and at Queen Mother Reservoir.

Information on the status of the species in earlier accounts is sparse. Noble (1906) described it as being fairly numerous, but the few records from early in the 20th century is likely to reflect a lack of coverage rather than any genuine change in population after 1906.

*Sponsored by Jon & Viv Wilding*

Tree Pipit *Dickie Duckett*

# Meadow Pipit

## *Anthus pratensis*

*Common migrant and winter visitor and locally common breeder*

The Meadow Pipit is a common passage migrant, winter visitor and locally common breeding species in Berkshire. Although its nesting habitat is generally rough grassland, heaths, moors and sand dunes, Meadow Pipits also breed in more cultivated areas and will utilise unploughed field margins, ditches or river banks and motorway embankments. Trees and scrub are not important, although the Meadow Pipit will occasionally take off or return to a tree or fence during its display flight. The species occurs in a wider range of habitats in Berkshire during the winter.

The distribution of the Meadow Pipit in Berkshire shown by the 2007–11 Tetrad Survey correlates well with these habitat preferences, with breeding being widespread in the downland areas in the north-west of the county, but with a contraction in breeding range over most of the county compared to the results of the 1987–89 survey. At that time, Meadow Pipits could still be found breeding in all but one of the 10 km squares covering Berkshire, but the latest survey revealed six

without records, with significant reductions in many others. Overall, the proportion of tetrads with evidence of breeding has fallen from 34% to just 13%. There has clearly been a decline in the status of the Meadow Pipit in Berkshire in recent years, reflecting BTO findings of a 50% decline nationally over the last 40 or so years, linked with loss of habitat. That the species was more widespread in summer before 1900, is indicated by a record of several nests beside the railway near Windsor before 1868 (Clark Kennedy, 1868).

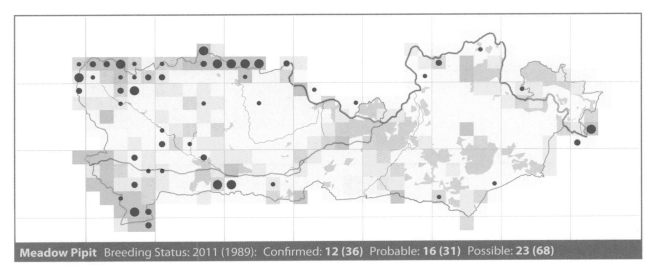

**Meadow Pipit** Breeding Status: 2011 (1989): Confirmed: **12 (36)** Probable: **16 (31)** Possible: **23 (68)**

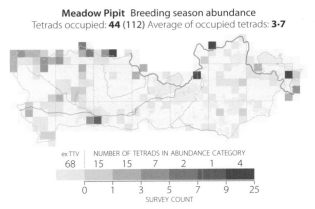

**Meadow Pipit** Breeding season abundance
Tetrads occupied: **44 (112)** Average of occupied tetrads: **3·7**

| exTTV | NUMBER OF TETRADS IN ABUNDANCE CATEGORY | | | | | |
|---|---|---|---|---|---|---|
| 68 | 15 | 15 | 7 | 2 | 1 | 4 |

| 0 | 1 | 3 | 5 | 7 | 9 | 25 |
SURVEY COUNT

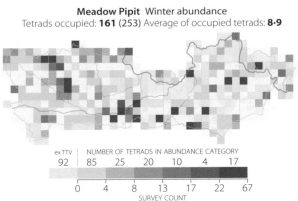

**Meadow Pipit** Winter abundance
Tetrads occupied: **161 (253)** Average of occupied tetrads: **8·9**

| exTTV | NUMBER OF TETRADS IN ABUNDANCE CATEGORY | | | | | |
|---|---|---|---|---|---|---|
| 92 | 85 | 25 | 20 | 10 | 4 | 17 |

| 0 | 4 | 8 | 13 | 17 | 22 | 67 |
SURVEY COUNT

Spring passage normally peaks from late March to early April, when counts of 30 to over 200 have been noted in a day, and as many as 1,800 over three hours at Queen Mother Reservoir on 14th April 2006. Autumn passage peaks from mid-September to early November, and often produces gatherings of 200 to 400, but the majority of these are recorded in central or eastern locations, not from the main breeding areas in west Berkshire. During winter, Meadow Pipits occur more widely across the county than during summer, including in river valley meadows, a habitat from which they are largely absent in the breeding season, as shown by the Winter Abundance Map from the 2007–11 Atlas Survey.

Although BTO nest record cards indicate that the Meadow Pipit is second only to the Dunnock as the favoured host of the Cuckoo (Glue and Morgan, 1972), no reports of such parasitism have been recorded in Berkshire. Meadow Pipits are however one of the most frequent species mentioned in accounts of Merlins chasing prey in Berkshire.

Berkshire's four ringing recoveries of Meadow Pipit ringed outside the county, all in the autumn or winter, involved birds ringed at Aberdeen, the Forest of Bowland in Lancashire, Spurn and one, recovered in September 2004, had been ringed the previous month in North Ronaldsay. All provide evidence of the influx from the north in winter. In 2007 a roost of Meadow Pipits was discovered at Padworth Common, used by typically 20 to 40 birds between October and March, considered to be birds from a few kilometres away. Birds from the roost were colour ringed during the following three winters and recoveries are awaited. No other roosts have been reported in the county.

*Sponsored by Tim Ball*

# Red-throated Pipit

*Anthus cervinus*

*Rare vagrant, one record*

The Red-throated Pipit is a scarce vagrant to Britain, its breeding range extending from north Norway to the Bering Straits. It has been recorded on just one occasion in Berkshire. This record was of a bird which was present at Theale Gravel Pits from 11th to 17th October 1979, and which spent much of its time on a weed-strewn embankment allowing observers excellent views. It apparently fed largely on grass seeds throughout its stay.

*Sponsored by Ken Moore*

# Rock Pipit          `Green`

*Anthus petrosus*

*Uncommon passage migrant and winter visitor*

The Rock Pipit is an uncommon passage migrant and winter visitor to Berkshire. The first county record was of a bird at Slough Sewage Farm on 30th September 1943. There was then a gap of 15 years until 1958 when a higher level of observer coverage resulted in birds being found at Ham Sewage Farm in January, October and November, and at Slough Sewage Farm in October and November. This heralded a succession of records from sewage farms and later from gravel pits, indicating that Rock Pipits were regular visitors. There have been records every winter from 1957/58 to 2012/13 except for 1963/64, 1979/80 and 1983/84.

Records from Ham and Reading Sewage Farms ceased in the 1970s as the sewage works were modernised, but Slough Sewage Farm continued to provide suitable habitat, and the bulk of the records from 1987 to 1994 came either from there or from Queen Mother Reservoir. Since the mid-1990s records from Slough Sewage Farm have dwindled and the great majority of records have been at Queen Mother Reservoir. The attraction of Queen Mother Reservoir to Rock Pipits is likely to be that it offers the largest area of open water in the county and has open bank-sides with concrete edges, offering the closest thing to the more typical coastal habitat of this species. Occasional passage birds are observed at gravel pits, and there is a scattering of records of over-flying birds from other sites including Silwood Park, Windsor Great Park, Dinton Pastures and Jealott's Hill. The vast majority of Rock Pipits records have come from east Berkshire, with only two county records from further west than Theale Gravel Pits, at Greenham Common and Lower Farm Gravel Pit respectively.

Figure 144 shows the average number of birds reported in each month. The earliest autumn arrival date was on 18th September 1961 at Slough Sewage Farm, and the latest post-winter departure date was on 22nd April at Pingewood Gravel Pits in 2001. The highest count was of eight at Queen Mother Reservoir on 11 October 1989, the next highest being five at the same site on 8th October 2008.

The variation in numbers of Rock Pipits recorded between years and decades is large (Figure 145). Whilst there appears to be no obvious reason for the high number of birds seen from 1966/67 to 1975/76, the high number recorded from 1986/87 is due, in part, to a series of records from Queen Mother Reservoir.

Closer attention to the species after 1960 revealed that some birds were lingering in autumn at suitable sites, such as sewage farms, and there were records during the 1960s from late September to the end of November. The first December record came from Ham Sewage Farm in 1970. Over-wintering birds were first noted during the winter of 1971/72 at Horton Gravel Pits and have been reported in six further winters subsequently: 1972/73, 1988/89, 1989/90, 1990/91, 1996/97 and 1998/99. In November 1990, a Rock Pipit at Slough Sewage Farm was seen going to roost in a patch of goosefoot *Chenopodium* spp. weeds alongside Water Pipits.

Seven of the county records up to 2012 have been of birds identified as exhibiting the characteristics of the

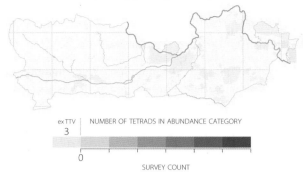

**Rock Pipit** Winter abundance
Tetrads occupied: **0** (3) Average of occupied tetrads: **0**

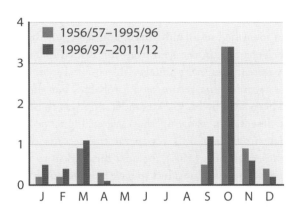

Figure 144: Rock Pipit: average number of birds recorded per month 1956/57–2011/12. Wintering birds are included for each month in which they occurred.

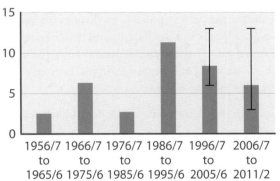

Figure 145: Rock Pipit: average number of birds per year 1956/57–2011/12. Bars show the interannual range for the last two periods.

Scandinavian race *A. p. littoralis*, although as this race is highly migratory, it may account for many more of the county records. Six of these have occurred between 1979 to 2008 in the early spring (1st March to 12th April), three at different gravel pits, one at Slough Sewage Farm and two at Queen Mother Reservoir. The seventh was one at Queen Mother Reservoir on 5th and 6th May 2011.

*Sponsored by Margaret Harrold*

# Water Pipit

*Anthus spinoletta*

*Uncommon passage migrant and winter visitor*

The Water Pipit is an uncommon passage migrant and winter visitor to Berkshire. Although it was formerly regarded as a race of the Rock Pipit, and only afforded species status in 1988, the two forms have always been treated separately in county reports.

The first reference to the Water Pipit in Berkshire related to a bird seen at Reading Sewage Farm on 11th October 1923. This was at a time when they had rarely been identified in inland Britain and were not thought to be separable in the field from the Rock Pipit unless they were in summer plumage. The county report at the time regarded the record as a "probable", but the bird had been seen by H. G. Alexander who was to become instrumental in showing that Water Pipits occurred widely in Britain. His review of the records of this species, Alexander (1974) includes this Berkshire record amongst those he considers to have been acceptable.

The next records did not occur until two were identified at Ham Sewage Farm on 14th October 1943, followed by further records from the same site in December and from Slough Sewage Farm in March 1944. H. G. Alexander had shown that it was possible to distinguish between the calls of Water and Rock Pipits and this characteristic was first used as a means of identification in the case of the birds recorded in February 1948 and February 1950; it has been used on many occasions since.

Figure 146 shows the average number of birds reported in each month. The earliest autumn arrival date was of one at Windsor Great Park on 24th September 1961 and the latest post-winter departure date was on 24th April 1995 at Eversley Gravel Pits.

Although Water Pipits may have over-wintered in Berkshire as early as 1944/45, when birds were seen in both January and February, it was not until January 1968 when, as part of a national Water Pipit survey organised by I. G. Johnson with the support of the BTO, a wintering bird was found at Reading Sewage Farm. This focused attention on the site and subsequently one or two birds were confirmed to have wintered there in ten of the 11 winters from 1967/68 to 1977/78, after which the habitat began to dry out.

The increased level of coverage generated by the 1966/67 and 1967/68 survey of the species was followed by a sharp rise in the number of Water Pipits recorded. In the ten winters up to 1965/66 only about ten birds were recorded, whereas in the following 20 winters at least 99 were reported. The survey showed how easy it

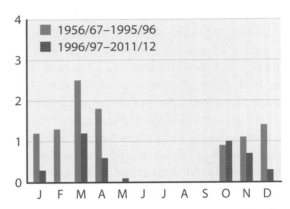

**Figure 146: Water Pipit: average number of birds recorded per month 1956/67–2011/12.** Wintering birds are included for each month in which they occurred.

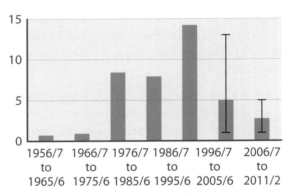

**Figure 147: Water Pipit: average number of birds per year 1956/57–2011/12.** Bars show the interannual range for the last two periods.

was to overlook this species, and Water Pipits are likely to have been under-recorded in Berkshire prior to 1968.

The records suggest that up to the mid-1990s, the relative consistency in the numbers recorded from October to January could indicate that many of the birds which arrived in October or November remained to winter. However, since the mid-1990s there have been far fewer records between December and February, with most records occurring during passage periods in autumn and spring. The reasons for this apparent change are not clear.

The increase in the number of records in March appears to be due to returning passage birds, with some of the wintering birds apparently leaving before these arrive. There have been a number of records of birds in full, or nearly full, summer plumage in the second half of March, and particularly in April, when they are more easily distinguished from the Rock Pipit. There is one May record in summer plumage, one at Pingewood Gravel Pit on the 5th in 2011.

The highest counts have been of five birds, at Dinton Pastures in March 1981, Theale Gravel Pits on 4th April 1992, and at Lower Farm Gravel Pit from 4th to 9th April 1996. Four occurred together at Reading Sewage Farm during April in consecutive years from 1973 to 1975, at Sandhurst Sewage Farm in March 1989 and at Moatlands Gravel Pit, Theale on 9th April 1996. The only party of more than three birds to occur before March was when up to four birds wintered at Slough Sewage Farm from 23rd December 1990 into 1991.

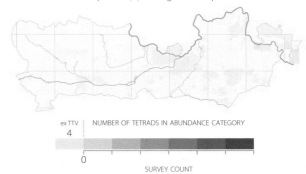

**Water Pipit** Winter abundance
Tetrads occupied: **0** (4) Average of occupied tetrads: **0**

ex TTV | NUMBER OF TETRADS IN ABUNDANCE CATEGORY
4

0

SURVEY COUNT

*Sponsored by Rebecca Clews-Roberts*

# Buff-bellied Pipit

## *Anthus rubescens*

*Rare vagrant, one record involving two birds*

There has been one record of this Nearctic bird in Berkshire, which involved two birds at Queen Mother Reservoir. It was remarkable for several reasons. It was only the second inland record in Britain, the length of stay enabled many observers to see the birds, and a fortnight after the first bird was seen it was joined by a second.

The first bird was first seen on 12th December 2012. It was present until Christmas, which enabled the BOC, which has permit arrangements at the site, to organise day permits which raised over £2,000 for club funds. On 26th December a second bird was found, and both birds were seen together. There were then no further sightings until both birds were again seen on 9th January 2013, and there were then further sightings of one or both birds until 26th January, either at the reservoir or at nearby Horton Gravel Pits.

By coincidence, the only previous inland record had been one at Farmoor Reservoir, Oxfordshire, in 2007, a site also owned by Thames Water, and which was in Berkshire prior the county boundary changes in 1974.

The nearest breeding population of Buff-bellied Pipit is found in Greenland and it has been suggested that this easily overlooked species may not be a vagrant, but has evolved a south-easterly migration route, similar to that of the Greenland Wheatear (Hudson *et al.*, 2012).

*Sponsored by Michael McKee*

Buff-bellied Pipit, Queen Mother Reservoir, 18th January 2013  *Michael McKee*

# Chaffinch

*Fringilla coelebs*

*Abundant resident and winter visitor*

The Chaffinch is an abundant resident and winter visitor in Berkshire. It is one of the commonest and most widespread birds in the county, occurring widely in gardens, farmland and woodland throughout the year. It is one of the most frequently reported birds in the BOC's Garden Bird survey and in BBS surveys carried out in Berkshire. In winter, flocks are often encountered in open country or woodland, often in the company of other finches or buntings.

During both Tetrad Surveys it was found in every tetrad in the county and was confirmed to have bred in 82%. There were slightly fewer confirmed breeding registrations in the more urban tetrads around Reading, Wokingham and Bracknell in the 2007–11 survey, and in the east of the county in 1987–89 than elsewhere. Both breeding season and winter abundance surveys carried out during 2007–11 show higher counts in the west of the county. Generally the results reflect the national population trend over the intervening period, with a general upward trend over recent decades levelling off towards the end of the first decade of the 21st century.

In winter, birds from northern Europe join resident birds, and there is some southward movement in Britain. There is an absence of reports of large scale diurnal movements of migrant birds from the continent as observed elsewhere in southern England in autumn. Ringing recoveries have produced evidence of arrivals from Norway and Sweden, with birds ringed or recovered in winter or early spring in Berkshire showing four birds moving to or from the former and three to or from the latter. There are also recoveries of birds ringed in Belgium and the Netherlands in Berkshire. The average counts in the TTV surveys indicate that winter numbers are perhaps 30 to 40% higher than in the breeding season.

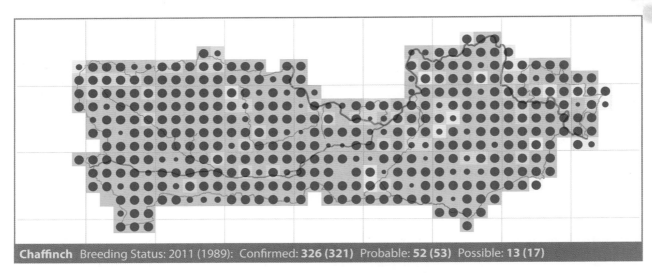

**Chaffinch** Breeding Status: 2011 (1989): Confirmed: **326 (321)** Probable: **52 (53)** Possible: **13 (17)**

**Chaffinch** Breeding season abundance
Tetrads occupied: **390 (394)** Average of occupied tetrads: **19·6**

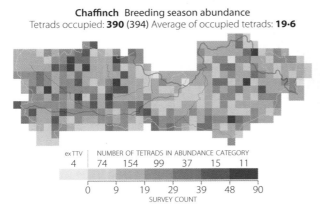

| exTTV | NUMBER OF TETRADS IN ABUNDANCE CATEGORY | | | | | |
|---|---|---|---|---|---|---|
| 4 | 74 | 154 | 99 | 37 | 15 | 11 |

| 0 | 9 | 19 | 29 | 39 | 48 | 90 |
|---|---|---|---|---|---|---|

SURVEY COUNT

**Chaffinch** Winter abundance
Tetrads occupied: **394 (394)** Average of occupied tetrads: **27·1**

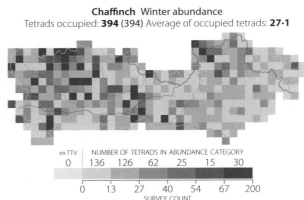

| exTTV | NUMBER OF TETRADS IN ABUNDANCE CATEGORY | | | | | |
|---|---|---|---|---|---|---|
| 0 | 136 | 126 | 62 | 25 | 15 | 30 |

| 0 | 13 | 27 | 40 | 54 | 67 | 200 |
|---|---|---|---|---|---|---|

SURVEY COUNT

The habitats favoured by Chaffinches during the winter include arable farmland, Beech *Fagus sylvatica* woods and sewage farms, and mixed flocks with Greenfinches, Yellowhammers and occasionally Bramblings are often encountered. Perhaps because it is so common, there are often few records in the county reports. Flocks of over a hundred are though widely reported where there is a suitable food supply, with peak counts usually occurring between November and February. The largest counts reported in recent decades were an estimated 600 in a mixed flock of finches at Kintbury on 22nd December 1983, and 500 among a mixed finch and bunting flock at Shinfield on 20th December 2005.

Noble (1906) described the Chaffinch as "very numerous and resident" at the turn of the 19th and 20th centuries.

*Sponsored by Renee Grayer*

# Brambling

`Green`  `Sch. 1`

## *Fringilla montifringilla*

*Uncommon winter visitor*

Bramblings are winter visitors to Berkshire. They usually arrive in Britain from Scandinavia in October or November, and their winter distribution is believed to be influenced primarily by the availability of Beech *Fagus sylvatica* mast, their favoured winter food source. As the Beech mast crop is irregular, Brambling numbers vary greatly from year to year and birds seldom spend successive winters in the same place (*1981–84 BTO Winter Atlas*). This is reflected in their occurrence in Berkshire, where the number, distribution and timing varies considerably from winter to winter. While typically a bird of woodland, it occurs widely in gardens and sometimes in varying numbers on open farmland.

Bramblings are regularly recorded from early to mid-October, although there have been seven September records from the east of the county up to 2012. The earliest record is of a bird at Silwood on 19th September 1960. In a typical year, numbers increase during November and December as more birds arrive, either to winter or on passage, although in a few years few are reported before the New Year. In 1979, for example, flocks of up to 350 were recorded in January and February, yet the highest count up to the end of December 1978 had been just 30 birds. The highest counts in Berkshire in the autumn have been (in October) 125 at Queen Mother Reservoir on 20th October 2010, and (in November) a flock of 400 at Windsor Great Park in 2005 and 300 birds at Silwood in 1970, but there have been several counts of smaller flocks of up to 200. Although in many years the size of the Brambling flocks in the county increases in January and February, two of the highest counts have been in December. In the winter of 1991/92, a flock of 2,000–3,000 birds was found feeding on linseed stubble at Combe Hill on 26th December, and on 20th December 1997 over 2,000 were counted feeding on beech mast in Windsor Great Park. These winter movements could be caused by cold weather or late passage movements

DA.Thelwell.

following the depletion of food supplies elsewhere in Britain or Europe. These birds may then disperse again during February and March, but in many years there is an increase in the number of Bramblings during March and April, particularly in the east of the county as returning passage birds pass through. The largest count from this time of year was about 1,000 in several flocks in Swinley Forest on 15th March 2003.

Birds are recorded well into April most years, and often into the last week of the month. The only later reports were of a male at Theale Gravel Pits on 1st May 1983, a male at Horton Gravel Pits on 1st May 1992, one in Windsor Great Park on 2nd May 1979, a male at Butter Hill on 7th May 1996, a male in full song on 12th May 2012 at Wishmoor Bottom, and singles on 31st May at Swinley in 1979 and Wishmoor in 2005. The only June record was a male seen and heard in full song in Windsor Great Park in June 1885 (Noble, 1906). Singing males have been reported on a number of other occasions on earlier dates and have often been observed in full summer plumage. In a flock of about 80 near Combe on 26th March 1974

449

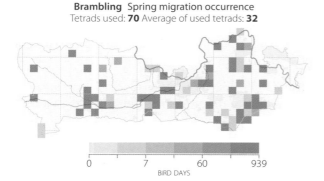

**Brambling** Spring migration occurrence
Tetrads used: **70** Average of used tetrads: **32**

0    7    60    939
BIRD DAYS

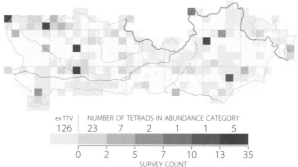

**Brambling** Winter abundance
Tetrads occupied: **39** (165) Average of occupied tetrads: **5·2**

ex TTV | NUMBER OF TETRADS IN ABUNDANCE CATEGORY
126 | 23    7    2    1    1    5

0    2    5    7    10    13    35
SURVEY COUNT

one in eight of the males were in summer plumage and several were in full song. Some of the flocks which have been recorded in Berkshire have been predominantly of male birds, such as a flock of 40–50 at Burghfield in February 1950 which comprised 75% males.

Although the availability of a good supply of Beech mast is generally considered to be the major factor influencing the timing of arrival and the size of winter flocks of Bramblings, other food sources may also attract large flocks. There have been several records of Bramblings from the Downs, most often in the early part of the winter where they feed, often with other finches, on farmland and grassland. In addition to the 1991 flock at Combe, at least 500 birds were seen in the same area during November the following year, and there were 500 at West Woodhay in January 2000, 200 at East Ilsley in November 1973, and about 260 at Compton in February 1979. However, the most important alternative local food source is the seed of conifers which falls to the ground in late winter and early spring. Large flocks of Brambling have been recorded from the coniferous woodlands of east and mid-Berkshire from January to March. In March 1931 there were reportedly large numbers in the pine woods at Burghfield Common, and in 1965 there were several large flocks in the Windsor/ Ascot/Silwood area in January and February which were estimated to total some 2,000 to 3,000 birds. There are numerous other counts of flocks of 100 to 200 birds from this habitat in late winter and early spring, and there were about 500 in the Ascot/Crowthorne area in late April 1994.

Bramblings have also been recorded in smaller numbers from sewage farms, and at Slough they were seen feeding on seeds of goosefoot *Chenopodium* spp. and burr-marigold *Bidens* spp. in 1949. More unusually, a flock of about 400 birds frequented a field of kale stubble at Finchampstead for some weeks in February 1956. Bramblings sometimes visit gardens, most commonly just one or two birds. However, garden records from Wokingham have occasionally produced substantial counts, with up to 100 in 1998 and 2000.

The variation in numbers between 'good' and 'poor' years for Brambling in Berkshire can be quite dramatic. In 'good' years there can be many reports of flocks of from 50 to 100 birds and usually two or three counts of 200–300 or more. In 'poor' years it can be difficult to find parties in excess of ten birds. After counts of up to 350 in the 1970s, for example, there was a period of 12 years from the winter of 1979/80 to the winter of 1990/91 when, with the exception of 1983/84 during which a flock of 150 was reported, there were no flocks in excess of 100 birds. During the 20th and 21st centuries, the winters during which the number of Brambling recorded in the county has been well above average have included 1930/31, 1964/65, 1975/76, 1978/79, 1991/92, 1992/93, 1993/94, 1994/95, 1997/98, 2002/03 and 2005/06. In some years there are large numbers in the forests of east Berkshire, associated with good crops of beech mast or conifer seeds, as mentioned above. In others there may be many records of small numbers from gardens throughout the county with no substantial counts. This was typical of the winters of the 2007–11 Atlas survey, and is reflected in the Winter Maps which show records from over 40% of tetrads, but an average count of just over five. A number of late wintering or passage birds were recorded during the 2007–11 breeding survey period, which are shown on the spring migration map, which shows a concentration of birds in April and early May in the south east of the county.

Ringing records reflect the nomadic nature of the species. Only one recovery involves a movement between Berkshire and the species' breeding areas in the boreal zone – a bird ringed in Norway in 2002 which was recovered at Jealott's Hill in 2004. The other two overseas records involved movements between the Netherlands and Berkshire in the same winter (2003/04), and one ringed at Lebbeke in Belgium in November 1979 which was recovered at Newbury in January 1982. Four records of birds ringed or recovered elsewhere in Britain all involved recoveries in different winters to the winter in which the birds were ringed, the birds having been ringed or recovered in Suffolk, Norfolk, Merseyside and Grampian.

Early ornithologists commented on the occurrence of periodic irruptions of Brambling in Berkshire. Lamb (1880) states that "vast flocks appeared in the severe winter, 1794, about Reading", and Palmer (1886) recalls immense flocks in the winter of 1864 when he killed "as many as 16 in one shot".

*Sponsored by Ted Rogers*

# Serin

Amber   Sch. 1

## *Serinus serinus*

*Rare vagrant, four records*

The Serin is a surprisingly recent addition to the Berkshire avifauna, given the considerable increase in records in southern Britain in the late 1960s. The first acceptable record was not until 1986, when an adult male was heard at Holyport on 8th September and seen on the ground with a small party of Goldfinches. A second record followed quickly in 1987 when an immature male was seen at Coley Park on 15th September. The next record was in 1988, during the Tetrad Survey, when a male was heard singing for two weeks in late May to early June 1988 just outside the county in Henley-on-Thames, although it was also recorded from the Berkshire side of the river. The most recent record, and only spring record, was one singing in a garden at Calcot from 22nd to 24th April 1996, at a time when there was a marked influx of the species into southern Britain.

*Sponsored by Renee Grayer*

# Greenfinch

Green

## *Chloris chloris*

*Common, widespread resident and winter visitor*

The Greenfinch is a common and widespread resident in Berkshire, where it breeds in hedgerows, along the edges of woodland, and in parks and gardens in rural, urban and suburban areas. It is a frequent visitor to gardens, and in winter forms flocks on farmland.

During the 2007–11 Tetrad Survey breeding evidence for the species was recorded in 376 tetrads in the county, eight fewer than in the 1987–89 survey, but breeding was confirmed in 243 of these, compared to 228 in 1987–89. In both surveys confirmed breeding records were obtained from both urban and rural areas, and included tetrads dominated by habitats with which Greenfinches are not usually associated, such as downland, heathland and coniferous woodland, although the few gaps in the species range in the county coincide with such habitat.

In contrast to many other seed-eating birds, it appears that the population of Greenfinches in Britain remained fairly constant during the 1970s and 1980s (*Population Trends*). Although numbers have fluctuated since, an increase up to the middle of the first decade of the 21st century reversed after an outbreak of trichomonosis, a disease to which the species seems particularly vulnerable.

The *1981–84 BTO Winter Atlas* suggests that although few continental birds appear to winter in Britain, there is a marked movement of British birds to the south-west in winter. Local evidence for this is provided by

451

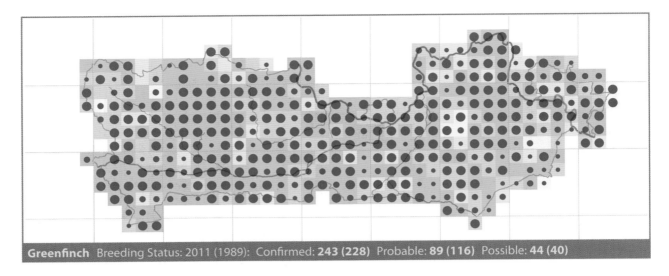

**Greenfinch** Breeding Status: 2011 (1989): Confirmed: **243 (228)** Probable: **89 (116)** Possible: **44 (40)**

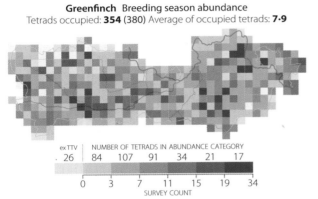

**Greenfinch** Breeding season abundance
Tetrads occupied: **354 (380)** Average of occupied tetrads: **7·9**

| ex TTV | NUMBER OF TETRADS IN ABUNDANCE CATEGORY | | | | | |
|---|---|---|---|---|---|---|
| · 26 | 84 | 107 | 91 | 34 | 21 | 17 |

0    3    7    11    15    19    34
SURVEY COUNT

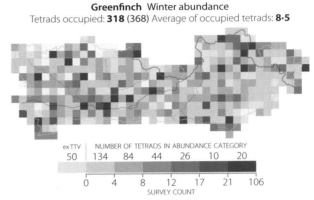

**Greenfinch** Winter abundance
Tetrads occupied: **318 (368)** Average of occupied tetrads: **8·5**

| ex TTV | NUMBER OF TETRADS IN ABUNDANCE CATEGORY | | | | | |
|---|---|---|---|---|---|---|
| 50 | 134 | 84 | 44 | 26 | 10 | 20 |

0    4    8    12    17    21    106
SURVEY COUNT

the pattern of ringing recoveries. Of the 398 recoveries involving birds moving into, or out of, the county, 276 were to or from five counties to the east or north; 66 from each of Surrey and Oxfordshire, 57 from Hertfordshire, 51 from Essex and 36 from Buckinghamshire. There are relative few from further afield to the north and east, with single recoveries involving movements to or from Nottinghamshire, Leicestershire and Lincolnshire the furthest, and relatively few involving movements to or from parts of Great Britain to the south or west of Berkshire. These imply a relatively short distance regular movement into the county in winter. The longest movement between ringing and recovery involved a bird that did not follow this pattern, a bird ringed in Colwyn Bay, Clwyd in March 1960 being found dead at Sunningdale the following April. There were also a series of three recoveries involving birds ringed or trapped in Devon between January and March 1976, possibly indicating a movement out of Berkshire that winter. Whilst there has not been a continental recovery of a Greenfinch ringed in Berkshire, one trapped at Denford in March 1982 was recovered on Guernsey the following December.

Outside the breeding season, flocks of Greenfinches can often be found on arable farmland, at sewage farms and other similar areas where there is suitable food available, sometimes in association with other finch species. Cover crops provided for game birds are often favoured. The species showed an increasing tendency to feed in gardens early in the winter from the 1970s (*1981–84 BTO Winter Atlas*), with numbers building as the winter progresses and the species is one of the most widely reported in the BOC's garden bird survey. The Winter Map indicates that the distribution is similar to that in summer, but with rather more gaps in the distribution on the Downs. Birds will also gather to feed in coniferous woodland, as indicated by the results of the *1981–84 BTO Winter Atlas* survey, which showed high numbers of birds in 10 km square SU86 to the south-east of Bracknell which contains considerable expanses of coniferous woodland. This was not however reflected in the results of the 2007–11 Atlas survey. In Berkshire the largest flocks are generally reported from October to March, although large gatherings are also recorded immediately after the breeding season. For example, there was a mixed flock of at least 300 Greenfinches and Linnets on Cookham Moor on 9th July 1988, and there were at least 600 Greenfinches at Cockmarsh on 25th August 1985. The largest winter flock since 1985 has been 500–600 feeding in flax fields between Cold Harbour and Kiln Green on 17th November 1991. Since then counts of 100 or more have been less frequent, the highest subsequent count being

200 at Bury Down on 9th November 2006. Despite the evidence of an influx of wintering birds in winter from ringing records, the average tetrad count from the 2007–11 TTV surveys indicate only a modest increase in numbers from the breeding season to winter.

The status of the Greenfinch in Berkshire in the 19th century appears to have been similar to its status today, being described in 1814 by Lamb (1880) as very common and by Noble (1906) as abundant.

*Sponsored by Brian Clews*

# Goldfinch

*Carduelis carduelis*

*Common and widespread resident*

The Goldfinch is a common and widespread resident in Berkshire. Since the early 1990s it has increased and spread within the county, and is now found throughout the county becoming a familiar sight at garden feeders and in urban areas.

The results of the 2007–11 Atlas Survey reveal Goldfinches to be present in almost all the tetrads in the county throughout the year, and confirmed to breed in 71% of those in which it was recorded. This represents a significant expansion of the range in the breeding season compared with the results of the 1987–89 survey, when Goldfinches were recorded in 87% of the tetrads in the county and were confirmed to have bred in some 44% of these. In the intervening period it has expanded into

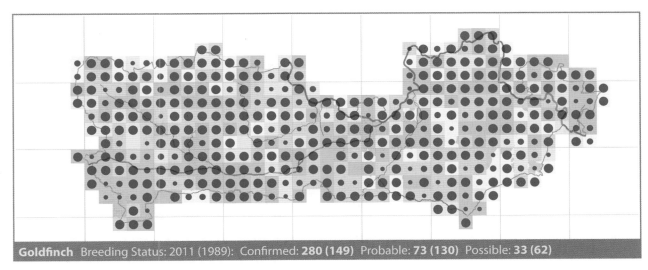

**Goldfinch** Breeding Status: 2011 (1989): Confirmed: **280 (149)** Probable: **73 (130)** Possible: **33 (62)**

**Goldfinch** Breeding season abundance
Tetrads occupied: **359 (392)** Average of occupied tetrads: **6·9**

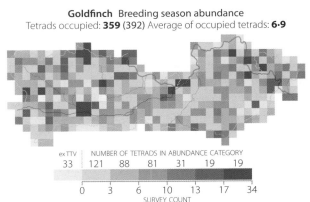

| exTTV | NUMBER OF TETRADS IN ABUNDANCE CATEGORY | | | | | |
|---|---|---|---|---|---|---|
| 33 | 121 | 88 | 81 | 31 | 19 | 19 |

0   3   6   10   13   17   34
SURVEY COUNT

**Goldfinch** Winter abundance
Tetrads occupied: **340 (388)** Average of occupied tetrads: **10·3**

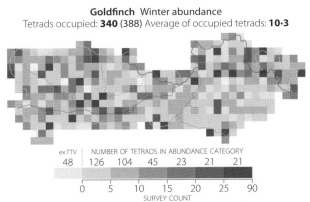

| exTTV | NUMBER OF TETRADS IN ABUNDANCE CATEGORY | | | | | |
|---|---|---|---|---|---|---|
| 48 | 126 | 104 | 45 | 23 | 21 | 21 |

0   5   10   15   20   25   90
SURVEY COUNT

the downland areas in the north west, and heaths of the south east of the county from which it was previously absent. This is consistent with the national population trend. After declines in the 1970s and early 1980s, the national population as estimated from CBC and BBS results has more than doubled, although the increase in south east England since the mid-1990s has been less marked, with a 36% increase calculated from BBS results between 1995 and 2010.

After the breeding season, Goldfinches gather in flocks, particularly in the early autumn and usually on rough ground where they feed on the seeds of thistles *Cirsium* spp. and other plants. In Berkshire, parties of from 50 to 100 birds are often reported from August, with the highest counts frequently being from gravel pits. The highest count in this season was 300 at Woolhampton Gravel Pits on 8th September 2004, and there have been counts of 250 or more birds in September 1981 at Theale Gravel Pits, and at Slough Sewage Farm in October 1996.

A large proportion of the British population of Goldfinches winters on the continent. However since the early 1990s winter flock counts have increased, with highest counts of 200 at Marsh Benham on 31st December 1996 and Eversley Gravel Pits on 5th

December 2004. Whereas the results of the *1981–84 BTO Winter Atlas* indicated that numbers are lowest in the open downland areas to the west of the county in winter, the 2007–11 Winter Map showed some of the highest counts from these tetrads. Goldfinches also began to use garden feeders widely in the early 1990s, and since then feeding Goldfinches have been recorded from 70% of gardens participating in the BOC Garden Bird Survey.

Ringing recoveries have indicated movement between Berkshire and south west Europe, and the movement of birds from the north west of England to (or through) Berkshire. There have been two records of movement between each of France and Spain, and four records involving movements between Lancashire (two), Merseyside and Cheshire and Berkshire, all of the latter being since 1990.

In the 19th century, the Goldfinch may well have been rather less common than it is at present, with Clark Kennedy (1868) indicating that the species was uncommon, and Noble (1906) noting a continued decline due to birdcatchers. The Goldfinch increased throughout the country after legislation banned trapping in the 1930s. (*1988–91 BTO Atlas*).

*Sponsored by Sally Wearing*

---

# Siskin

## *Carduelis spinus*

*Common winter visitor and passage migrant, scarce summer visitor*

The Siskin is a scarce summer visitor to Berkshire, breeding in only small numbers, but a widespread winter visitor in variable numbers, feeding gregariously in riverside or waterside Alders *Alnus glutinosa* or more widely on birch *Betula* spp. seed, often in the company of Redpolls. Since 1963, Siskins have been recorded nationally coming to garden feeders (*1968–72 BTO Atlas*). This practice was first reported in Berkshire in 1969, when birds were observed coming to peanuts at Burghfield Common, but is now an annual feature, particularly later in winter, giving many more observers the pleasure of watching the species at close range.

Clark Kennedy (1868) records its arrival as the end of November, and the county reports from 1925 to 1946 indicate that the earliest of the few Berkshire records was on 14th November 1935. The increase in the number of observers submitting records from the 1950s has provided a more detailed picture and shown that passage commonly begins in September or October,

followed in good years by further influxes in the period from November to January. Analysis of available information on arrival dates for the 24 years from 1961 to 1984 shows that in seven of these years birds arrived in September, the earliest on the 3rd. Since then Siskins appear to be showing an increasing tendency to arrive early, with September records in 29 of the 28 years from 1985 to 2012, 1988 being particularly notable with ten

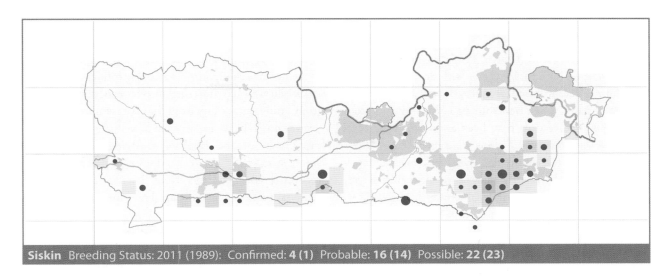

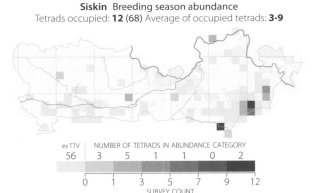

**Siskin**  Breeding season abundance
Tetrads occupied: **12 (68)** Average of occupied tetrads: **3·9**

| exTTV | NUMBER OF TETRADS IN ABUNDANCE CATEGORY | | | | | |
|---|---|---|---|---|---|---|
| 56 | 3 | 5 | 1 | 1 | 0 | 2 |

| 0 | 1 | 3 | 5 | 7 | 9 | 12 |

SURVEY COUNT

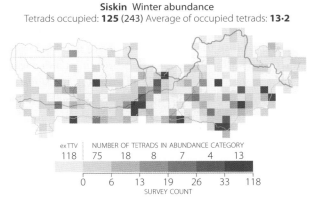

**Siskin**  Winter abundance
Tetrads occupied: **125 (243)** Average of occupied tetrads: **13·2**

| exTTV | NUMBER OF TETRADS IN ABUNDANCE CATEGORY | | | | | |
|---|---|---|---|---|---|---|
| 118 | 75 | 18 | 8 | 7 | 4 | 13 |

| 0 | 6 | 13 | 19 | 26 | 33 | 118 |

SURVEY COUNT

different sightings from the 3rd to the 22nd. There has been just one August record away from the breeding range in Berkshire, a sickly juvenile at Emmer Green on 28th August 2007. During some winters further dispersal takes place, either as a consequence of hard weather or shortage of food, resulting in lower numbers until the return passage occurs in March and April leading to an upsurge in numbers.

The number of Siskins wintering in Berkshire appears always to have been extremely variable. In some years they have been regarded as abundant, as in the winters of 1857/58 and 1866/67 (Clark Kennedy, 1868) and 1925/26, 1942/43, 1985/86, 1994/95 and 1997/98. In years when they are more abundant, flocks of over 100 birds have been reported regularly, and on occasion flocks of up to 400 birds have occurred. Higher concentrations are exceptional, the largest flocks recorded being: between 500 and 1,000 in the Rapley/Surrey Hill area on 21st March 1998, about 500 at Burghfield Mill on 28th January 1995, about 500 at Thatcham Marsh and at least 400 at Dinton Pastures in January 1986, part of a large influx that winter which by January totalled over 1,800 birds; 500–700 near Mortimer in December 1942; and a sudden influx at Upper Woolhampton on 13th March 1984 which brought numbers up to about 750. In 1990 there was an unprecedented fall of Siskins

at Theale on 26th January following severe gales which produced the largest flock ever recorded in Berkshire, at least 1,000 and probably many more. In 'poor' years flock sizes are smaller, usually from ten to 50 birds, and Siskins may be virtually absent from some areas for much of the winter, as in mid-Berkshire in the winter of 1976/77 when the highest count was just ten birds. Even in poor years however, larger parties of passage birds can occur briefly. As the Winter abundance map shows, Siskins occur widely in winter away from open arable areas in the centre and north west of the county, with highest concentrations tending to occur in the river valleys.

In some years return passage is well marked with a number of records. When there is a good supply of birch and conifer seed many birds remain throughout April and into early May. There have been few years since 1946 without reports of Siskins in April, but since the mid-1970s there has been an increasing tendency towards late departure or more frequent summering. The majority of records shown on the 2007–11 Breeding Season abundance map are likely to relate to late departing winter visitors.

The first June record for Berkshire was in 1955 and was followed in 1956 by the first record of birds apparently breeding within the county, an adult and two juveniles being seen in east Berkshire in early June. In the following 37 years from 1958 to 1994, Siskins were seen in late May or June in 13 years, with reports coming from four different localities in 1978, and with a small number of pairs in east Berkshire in 1985, and since the mid-1990s such records have been annual. During the 1987–89 Tetrad Survey, Siskins were recorded in 10% of the tetrads in the county and were confirmed to have bred in one, with recently fledged young being seen. They probably bred in a further 14 tetrads. In the 2007–11 survey, breeding was confirmed in four tetrads, and probably occurred in another 23. The possible breeding records may also relate to late wintering birds.

A small breeding population has now been established, largely concentrated in the coniferous woodlands of the south east of the county, but with occasional records from elsewhere. Since the nest of this species is notoriously difficult to find it is possible that breeding pairs could easily go undetected. The *1988–91 BTO Atlas* indicates that the colonisation of Berkshire by Siskins is part of a more extensive spread into southern England since the 1970s.

The movements of Siskins in Britain have been shown from ringing recoveries to be quite complex. The species is irruptive and the extent and direction of its movements is thought to be strongly influenced by food availability. Birds wintering in one year may originate from a different locality from those present the following year. Scottish birds are believed to make up a substantial proportion of the English wintering population in some years (*1981–84 BTO Winter Atlas*). The ringing recoveries and controls from Berkshire reflect this national picture and indicate that wintering Siskins in Berkshire are a mix of continental and Scottish birds. Nine have involved birds ringed or recovered in Belgium, three from Norway, two each from France and Germany and singles from Denmark, the Netherlands and Italy. Of over 300 Siskins trapped for ringing at Wash Common from January to April 1989, three were found to have been ringed in Scotland, two in May 1986 and one in September 1988, one in Belgium the previous October and one in Devon in March 1986. Of the birds ringed at Wash Common that year, one was re-trapped the following February in Aberdeen and another in the same month in Carlisle.

*Sponsored by Jim Burnett*

# Linnet

`Red`

*Carduelis cannabina*

*Common Resident and migrant*

The Linnet is a common but unevenly distributed resident in Berkshire, favouring a wide variety of open habitats with thorny bushes in which it builds its nest. It occurs most frequently on farmland, where it breeds in hedgerows, on heathland and commons and in areas of scrub, young plantations and rural gardens. During migration and in winter flocks are encountered in open country, especially fallow land and stubble, and overgrown margins of sites such as gravel pits and sewage farms. There does seem to have been a shift in the species distribution in recent decades, with more concentration in arable areas, particularly on the Downs.

The shift in distribution is revealed by the results of the Tetrad Surveys. Although the number of tetrads from which breeding evidence was recorded did not change greatly, with a decline of 16 tetrads between the two surveys, but breeding confirmed in eight more, the geographic distribution within the county changed markedly. In the 1987–89 survey it was more evenly, if somewhat patchily, distributed. In the 2007–11 survey, it was absent from many tetrads in the east, centre and south of the county, but was more widespread in

the north west of the county, and had also colonised other tetrads with arable cultivation east of Reading and west of Maidenhead. The heaths of the south east of Berkshire had largely been deserted. Nationally, Linnets have declined by about 75% since the mid-1960s, although the decline has been less rapid in more recent years, the CBC/BBS index for the species having declined by 20% between 1989 and 2009. There is some evidence that the spread of cultivation of oilseed rape has mitigated the loss of weed seeds as a food source, although the evidence is not conclusive (Moorcroft *et al.*,

1997, Siriwardena *et al.*, 2001). Anecdotally, observers in the latest Berkshire Atlas survey indicated that the crop was often associated with breeding Linnets.

After the breeding season, Linnets vacate many of their summer haunts, leaving large gaps in their distribution. Some migrate out of Britain to France and Spain in winter, as indicted by ringing recoveries. There have been eight recoveries of Linnets ringed in Berkshire from these two countries, six from France and two from Spain, which matches the pattern from Britain as a whole. However clearly many remain, and the Winter Map shows that although the number of tetrads from which Linnets were recorded was just under 60% of the number occupied in the breeding season, the average count was over four times higher in occupied tetrads, possibly indicating an influx of wintering birds. There is however very little information on the source of Berkshire's winter and passage birds. As a bird of open country, there has been relatively little ringing of the species, with just 16 recoveries involving movements within the UK, the furthest being from Dorset and Hertfordshire.

The flocks which form in autumn and winter frequently number from 100 to 300, although the numbers vary considerably from year to year. The highest monthly counts from 1981 to 2011 are shown in Table 9. Despite

|     | Count | Year          |
|-----|-------|---------------|
| Jan | 500   | 2010          |
| Feb | 500   | 1992 and 2003 |
| Mar | 500   | 1994          |
| Apr | 600   | 2004          |
| May | –     | –             |
| Jun | –     | –             |
| Jul | 103   | 2009          |
| Aug | 400   | 2006          |
| Sep | 420+  | 1993          |
| Oct | 500   | 1992          |
| Nov | 300+  | 1989          |
| Dec | 1,000 | 1991          |

**Table 9: Linnet: highest monthly counts 1981–2011.**

the decline in the UK's breeding population over this period, this does not indicate that there has been a decrease in the size of Linnet flocks in Berkshire in recent decades.

In some years the size of flocks increase during the autumn, but it is unclear what proportion is made up of migrants passing through or birds remaining during the winter. The exceptional flock of about 1,000 at Combe on 26th December 1991 arrived with an even larger number of Bramblings, pointing to the continental origin of at

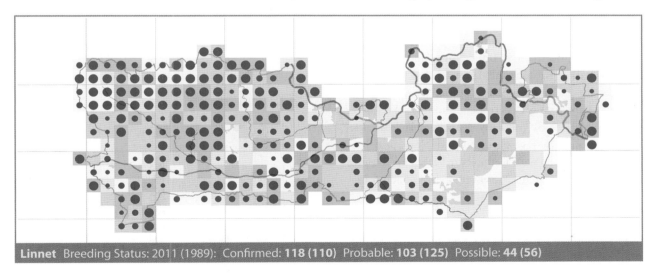

**Linnet** Breeding Status: 2011 (1989): Confirmed: **118 (110)** Probable: **103 (125)** Possible: **44 (56)**

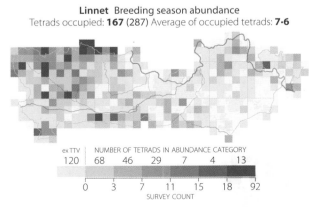

**Linnet** Breeding season abundance
Tetrads occupied: **167 (287)** Average of occupied tetrads: **7·6**

| exTTV | NUMBER OF TETRADS IN ABUNDANCE CATEGORY | | | | | |
|-------|----|----|----|---|---|----|
| 120   | 68 | 46 | 29 | 7 | 4 | 13 |

| 0 | 3 | 7 | 11 | 15 | 18 | 92 |
SURVEY COUNT

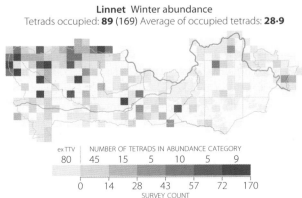

**Linnet** Winter abundance
Tetrads occupied: **89 (169)** Average of occupied tetrads: **28·9**

| exTTV | NUMBER OF TETRADS IN ABUNDANCE CATEGORY | | | | | |
|-------|----|----|---|----|---|---|
| 80    | 45 | 15 | 5 | 10 | 5 | 9 |

| 0 | 14 | 28 | 43 | 57 | 72 | 170 |
SURVEY COUNT

least a proportion of the Linnets. Winter flocks often remain for several weeks in a favoured feeding area, their numbers sometimes being augmented by other finches, buntings and skylarks. Comparison between the Winter Map and the results of the *1981–84 BTO Winter Atlas* survey indicate that there may have been a similar shift in the distribution in winter to the one in the breeding season. The earlier atlas showed some of the highest counts in 10 km squares SU67 west of Reading and SU86 which includes the heaths south of Bracknell from which the species was largely absent in 2007–11, and the latest atlas shows the largest concentrations on the Downs in the north west of the county.

The population of Linnets in Britain fluctuated considerably during the 20th century and it seems likely that this pattern has been reflected in Berkshire. Numbers recovered in the early part of the century after the species ceased to be trapped and caged on a large scale. Since the 1940s there has been a loss of habitat due to the cultivation of marginal land and, more recently, the use of selective herbicides has reduced the availability of its favoured food source, weed seeds. The Linnet was evidently a common resident during the 19th century as noted by Clark Kennedy (1868) and Palmer (1886), and Noble (1906) recalls finding 14 nests in one day in box *Buxus* sp. bushes in less than a quarter of an acre of his garden.

*Sponsored by Berks, Bucks and Oxford Wildlife Trust*

# Twite
`Red`

## *Carduelis flavirostris*

*Rare and decreasing passage migrant and winter visitor*

The Twite is a scarce passage migrant and winter visitor in Berkshire, with just one record since 1984. Its preference for fields and uncultivated areas where it feeds on seeds, often in association with Linnets, may lead to some birds being overlooked since such areas are not regularly frequented by birdwatchers.

The difficulty in identifying Twite probably accounts for the fact that there was only one record of the species in Berkshire prior to the 20th century, one caught in a timber wharf at Reading in March 1794 (Lamb, 1880). A statement by Clark Kennedy (1868) that the species was a regular winter visitor is erroneous and was considered so by Noble (1906). Similarly, reports of at least three birds at Slough Sewage Farm on 2nd November 1952 and one associating with Redpolls at Barkham Common from January to March 1958 are considered doubtful.

From 1960 to 1984 there were 18 records of Twite in Berkshire, involving a total of at least 34 birds. Three were reliably reported from the Downs at Compton in March 1960 and a further three were in the Compton area on 25th November 1961. A party of six were identified by call in Windsor Great Park on 25th October 1964, the earliest arrival date for Berkshire, although the location is not specific enough to establish whether the birds were actually seen in Berkshire or in Surrey. One was also heard calling over Ham Island on 7th November that year. The following year one was reported calling over Fifield on 21st November 1965, and one was roosting with Linnets in Windsor Great Park on 11th March 1966. One, or possibly two, were at Theale Gravel Pits from 11th to 12th December 1971, with another there with Goldfinches and Linnets on

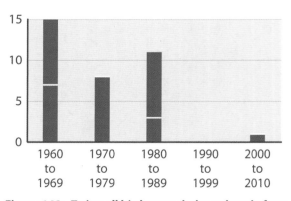

**Figure 148: Twite: all birds recorded per decade from 1960.** Bar – birds; white line – records.

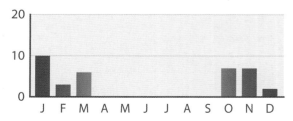

**Figure 149: Twite: all birds recorded 1960–2012, by month of arrival.**

458

22nd January 1972. A male was at Horton Gravel Pits on 12th March 1975 and one was on the Lambourn Downs on 4th November 1975. In 1976 a male was caught and ringed with Linnets at Jealott's Hill on 8th November and one was seen and heard that year at Reading Sewage Farm on 2nd December. One was at Wraysbury Gravel Pits on 27th March 1978, the latest date for departure in Berkshire, and a female was with Chaffinches at Thatcham Marsh on 31st January 1979, ending a sequence of records in six of the nine years from 1971 to 1979.

In 1982, six males and possibly some females which were not specifically identified, were in a flock of about 200 Linnets at Lower Earley on 11th January and two were at Farley Hill on 26th January. The last county record in the 20th century was of three at Wraysbury Gravel Pits on 23rd February 1984. It appears that the population of Twite declined nationally (*Population Trends*) and the pattern of records for Berkshire would seem to support this trend (Figure 148). There was a similar decrease in the number of records of Twite in Hampshire during the 1980s (Clark & Eyre, 1993). The only 21st century record was one at Slough Sewage Farm on 18th November 2006, which was relocated at Cippenham later that day.

The records of Twite in Berkshire match the national picture for southern England, with the first arrivals appearing from September to November, with further arrivals in the period from December to January, and returning birds occurring from the end of January to the middle of March (*1981–84 BTO Winter Atlas*). A summary of the monthly distribution of records in Berkshire from 1960 to 2012 is shown in Figure 149.

*Sponsored by Duncan Spence*

# Lesser Redpoll

`Red`

## Carduelis cabaret

*Locally common passage migrant and winter visitor and formerly sporadic breeder*

The Redpoll is a locally common passage migrant and winter visitor to Berkshire, which has bred sporadically in small numbers. As indicated by the Winter abundance map, it occurs widely in most areas but is scarcest in open arable areas, and commonest in river valleys in waterside vegetation, and the coniferous forests and heaths of south east Berkshire. In recent years Redpolls have started to feed in gardens, showing a particular liking for nyjer seed feeders.

The species' fortunes as a breeding bird in Berkshire reflect its fluctuating status nationally. An increase in the population of Redpolls in Britain occurred from 1950, considerably aided by coniferous afforestation, the CBC showing a four-fold increase from 1967 to 1977. Numbers declined subsequently and by 2009 the CBC/BBS Index indicated a decline of nearly 90% since the mid-1960s. (Baillie *et al.*, 2012). In Berkshire, summering birds were reported in 1947, 1950 and 1956, when there was a possible family party at Earley, and in five of the 13 years from 1957 to 1969. Summer records were annual in the 1970s and 1980s and breeding was confirmed in three 10km squares in the *1968–72 BTO Atlas*. A study was carried out in a recently afforested area at Sulham Woods in 1974, which established that the size of each territory was in the order of 3·5 to 4·0 hectares. In that area in 1975 four pairs were present and a nest containing young was found.

During the 1987–89 Tetrad Survey, Redpolls were confirmed to have bred in seven tetrads in Berkshire and were recorded as probably occurring in a further 16. Birds were also present in an additional 23 tetrads, but many of these are likely to have been late departing migrants which occur quite often on passage in Berkshire well into May. These breeding records showed a strong correlation with the distribution of heathland and conifer plantations, bearing out the observation that acid heath with birch *Betula* spp. and mixed scrub are favoured by summering Redpolls in England (*1968–72 BTO Atlas*). This is in contrast to the recorded habitat of breeding birds in Berkshire between 1900 and 1950, which was either river valley osier *Salix* spp. beds or suburban gardens or parks, and during the 1987–89 Tetrad Survey a nest was found in an old hedgerow at Dinton Pastures in 1987.

In the years since the 1987–89 Tetrad survey, Lesser Redpolls may have been lost to the county as a breeding species, the last confirmed breeding record being at Crowthorne in 1997. There were no confirmed breeding records from the 2007–11 Atlas survey, and many of the spring records almost certainly relate to departing wintering birds.

The usual pattern of records indicates that there is a post-breeding dispersal of summering birds before the arrival of passage or wintering birds in the autumn. The autumn arrival begins in September and continues through October, with a further distinct influx in some years in November after earlier arrivals have apparently continued their migration. There is almost invariably an increase in numbers in spring as returning birds pass through the county during April and early May, occasionally forming large flocks. Numbers fluctuate considerably from year to year. The largest parties reported each month over the period from 1979 to 2011 are shown in Table 10 and reflect the peaks of passage which occur in November and April. The highest counts tend to be from the forests of south east Berkshire during the spring passage, where the highest count of about 1,000 occurred in April 2002 in Swinley Forest. This area usually produces counts of more than 200 at this time of year, but numbers seem dependant on the pine cone crop. When this failed in 2008 few birds were seen.

Ringing recoveries have shown that some wintering birds are from northern England. Movements between Berkshire and Durham, Northumberland, Cumbria and West Yorkshire have been disclosed, and there is one record of a bird from Scotland, ringed at Blackburn, Lothian in September 2009 and recovered at Padworth Common the following February. There has been one overseas recovery, a bird ringed at Thatcham Marsh in January 1965 being reported from Belgium the following October.

Clark Kennedy (1868) observed the species to be only a winter visitor and "never been able to meet with an authenticated nest in Berkshire", but after being recorded breeding at Finchampstead in 1887 (Noble, 1906), Maidenhead Thicket in 1897 (Proctor, 1908), Wellington College in 1898, and probably at Reading in 1901 (Noble, 1906), there was an increase in records from 1905, with several pairs regularly reported breeding in osier *Salix* spp. plantations along the Thames Valley below Reading (Kerr, 1916). Breeding was also reported at Leighton Park School from 1905 to 1909.

This increase in breeding records in Berkshire coincided with a national increase in Redpolls in lowland Britain

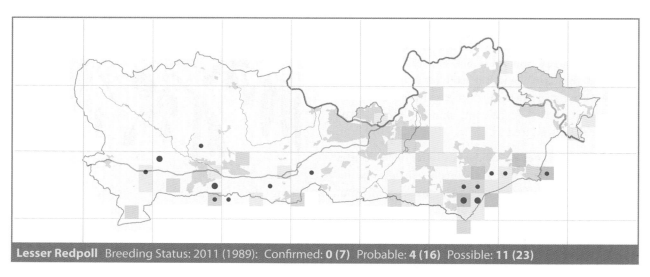

**Lesser Redpoll**  Breeding Status: 2011 (1989):  Confirmed: **0 (7)**  Probable: **4 (16)**  Possible: **11 (23)**

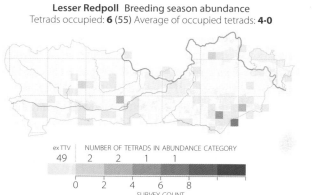

**Lesser Redpoll**  Breeding season abundance
Tetrads occupied: **6 (55)** Average of occupied tetrads: **4·0**

| ex TTV | NUMBER OF TETRADS IN ABUNDANCE CATEGORY | | | |
|---|---|---|---|---|
| 49 | 2 | 2 | 1 | 1 |

0    2    4    6    8
SURVEY COUNT

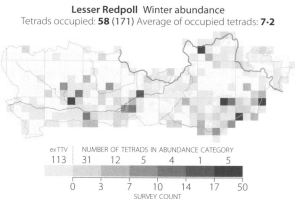

**Lesser Redpoll**  Winter abundance
Tetrads occupied: **58 (171)** Average of occupied tetrads: **7·2**

| ex TTV | NUMBER OF TETRADS IN ABUNDANCE CATEGORY | | | | | |
|---|---|---|---|---|---|---|
| 113 | 31 | 12 | 5 | 4 | 1 | 5 |

0    3    7    10    14    17    50
SURVEY COUNT

from 1900 to 1910, which was followed by a crash in numbers in 1917 and their disappearance from many areas from 1920 (*1968–72 BTO Atlas*). The 1917 crash followed the great freeze from January to March of that year and although breeding numbers in Berkshire were claimed to have recovered by 1922, supporting information is lacking. In the 20 years from 1923 to 1942 breeding was only reported in 1924, 1927, 1929, 1932, 1933 and in 1940 when a late nest and eggs were found at Eton in August. No more than one pair was reported in any year except for 1932 when three sites were occupied, one of which, Ascot Heath, still had breeding Redpolls in the 1990s.

*Sponsored by Dick Haydon*

|  | Count | Year |
|---|---|---|
| Jan | 200 | 1996 |
| Feb | 300 | 1982 |
| Mar | 400 | 1990 |
| Apr | 1,000 | 2002 |
| May | 250 | 2004 |
| Jun | – | – |
| Jul | – | – |
| Aug | – | – |
| Sep | – | – |
| Oct | 110 | 2006 |
| Nov | 600 | 1984 |
| Dec | 100 | 1980, 1985, 1995, 2010 |

**Table 10: Lesser Redpoll: highest monthly counts 1979–2011.**

# Common Redpoll  Green

*Carduelis flammea*

*Scarce winter visitor*

Until 2001, Lesser Redpolls were considered to be the race of Common Redpoll native to north west and central Europe, the latter being present in much of the boreal zone of the northern hemisphere. The decision was taken to allocate full species status to Lesser Redpolls, which are distinguishable by their smaller size and darker plumage (Knox *et al.*, 2001), although subsequently DNA analysis has shown no significant difference between individuals attributed to both species, and some individuals have proved impossible to separate even when handled by ringers (Collar, 2013). Nonetheless both species remain on the BOU's British List, so are treated as separate species in this book.

During winter, birds exhibiting the characteristics of the Mealy Redpoll *C. f flammea*, the race of Common Redpoll present in central and northern Scandanavia, are occasionally observed in Berkshire. Many records have been of birds associating with Lesser Redpolls. There are county records for 1936, 1963, 1972 (two birds), 1975, 1976 (four birds), 1985, 1986 (two birds), 1988, 1994, 1995, 1998 (a record of two birds at Brimpton), 2002 and 2005 (two records). There was an influx in January and February 2006, with records from five locations, including up to three at Sonning and two at Bucklebury. A second influx produced records from four sites in February and March 2010, including the highest count of 10 at Padworth Common on 1st March, followed by another the following January to March, which produced records from five sites, including up to four at Greenham Common. There were also three at Padworth Common on 31st December 2011, and two at each of

**Common Redpoll** Winter abundance
Tetrads occupied: **0** (2) Average of occupied tetrads: **0**

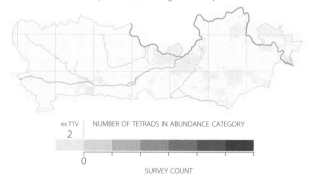

exTTV    NUMBER OF TETRADS IN ABUNDANCE CATEGORY
2

0
SURVEY COUNT

Bracknell and Ashley Hill in the following two months. The increase in the number of records in recent years probably results from an increased awareness amongst observers of the characteristics of this species, and from birds caught for ringing. The earliest autumn arrival was one at Queen Mother Reservoir on 3rd November 2005.

*Sponsored by Hugh Netley*

461

# Two-barred Crossbill

## *Loxia leucoptera*

*Rare vagrant, one record of four birds*

The Two-barred Crossbill is a rare vagrant to Berkshire, its normal range being the northern parts of Europe, Asia and North America. It has only been recorded in the 19th century. Following an invasion of the species into Britain in 1889, four were seen near Wellington College on 27th February 1890 and were reported in the Wellington College Natural Science Report for that year (Noble, 1906). One bird, presumably of this four, was killed in the same district and reported in *The Field* on 8th March 1890.

*Sponsored by Brian Clews*

# Crossbill

## *Loxia curvirostra*

*Regular winter visitor in variable numbers and sporadic breeder*

The Crossbill is an annual winter visitor to Berkshire in highly variable numbers and often summers after 'irruptions'. With extensive areas of coniferous woodland in the south-east of the county, particularly along the Surrey and Hampshire borders, and to the north of Newbury, Berkshire is well placed to attract Crossbills during their periodic irruptions and to provide them with suitable habitat in which to remain and breed. Records have been annual since 1953 and birds have been reported in all months of the year.

The earliest county records include a reference to this irruptive behaviour, with Lamb (1880) commenting on the scale of an invasion of Crossbills in July 1810 when "vast flocks were seen, particularly in the area of Hungerford". The likelihood of breeding occurring after invasions was referred to by Noble (1906). He mentions a nest found in Windsor Forest in 1882, beneath which an unfledged bird was found dead on 13th May, and birds building a nest near Virginia Water in 1889. A very young Crossbill, which had probably been reared locally, was reported from Aldermaston in 1898 where they had been very abundant earlier that year (Witherby and Ticehurst, 1908).

There was a vast irruption of Crossbills into Britain in the winter of 1909/10. Birds first began arriving in Berkshire about mid-August 1909 and were reported in small parties from several places during the winter. In February 1910 Crossbill nests containing four and five eggs were found near Aldermaston (Gilroy, 1910),

and from 16th March to 20th April no less than seven nests, all with three or four eggs, were found in south Berkshire pine *Pinus* spp. woods. Two nests with young were also reported and a few pairs had "still not quite finished nesting" by 18th May (Tomlinson, 1910).

Smaller invasions occurred in 1929; 1935, after which birds bred at West Woodhay in 1936; in 1953, after which a nest was found at Cold Ash in January 1954; and in 1956, after which breeding was recorded at Hermitage in 1957 and 1958. Irruptions since 1960 have been occurring with increasing frequency; in 1962, 1966, 1972, 1979, and in eleven of the 29 years from 1983 to 2011. These periodic irruptions have resulted in a cycle of records which is broadly repeated with each irruption.

The first invading birds are usually seen in June, following which flocks of up to 60 birds are not uncommon. It is not easy to establish the total number present in Berkshire at any one time from published reports, but this certainly varies depending upon the size of the irruption. In years when large invasions occur, such as in 1979 and 1990, the number of birds reaching Berkshire may be up to 100. In some years the number of birds reported declines during the winter, although this may be a reflection of flocks breaking down into pairs which are then more difficult to detect. A study in 1936 showed that, following the 1935/36 invasion, birds began to appear in pairs about the 7th February (Monk & Southern, 1937). Some regrouping of these pairs then takes place from April, often with numbers supplemented by juveniles following successful breeding, although family parties may continue to occur until September. In other years numbers may be supplemented by further arrivals during the autumn and winter. Following the particularly large irruption in 1990 there were an estimated 400 birds in the county in May 1991, which appeared to be flocking prior to departure. This included the largest concentration of Crossbills recorded in Berkshire, about 200 birds in the coniferous woodland to the east of Crowthorne in April and May 1991. In 2003 on the other hand, very high numbers (flocks of between 100 and 165 birds) were recorded from March right into May, despite very few records in the latter part of 2002. Observations of birds on passage have been relatively few in Berkshire, with 16 seen flying south-west over Queen Mother Reservoir in November 1986 being one of the few examples. By the

second summer after an irruption Crossbills can become relatively scarce; for example no more than three birds were reported in 1969, 1970, 1974 and 1982. Similarly, no records were received before June in 1999.

After the 1962 invasion breeding was recorded at Barkham Common and probably in the Windsor/ Ascot area in 1963, and there were six nests in the Windsor Great Park area in 1964. The 1979 invasion was followed by reports in 1980 of probably ten pairs in the Windsor Great Park area, and of three juveniles at Bucklebury Common. Similarly, after the 1983 irruption there were estimated to be up to seven pairs in 1984, where nest building was seen in the Windsor Forest and Crowthorne areas.

In view of this link between breeding and invasion years, the distribution of the Crossbill as revealed by a breeding bird survey depends very much upon whether there has been a recent invasion. The 1987–89 Atlas Survey period spanned the irruption of June 1988, and Crossbills were located in 14 tetrads with 12 of these in east Berkshire (predominantly in 10 km square SU86) and confirmed breeding in two tetrads. There were also indications of probable breeding in seven tetrads, including one observation of a nest being built, and breeding was confirmed at two sites in coniferous woodland near Crowthorne where fledged young were

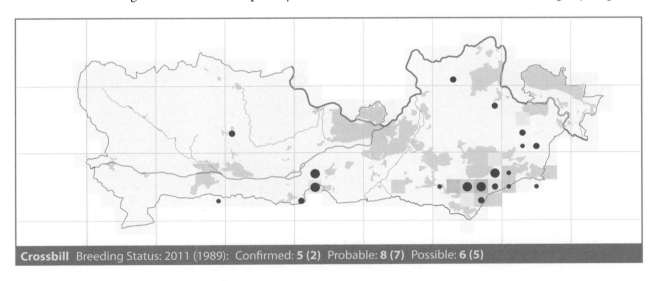

**Crossbill** Breeding Status: 2011 (1989): Confirmed: **5 (2)** Probable: **8 (7)** Possible: **6 (5)**

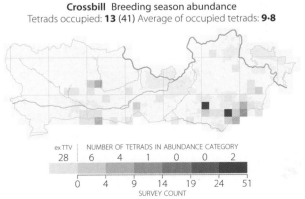

**Crossbill** Breeding season abundance
Tetrads occupied: **13 (41)** Average of occupied tetrads: **9·8**

| exTTV | NUMBER OF TETRADS IN ABUNDANCE CATEGORY | | | | | |
|---|---|---|---|---|---|---|
| 28 | 6 | 4 | 1 | 0 | 0 | 2 |

0    4    9    14    19    24    51
SURVEY COUNT

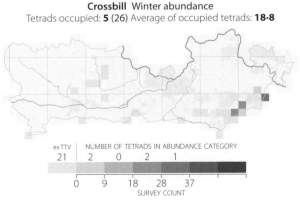

**Crossbill** Winter abundance
Tetrads occupied: **5 (26)** Average of occupied tetrads: **18·8**

| exTTV | NUMBER OF TETRADS IN ABUNDANCE CATEGORY | | | |
|---|---|---|---|---|
| 21 | 2 | 0 | 2 | 1 |

0    9    18    28    37
SURVEY COUNT

seen. However, the difficulty in proving breeding means that the species is probably under-recorded. After the 1987–89 Atlas Survey, juvenile birds were reported in almost all years up to the 2007–11 Atlas Survey.

The 2007–11 Atlas Survey revealed the presence of this species in 41 tetrads, with breeding confirmed in five of these. There were signs of probable breeding in another eight and possible breeding in a further six. The distribution of these tetrads broadly reflects that recorded by the 1987–89 Atlas Survey, with a concentration in the 10 km square SU86. However possible and probable breeding was recorded in several new tetrads in north-east Berkshire. This Atlas Survey spanned the 2008 influx.

Nests have been found in Berkshire as early as 21st January in 1954 and as late as 22nd April in 1960, although one which was 13 metres up in a Scots Pine *Pinus sylvestris* at West Woodhay in 1936 was not started until 19th April. In 1984 a female was seen removing material from a nest in order to build another nearby. Because of the difficulty of confirming breeding there is little information on which to base an estimate of the breeding population of Crossbills in a post-invasion year. The highest estimate has been of up to ten pairs in the Windsor Great Park area in 1980. However large flocks in the breeding season following irruption years have been recorded, including about 100 birds at Swinley Forest on 12th March 2000, about 50 on 9th March 2002 at Caesars Camp, and 89 on 22nd April 2006 in the same area.

Crossbills feed readily on larch *Larix* spp. seed in winter, and a study which was undertaken following the invasion of 1935/36 found that where larch seed was available the birds fed on this first, resorting to Scots Pine later in the season (Monk & Southern, 1937). In April, Crossbills have been reported feeding in oak *Quercus* spp. trees, presumably on the emerging buds.

*Sponsored by Bill Nicoll*

Crossbills, Swinley Forest *David Lowther*

# Parrot Crossbill

Amber    Sch. 1

*Loxia pytyopsittacus*

*Rare vagrant, one record involving four birds*

Although Parrot Crossbills were thought to have been present in Berkshire during the Crossbill invasion of 1962, the first and only acceptable county record is of four birds, including a male, which were found near Crowthorne on 29th January 1983. These birds occurred in the wake of an influx of Crossbills into Britain and were first located by their call. They remained in the area until last reported on 27th February.

*Sponsored by Audrey Springate*

# Common Rosefinch

Sch. 1

*Carpodacus erythrinus*

*Rare vagrant, two records*

There have been two Berkshire records of Common Rosefinch (formerly known as Scarlet Rosefinch) in Berkshire. The first was of a male seen in a small garden at Earley on 29th May 1982, the same year in which the species first bred in Scotland, following a period of expansion of the species' range westward across Europe. The bird was watched for half an hour feeding mainly on the seeds of cranesbill *Geranium* spp. before it was disturbed and flew away. The second was a male seen and heard by the Kennet and Avon Canal near Aldermaston between 6th and 23rd June 1997.

*Sponsored by Rachel Edwards*

# Pine Grosbeak

*Pinicola enucleator*

*Rare vagrant, one record*

The Pine Grosbeak is a rare vagrant to Britain and there is just a single Berkshire record of one seen by two observers on several separate occasions in woods near Wellington College in early December 1901 (Noble, 1906). The record was written up briefly by one of the observers in the 12th December 1901 issue of Nature (Rogers, 1901), and describes how the bird was first seen from a window, apparently either eating Beech *Fagus sylvatica* buds or else hunting for insects on them. Although not listed by some authorities, there appear to be reasonable grounds for treating this record as reliable.

*Sponsored by Renton Righelato*

# Bullfinch

Amber

*Pyrrhula pyrrhula*

*Widespread resident, occasional passage migrant and winter visitor.*

The Bullfinch is a widespread resident in Berkshire occurring in a wide range of habitats where sufficient cover is available, habitats such as woodland edge, open farmland with hedgerows, areas of scrub, town parks, allotments and suburban gardens. It is commonest in the west of the county.

The results of the Tetrad Surveys indicate a substantial decline in Berkshire between the 1987–89 and 2007–11 surveys. Breeding evidence of Bullfinches was recorded in 87% of the tetrads in Berkshire in the former, but only 68% in the latter, with the species apparently lost from many tetrads in the centre and east of the county. Breeding was only confirmed in just over one third of the tetrads in which they were recorded in both surveys. The breeding season abundance map confirms that numbers are also higher in the west of the county.

These results indicate that the species' recent fortunes in Berkshire seem to be worse than the picture nationally. The population of the Bullfinch has been monitored, and its food preferences and habitat requirements

studied, for many years due to the species' depredations in orchards (Newton, 1972). After an increase in the 1940s and 1950s, when the Bullfinch appears to have colonised more open farmland, its numbers declined considerably from the mid-1970s until the early 1990s (*Population Trends*), and Marchant and Musty (1992) included the Bullfinch among the 20 common species whose numbers had declined markedly in the previous two years. However, results from the BBS indicate that after a considerable decline in the previous two decades, numbers stabilised in the 1990s, and have recovered a little since. It is unclear why Bullfinches in east and central Berkshire have declined, although the pattern matches a similar contraction of range between the

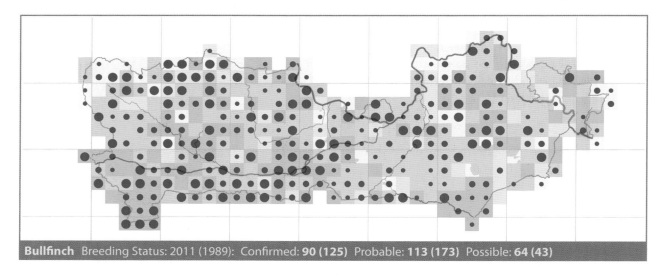

**Bullfinch** Breeding Status: 2011 (1989): Confirmed: **90 (125)** Probable: **113 (173)** Possible: **64 (43)**

**Bullfinch** Breeding season abundance
Tetrads occupied: **138 (289)** Average of occupied tetrads: **2·0**

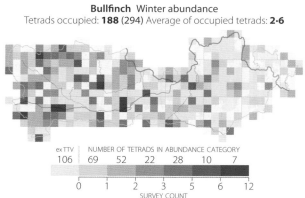

| | ex TTV | NUMBER OF TETRADS IN ABUNDANCE CATEGORY | | | | | |
|---|---|---|---|---|---|---|---|
| | 151 | 57 | 46 | 20 | 9 | 2 | 4 |

0  1  2  3  4  5  6
SURVEY COUNT

**Bullfinch** Winter abundance
Tetrads occupied: **188 (294)** Average of occupied tetrads: **2·6**

| | ex TTV | NUMBER OF TETRADS IN ABUNDANCE CATEGORY | | | | | |
|---|---|---|---|---|---|---|---|
| | 106 | 69 | 52 | 22 | 28 | 10 | 7 |

0  1  2  3  5  6  12
SURVEY COUNT

results of tetrad surveys carried out in 1988–92 and 2008–11 in Hertfordshire, with losses mostly in the centre and east of that county too.

The Bullfinch is a largely sedentary species and ringing studies in Berkshire have shown that the majority of birds recovered have been within 9 km from where they were ringed. The most distant recovery involved a bird ringed at Thatcham Marsh in April 1976 which was found on 17th June 1978 near Taunton, 126 km WSW. In winter, Bullfinches appear to remain close to the area where they bred, the Winter Map indicating a broadly similar distribution to that revealed by the Breeding TTV Survey. However, there is some evidence of passage movements with, for example, ten being caught and ringed at Wraysbury Gravel Pits in July 1986. There are also occasional influxes of continental (especially Scandinavian) birds into Britain in winter, often associated with larger scale irruptions. One such irruption in the winter of 1995/96 coincided with four counts of 10 or more in central and eastern Berkshire.

After the breeding season the species is often recorded in small, family parties of six or seven. The largest flocks reported since 1980 have been of 23 at a garden centre in Binfield in January 1993, and 30 at Wraysbury Gravel Pits in January 1992, although the highest count since 2000 has been just 18, at Upper Bucklebury on 18th February 2012. The highest number recorded in Berkshire was a flock of at least 64 which were seen sunning themselves on some thorns near Bradfield on 6th March 1932.

Bullfinches appear to have been common in Berkshire since at least the 19th century, accounts from the era reflecting its reputation as a pest of orchards. Noble (1906) suggests that it was increasing at the beginning of the 20th century and comments: "I have known 27 killed in three weeks (in a kitchen garden), the owner being oblivious of the fact that each ounce of shot poured into his fruit tree would do more damage than his victims." Palmer (1886) described it as "A jolly sight too common for buds."

*Sponsored by Peter Driver*

# Hawfinch

*Coccothraustes coccothraustes*

*Rare visitor, formerly uncommon local resident*

The Hawfinch used to be an uncommon local resident in Berkshire, but it has been lost to the county as a breeding species since the 1990s.

Both Clark Kennedy (1868) and Noble (1906) considered that there had been a marked increase in the size of the Hawfinch population in Berkshire during the 19th century. They recorded breeding from Windsor Forest, where it was "abundant", Cookham, Bradfield, Reading, Aldermaston, Bucklebury and Newbury, all sites which still held the species a century later. Since the 1970s, the species has disappeared from the county, being lost first from the west, then the centre and finally its remaining stronghold in Windsor Great Park.

During the 1987–89 Tetrad Survey, Hawfinches were located in 16 tetrads. Of the four confirmed breeding records, three were in the Windsor Great Park area and one was at Purley, and the eight tetrads in which breeding probably occurred were divided equally between west Berkshire and east Berkshire. None were confirmed to have bred in Berkshire in the 2007–11 Atlas Survey, though in 2009 up to four birds were present in the Combe area during March.

Hawfinches were always very local in the west of the county in summer, with breeding or summering birds being reported during the period from 1950 to 1994

only from Inkpen, Frilsham, Hermitage, Fence Wood, Newbury, Wash Common, Aldermaston Court and Upper Woolhampton. Records from at least three of these localities came from observers living in the immediate vicinity and ceased when the observers concerned departed. After 1980, Hawfinches were only reported in west Berkshire in summer from the Hermitage area, Upper Woolhampton and Shefford Woodlands.

In west Berkshire, outside the breeding season, Hawfinches occured much more widely and have

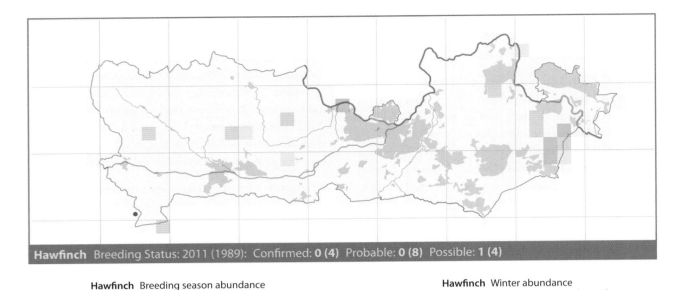

**Hawfinch** Breeding Status: 2011 (1989): Confirmed: **0 (4)** Probable: **0 (8)** Possible: **1 (4)**

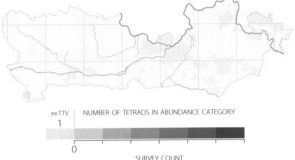

**Hawfinch** Breeding season abundance
Tetrads occupied: **0 (1)** Average of occupied tetrads: **0**

ex TTV | NUMBER OF TETRADS IN ABUNDANCE CATEGORY
1

0

SURVEY COUNT

**Hawfinch** Winter abundance
Tetrads occupied: **0 (6)** Average of occupied tetrads: **0**

ex TTV | NUMBER OF TETRADS IN ABUNDANCE CATEGORY
6

0

SURVEY COUNT

been reported from at least 16 different localities since 1950, although from far fewer areas since about 1970. Numbers were usually small, involving only one or two birds. The only large count was of a party of about 50 birds at Aldermaston Court in December 1960, a site from which records were not received for many years because of restricted access. The highest count since 1960 was of nine at Upper Woolhampton in July 1985.

In mid-Berkshire the number of places from which birds were recorded in winter remained fairly consistent until the early 1980s, after which the number of records fell. Records also used to be frequent from various parts of Reading. Leighton Park used to be a regular site for the species. There were reports in 1930 of noisy gatherings there in March and considerable numbers in June, a record of up to about 30 birds in 1949, and several reports of successful breeding up to 1966. There were then only scattered records until 1980 with none since. In 1971 records were received from Maiden Erleigh, Prospect Park, Whiteknights Park and Tilehurst, but in the 14 years from 1981 to 1994 records came only from Tilehurst in 1983 and Coley Park in 1987. Elsewhere in mid-Berkshire there used to be fairly frequent records from Bradfield, Upper Basildon and Pangbourne. In 1950 six nests were found close together in the grounds of the Pangbourne Nautical College. Records from these

areas ceased after 1982 except that summering birds were located at Burnt Hill and at Purley during the 1987–89 Tetrad Survey.

The east of the county, especially Windsor Great Park, was the last stronghold of the species in Berkshire. Because this area is largely inaccessible, however, there is little information on breeding numbers. There were several isolated records of successful breeding from Windsor Great Park and the adjacent area, including three during the 1987–89 Tetrad Survey. Two adults were feeding a young bird at Virginia Water on 16th May 1988.

In the Windsor Great Park area, in spite of some disturbance by birdwatchers, as many as 40 birds could still be seen in winter into the 1990s, and there were 52 in February 1994. Counts of more than 20 were reported from this site in 16 of the 45 years from 1950 to 1994. A flock of 95 at Cheapside in January 1974 is the highest number recorded together in Berkshire, although numbers approaching this may have been reached in other years when birds were dispersed more widely. In 1957, in addition to 50 birds in Windsor Great Park, there were a further 20 to 30 at a second site nearby. Elsewhere in east Berkshire, Hawfinches were reported quite widely in small numbers from a variety of sites, including gravel pits, although there are no recent summer records. The only large count was of 34 at Cockmarsh in January

1974. Away from the Windsor Great Park area, most of the records came from Remenham and the Maidenhead and Cookham areas.

The mid-1990s saw a sharp reduction in records with none after March in 1994, and no records in 1995, and none again in 1999, 2001 or 2004. The species is now an occasional winter visitor, with most records being of single birds from the east of the county, or the south-west. The species does however sometimes undertake irruptive movements, which probably explain three records in late 2005. Hawfinches were seen in only six tetrads in the winter during the 2007–11 Atlas survey, with most records in the south west of the county, where up to seven were present in January 2013.

Nationally, Hawfinches have been placed on the Red List of birds of conservation concern due to the decline in numbers. This has clearly been reflected in the loss of the species as a breeding and regular wintering species in Berkshire.

*Sponsored by Linda & Roger Dobbs*

# Snow Bunting

Amber  Sch. 1

*Plectrophenax nivalis*

*Scarce winter visitor*

The Snow Bunting is a scarce winter visitor to Berkshire, being recorded largely from open sites, especially gravel pits, reservoirs and the Downs, although this may be a reflection of observer coverage as well as habitat preference. The winter population of Snow Buntings in Britain is extremely variable, with high numbers occurring for a number of years, followed by a marked decline over a similar period (*1981–84 BTO Winter Atlas*).

The records in Berkshire this century have all been since 1957, when one was seen on the Downs near Aldworth on 20th October, which remained the earliest autumn arrival date until 1996. This was followed by a small influx in November 1959 when single birds were seen south of Lowbury Hill, at Ham Island and over Silwood. Snow Buntings were seen again in the winters of 1961/62 when in January there was one at Shaw and six flew over Ham Fields, and in 1962/63 when there were single birds at Lambourn in December and Shinfield in January. There was then a significant gap of nine winters with no records until single birds were seen in 1972, at Theale Gravel Pits in November and at Reading Sewage Farm in December. There was then a remarkable run of records in nine of the twelve winters from 1976/77 to 1987/78, involving just one bird in four of those winters, two birds in 1977/78, 1980/81, 1981/82 and 1984/85 and up to three birds in 1985/86. Records then ceased until one was seen at Walbury Hill in December 1991, and there was at least one at Queen Mother Reservoir, Datchet in November 1995. Since then all records apart from two have been from this latter site, with records in 1996, 1999, 2003, 2004, 2007, 2010, 2011 and 2012. All were of single birds, except two in November 2010 and 2011. The only other site with any accepted record in this period has been the area around Combe Gibbet and Inkpen Beacon, with two in November 2004 and one in December 2005, although at the time of publication

a record of one flying over Ascot Heath in November 2012 awaits consideration by the Berkshire Records Committee.

Figure 150 shows the monthly distribution of arrival dates of Snow Bunting from the winter of 1956/57 to 2012/13. The earliest was one at Queen Mother Reservoir on 17th November 1996. None of the records since 1990 have been of birds arriving after New Year.

The latest departing bird was a male in summer plumage at Theale Gravel Pits on 18th and 19th March 1981. The only birds reported to have remained for longer than two days were at Theale Gravel Pits from 27th October to 2nd November 1981, in the Slough Sewage Farm area from 11th February 1985 to 27th February, at Inkpen from 3rd to 28th December 2005, and a female or immature at Queen Mother Reservoir from 9th to

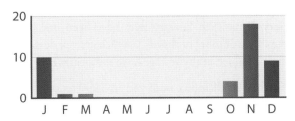

**Figure 150: Snow Bunting: all birds recorded 1956/57– 2012/13, by month of arrival.**

24th December 2011, although the two birds seen there on 6th November that year were also female or immature birds, so the stay may have been longer. Over-wintering occurred at Queen Mother Reservoir from November 1985 to February 1986 when, after a single female was seen on 6th November 1985, there were reports of one to two birds on many dates until 25th February 1986, with three being seen on 17th December and 11th February.

The Snow Buntings which have been seen in Berkshire have usually been solitary, but on a few occasions they have been seen associating with other species, including Skylarks, House Sparrows and a mixed finch flock.

Records of Snow Buntings in Berkshire prior to 1900 are few. Two were shot at Reading in January 1795 (Lamb, 1880), one is said to have been killed near Cookham before 1868 (Clark Kennedy, 1868), one is reported to have been shot in the Enborne area in the 1880s, and a male and a female were seen near Enborne Church during the winter of 1885 (Palmer, 1886).

*Sponsored by Mrs L J Taylor*

# Lapland Bunting
Amber  Sch. 1

*Calcarius lapponicus*

*Rare winter visitor and passage migrant*

The Lapland Bunting is a rare visitor to Berkshire from October to April. The first county record appears in an appendix to Noble's account of the birds of Berkshire (1906), and was of a party of four birds seen near Wellington College on 2nd February 1905, with a further bird, presumably one of the same party, seen in the same area on 26th February.

There were no further records until one was found dead at East Ilsley in early April 1967. A record of two with Corn and Reed Buntings in a mustard field on 22nd September 1963, which were reported to have been seen near Lambourn were in fact at Green Down, now in Oxfordshire, although the record does not appear in Brucker *et al.*, (1992).

The Lapland Bunting has a distinctive flight note and contact call and it is significant that the many records since 1967 have come from observers familiar with these calls. During a cold-weather movement on 1st January 1979, one was observed flying south-west with Skylarks at Summerleaze Gravel Pits, landing only briefly. A further bird was seen at Queen Mother Reservoir on 27th and 28th January that year. In 1984, two were found among Skylarks at Slough Sewage Farm on 11th October. There was then a small influx in 1987, also at Slough Sewage Farm, when an adult which was present on 13th January was joined by a second adult and a first-winter bird the next day. Two first-winter birds were present at this site on 17th January, and a bird at Queen Mother Reservoir on 19th January may have been one of this group. One or more of the birds which arrived during this influx remained at the sewage farm until early February.

A further small influx occurred in 1990 as part of the arrival into Britain in October of much larger numbers of Lapland Buntings than usual. A female or first-winter bird was seen in Windsor Great Park on 2nd October, and one, or possibly two, were heard calling over Holyport on 16th October. A further bird was heard calling as it flew south over Summerleaze Gravel Pits on 9th December. Queen Mother Reservoir has provided further records of single birds since, on 15th October 1993, from 2nd to 7th October 2002, 4th October 2003 and 19th October 2011, and one was nearby at Horton on 13th and 14th October 1998. Remenham has produced records of single birds from 20th to 22nd October 2007 and on 16th and 17th October 2010. There was another record from Slough Sewage Farm on 7th October 1998, and records of single birds from South Ascot on the late date of 4th April 1995, Eton Wick on 20th October 2002, Widbrook Common, Cookham on 6th October 2003, and Bury Down, West Ilsley on 21nd December 2007, the last being seen just over the Oxfordshire boundary into January 2008.

Of the 23 birds recorded since 1967, 14 have been on passage in October and eight have been reported in December or January. During this period there has been just one record from the Berkshire Downs, and it is possible that the species is under-recorded in that part of the county.

*Sponsored by Dick Haydon*

470

# Yellowhammer

*Emberiza citrinella*

Common resident

The Yellowhammer is a widespread resident of farmland throughout Berkshire. During the 1987–89 Tetrad Survey breeding evidence was recorded in 88% of the tetrads in the county. However the 2007–11 breeding map shows a marked decline in the number of tetrads with breeding evidence to 59%, with significant gaps in the range within the county in the southeast and east of the county. The highest concentrations remain in west Berkshire, where the species was found to be well distributed throughout open farmland. The species was absent from the larger towns and forested areas, although nesting was confirmed both near the centre of Windsor and from areas of predominantly coniferous woodland near Bracknell in 1987–89 but not in 2007–11. It was not recorded from parts of Windsor Forest or from the tetrads in east Berkshire which are dominated by Queen Mother Reservoir and Wraysbury Reservoir nor from the south-west of Wokingham in either survey, and it appears to have disappeared between 1987–89 and 2007–11 from the heathland areas with which the species had often been associated.

Yellowhammers are rather sedentary and seldom move far from their breeding areas, even in severe winters. Indeed, ringing studies have shown that 70% of adults winter less than 5 km from their breeding territory (*1981–84 BTO Winter Atlas*) and just two

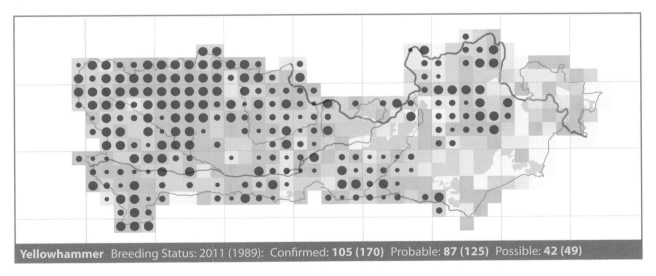

**Yellowhammer** Breeding Status: 2011 (1989): Confirmed: **105 (170)** Probable: **87 (125)** Possible: **42 (49)**

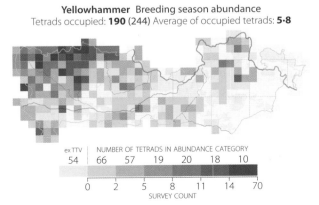

**Yellowhammer** Breeding season abundance
Tetrads occupied: **190 (244)** Average of occupied tetrads: **5·8**

| exTTV | NUMBER OF TETRADS IN ABUNDANCE CATEGORY | | | | | |
|---|---|---|---|---|---|---|
| 54 | 66 | 57 | 19 | 20 | 18 | 10 |

0   2   5   8   11   14   70
SURVEY COUNT

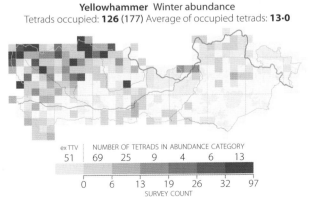

**Yellowhammer** Winter abundance
Tetrads occupied: **126 (177)** Average of occupied tetrads: **13·0**

| exTTV | NUMBER OF TETRADS IN ABUNDANCE CATEGORY | | | | | |
|---|---|---|---|---|---|---|
| 51 | 69 | 25 | 9 | 4 | 6 | 13 |

0   6   13   19   26   32   97
SURVEY COUNT

of the 12 ringing recoveries from Berkshire have been of movements beyond the county and neighbouring counties, involving movements to Warwickshire and Bedfordshire. Winter flocks numbering from 20 to 100 birds occur widely in Berkshire, especially on the Downs, in weedy areas around gravel pits and sewage-farms, in cereal fields which have been left uncultivated and in the vicinity of farmyards where poultry or cattle are being fed on grain. Often Yellowhammers are noted in mixed species flocks with finches or other buntings. As might be expected for such a sedentary species, the distribution shown by the Winter Map broadly matches the breeding distribution, although as with Corn Buntings, the range in winter is rather smaller than in the breeding season.

A decline in the population of Yellowhammer nationally was recorded in the 1950s and, although this is believed to have been mainly due to the use of organochlorines as seed dressing (*Population Trends*), it is possible that the species had started to decline prior to this period as it was evidently abundant in the latter part of the 19th century (*Historical Atlas*). In 1990, the Yellowhammer population was described as being subject to "long-term overall stability" despite general declines in most seed-eating birds (*Population Trends*), but there has been a marked fall in the population as monitored by national surveys, particularly between the late 1980s and the beginning of the 21st century, when the population in Britain appears to have declined by 50%. As a result, the species is now on the Red List of species of conservation concern. It appears therefore that the decline in Berkshire indicated by the contraction in its range reflects the national trend.

In the 19th century the Yellowhammer was reported by both Clark Kennedy (1868) and Noble (1906) as the commonest bunting and was clearly widespread and common.

*In Memory of Ian Bell*

# Cirl Bunting

`Red`　`Sch. 1`

*Emberiza cirlus*

*Former resident*

The Cirl Bunting was once a resident in Berkshire, but has not been recorded since 1981. Its disappearance from the county is consistent with the national pattern in which it has retreated from much of southern England and it is now confined to south Devon (*1988–91 BTO Atlas*).

Cirl Buntings do not appear ever to have been common in Berkshire. The earliest record is of a nest and an adult procured by the Rev F. O. Morris in the garden of East Garston vicarage in 1826 or 1827 (Clark Kennedy, 1868), only about 25 years after the species was added to the British List. Records from between about 1850 and 1950 show that the Cirl Bunting was fairly widely but thinly distributed in Berkshire, with reports coming from four areas. In the Newbury area the species was found nesting near Speen in 1884, where two were shot in 1885, at Aldermaston before 1900 (Noble, 1906) and a singing male was at Shaw in 1951. On the Downs, Cirl Buntings were reported from Aldworth before 1906 (Noble, 1906) and a nest with young was found at Streatley in 1943. In the Reading area, there were records from Tilehurst in 1934, a singing male at Reading in 1946, and an adult and a juvenile at Burghfield Gravel Pits in 1950. The fourth area, around Cookham and Maidenhead, produced most records and the species was said to have been observed most summers (Clark Kennedy, 1868), with two being killed near Maidenhead

in 1875 (Noble, 1906). A singing male was present by the Marlow to Maidenhead road in 1924, and one was reported from Maidenhead Golf Course in April 1950.

An increase in observer coverage from about 1950 showed that Cirl Buntings moved short distances into adjacent areas after the breeding season. There were records in the period from October to December in 1956 and 1958 from Slough, in 1961 from Hurley, and in 1969 from Burghfield Gravel Pits and Tilehurst. There were also records from a small number of other areas in the period from January to March. The only reports of more than one bird during the winter were of six at Burghfield in January 1962, three at Earley Sewage Farm in 1966, four males and two females at Warfield in October 1971, and four at Hurley in November 1974, the last occasion when more than one bird was seen in Berkshire.

Male Cirl Buntings are known to sing outside the breeding season and the presence of a singing bird does not necessarily indicate an occupied breeding territory. Singing males were reported from a wide range of sites during the 1960s and 1970s. The Downs above Streatley seem to have been a favoured area, with records in 1961, 1967, 1972, 1973 and 1974. Elsewhere, downland records were received from Compton in 1976, Upper Lambourn, where there was a pair in July 1963, Walbury Hill in 1973 and Inkpen Hill in September 1976. There were also records from the Kennet Valley, with birds being reported from Upper Woolhampton in 1968, 1969 and 1981, Aldermaston where there was a pair in April 1971, Theale in 1974 and Greenham Common in 1975 and 1976. In addition, there were records from Pangbourne in 1972, Cookham in 1969 and Crowthorne in 1972, where a bird was present for three weeks in February and March.

It is likely that Cirl Buntings bred successfully at Streatley during the 1950s and possibly the 1960s. The last confirmed breeding records in Berkshire were near Upper Woolhampton when a pair, which had been first seen on 11th April 1968, were subsequently seen carrying food on 1st June, and in 1971, when a family party was seen at Englefield. Although there were singing males at Greenham Common, Compton and Inkpen Hill in 1976, there was only one subsequent record, a singing male at Upper Woolhampton on 22nd March 1981.

*Sponsored by Raptormania in Andalucia April 2011*

# Ortolan Bunting

## *Emberiza hortulana*

*Rare vagrant, three records involving five birds*

The Ortolan Bunting is a rare vagrant to Berkshire. Although widely distributed across Europe, it is a scarce passage vagrant in Britain, with most records from the south-west of England or the Northern Isles (Brown & Grice, 2005). Witherby *et al.*, (1938) noted that in Britain this species occasionally occurs in small parties, which lends credibility to an early, second-hand record of three being shot near Cookham in the early 1860s (Clark Kennedy, 1868). The author had been informed of this record by the eminent Victorian naturalist Richard Bowdler Sharpe, with the accompanying statement that "these specimens were well identified but were unfortunately not preserved". Since then there have been two county records. The first was of one seen at Silwood Park, Sunninghill on 28th October 1958, the

second of a juvenile trapped and ringed at Wraysbury on 5th September 2007.

*Sponsored by Tim Alexander*

# Little Bunting

## *Emberiza pusilla*

*Rare vagrant, one record*

The only Berkshire record of this species, whose usual range stretches east from northern Finland to eastern Siberia, was a single bird at Datchet Common Gravel Pit from 18th to 31st January 1987. The bird was first heard calling as it flew over the observer who subsequently located it in bushes beside the gravel pit.

*Sponsored by Johanna Fewtrell, WSP Environment & Energy*

# Reed Bunting

## *Emberiza schoeniclus*

*Common resident and passage migrant*

The Reed Bunting is a common resident of waterside vegetation and damp areas throughout Berkshire, with some birds also occurring in arable areas.

The *1968–72 BTO Atlas* suggested that the Reed Bunting was widely and evenly distributed throughout Berkshire in the late 1960s and early 1970s. This would seem to be consistent with the well documented expansion of the species' range into drier habitats after the 1950s with, for example, birds increasingly being found nesting in young conifer plantations and hawthorn *Crataegus* spp. scrub on downland (1968–72 Atlas). However, the 1987–89 Tetrad Survey presented a very different picture. From 1975 to 1983 a steep decline in the national population was recorded (*Population Trends*), and the Tetrad Survey showed the species to be present in only about half the tetrads in the county. It was largely absent from the northern half of west Berkshire, the area above 200 metres in the south-west around Combe, the Burghfield/Beech Hill area south of Reading, and from the well-drained agricultural land south of the Thames and west of Maidenhead.

The 2007–11 Berkshire Atlas surveys do not indicate any overall improvement in the species' fortunes, with a comparable number of tetrads where breeding was confirmed (66 in 2007–11, 69 in 1987–89), but fewer where breeding was probable (only 42 in 2007–11, 75 in 1987–89). However the geographical distribution has changed, with an increase of use of tetrads on the Downs in north-west Berkshire and a loss from many of the lower farmland tetrads.

The population of Reed Buntings fluctuates in response to weather conditions. Numbers decline after severe winters, particularly when there is persistent snow cover which prevents the birds from feeding, and increase after a run of mild winters. The increase in the population in the mid-1950s, for example, followed a series of mild winters (*Population Trends*), whilst the decline and withdrawal from former favoured habitats, as demonstrated by the 1987–89 Tetrad Survey, may be due in part to the sequence of cold winters between 1978 and 1987. Since the 1980s, the British population has stabilized and even begun to increase again, partly attributed to the use of oilseed rape crops in the breeding season, a habitat used by the species in north west Berkshire. Studies have shown that densities in this crop can be up to four times higher than other breeding habitats (Gruar *et al.*, 2006). It is unclear why the Berkshire range has apparently contracted, although

the latter part of the 2007–11 Atlas survey coincided with years of low rainfall, possibly resulting in the drying out of some suitable habitat.

In favoured habitat alongside the River Kennet near Thatcham, a total of some 120 breeding pairs was estimated in 1984, and in the Theale and Burghfield Gravel Pits area the population was estimated to be 30–35 breeding pairs in 1996.

Flocks occur in the spring and autumn migration periods and in winter, and Reed Buntings sometimes occur in mixed finch and bunting flocks in winter. The pattern seems to vary from year to year, but flocks of about 50 are often reported out of the breeding season. The highest counts since 1980 include some 100 birds at Thatcham Marsh in November 1987, about 100 at Cookham Rise on 19th November 2005, and about 150 at Remenham on 11th December 2005. There is some evidence of immigration of Reed Buntings into Berkshire during the winter, including birds from the continent. One which had been ringed in Holland was trapped and released at Brimpton in November 1986. There have also been five movements of more than 100 km within Britain disclosed by ringing recoveries, a bird ringed in Newcastle-upon-Tyne, and two at Woolston Eyes in Cheshire, have been recovered in Berkshire, and birds ringed in Berkshire have been recovered in Nottinghamshire and at Dungeness in Kent. However, the British population is mainly resident and birds do not winter far from their breeding areas (*BWP IX*). There have been 100 recoveries of birds either ringed

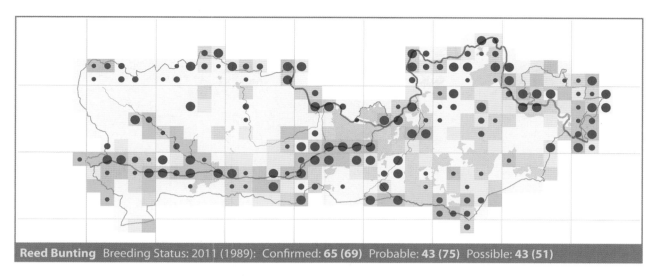

**Reed Bunting** Breeding Status: 2011 (1989): Confirmed: **65 (69)** Probable: **43 (75)** Possible: **43 (51)**

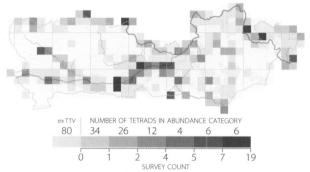

**Reed Bunting** Breeding season abundance
Tetrads occupied: **88 (168)** Average of occupied tetrads: **2·9**

| ex TTV | NUMBER OF TETRADS IN ABUNDANCE CATEGORY | | | | | |
|---|---|---|---|---|---|---|
| 80 | 34 | 26 | 12 | 4 | 6 | 6 |

0   1   2   4   5   7   19
SURVEY COUNT

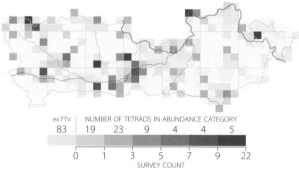

**Reed Bunting** Winter abundance
Tetrads occupied: **64 (147)** Average of occupied tetrads: **3·8**

| ex TTV | NUMBER OF TETRADS IN ABUNDANCE CATEGORY | | | | | |
|---|---|---|---|---|---|---|
| 83 | 19 | 23 | 9 | 4 | 4 | 5 |

0   1   3   5   7   9   22
SURVEY COUNT

or recovered ringed in Berkshire, 68 of which involved movements within the county.

It is not surprising, therefore, that the distribution of the species during the winter, as indicated by the winter map, is similar to the distribution revealed by the Tetrad Survey and breeding season abundance map.

Since the 1970s, Reed Buntings have taken to visiting feeding stations in various parts of Britain, including Berkshire, especially in hard winter weather. In the early 1980s, they were regular in gardens in the City Road and Park Lane area of Tilehurst and in Mortimer.

In the 19th century the Reed Bunting was common in wetland areas in Berkshire (Noble, 1906), but there is no reference to it occurring on higher ground in the county.

*Sponsored by Berks, Bucks and Oxford Wildlife Trust*

# Corn Bunting

*Emberiza calandra*

*Locally common but declining resident*

The Corn Bunting is a locally common resident in Berkshire, which has declined in numbers and contracted in range in recent years. It favours arable farming areas, especially on the chalk, where there are large fields and suitable song perches such as isolated bushes. During the late 1920s Corn Buntings were commonly found along the Ridgeway and at Aldworth, although records from other localities were sparse. In the 1940s Summers-Smith (1951) indicates that it was resident but very locally distributed, occurring on the more open Downs and in small numbers to the west of Aldermaston.

During the 1987–89 Tetrad Survey, Corn Buntings were recorded as confirmed or probably breeding in 99 of the tetrads in Berkshire, but were confirmed to have

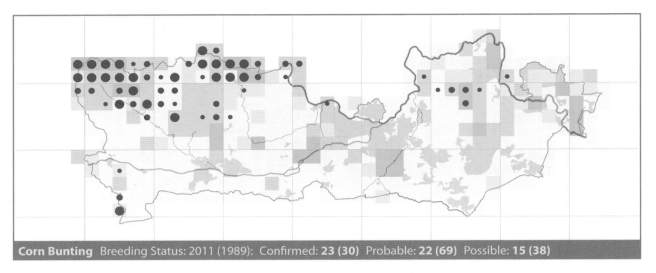

**Corn Bunting** Breeding Status: 2011 (1989): Confirmed: **23 (30)** Probable: **22 (69)** Possible: **15 (38)**

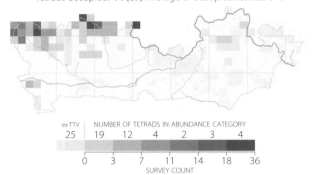

**Corn Bunting** Breeding season abundance
Tetrads occupied: **44 (69)** Average of occupied tetrads: **7·4**

| ex TTV | NUMBER OF TETRADS IN ABUNDANCE CATEGORY | | | | | |
|---|---|---|---|---|---|---|
| 25 | 19 | 12 | 4 | 2 | 3 | 4 |

| 0 | 3 | 7 | 11 | 14 | 18 | 36 |

SURVEY COUNT

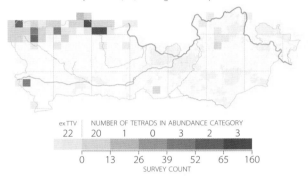

**Corn Bunting** Winter abundance
Tetrads occupied: **29 (51)** Average of occupied tetrads: **26·0**

| ex TTV | NUMBER OF TETRADS IN ABUNDANCE CATEGORY | | | | | |
|---|---|---|---|---|---|---|
| 22 | 20 | 1 | 0 | 3 | 2 | 3 |

| 0 | 13 | 26 | 39 | 52 | 65 | 160 |

SURVEY COUNT

bred in only 30 of these. In the 2007–11 survey, this had declined to 45 for both categories, but still 23 tetrads where breeding was confirmed. The stronghold for the species in the county remains the arable land in the north-west. Elsewhere there were no confirmed breeding records, and only two tetrads with probable breeding, both from the area west of Maidenhead from which records of a diminishing population have appeared in the county reports in the intervening years. During the period from 1992 to 1994 the species was still present in east Berkshire, with birds reported from at least nine sites, including Slough Sewage Farm, where there were four singing males, and Cold Harbour where there were five singing males. However, in 2008 there were reports from just four sites, with a maximum total of 11 singing males at all four together. A comparison between the *1968–72 BTO Atlas* and the Tetrad Surveys indicates that Corn Buntings have disappeared from extensive areas in the south, centre and east of Berkshire in the intervening years, in line with a steady decline nationally since the 1970s, and more markedly since 1981 (Stroud and Glue, 1991). The Breeding Season Abundance Map does indicate that good numbers still occur in the main downland breeding areas.

In winter, flocks of Corn Buntings still occur on the Downs with counts of between 50 and 150 usually received from at least one site, often as part of a larger mixed finch and bunting flock. The location of such flocks varies from year to year, but favoured sites include Bury Down near West Illsley, and the Compton and Lambourn Downs. There used to be other roosts, such as at Thatcham Marsh and, until 1991, Slough Sewage Farm, where 60–90 birds were often recorded and a maximum of 260+ was reported on 20th January 1979. Since 1991 there have only been up to eight birds at Slough Sewage Farm in the winters of 1992/93 and 1993/94, although at Cold Harbour, Binfield there was a flock of 60–70 in November 1993. In recent years however counts of more than ten have seldom been recorded away from the Downs, a record of about 40 at Remenham Hill on 18th October 2007 being the highest recent count. Since the species is rather sedentary it is not surprising that the distribution shown by the Winter Map is similar to the breeding distribution, although perhaps surprisingly the winter range seems even more confined to the highest areas along the northern county boundary.

In common with the majority of farmland birds, the Corn Bunting has suffered from changes in agricultural practice, chiefly the conversion from spring-sown to winter-sown cereals. The lack of stubble during the winter months has significantly reduced the availability of food, although the set-aside programme may well have had a short-term beneficial effect. O'Connor and Shrubb (1986) commented that the population of Corn Buntings nationally has a close correlation with the rise and fall of the acreage of barley cultivation.

Prior to the 20th century, the Corn Bunting was evidently much more widespread in Berkshire than it is today. Clark Kennedy (1868) referred to it as "a common resident and very generally dispersed", and Herbert (1871) and Palmer (1886) also referred to it as common. Hewett (1875) intimates that it was common all year in the Compton district, whilst Noble (1906) states that it was a common resident on the high ground, though seldom seen near the river.

*Sponsored by Berkshire Downs Ringing Group*

Corn Bunting, Bury Down *David Lowther*

# Category 'D' species and Escapes

The British List, compiled by the BOU, comprises three categories. Category A (species recorded in an apparently natural state since 1st January 1950), Category B (as Category A, for species recorded between 1800 and 1949 but not since) and Category C (introduced species which have established self-sustaining populations). Two other lists are maintained of species not accepted for the full British List, namely Category D (where there is doubt that any records are of birds occurring in a natural state) and Category E (introduced species which are thought not to have established a self-sustaining population; escapes; or birds considered to have occurred as a result of human-assisted transportation).

Category D is a holding category and is not intended to be a long-term assignment of any species. These species are reviewed regularly with a view to assign them to either A or E.

The records set out in this section almost certainly represent an incomplete list due to under-recording, but do indicate the number of 'unusual' birds that can be found from time to time. As the species are not included on the full British List, they are not included on the Berkshire List.

---

## Category D species

## White Pelican

*Pelecnnus oncrotnizis*

Two adult birds were seen from Wraysbury Reservoir in Surrey on 10th November 1972 departing in a southerly direction over Wraysbury Gravel Pits. This record has been accepted by BBRC but is included on Category 'D' of the British List on the grounds that there is reasonable doubt that they were truly wild birds.

Two were at Hosehill, Theale, reported by a local resident on 10th May 1998, and seen later the same day by at least three local birders. One was seen circling the lake, and briefly landing on both Main and Moatlands Pits, until 20:00 hrs. A single bird was also seen at Sulhamstead on the following day, and at Sonning cricket field. In addition, local residents in East Reading reported 'two White Storks' on 11th May 1998.

*Sponsored by Mark Poynter*

---

## Category E, Escapees

These are species recorded as introductions, human-assisted transportees or escapees from captivity, and whose breeding populations (if any) are thought not to be self-sustaining. Species in Category E that have bred in the wild in Britain are designated as E*.

Category E species form no part of the British List (unless already included within Categories A, B or C). Doubtful cases have generally been excluded, except where there is doubt as to the actual species, but the genus indicated a record of interest, or where there is reasonable certainty of identification. In some cases, where species are regularly present, are also genuinely wild species which occur in the county, or breeding has occurred, full species accounts have been prepared.

It has long been recognised that the recording of escapes and "introduced species" has been haphazard. There have been a number of calls for birdwatchers to record escapes as they have been often over-looked until there is a perceived need for action, such as in the case of the Ruddy Duck. It is perhaps indicative of the state of such records that a number of species recorded below are not on the list of species in category E currently (2013) published on the BOU website.

The following list contains details from the county reports of sightings of species which are believed to have escaped from captivity and which have been in a free flying state in Berkshire between 1974 and 2011, with some earlier records. The Nomenclature follows the latest (2011) BOU listing (http://www.bou.org.uk/british-list/category-e-species/). Where species are not listed by the BOU, they are marked by an asterisk (*), and names are taken from the BirdLife list (2013) (http://www.birdlife.org/datazone/info/taxonomy/). The taxonomic order in the BirdLife List is used. Note that this differs in some respects from the 2013 BOU list used for the main species accounts, for example, the gamebirds preceded (rather than follow) the wildfowl.

**Helmeted (?) Guineafowl** *Numida meleagris(?)* – raised as domestic fowl for food, records from White Waltham (four in 2007) and Beenham (two in 2010)

**Silver Pheasant** *Lophura nycthemera* – Cock between Catmore and West Ilsley, April 1991

**Reeve's Pheasant** *Syrmaticus reevesii* – Five records, Hungerford/Brimpton/Theale/Twyford 1984 to 2005.

**Golden Pheasant** *Chrysolophus pictus* – see species account page 168.

**Indian Peafowl** *Pavo cristatus* – commonly kept as a pet/collection bird. Two definite records (one dead, Dunford, 1988; one, Greenham Common 2011) and probably this species at Hungerford Common and Eversley Gravel Pits (both 2004).

**Black-bellied Whistling Duck\*** *Dendrocygna autumnalis* – Streatley, 2007 (2), 2008 (1) and 2013 (1).

**Black Swan** *Cygnus atratus* – see species account page 108.

**Black-necked Swan** *Cygnus melanocoryphus* – one, Hurley, 1983.

**Swan (Chinese) Goose** *Anser cygnoides* – both "wild" types and domestic variety ("Chinese") often kept in collections. Some 11 records from throughout county from 1997 to 2012, with records of two together at Newbury (1997), Datchet (2007), Hungerford (2011) and Padworth Lane Gravel Pit (2012), and three at Bracknell from 2002 to 2004.

**Lesser White-fronted Goose** *Anser erythropus* – records of individuals from Loddon/Blackwater Valley 1986 to 1990, and Kennet Valley, Theale to Lower Farm Gravel Pit, 1997 to 2005. One with colour ring, Eversley Gravel Pits, 2006.

**Bar-headed Goose** *Anser indicus* – see species account, page 116.

**Snow Goose** *Chen caerulescens* – see species account, page 116.

**Ross's Goose** *Chen rossii* – Records of single birds from 1997–99, 2002–07, 2011 and 2013, possibly involving five or six birds, mostly from Loddon and Kennet valleys and east of county.

**Emperor Goose** *Chen canagica* – records of singles from 1981, 1997, 2004, 2009 and 2010 from Dinton Pastures, Theale Gravel Pits, Lower Farm Gravel Pit, Windsor Great Park and Queen Mother Reservoir.

**Cackling Goose** *Branta hutchinsii* – singles in 1981, 1990, 1995 and 1996 from Thames at Henley, Eversley Gravel Pits, Burghfield Mill Gravel Pit at Theale and Bray Gravel Pits.

**Barnacle Goose** *Branta leucopsis* – see species account page 119.

**Red-Breasted Goose** *Branta ruficollis* – see species account page 121.

**Ruddy-headed Goose\*** *Chloephaga rubidiceps* – Two, Twyford Gravel Pits, 2003.

**Ruddy Shelduck** *Tadorna ferruginea* – see species account page 124.

**Australian Shelduck** *Tadorna tadornoides* – Pair, Slough Sewage Farm, 1998.

**Raja Shelduck** *Tadorna radjah* – One, Binfield, 1993.

**Muscovy Duck** *Cairina moschata* – common domestic fowl, records of one to four at various sites, 2000, 2003–05, 2008 and 2011.

**Ringed Teal** *Callonetta leucophyrus* – singles at various sites from Queen Mother Reservoir to Woolhampton Gravel Pits, 1984, 1997, 2000, 2007 and 2012.

**Wood Duck** *Aix sponsa* – see species account page 127.

**Maned Duck** *Chenonetta jubata* – one, Eversley Gravel Pits, 2009.

**Cape Teal** *Anas capensis* – singles at Streatley (1998) and East Ilsley (2001).

**Chiloe Wigeon** *Anas sibilatrix* – between one and three at various sites, principally gravel pits in the Kennet Valley, in 1987–88, 1992–93, 1997–98, 2000–01 and 2003.

**Laysan Duck\*** *Anas laysanensis* – one, Lower Farm Gravel Pit, 2006.

**Cinnamon Teal** *Anas cyanoptera* – six records, all singles except two drakes at Brimpton Gravel Pits (1991) from Eversley, Theale, Brimpton , Lower Farm and Wraysbury Gravel Pits and Fobney Water Meadows in 1990, 1991, 1993, 1994, 2000 and 2001.

**Red Shoveler** *Anas platalea* – singles at Bray Gravel Pits (1990) and Queen Mother Reservoir and Horton Gravel Pits (1997).

**Chestnut Teal** *Anas castanea* – female, Ruscombe , 2000.

**White-cheeked Pintail** *Anas bahamensis* – singles, Dinton Pastures (1998), Thatcham area (1996) and Slough Sewage Farm (2010); up to two at Twyford Gravel Pits (2003–04).

**Red-billed Teal** *Anas erythrorhyncha* – two, Reading Sewage Farm, 1976.

**Silver Teal** *Anas versicolor* – singles at Bullbrook (1990) and River Thames at Cliveden Reach (1997).

**Rosy-billed Pochard** *Netta peposaca* – two, Dinton Pastures, 1992; female, Summerleaze Gravel Pit , 2002 and a pair, Muddy Lane Gravel Pits, 2003.

**Ferruginous Duck** *Aythya nyroca* – see species account page 146.

**Greater Flamingo** *Phoenicopterus roseus* – an escape from Marwell Zoo, Hampshire at Lower Farm Gravel Pit and then Streatley, April/May 2011. Having last been seen at 21:00 on 10th May, the bird was seen at the RSPB Strumpshaw Fen Reserve, Norfolk, the following day. Also five birds only identified as "Flamingo species", various sites, 1975 to 1989.

**Chilean Flamingo** *Phoenicopterus chilensis* – singles at Theale Gravel Pits (1980–81) and Brimpton Gravel Pits (1989).

**Sacred Ibis** *Threskiornis aethiopicus* – introduced breeding population in France. Singles (the same bird?) from Hungerford area, Burghfield, Theale and Wraysbury Gravel Pits, (1982–83), and from Theale Gravel Pits, (1987) and Finchampstead, (1993).

**Pink-backed Pelican(?)** *Pelecanus rufescens,* one, Burghfield Gravel Pits in 1990 when there were several other reports from southern England.

**Northern Crested Caracara** *Cararara cheriway* – one, Donnington, 2011.

**Lanner Falcon** *Falco biarmicus* – kept as a falconry bird. Singles at Windsor Park (1998), Lea Farm Gravel Pit and Compton (2008), Sonning and Charvil (2009) and Queen Mother Reservoir (2010).

**Barbary Falcon** *Falco pelegrinoides* – kept as a falconry bird. Singles at Horton, Queen Mother Reservoir and Lower Earley, 2008.

**Goshawk** *Accipiter gentilis* – see species account *page 200*.

**Bald Eagle** *Haliaeetus leucocephalus* – one from Whipsnade Zoo recaptured at Brightwalton Common, 2010.

**Harris's Hawk** *Parabuteo unicinctus* – used by pest control industry for pigeon control. One Langley/Cippenham area, 2000. One present Streatley/Moulsford area, 2008–09, joined by second bird in March 2009. One at Cookham, 2011.

**Grey Crowned Crane** *Balearica pavonina* – one, Reading Sewage Farm, October 1976.

**Patagonian Conure** *Cyanoliseus patagonus* one, Summerleaze Gravel Pit, 1985–86.

**Barbary Dove** *Streptopelia roseogrisea 'risoria'* – domestic bird, singles at Tilehurst (1975) and Dinton Pastures (1993).

**Rainbow Lorikeet*** *Trichoglossus haematodus* – one or two at Cookham, 1991 to 1993.

**Lorikeet** sp. – one, Maidenhead Court, 2007.

**Sulphur-crested Cockatoo** *Cacatua galerita* – singles at Bradfield in 1980 and Maidenhead in 2009.

**Cockatiel** *Nymphicus hollandicus* – popular cagebird, widely reported, with 35 records from all parts of the county between 1975 and 2013, all of single birds.

**Eastern Rosella*** *Platycercus eximius* – one was reported from Sandhurst during January and February 2002.

**Budgerigar** *Melopsittacus undulatus* – perhaps under-recorded? Six records, 1993 to 2013, from various sites from Kintbury to Queen Mother Reservoir, three of these were in 1993 or 1994.

**Rosy-faced Lovebird** *Agapornis roseicollis* – one, Summerleaze Gravel Pits, 1990.

**Yellow-collared Lovebird*** *Agapornis personatus* – One at Woosehill, Wokingham, 2008.

**African Grey Parrot** *Psittacus erithacus* – one, Dorney Wetlands, 2013.

**Senegal Parrot** *Poicephalus senegalus* – one, Summerleaze Gravel Pits and Braywick Park, 1990–91.

**Burrowing Parrot** *Cyanoliseus patagonus* – one, Summerleaze Gravel Pits, 1985–86.

**Nanday Parakeet*** *Nandayus nenday* – two, Compton, 2000, and one possibly this species, Greenham Common, 2005. The County Report for 2000 noted that this species could be found living ferally in Windsor Great Park 20 years ago.

**Monk Parakeet** *Myiopsitta monachus* – one at Wraysbury Gravel Pits, 2008.

**Hartlaub's Turaco** *Tauraco hartlaubi* – one, Eversley Gravel Pits, 2005 (The British Turaco Society was once based in Berkshire).

**Red-billed Ground Cuckoo** (?)* *Neomorphus spucheranii* – one, possibly this species, Sandford, 1979.

**Eagle Owl** *Bubo bubo* – two, Langley/Cippenham area, 2000, escaped from captivity in Greenford, west London.

**Azure-winged Magpie** *Cyanopica cyana* – one, possibly from Paignton Zoo, Reading Motorway Services, 2006.

**Red-vented Bulbul** *Pycnonotus cafer* – one, Tilehurst, 1979.

**White-browed Laughing Thrush*** *Garrulax sannio* – one, Twyford and Woodley, 1999.

**Glossy Starling sp** *Lamprotornis sp* – two "East African Starlings", Tilehurst, 1974. were most likely to have been this genus.

**Chestnut-backed Thrush*** *Zoothera dohertyi* – one bearing an aviary-style ring, Wraysbury Gravel Pits, 2009.

**Oriental Magpie-robin*** *Copsychus saularis* – one, Datchet, 1990.

**White-capped Redstart** *Chaimarrornis leucocephalus* – one, Peasemore, 2000.

**Lesser Green Leafbird*** *Chloropsis cyanopogon* – one, Twyford, 2005.

**Black-headed Weaver** *Ploceus melanocephalus* – one, Mortimer, 1975.

**Northern Masked Weaver** (?) *Ploceus taeniopterus* – one, thought to be this species, Twyford, 1996.

**Orange-cheeked Waxbill** *Estrilda melpoda* – one, Warfield, 2001.

**Common Waxbill** *Estrilda astrild* – one, Wraysbury Gravel Pits, 1999.

**Zebra Finch** *Taeniopygia guttata* – commonly-kept cagebird. Singles at Bearwood (1974), Reading 1986), Maidenhead and Twyford (1997), Cold Ash (2000) and Cookham (2006).

**Java Sparrow*** *Padda oryzivora* – one was found dead in Reading, 1979.

**Trumpeter Finch** *Bucanetes githagineus* – one, Woodley, 1991, assumed by observer to be an escaped bird.

**Atlantic Canary** *Serinus canaria* – Singles at Woosehill, Wokingham and Langley, 2008.

**Red-winged Blackbird** *Agelaius phoeniceus* – one at Reading Sewage Farm, 1927 – possibly a vagrant rather than an escaped bird, seen in October or November, but the observer dismissed it as an escape from captivity.

**Cinnamon-breasted Rock Bunting*** *Emberiza tahapisi* – one, Crowthorne, 1986.

**Black-headed Bunting** *Emberiza melanocephala* – one, Kintbury, 1989.

**Red-headed Bunting** *Emberiza bruniceps* – singles at Reading and Maidenhead, both 1975.

# Summary of records of hybrids in Berkshire

## Introduction

This section summarises records of inter-specific hybrid birds published for Berkshire in recent years. Hybrids between races or subspecies of the same species are dealt with in the relevant species accounts (for example, Yellow Wagtail and Pied/White Wagtail).

Although hybrids in birds are more often viable than in other taxa, and hybrid males (but not females) can be fertile, in most cases hybrid birds do not persist. They may have conservation implications, for example when feral Ruddy Ducks, a North American species, started to interbreed with the threatened western European White-headed Duck. Most of the interest amongst birdwatchers arises from the potential identification problems they can cause.

In this summary, the attribution of parentage provided by observers is given, although caution is needed, as, except in the case of geese, the parents are rarely seen with young. Records of birds without attribution of both parents are not included. Records reviewed are up to 2011, but some later records have been included. The English vernacular names used are the same as used in the main species accounts above, or the section on escapes (*pages 478–480*). Please see these sections for the relevant scientific names.

## Wildfowl – general

Most records relate to wildfowl, particularly geese and diving ducks of the genus *Aythya*. Hybridisation is frequently associated with captive bred birds. Small garden or park collections of ornamental wildfowl often only have one or two examples of each species, leading to inter-specific mating, and ornamental geese escaping from captivity have a ready supply of potential mates from the large local population of geese derived from introduced birds.

The records do not include those relating to farmyard geese or ducks, both of which are derived from domesticated Mallard and Greylag Geese. The former comprise a wide variety of forms, of different colours, sizes and shapes, so care needs to be taken when considering "odd" dabbling ducks. Often hybridisation amongst geese involves farmyard-type Greylags, and in this summary all records involving either form are shown as Greylag.

## Geese

**Greylag hybrids** – Crosses between Greylag and **Canada Geese** are frequently encountered, with records in the County Reports almost every year.

There have been two reports of hybrid Greylag × **White-fronted Goose**, one around Moor Green Lakes from 1995 to 1999, and a mixed pair which bred at Great Meadow Pond, Windsor Great Park in 2006, with records up to 2010.

Greylag × **Bar-headed Geese** have been reported from Windsor Great Park. After one in 2004, a mixed pair raised two young in 2008, resulting in records from various east Berkshire sites persisting until early 2011.

Greylag × **Snow Geese** have been reported from Wargrave Marsh in 2007 and Bearwood Lake in 2008. A Greylag × **Emperor Goose** was at Horton Gravel Pits in December 2002, and a Greylag × **Barnacle Goose** reported from Windsor Great Park in January 2011.

**Canada hybrids** – in addition to Greylag hybrids, there have been records of hybridisation with three other species.

A mixed pair of a Canada and a **Barnacle Goose** bred on the Thames at Caversham in 2008 produced four goslings. Single birds were also reported from various sites, mostly in the Kennet valley, between 1997 and 2005.

Canada × **Bar-headed Goose** crosses were reported from Lower Farm and Summerleaze Gravel Pits in 2006, and a Canada × **Emperor Goose** was reported from Cockmarsh in 2003.

**Other goose hybrids** – **Snow × Barnacle Goose** hybrids have been reported from Eversley Gravel Pits in 2001, and a mixed pair with possibly three progeny from two broods was at Summerleaze Gravel Pits in 2007. A **Barnacle × Bar-headed Goose** was reported from Charvil in March 2010.

There are a number of birds apparently involving **Emperor Goose** hybrids. In addition to the **Canada** and **Greylag Goose** hybrids noted above, hybrids with **Bar-headed Goose** (the same bird?) were reported from various sites in the east of the county between 2007 and 2010, and a hybrid with **Snow Goose** was at Eversley Gravel Pits in 2006 and 2007.

## Diving Duck (*Aythya*)

Although there are no records of mixed pairs, observers have tended to group records of these hybrids according to appearance as set out in this summary, with assumptions made as to parentage. Some "second cross" (birds with one hybrid parent) reports appear, but these are likely simply to reflect the variability of hybrid forms. An examination of records over the years indicates that many records may actually refer to individuals present in an area for a considerable period.

**"Ferruginous" types** – these can cause problems with identifying true records of Ferruginous Duck. However hybrids are larger than the small pure-bred birds. Most are attributed to **Pochard × Ferruginous Ducks ("Paget's Pochard")**. Ducks (females) were present in the Kennet valley between February 2003 and December 2004, at Bray and Wraysbury Gravel Pits from 2003 to 2005, and at Woolhampton and Padworth Lane Gravel Pits in late 2009 and early 2010. A drake was at various east Berkshire sites from November 2006 to January 2011, and an unsexed bird on the Jubilee River for "some years" from 2006. There have also been occasional records elsewhere. A male **Tufted × Ferruginous Duck** ("Baer's Pochard") was first noted as a juvenile at Wraysbury Gravel Pits in 2007, and was seen there and at Bray Gravel Pits up to 2010. One at Old Slade and Wraysbury Gravel Pits in 2000 resembled a bird identified as a cross between a Ferruginous Duck and a Baer's Pochard at Chew Valley Reservoir, Somerset.

**"Lesser Scaup" types** – these are normally considered to be **Pochard × Tufted Duck** hybrids, and have been recorded every year since 1997 to 2010 except 2002. The resemblance to the rare North American vagrant, **Lesser Scaup,** may mean records of the latter have been overlooked. Most records are of single birds, and come from the gravel pits in the Kennet valley from Burghfield west to Woolhampton, or from Wraysbury, Horton and Bray Gravel Pits in the east, although there are a few from elsewhere. Observers sometimes become familiar with the characteristics of individuals, so that in 2008 it was reported that at least four different birds were present in the lower Kennet valley, comprising two different ducks and two different drakes.

**"Scaup" types** – these are normally attributed to crosses between **Scaup** and either **Pochard** or **Tufted Duck.** Notably, where these birds have been sexed, the drakes have been attributed to Tufted Duck crosses, and the ducks to Pochard crosses. Females were at Wraysbury in 1992, 2001 and various dates in 2006 and 2007, and one at Bray and Dorney late in 2008. Another was at Crowthorne, Eversley and Twyford in 1998 or 1999. One was at various Kennet valley sites between Moatlands Pit at Theale and Woolhampton between 2002 and 2007, and there was speculation that this may also have been the bird present in east Berkshire at this time. A drake was at various sites between Burghfield and Woolhampton Gravel Pits from 2008 to 2011, and one also at Wraysbury in 2008.

## Other duck hybrids

**Shelduck** (*Tadorna*) **hybrids** – for **Cape × Ruddy Shelduck** hybrids, see the Ruddy Shelduck species account. An **Egyptian Goose × Ruddy Shelduck** was reported from Dinton Pastures in July 2004.

**Mallard hybrids** – a hybrid with **Wigeon** was present between April and November 1999 at Dinton Pastures. A **Gadwall** hybrid, a drake, was present at Wraysbury Gravel Pits and Windsor Great Park from November 2002 to December 2007. A **Pochard** hybrid was at Hurst landfill site in 1999, and another at Woolhampton and Midgham in 2006 and 2007. One, identified as a hybrid with **American Black Duck** at Slough Sewage Farm, may have been a bird with domestic origins.

**Wigeon hybrids** – apart from the Mallard cross, there was a bird identified as a **Wigeon × American Wigeon** at Dinton Pastures from 1993 to 1996, and another at Summerleaze Gravel Pit in November 2006. One thought to be a **Wigeon × Gadwall** was at Orlitts Lake in the same month.

**Other duck hybrids** – a drake **Red-crested Pochard × Pochard** was at Wraysbury Gravel Pits at various dates between November 2006 and December 2011. A **Red-crested Pochard × Gadwall** was at Field Farm pit, Theale in 2000, and two **White-cheeked Pintail × Wood Duck** were at Whistley Mill, Twyford, in July 2001.

## Gamebirds

For **Chukar × Red-legged Partridge** ("Ogridges") – see the Chukar species account *page 161*.

Two birds in a mixed covey of **Partridge** and **Red-legged Partridge** at Pingewood Gravel Pit in December 2002 were thought to be hybrids.

## Raptors

Hybrids of **Peregrine** with **Lanner, Saker** or **Gyr Falcon** are sometimes bred to produce large falconer's birds, which might explain one with falconer's jesses at Queen Mother Reservoir in November 2003 and a "large Peregrine type" attacking a Cormorant at Lower Farm Gravel Pits in September 2011. A bird identified as a Lanner hybrid was at Greenham Common in 2002, and one as a Saker hybrid was present at various sites in the east of the county from April 2007 to December 2008.

## Gulls

**Mediterranean × Black-headed Gull** – For details of the two records, see the main Mediterranean Gull species account *page 289*.

**Large "*Larus*" Gull hybrids** – **Herring × Lesser Black-backed Gull** hybrids were reported from Smallmead Gravel Pit, Reading in 2006 and Queen Mother Reservoir in 2010. **Herring × Glaucous Gulls** occur widely in Iceland, which may be the source of a number of records, all in late winter or early spring between January and April. There was one at Maidenhead in 1978, different birds at Wraysbury Gravel Pits and Cockmarsh in 1985, singles at Queen Mother Reservoir in 2000 and 2001, two there in 2003, and one at Hurst Tip and Moatlands Gravel Pit, Theale in 2004. There have been other records which might also be hybrids of other large gulls, of which one identified as a **Herring × Caspian Gull** at Queen Mother Reservoir in August and September 2007 seems the most definite.

## Others

**Stock × Collared Dove** – a juvenile at Queen Mother Reservoir on 25th May 2005

**Carrion × Hooded Crow** – these occur widely in the extensive zones where the range of the two species overlap. One at Aldworth and Compton in June 2010 may originate from the nearest such zones in Scotland or Ireland.

**Goldfinch × Canary** – one at Wraysbury in April 2010 may originate from captive bred birds.

# Appendix I

## Participants in the 2007–11 Atlas Surveys

S. Abbott
G. Alder
M. Alexander
M. G. Allderidge
C. Allen
R. M. Alliss
K. Anckorn
K. Anderson
G. P. Anderson
R. Andrews
M. Andrews
B. Archer
R. Arnold
K. Ashbrook
H. Baker
J. Baker
T. Ball
D. E. Balmer
M. Bamber
P. S. Banks
D. Barker
J. Barker
S. R. J. Barker
P. Barrow
L. Bateman
W. H. Beglow
I. C. Bell
C. Bendickson
S. Bentall
N. W. Beswick
K. F. Betton
R. Billingsley
A. Binham
J. Birkett
J. Bishop
L. Bizley
A. Bluett
L. Blundell
D. Boddington
A. Bolton
M. Bonham
S. Boswell
B. Boyland
Y. Bramley
P. Bright-Thomas
M. Britnell
M. Brocklesby
C. Brooks
S. Brown
V. Brown
W. Brown
M. Bryant
N. J. Bucknell
P. A. Budd
P. Burden
G. Burfoot
J. Burnett
I. Burrus
D. Burt
N. J. Buxton
A. Camp
B. Carpenter
D. G. Carr
P. E. Castle
W. R. Chapman
S. Chatten
G. Cheetham
J. Chivers
R. Claridge

B. Clark
J. Clark
K. G. Clark
D. Cleal
B. D. Clews
M. Collard
M. Collings
S. Conyers
P. Cook
R. Cook
R. Coombes
I. Corbett
F. Cottington
P. Couch
H. Crabtree
B. Crathorne
R. Crawford
A. Cronin
P. Crowley
M. Crutch
T. Dalton
N. Daly
L. Daniells
P. Davies
S. Davies
C. Dee
J. Dellow
G. Dennis
B. Dennison
R. A. Denyer
N. J. Donnithorne
J. Downes
I. Downie
E. Drewitt
P. Driver
R. Dryden
C. du Feu
K. Duncan
E. Dunford
M. P. Dyer
J. Edwards
S. Edwards
E. J. Edwards
J. Elkin
I. Ellis
I. M. Elphick
S. Elstub
P. M. D. Etherington
H. Evans
J. Eyre
F. M. Farnsworth
S. J. Farnsworth
M. Fellowes
D. M. Ferguson
P. N. Field
M. Fielker
M. J. Finch
K. Fleming
J. Ford
N. Foster
O. Fox
R. J. Fox
R. Frankum
D. Free
D. V. Free
S. Freeman
E. Fricker
D. Fuller
V. Fullforth

C. Furley
D. Galloway
L. Garvey
J. Gates
C. Gent
I. Gerrard
S. Giddens
D. Gilby
S. Ginnaw
J. G. Gissing
D. R. Glover
R. J. Godden
C. Good
H. M. Goodship
P. Goriup
S. J. Gough
M. Gould
C. Gowing
S. A. Graham
M. Grantham
S. Greer
G. M. Gregory
M. Griffiths
R. Griffiths
R. Grimmond
R. D. Gross
P. Hadland
A. P. S. Hale
R. Hall
J. M. Halls
P. Hancocks
R. Hardy
R. P. Harley
R. Harper
I. Hartley
C. Haworth-Booth
R. Haydon
B. Haynes
A. Hayward
A. Hickman
P. Hickman
R. Hicks
T. Hodge
M. Holehouse
J. Holland
K. Holt
W. D. Hopkins
A. Horscroft
K. Horsepool
T. Hounsome
D. Housley
B. Howes
P. Hughes
C. Humphrey
D. J. Humphries
E. Hutchings
A. Hutchison
K. A. Imber
R. Ison
R. Jacobs
K. Jenks
G. John
K. Johns
B. Jones
B. Jones
C. Jones
C. Jones
D. S. Jones
N. Kaduck

M. Keates
M. M. Kettell
G. R. Kirk
G. Knass
A. Kydd
C. Lamsdell
M. J. Latham
A. Lawrence
A. Lawson
D. Lee
J. Legg
M. D. Lenney
R. J. Lerpiniere
S. Lewington
G. Lewis
G. H. Lewis
J. K. Lewis
R. Long
D. F. Long
K. J. Lovett
I. Loyd
G. Lucraft
K. Lugg
J. Lunn
B. Macdonald
M. Macgregor
L. Mann
S. Mansfield
N. Manthorpe
R. Marchant
R. Marsh
P. Marston
J. P. Martin
C. Mason
K. May
S. May
J. McCaig
D. McEwan
E. K. McMahon
G. Megson
J. Melling
D. Mellor
D. Melville
J. H. Mercer
M. Merritt
A. Meurer
G. Michelmore
M. Milan
J. Mitchell
P. Montgomery
D. Montier
A. Moore
K. E. Moore
R. Morris
R. Murfitt
A. J. Murray
H. R. Netley
P. Newbound
G. Newport
W. A. Nicoll
G. Noble
T. Norton
P. Ogden
D. Orr-Ewing
G. Osborne
M. Painter
J. Palmer
R. B. Palmer
K. Panchen

A. Parfitt
N. Parish
A. Parkes
A. Payne
K. Pearce
R. Pearson
L. Pemble
J. Peters
N. J. Phillips
B. Philpott
I. Pilling
L. Pitt
M. Pitt
P. Potts
S. Poulston
G. Pratt
I. Prentice
J. S. Pritchard
R. Pyrah
W. Quantrill
A. Quinn
M. Rafter
I. Ralphs
R. Reedman
D. J. Reynolds
M. J. Ridley
R. Righelato
D. Rimes
P. Roberts
M. Robertson
C. Robinson
P. Robinson
R. Robinson
S. Roddis
T. Rogers
D. Rogerson
J. E. Rose
J. Rosser
G. J. S. Rowland
P. Rowse
C. Ryall
K. Rylands
A. Rymer
J. R. Samuel
S. P. Satterthwaite
I. Saunders
G. Scholey
D. Scott
E. Scott
P. G. Scudamore
B. Sealy
P. Seligman
M. R. W. Sell
B. Sharkey
N. Sharkey
P. R. Shepley
M. Shurmer
A. Slater
M. Smith
M. Smith
N. Smith
S. Smith
W. Smith
R. G. Smith
W. L. Smith
S. Smithee
M. Spencer
B. Stacey
G. Stacey

R. Stansfield
L. Staves
P. J. Stevens
G. Stewart
A. Stow
P. Strangeman
P. Stronach
G. Studd
M. Sullivan
D. J. Sussex
J. L. Swallow
A. Sweetland
S. Szary
A. Taylor
M. J. Taylor
T. Taylor
A. J. Taylor
G. Tedbury

K. Thomas
S. Thomson
S. Thomson
I. Tomankova
A. B. Tomczynski
I. Traynor
K. Tucker
S. Tucker
K. Tucker
D. H. Tulley
M. Turton
C. Tyas
G. Uney
M. Vokes
M. Walford
B. J. Walker
M. J. Wall
P. Walley

J. J. Walling
J. Wardell
K. Warden
J. Warren
R. Warren
M. Watson
P. Watson
R. Watson
I. L. G. Weston
E. Whalley
D. Wheeler
M. Whitaker
K. White
S. White
J. Wilding
M. Wildish
C. Wilkinson
C. Wilks

J. Williams
P. Williams
R. Williams
C. S. Williamson
R. Willows
K. Wills
C. R. Wilson
G. E. Wilson

J. Wilson
J. M. Winyard
D. Withrington
T. J. Wood
I. Woodward
I. Woolsey
N. M. Wright

Berkshire Ornithological Club
British Trust for Ornithology
Buckinghamshire Bird Club
Game & Wildlife Conservation Trust
Hampshire Ornithological Society
London Bird Club
Newbury District Ornithological Club
Oxford Ornithological Society

## Participants in the 1987–89 Atlas Surveys

B. K. Abbott
S. Abbott
S. P. Adam
V. J. Adam
Y. Adams
B. R. Allen
P. Andrew
E. M. Angelo
P. Arthur
S. Ball
C. Barnes
E. G. Beard
I. C. Bell
B. Bennett
T. Billington
C. R. Bishop
J. C. Booth
S. Bowden
P Bowler
R. Bowles
Bracknell. D. C. Rangers
A. H. Brampton
N. Brine
C. N. Brown
M. Brown
T. Brownlie
J. Brucker
J. C. Buchanan
S. R. Buchanan
N. J. Bucknell
B. Budd
R. A. Budd
J. Bunce
J. Bundy
S. F. Burch
L. H. Cady
E. Cane
F. R. Cannings
D. Carter
R. Castle
P. Chandler
D. Cherry
B. A. J. Clark
J. M. V. Clark
M. Clarke
N. Cleere
B. D. Clews
C. B. Cole
I. D. Collins
W. J. Cook
B. Cooper

R. Cooper
D. L. Copas
J. Cordingley
D. Cowlrick
R. S. Cowlrick
P. Cox
B. Crockford
R. Crockford
M. G. Culley
T. J. Culley
R. Curtis
J. Dalgleish
N. A. Dalton
M. Daniel
C. Davis
S. Day
J. B. Dellow
A. M. Dew
H. Ennion
F. M. Farnsworth
S. J. Farnsworth
J. Field
O. Field
L. J. Finch
B. Finnigan
T. M. Finnigan
J. Fletcher
J. H. Flint
R. Flood
C. H. Flower
A. Forbes
D. Foskett
I. Francis
M. Fry
J. Gearing
C. Gent
M. Gibson
P. Gipson
A. Gladstone
L. J. Goatley
E. A. Godden
R. J. Godden
G. Goldsmith
H. M. Goodship
J. Gould
C. Gray
E. Green
P. N. Grove
M. E. Harper
T. Harris
M. Harrison

M. Hart
J. Hartnell
J. Hazzard
K. Herber
R. Hirons
J. Hobson
D. Holloway
G. J. Holloway
J. Hopkins
R. J. Hornby
J. A. Horsfall
J. Howard
M. T. Howarth
Sir H. Hudson
H. Hughes
D. H. Humphries
E. Hyams
K. P. Irish
G. James
John O'Gaunt School
P. Johns
D. Jowett
K. Jowett
P. Jowett
R. Kehyaian
D. Kerrell
J. King
P. King
G. B. Langley
R. Laugher
S. M. Lawrence
J. Legg
R. M. Lemcke
L. R. Lewis
S. Lock
D. Long
R. A. Lyle
P. D. Mann
P. Martin
D. Massie
N. Massie
L. M. Matthews
A. S. Melville
P. Meredith
A. N. Meyer
R. H. A. Mills
T. Newman
W. A. Nicoll
J. Nickson
K. J. Norledge
M. North

J. Norton
E. Norvell
T. G. Osmond
E. Padmore
F. Palmer
D. Parker
B. Parsons
I. M. Phillips
J. Pomroy
P. Pool
I. Powell
K. Pritchard
P. Puckering
A. K. Puffett
B. Ratcliffe
E. Reeves
J. H. K. Reeves
D. Reid
D. J. Reynolds
J. Roberts
C. Robinson
The late Lord Rootes
J. Rowland
R. Rowland
Runnymede Ringing
  Group
M. A. Sales
P. Schofield
J. Sears
M. R. W. Sell
J. Sharp
G. N. Shaw
D. Shephard
J. R. Simmons
J. A. Simpson
D. Sinclair
T. J. Skeates
A. Smith
C. Smith
E. M. Smith
L. Smith
R. G. Smith
D. K. Sparrow
M. Stabler
M. Stacey
P. E. Standley
W. Stanford
J. R. Stevens
P. Stevens
T. A. Stevenson
A. Stewart

G. J. Stewart
R. Still
J. R. Stockbridge
R. Stockhausen
J. Stollery
G. L. Stuart
G. Sumner
M. Sutton
A. R. H. Swash
G. D. Swash
A. Symonowicz
M. J. Taylor
R. Taylor
A. J. Thomas
J. W. Thomas
L. W. Thomas
T. Thompson
D. Thorley
P. Thumwood
A. Todd
I. Todd
The late M. W. Tucker
B. Uttley
J. J. Walling
T. Warnes
B. L. Wastie
P. R. Watkins
E. A. Watson
E. V. Watson
J. L. Watson
G. Webb
F. J. Webbing
J. M. Webbing
C. Weeks
I. L. G. Weston
C. W. Westwood
R. Wheeler
D. J. White
P. J. White
A. Whitehead
J. Whitlock
M. A. Wilkins
B. Williams
A. E. Wills
C. R. Wilson
G. E. Wilson.
R. D. Wilson

# Appendix II

## Site Gazetteer

This gazetteer gives four-figure Ordnance Survey grid references for each place in or adjacent to Berkshire which is mentioned in the text of this book or recent County Reports. The grid reference given for larger towns or sites is for the centre of the area concerned and is indicated with a '(C)'. Places or sites in adjoining counties near the county boundary are shown with the county name in brackets. Alternative names for sites, or the suffix '-on-Thames', which are sometimes used are given in brackets. It should be borne in mind that some sites, particularly those referred to in earlier records, such as substantial country houses or private estates, no longer exist and are not found on contemporary maps. For larger, regularly-visited sites, additional information is provided on section names, such as lakes or gravel pits. The inclusion of sites in this gazetteer does not necessarily imply that they are accessible to the public. A map of Berkshire appears in this Gazetteer and shows the Ordnance Survey 10 km National Grid lines to assist in locating the places listed.

Regional sections – West Berkshire – west of SU60. Central Berkshire – SU60 to SU80. East Berkshire – east of SU80.

| A | |
|---|---|
| Aldermaston | SU 5965 |
| Aldermaston Gravel Pits | SU 5966 |
| Aldermaston Park (Aldermaston Court) | SU 5964 |
| Aldermaston Soke | SU 6163 |
| Aldworth | SU 5579 |
| Arborfield | SU 7567 |
| Ascot | SU 9268 |
| Ascot Heath | SU 9269 |
| Ashampstead | SU 5676 |
| Ashampstead Common | SU 5875 |
| Ashmansworth (Hants) | SU 4157 |
| Ashley Hill | SU 8281 |
| Aston | SU 7884 |
| Aston Upthorpe Downs (Oxon) | SU 5483 |
| Avington | SU 3768 |

| B | |
|---|---|
| Bagnor (Cress Beds) | SU 4569 |
| Ball Hill (Hants) | SU 4263 |
| Barkham | SU 7867 |
| Basildon (House) | SU 6178 |
| Baynes Wood (Baynes Reserve) | SU 5165 |
| Bearwood (Lake) | SU 7768 |
| Beech Hill | SU 6964 |
| Beedon | SU 4877 |
| Beenham | SU 5868 |
| Beenham Gravel Pit (Marley Tiles Gravel Pit) | SU 6068 |
| Benham Park | SU 4367 |
| Bill Hill | SU 8071 |
| Billingbear | SU 8472 |
| Binfield | SU 8471 |
| Binfield Manor | SU 8571 |
| Bisham | SU 8485 |
| Bisham Woods | SU 8584 |
| Black Swan Lake (Dinton Pastures) | SU 7872 |
| Blacknest Gate | SU 9568 |
| Blackwater River (from Swallowfield to Blackwater) | SU 7265 to SU 8559 |
| Borough Marsh, Wargrave | SU 7777 |
| Bothampstead | SU 5076 |
| Bottom Lane GP | SU 6469 |
| Boulters Lock | SU 9082 |

| Bourne End (Bucks) | SU 8987 |
|---|---|
| Boveney (Bucks) | SU 9377 |
| Bowsey Hill | SU 8080 |
| Boxford | SU 4271 |
| Bracknell | SU 8769(C) |
| Bradfield | SU 6072 |
| Bramshill Forest (Hants) | SU 7562 |
| Bray | SU 9079 |
| Brayfield Farm | SU 9177 |
| Bray Gravel Pits | SU 9178 |
| Bray Wick | SU 8979 |
| Brightwalton | SU 4279 |
| Brimpton | SU 5564 |
| Brimpton Common | SU 5763 |
| Brimpton Gravel Pits | SU 5665 |
| Broadmoor | SU 8563 |
| Broadmoor Bottom | SU 8562 |
| Bucklebury | SU 5568 |
| Bucklebury Common | SU 5569 |
| Bucklebury Ford | SU 5471 |
| Bullbrook | SU 8869 |
| Bulmershe (Lake) | SU 7572 |
| Burchett's Green | SU 8481 |
| Burghfield | SU 6668 |
| Burghfield Common | SU 6566 |
| Burghfield Gravel Pits | SU 6870 |
| Hotel Gravel Pit | SU 6870 |
| Kirton's Farm Gravel Pit | SU 6870 |
| Knights Farm Gravel Pit | SU 6870 |
| Searles Farm Gravel Pit | SU 6870 |
| Burghfield Mill Gravel Pit | SU 6770 |
| Burnham (Bucks) | SU 9282 |
| Burnt Hill | SU 5774 |
| Burnthouse Lane Gravel Pits | SU 6868 |
| Bury Down (Ridgeway) | SU 4884 |

| C | |
|---|---|
| Calcot (Calcot Row) | SU 6671 |
| California Country Park | SU 7865 |
| Caesar's Camp (Swinley Forest) | SU 8665 |
| Car Park Lake (Moatlands Gravel Pits) | SU 6770 |
| Catmore | SU 4580 |
| Caversham | SU 7175(C) |

| | |
|---|---|
| Caversham Lakes/Henley Road Gravel Pits (Oxon) | SU 7374 |
| Chaddleworth | SU 4177 |
| Chamberhouse Marsh | SU 5266 |
| Chapel Row | SU 5769 |
| Charvil | SU 7776 |
| Chavey Down | SU 8969 |
| Cheapside | SU 9369 |
| Chieveley | SU 4774 |
| Child-Beale Wildlife Park | SU 6178 |
| Churn (Oxon) | SU 5183 |
| Cippenham | SU 9480 |
| Clayfield Copse, Caversham | SU 7277 |
| Clewer | SU 9577 |
| Clewer Point | SU 9577 |
| Cliveden (Bucks) | SU 9185 |
| Cliveden Reach (Cookham) | SU 9084 |
| Cockpole Green | SU 7981 |
| Cockmarsh | SU 8886 |
| Cold Ash | SU 6169 |
| Cold Harbour | SU 8378 |
| Colebrook Lake (Moor Green) | SU 8062 |
| Coley Park | SU 7072 |
| Colne Mere (Wraysbury) | TQ 0173 |
| Colnbrook | TQ 0277 |
| Colthrop | SU 5366 |
| Combe | SU 3760 |
| Combe Gibbet | SU 3662 |
| Combe Hill | SU 3860 |
| Combe Wood | SU 3559 |
| Compton | SU 5279 |
| Compton Downs | SU 5182 |
| Cookham | SU 8985 |
| Cookham Dean | SU 8684 |
| Cookham Rise | SU 8885 |
| Cow Down (Ridgeway) | SU 4784 |
| Cox Green | SU 8679 |
| Cranbourne | SU 9272 |
| Cranemoor Lake (Englefield) | SU 6271 |
| Cranswell Lake (Woolhampton Gravel Pits) | SU 5666 |
| Crookham | SU 5464 |
| Crookham Common | SU 5264 |
| Crowthorne | SU 8364 |
| Culham Court | SU 7883 |
| Curridge | SU 4871 |

| **D** | |
|---|---|
| Datchet | SU 9877 |
| Datchet Common Gravel Pits | SU 9976 |
| Datchet Reservoir (Queen Mother Reservoir) | TQ 0076 |
| Dedworth | SU 9376 |
| Denford | SU 3669 |
| Denford Mill | SU 3568 |
| Dinton Pastures Country Park | SU 7872 |
| Black Swan Lake | SU 7872 |
| Sandford Lake | SU 7872 |
| White Swan Lake | SU 7872 |
| Discovery Centre (Thatcham) | SU 5066 |
| Ditton Park | SU 9978 |
| Donnington | SU 4668 |
| Donnington Grove | SU 4568 |
| Dorney (Bucks) | SU 9279 |

| | |
|---|---|
| Dorney Wetlands (Jubilee River) | SU 9379 |
| Dunford | SU 8471 |

| **E** | |
|---|---|
| Earley | SU 7571 |
| Eastbury | SU 3477 |
| East Garston | SU 3676 |
| Easthampstead | SU 8667 |
| Easthampstead Park (Bracknell) | SU 8467 |
| East Hendred Down | SU 4685 |
| East Ilsley | SU 4981 |
| Easton | SU 4172 |
| Eastwick | SU 3960 |
| Edgebarrow Heath (Wildmoor Heath) | SU 8462 |
| Elephant Lake(Wigmore Lane) | SU 6370 |
| Emmbrook | SU 7969 |
| Emmer Green | SU 7276 |
| Enborne | SU 4365 |
| Englefield | SU 6271 |
| Englemere Pond | SU 9068 |
| Erleigh | SU 7471 |
| Eton | SU 9677 |
| Eton Wick | SU 9478 |
| Eversley (Hants) | SU 7861 |
| Eversley Gravel Pits/Moor Green Lakes | SU 8062 |
| Colebrook Lake | SU 8062 |
| Grove Lake | SU 8162 |
| Horseshoe Lake | SU 8162 |
| New Workings | SU 8062 |

| **F** | |
|---|---|
| Fairmile (The Fair Mile: Oxon) | SU 5482(C) |
| Farley Hill | SU 7564 |
| Farnborough | SU 4381 |
| Farnborough Down | SU 4181 |
| Fawley | SU 3981 |
| Fence Wood | SU 5171 |
| Field Farm Gravel Pit (infill site) | SU 6770 |
| Fifield | SU 9076 |
| Finchampstead | SU 7963 |
| Finchampstead Ridges | SU 8063 |
| Fobney Island Nature Reserve | SU 7070 |
| Fobney Lock | SU 7071 |
| Foliejon Park | SU 9074 |
| Formosa | SU 9085 |
| Fox and Hounds Gravel Pit (Hosehill Lake Nature Reserve) | SU 6569 |
| Freemens Marsh | SU 3268 |
| Frilsham | SU 5473 |
| Frogmill | SU 8183 |
| Frogmore (Hants) | SU 8360 |
| Frogmore House | SU 9776 |

| **G** | |
|---|---|
| Goring (-on-Thames: Oxon) | SU 6081 |
| Grazeley | SU 6966 |
| Great Hollands | SU 8567 |
| Great Meadow Pond | SU 9670 |
| Great Shefford | SU 3875 |
| Green Down (Oxon) | SU 3484 |
| Green Park | SU 7070 |

| | |
|---|---|
| Greenham | SU 4865 |
| Greenham Common | SU 5064(C) |
| Greenlands (Bucks) | SU 7785 |
| Grove Lake (Moor Green) | SU 8162 |

| H | |
|---|---|
| Halfway | SU 4068 |
| Hall Place | SU 8381 |
| Ham (Ham Island) | SU 9975 |
| Ham (Island) Sewage Farm | SU 9975 |
| Ham Spray (Wilts) | SU 3463 |
| Hambridge Lake | SU 4867 |
| Hamstead Marshall | SU 4165 |
| Hampstead Norreys (Hampstead Norris) | SU 5276 |
| Hampstead Park | SU 4266 |
| Hare Hatch | SU 8077 |
| Harman's Water | SU 8868 |
| Hartshill Gravel Pit | SU 5368 |
| Hawards Lake (Wigmore Lane) | SU 6370 |
| Hawthorn Hill | SU 8774 |
| Hay Mill Pond | SU 9481 |
| Hennerton | SU 7880 |
| Henley Road Gravel Pits/Caversham Lakes (Oxon) | SU 7374 |
| Heron Lake (Wraysbury) | TQ 0273 |
| Herschel Park Nature Reserve | SU 9779 |
| Hermitage | SU 5073 |
| Highclere (Hants) | SU 4360 |
| Highstanding Hill | SU 9374 |
| Hillgreen | SU 4576 |
| Hobby Lake (Wigmore Lane) | SU 6370 |
| Holyport | SU 8977 |
| Holyport Gravel Pits (now filled in) | SU 9077 |
| Horseshoe Lake (Moor Green) | SU 8162 |
| Horseshoe Lake (Wigmore Lane) | SU 6370 |
| Horton | TQ 0175 |
| Horton Fields | TQ 0176 |
| Horton Gravel Pits | TQ 0175 |
| Hosehill Lake Nature Reserve (Fox and Hounds Gravel Pit) | SU 6569 |
| Hotel Lake (Burghfield Gravel Pits) | SU 6969 |
| Hungerford | SU 3368 |
| Hungerford Common | SU 3467 |
| Hungerford Marsh | SU 3368 |
| Hungerford Newtown | SU 3571 |
| Hurley | SU 8283 |
| Hurst | SU 7973 |
| Hurst Green Lake (Twyford) | SU 7874 |
| Hythe End | TQ 0272 |
| Hythe Lake (Wraysbury) | TQ 0173 |

| I | |
|---|---|
| Ilsley (see East Ilsley, West Ilsley) | |
| Inkpen | SU 3764 |
| Inkpen Beacon (Inkpen Hill) | SU 3561 |
| Inkpen Common | SU 3863 |

| J | |
|---|---|
| Jealott's Hill | SU 8673 |
| Jubilee River | SU 9379(C) |
| – Cookham to Dorney (Bucks) | SU 9082 to SU 9279 |
| – Lake End Road to Datchet (Berks) | SU 9379 to SU 9778 |
| – Dorney Wetlands (Berks) | SU 9379 |

| K | |
|---|---|
| Kiln Green | SU 8178 |
| Kintbury | SU 3866 |
| Kirton's Farm Lake (Burghfield Gravel Pits) | SU 6869 |
| Knights Farm Lake (Burghfield Gravel Pits) | SU 6869 |
| Knowl Hill | SU 8279 |

| L | |
|---|---|
| Lambourn | SU 3278 |
| Lambourn Downs | SU 3481(C) |
| Lambourn Woodlands | SU 3275 |
| Langley | TQ 0079 |
| Lavell's Lake | SU 7872 |
| Lea Farm, Lavell's | SU 7873 |
| Leckhampstead | SU 4376 |
| Leighton Park (School) | SU 7371 |
| Lilley | SU 4479 |
| Littlecote (Wilts) | SU 3070 |
| Littlewick Green | SU 8480 |
| Loddon Reserve (BBOWT) Twyford | SU 7875 |
| Lowbury Hill | SU 5482 |
| Lower Basildon | SU 6179 |
| Lower Chance Farm (Oxon) | SU 5282 |
| Lower Common | SU 5569 |
| Lower Denford | SU 3568 |
| Lower Earley | SU 7571(C) |
| Lower Farm Gravel Pits (Newbury) | SU 4966 |
| Lower Farm Gravel Pit (with hide) | SU 4966 |
| Lower Farm Trout Lake/Racecourse GP | SU 5066 |
| Lower Green | SU 3564 |
| Lower Whitley | SU 7169 |

| M | |
|---|---|
| Maiden Erleigh | SU 7471 |
| Maidenhead | SU 8881(C) |
| Maidenhead Thicket | SU 8580 |
| Maiden's Green | SU 8972 |
| Magna Carta Island | SU 9973 |
| Main Lake (Moatlands Gravel Pits) | SU 6670 |
| Manor Farm Sewage Farm (Reading Sewage Farm) | SU 7070 |
| Mapledurham (Oxon) | SU 6776 |
| Marlow (Bucks) | SU 8586(C) |
| Marsh Benham | SU 4267 |
| Medmenham (Bucks) | SU 8084 |
| Midgham | SU 5567 |
| Mill Pond, Bracknell | SU 8568 |
| Moatlands Gravel Pit | SU 6670 |
| Monkey Island | SU 9178 |
| Mortimer | SU 6564 |
| Mortimer Common | SU 6465 |
| Moor Copse | SU 6374 |
| Moors Farm Gravel Pit (Pingewood Gravel Pits) | SU 6969 |
| Motorway Lake (Moatlands Gravel Pits) | SU 6670 |
| Moor Green Lakes/ Eversley Gravel Pits | SU 8062 |
| Colebrook Lake | SU 8062 |
| Grove Lake | SU 8162 |
| Horseshoe Lake | SU 8162 |
| New Workings | SU 8062 |
| Muddy Lane Gravel Pit | SU 5066 |

| N | |
|---|---|
| New Workings (Moor Green) | SU 8062 |
| Newbury | SU 4767(C) |
| Newell Green | SU 8771 |
| Nine Mile Ride | SU 8265(C) |
| North Ascot | SU 9069 |
| North Standen | SU 3167 |
| Northcroft | SU 4667 |
| Northerams Wood | SU 8568 |

| O | |
|---|---|
| Oaken Copse, Yattendon | SU 5574 |
| Oare | SU 5074 |
| Oare Common | SU 5074 |
| Obelisk Pond (Surrey) | SU 8562 |
| Ockwells Manor | SU 8778 |
| Olddean Common (part Surrey) | SU 8762 |
| Old Slade | TQ 0378 |
| Old Slade Lake | TQ 0378 |
| Orlitts Lake North | TQ 0377 |
| Orlitts Lake South | TQ 0377 |
| Old Wader Pit (Moatlands Gravel Pits) | SU 6670 |
| Old Windsor | SU 9874 |
| Owlsmoor | SU 8462 |
| Oxlease Lake Woolhampton Gravel Pits) | SU 5666 |

| P | |
|---|---|
| Padworth | SU 6166 |
| Padworth Common | SU 6264 |
| Padworth Lane GP | SU 6066 |
| Paices Wood, Aldermaston | SU 5864 |
| Pamber Heath (Hants) | SU 6162 |
| Pangbourne | SU 6376 |
| Park Place | SU 7782 |
| Peasemore | SU 4577 |
| Pilot Hill (Hants) | SU 3959 |
| Pinal Wood (Oxon) | SU 3882 |
| Pingewood | SU 6969 |
| Pingewood Gravel Pits | SU 6969 |
| Burnthouse Lane Gravel Pits | SU 6868 |
| Moors Farm Gravel Pit | SU 6969 |
| Pingewood Jet Ski Pit | SU 6969 |
| Pinkneys Green | SU 8682 |
| Purley (-on-Thames) | SU 6676 |
| Pylon Pit (Wraysbury) | TQ 0173 |

| Q | |
|---|---|
| Quarry Wood | SU 8685 |
| Queen Mother Reservoir | TQ 0076 |

| R | |
|---|---|
| Racecourse Gravel Pit | SU 5066 |
| Rapley | SU 8965 |
| Rapley Lake | SU 8964 |
| Reading | SU 7173(C) |
| Reading Motorway Services | SU 6769 |
| Reading Sewage Farm (Manor Farm) | SU 7170 |
| Remenham | SU 7784 |
| Remenham Hill | SU 7882 |
| Riseley | SU 7263 |
| Rowney Predator Lake (Woolhampton Gravel Pits) | SU 5666 |
| Ruscombe | SU 7976 |

| S | |
|---|---|
| Sandford | SU 7873 |
| Sandford Lake, (Dinton Pastures) | SU 7872 |
| Sandhurst (Sewage Farm) | SU 8361 |
| Sandleford | SU 4764 |
| Searles Farm Gravel Pit | SU 6870 |
| Shaw | SU 4868 |
| Shaw Marsh | SU 4867 |
| Sheepdrove Farm (Lambourne) | SU 3582 |
| Shefford Woodlands | SU 3673 |
| Shinfield | SU 7368 |
| Shiplake (Oxon) | SU 7678 |
| Shottesbrooke | SU 8478 |
| Shurlock Row | SU 8374 |
| Silchester (Hants) | SU 6262 |
| Silverwings Sailing (BA) Lake (Wraysbury) | TQ 0173 |
| Silwood | SU 9468 |
| Silwood Park | SU 9468 |
| Sindlesham | SU 7769 |
| Slough | SU 9780(C) |
| Slough Sewage Farm | SU 9479 |
| Slough Trading Estate | SU 9581 |
| Smallmead (Farm) Gravel Pit | SU 6970 |
| Smallmead Rubbish Tip | SU 7070 |
| Snelsmore Common | SU 4670 |
| Sole Common | SU 4170 |
| Sonning ('Sunning' historic) | SU 7575 |
| Sonning Cutting | SU 7574 |
| Sonning Eye Gravel Pits (Oxon) | SU 7475 |
| Sots Hole | SU 6277 |
| Southcote (Lock) | SU 6871 |
| South Ascot | SU 9267 |
| South Fawley | SU 3980 |
| South Hill Park | SU 8766 |
| South Lake, Woodley | SU 7572 |
| Spade Oak | SU 8887 |
| Sparrows' Copse | SU 4082 |
| Speen (Berks) | SU 4568 |
| Spencers Wood | SU 7166 |
| Stanford Dingley | SU 5771 |
| Stratfield Saye (Hants) | SU 6961 |
| Streatley (-on-Thames) | SU 5980(C) |
| Streatley Warren | SU 5580 |
| Sulham | SU 6474 |
| Sulham Wood | SU 6474(C) |
| Sulhamstead | SU 6368 |
| Summerleaze Gravel Pits | SU 8982 |
| Sunning (Historic name for Sonning) | SU 7575 |
| Sunninghill | SU 9467 |
| Sunnymeads GP | TQ 0175 |
| Surley Hall (near Windsor) | SU 9477 |
| Surrey Hill (part Surrey) | SU 8964 |
| Swallowfield | SU 7264 |
| Swinley | SU 8967 |
| Swinley Forest (Wishmoor area) | SU 8763 |
| Swinley Forest (Caesar's Camp) | SU 8765 |
| Swinley Park | SU 8967 |

| T | |
|---|---|
| Taplow Lake (Bucks) | SU 9180 |
| Taxi Pit (Theale Gravel Pits) | SU 6770 |
| Temple Island | SU 7784 |

| | |
|---|---|
| Thatcham | SU 5167(C) |
| Thatcham (Marsh) Gravel Pits | SU 5061 |
| Muddy Lane | SU 5061 |
| Discovery Centre | SU 5061 |
| Thatcham Marsh | SU 5161 |
| The Lookout (Bracknell) | SU 8765 |
| Theale | SU 6471 |
| Theale Gravel Pits | SU 6570(C) |
| Burghfield Mill | SU 6770 |
| Car Park Lake | SU 6770 |
| Field Farm (infill) | SU 6770 |
| Hosehill Lake (Fox & Hounds Gravel Pit) | SU 6569 |
| Main Lake | SU 6670 |
| Moatlands Gravel Pit | SU 6670 |
| Motorway Lake | SU 6670 |
| Old Wader Pit | SU 6670 |
| Taxi Pit | SU 6770 |
| Theale Bottom Lane Pit | SU 6469 |
| Theale Main Pit | SU 6470 |
| Theale Wigmore Lane Pits | SU 6370 |
| Thurle Down | SU 5781 |
| Tickleback Row | SU 8673 |
| Tidmarsh | SU 6374 |
| Tilehurst | SU 6673(C) |
| Titness Park | SU 9568 |
| Trout Fishery Lake (Wigmore Lane) | SU 6370 |
| Twyford Gravel Pits | SU 7875 |
| Hurst Green Lake | SU 7874 |
| Loddon Reserve (BBOWT) | SU 7875 |

| U | |
|---|---|
| Ufton Nervet | SU 6367 |
| Unhill Wood (Oxon) | SU 5682 |
| Upper Basildon | SU 5976 |
| Upper Bucklebury | SU 5468 |
| Upper Green | SU 3663 |
| Upper Lambourn | SU 3180 |
| Upper Woolhampton | SU 5767 |

| V | |
|---|---|
| Village Lake (Wraysbury) | TQ 0173 |
| Virginia Water (part Surrey) | SU 9669 |

| W | |
|---|---|
| Walbury | SU 3761 |
| Walbury Hill | SU 3761 |
| Waltham Grove | SU 8577 |
| Waltham St Lawrence | SU 8377 |
| Warfield | SU 8870 |
| Wargrave | SU 7878 |
| Warren Row | SU 8180 |
| Wash Common | SU 4564 |
| Wasing | SU 5764 |
| Welford | SU 4073 |
| Wellington College | SU 8363 |

| | |
|---|---|
| Wellington Country Park (Hants) | SU 7363 |
| West Bradfield | SU 6072 |
| West Ilsley | SU 4782 |
| West Woodhay | SU 3963 |
| Whitchurch (Oxon) | SU 6377 |
| White Swan Lake (Dinton Pastures) | SU 7772 |
| Whiteknights Lake | SU 7372 |
| Whiteknights Park | SU 7371 |
| White Waltham | SU 8577 |
| White Waltham Aerodrome | SU 8578 |
| Whitley | SU 7170 |
| Whitley Wood | SU 7269 |
| Wickham | SU 3971 |
| Wickham Heath | SU 4269 |
| Widbrook Common | SU 8984 |
| Wigmore Lane Gravel Pits | SU 6370 |
| Elephant Lake | SU 6370 |
| Hawards Lake | SU 6370 |
| Hobby Lake | SU 6370 |
| Horseshoe Lake | SU 6370 |
| Trout Fishery Lake | SU 6370 |
| Wilderness (Kintbury) | SU 3866 |
| Wildmoor Heath (Edgebarrow Heath) | SU 8462 |
| Windsor | SU 9677(C) |
| Windsor Forest | SU 9372(C) |
| Windsor Great Park | SU 9672(C) |
| Winkfield | SU 9072 |
| Winkfield Row | SU 8971 |
| Winnersh | SU 7871 |
| Winter Hill | SU 8786 |
| Winterbourne | SU 4572 |
| Wishmoor Bottom (part Surrey) | SU 8762 |
| Woolley Down | SU 4081 |
| Woolhampton | SU 5766 |
| Woolhampton Gravel Pits | SU 5666 |
| Cranswell Lake | SU 5666 |
| Oxlease Lake | SU 5666 |
| Rowney Predator Lake | SU 5666 |
| Woolwich Green Gravel Pit (west of Hosehill NR) | SU 6469 |
| Woosehill | SU 7968 |
| Wraysbury | TQ 0074 |
| Wraysbury Gravel Pits | TQ 0173(C) |
| Silverwings Sailing (BA) Lake | TQ 0173 |
| Colne Mere | TQ 0173 |
| Hythe Lake | TQ 0173 |
| Heron Lake | TQ 0273 |
| Pylon Pit | TQ 0173 |
| Village Lake | TQ 0173 |
| Wraysbury Reservoir (Surrey) | TQ 0274 |

| Y | |
|---|---|
| Yateley (Hants) | SU 8160 |
| Yateley Gravel Pits (Hants) | SU 8261 |
| Yattendon | SU 5574 |
| Yeoveney Gravel Pits | TQ 0272 |

# Appendix III

## Tetrad Survey Data

### Table A1: Tetrad surveys: breeding status summary

Table shows the number of tetrads with the level of breeding evidence indicated: 2007–11 (1987–89)

| Species | Number of tetrads | | | % Tetrads | |
|---|---|---|---|---|---|
| | Confirmed | Probable | Possible | All categories | Confirmed |
| Mute Swan | 131 (101) | 20 (17) | 17 (34) | 42·6 (38·8) | 33·2 (25·8) |
| Greylag Goose | 55 (12) | 23 (6) | 13 (11) | 23·1 (7·4) | 14 (3·1) |
| Canada Goose | 147 (116) | 22 (36) | 17 (40) | 47·2 (49) | 37·3 (29·6) |
| Barnacle Goose | 1 (1) | 0 (0) | 2 (0) | 0·8 (0·3) | 0·3 (0·3) |
| Egyptian Goose | 87 (4) | 30 (1) | 12 (2) | 32·7 (1·8) | 22·1 (1) |
| Shelduck | 17 (5) | 15 (6) | 8 (2) | 10·2 (3·3) | 4·3 (1·3) |
| Wood Duck | 1 (0) | 1 (0) | 1 (3) | 0·8 (0) | 0·3 (0) |
| Mandarin Duck | 67 (25) | 31 (13) | 20 (13) | 29·9 (13) | 17 (6·4) |
| Wigeon | 0 (0) | 0 (0) | 2 (1) | 0·5 (0) | 0 (0) |
| Gadwall | 24 (6) | 33 (6) | 5 (11) | 15·7 (5·9) | 6·1 (1·5) |
| Teal | 0 (2) | 5 (6) | 10 (17) | 3·8 (6·4) | 0 (0·5) |
| Mallard | 217 (232) | 55 (50) | 24 (37) | 75·1 (81·4) | 55·1 (59·2) |
| Garganey | 0 (1) | 1 (0) | 3 (1) | 1 (0·5) | 0 (0·3) |
| Shoveler | 0 (2) | 15 (1) | 5 (4) | 5·1 (1·8) | 0 (0·5) |
| Red-crested Pochard | 3 (0) | 3 (0) | 1 (0) | 1·8 (0) | 0·8 (0) |
| Pochard | 3 (1) | 7 (9) | 7 (10) | 4·3 (5·1) | 0·8 (0·3) |
| Tufted Duck | 43 (54) | 60 (58) | 9 (17) | 28·4 (32·9) | 10·9 (13·8) |
| Ruddy Duck | 0 (1) | 2 (1) | 1 (1) | 0·8 (0·8) | 0 (0·3) |
| Chukar | 0 (6) | 0 (21) | 0 (19) | 0 (11·7) | 0 (1·5) |
| Red-legged Partridge | 37 (72) | 119 (113) | 50 (47) | 52·3 (59·2) | 9·4 (18·4) |
| Grey Partridge | 20 (97) | 42 (112) | 24 (42) | 21·8 (64) | 5·1 (24·7) |
| Quail | 2 (2) | 11 (9) | 18 (14) | 7·9 (6·4) | 0·5 (0·5) |
| Pheasant | 93 (216) | 138 (86) | 93 (61) | 82·2 (92·6) | 23·6 (55·1) |
| Golden Pheasant | 0 (1) | 0 (1) | 0 (3) | 0 (1·3) | 0 (0·3) |
| Cormorant | 4 (0) | 6 (0) | 28 (16) | 9·6 (4·1) | 1 (0) |
| Little Egret | 2 (0) | 5 (0) | 15 (0) | 5·6 (0) | 0·5 (0) |
| Grey Heron | 35 (18) | 8 (12) | 67 (128) | 27·9 (40·3) | 8·9 (4·6) |
| Little Grebe | 41 (83) | 13 (22) | 25 (16) | 20·1 (30·9) | 10·4 (21·2) |
| Great Crested Grebe | 88 (71) | 12 (13) | 7 (13) | 27·2 (24·7) | 22·3 (18·1) |
| Red Kite | 67 (0) | 118 (0) | 102 (0) | 72·8 (0) | 17 (0) |
| Montagu's Harrier | 0 (0) | 1 (0) | 4 (1) | 1·3 (0·3) | 0 (0) |
| Goshawk | 0 (0) | 1 (1) | 0 (6) | 0·3 (1·5) | 0 (0) |
| Sparrowhawk | 71 (97) | 55 (55) | 104 (142) | 58·4 (75) | 18 (24·7) |
| Buzzard | 133 (3) | 129 (4) | 74 (20) | 85·3 (6·9) | 33·8 (0·8) |
| Kestrel | 115 (92) | 69 (112) | 113 (138) | 75·4 (87·2) | 29·2 (23·5) |
| Hobby | 24 (8) | 22 (10) | 91 (50) | 34·8 (17·3) | 6·1 (2) |
| Peregrine | 4 (0) | 3 (0) | 13 (0) | 5·1 (0) | 1 (0) |
| Water Rail | 5 (1) | 3 (2) | 12 (19) | 5·1 (5·6) | 1·3 (0·3) |
| Corncrake | 0 (0) | 1 (0) | 0 (0) | 0·3 (0) | 0 (0) |
| Moorhen | 228 (251) | 21 (27) | 30 (33) | 70·8 (79·3) | 57·9 (64) |
| Coot | 173 (169) | 4 (16) | 17 (19) | 49·2 (52) | 43·9 (43·1) |
| Stone-curlew | 7 (4) | 2 (4) | 0 (5) | 2·3 (3·3) | 1·8 (1) |
| Oystercatcher | 3 (0) | 2 (0) | 2 (0) | 1·8 (0) | 0·8 (0) |
| Lapwing | 124 (156) | 65 (101) | 31 (41) | 55·8 (76) | 31·5 (39·8) |
| Little Ringed Plover | 25 (21) | 3 (14) | 6 (4) | 8·6 (9·9) | 6·3 (5·4) |
| Ringed Plover | 9 (10) | 5 (9) | 4 (9) | 4·6 (7·1) | 2·3 (2·6) |
| Curlew | 2 (1) | 8 (0) | 5 (7) | 3·8 (2) | 0·5 (0·3) |
| Common Sandpiper | 0 (0) | 0 (1) | 0 (17) | 0 (4·6) | 0 (0) |
| Redshank | 9 (10) | 12 (21) | 10 (18) | 7·9 (12·5) | 2·3 (2·6) |
| Woodcock | 1 (17) | 52 (85) | 18 (35) | 18 (34·9) | 0·3 (4·3) |
| Snipe | 0 (1) | 2 (25) | 14 (31) | 4·1 (14·5) | 0 (0·3) |
| Common Tern | 27 (15) | 6 (1) | 14 (20) | 11·9 (9·2) | 6·9 (3·8) |

| Species | Number of tetrads | | | % Tetrads | |
|---|---|---|---|---|---|
| | Confirmed | Probable | Possible | All categories | Confirmed |
| Black-headed Gull | 12 (2) | 7 (1) | 16 (84) | 8·9 (22·2) | 3 (0·5) |
| Lesser Black-backed Gull | 5 (0) | 1 (0) | 7 (0) | 3·3 (0) | 1·3 (0) |
| Herring Gull | 4 (0) | 3 (0) | 4 (0) | 2·8 (0) | 1 (0) |
| Feral Pigeon | 45 (76) | 38 (67) | 57 (97) | 35·5 (61·2) | 11·4 (19·4) |
| Stock Dove | 112 (86) | 148 (147) | 69 (74) | 83·5 (78·3) | 28·4 (21·9) |
| Woodpigeon | 303 (308) | 69 (63) | 21 (19) | 99·7 (99·5) | 76·9 (78·6) |
| Collared Dove | 126 (189) | 158 (146) | 42 (34) | 82·7 (94·1) | 32 (48·2) |
| Turtle Dove | 3 (23) | 13 (117) | 25 (88) | 10·4 (58·2) | 0·8 (5·9) |
| Ring-necked Parakeet | 34 (5) | 25 (3) | 29 (8) | 22·3 (4·1) | 8·6 (1·3) |
| Cuckoo | 9 (36) | 42 (137) | 153 (154) | 51·8 (83·4) | 2·3 (9·2) |
| Barn Owl | 76 (11) | 7 (15) | 43 (28) | 32 (13·8) | 19·3 (2·8) |
| Little Owl | 51 (59) | 26 (68) | 67 (98) | 36·5 (57·4) | 12·9 (15·1) |
| Tawny Owl | 81 (57) | 22 (94) | 94 (119) | 50 (68·9) | 20·6 (14·5) |
| Long-eared Owl | 1 (0) | 0 (0) | 1 (3) | 0·5 (0·3) | 0·3 (0) |
| Short-eared Owl | 1 (0) | 0 (0) | 1 (9) | 0·5 (2·3) | 0·3 (0) |
| Nightjar | 10 (7) | 21 (13) | 12 (5) | 10·9 (6·4) | 2·5 (1·8) |
| Swift | 53 (109) | 57 (51) | 101 (169) | 53·6 (83·9) | 13·5 (27·8) |
| Kingfisher | 44 (40) | 25 (41) | 56 (64) | 31·7 (37) | 11·2 (10·2) |
| Green Woodpecker | 158 (97) | 75 (105) | 101 (98) | 84·8 (76·5) | 40·1 (24·7) |
| Great Spotted Woodpecker | 274 (183) | 45 (92) | 56 (77) | 95·2 (89·8) | 69·5 (46·7) |
| Lesser Spotted Woodpecker | 1 (22) | 10 (33) | 25 (61) | 9·1 (29·6) | 0·3 (5·6) |
| Magpie | 282 (304) | 52 (58) | 45 (26) | 96·2 (99) | 71·6 (77·6) |
| Jay | 141 (164) | 88 (110) | 98 (73) | 83 (88·5) | 35·8 (41·8) |
| Jackdaw | 283 (224) | 54 (77) | 37 (58) | 94·9 (91·6) | 71·8 (57·1) |
| Rook | 211 (218) | 21 (23) | 30 (79) | 66·5 (81·6) | 53·6 (55·6) |
| Carrion Crow | 302 (262) | 55 (80) | 23 (49) | 96·4 (99·7) | 76·6 (66·8) |
| Raven | 8 (0) | 22 (0) | 23 (0) | 13·5 (0) | 2 (0) |
| Goldcrest | 151 (118) | 85 (119) | 83 (80) | 81 (80·9) | 38·3 (30·1) |
| Firecrest | 11 (2) | 17 (14) | 11 (4) | 9·9 (5·1) | 2·8 (0·5) |
| Blue Tit | 385 (371) | 6 (15) | 1 (5) | 99·5 (99·7) | 97·7 (94·6) |
| Great Tit | 377 (348) | 9 (31) | 7 (10) | 99·7 (99·2) | 95·7 (88·8) |
| Coal Tit | 184 (151) | 38 (68) | 65 (74) | 72·8 (74·7) | 46·7 (38·5) |
| Willow Tit | 5 (52) | 4 (33) | 8 (39) | 4·3 (31·6) | 1·3 (13·3) |
| Marsh Tit | 69 (76) | 27 (58) | 46 (64) | 36 (50·5) | 17·5 (19·4) |
| Bearded Tit | 0 (1) | 0 (0) | 0 (0) | 0 (0·3) | 0 (0·3) |
| Woodlark | 14 (7) | 9 (3) | 11 (1) | 8·6 (2·8) | 3·6 (1·8) |
| Skylark | 93 (90) | 160 (196) | 68 (56) | 81·5 (87·2) | 23·6 (23) |
| Sand Martin | 29 (19) | 4 (5) | 19 (50) | 13·2 (18·9) | 7·4 (4·8) |
| Swallow | 259 (271) | 47 (47) | 34 (51) | 86·3 (94·1) | 65·7 (69·1) |
| House Martin | 186 (306) | 36 (26) | 61 (40) | 71·8 (94·9) | 47·2 (78·1) |
| Cetti's Warbler | 13 (1) | 17 (1) | 16 (6) | 11·7 (2) | 3·3 (0·3) |
| Long-tailed Tit | 331 (287) | 30 (51) | 11 (29) | 94·4 (93·6) | 84 (73·2) |
| Wood Warbler | 0 (4) | 1 (19) | 9 (19) | 2·5 (10·7) | 0 (1) |
| Chiffchaff | 210 (140) | 98 (163) | 76 (62) | 97·5 (93·1) | 53·3 (35·7) |
| Willow Warbler | 60 (191) | 70 (122) | 135 (61) | 67·3 (95·4) | 15·2 (48·7) |
| Blackcap | 273 (167) | 77 (153) | 41 (52) | 99·2 (94·9) | 69·3 (42·6) |
| Garden Warbler | 59 (82) | 77 (125) | 101 (82) | 60·2 (73·7) | 15 (20·9) |
| Lesser Whitethroat | 25 (56) | 33 (82) | 111 (68) | 42·9 (52·6) | 6·3 (14·3) |
| Whitethroat | 248 (148) | 63 (119) | 48 (57) | 91·1 (82·7) | 62·9 (37·8) |
| Dartford Warbler | 11 (0) | 1 (0) | 3 (0) | 3·8 (0) | 2·8 (0) |
| Grasshopper Warbler | 2 (5) | 5 (7) | 22 (14) | 7·4 (6·6) | 0·5 (1·3) |
| Icterine Warbler | 0 (0) | 0 (0) | 0 (1) | 0 (0·3) | 0 (0) |
| Sedge Warbler | 34 (49) | 26 (48) | 39 (31) | 25·1 (32·7) | 8·6 (12·5) |
| Reed Warbler | 52 (40) | 30 (21) | 24 (12) | 26·9 (18·6) | 13·2 (10·2) |
| Nuthatch | 230 (164) | 36 (84) | 57 (58) | 82 (78·1) | 58·4 (41·8) |
| Treecreeper | 149 (150) | 40 (75) | 76 (86) | 67·3 (79·3) | 37·8 (38·3) |
| Wren | 302 (305) | 70 (62) | 22 (24) | 100 (99·7) | 76·6 (77·8) |
| Starling | 273 (364) | 15 (15) | 30 (8) | 80·7 (98·7) | 69·3 (92·9) |
| Blackbird | 371 (362) | 17 (23) | 6 (5) | 100 (99·5) | 94·2 (92·3) |

| Species | Number of tetrads | | | % Tetrads | |
|---|---|---|---|---|---|
| | Confirmed | Probable | Possible | All categories | Confirmed |
| Fieldfare | 0 (1) | 0 (0) | 2 (9) | 0·5 (2·6) | 0 (0·3) |
| Song Thrush | 241 (290) | 90 (67) | 57 (25) | 98·5 (97·4) | 61·2 (74) |
| Mistle Thrush | 187 (277) | 68 (66) | 87 (32) | 86·8 (95·7) | 47·5 (70·7) |
| Spotted Flycatcher | 49 (152) | 41 (58) | 32 (66) | 31 (70·4) | 12·4 (38·8) |
| Robin | 366 (339) | 14 (36) | 11 (16) | 99·2 (99·7) | 92·9 (86·5) |
| Nightingale | 10 (11) | 5 (32) | 19 (36) | 8·6 (20·2) | 2·5 (2·8) |
| Pied Flycatcher | 0 (0) | 0 (0) | 0 (7) | 0 (1·8) | 0 (0) |
| Black Redstart | 1 (1) | 0 (0) | 2 (2) | 0·8 (0·8) | 0·3 (0·3) |
| Redstart | 5 (7) | 4 (8) | 4 (19) | 3·3 (8·7) | 1·3 (1·8) |
| Whinchat | 0 (0) | 0 (26) | 1 (2) | 0·3 (7·1) | 0 (0) |
| Stonechat | 16 (10) | 2 (2) | 10 (3) | 7·1 (3·8) | 4·1 (2·6) |
| Wheatear | 0 (0) | 1 (3) | 0 (31) | 0·3 (0·9) | 0 (0) |
| Dunnock | 271 (270) | 79 (88) | 39 (29) | 98·7 (98·7) | 68·8 (68·9) |
| House Sparrow | 306 (332) | 25 (29) | 20 (19) | 89·1 (96·9) | 77·7 (84·7) |
| Tree Sparrow | 0 (24) | 0 (16) | 0 (21) | 0 (15·6) | 0 (6·1) |
| Yellow Wagtail | 38 (33) | 12 (21) | 16 (39) | 16·8 (23·7) | 9·6 (8·4) |
| Grey Wagtail | 77 (75) | 28 (41) | 29 (38) | 34 (39·3) | 19·5 (19·1) |
| Pied Wagtail | 222 (244) | 38 (65) | 65 (52) | 82·5 (92·1) | 56·3 (62·2) |
| Tree Pipit | 9 (26) | 11 (37) | 10 (24) | 7·6 (22·2) | 2·3 (6·6) |
| Meadow Pipit | 12 (36) | 16 (31) | 23 (68) | 12·9 (34·4) | 3 (9·2) |
| Chaffinch | 326 (321) | 52 (53) | 13 (17) | 99·2 (99·7) | 82·7 (81·9) |
| Brambling | 0 (0) | 0 (0) | 2 (0) | 0·5 (0) | 0 (0) |
| Serin | 0 (0) | 0 (1) | 0 (0) | 0 (0·3) | 0 (0) |
| Greenfinch | 243 (228) | 89 (116) | 44 (40) | 95·4 (98) | 61·7 (58·2) |
| Goldfinch | 280 (149) | 73 (130) | 33 (62) | 98 (87) | 71·1 (38) |
| Siskin | 4 (1) | 16 (14) | 22 (23) | 10·7 (9·7) | 1 (0·3) |
| Linnet | 118 (110) | 103 (125) | 44 (56) | 67·3 (74·2) | 29·9 (28·1) |
| Lesser Redpoll | 0 (7) | 4 (16) | 11 (23) | 3·8 (11·7) | 0 (1·8) |
| Crossbill | 5 (2) | 8 (7) | 6 (5) | 4·8 (3·6) | 1·3 (0·5) |
| Bullfinch | 90 (125) | 113 (173) | 64 (43) | 67·8 (87) | 22·8 (31·9) |
| Hawfinch | 0 (4) | 0 (8) | 1 (4) | 0·3 (4·1) | 0 (1) |
| Yellowhammer | 105 (170) | 87 (125) | 42 (49) | 59·4 (87·8) | 26·6 (43·4) |
| Reed Bunting | 65 (69) | 43 (75) | 43 (51) | 38·3 (49·7) | 16·5 (17·6) |
| Corn Bunting | 23 (30) | 22 (69) | 15 (38) | 15·2 (34·9) | 5·8 (7·7) |

## Table A2: **Summary of species totals by tetrad**

Table shows the number of species recorded in the tetrad indicated: 2007–11 (1987–89)

1 Tetrad not surveyed in 1987-89

2 Tetrad added following boundary changes in 1995

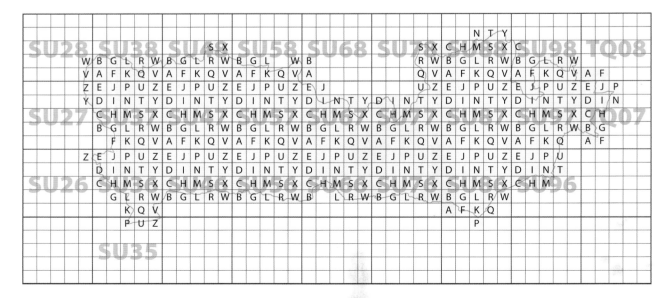

| Tetrad | Tetrad name | Breeding Season: species with maximum breeding evidence 2007–11 (1987–89) | | | | Summer All species 2007–11 | Winter All species 2007–11 |
|---|---|---|---|---|---|---|---|
| | | Confirmed | Probable | Possible | All levels | | |
| | Berkshire total | 121 (121) | 11 (5) | 4 (8) | 136 (137) | 202 | 187 |
| SU26 Z | Littlecote Park Farm | 29 (51) | 9 (13) | 19 (14) | 57 (78) | 60 | 44 |
| SU27 Y | Baydon | 23 (14) | 12 (16) | 10 (23) | 45 (53) | 46 | 40 |
| SU27 Z | Baydon Hole | 26 (22) | 14 (10) | 10 (9) | 50 (41) | 52 | 42 |
| SU28 V | Park Farm, Lambourn | 21 (12) | 11 (25) | 14 (10) | 46 (47) | 50 | 47 |
| SU28 W | Knighton Bushes | 11 (24) | 15 (13) | 15 (10) | 41 (47) | 55 | 49 |
| SU35 P | Combe Wood | 27 (35) | 13 (15) | 8 (11) | 48 (61) | 50 | 47 |
| SU35 U | Linkenholt | 28 (44) | 13 (10) | 8 (16) | 49 (70) | 51 | 44 |
| SU35 Z | Faccombe | 28 (43) | 19 (15) | 9 (12) | 56 (70) | 56 | 56 |
| SU36 C | Stype Grange | 15 (52) | 13 (11) | 16 (16) | 44 (79) | 45 | 39 |
| SU36 D | North Standen House | 14 (59) | 18 (10) | 15 (25) | 47 (94) | 64 | 47 |
| SU36 E | Cake Wood | 13 (53) | 9 (20) | 10 (12) | 32 (85) | 52 | 41 |
| SU36 G | Ham | 15 (42) | 6 (10) | 15 (18) | 36 (70) | 47 | 34 |
| SU36 H | Prosperous House Farm | 11 (33) | 6 (11) | 23 (22) | 40 (66) | 40 | 39 |
| SU36 I | Standen Manor | 16 (50) | 6 (10) | 25 (15) | 47 (75) | 56 | 29 |
| SU36 J | Freeman's Marsh | 45 (55) | 11 (2) | 15 (22) | 71 (79) | 92 | 83 |
| SU36 K | Buttermere | 17 (45) | 11 (9) | 11 (11) | 39 (65) | 55 | 44 |
| SU36 L | Ham Spray House | 21 (38) | 18 (10) | 9 (18) | 48 (66) | 51 | 48 |
| SU36 M | Lower Green | 18 (39) | 10 (17) | 24 (12) | 52 (68) | 58 | 40 |
| SU36 N | Hungerford Common | 14 (46) | 5 (11) | 23 (20) | 42 (77) | 51 | 35 |
| SU36 P | Denford Hill | 44 (64) | 11 (5) | 11 (18) | 66 (87) | 91 | 78 |
| SU36 Q | Walbury Hill | 22 (33) | 17 (10) | 8 (19) | 47 (62) | 65 | 64 |
| SU36 R | Combe Gibbet | 27 (44) | 10 (15) | 15 (5) | 52 (64) | 65 | 58 |
| SU36 S | Inkpen | 41 (52) | 19 (12) | 7 (9) | 67 (73) | 71 | 60 |
| SU36 T | Inglewood Hydro | 45 (46) | 11 (18) | 14 (10) | 70 (74) | 91 | 69 |
| SU36 U | Avington | 21 (36) | 33 (25) | 10 (5) | 64 (66) | 71 | 60 |
| SU36 V | Eastwick | 30 (44) | 11 (12) | 16 (15) | 57 (71) | 73 | 52 |
| SU36 W | West Woodhay | 31 (48) | 11 (15) | 12 (7) | 54 (70) | 63 | 56 |
| SU36 X | Inkpen Common | 40 (60) | 6 (10) | 10 (3) | 56 (73) | 63 | 55 |
| SU36 Y | Kintbury | 32 (41) | 24 (21) | 25 (13) | 81 (75) | 94 | 79 |
| SU36 Z | Elcot | 21 (45) | 15 (11) | 20 (19) | 56 (75) | 62 | 44 |
| SU37 B | Foxbury Wood | 20 (27) | 8 (22) | 12 (12) | 40 (61) | 43 | 41 |
| SU37 C | Membury | 17 (28) | 15 (22) | 10 (9) | 42 (59) | 45 | 34 |
| SU37 D | Coppington Down | 27 (13) | 5 (26) | 4 (17) | 36 (56) | 41 | 35 |
| SU37 E | Row Down | 18 (6) | 7 (23) | 7 (3) | 32 (32) | 42 | 43 |
| SU37 F | Chilton Foliat | 37 (25) | 11 (20) | 15 (14) | 63 (59) | 65 | 69 |
| SU37 G | Straight Soley | 35 (23) | 7 (18) | 7 (11) | 49 (52) | 53 | 43 |
| SU37 H | Woodlands St Mary | 25 (31) | 6 (16) | 15 (6) | 46 (53) | 46 | 34 |
| SU37 I | Cleeve Hill | 20 (21) | 19 (18) | 12 (18) | 51 (57) | 54 | 44 |
| SU37 J | Lambourn | 22 (27) | 7 (19) | 14 (5) | 43 (51) | 49 | 42 |
| SU37 K | Hungerford Newtown | 28 (28) | 10 (24) | 10 (7) | 48 (59) | 57 | 47 |
| SU37 L | North Hidden Farm | 16 (24) | 9 (19) | 6 (7) | 31 (50) | 44 | 38 |
| SU37 M | East Garston Wood | 25 (27) | 15 (14) | 7 (9) | 47 (50) | 51 | 35 |
| SU37 N | Eastbury | 26 (34) | 10 (16) | 7 (14) | 43 (64) | 48 | 44 |
| SU37 P | Eastbury Down | 17 (17) | 12 (15) | 15 (14) | 44 (46) | 53 | 42 |
| SU37 Q | Radley Farm | 23 (24) | 10 (21) | 7 (12) | 40 (57) | 47 | 39 |
| SU37 R | Shefford Woodlands | 26 (20) | 14 (19) | 3 (17) | 43 (56) | 44 | 39 |
| SU37 S | South Hidden Farm | 17 (22) | 18 (25) | 9 (15) | 44 (62) | 57 | 51 |
| SU37 T | East Garston | 28 (19) | 12 (6) | 8 (26) | 48 (51) | 54 | 44 |
| SU37 U | East Garston Down | 30 (39) | 12 (11) | 7 (9) | 49 (59) | 50 | 50 |
| SU37 V | Wickham | 21 (27) | 4 (19) | 17 (7) | 42 (53) | 48 | 40 |
| SU37 W | Weston | 15 (28) | 15 (27) | 17 (11) | 47 (66) | 52 | 45 |
| SU37 X | Great Shefford | 32 (30) | 18 (19) | 10 (12) | 60 (61) | 68 | 77 |
| SU37 Y | Northfield Farm | 19 (15) | 7 (23) | 8 (10) | 34 (48) | 37 | 38 |
| SU37 Z | Whatcombe | 32 (12) | 12 (26) | 7 (7) | 51 (45) | 52 | 52 |
| SU38 A | Upper Lambourn | 23 (11) | 8 (23) | 16 (7) | 47 (41) | 48 | 43 |
| SU38 B | Maddle Farm | 23 (25) | 12 (7) | 17 (7) | 52 (39) | 60 | 48 |

| Tetrad | Tetrad name | Breeding Season: species with maximum breeding evidence 2007–11 (1987–89) | | | | Summer All species 2007–11 | Winter All species 2007–11 |
|---|---|---|---|---|---|---|---|
| | | Confirmed | Probable | Possible | All levels | | |
| SU38 F | Wether Down | 25 (11) | 10 (14) | 6 (13) | 41 (38) | 52 | 44 |
| SU38 G | Seven Barrows | 25 (28) | 12 (8) | 14 (9) | 51 (45) | 56 | 41 |
| SU38 K | Bockhampton Down | 32 (20) | 6 (17) | 12 (7) | 50 (44) | 61 | 47 |
| SU38 L | Stancombe Farm | 26 (29) | 11 (6) | 10 (6) | 47 (41) | 54 | 45 |
| SU38 Q | Warren Farm | 30 (17) | 9 (5) | 16 (25) | 55 (47) | 60 | 46 |
| SU38 R | Nutwood Down | 7 (21) | 15 (15) | 20 (11) | 42 (47) | 49 | 46 |
| SU38 V | Fawley | 23 (24) | 12 (17) | 16 (6) | 50 (47) | 55 | 53 |
| SU38 W | Letcombe Bowers | 4 (19) | 22 (26) | 10 (6) | 36 (51) | 38 | 40 |
| SU46 B | North End | 12 (34) | 9 (16) | 13 (11) | 34 (61) | 61 | 50 |
| SU46 C | Hamstead Marshall | 30 (36) | 9 (24) | 14 (3) | 53 (63) | 57 | 43 |
| SU46 D | Irish Hill | 54 (46) | 16 (25) | 5 (4) | 75 (75) | 91 | 73 |
| SU46 E | Bradfords Farm | 24 (25) | 16 (23) | 13 (13) | 53 (61) | 70 | 34 |
| SU46 G | Ball Hill | 34 (34) | 6 (5) | 7 (12) | 47 (51) | 50 | 40 |
| SU46 H | Enbourne | 14 (25) | 14 (27) | 15 (9) | 43 (61) | 50 | 39 |
| SU46 I | Marsh Benham | 43 (52) | 18 (22) | 11 (7) | 72 (81) | 78 | 59 |
| SU46 J | Stockcross | 15 (16) | 18 (19) | 15 (22) | 48 (57) | 55 | 50 |
| SU46 L | Great Pen Wood | 12 (16) | 18 (22) | 12 (9) | 42 (47) | 54 | 36 |
| SU46 M | Skinners Green | 27 (13) | 14 (27) | 9 (15) | 49 (55) | 61 | 61 |
| SU46 N | Speen Moor | 43 (51) | 6 (12) | 7 (12) | 56 (75) | 67 | 55 |
| SU46 P | Bagnor Village | 44 (57) | 10 (11) | 11 (7) | 65 (75) | 76 | 74 |
| SU46 R | Newtown Common | 15 (30) | 17 (15) | 9 (13) | 41 (58) | 49 | 38 |
| SU46 S | Sandleford | 40 (37) | 5 (13) | 5 (7) | 50 (57) | 60 | 61 |
| SU46 T | Newbury | 31 (44) | 4 (13) | 8 (6) | 43 (63) | 66 | 59 |
| SU46 U | Donnington | 41 (61) | 21 (6) | 10 (8) | 72 (75) | 75 | 58 |
| SU46 W | Sydmonton Common | 27 (16) | 21 (31) | 13 (11) | 61 (58) | 70 | 65 |
| SU46 X | Greenham | 28 (33) | 23 (23) | 15 (5) | 66 (61) | 111 | 75 |
| SU46 Y | Hambridge Lake | 56 (37) | 23 (16) | 6 (21) | 85 (74) | 129 | 106 |
| SU46 Z | Henwick | 25 (23) | 11 (22) | 8 (16) | 44 (61) | 52 | 45 |
| SU47 A | Sole Common | 35 (38) | 8 (15) | 2 (9) | 45 (62) | 46 | 52 |
| SU47 B | Welford Park | 35 (44) | 12 (15) | 11 (7) | 58 (66) | 63 | 66 |
| SU47 C | Poughly Farm | 33 (33) | 7 (5) | 11 (11) | 51 (49) | 57 | 37 |
| SU47 D | Chaddleworth | 40 (38) | 8 (11) | 4 (6) | 52 (55) | 54 | 42 |
| SU47 E | Wooley Farm | 38 (35) | 10 (12) | 7 (10) | 55 (57) | 55 | 49 |
| SU47 F | Boxford | 38 (52) | 8 (16) | 9 (10) | 55 (78) | 66 | 61 |
| SU47 G | Westbrook Farm | 34 (38) | 12 (21) | 14 (5) | 60 (64) | 70 | 63 |
| SU47 H | Rowbury | 32 (30) | 13 (16) | 4 (14) | 49 (60) | 52 | 29 |
| SU47 I | Leckhampstead | 37 (27) | 5 (19) | 10 (7) | 52 (53) | 52 | 42 |
| SU47 J | Brightwalton | 41 (37) | 9 (12) | 7 (16) | 57 (65) | 57 | 52 |
| SU47 K | Winterbourne Holt | 51 (59) | 6 (9) | 8 (8) | 65 (76) | 84 | 71 |
| SU47 L | Winterbourne | 37 (33) | 10 (23) | 9 (10) | 56 (66) | 59 | 47 |
| SU47 M | North Heath | 42 (37) | 8 (17) | 6 (8) | 56 (62) | 60 | 53 |
| SU47 N | Peasemore | 34 (37) | 10 (15) | 5 (6) | 49 (58) | 54 | 41 |
| SU47 P | Lilley | 33 (39) | 7 (9) | 2 (6) | 42 (54) | 48 | 39 |
| SU47 Q | Snelsmore Common | 35 (53) | 18 (8) | 9 (4) | 62 (65) | 68 | 53 |
| SU47 R | Chieveley | 41 (40) | 3 (16) | 6 (5) | 50 (61) | 54 | 50 |
| SU47 S | Downend | 31 (32) | 9 (21) | 6 (9) | 46 (62) | 58 | 49 |
| SU47 T | Beedon Common | 31 (31) | 7 (18) | 8 (10) | 46 (59) | 46 | 44 |
| SU47 U | Stanmore | 39 (42) | 8 (11) | 6 (8) | 53 (61) | 63 | 50 |
| SU47 V | Fishers Farm | 34 (37) | 10 (18) | 9 (7) | 53 (62) | 58 | 47 |
| SU47 W | Curridge | 39 (39) | 5 (23) | 4 (10) | 48 (72) | 53 | 39 |
| SU47 X | Bradley Court | 34 (25) | 8 (23) | 8 (13) | 50 (61) | 55 | 34 |
| SU47 Y | Beedon | 37 (29) | 16 (19) | 13 (11) | 66 (59) | 71 | 55 |
| SU47 Z | Shrill Down | 30 (22) | 5 (19) | 5 (5) | 40 (46) | 47 | 40 |
| SU48 A | Woolley Down | 37 (29) | 7 (3) | 13 (6) | 57 (38) | 60 | 57 |
| SU48 B | Latin Down Farm | 32 (16) | 8 (26) | 10 (10) | 50 (52) | 51 | 49 |
| SU48 F | Brightwalton Common | 51 (34) | 8 (1) | 1 (10) | 60 (45) | 66 | 58 |
| SU48 G | Lockinge Kiln Farm | 37 (14) | 13 (23) | 4 (7) | 54 (44) | 56 | 50 |

| Tetrad | Tetrad name | Breeding Season: species with maximum breeding evidence 2007–11 (1987–89) | | | | Summer All species 2007–11 | Winter All species 2007–11 |
|--------|-------------|-----------|----------|----------|------------|---|---|
| | | Confirmed | Probable | Possible | All levels | | |
| SU48 K | Catmore | 36 (31) | 9 (0) | 7 (15) | 52 (46) | 53 | 52 |
| SU48 L | West Ginge Down | 31 (37) | 11 (5) | 8 (10) | 50 (52) | 54 | 53 |
| SU48 Q | Hodcott Farm | 36 (12) | 11 (32) | 11 (7) | 58 (51) | 61 | 51 |
| SU48 R | West Ilsley | 23 (12) | 7 (20) | 6 (11) | 36 (43) | 58 | 54 |
| SU48 S | East Hendred Down | 24 (11) | 19 (13) | 16 (21) | 59 (45) | 69 | 57 |
| SU48 V | East Ilsley | 34 (21) | 6 (16) | 8 (3) | 48 (40) | 51 | 47 |
| SU48 W | Gore Hill | 23 (14) | 8 (14) | 12 (21) | 43 (49) | 50 | 50 |
| SU48 X | Chilton | 25 (11) | 10 (25) | 10 (17) | 45 (53) | 49 | 53 |
| SU56 B | Headley | 33 (50) | 14 (11) | 14 (9) | 61 (70) | 70 | 60 |
| SU56 C | Goldfinch Bottom | 45 (42) | 22 (16) | 13 (14) | 80 (72) | 112 | 68 |
| SU56 D | Thatcham West | 48 (68) | 20 (8) | 19 (23) | 87 (99) | 108 | 91 |
| SU56 E | Cold Ash | 23 (19) | 7 (7) | 14 (27) | 44 (53) | 46 | 43 |
| SU56 G | Mill Green | 40 (35) | 7 (18) | 3 (8) | 50 (61) | 68 | 67 |
| SU56 H | Crookham Common | 30 (40) | 25 (26) | 17 (7) | 72 (73) | 94 | 67 |
| SU56 I | Thatcham East | 21 (33) | 6 (16) | 20 (10) | 47 (59) | 61 | 50 |
| SU56 J | Harts Hill Farm | 37 (31) | 9 (21) | 8 (19) | 54 (71) | 62 | 34 |
| SU56 L | Ashford Hill | 28 (27) | 13 (16) | 10 (22) | 51 (65) | 59 | 38 |
| SU56 M | Brimpton Village | 34 (27) | 17 (24) | 12 (19) | 63 (70) | 81 | 57 |
| SU56 N | Midgham | 25 (54) | 24 (5) | 11 (5) | 60 (64) | 78 | 49 |
| SU56 P | Bucklebury Common | 21 (39) | 17 (14) | 15 (7) | 53 (60) | 59 | 51 |
| SU56 R | Brimpton Common | 30 (40) | 10 (14) | 14 (12) | 54 (66) | 64 | 39 |
| SU56 S | Brimpton Gravel Pits | 52 (58) | 21 (19) | 18 (31) | 91 (108) | 107 | 91 |
| SU56 T | Woolhampton | 52 (38) | 17 (8) | 17 (17) | 86 (63) | 126 | 93 |
| SU56 U | Upper Woolhampton | 21 (49) | 12 (0) | 19 (8) | 52 (57) | 56 | 51 |
| SU56 W | Heath End | 24 (32) | 20 (9) | 9 (19) | 53 (60) | 69 | 49 |
| SU56 X | Aldermaston Village | 21 (14) | 13 (18) | 30 (24) | 64 (56) | 74 | 61 |
| SU56 Y | Aldermaston Gravel Pits | 41 (39) | 23 (20) | 18 (11) | 82 (70) | 87 | 66 |
| SU56 Z | Beenham | 36 (37) | 7 (0) | 15 (12) | 58 (49) | 68 | 50 |
| SU57 A | Fence Wood | 21 (24) | 14 (25) | 12 (14) | 47 (63) | 51 | 42 |
| SU57 B | Hermitage | 29 (45) | 11 (18) | 8 (6) | 48 (69) | 62 | 49 |
| SU57 C | Trumpletts Farm | 23 (29) | 14 (14) | 13 (14) | 50 (57) | 57 | 38 |
| SU57 D | Oakhouse Farm | 22 (27) | 12 (16) | 11 (10) | 45 (53) | 47 | 42 |
| SU57 E | Cheseridge Farm | 24 (12) | 7 (21) | 7 (26) | 38 (59) | 38 | 54 |
| SU57 F | Withers Farm | 17 (24) | 4 (17) | 19 (22) | 40 (63) | 41 | 43 |
| SU57 G | Frilsham Church | 36 (24) | 6 (18) | 11 (19) | 53 (61) | 59 | 61 |
| SU57 H | Eling | 34 (28) | 21 (19) | 9 (11) | 64 (58) | 68 | 42 |
| SU57 I | Hampstead Norreys | 19 (21) | 22 (18) | 7 (12) | 48 (51) | 53 | 46 |
| SU57 J | New Farm, Compton | 28 (22) | 10 (14) | 8 (11) | 46 (47) | 47 | 47 |
| SU57 K | Bucklebury | 17 (24) | 4 (23) | 24 (19) | 45 (66) | 53 | 48 |
| SU57 L | Frilsham Common | 33 (20) | 6 (22) | 14 (12) | 53 (54) | 64 | 50 |
| SU57 M | Yattendon | 29 (30) | 13 (14) | 5 (12) | 47 (56) | 49 | 40 |
| SU57 N | Haw Farm | 26 (35) | 9 (10) | 10 (11) | 45 (56) | 48 | 39 |
| SU57 P | Aldworth | 26 (22) | 16 (21) | 8 (11) | 50 (54) | 53 | 39 |
| SU57 Q | Stanford Dingley | 23 (39) | 16 (17) | 17 (14) | 56 (70) | 63 | 55 |
| SU57 R | Maselands Farm | 30 (29) | 12 (22) | 11 (2) | 53 (53) | 56 | 52 |
| SU57 S | Burnt Hill | 25 (31) | 13 (20) | 10 (6) | 48 (57) | 57 | 42 |
| SU57 T | Ashampstead | 24 (21) | 14 (18) | 12 (11) | 50 (50) | 52 | 49 |
| SU57 U | Southridge Farm | 30 (30) | 8 (17) | 6 (6) | 44 (53) | 55 | 44 |
| SU57 V | Bradfield Southend | 25 (29) | 13 (24) | 13 (17) | 51 (70) | 52 | 53 |
| SU57 W | Greathouse Wood | 29 (26) | 25 (25) | 6 (11) | 60 (62) | 70 | 58 |
| SU57 X | Ashampstead Common | 25 (22) | 17 (18) | 6 (9) | 48 (49) | 49 | 42 |
| SU57 Y | Upper Basildon | 33 (35) | 13 (17) | 6 (8) | 52 (60) | 55 | 46 |
| SU57 Z | Stitchens Green | 18 (29) | 18 (14) | 11 (14) | 47 (57) | 50 | 52 |
| SU58 A | Superity Farm | 31 (16) | 7 (9) | 10 (21) | 48 (46) | 56 | 49 |
| SU58 B | Churn Farm | 27 (25) | 15 (5) | 7 (18) | 49 (48) | 63 | 56 |
| SU58 F | Stocks/Roden Farm | 28 (35) | 9 (11) | 12 (17) | 49 (63) | 55 | 46 |
| SU58 G | Lower Chance Farm | 27 (25) | 8 (22) | 13 (19) | 48 (66) | 55 | 44 |

| Tetrad | Tetrad name | Breeding Season: species with maximum breeding evidence 2007–11 (1987–89) | | | | Summer All species 2007–11 | Winter All species 2007–11 |
|--------|-------------|-----------|----------|----------|------------|---------|---------|
| | | **Confirmed** | **Probable** | **Possible** | **All levels** | | |
| SU58 K | Starveall Farm | 28 (30) | 8 (15) | 16 (11) | 52 (56) | 60 | 54 |
| SU58 L | Fair Mile | 21 (32) | 19 (15) | 12 (19) | 52 (66) | 66 | 42 |
| SU58 Q | Thurle Down | 26 (31) | 15 (7) | 11 (21) | 52 (59) | 55 | 47 |
| SU58 V | Streatley | 48 (31) | 13 (24) | 6 (15) | 67 (70) | 79 | 79 |
| SU58 W | Moulsford | 41 (49) | 16 (12) | 11 (17) | 68 (78) | 89 | 89 |
| SU66 B | Pamber Heath | 32 (54) | 19 (12) | 10 (7) | 61 (73) | 74 | 58 |
| SU66 C | Upper Padworth | 34 (31) | 13 (13) | 11 (9) | 58 (53) | 62 | 53 |
| SU66 D | Aldermarston Wharf | 36 (42) | 20 (19) | 29 (18) | 85 (79) | 105 | 87 |
| SU66 E | Bath Road Beenham | 33 (45) | 11 (18) | 7 (12) | 51 (75) | 65 | 65 |
| SU66 H | Padworth Common | 39 (37) | 18 (21) | 12 (6) | 69 (64) | 84 | 60 |
| SU66 I | Ufton Nervet | 21 (44) | 20 (9) | 16 (9) | 57 (62) | 66 | 53 |
| SU66 J | Sulhamstead | 48 (35) | 8 (21) | 14 (15) | 70 (71) | 87 | 64 |
| SU66 L | South Mortimer | 24 (36) | 16 (12) | 6 (9) | 46 (57) | 47 | 50 |
| SU66 M | Mortimer | 28 (31) | 8 (17) | 14 (14) | 50 (62) | 54 | 40 |
| SU66 N | Burghfield Common | 24 (34) | 2 (11) | 17 (12) | 43 (57) | 53 | 41 |
| SU66 P | Trash Green | 47 (44) | 7 (13) | 12 (20) | 66 (77) | 105 | 83 |
| SU66 R | Butler's Lands | 22 (37) | 14 (10) | 19 (11) | 55 (58) | 60 | 38 |
| SU66 S | Wokefield Park | 29 (34) | 11 (15) | 13 (11) | 53 (60) | 66 | 55 |
| SU66 T | Goddard's Green | 23 (34) | 4 (22) | 17 (8) | 44 (64) | 50 | 53 |
| SU66 U | Burghfield | 30 (28) | 17 (14) | 21 (17) | 68 (59) | 83 | 53 |
| SU66 W | Fair Cross | 27 (20) | 15 (17) | 7 (13) | 49 (50) | 50 | 43 |
| SU66 X | Beech Hill | 29 (27) | 4 (14) | 14 (9) | 47 (50) | 49 | 49 |
| SU66 Y | Grazeley | 21 (27) | 1 (17) | 14 (7) | 36 (51) | 53 | 39 |
| SU66 Z | Pingewood | 33 (35) | 15 (13) | 22 (15) | 70 (63) | 102 | 84 |
| SU67 A | Bournefield Farm | 48 (16) | 9 (17) | 5 (19) | 62 (52) | 71 | 67 |
| SU67 B | Bradfield | 24 (33) | 9 (24) | 17 (5) | 50 (62) | 63 | 53 |
| SU67 C | Great Bear | 26 (29) | 8 (9) | 9 (7) | 43 (45) | 48 | 41 |
| SU67 D | Basildon Park | 28 (26) | 11 (11) | 10 (13) | 49 (50) | 50 | 45 |
| SU67 E | Lower Basildon | 33 (39) | 8 (14) | 14 (12) | 55 (65) | 64 | 70 |
| SU67 F | Englefield Park | 60 (46) | 3 (16) | 10 (5) | 73 (67) | 95 | 93 |
| SU67 G | Hogmoor | 37 (25) | 12 (18) | 9 (14) | 58 (57) | 62 | 41 |
| SU67 H | Tidmarsh | 32 (28) | 8 (9) | 13 (7) | 53 (44) | 71 | 50 |
| SU67 I | Pangbourne | 47 (25) | 5 (18) | 7 (14) | 59 (57) | 67 | 60 |
| SU67 J | Coombe End Farm | 29 (26) | 14 (21) | 13 (9) | 56 (56) | 60 | 49 |
| SU67 K | Theale | 57 (50) | 4 (15) | 15 (4) | 76 (69) | 105 | 95 |
| SU67 L | Nunhide Farm | 25 (30) | 12 (19) | 5 (13) | 42 (62) | 54 | 50 |
| SU67 M | Sulham | 29 (20) | 8 (16) | 16 (7) | 53 (43) | 59 | 61 |
| SU67 N | Purley Rise | 30 (36) | 15 (24) | 12 (4) | 57 (64) | 71 | 73 |
| SU67 Q | Burghfield Mill | 40 (54) | 9 (20) | 27 (10) | 76 (84) | 105 | 91 |
| SU67 R | Tilehurst | 25 (28) | 2 (10) | 13 (9) | 40 (47) | 46 | 54 |
| SU67 S | Scours Lane | 31 (40) | 4 (13) | 7 (14) | 42 (67) | 69 | 54 |
| SU67 T | Purley Village | 35 (32) | 13 (16) | 9 (9) | 57 (57) | 65 | 62 |
| SU67 V | Searles Farm | 34 (40) | 3 (13) | 32 (16) | 69 (69) | 89 | 90 |
| SU67 W | Prospect Park | 28 (25) | 7 (12) | 3 (7) | 38 (44) | 44 | 38 |
| SU67 X | Warren Lane | 28 (11) | 11 (22) | 24 (23) | 63 (56) | 68 | 66 |
| SU67 Y | Chazey Heath | 31 (21) | 6 (18) | 15 (11) | 52 (50) | 53 | 52 |
| SU68 A | Goring | 33 (18) | 10 (22) | 17 (11) | 60 (51) | 66 | 68 |
| SU68 B | South Stoke | 31 (18) | 17 (12) | 12 (29) | 60 (59) | 65 | 70 |
| SU76 B | Stanford End | 31 (37) | 24 (23) | 10 (3) | 65 (63) | 71 | 64 |
| SU76 C | Loddon Court | 37 (27) | 12 (19) | 5 (19) | 54 (65) | 58 | 49 |
| SU76 D | Spencers Wood | 27 (30) | 11 (17) | 3 (16) | 41 (63) | 46 | 49 |
| SU76 E | Great Lea Common | 29 (31) | 10 (20) | 13 (18) | 52 (69) | 71 | 60 |
| SU76 G | Riseley | 43 (34) | 12 (26) | 5 (7) | 60 (67) | 68 | 67 |
| SU76 H | Swallowfield | 42 (39) | 15 (14) | 7 (15) | 64 (68) | 70 | 55 |
| SU76 I | Hyde End | 26 (20) | 18 (18) | 16 (14) | 60 (52) | 73 | 67 |
| SU76 J | Shinfield Park | 26 (31) | 8 (14) | 18 (14) | 52 (59) | 60 | 55 |
| SU76 L | Bramshill | 48 (39) | 12 (23) | 8 (3) | 68 (65) | 79 | 65 |

| Tetrad | Tetrad name | Breeding Season: species with maximum breeding evidence 2007–11 (1987–89) | | | | Summer All species 2007–11 | Winter All species 2007–11 |
|--------|-------------|-----------|----------|----------|------------|--------|--------|
| | | Confirmed | Probable | Possible | All levels | | |
| SU76 M | Farley Hill | 32 (35) | 13 (8) | 13 (25) | 58 (68) | 65 | 45 |
| SU76 N | Arborfield | 32 (32) | 7 (12) | 20 (23) | 59 (67) | 71 | 61 |
| SU76 P | Rushy Mead | 41 (48) | 8 (17) | 6 (6) | 55 (71) | 58 | 78 |
| SU76 R | Eversley | 29 (27) | 12 (25) | 9 (11) | 50 (63) | 57 | 43 |
| SU76 S | Arborfield Green | 23 (34) | 5 (21) | 17 (8) | 45 (63) | 49 | 40 |
| SU76 T | Arborfield Cross | 23 (26) | 7 (15) | 17 (12) | 47 (53) | 47 | 45 |
| SU76 U | Bearwood | 46 (25) | 17 (14) | 2 (14) | 65 (53) | 68 | 75 |
| SU76 W | Finchampstead | 22 (31) | 10 (20) | 26 (9) | 58 (60) | 84 | 64 |
| SU76 X | California | 23 (40) | 12 (23) | 21 (3) | 56 (66) | 63 | 55 |
| SU76 Y | Barkham | 30 (17) | 9 (8) | 10 (22) | 49 (47) | 53 | 52 |
| SU76 Z | Woosehill | 21 (24) | 4 (17) | 10 (22) | 35 (63) | 52 | 57 |
| SU77 A | Smallmead | 39 (31) | 11 (9) | 11 (8) | 61 (48) | 70 | 66 |
| SU77 B | Central Reading | 27 (28) | 9 (9) | 12 (21) | 48 (58) | 51 | 51 |
| SU77 C | Caversham | 26 (23) | 10 (9) | 14 (14) | 50 (46) | 55 | 66 |
| SU77 D | Emmer Green | 33 (21) | 4 (17) | 10 (8) | 47 (46) | 53 | 51 |
| SU77 F | Reading University (Whiteknights) | 32 (31) | 9 (9) | 10 (6) | 51 (46) | 54 | 52 |
| SU77 G | Redlands | 33 (36) | 10 (11) | 8 (16) | 51 (63) | 65 | 61 |
| SU77 H | Henley Road | 41 (28) | 14 (21) | 11 (24) | 66 (73) | 74 | 82 |
| SU77 I | Caversham Park | 22 (14) | 12 (15) | 13 (16) | 47 (45) | 55 | 56 |
| SU77 K | Lower Earley | 25 (31) | 5 (15) | 11 (11) | 41 (57) | 49 | 47 |
| SU77 L | South Lake | 34 (30) | 13 (9) | 8 (7) | 55 (46) | 67 | 64 |
| SU77 M | Sonning | 33 (31) | 23 (25) | 12 (12) | 68 (68) | 74 | 89 |
| SU77 N | Sonning Eye | 22 (16) | 17 (24) | 16 (16) | 55 (56) | 61 | 71 |
| SU77 Q | Loddon Bridge | 30 (23) | 7 (16) | 7 (19) | 44 (58) | 53 | 57 |
| SU77 R | Woodley | 45 (37) | 4 (13) | 19 (26) | 68 (76) | 76 | 80 |
| SU77 S | Charvil South | 32 (9) | 13 (35) | 15 (4) | 60 (48) | 64 | 68 |
| SU77 T | Charvil North | 43 (26) | 20 (30) | 14 (9) | 77 (65) | 103 | 95 |
| SU77 U | Shiplake | 25 (22) | 16 (17) | 22 (21) | 63 (60) | 82 | 75 |
| SU77 V | Winnersh | 28 (33) | 9 (24) | 8 (17) | 45 (74) | 47 | 64 |
| SU77 W | Dinton Pastures | 53 (63) | 21 (9) | 14 (11) | 88 (83) | 125 | 109 |
| SU77 X | Whistley Green | 42 (55) | 12 (9) | 24 (12) | 78 (76) | 96 | 88 |
| SU77 Y | Twyford | 37 (29) | 7 (6) | 4 (16) | 48 (51) | 72 | 66 |
| SU77 Z | Wargrave | 32 (39) | 22 (9) | 1 (9) | 55 (57) | 59 | 56 |
| SU78 Q | Bolney | 20 (25) | 27 (16) | 8 (10) | 55 (51) | 68 | 52 |
| SU78 R | Remenham Court | 28 (20) | 26 (14) | 7 (17) | 61 (51) | 69 | 64 |
| SU78 S | Temple Island | 22 (28) | 18 (19) | 17 (15) | 57 (62) | 70 | 68 |
| SU78 V | Crazies Hill | 25 (28) | 19 (18) | 9 (14) | 53 (60) | 57 | 57 |
| SU78 W | Remenham Hill | 44 (12) | 16 (10) | 12 (33) | 72 (55) | 82 | 64 |
| SU78 X | Aston | 34 (11) | 19 (9) | 14 (22) | 67 (42) | 72 | 66 |
| SU85 P | Yorktown | 29 (41) | 11 (14) | 16 (9) | 56 (64) | 64 | 64 |
| SU86 A | Yateley | 42 (40) | 9 (16) | 4 (13) | 55 (69) | 67 | 71 |
| SU86 B | Finchampstead Ridge | 50 (48) | 19 (20) | 16 (8) | 85 (76) | 124 | 109 |
| SU86 C | Wick Hill | 31 (20) | 8 (17) | 20 (13) | 59 (50) | 62 | 54 |
| SU86 D | Eastheath | 27 (30) | 7 (13) | 11 (6) | 45 (49) | 56 | 51 |
| SU86 E | Wokingham | 24 (15) | 3 (15) | 10 (11) | 37 (41) | 48 | 56 |
| SU86 F | Sandhurst | 43 (42) | 9 (11) | 6 (16) | 58 (69) | 70 | 78 |
| SU86 G | Wellington College | 27 (30) | 7 (10) | 5 (10) | 39 (50) | 46 | 51 |
| SU86 H | Nine Mile Ride | 35 (32) | 4 (9) | 9 (6) | 48 (47) | 59 | 64 |
| SU86 I | Holme Green | 27 (24) | 8 (16) | 8 (18) | 43 (58) | 61 | 53 |
| SU86 J | Amen Corner | 32 (14) | 4 (20) | 6 (22) | 42 (56) | 51 | 47 |
| SU86 K | College Farm | 29 (20) | 7 (18) | 10 (19) | 46 (57) | 59 | 57 |
| SU86 L | Owlsmoor | 25 (50) | 14 (10) | 20 (12) | 59 (72) | 64 | 46 |
| SU86 M | Crowthorne | 36 (50) | 7 (12) | 16 (10) | 59 (72) | 64 | 43 |
| SU86 N | Great Hollands | 29 (14) | 3 (20) | 14 (11) | 46 (45) | 56 | 51 |
| SU86 P | Popeswood | 34 (25) | 9 (22) | 12 (18) | 55 (65) | 64 | 53 |
| SU86 Q | RMA Sandhurst | 26 (41) | 7 (12) | 23 (5) | 56 (58) | 65 | 56 |
| SU86 R | Poppy Hills | 29 (30) | 11 (16) | 14 (9) | 54 (55) | 66 | 49 |

497

| Tetrad | Tetrad name | Breeding Season: species with maximum breeding evidence 2007–11 (1987–89) | | | | Summer All species 2007–11 | Winter All species 2007–11 |
|---|---|---|---|---|---|---|---|
| | | Confirmed | Probable | Possible | All levels | | |
| SU86 S | Caesar's Camp | 26 (34) | 22 (12) | 3 (13) | 51 (59) | 61 | 45 |
| SU86 T | Easthampstead | 27 (22) | 9 (12) | 9 (12) | 45 (46) | 50 | 57 |
| SU86 U | Bracknell | 21 (25) | 5 (14) | 8 (3) | 34 (42) | 44 | 48 |
| SU86 W | Olddean Common | 24 (28) | 14 (11) | 5 (15) | 43 (54) | 52 | 44 |
| SU86 X | Surrey Hill | 28 (32) | 14 (14) | 12 (25) | 54 (71) | 62 | 48 |
| SU86 Y | Swinley Park | 36 (33) | 11 (13) | 9 (9) | 56 (55) | 67 | 52 |
| SU86 Z | Chavey Down | 21 (23) | 10 (12) | 15 (16) | 46 (51) | 49 | 51 |
| SU87 A | Bill Hill Park | 35 (36) | 11 (18) | 10 (7) | 56 (61) | 71 | 50 |
| SU87 B | Buckland Farm | 23 (11) | 12 (5) | 9 (30) | 44 (46) | 51 | 42 |
| SU87 C | Stanlake Park | 32 (7) | 15 (13) | 13 (15) | 60 (35) | 67 | 44 |
| SU87 D | Hare Hatch | 28 (6) | 7 (26) | 11 (16) | 46 (48) | 52 | 53 |
| SU87 E | Kiln Green | 27 (40) | 8 (17) | 11 (6) | 46 (63) | 56 | 53 |
| SU87 F | Kingscote | 30 (6) | 4 (2) | 10 (27) | 44 (35) | 47 | 49 |
| SU87 G | Billingbear | 28 (18) | 12 (10) | 11 (22) | 51 (50) | 60 | 48 |
| SU87 H | Shurlock Row | 36 (2) | 10 (7) | 6 (22) | 52 (31) | 65 | 53 |
| SU87 I | Waltham St Lawrence | 39 (16) | 12 (17) | 11 (14) | 62 (47) | 66 | 61 |
| SU87 J | Knowle Hill | 40 (32) | 8 (17) | 10 (7) | 58 (56) | 65 | 66 |
| SU87 K | Binfield | 33 (28) | 5 (16) | 13 (11) | 51 (55) | 64 | 64 |
| SU87 L | Binfield Lodge | 26 (41) | 20 (16) | 7 (13) | 53 (70) | 59 | 60 |
| SU87 M | Beenham's Heath | 28 (35) | 24 (17) | 6 (7) | 58 (59) | 62 | 64 |
| SU87 N | White Waltham | 41 (49) | 14 (8) | 10 (6) | 65 (63) | 68 | 64 |
| SU87 P | Waltham Airfield | 32 (41) | 8 (10) | 9 (3) | 49 (54) | 60 | 59 |
| SU87 Q | Newell Green | 32 (36) | 4 (25) | 16 (4) | 52 (65) | 57 | 46 |
| SU87 R | Jealott's Hill | 40 (43) | 10 (21) | 9 (8) | 59 (72) | 67 | 62 |
| SU87 S | Braywoodside | 36 (31) | 20 (8) | 12 (14) | 68 (53) | 79 | 64 |
| SU87 T | Paley Street | 35 (33) | 9 (21) | 3 (7) | 47 (61) | 59 | 56 |
| SU87 U | Cox Green | 33 (32) | 9 (19) | 9 (15) | 51 (66) | 68 | 62 |
| SU87 V | Winkfield Row | 37 (44) | 15 (14) | 11 (8) | 63 (66) | 71 | 64 |
| SU87 W | Maiden's Green | 32 (32) | 9 (19) | 18 (4) | 59 (55) | 66 | 58 |
| SU87 X | Drift Road | 26 (38) | 13 (15) | 15 (5) | 54 (58) | 60 | 46 |
| SU87 Y | Holyport | 35 (28) | 13 (14) | 8 (12) | 56 (54) | 61 | 56 |
| SU87 Z | Bray Wick | 37 (32) | 8 (16) | 5 (14) | 50 (62) | 58 | 63 |
| SU88 A | Warren Row | 37 (6) | 3 (7) | 12 (25) | 52 (38) | 52 | 51 |
| SU88 B | Frogmill | 55 (36) | 17 (15) | 11 (22) | 83 (73) | 92 | 85 |
| SU88 C | Medmenham | 31 (3) | 9 (15) | 13 (16) | 53 (34) | 66 | 63 |
| SU88 F | Ashley Hill | 43 (35) | 9 (15) | 11 (3) | 63 (53) | 68 | 64 |
| SU88 G | Hurley | 33 (8) | 7 (4) | 10 (26) | 50 (38) | 54 | 66 |
| SU88 H | Temple Lock | 26 (11) | 20 (18) | 7 (17) | 53 (46) | 62 | 59 |
| SU88 K | Maidenhead Thicket | 38 (30) | 4 (18) | 6 (11) | 48 (59) | 54 | 54 |
| SU88 L | Pinkney's Green | 43 (28) | 6 (16) | 5 (8) | 54 (52) | 60 | 55 |
| SU88 M | Bisham | 35 (35) | 25 (20) | 7 (11) | 67 (66) | 79 | 75 |
| SU88 N | Marlow | 28 (5) | 15 (6) | 5 (20) | 48 (31) | 61 | 63 |
| SU88 Q | Boyn Hill | 22 (10) | 4 (0) | 1 (13) | 27 (23) | 41 | 47 |
| SU88 R | Furze Platt | 31 (19) | 12 (20) | 8 (5) | 51 (44) | 68 | 67 |
| SU88 S | Cookham Dean | 36 (40) | 14 (12) | 13 (1) | 63 (53) | 71 | 68 |
| SU88 T | Winter Hill | 47 (42) | 21 (16) | 10 (23) | 78 (81) | 121 | 108 |
| SU88 V | Maidenhead | 33 (22) | 4 (14) | 8 (10) | 45 (46) | 54 | 58 |
| SU88 W | North Town | 46 (51) | 8 (6) | 10 (9) | 64 (66) | 89 | 83 |
| SU88 X | Cookham Rise | 53 (40) | 4 (13) | 11 (12) | 68 (65) | 75 | 74 |
| SU88 Y | Bourne End | 48 (25) | 9 (20) | 8 (19) | 65 (64) | 89 | 91 |
| SU96 C | Bagshot Park | 26 (17) | 12 (19) | 11 (18) | 49 (54) | 52 | 36 |
| SU96 D | Tower Hill | 26 (30) | 12 (14) | 12 (8) | 50 (52) | 52 | 40 |
| SU96 E | Englemere Pond | 30 (15) | 12 (10) | 8 (15) | 50 (40) | 64 | 54 |
| SU96 H | Windlesham Hall | 23 (25) | 5 (14) | 10 (14) | 38 (53) | 45 | 41 |
| SU96 I | South Ascot | 23 (28) | 9 (7) | 3 (9) | 35 (44) | 44 | 38 |
| SU96 J | Ascot | 32 (40) | 7 (10) | 10 (13) | 49 (63) | 64 | 64 |
| SU96 M [1] | Sunningdale Golf Course | 35 (–) | 9 (–) | 13 (–) | 57 (–) | 65 | 30 |

| Tetrad | Tetrad name | Breeding Season: species with maximum breeding evidence 2007–11 (1987–89) | | | | Summer All species 2007–11 | Winter All species 2007–11 |
|---|---|---|---|---|---|---|---|
| | | Confirmed | Probable | Possible | All levels | | |
| SU96 N | Sunningdale | 26 (25) | 12 (16) | 9 (7) | 47 (48) | 52 | 35 |
| SU96 P | Cheapside | 22 (45) | 6 (11) | 9 (12) | 37 (68) | 41 | 67 |
| SU96 T | Broomhall | 33 (28) | 15 (16) | 11 (13) | 59 (57) | 67 | 34 |
| SU96 U | Virginia Water | 22 (45) | 20 (11) | 4 (12) | 46 (68) | 48 | 67 |
| SU97 A | Brookside | 32 (30) | 12 (5) | 14 (15) | 58 (50) | 65 | 51 |
| SU97 B | Winkfield | 25 (27) | 11 (13) | 18 (13) | 54 (53) | 58 | 53 |
| SU97 C | New Lodge | 29 (47) | 19 (12) | 13 (13) | 61 (72) | 65 | 52 |
| SU97 D | Fifield | 32 (27) | 7 (22) | 10 (17) | 49 (66) | 57 | 53 |
| SU97 E | Bray | 44 (27) | 13 (15) | 15 (27) | 72 (69) | 89 | 87 |
| SU97 F | Woodside | 44 (30) | 18 (12) | 9 (11) | 71 (53) | 76 | 54 |
| SU97 G | Cranbourne | 34 (24) | 15 (11) | 6 (19) | 55 (54) | 63 | 57 |
| SU97 H | St Leonard's | 26 (20) | 17 (14) | 13 (20) | 56 (54) | 61 | 47 |
| SU97 I | Oakley Green | 38 (17) | 12 (15) | 16 (24) | 66 (56) | 110 | 98 |
| SU97 J | Dorney | 55 (40) | 9 (16) | 13 (12) | 77 (68) | 123 | 108 |
| SU97 K | Home Farm | 37 (18) | 17 (8) | 10 (21) | 64 (47) | 71 | 70 |
| SU97 L | Ranger's Lodge | 35 (32) | 22 (21) | 12 (5) | 69 (58) | 77 | 55 |
| SU97 M | Clewer Green | 33 (29) | 12 (8) | 12 (11) | 57 (48) | 61 | 51 |
| SU97 N | Clewer Village | 35 (42) | 2 (18) | 5 (15) | 42 (75) | 58 | 65 |
| SU97 P | Slough Sewage Farm | 36 (32) | 19 (5) | 12 (22) | 67 (59) | 84 | 89 |
| SU97 Q | Great Meadow Pond | 58 (56) | 11 (16) | 11 (6) | 80 (78) | 102 | 85 |
| SU97 R | Snow Hill | 47 (45) | 10 (6) | 4 (5) | 61 (56) | 65 | 63 |
| SU97 S | Shaw Farm | 34 (31) | 12 (12) | 5 (17) | 51 (60) | 57 | 53 |
| SU97 T | Windsor Castle | 32 (34) | 5 (9) | 10 (8) | 47 (51) | 61 | 63 |
| SU97 U | Agars Plough | 41 (14) | 13 (6) | 11 (15) | 65 (35) | 74 | 80 |
| SU97 W | Runnymede | 35 (36) | 11 (17) | 6 (16) | 52 (69) | 64 | 66 |
| SU97 X | Ham Island | 41 (23) | 14 (16) | 5 (11) | 60 (50) | 69 | 76 |
| SU97 Y | Datchet | 35 (28) | 13 (7) | 8 (28) | 56 (63) | 69 | 67 |
| SU97 Z | Upton | 30 (35) | 7 (10) | 10 (14) | 47 (59) | 53 | 55 |
| SU98 A | Amerden Ponds | 51 (30) | 7 (14) | 13 (6) | 71 (50) | 95 | 95 |
| SU98 B | Taplow | 46 (22) | 10 (12) | 10 (28) | 66 (62) | 77 | 75 |
| SU98 C | Cliveden | 49 (16) | 4 (9) | 4 (35) | 57 (60) | 64 | 73 |
| SU98 F | Huntercombe Manor | 23 (13) | 1 (8) | 3 (20) | 27 (41) | 34 | 43 |
| SU98 G | Burnham | 29 (6) | 6 (10) | 9 (15) | 44 (31) | 50 | 46 |
| SU98 K | Cippenham | 16 (33) | 8 (10) | 4 (13) | 28 (56) | 40 | 44 |
| SU98 L | Britwell | 28 (30) | 4 (8) | 14 (6) | 46 (44) | 48 | 42 |
| SU98 Q | Central Slough | 25 (33) | 3 (16) | 11 (15) | 39 (64) | 48 | 49 |
| SU98 R | Stoke Park | 26 (43) | 13 (10) | 8 (2) | 47 (55) | 53 | 54 |
| SU98 V | Slough North East | 36 (32) | 9 (9) | 7 (15) | 52 (56) | 62 | 50 |
| SU98 W | Wexham Street | 31 (27) | 2 (14) | 8 (14) | 41 (55) | 55 | 50 |
| TQ07 A | Egham | 33 (22) | 12 (14) | 11 (11) | 56 (47) | 67 | 57 |
| TQ07 B | Wraysbury Gravel Pits | 43 (74) | 18 (7) | 8 (10) | 69 (91) | 88 | 101 |
| TQ07 C | Horton | 37 (67) | 23 (9) | 13 (1) | 73 (77) | 104 | 83 |
| TQ07 D | Queen Mother Reservoir | 26 (53) | 9 (6) | 17 (7) | 52 (66) | 117 | 113 |
| TQ07 E | Langley | 25 (9) | 11 (31) | 8 (16) | 44 (56) | 46 | 45 |
| TQ07 F | Egham Hythe | 30 (15) | 17 (7) | 12 (16) | 59 (38) | 65 | 60 |
| TQ07 G | Staines Moor | 42 (48) | 14 (7) | 12 (15) | 68 (70) | 95 | 85 |
| TQ07 H | Stanwell Moor | 41 (63) | 15 (8) | 12 (7) | 68 (78) | 83 | 73 |
| TQ07 I | Colnbrook | 31 (14) | 9 (32) | 12 (15) | 52 (61) | 74 | 62 |
| TQ07 J | Sutton | 30 (6) | 10 (39) | 16 (8) | 56 (53) | 67 | 70 |
| TQ07 N [2] | Longford | 35 (–) | 14 (–) | 5 (–) | 54 (–) | 59 | 56 |
| TQ07 P [2] | Thorney | 33 (–) | 12 (–) | 13 (–) | 58 (–) | 67 | 68 |
| TQ08 A | Langley Park | 30 (49) | 9 (16) | 12 (6) | 51 (71) | 58 | 57 |
| TQ08 F | Iver | 26 (28) | 8 (11) | 8 (8) | 42 (47) | 49 | 50 |

## Table A3: **Rank order of distribution of species in the winter season**

| Species | | Species | | Species | |
|---|---|---|---|---|---|
| Woodpigeon | 100 | Red-legged Partridge | 47 | Yellow-legged Gull | 8 |
| Robin | 100 | Canada Goose | 45 | Woodlark | 8 |
| Blue Tit | 100 | Marsh Tit | 45 | Jack Snipe | 8 |
| Great Tit | 100 | Yellowhammer | 45 | Pintail | 7 |
| Chaffinch | 100 | Coot | 45 | Red-crested Pochard | 7 |
| Blackbird | 100 | Mute Swan | 44 | Crossbill | 7 |
| Carrion Crow | 100 | Grey Wagtail | 44 | Bittern | 6 |
| Magpie | 99 | Lesser Redpoll | 43 | Scaup | 6 |
| Wren | 99 | Linnet | 43 | Ruddy Duck | 6 |
| Dunnock | 98 | Brambling | 42 | Hen Harrier | 6 |
| Goldfinch | 98 | Cormorant | 42 | White-fronted Goose | 5 |
| Long-tailed Tit | 97 | Herring Gull | 39 | Willow Tit | 5 |
| Redwing | 97 | Reed Bunting | 37 | Smew | 5 |
| Jackdaw | 96 | Egyptian Goose | 36 | Curlew | 5 |
| Song Thrush | 95 | Stonechat | 36 | Firecrest | 5 |
| Great Spotted Woodpecker | 93 | Blackcap | 35 | Barnacle Goose | 5 |
| Jay | 93 | Tufted Duck | 34 | Short-eared Owl | 5 |
| Greenfinch | 93 | Woodcock | 34 | Dartford Warbler | 5 |
| Fieldfare | 93 | Kingfisher | 31 | Mediterranean Gull | 4 |
| Buzzard | 91 | Raven | 30 | Caspian Gull | 4 |
| Pied Wagtail | 90 | Golden Plover | 30 | Dunlin | 4 |
| Red Kite | 90 | Barn Owl | 30 | Redshank | 3 |
| Mistle Thrush | 89 | Little Grebe | 29 | Bewick's Swan | 2 |
| Starling | 89 | Snipe | 29 | Ferruginous Duck | 2 |
| Green Woodpecker | 86 | Ring-necked Parakeet | 29 | Common Sandpiper | 2 |
| Kestrel | 86 | Little Owl | 29 | Tree Sparrow | 2 |
| Rook | 86 | Teal | 26 | Common Redpoll | 2 |
| Pheasant | 85 | Waxwing | 26 | Snow Goose | 2 |
| Goldcrest | 85 | Great Crested Grebe | 26 | Black-necked Grebe | 2 |
| House Sparrow | 84 | Little Egret | 26 | Oystercatcher | 2 |
| Collared Dove | 84 | Peregrine | 25 | Hawfinch | 2 |
| Nuthatch | 81 | Gadwall | 24 | Pink-footed Goose | 2 |
| Coal Tit | 80 | Greylag Goose | 23 | Common Scoter | 2 |
| Black-headed Gull | 78 | Pochard | 23 | Great Northern Diver | 2 |
| Bullfinch | 75 | Water Rail | 21 | Great White Egret | 2 |
| Sparrowhawk | 72 | Grey Partridge | 21 | Marsh Harrier | 2 |
| Skylark | 70 | Chiffchaff | 21 | Black Redstart | 2 |
| Moorhen | 69 | Wigeon | 20 | Brent Goose (Dark-bellied) | 1 |
| Mallard | 68 | Shoveler | 18 | Slavonian Grebe | 1 |
| Stock Dove | 66 | Mandarin Duck | 16 | Goshawk | 1 |
| Meadow Pipit | 64 | Goosander | 15 | Great Grey Shrike | 1 |
| Siskin | 62 | Lesser Spotted Woodpecker | 13 | Whooper Swan | 1 |
| Treecreeper | 60 | Corn Bunting | 13 | Red-breasted Merganser | 1 |
| Grey Heron | 59 | Green Sandpiper | 12 | Ringed Plover | 1 |
| Lesser Black-backed Gull | 54 | Shelduck | 11 | Black-tailed Godwit | 1 |
| Feral Pigeon | 54 | Merlin | 11 | Iceland Gull | 1 |
| Lapwing | 52 | Great Black-backed Gull | 10 | Water Pipit | 1 |
| Tawny Owl | 51 | Goldeneye | 9 | Wood Duck | 1 |
| Common Gull | 49 | Cetti's Warbler | 8 | Garganey | 1 |

| | | | | | |
|---|---|---|---|---|---|
| Red-necked Grebe | 1 | Long-eared Owl | 1 | Spotted Redshank | 0.3 |
| Rough-legged Buzzard | 1 | Sand Martin | 1 | Grey Phalarope | 0.3 |
| Grey Plover | 1 | Yellow Wagtail | 1 | Kittiwake | 0.3 |
| Sanderling | 1 | American Wigeon | 1 | House Martin | 0.3 |
| Ruff | 1 | Glossy Ibis | 1 | Dipper | 0.3 |
| Swallow | 1 | Siberian Chiffchaff | 1 | Yellow-browed Warbler | 0.3 |
| Rock Pipit | 1 | Brown Shrike | 1 | Velvet Scoter | 0.3 |
| White Wagtail (*alba*) | 1 | Bean Goose | 0.3 | Kumlien's Gull | 0.3 |
| Bearded Tit | 1 | Gannet | 0.3 | Little Auk | 0.3 |
| Long-tailed Duck | 1 | Shag | 0.3 | Crane | 0.3 |
| Lesser Scaup | 1 | Spoonbill | 0.3 | Spoonbill | 0.3 |
| Greenshank | 1 | Avocet | 0.3 | Pomarine Skua | 0.3 |
| Little Gull | 1 | Knot | 0.3 | Lapland Bunting | 0.3 |
| Glaucous Gull | 1 | Bar-tailed Godwit | 0.3 | | |

## Table A4: Rank order of distribution of species with evidence of breeding

| Species | % of tetrads occupied | | % tetrads confirmed | | Species | % of tetrads occupied | | % tetrads confirmed | |
|---|---|---|---|---|---|---|---|---|---|
| | 2007 –2011 | 1987 –1989 | 2007 –2011 | 1987 –1989 | | 2007 –2011 | 1987 –1989 | 2007 –2011 | 1987 –1989 |
| Wren | 100 | 100 | 77 | 78 | Pheasant | 82 | 93 | 24 | 55 |
| Blackbird | 100 | 99 | 94 | 92 | Nuthatch | 82 | 78 | 58 | 42 |
| Woodpigeon | 100 | 99 | 77 | 79 | Skylark | 81 | 87 | 24 | 23 |
| Great Tit | 100 | 99 | 96 | 89 | Goldcrest | 81 | 81 | 38 | 30 |
| Blue Tit | 99 | 100 | 98 | 95 | Starling | 81 | 99 | 69 | 93 |
| Robin | 99 | 100 | 93 | 86 | Kestrel | 75 | 87 | 29 | 23 |
| Blackcap | 99 | 95 | 69 | 43 | Mallard | 75 | 81 | 55 | 59 |
| Chaffinch | 99 | 100 | 83 | 82 | Red Kite | 73 | 0 | 17 | 0 |
| Dunnock | 99 | 99 | 69 | 69 | Coal Tit | 73 | 75 | 47 | 39 |
| Song Thrush | 98 | 97 | 61 | 74 | House Martin | 72 | 95 | 47 | 78 |
| Goldfinch | 98 | 87 | 71 | 38 | Moorhen | 71 | 79 | 58 | 64 |
| Chiffchaff | 97 | 93 | 53 | 36 | Bullfinch | 68 | 87 | 23 | 32 |
| Carrion Crow | 96 | 100 | 77 | 67 | Willow Warbler | 67 | 95 | 15 | 49 |
| Magpie | 96 | 99 | 72 | 78 | Treecreeper | 67 | 79 | 38 | 38 |
| Greenfinch | 95 | 98 | 62 | 58 | Linnet | 67 | 74 | 30 | 28 |
| Great Spotted Woodpecker | 95 | 90 | 70 | 47 | Rook | 66 | 82 | 54 | 56 |
| Jackdaw | 95 | 92 | 72 | 57 | Garden Warbler | 60 | 74 | 15 | 21 |
| Long-tailed Tit | 94 | 94 | 84 | 73 | Yellowhammer | 59 | 88 | 27 | 43 |
| Whitethroat | 91 | 83 | 63 | 38 | Sparrowhawk | 58 | 75 | 18 | 25 |
| House Sparrow | 89 | 97 | 78 | 85 | Lapwing | 56 | 76 | 31 | 40 |
| Mistle Thrush | 87 | 96 | 47 | 71 | Swift | 54 | 84 | 13 | 28 |
| Swallow | 86 | 94 | 66 | 69 | Red-legged Partridge | 52 | 59 | 9 | 18 |
| Buzzard | 85 | 7 | 34 | 1 | Cuckoo | 52 | 83 | 2 | 9 |
| Green Woodpecker | 85 | 77 | 40 | 25 | Tawny Owl | 50 | 69 | 21 | 15 |
| Stock Dove | 84 | 78 | 28 | 22 | Coot | 49 | 52 | 44 | 43 |
| Jay | 83 | 89 | 36 | 42 | Canada Goose | 47 | 49 | 37 | 30 |
| Collared Dove | 83 | 94 | 32 | 48 | Lesser Whitethroat | 43 | 53 | 6 | 14 |
| Pied Wagtail | 82 | 92 | 56 | 62 | Mute Swan | 43 | 39 | 33 | 26 |

| Species | % of tetrads occupied | | % tetrads confirmed | |
|---|---|---|---|---|
| | 2007 –2011 | 1987 –1989 | 2007 –2011 | 1987 –1989 |
| Reed Bunting | 38 | 50 | 16 | 18 |
| Little Owl | 37 | 57 | 13 | 15 |
| Marsh Tit | 36 | 51 | 18 | 19 |
| Feral Pigeon | 36 | 61 | 11 | 19 |
| Hobby | 35 | 17 | 6 | 2 |
| Grey Wagtail | 34 | 39 | 20 | 19 |
| Egyptian Goose | 33 | 2 | 22 | 1 |
| Barn Owl | 32 | 14 | 19 | 3 |
| Kingfisher | 32 | 37 | 11 | 10 |
| Spotted Flycatcher | 31 | 70 | 12 | 39 |
| Mandarin Duck | 30 | 13 | 17 | 6 |
| Tufted Duck | 28 | 33 | 11 | 14 |
| Grey Heron | 28 | 40 | 9 | 5 |
| Great Crested Grebe | 27 | 25 | 22 | 18 |
| Reed Warbler | 27 | 19 | 13 | 10 |
| Sedge Warbler | 25 | 33 | 9 | 13 |
| Greylag Goose | 23 | 7 | 14 | 3 |
| Ring-necked Parakeet | 22 | 4 | 9 | 1 |
| Grey Partridge | 22 | 64 | 5 | 25 |
| Little Grebe | 20 | 31 | 10 | 21 |
| Woodcock | 18 | 35 | 0 | 4 |
| Yellow Wagtail | 17 | 24 | 10 | 8 |
| Gadwall | 16 | 6 | 6 | 2 |
| Corn Bunting | 15 | 35 | 6 | 8 |
| Raven | 13 | 0 | 2 | 0 |
| Sand Martin | 13 | 19 | 7 | 5 |
| Meadow Pipit | 13 | 34 | 3 | 9 |
| Common Tern | 12 | 9 | 7 | 4 |
| Cetti's Warbler | 12 | 2 | 3 | 0.3 |
| Nightjar | 11 | 6 | 3 | 2 |
| Siskin | 11 | 10 | 1 | 0.3 |
| Turtle Dove | 10 | 58 | 1 | 6 |
| Shelduck | 10 | 3 | 4 | 1 |
| Firecrest | 10 | 5 | 3 | 1 |
| Cormorant | 10 | 0 | 1 | 0 |
| Lesser Spotted Woodpecker | 9 | 30 | 0.3 | 6 |
| Black-headed Gull | 9 | 22 | 3 | 1 |
| Little Ringed Plover | 9 | 10 | 6 | 5 |
| Woodlark | 9 | 3 | 4 | 2 |
| Nightingale | 9 | 20 | 3 | 3 |
| Quail | 8 | 6 | 1 | 1 |

| Species | % of tetrads occupied | | % tetrads confirmed | |
|---|---|---|---|---|
| | 2007 –2011 | 1987 –1989 | 2007 –2011 | 1987 –1989 |
| Redshank | 8 | 13 | 2 | 3 |
| Tree Pipit | 8 | 22 | 2 | 7 |
| Grasshopper Warbler | 7 | 7 | 1 | 1 |
| Stonechat | 7 | 4 | 4 | 3 |
| Little Egret | 6 | 0 | 1 | 0 |
| Shoveler | 5 | 2 | 0 | 1 |
| Peregrine | 5 | 0 | 1 | 0 |
| Water Rail | 5 | 6 | 1 | 0.3 |
| Crossbill | 5 | 4 | 1 | 1 |
| Ringed Plover | 5 | 7 | 2 | 3 |
| Pochard | 4 | 5 | 1 | 0 |
| Willow Tit | 4 | 32 | 1 | 13 |
| Snipe | 4 | 15 | 0 | 0.3 |
| Teal | 4 | 6 | 0 | 1 |
| Curlew | 4 | 2 | 1 | 0.3 |
| Dartford Warbler | 4 | 0 | 3 | 0 |
| Lesser Redpoll | 4 | 12 | 0 | 2 |
| Lesser Black-backed Gull | 3 | 0 | 1 | 0 |
| Redstart | 3 | 9 | 1 | 2 |
| Herring Gull | 3 | 0 | 1 | 0 |
| Wood Warbler | 3 | 11 | 0 | 1 |
| Stone-curlew | 2 | 3 | 2 | 1 |
| Red-crested Pochard | 2 | 0 | 1 | 0 |
| Oystercatcher | 2 | 0 | 1 | 0 |
| Montagu's Harrier | 1 | 0 | 0 | 0 |
| Garganey | 1 | 1 | 0.0 | 0.3 |
| Barnacle Goose | 1 | 0.3 | 0.3 | 0.3 |
| Wood Duck | 1 | 0.0 | 0.3 | 0 |
| Ruddy Duck | 1 | 1 | 0.0 | 0.3 |
| Black Redstart | 1 | 1 | 0.3 | 0.3 |
| Wigeon | 1 | 0 | 0 | 0 |
| Long-eared Owl | 1 | 0.0 | 0.3 | 0 |
| Short-eared Owl | 1 | 0.0 | 0.3 | 0 |
| Fieldfare | 1 | 3 | 0.0 | 0.3 |
| Brambling | 1 | 0 | 0 | 0 |
| Goshawk | 0.3 | 0.3 | 0.0 | 0.3 |
| Corncrake | 0.3 | 0 | 0 | 0.0 |
| Whinchat | 0.3 | 0 | 0 | 0 |
| Wheatear | 0.3 | 0 | 0 | 0 |
| Hawfinch | 0.3 | 4 | 0 | 1 |

# Appendix IV

## Berkshire Bird Population Estimates

Knowledge of the populations of birds is important in assessing the ecological significance of a species and in conservation decisions. However, particularly for the more abundant and less readily detected species, quantifying populations is difficult. The Avian Population Estimates Panel (APEP) estimates the national population of most species that breed or winter in Great Britain using a wide range of data and has recently published its latest assessment (Musgrove *et al.*, 2013).

The abundance estimates made during timed counts in the 2007–11 Atlas surveys locally and nationally allow the APEP national estimates to be apportioned to counties, or other units of area, on the basis of the proportion of the total British abundance to the abundance observed locally. The following table summarises these estimates for many species in Berkshire.

For a number of species for which independent estimates could be made, they are included in the table for comparison. This could only be done for the less abundant species and those whose detection rate is likely to have been high, *i.e.* a substantial proportion of the birds present are likely to have been counted in surveys. For the majority of breeding species for which independent estimates were made, there was reasonable accord with the estimates derived from the APEP data. Notable exceptions are the owls, for which the abundance estimates, based on daytime surveys, are likely to be poor; and the large gulls, a substantial proportion of which are likely to have been non-breeding birds.

Berkshire, whose land area is 0.5% of that of Great Britain, has nationally significant breeding populations (more than 5% of Great Britain) of the following species: Egyptian Goose, Mandarin Duck, Red Kite, Ring-necked Parakeet, Woodlark and Firecrest, and important populations (more than 2% of Great Britain) of Mute Swan, Canada Goose, Great Crested Grebe, Coot, Green Woodpecker, Nightingale, Cetti's Warbler and Corn Bunting.

The estimates of wintering species are more problematic: many are highly mobile, driven by weather conditions, changing food sources and disturbance. The independent estimates rely largely on counts made at the major sites for a species and hence are likely to be underestimates for the more widespread species. Nonetheless, the independent estimates are largely within the range of 0.5 to 2.0 times the APEP-derived estimates. Berkshire held more than 5% of the national population of Egyptian Goose, Gadwall and Mandarin Duck. Species for which the county held more than 2% of the national population are Canada Goose, Shoveler, Pochard, Tufted Duck, Great Crested Grebe, Coot and Lesser Black-backed Gull. In surveys from 2003/04 to 2005/06, the gull roosts the lower Kennet valley held over 1% of the international population of Lesser Black-backed Gull (Burton *et al.*, 2013).

## References

Musgrove, A., Aebischer, N., Eaton, M., Hearn, R., Newson, S., Noble, D., Parsons, M., Risely, K. and Stroud, D., 2013. Population estimates of birds in Great Britain and the United Kingdom. *British Birds* **106**: 64–100.

Burton, N. H. K., Banks, A. N., Calladine, J. R. and Austin, G. E., 2013. The importance of the United Kingdom for wintering gulls: population estimates and conservation requirements. *Bird Study* **60**: 87–101.

## Table notes

**Units:** I, individuals; P, pairs; T, territories; M, males

**Reliability:** 1, good; 2, moderate; 3, poor

### Notes

1. For species with a high detection rate, Atlas breeding data have been used to estimate the population. The lower number is [confirmed tetrads x average number of birds per occupied tetrad/2]; the higher [confirmed+probable tetrads × average number of birds per occupied tetrad/2].

2. Nocturnal species were understimated in tetrad surveys: the total number of tetrads occupied is given as a minimum figure for likely breeding pairs.

3. Assumes only singing males detected.

4. Assumes 50% of Mute Swans recorded in timed surveys were non-breeders.

5. Estimate based on abundance data includes non-breeding birds.

| BREEDING SEASON | GREAT BRITAIN | | | | BERKSHIRE | | | |
|---|---|---|---|---|---|---|---|---|
| Species | GB population | unit | reliability | Ref· yrs | Berks/GB abundance % | Berkshire population | Independent estimate [1] | |
| Mute Swan | 6,000 | P | 2 | 2009 | 2.3 | 140 | 260–300 | Atlas breeding data [4] |
| Greylag Goose | 46,000 | P | 3 | 2004–08 | 0.7 | 340 | | |
| Canada Goose | 62,000 | P | 3 | 2004–08 | 3.1 | 1,900 | | |
| Egyptian Goose | 1,100 | P | 3 | 2004–08 | 14.0 | 150 | | |
| Shelduck | 15,000 | P | 2 | 2009 | 0.2 | 24 | | |
| Mandarin Duck | 2,300 | P | 3 | 1988 | 8.0 | 190 | 114–166 | Atlas breeding data |
| Gadwall | 1,190 | P | 2 | 2006–09 | 1.5 | 18 | 24–68 | Atlas breeding data |
| Mallard | 100,500 | P | 3 | 2009 | 1.2 | 1,200 | | |
| Tufted Duck | 17,000 | P | 3 | 2009 | 1.5 | 250 | | |
| Red–legged Partridge | 82,000 | T | 2 | 2009 | 1.0 | 850 | | |
| Grey Partridge | 43,000 | T | 2 | 2009 | 0.6 | 250 | | |
| Pheasant | 2,200,000 | F | 2 | 2009 | 0.9 | 20,000 | | |
| Cormorant | 8,400 | P | 2 | 1998–2002 | 1.3 | 110 | | |
| Grey Heron | 12,000 | P | 1 | 2007–11 | 0.9 | 110 | | |
| Little Grebe | 5,300 | P | 2 | 2009 | 0.7 | 37 | 41–54 | Atlas breeding data |
| Great Crested Grebe | 4,600 | P | 2 | 2009 | 3.2 | 150 | 220–250 | Atlas breeding data |
| Red Kite | 1,600 | P | 2 | 2006–10 | 7.5 | 120 | 67–185 | Atlas breeding data |
| Sparrowhawk | 33,000 | P | 2 | 2009 | 0.6 | 210 | | |
| Buzzard | 66,500 | P | 2 | 2009 | 0.8 | 520 | 618–873 | Atlas breeding data |
| Kestrel | 45,000 | P | 2 | 2009 | 1.0 | 450 | | |
| Hobby | 2,800 | P | 2 | 2009 | 1.9 | 54 | 24–46 | Atlas breeding data |
| Water Rail | 1,100 | T | 3 | 2006–10 | 1.1 | 12 | | |
| Moorhen | 260,000 | T | 2 | 2009 | 1.4 | 3,500 | | |
| Coot | 30,000 | P | 3 | 2009 | 2.3 | 690 | | |
| Lapwing | 130,000 | P | 2 | 2009 | 0.8 | 1,000 | 546–831 | Atlas breeding data |
| Little Ringed Plover | 1,250 | P | 1 | 2007 | 1.3 | 17 | 27–30 | Atlas breeding data |
| Redshank | 24,000 | P | 2 | 2009 | 0.1 | 25 | | |
| Woodcock | 78,000 | M | 2 | 2003 | 0.5 | 400 | > 85 | Atlas distribution data [2] |
| Common Tern | 10,000 | P | 1 | 2000 | 1.7 | 170 | | |
| Black–headed Gull | 130,000 | P | 1 | 1998–2002 | 0.3 | 450 | | |
| Lesser Black–backed Gull | 110,000 | P | 1 | 1998–2002 | 0.2 | 200 | 5–6 | Atlas breeding data [5] |
| Herring Gull | 130,000 | P | 1 | 1998–2002 | 0.1 | 110 | 20–35 | Atlas breeding data |
| Feral Pigeon | 540,000 | P | 2 | 2006–10 | 0.9 | 4,700 | | |
| Stock Dove | 260,000 | T | 2 | 2009 | 1.1 | 3,000 | | |
| Woodpigeon | 5,300,000 | P | 2 | 2009 | 1.4 | 76,000 | | |
| Collared Dove | 975,000 | P | 2 | 2009 | 0.8 | 8,200 | | |
| Turtle Dove | 14,000 | T | 2 | 2009 | 0.4 | 62 | | |
| Ring–necked Parakeet | 8,600 | P | | 2012 | – | 8·7 | 750 | |
| Cuckoo | 15,500 | P | 3 | 2009 | 0.5 | 75 | | |
| Barn Owl | 4,000 | P | 3 | 1995–97 | 0.5 | 20 | 60–100 | See species account |
| Little Owl | 5,700 | P | 2 | 2009 | 1.0 | 57 | 51–77 | Atlas breeding data |
| Tawny Owl | 50,000 | P | 2 | 2005 | 0.8 | 400 | >232 | Atlas distribution data [2] |
| Swift | 87,000 | P | 2 | 2009 | 0.9 | 750 | | |
| Kingfisher | 4,850 | P | 3 | 2009 | 1.5 | 71 | 44–69 | Atlas breeding data |
| Green Woodpecker | 52,500 | P | 2 | 2009 | 2.1 | 1,100 | | |
| Great Spotted Woodpecker | 140,000 | P | 2 | 2009 | 1.8 | 2,500 | | |
| Magpie | 550,000 | P | 2 | 2009 | 1.5 | 8,000 | | |
| Jay | 170,000 | T | 2 | 2009 | 1.9 | 3,200 | | |
| Jackdaw | 1,250,000 | P | 2 | 2009 | 1.2 | 14,000 | | |
| Rook | 990,000 | P | 2 | 2009 | 1.2 | 12,000 | | |
| Carrion Crow | 1,000,000 | T | 2 | 2009 | 0.9 | 8,600 | | |
| Goldcrest | 520,000 | T | 2 | 2009 | 1.0 | 5,100 | | |
| Firecrest | 550 | T | 2 | 2006–10 | 14.4 | 79 | 81 | Annual report, 2008 |
| Blue Tit | 3,400,000 | T | 2 | 2009 | 1.3 | 44,000 | | |
| Great Tit | 2,500,000 | T | 2 | 2009 | 1.4 | 35,000 | | |

| BREEDING SEASON | GREAT BRITAIN | | | | BERKSHIRE | | | |
| --- | --- | --- | --- | --- | --- | --- | --- | --- |
| Species | GB population | unit | reliability | Ref· yrs | Berks/GB abundance % | Berkshire population | Independent estimate [1] | |
| Coal Tit | 680,000 | T | 2 | 2009 | 0.7 | 5,000 | | |
| Willow Tit | 3,400 | P | 2 | 2009 | 0.5 | 16 | | |
| Marsh Tit | 41,000 | T | 2 | 2009 | 1.5 | 610 | | |
| Woodlark | 3,100 | P | 1 | 2006 | 5.2 | 160 | | |
| Skylark | 1,400,000 | T | 2 | 2009 | 0.7 | 9,800 | | |
| Sand Martin | 104,000 | N | 3 | 2009 | 0.1 | 150 | | |
| Swallow | 760,000 | T | 2 | 2009 | 0.4 | 2,700 | | |
| House Martin | 510,000 | P | 2 | 2009 | 0.6 | 3,200 | | |
| Cetti s Warbler | 2,000 | M | 2 | 2006–10 | 2.3 | 46 | 44–78 | Atlas breeding data [3] |
| Long–tailed Tit | 330,000 | T | 2 | 2009 | 1.6 | 5,400 | | |
| Chiffchaff | 1,100,000 | T | 2 | 2009 | 1.0 | 11,000 | | |
| Willow Warbler | 2,200,000 | T | 2 | 2009 | 0.2 | 3,500 | | |
| Blackcap | 1,100,000 | T | 2 | 2009 | 1.4 | 15,000 | | |
| Garden Warbler | 170,000 | T | 2 | 2009 | 0.9 | 1,600 | | |
| Lesser Whitethroat | 74,000 | T | 2 | 2009 | 0.3 | 250 | | |
| Whitethroat | 1,400,000 | T | 2 | 2009 | 0.8 | 11,000 | | |
| Dartford Warbler | 3,250 | P | 1 | 2009 | 1.6 | 53 | 40 | Annual report, 2008 |
| Sedge Warbler | 260,000 | T | 2 | 2009 | 0.8 | 2,100 | | |
| Reed Warbler | 130,000 | P | 2 | 2009 | 1.0 | 1,400 | | |
| Nuthatch | 220,000 | T | 2 | 2009 | 1.9 | 4,200 | | |
| Treecreeper | 180,000 | T | 2 | 2009 | 1.4 | 2,600 | | |
| Wren | 7,700,000 | T | 2 | 2009 | 1.0 | 76,000 | | |
| Starling | 1,800,000 | P | 2 | 2009 | 0.6 | 12,000 | | |
| Blackbird | 4,900,000 | P | 2 | 2009 | 1.0 | 48,000 | | |
| Song Thrush | 1,100,000 | T | 2 | 2009 | 1.0 | 11,000 | | |
| Mistle Thrush | 160,000 | T | 2 | 2009 | 0.8 | 1,300 | | |
| Spotted Flycatcher | 33,000 | T | 3 | 2009 | 0.4 | 130 | | |
| Robin | 6,000,000 | T | 2 | 2009 | 1.2 | 70,000 | | |
| Nightingale | 7,500 | M | 3 | 1999 | 2.3 | 170 | 166 | BTO survey 2012 |
| Redstart | 100,000 | P | 2 | 2009 | 0.1 | 60 | | |
| Stonechat | 56,000 | P | 2 | 2009 | 0.1 | 77 | 42 | Annual Report, 2008 |
| Dunnock | 2,300,000 | T | 2 | 2009 | 0.9 | 20,000 | | |
| House Sparrow | 5,150,000 | P | 2 | 2009 | 0.4 | 23,000 | | |
| Yellow Wagtail | 15,000 | T | 2 | 2009 | 0.3 | 45 | 38–51 | Atlas breeding data |
| Grey Wagtail | 35,000 | P | 3 | 2009 | 0.7 | 260 | | |
| Pied Wagtail | 455,000 | P | 2 | 2009 | 0.5 | 2,500 | | |
| Tree Pipit | 88,000 | P | 2 | 2009 | 0.4 | 340 | | |
| Meadow Pipit | 1,850,000 | P | 2 | 2009 | 0.0 | 460 | | |
| Chaffinch | 5,800,000 | T | 2 | 2009 | 0.8 | 48,000 | | |
| Greenfinch | 1,700,000 | P | 2 | 2009 | 1.1 | 19,000 | | |
| Goldfinch | 1,200,000 | P | 2 | 2009 | 0.8 | 9,300 | | |
| Siskin | 410,000 | P | 3 | 2009 | 0.1 | 230 | | |
| Linnet | 41,000 | T | 2 | 2009 | 0.6 | 230 | | |
| Bullfinch | 190,000 | T | 2 | 2009 | 0.5 | 960 | | |
| Yellowhammer | 700,000 | T | 2 | 2009 | 0.7 | 5,000 | | |
| Reed Bunting | 230,000 | T | 2 | 2009 | 0.5 | 1,200 | | |
| Corn Bunting | 11,000 | T | 2 | 2009 | 2.7 | 290 | | |

| WINTER | GREAT BRITAIN | | | | BERKSHIRE | | |
|---|---|---|---|---|---|---|---|
| Species | GB population | unit | reliability | Ref· yrs | Berks/GB abundance % | Berkshire population | Independent estimate [1] |
| Mute Swan | 74,000 | I | 2 | 2004/5–2008/9 | 1·88 | 1,400 | |
| Greylag Goose | 220,000 | I | 2 | 2004/5–2008/9 | 0·28 | 630 | |
| Canada Goose | 190,000 | I | 2 | 2004/5–2008/9 | 2·32 | 4,400 | |
| Egyptian Goose | 3,400 | I | 2 | 2004/5–2008/9 | 7·71 | 260 | |
| Mandarin Duck | 7,000 | I | 3 | 1988 | 6·15 | 430 | |
| Wigeon | 440,000 | I | 1 | 2004/5–2008/9 | 0·35 | 1,500 | |
| Gadwall | 25,000 | I | 1 | 2004/5–2008/9 | 6·01 | 1,500 | |
| Teal | 210,000 | I | 2 | 2004/5–2008/9 | 0·21 | 450 | |
| Mallard | 680,000 | I | 3 | 2004/5–2008/9 | 0·91 | 6,200 | 4,196 Atlas survey count |
| Shoveler | 18,000 | I | 1 | 2004/5–2008/9 | 2·65 | 480 | |
| Pochard | 38,000 | I | 1 | 2004/5–2008/9 | 2·49 | 950 | 1,071 Annual report, 2008 |
| Tufted Duck | 110,000 | I | 1 | 2004/5–2008/9 | 3·26 | 3,600 | 3,000 Annual report, 2008 |
| Goldeneye | 20,000 | I | 2 | 2004/5–2008/9 | 0·18 | 36 | 75 Annual report, 2008 |
| Little Egret | 4,500 | I | 2 | 2004/5–2008/9 | 0·34 | 15 | |
| Grey Heron | 61,000 | I | 2 | 2004/5–2008/9 | 0·93 | 570 | |
| Little Grebe | 16,000 | I | 2 | 2004/5–2008/9 | 0·92 | 150 | |
| Great Crested Grebe | 19,000 | I | 1 | 2004/5–2008/9 | 4·37 | 830 | |
| Moorhen | 320,000 | I | 3 | 2004/5–2008/9 | 1·42 | 4,600 | |
| Coot | 180,000 | I | 1 | 2004/5–2008/9 | 2·48 | 4,500 | |
| Golden Plover | 400,000 | I | 2 | 2006/7 | 0·29 | 1,200 | |
| Lapwing | 620,000 | I | 2 | 2006/7 | 0·49 | 3,000 | |
| Green Sandpiper | 910 | I | 3 | 2004/5–2008/9 | 1·40 | 13 | |
| Woodcock | 1,400,000 | I | 3 | 2003/4 | 0·13 | 1,800 | |
| Snipe | 1,000,000 | I | 3 | 2004/5 | 0·41 | 4,100 | |
| Black-headed Gull | 2,150,000 | I | 2 | 2003/4–2005/6 | 1·22 | 26,000 | |
| Common Gull | 700,000 | I | 2 | 2003/4–2005/6 | 0·19 | 1,300 | |
| Lesser Black-backed Gull | 125,000 | I | 2 | 2003/4–2005/6 | 4·10 | 5,100 | |
| Herring Gull | 730,000 | I | 2 | 2003/4–2005/6 | 0·29 | 2,100 | |
| Great Black-backed Gull | 76,000 | I | 2 | 2003/4–2005/6 | 0·12 | 87 | |
| Fieldfare | 680,000 | I | 3 | 1981–4 | 0·82 | 5,600 | |
| Redwing | 650,000 | I | 3 | 1981–4 | 0·93 | 6,000 | |
| Brambling | 922,500 | I | 3 | 1981–4 | 0·32 | 2,900 | High inter-annual variation |

# Appendix V

## The Berkshire List

We are grateful to Marek Walford for permission to use as our basis the list maintained on www.berksbirds.co.uk. The list, as at 17th August, was reorganised in the BOU sequence published in 2013 and amended where further information has been provided for this avifauna. For species with fewer than 10 records, the years of the first and last records are listed here, together with the total number to July 2013. Records subject to review by county or national records committee are shown in parenthesis.

| Species | First record | Last record | No. of Records | Birds |
|---|---|---|---|---|
| Mute Swan | | | | |
| Bewick's Swan | | | | |
| Whooper Swan | | | | |
| Bean Goose | | | | |
| Pink-footed Goose | | | | |
| White-fronted Goose | | | | |
| Greylag Goose | | | | |
| Canada Goose | | | | |
| Barnacle Goose | | | | |
| Brent Goose | | | | |
| Egyptian Goose | | | | |
| Shelduck | | | | |
| Mandarin Duck | | | | |
| Wigeon | | | | |
| American Wigeon | 1985 | 2008 | 3 | 6 |
| Gadwall | | | | |
| Teal | | | | |
| Green-winged Teal | 1990 | 2004 | 3 | 3 |
| Mallard | | | | |
| Pintail | | | | |
| Garganey | | | | |
| Blue-winged Teal | 1988 | 1990 | 2 | 2 |
| Shoveler | | | | |
| Red-crested Pochard | | | | |
| Pochard | | | | |
| Ring-necked Duck | 1959 | 2007 | 9 | 10 |
| Ferruginous Duck | | | | |
| Tufted Duck | | | | |
| Scaup | | | | |
| Lesser Scaup | 2007 | 2008 | 2 | 2 |
| Eider | | | | |
| Long-tailed Duck | | | | |
| Common Scoter | | | | |
| Velvet Scoter | | | | |
| Goldeneye | | | | |
| Smew | | | | |
| Red-breasted Merganser | | | | |
| Goosander | | | | |
| Ruddy Duck | | | | |
| Red-legged Partridge | | | | |
| Grey Partridge | | | | |
| Quail | | | | |
| Pheasant | | | | |
| Red-throated Diver | | | | |
| Black-throated Diver | | | | |
| Great Northern Diver | | | | |
| Fulmar | 1971 | 2003 | 4 | 4 |
| Manx Shearwater | | | | |
| Storm Petrel | 1929 | 2003 | 8 | 8 |

| Species | First record | Last record | No. of Records | Birds |
|---|---|---|---|---|
| Leach's Petrel | | | | |
| Gannet | | | | |
| Cormorant | | | | |
| Shag | | | | |
| Bittern | | | | |
| Little Bittern | 1826 | 1972 | 3 | 4 |
| Night Heron | 1976 | 1987 | 3 | 3 |
| Cattle Egret | 2007 | 2012 | 4 | 5 |
| Little Egret | | | | |
| Great White Egret | 2003 | 2007 (2012) | 3 (5) | 3 (5) |
| Grey Heron | | | | |
| Purple Heron | 1861 | 2000 | 6 | 6 |
| White Stork | 1968 | 2004 | 4 | 4 |
| Glossy Ibis | 1793 | 1793 (2011) | 4 | 4 |
| Spoonbill | | | | |
| Little Grebe | | | | |
| Great Crested Grebe | | | | |
| Red-necked Grebe | | | | |
| Slavonian Grebe | | | | |
| Black-necked Grebe | | | | |
| Honey Buzzard | | | | |
| Black Kite | 2001 | 2001 | 1 | 1 |
| Red Kite | | | | |
| White-tailed Eagle | 1851 | 1865 | 5 | 6 |
| Marsh Harrier | | | | |
| Hen Harrier | | | | |
| Montagu's Harrier | | | | |
| Goshawk | | | | |
| Sparrowhawk | | | | |
| Buzzard | | | | |
| Rough-legged Buzzard | | | | |
| Greater Spotted Eagle | 1872 | | 1 | 1 |
| Golden Eagle | 1924 | 1924 | 1 | 1 |
| Osprey | | | | |
| Kestrel | | | | |
| Red-footed Falcon | 1973 | 2008 | 9 | 10 |
| Merlin | | | | |
| Hobby | | | | |
| Gyr Falcon | 1970 | 1971 | 2 | 2 |
| Peregrine | | | | |
| Water Rail | | | | |
| Spotted Crake | | | | |
| Sora Rail | 1864 | 1864 | 1 | 1 |
| Baillon's Crake | 1972 | 1972 | 1 | 1 |
| Corncrake | | | | |
| Moorhen | | | | |
| Coot | | | | |
| Crane | 1976 | 2003 (2012) | 8 | 24 |
| Little Bustard | 1958 | 1958 | 1 | 1 |

| Species | First record | Last record | No. of Records | Birds |
|---|---|---|---|---|
| Great Bustard | 1856 | 1856 | 1 | 1 |
| Stone Curlew | | | | |
| Black-winged Stilt | 1922 | 1945 | 2 | 6 |
| Avocet | | | | |
| Oystercatcher | | | | |
| Golden Plover | | | | |
| Grey Plover | | | | |
| Sociable Plover | 1991 | 1991 | 1 | 1 |
| Lapwing | | | | |
| Little Ringed Plover | | | | |
| Ringed Plover | | | | |
| Killdeer | 1984 | 1984 | 1 | 1 |
| Kentish Plover | 1935 | 1986 | 6 | 6 |
| Dotterel | | | | |
| Whimbrel | | | | |
| Curlew | | | | |
| Black-tailed Godwit | | | | |
| Bar-tailed Godwit | | | | |
| Turnstone | | | | |
| Knot | | | | |
| Ruff | | | | |
| Sharp-tailed Sandpiper | 1975 | 1975 | 1 | 1 |
| Broad-billed Sandpiper | 1956 | 1956 | 1 | 1 |
| Curlew Sandpiper | | | | |
| Temminck's stint | | | | |
| Sanderling | | | | |
| Dunlin | | | | |
| Purple Sandpiper | 1983 | 2011 | 5 | 5 |
| Little Stint | | | | |
| Least Sandpiper | 1975 | 1975 | 1 | 1 |
| Pectoral Sandpiper | | | | |
| Wilson's Phalarope | 1979 | 1987 | 2 | 2 |
| Red-necked Phalarope | 1932 | 2001 | 5 | 7 |
| Grey Phalarope | | | | |
| Common Sandpiper | | | | |
| Green Sandpiper | | | | |
| Spotted Redshank | | | | |
| Greenshank | | | | |
| Lesser Yellowlegs | 1953 | 1953 | 1 | 1 |
| Wood Sandpiper | | | | |
| Redshank | | | | |
| Jack Snipe | | | | |
| Woodcock | | | | |
| Snipe | | | | |
| Great Snipe | <1868 | 1956 | 5 | 5 |
| Black-winged Pratincole | 1976 | 1976 | 1 | 1 |
| Pomarine Skua | 1877 | 2007 | 6 | 18 |
| Arctic Skua | | | | |
| Long-tailed Skua | 1978 | 2013 | 7 (1) | 7 (1) |
| Great Skua | 1980 | 2011 | 9 | 11 |
| Puffin | | | | |
| Razorbill | 1948 | 1948 | 1 | 1 |
| Little Auk | | | | |
| Guillemot | 1904 | 1986 | 7 | 7 |
| Little Tern | | | | |
| Caspian Tern | 1979 | 1979 | 1 | 1 |
| Whiskered Tern | 2005 | 2005 | 1 | 1 |
| Black Tern | | | | |
| White-winged Black Tern | 1948 | 1994 | 8 | 9 or 10 |

| Species | First record | Last record | No. of Records | Birds |
|---|---|---|---|---|
| Sandwich Tern | | | | |
| Common Tern | | | | |
| Roseate Tern | 1967 | 1984 (2013) | 4 (3) | 4 (4) |
| Arctic Tern | | | | |
| Sabine's Gull | | | | |
| Kittiwake | | | | |
| Bonaparte's Gull | 2013 | 2013 | 1 | 1 |
| Black-headed Gull | | | | |
| Little Gull | | | | |
| Laughing Gull | 2005 | 2005 | 1 | 1 |
| Mediterranean Gull | | | | |
| Common Gull | | | | |
| Ring-billed Gull | 1984 | 2005 | 10 | 10 |
| Lesser Black-backed Gull | | | | |
| Herring Gull | | | | |
| Yellow –legged Gull | | | | |
| Caspian Gull | | | | |
| Iceland Gull | | | | |
| Glaucous Gull | | | | |
| Great Black-backed Gull | | | | |
| Pallas's Sandgrouse | 1888 | 1908 | 5 | 37 |
| Feral Pigeon | | | | |
| Stock Dove | | | | |
| Woodpigeon | | | | |
| Collared Dove | | | | |
| Turtle Dove | | | | |
| Ring-necked Parakeet | | | | |
| Cuckoo | | | | |
| Barn Owl | | | | |
| Little Owl | | | | |
| Tawny Owl | | | | |
| Long-eared Owl | | | | |
| Short-eared Owl | | | | |
| Tengmalm's Owl | 1864 | 1864 | 1 | 1 |
| Nightjar | | | | |
| Swift | | | | |
| Alpine Swift | 1955 | 2010 | 6 | 6 |
| Kingfisher | | | | |
| Roller | 1927 | 1927 | 1 | 1 |
| Hoopoe | | | | |
| Wryneck | | | | |
| Green Woodpecker | | | | |
| Great Spotted Woodpecker | | | | |
| Lesser Spotted Woodpecker | | | | |
| Golden Oriole | | | | |
| Red-backed Shrike | | | | |
| Great Grey Shrike | | | | |
| Woodchat Shrike | 1989 | 1991 | 2 | 2 |
| Magpie | | | | |
| Jay | | | | |
| Nutcracker | 1968 | 1968 | 3 | 4 |
| Jackdaw | | | | |
| Rook | | | | |
| Carrion Crow | | | | |
| Hooded Crow | | | | |
| Raven | | | | |
| Goldcrest | | | | |
| Firecrest | | | | |
| Penduline Tit | 1988 | 1988 | 1 | 1 |

| Species | First record | Last record | No. of Records | Birds |
|---|---|---|---|---|
| Blue Tit | | | | |
| Great Tit | | | | |
| Coal Tit | | | | |
| Willow Tit | | | | |
| Marsh Tit | | | | |
| Bearded Tit | | | | |
| Short-toed Lark | 1987 | 1987 | 1 | 1 |
| Woodlark | | | | |
| Skylark | | | | |
| Shore Lark | 1973 | 1998 | 2 | 2 |
| Sand Martin | | | | |
| Swallow | | | | |
| House Martin | | | | |
| Red-rumped Swallow | 1992 | 1999 | 3 | 3 |
| Cetti's Warbler | | | | |
| Long-tailed Tit | | | | |
| Pallas's Warbler | 2013 | 2013 | 1 | 1 |
| Yellow-browed Warbler | 1986 | 2007 (2012) | 3 (2) | 3 (2) |
| [Western] Bonelli's Warbler | 1975 | 1975 | 1 | 1 |
| Wood Warbler | | | | |
| Chiffchaff | | | | |
| Willow Warbler | | | | |
| Blackcap | | | | |
| Garden Warbler | | | | |
| Lesser Whitethroat | | | | |
| Whitethroat | | | | |
| Dartford Warbler | | | | |
| Grasshopper Warbler | | | | |
| Savi's Warbler | 1968 | 1968 | 1 | 1 |
| Icterine Warbler | 1963 | 1989 | 3 | 3 |
| Melodious Warbler | 1972 | | 1 | 1 |
| Aquatic Warbler | 1944 | 1991 | 5 | 5 |
| Sedge Warbler | | | | |
| Paddyfield Warbler | 1997 | 1997 | 1 | 1 |
| Marsh Warbler | | | | |
| Reed Warbler | | | | |
| Great Reed Warbler | 1960 | 1990 | 3 | 3 |
| Waxwing | | | | |
| Nuthatch | | | | |
| Treecreeper | | | | |
| Wren | | | | |
| Starling | | | | |
| Rose-coloured Starling | 1810 | 1975 | 3 | 3 |
| Dipper | | | | |
| Ring Ouzel | | | | |
| Blackbird | | | | |
| Black-throated Thrush | 1998 | 1998 | 1 | 1 |
| Fieldfare | | | | |
| Song Thrush | | | | |
| Redwing | | | | |
| Mistle Thrush | | | | |
| Spotted Flycatcher | | | | |
| Robin | | | | |
| Nightingale | | | | |
| Bluethroat | 1972 | 2009 | 3 | 3 |
| Pied Flycatcher | | | | |
| Black Redstart | | | | |
| Redstart | | | | |
| Whinchat | | | | |

| Species | First record | Last record | No. of Records | Birds |
|---|---|---|---|---|
| Siberian Stonechat | 1986 | 1986 | 1 | 1 |
| Stonechat | | | | |
| Wheatear | | | | |
| Dunnock | | | | |
| House Sparrow | | | | |
| Tree Sparrow | | | | |
| Yellow Wagtail | | | | |
| Grey Wagtail | | | | |
| Pied Wagtail | | | | |
| Richard's Pipit | 1967 | 2002 (2012) | 5 (2) | 5 (2) |
| Tawny Pipit | 1975 | 1975 | 1 | 1 |
| Olive-backed Pipit | 1984 | 1984 | 1 | 1 |
| Tree Pipit | | | | |
| Meadow Pipit | | | | |
| Red-throated Pipit | 1979 | 1979 | 1 | 1 |
| Rock Pipit | | | | |
| Water Pipit | | | | |
| Buff-bellied Pipit | 2012 | 2012 | 1 | 2 |
| Chaffinch | | | | |
| Brambling | | | | |
| Serin | 1986 | 1996 | 4 | 4 |
| Greenfinch | | | | |
| Goldfinch | | | | |
| Siskin | | | | |
| Linnet | | | | |
| Twite | | | | |
| Lesser Redpoll | | | | |
| Mealy Redpoll | | | | |
| Two-barred Crossbill | 1890 | 1890 | 1 | 4 |
| Crossbill | | | | |
| Parrot Crossbill | 1983 | 1983 | 1 | 4 |
| Common Rosefinch | 1982 | 1997 | 2 | 2 |
| Pine Grosbeak | 1901 | 1901 | 1 | 1 |
| Bullfinch | | | | |
| Hawfinch | | | | |
| Snow Bunting | | | | |
| Lapland Bunting | | | | |
| Yellowhammer | | | | |
| Cirl Bunting | | | | |
| Ortolan Bunting | 1860s | 2007 | 3 | 5 |
| Little Bunting | 1987 | 1987 | 1 | 1 |
| Reed Bunting | | | | |
| Corn Bunting | | | | |

**The following species with accounts in the Avifauna are considered to be escapes, not admitted into Category C of the British List or not proven:**

Black Swan
Bar-headed Goose
Snow Goose
Red-breasted Goose
Ruddy Shelduck
Wood Duck
Black Grouse
Chukar
Golden Pheasant
Lady Amherst's Pheasant
Marsh Sandpiper
Chough

# Appendix VI

## Habitat areas

The habitat maps shown in Chapter 3 were compiled from phase 1 habitat assignments by the Thames Valley Environmental Centre (TVERC) in 2006. Forty five Phase 1 habitat categories were combined into nine main classes, as shown below.

The total built area was assessed by inspection of Ordnance Survey 1:50,000 maps to be approximately 16,000 ha. Gardens were separately measured as approximately 11,000 ha (TVERC). These measurements, together with the nine main habitat classes, amount to 98% of the county area.

The total length of hedgerows in Berkshire was measured from aerial photographs of each tetrad as approximately 976 km of hedgerow with trees and 662 of hedgerow without trees.

| Habitat type | Area | Phase 1 habitat category |
|---|---|---|
| **Arable** | 42,582 ha | Cultivated/disturbed land – arable |
| | | Cultivated/disturbed land – ephemeral/short perennial |
| **Grassland** (of which unimproved < 2%) | 31,522 ha | Acid grassland – semi–improved |
| | | Acid grassland – unimproved |
| | | Calcareous grassland – semi–improved |
| | | Calcareous grassland – unimproved |
| | | Cultivated/disturbed land – amenity grassland |
| | | Neutral grassland – semi–improved |
| | | Neutral grassland – unimproved |
| | | Improved grassland |
| **Broadleaved woodland** | 10,761 ha | Broadleaved woodland – plantation |
| | | Broadleaved woodland – semi–natural |
| | | Recently felled woodland – broadleaved |
| | | Parkland and scattered trees – broadleaved |
| **Mixed woodland** | 3,431 ha | Mixed woodland – plantation |
| | | Mixed woodland – semi–natural |
| | | Recently felled woodland – mixed |
| | | Parkland and scattered trees – mixed |
| **Coniferous woodland** | 3,176 ha | Coniferous woodland – plantation |
| | | Coniferous woodland – semi–natural |
| | | Recently felled woodland – coniferous |
| | | Parkland and scattered trees – coniferous |
| **Scrub** | 1,507 ha | Dry dwarf shrub heath |
| | | Scrub – scattered |
| | | Scrub – dense/continuous |
| **Heath** | 534 ha | Dry heath/acid grassland mosaic |
| | | Wet dwarf shrub heath |
| **Wetland** | 349 ha | Fen – flood plain mire |
| | | Fen – valley mire |
| | | Marginal/inundation – inundation |
| | | Flush and spring – acid/neutral flush |
| | | Marginal/inundation – marginal |
| | | Marsh/marshy grassland |
| **Water** | 1,984 ha | Running water – eutrophic |
| | | Running water – mesotrophic |
| | | Standing water – eutrophic |
| | | Standing water – mesotrophic |

# Appendix VII

## Museums

There are three museums in the county that have sections of interest to ornithologists.

Reading Museum has a general Natural History section whilst Eton College hosts an impressive Natural History Museum. The Zoological Museum at the University of Reading holds yet another excellent natural history collection.

### Reading Museum

The museum is housed in an historic Grade II listed building and holds a collection of over 200,000 biological and geological specimens accumulated since 1883, in addition to extensive art, historic and archaeological collections. The Natural History collections reflect the biodiversity and environment of Reading, with specimens from Berkshire, south Oxfordshire and elsewhere in southern England and also from other parts of the world. They include an Entomology section holding an estimated 150,000 insects. Of the other wildlife items, approximately 8,500 are birds.

The museum's main natural history display is the Green Space Gallery which charts the immediate environment from the distant past to the present day, and includes exhibits of birds and other animals that have featured in this local history.

The Box Room hosts a good number of mounted bird specimens in protective boxes which are available for loan to schools and can be viewed upon request.

Collections in store include 136 specimens of definite Berkshire provenance, including the 1916 Glossy Ibis, a Hooded Crow from Fobney Water Works (1955) and the Nutcracker which was found dead in Windsor Great Park in 1968. Some of the 'Hastings Rarities' are held in the collection, together with around 300 skins, a small number of skulls and other skeletal elements, nests, feathers and other traces, and some 7,000 eggs. These can be viewed by appointment.

*Address and contact details:* Blagrave Street, Reading, RG1 1QH, tel. 01189 373400 www.readingmuseum.org.uk  Open daily except on Mondays, check the website for details.

### Eton College Natural History Museum

The museum and has been at its present site since 1895. It houses 15,000 specimens in 77 displays spread over two floors, with exhibits donated from the nineteenth century onwards. Whilst being used extensively for teaching biology and geology, it is available for public and group visits.

Amongst the many exhibits is one denoting the voyage of the Endeavour by Etonian Sir Joseph Banks, whilst other notable biologists, naturalists and explorers are also featured. Another significant display covers the work of Charles Darwin and includes an original handwritten page from his manuscript, one of only 45 such pages remaining.

One of the larger exhibits is the collection of mounted British Birds donated by Rev Dr George Thackeray (1777–1850), including examples of several rare New Zealand ground birds, whilst the egg collection of William Newall, comprising 3,000 eggs of 400 species, was donated by him in memory of his two sons who both died in WWI. Themed display cases cover such topics as 'What is a Species', 'Life and Climate', 'Migration', 'The Wild Wood' and several others, all involving ornithological aspects. There are additional sections covering Genetics and Biogeography.

The museum can host up to 60 visitors and has a lecture area seating 30, toilet facilities and a licensed meeting area.

*Address and contact details:-* Keats Lane, Eton, SL6 6EN (tel 01753 671288) http://etonnhm.com/ Open Sunday 2.30 to 5pm (during term time). Other times by appointment.

### Cole Museum of Zoology

The Museum was established in the early 20th century by Francis J. Cole, Professor of Zoology from 1907 to 1939. The Collection was originally housed at the London Road campus of University of Reading until the early 1970s when it was transported to its present location at Whiteknights. The Cole Museum of Zoology contains some 3,500 specimens of which about 400 are on display at any one time. Specimens are arranged in taxonomic sequence enabling a complete tour of the diversity of the Animal Kingdom to be completed in less than one hour. All displays are contained on the ground floor level.

The displays are designed for all ages, many created to support the national school's curriculum, and although extensive, only represent some 15% of the total collection. The remainder can be viewed by students upon request. The ornithological section incorporates a bird skull collection with 168 items and a couple of dioramas, one Victorian with Toucans and another with a mix of birds. There is also a small collection of eggs.

There is also a significant beetle, moth and butterfly collection.

*Address and contact details:* AMS building (building 30), School of Biological Sciences, Whiteknights Campus, University of Reading. Open 9am to 4.30pm, Mondays to Fridays, except Bank Holidays.

# References

Alexander, W.B. 1952. *An Annotated List of the Birds of Berkshire.* Oxfordshire Ornithological Society.

Alexander, H.G. 1974. *Seventy Years of Birdwatching.* T. & A.D. Poyser, Berkhampstead.

Allen, R.C.R. 1946. Account of breeding Marsh Warblers. In systematic list in the *Report of the Oxford Ornithological Society on the Birds of Oxfordshire, Berkshire and Buckinghamshire 1944.*

Allen, R.C.R. 1945. Ring Ouzels in Berkshire. *British Birds* 38: 256.

Anon. 1895. *Curator's report of Leighton Park School Natural History Society for 1895.* Unpublished manuscript.

Aplin, O.V. 1889. *The Birds of Oxfordshire.* Clarendon Press, Oxford.

Baillie, S.R., Marchant, J.H., Leech, D.I., Renwick, A.R., Eglington, S.M., Joys, A.C., Noble, D.G., Barimore, C., Conway, G.J., Downie, I.S., Risely, K. & Robinson, R.A. 2012. *BirdTrends 2011.* BTO Research Report 609. BTO, Thetford. **http://www.bto.org/ birdtrends.**

Balch, C.C. 1951. *Provisional List of the Birds of Reading.* Reading Ornithological Club.

Banks, A.N., Coombes, R.H. and Crick, H.Q.P. 2003. *The Peregrine Falcon breeding population of the U.K. and the Isle of Man in 2002.* BTO Research Report 330.

Bibby, C.J. 1982. Polygyny and Breeding Ecology of the Cetti's Warbler. *Ibis* **124:** 288–301.

Bibby, C.J. 1989. A survey of breeding Wood Warblers *Phylloscopus sibilatrix* in Britain, 1984–1985. *Bird Study* **36:** 56–72.

Bircham, P.M.M. 1989. *The Birds of Cambridgeshire.* Cambridge University Press, Cambridge.

BirdLife International. 2004. *Birds in Europe: population estimates, trends and conservation status.* BirdLife Conservation Series No. 12. BirdLife International, Cambridge. (BiE04) (**www.birdlife.org/ action/science/species/birds_in_europe/species_search.html**).

Blaker, G.B. 1934. *The Barn Owl in England and Wales.* RSPB, London.

Bland, H.M. 1935. *Birds in an Eton Garden.* J.M. Dent and Sons, London.

Bland, R. 1989. Feeding Garden Birds. The View from Avon. *BTO News* 164: 8.

Brooke, M. de L. 1990. *The Manx Shearwater.* T. & A.D. Poyser, London.

Broom, D.M., Dick, W.J.A., Johnson, C.E., Sales, D.I. and Zahavi, A. 1976. Pied Wagtail roosting and feeding behaviour. *Bird Study* **23:** 267–279.

Brown, A. and Grice, P. 2005. *Birds in England.* Poyser, London.

Brown, G. 1935. Black-throated Diver in Berkshire. *British Birds* **28:** 370.

Brucker, J.W., Gosler, A.G., Heryet, A.R. 1992. *Birds of Oxfordshire.* Pisces Publications, Newbury.

Burton, N.H.K..2007. Influences of restock age and habitat patchiness on Tree Pipits *Anthus trivialis* breeding in Breckland pine plantations. *Ibis* **149:** 193–204.

Burton, N.H.K., Banks, A.N., Calladine, J.R., Austin, G.E., 2013. The importance of the U.K. for wintering gulls: population estimates and conservation requirements. *Bird Study* **60:** 87–101.

Burton, N.H.K. and Conway, G.J. 2008. *Assessing population change of breeding Ringed Plovers in the UK between 1984 and 2007.* BTO Research Report 503.

Clark, J.M. 1984. *Birds of the Hants/Surrey Border.* Hobby Books, Fleet.

Clark, J.M. 2009. Feral Barnacle and Snow Geese in the Upper Loddon and Blackwater Valleys. *The Birds of Berkshire Annual Report 2005:* 11–14.

Clark, J.M. and Eyre, J.A. 1993. *The Birds of Hampshire.* Hampshire Ornithological Society.

Clark Kennedy, A.W.M. 1868. *The Birds of Berkshire and Buckinghamshire.* Simpkin, Marshall and Co., London.

Clews, B.D. 2006. *Birds in a Village – A Century On.* WILDGuides, Old Basing.

Clews, B., Heryat, A. and Trodd, P. 1994. *Where to Watch Birds in Bedfordshire, Berkshire, Buckinghamshire, Hertfordshire and Oxfordshire.* Second Edition. Helm, London.

Collar, N. 2013. A species is whatever I say it is. *British Birds* **106:** 130–142.

Collings, D.W. 1911. Puffin in Berkshire. *British Birds* **5:** 197.

Conway, G., Wotton, S., Henderson, I., Eaton, M., Drewitt, A. & Spencer, J. 2009. The status of breeding Woodlarks *Lullula arborea* in Britain in 2006. *Bird Study* **56:** 310–325.

Cranswick. P.A., Kirby, J.S. and Waters, R.J. 1992. *Wildfowl and Wader Counts 1991–92: the Results of the National Waterfowl Counts and Birds of Estuaries Enquiry in the United Kingdom.* Wildfowl and Wetlands Trust and British Trust for Ornithology, Slimbridge.

Cranswick, P.A., Waters, R.J., Evans, J. and Pollitt, M.S. 1995. *The Wetland Bird Survey 1993–94, Wildfowl and Wader Counts.* Wildfowl and Wetlands Trust, Slimbridge.

Cramp, S., Pettet, R. and Sharrock, J.T.R. 1960. The irruption of tits in autumn 1957. *British Birds* **53:** 49–77, 99–117, 176–192.

Cramp, S. and Simmons, K.E.L. (eds.) 1977–83. *The Handbook of the Birds of Europe, the Middle East and North Africa: the Birds of the Western Palaearctic.* Volumes **I–III.** Oxford University Press, Oxford.

Cramp, S. (ed.) 1985–92. *The Handbook of the Birds of Europe, the Middle East and North Africa: the Birds of the Western Palaearctic.* Volumes **IV–VI.** Oxford University Press, Oxford.

Cramp, S. and Perrins, C.M. (eds.) 1993–94. *The Handbook of the Birds of Europe, the Middle East and North Africa: the Birds of the Western Palaearctic.* Volumes **VII–IX.** Oxford University Press, Oxford.

Cramp, S., Bourne, W.R.P. and Saunders, D. 1974. *The Seabirds of Britain and Ireland.* Collins, London.

Crawford, R. 2007. Unprecedented Numbers of Yellow Wagtails at Englefield in Autumn 2001. *The Birds of Berkshire Annual Report 2001:* 12–13.

Crowley, P. 2010. *Berkshire Bird Index (BBI) Report for 2008.* Maidenhead.

Davies, A.K. 1988. The Distribution and Status of the Mandarin Duck *Aix galericulata* in Britain. *Bird Study* **35:** 203–208.

Dawson, I. and Allsopp, K. 1994. The ornithological year 1993. *British Birds* **87:** 462.

Dean, A.R. 1985. Review of British status and identification of Greenish Warbler. *British Birds* **78:** 437–451.

Delaney, S. 1992. *Survey of Introduced Geese in Britain, Summer 1991: Provisional Results.* Wildfowl and Wetlands Trust, Slimbridge.

Dudley, S. 1991. To Russia – a dove. *BTO News* **176:** 6.

Dymond, J.N., Fraser, P.A., and Gantlett, S.J.M. 1989. *Rare Birds in Britain and Ireland.* T. & A.D. Poyser, Calton.

Eaton M.A., Balmer D.E.,Cuthbert R., Grice P.V., Hall J., Hearn R.D., Holt C.A., Musgrove A.J., Noble D.G., Parsons M., Risely K., Stroud D.A. & Wotton S. 2011. *The state of the UK's birds 2011.* RSPB, BTO, WWT,CCW, JNCC, NE, NIEA and SNH, Sandy, Bedfordshire.

Eaton, M.A., Brown, A.F., Noble, D.G., Musgrove, A.J., Hearn, R.D., Aebischer, N.J., Gibbons, D.W., Evans, A. & Gregory, R.D. 2009. Birds of Conservation Concern 3: the population status of birds in the United Kingdom, Channel Islands and Isle of Man. *British Birds* **102:** 296–341.

Evans, K.L. & Robinson, R.A. 2004. Barn Swallows and agriculture. *British Birds* **97:** 218–230.

Ewing, S.R., Rebecca, G.W., Heavisides, A., Court, I., Lindley, P., Ruddock, M., Cohen, S. & Eaton, M.A. 2011. Breeding status of the Merlin *Falco columbarius* in the UK in 2008. *Bird Study* **58:** 379–389.

Ferguson, D. *The Birds of Buckinghamshire*. second edition. 2013. Buckinghamshire Bird Club,.

Ferguson-Lees, J., Castle, P., Cranswick, P., Edwards, S., Combridge, P., Turner, R., Cady, L. 2007. *The Birds of Wiltshire*, Wiltshire Ornithological Society, Devizes.

Fleure, H.J. and Davies, M. 1951. *A Natural History of Man in Britain*. Collins, London.

Fox, A.D. and Salmon, D.G. 1989. The winter status and distribution of Gadwall in Britain and Ireland. *Bird Study* **36**: 37–44.

Fraser, A.C. 1954. *The Birds of the Middle Thames*. The Middle Thames Natural History Society.

Fraser, A.C. and Youngman, R.E. 1976. *The Birds of Buckinghamshire and East Berkshire*. The Middle Thames Natural History Society.

Frankum, R.G. 1985. *The Birds and Plants of Hungerford Common 1980–1984*. Private publication.

Frankum, R.G. and Frankum, M. 1975. *The Birds and Plants of Freemen's Marsh Hungerford 1970–1974*. Private publication.

Frankum, R.G. and Frankum, M. 1980. *The Birds and Plants of Freemens Marsh Hungerford 1975–979*. Private publication.

Fraser, P.A. and Rogers, M.J. 2002. Report on scarce migrants in Britain in 2000. *British Birds* **95**: 606–630.

Fraser, P.A., Rogers, M.J. 2006. Report on Scarce Migrant Birds in Britain in 2003. *British Birds* **99**: 74–91.

Frederiksen, M., Harris, M.P., Daunt, F., Rothery, P. and Wanless, S. 2004. The role of industrial fisheries and oceanographic change in the decline of North Sea black-legged kittiwakes. *Journal of Applied Ecology* **41**: 1129–1139.

Freeman, S., Balmer, D. & Crick, H. 2007. Tawny Owl Survey 2005. *BTO News* **268**: 6–7.

French, P.R., 2009. Identification of Dark-breasted Barn Owl in Britain. *British Birds* **102**: 494.

Fuller, R.J. 1982. *Bird Habitats in Britain*. T. & A.D. Poyser, Calton.

Fuller, R.J., Smith, K.W., Grice, P.V., Currie, F.A., Quine, C.P., 2007. Habitat change and woodland birds in Britain: implications for management and future research. *Ibis* **149**: (Suppl. 2) 261–268.

Giles, E. 1946. Account of the status of the Wryneck. In systematic list in the *Report of the Oxford Ornithological Society on the Birds of Oxfordshire, Berkshire and Buckinghamshire 1945*.

Gilroy, N. 1910. Crossbills nesting in Berkshire. *British Birds* **3**: 371–2.

Glue, D.E. and Morgan, R. 1972. Cuckoo hosts in British Habitats. *Bird Study* 19:187–192

Gray, D.B. 1974. Breeding behaviour of Whinchats. *Bird Study* 21: 280–282. Green, M.S. and Ramsden, D.J. 2001. *Barn Owl Trust Second Reintroduction Report*. Barn Owl Trust, Ashburton, Devon.

Green, R.E. 1988. Stone Curlew Conservation. *RSPB Conservation Review* 2: 30–33.

Gruar, D., Barritt, D. & Peach, W.J. 2006. Summer utilization of Oilseed Rape by Reed Buntings Emberiza schoeniclus and other farmland birds. *Bird Study* **53**: 47–54.

Harrison, G.R., Dean, A.R., Richards, A.J. and Smallshire, D. 1982. *The Birds of the West Midlands*. West Midlands Bird Club, Studley.

Hastings, R.B. 1986. The 1986 Guillemot 'wreck'. *London Bird Report* 51.

Hawkins, J.L. 1933. Birds in the Neighbourhood of Reading. *Quaestiones Naturales* (Proceedings of the Reading and District Natural History Society) **1**: 81–85.

Hawthorn, I. 1975. Wrens wintering in a Reed-bed. *Bird Study* **22**: 19–23.

Hawthorn, I. and Mead C.J. 1975. Wren Movement and Survival. *British Birds* 68: 349–358.

Hawthorn, I., Weston, I., Crockford, R. and Smith, R.G. 1971. Wrens wintering in a Reed-bed at Thatcham, Berkshire. *Bird Study* **18**: 27–29.

Heard, C.D.R. 1989. Hybrid Glaucous x Herring Gulls in Berkshire. *The Birds of Berkshire Annual Report 1986–7*: 7–8.

Heard, C.D.R. 1989. Racial identification of wintering Chiffchaffs. *Birding World* **2**: 60–65.

Heard, C.D.R. 1997. Kittiwake movements in East Berkshire on 25th January 1993. *The Birds of Berkshire Annual Report 1992–93*: 5–6.

Heard, C.D.R. 2012. Siberian Chiffchaffs in Berkshire. *The Birds of Berkshire Annual Report 2008*: 17–21.

Henderson, I.G. & Hart, P.J.B. 1993. Provisioning, parental investment and reproductive success in Jackdaws Corvus monedula. *Ornis Scandinavica* 24: 142–148.

Herbert, W.H. 1871. Notes on Some Rarer Birds Observed in the Neighbourhood of Newbury. *Transactions of the Newbury District Field Club* 1 (1870–71).

Herbert, W.H. 1875. Notes on Some Rarer Birds Observed in the Neighbourhood of Newbury. *Transactions of the Newbury District Field Club* 2 (1872–75).

Hewett, W. Jr. 1844. *The History and Antiquities of the Hundred of Compton Berkshire*. John Snare, Reading.

Hewett, W. 1895–1911. Notes on the Natural History of the Compton District. *Transactions of the Newbury District Field Club* **5**: 29–41.

Holling, M and the Rare Birds Breeding Panel, 2011. Rare breeding birds in the United Kingdom in 2009. *British Birds* **104**: 476–537.

Holling, M. and the Rare Birds Breeding Panel, 2012. Rare breeding birds in the United Kingdom in 2010. *British Birds* **105**: 352–416.

Holloway, S. 1996. *The Historical Atlas of Breeding Birds in Britain and Ireland 1875–1900*. T. & A.D. Poyser, London.

Holt, C. A., Austin, G.E., Calbrade, N.A., Mellan, H.J., Mitchell, C., Stroud, D.A., Wotton, S.R. and Musgrove, A.J. 2011. *Waterbirds in the UK 2009/10: The Wetlands Bird Survey*. BTO/RSPB/JNCC, Thetford.

Holt, C.A., Austin, G.E., Calbrade, N.A., Mellan, H.J., Hearn, R.D., Stroud, D.A., Wotton, S.R. & Musgrove, A.J. 2012. *Waterbirds in the UK 2010/11: the Wetland Bird Survey*. BTO/RSPB/JNCC, Thetford.

Holt, C. A., Hewson, C. M., and Fuller, R.J. 2012. The Nightingale in Britain: status, ecology and conservation needs. *British Birds* **105**: 172–187.

Howard, R. and Moore, A. 1991. *A Complete Checklist of the Birds of the World*. Second Edition. Academic Press Ltd., London

Hudson, N and the Rarities Committee, 2012. Report on rare birds in Great Bitain in 2011. *British Birds* **105**: 556–625. [this entry was p 613].

Hudson, W.H. 1893. *Birds in a Village*. Chapman & Hall, London.

Hudson, W.H. 1919. *Birds in Town and Village*. J.M. Dent and Sons, London.

Hughes, S.W.M. 1972. The breeding distribution and status of the Tree Pipit in Sussex. *Sussex Bird Report* **24**: 68–79.

James, P. (ed.). 1996. *Birds of Sussex*. Sussex Ornithological Society.

John, A.W.G. and Roskell, J. 1985. Jay movements in autumn 1983. *British Birds* 78: 611.

Jonzen N., Linden A., Ergon, T.,Knudsen, E., Vik, J., Rubolini, D., Piacentini, D., Brinch, C., Spina, F., Karlsson, L:, Stervander, M., Andersson, A., Waldenstrom, J., Lehikoinen, A., Edvardsen, E., Solvang, R., Stenseth, N., 2006. Rapid Advance of Spring Arrival Dates in Long-Distance Migratory Birds. *Science* **312**: 1959–1961.

Karpowicz, Z.J. 1975. The Grasshopper Warbler in the Sulham area during 1968–71. *Reading Ornithological Club Report* **27**: 29–33.

Kerr, G.W. 1909. Marsh Warblers' nests with Cuckoos' eggs in Buckinghamshire. *British Birds* **3**: 232.

Kerr, G.W. 1916. The Lesser Redpoll in the Thames Valley. *Wild Life* 8 (3).

Knox, A.G. 1992. *Checklist of Birds of Britain and Ireland*. 6th Edition. British Ornithologists' Union, Tring.

Knox, A.G., Helbig, A.J., Parkin, D.T. and Sangster, G. 2002. The taxonomic status of Lesser Redpoll. *British Birds* **94**: 260–267.

Lack, D. 1956. *Swifts in a Tower*. Methuen, London.

Lack, P. 1986. *The Atlas of Wintering Birds in Britain and Ireland*. T. & A.D. Poyser, Calton.

Lack, P. 1992. *Birds on Lowland Farms*. HMSO, London.

Lack, P. and Ferguson, D. 1993. *The Birds of Buckinghamshire*. Buckinghamshire Bird Club.

Lamb, T. 1880. Ornithologia Bercheria. *The Zoologist* **4**: 313–325. Lever, C. 1987. *Naturalised Birds of the World*. Longman, Marlow.

Lever, C. 1990. *The Mandarin Duck*. Shire Natural History, Princes Risborough.

Lewis, L.R. 1958. Birds of the Newbury District 1954–58. *Transactions of the Newbury District Field Club* **10**: 14–30.

Lewis, L.R. 1960. An Interim Report – Gulls in Newbury District 1950 to February 1960. *Transactions of the Newbury District Field Club* **11**: 32–38.

Lewis, L.R. 1981. Willow Warblers on Bucklebury/Lower Common – 1981. *Newbury District Ornithological Club Annual Report 1981*.

Lloyd, C., Tasker, M.L. and Partridge, K. 1991. *The Status of Seabirds in Britain and Ireland*. T. & A.D. Poyser, London.

Lucas, J.A. and Standley, P.E. 1967. Autumn passage of terns at Theale Gravel Pits 1967. *Reading Ornithological Club Report* **21**: 50–53.

Marchant, J.H. and Musty, L. 1992. Common Bird Census 1990–91 index report. *BTO News* **182**: 9–12.

Marchant, J.H., Hudson, R., Carter, S.P. and Whittington, P. 1990. *Population Trends in British Breeding Birds*. BTO, Tring.

Mason, C.F. 1995. Long-term trends in the arrival of spring migrants. *Bird Study* 42: 182.

Mead, C. 1992. Bye Bye Blackbird. *BTO News* **181**: 1.

Murton, R.K. and Ridpath, M.G. 1962. The autumn movements of the Woodpigeon. *Bird Study* **9**: 7–41.

Montier, D. (ed.) 1977. *Atlas of Breeding Birds of the London Area*. Batsford, London. Moon, A.V. (ed.) 1985. *London Bird Report 1985*. London Natural History Society.

Monk, J.F. and Southern, H.N. 1937. Report of Crossbill Enquiry (1936). *Report of the Oxfordshire Ornithological Society on the Birds of Oxfordshire, Berkshire and Buckinghamshire 1936*. Oxfordshire Ornithological Society.

Moon, A.V. (ed.) 1990. *London Bird Report 1990*. London Natural History Society.

Moorcroft, D., Bradbury, R.B. & Wilson, J.D. 1997. The diet of nestling Linnets *Carduelis cannabina* before and after agricultural intensification. 1997 Brighton Crop Protection Conference – Weeds, *Conference Proceedings* vols **1–3**: 923–928.

Morris, Rev F.O. 1851–57. *A History of British Birds*. Volumes **I–VI**. G. Bell and Sons, London.

Morley, A. 1940. Special Reports: Scheduled Species. *Report of the Oxfordshire Ornithological Society on the Birds of Oxfordshire, Berkshire and Buckinghamshire 1939*. Oxfordshire Ornithological Society.

Musgrove, A.J., Austin, G.E., Hearn, R.D., Holt, C.A., Stroud, D.A. and Wotton, S.R. 2011. Overwinter population estimates of British waterbirds. *British Birds* **104**: 364.

Newson, S. E., Johnston, A., Parrott, D., Leech, D. I. 2011. Evaluating the population-level impact of an invasive species, Ring-necked Parakeet *Psittacula krameri*, on native avifauna. *Ibis* **153**: 509–516.

Newson, S.E., Marchant, J.H., Ekins, G.R. & Sellers, R.M. 2007. The status of inland-breeding Great Cormorants in England. *British Birds* **100**: 289–299.

Newton, I. 1972. *Finches*. Collins, London.

Nightingale, B. and Allsop, K. 1994. Invasion of Red-footed Falcons in spring 1992. *British Birds* **87**: 223–231.

Noble, H. 1906. *The Victoria County History of Berkshire: Birds*. Archibald Constable, London.

Noble, H. 1909. Manx Shearwater in Berkshire. *British Birds* **3**: 321.

Noble, H. 1912. Montagu's Harrier in Berkshire. *British Birds* **5**: 245.

O'Connnor, R.J. and Mead, C.J. 1984. The Stock Dove in Britain, 1930–80. *British Birds* **77**: 181201.

O'Connor, R.J. and Shrubb, M. 1986. *Fanning and Birds*. Cambridge University Press, Cambridge.

Osborne, P. 1982. Some effects of Dutch elm disease on nesting farmland birds. *Bird Study* **29**: 2–16.

Owen, M., Atkinson-Willes, G.L. and Salmon, D.G. 1986. *Wildfowl in Great Britain*. Second Edition. Cambridge University Press, Cambridge.

Owen, M. and Salmon, D.G. 1988. Feral Greylag Geese *Anser anser* in Britain and Ireland. *Bird Study* **35**: 37–45.

PACEC. 2006. The Economic and Environmental Impact of Sporting Shooting. Public and Corporate Economic Consultants, Cambridge.

Palmer, M.H. 1886. The Birds of Newbury. *Newbury Weekly News*. Issues from 20th May to 10th June 1886.

Parrinder, E.D. 1989. Little Ringed Plovers *Charadrius dubius* in Britain in 1984. *Bird Study* **36**: 147–153.

Partridge. F.H. 1908. Pallas's Sand-Grouse in England. *British Birds* **2**: 98.

Perrins, C.M. and Owen, D.F. 1958. Mésange noire au large de Dieppe en septembre. *Alauda* **26**: 69.

Proctor, Major F.W. 1908. The Lesser Redpoll as a Breeding Species in Berkshire. *British Birds* **1**: 312–313.

Radford, M.C. 1966. *The Birds of Berkshire and Oxfordshire*. Longmans, London.

Rackham, O., 2006. *Woodlands*. Collins, London.

Rebecca, G.W. & Bainbridge, I.P. 1998. The breeding status of the Merlin *Falco columbarius* in Britain in 1993–94. *Bird Study* **45**: 172–187.

Rehfisch, M.M, Austin, G.E., Holloway, S.J., Allan, J.R. & O'Connell, M. 2002. An approach to the assessment of change in the numbers of Canada Geese *Branta canadensis* and Greylag Geese *Anser anser* in southern Britain. *Bird Study* **49**: 50–59.

Reille, A. 1993. Le Grand Cormoran est Revenu. *L'Oiseau* 30: 36–37.

Righelato, R., 2012. Dark-breasted Barn Owl in Berkshire – a re-examination. *The Birds of Berkshire Annual Report 2008*: 13–15.

Robb, G.N., McDonald, R.A., Chamberlain, D.E., Reynolds, S.J., Harrison, T.J.E., Bearhop, S., 2008. Winter feeding of birds increases productivity in the subsequent breeding season. *Biology. Letters* **4**: 220–223.

Robertson,H.A. 1990. Breeding of Collared Doves *Streptopelia decaocto* in Rural Oxfordshire, England. *Bird Study*, **37**: 73.

Robinson, C. 2006. The growth of herons in Berkshire 1992 – 2003. *The Birds of Berkshire Annual Report 2003*: 13–14.

Robinson, C. 2009. The Berkshire Kingfisher Survey 2005. *The Birds of Berkshire Annual Report 2005*: 20–25.

Robinson,C., 2007. *Red Kites and Buzzards in Berkshire, 2006*. published online at http://www.berksoc.org.uk/surveys/kites_and_buzzards_2006_results.shtml.

Rogers, C.M. 1901. Pine Grosbeak in Berkshire. *Nature* **65**: 129.

Rogers, M.J. and The Rarities Committee. 1992. Report on Rare Birds in Great Britain 1991. *British Birds* 85: 507–554.

Rogers, M.J. and The Rarities Committee. 1993. Report on Rare Birds in Great Britain 1992. *British Birds* 86: 447–540.

RSBP. 1995. *Stone Curlews in Central Southern England, Annual Report*. RSPB, Sandy.

RSPB. 1996. *Birds of Conservation Concern in the United Kingdom, Channel Island and Isle of Man*. RSPB, Sandy.

Sangster, G, Collinson, M, Crochet, P-A, Knox, A, Parkin, D T, Svensson, L and Votier, S. 2011. Taxonomic recommendations for British birds: seventh report. *Ibis* **153**: 883–892.

Sangster, G., Collinson, J. M., Knox, A.G., Parkin, D. T. and Svensson, L. 2007. Taxonomic recommendations for British birds: fourth report. *Ibis* 149: 853.

Sears, J. 1989. A review of lead poisoning among the River Thames Mute Swan *Cygnus olor* population. *Wildfowl* **40**: 151–152.

Sharrock, J.T.R. and Sharrock, E. M. 1976 *Rare Birds in Britain and Ireland*. T. & A.D. Poyser, Berkhamsted.

Sharrock, J.T.R. 1976. *The Atlas of Breeding Birds in Britain and Ireland.* T. & A.D. Poyser, Berkhamsted.

Shawyer, C.R. 1987. *The Barn Owl in the British Isles – Its Past, Present and Future.* The Hawk Trust.

Shrubb, M. 1990. Effects of agricultural change on nesting Lapwings *Vanellus vanellus* in England and Wales. *Bird Study* **37**: 115–127.

Shrubb, M., 2003. Birds, *Scythes and Combines – A history of birds and agricultural change.* Cambridge University Press, Cambridge.

Sim, I. M.W., Dillon, I. A., Eaton, M. A., Etheridge, B., Lindley, P., Riley, H., Saunders, R., Sharpe, C., & Tickner, M. 2007. Status of the Hen Harrier *Circus cyaneus* in the UK and Isle of Man in 2004, and a comparison with the 1988/89 and 1998 surveys. *Bird Study* **54**: 256–267.

Sim, I., Rollie, C., Arthur, D., Benn, S., Booker, H., Fairbrother, V., Green, M., Hutchinson, K., Ludwig, S., Nicoll, M., Poxton, I., Rebecca, G., Smith, L., Stanbury, A. & Wilson, P. 2010. The decline of the Ring Ouzel in Britain. *British Birds* **103**: 229–239.

Siriwardena, G., Baillie, S., Crick, H. & Wilson, J. (2001) Changes in agricultural land-use and breeding performance of some granivorous farmland passerines in Britain. *Agriculture, Ecosystems & Environment* **84**: 191–206.

Sitters, H.P. 1986. Woodlarks in Britain, 1968–83. *British Birds* **79**: 105–116.

Sitters, H.P. 1988. *Tetrad Atlas of the Breeding Birds of Devon.* Devon Birdwatching and Preservation Society, Yelverton.

Snow, D.W. 1966. The migration and dispersal of British Blackbirds. *Bird Study* **13**: 237–255.

Spencer, J.W., and Kirby, K.J. 1992. An inventory of ancient woodland for England and Wales. *Biological Conservation* **62**: 77–93.

Spencer, R. and the Rare Birds Breeding Panel. 1986. Rare Breeding Birds in the United Kingdom in 1984. *British Birds* 79: 470–495.

Spencer, R. and the Rare Birds Breeding Panel. 1988. Rare Breeding Birds in the United Kingdom in 1986. *British Birds* **81**: 417–444.

Spencer, R. and the Rare Birds Breeding Panel. 1990. Rare Breeding Birds in the United Kingdom in 1988. *British Birds* **83**: 353–390.

Spencer, R. and the Rare Birds Breeding Panel. 1991. Rare Breeding Birds in the United Kingdom in 1989. *British Birds* **84**: 349–370.

Spencer, R. and the Rare Birds Breeding Panel. 1993. Rare Breeding Birds in the United Kingdom in 1990. *British Birds* **86**: 62–90

Standley, P.E. 1991. The incidence of Fieldfares in Berkshire from May to September. *The Birds of Berkshire Annual Report 1989*: 10–13.

Standley, P.E. 1999. *The Birds of Berkshire Annual Report 1994–95.*

Stroud, D.A. and Glue, D. 1991. *Britain's Birds in 1989/90: the conservation and monitoring review.* BTO/NCC, Thetford.

Strubbe, D., Matthysen, E., 2011. A radiotelemetry study of habitat use by the exotic Ring-necked Parakeet *Psittacula krameri* in Belgium. *Ibis* **153**: 180–184.

Stubbs, C.E. 1867. *A Slight Sketch of the Ornithology of Henley-on-Thames.* Unpublished manuscript.

Summers-Smith, D. 1951. A History of the Birds of the Newbury District. *Transactions of the Newbury District Field Club* **9**: 59–85.

Summers-Smith, D. 1954. Birds of the Newbury District 1951–53. *Transactions of the Newbury District Field Club* **10**: 26–31.

Summers-Smith, J.D. 2005. *On Sparrows and Man.* J Dennis Summers-Smith, Guisborough.

Swaine, C.M. 1982. *Birds of Gloucestershire.* Alan Sutton, Gloucester.

Taylor, I., 1994. Barn *Owls: Predator-prey relationships and conservation.* Cambridge University Press, Cambridge.

Taylor, K., Hudson, R. and Home, G. 1983. Buzzard breeding distribution and abundance in Britain and Northern Ireland in 1983. *Bird Study* **35**: 109–118.

Thackeray, S., Sparks, T., Frederiksen M., Burthe S., Bacon, P., Bell, J., Botham, M., Brereton, T., Bright P., Carvalhos, L., Clutton-Brock, T., Dawson, A., Edwards, M., Elliott, M.,Harrington, R., Johns, D., Jones, I., Jones, J., Leech, D., Roy, D., Scott, A., Smith, Smithers,

R., Winfield, I., Wanless, S., 2010. Trophic level asynchrony in rates of phenological change for marine, freshwater and terrestrial environments. *Global Change Biology* **16**: 3304–3313.

Tomlinson. A.S. 1910. Crosbills nesting in Berkshire. *British Birds* **4**:20.

Turner, R., Castle, P.E. and Edwards, S.B. 1995. Birds in Wiltshire 1994. *Hobby* **21**: 70.

Tyler, S. J. 1979. Mortality and movements of the Grey Wagtail. *Ringing and Migration* 2: 122131.

Van de Weyer, B. 1911. Probable breeding of the Little Owl in Berkshire. *British Birds* 5: 138.

Veysey, C.M. 1953. Lesser Yellowlegs at Ham Island 1953. *The Middle-Thames Naturalist* 6: 20.

Veysey, C.M. 1954. Little Gull's prolonged stay. *The Middle-Thames Naturalist* 7: 18.

Voous, K.H. 1973. List of Recent Holarctic Bird Species, Non-passerines. *Ibis* 115: 612–638.

Voous, K.H. 1977. *List of Recent Holarctic Bird Species.* British Ornithologists' Union, London.

Walford, N.T. 1935. Nightjar Census. *Report of the Oxfordshire Ornithological Society on the Birds of Oxfordshire, Berkshire and Buckinghamshire for 1934:* 47–49.

Wallis, H.M. 1916. Dark-breasted Barn Owl in Berkshire. *British Birds* 9: 210.

Wallis, H.M. and Wood, J.D. 1933. Bird life at Reading Sewage Farm 1922–1932. *Report of the Oxfordshire Ornithological Society on the Birds of Oxfordshire, Berkshire and Buckinghamshire for 1932.*

Watson, D. 1977. *The Hen Harrier.* T. & A.D.Poyser, Berkhamsted.

Webb, G. 1991. Rookery Survey. *Newbury District Ornithlological Club 1991 Annual Report.*

Wernham, C.V., Toms M.P., Marchant, J.H., Clark, J.A., Siriwardena, G.M. & Baillie, S.R. (eds) 2002. *The Migration Atlas: movements of the birds of Britain and Ireland.* T. & A.D. Poyser, London.

Wheatley, J. J. 2007. *The Birds of Surrey.* Surrey Bird Club, Hersham.

White, G. 1788–9. *The Natural History of Selborne.* Benjamin White & Son, London.

Wilson, A. M., Henderson, A.C.B., and Fuller, R. J. 2002. Status of the Nightingale in Britain at the end of the 20th Century with particular reference to climate change. *Bird Study* **49**: 193–2.

Wilson, A.M., Vickery, J.A., Brown, A., Langston, R.H.W., Smallshire, D., Wotton, S. & Vanhinsbergh, D. 2005. Changes in the numbers of breeding waders on lowland wet grasslands in England and Wales between 1982 and 2002. *Bird Study* **52**: 55–69.

Wilson, G.E. 1977. 1975 census of rookeries in Berkshire. *The Birds of Berkshire Second Annual Report.*

Wingfield Gibbons, D., Reid, J. and Chapman, R. 1993. *The New Atlas of Breeding Birds in Britain and Ireland 1988–91.* T. & A.D. Poyser London.

Winnall, R.N. and Yeates, J.K. 1932. *Bird Haunts in Wild Britain.* Philip Allan, London.

Witherby, H.F. and Ticehurst, N.F. 1908. On the more important additions to our knowledge of British birds since 1899. *British Birds* **1**: 247.

Witherby, H.F. and Ticehurst, N.F. 1908. The spread of the Little Owl from the chief centres of its introduction. *British Birds* **1**: 335–342.

Witherby, H.F., Jourdain, F.C.R., Ticehurst, N.F. and Tucker, B.W. 1938–41. *The Handbook of British Birds.* Vols. **1–5.** Witherby, London.

Wood, J.D. and Barlow, F.R. 1932. *Birds of Leighton Park School Grounds and Neighbourhood.* Leighton Park School.

Wotton, S., Conway, G., Eaton, M., Henderson, I. & Grice, P. 2009. The status of the Dartford Warbler in the UK and the Channel Islands in 2006. *British Birds* **102**: 230–246.

# Index

This index includes the common English and *scientific* names of all the birds included in the Species Accounts (Chapter 6, *pages 105–478*).

**Bold figures** indicates the page number of the main text for the species.
*Italicised figures* indicate a page where a photograph of the species can be found.